SPORT
IN THE
SOCIO-
CULTURAL
PROCESS

SPORT IN THE SOCIO- CULTURAL PROCESS

Edited by

M. MARIE HART

California State College at Hayward

wcb

WM. C. BROWN COMPANY PUBLISHERS
Dubuque, Iowa

PHYSICAL EDUCATION

Consulting Editor
Aileene Lockhart
University of Southern California

PARKS AND RECREATION

Consulting Editor
David Gray
California State College, Long Beach

HEALTH

Consulting Editor
Robert Kaplan
Ohio State University

Copyright © 1972 by Wm. C. Brown Company Publishers

Library of Congress Catalog Card Number: 72—170716

ISBN 0—697—07157—X

Second Printing, 1972

Printed in the United States of America

Contents

Preface ix

PART I. CULTURAL CONTEXT

Section A. Theories and Definitions   3

The Play-Element in Contemporary Civilization   5
Johan Huizinga

The Interdependence of Sport and Culture   22
Günther Lüschen

Theories of Why and How   36
Peter C. McIntosh

Section B. Sport and Social Organization   49

The Nature of Sport: A Definitional Effort   50
John W. Loy, Jr.

Small Group Research and the Group in Sport   67
Günther Lüschen

Reaction to Lüschen Paper   78
John W. Loy, Jr.

Section C. Thechnology—A Perspective   89

Forbidden Games   91
Theodore Roszak

The Theatre of Sports   105
John Lahr

The Technological Revolution and the Rise of Sport, 1850-1900   **116**
John Rickards Betts

PART II. PEOPLE IN THE PROCESS

Section A. Sport and Games: American Style   **143**

Games: The Extensions of Man   **145**
Marshall McLuhan

Some Meanings of American Sport: An Extended View   **155**
Gregory P. Stone

Reaction to Stone Paper   **168**
Charles H. Page

Foreword to *Man, Sport and Existence*   **180**
Edgar Z. Friedenberg

The City Game   **187**
Pete Axthelm

Football in America: A Study in Culture Diffusion   **206**
David Riesman and Reuel Denney

Section B. Rites of Passage and Sexual Identity   **222**

Introduction to *Children's Games in Street and Playground*   **224**
Iona and Peter Opie

Pigskin Review: An American Initiation   **241**
Shirley Fiske

The American Seasonal Masculinity Rites   **259**
Arnold R. Beisser

Symbolic Forms of Movement: The Olympic Games   **269**
Eleanor Metheny

Symbolic Forms of Movement: The Femine Image in Sports   **277**
Eleanor Metheny

On Being Female in Sport   **291**
M. Marie Hart

Section C. Ethnic Group Patterns   **303**

Preface to *The Revolt of the Black Athlete*   **304**
Harry Edwards

Contents

Racial Segregation in American Sport   308
John W. Loy and Joseph F. McElvogue

Ethnic Soccer Clubs in Milwaukee: A Study in Assimilation   328
John C. Pooley

The Native American Ball Games   346
Jerald C. Smith

PART III. BEYOND THE PEOPLE WHO PLAY: SYSTEMS WHICH CONTROL

Section A. Media and the Sports Message   361

Sports and the Mass Media   363
Harry Edwards

American Sports Magazines: One Part of the Media Message   369
M. Marie Hart

Take Me In to the Ball Game   378
Stan Opotowsky

Television's Effects on Spectator Sports   386
Leo Bogart

Section B. Economics or Education: Dedication and Dollars   397

Pro Football's Profit Explosion   399
Stephen Mahoney

Pro Football's 110% Coaches   411
Bill Braucher

Student Unrest and Athletic Dollars   418
Alfred R. Mathews, Jr.

Trends in the Sporting Goods Market   423
Richard Snyder

The Sporting Goods Market at the Threshold of the Seventies   438
Richard Snyder

Section C. Politics: National and International Positions   443

The Growing Crisis in College Sports   445
David Wolf

The Olympics That Almost Weren't   473
    Don Schollander and Duke Savage

Sports and Politics   482
    Sir Arnold Lunn

Sport, Politics and Internationalism   486
    Peter C. McIntosh

PART IV

Suggestions for Further Readings   501

Preface

What is the essence of sport in society—its meaning and function? How can the study of sport be approached in a total yet non-normative way? It is imperative when studying any social or cultural phenomenon to examine it within its total cultural context. To gain the most complete understanding and knowledge of the why, who, and how of any group being studied calls for a careful look at all aspects of their living. If a folklorist were studying proverbs in a culture and only considered them in their literary form, devoid of contextual information, it would not assist him in understanding a specific culture or subculture. How the proverb is used, who is allowed to say it and to whom, and under what circumstances it is used are all significant. Only in recent years have we considered sport in this light. Sport as a socio-cultural phenomenon must be studied in its contextual setting. How the sport is performed, under what circumstances, and who performs and who observes it, are all of prime importance in understanding the meaning of sport.

Often sport has been referred to as something operating outside of or separate from other cultural forms. It has been considered outside of ordinary life and responsibility, outside of the scrutiny that other values and norms receive. The ritual, costumes, and space especially set aside for the game have often given the environment and experience of sport a semi-sacred aura. As a student recently stated in all seriousness, "It is tantamount to the divine." "It is our sacred trust" is another phrase heard in the conversation of those working with athletes in games and sports.

This kind of romanticism has kept us from thoroughly investigating sport in its positive and negative aspects. We have believed and trusted, but not studied and researched. True, we have given scholarly consideration to aspects of improving the performance, but we have not studied the total sport expression as it occurs for the individual in his life experience. The situation within which each sport occasion—each specific one—occurs needs to be more fully explored. The people involved, the things said and done, before, during and after the game, all need attention.

We have often stated generalizations regarding the positive functions and social rewards of sport while avoiding the study of its negative outcomes. It is because these generalizations are made without knowledge of the specific setting, identity of participants and spectators, and goings-on of the supporting and promoting groups that we continue to be vaguely positive about values in sport. When, for instance, do we ask and pursue the question: What is the relationship between one's acceptance in sport and acceptance in other social situations? That a second baseman is respected on the field for his skill but is rejected socially off the field is no longer justifiable in American society.

Throughout time, there appears to have been an intricate mutual interdependence between sport and culture. Sport may be differently structured in various cultures and probably in different time periods of the same culture. It is only by looking at the sport of a particular culture, at a particular place and time, that comparisons can be made and patterns can be established, and that vague, perhaps untrue, generalizations can be avoided. Is part of the present controversy in sport because the verbalized idealized goals and images of sport are not serving the social functions long attributed to them? Recent turmoil and questioning in sport may indicate that sport has become more socially relevant, that sport has more meaning in the everyday ordinary life of people and cannot be held apart in a sacrosanct vacuum.

It is possible that achievement, social status, social mobility (upward always inferred), and equality—the American values claimed as part of the sport experience—may not have been operable because sport has been set apart, separate from other social processes. It cannot function as a social system whereby man enters into a full participation of American life. Until the sports system is more open to various ethnic groups, all people of color, and to women, it will continue to function effectively only for a few, embodying the disillusionment of a dream for the others.

A pay raise in professional sport does not necessarily mean a social raise. The experience of well-known, professional black athletes as they miss out on advertising revenue or try to buy homes in white suburbia provide ample proof of this. The negative social connotations often attached to the female athlete can isolate her socially, limiting her status and mobility altogether. These examples and many more create an awareness that we need to study both the functions and dysfunctions of sport in American society, especially if we accept the principle that sport can function as a part of the social system, as a means of maintaining norms, serving goal attainment and providing one way for individuals to adapt to society.

At this present time of questioning and redefinition of cultural values and norms, it seems crucial to be open to investigating and, in fact, energetically pursuing the place of sport in American society. It is important for the people in the center of studying, performing and producing sport to be also in the middle of the reformulation of understandings of it. Formerly, because of the normative approach to the study of sport from those within it, many of the present criticisms were levied only by those outside the area. Coaches and physical educators took these questions as anti-sport and did not feel obligated to seriously consider them.

Now, finally, the era of economic expansionism and the exclusively promotional approach to sport seem to be coming to an end. Now, finally, the era of self-criticism and the examination of sport from within is approaching. It is in support of this reformation that these articles by many of those asking the questions were collected. These are authors who have sought to understand sport in other than its performance aspects. Some of the authors included here present theoretical positions and constructs, while others have collected data on people in sport.

Part one of the book is organized to give the reader a cultural framework, a series of definitions and some understanding of the social organization of sport, as an orientation to the subsequent topics discussed. It is in the second part of the book that people in American sport are considered. What sports occur in the cities and in suburbia? Why? How are these games an extension of our social selves? "Coming of age" in America as a process of sport is a topic thoughtfully presented by several authors.

The second section also looks at sport "American style." Does this really mean that the many faces of sport are expressed by a multitude of ethnic groups? "The American way of sport" may actually be the many ways of American sport, exemplified by the various ethnic groups involved. Might it be that this means a use of sport to retain one's ethnic identity rather than as a means for moving into the main stream of American life? Several authors discuss this point.

How do social systems affect the people who operate within them? The media, economics, education and politics all seem to have direct and dynamic effect on the sports life of the American public. In the third and last part of the book, many authors give the reader an inside view of these systems. Do they assist or trap the person in sport? How controlled by these powerful factors is the participating spectating public? What are the effects of the "system" on sport? Although there are many strong feelings about this, there is very little research and documented knowledge on the subject. It is even said that sport may be its own "system." How does sport as a "system" affect the individual engaged in it in American life?

This anthology does not include material relevant to the psychology of the sport experience. Recognizing the relationship of the psychological to the sociological aspects of consideration, the author omits this topic only because there is sufficient and significant material in this area to extend it into a full volume of materials on its own.

These presentations are only a starting place for thoughtful discussion, leading, it is hoped, toward active research. This book is intended for those who are somewhat new to the socio-cultural study of sport, whether that be in physical education, sociology, anthropology or any other study of human behavior in the social process. It is hoped that the student will also concurrently be actively involved with courses in research procedures and seminars in specific aspects of sport in culture.

The author wishes to thank Barbara Vukman, June Wainwright, and Gay Cheney for their assistance in preparing the manuscript. And to those represented in this anthology she expresses her appreciation. Their response and assistance were encouraging. Recognition is also given to the many editors and authors who granted permission to reprint their work.

PART I

**CULTURAL
CONTEXT**

SECTION

A

THEORIES AND
DEFINITIONS

It seems important in considering "sport in the socio-cultural process" to present first those theories of sport, games and play that are culturally based as differentiated from those that are concerned with biological function. As an introduction to this section, an article by Huizinga considers play not only as pre-cultural and pervading all of life, but also as the recreating and dynamic force which brings about new cultural forms. Stated in his own words:

> The spirit of playful competition is, as a social impulse, older than culture itself and pervades all life like a veritable ferment. Ritual grew up in sacred play; poetry was born in play and nourished on play; music and dancing were pure play. Wisdom and philosophy found expression in words and forms derived from religious contests. The rules of warfare, the conventions of noble living were built up in play patterns. We have to conclude, therefore, that civilization is, in its earliest phases, played. It does not come from play like a babe detaching itself from the womb; it arises in and as play, and never leaves it.[1]

The second article in this section, by Lüschen, helps the reader make a transition from Huizinga's more sweeping descriptions of play, sport and culture to specific examples and discussion of the interdependence of these phenomena. Lüschen first asks the question, "What factors make for the appearance of sport? Or more specifically, what are the underlying cultural values?" In considering this question, his discussion of cultural values in relation to technology, Protestantism, and achievement orientation create a framework within which a clearer, more systematic understanding of sport can be developed. The second question asked is: "How does sport influence the socio-cultural system at large?" Because sport has often been considered apart from culture or specifically apart

---

1. Johan Huizinga, *Homo Ludens: A Study of the Play Element in Culture* (Boston, Mass.: Beacon Press, 1950), p. 173.

3

from "higher" culture, Lüschen's second question takes on importance for the study of sport and cultural process.

McIntosh synthesizes several theories and adds to these some of his own ideas about categorizing and analyzing sport. In considering the state of sport in the early 1960's, he does not see that concentration on technique or technical knowledge will necessarily obscure the play element in sport or corrupt those who play. In consideration of both the Huizinga and the McIntosh points of view, one might still ask: Has the concentration on technique, technical knowledge and the body as a technical object been responsible for some of the storm of protest in American sport?

THE PLAY-ELEMENT IN CONTEMPORARY CIVILIZATION

JOHAN HUIZINGA

Let us not waste time arguing about what is meant by "contemporary." It goes without saying that any time we speak of has already become an historical past, a past that seems to crumble away at the hinder end the further we recede from it. Phenomena which a younger generation is constantly relegating to "former days" are, for their elders, part of "our own day," not merely because their elders have a personal recollection of them but because their culture still participates in them. This different time-sense is not so much dependent on the generation to which one happens to belong as on the knowledge one has of things old and new. A mind historically focussed will embody in its idea of what is "modern" and "contemporary" a far larger section of the past than a mind living in the myopia of the moment. "Contemporary civilization" in our sense, therefore, goes deep into the nineteenth century.

The question to which we address ourselves is this: To what extent does the civilization we live in still develop in play-forms? How far does the play-spirit dominate the lives of those who share that civilization? The nineteenth century, we observed, had lost many of the play-elements so characteristic of former ages. Has this leeway been made up or has it increased?

It might seem at first sight that certain phenomena in modern social life have more than compensated for the loss of play-forms. Sport and athletics, as social functions, have steadily increased in scope and conquered ever fresh fields both nationally and internationally.

Johan Huizinga, *Homo Ludens: A Study of the Play Element in Culture* (Boston: The Beacon Press. Copyright 1950 by Roy Publishers. Reprinted by permission of Beacon Press.) Chapter 12. Reprinted by permission of Routledge and Kegan Paul, Ltd.

5

Contests in skill, strength and perseverance have, as we have shown, always occupied an important place in every culture either in connection with ritual or simply for fun and festivity. Feudal society was only really interested in the tournament; the rest was just popular recreation and nothing more. Now the tournament, with its highly dramatic staging and aristocratic embellishments, can hardly be called a sport. It fulfilled one of the functions of the theatre. Only a numerically small upper class took active part in it. This one-sidedness of mediaeval sporting life was due in large measure to the influence of the Church. The Christian ideal left but little room for the organized practice of sport and the cultivation of bodily exercise, except insofar as the latter contributed to gentle education. Similarly, the Renaissance affords fairly numerous examples of body-training cultivated for the sake of perfection, but only on the part of individuals, never groups or classes. If anything, the emphasis laid by the Humanists on learning and erudition tended to perpetuate the old under-estimation of the body, likewise the moral zeal and severe intellectuality of the Reformation and Counter-Reformation. The recognition of games and bodily exercises as important cultural values was withheld right up to the end of the eighteenth century.

The basic forms of sportive competition are, of course, constant through the ages. In some the trial of strength and speed is the whole essence of the contest, as in running and skating matches, chariot and horse races, weight-lifting, swimming, diving, marksmanship, etc.[1] Though human beings have indulged in such activities since the dawn of time, these only take on the character of organized games to a very slight degree. Yet nobody, bearing in mind the agonistic principle which animates them, would hesitate to call them games in the sense of play —which, as we have seen, can be very serious indeed. There are, however, other forms of contest which develop of their own accord into "sports." These are the ball-games.

What we are concerned with here is the transition from occasional amusement to the system of organized clubs and matches. Dutch pictures of the seventeenth century show us burghers and peasants intent upon their game of *kolf;* but, so far as I know, nothing is heard of games being organized in clubs or played as matches. It is obvious that a fixed organization of this kind will most readily occur when two groups play against one another. The great ball-games in particular require the existence of permanent teams, and herein lies the starting-point of modern sport. The process arises quite spontaneously in the meeting of vil-

---

1. A happy variation of the natatorial contest is found in *Beowulf,* where the aim is to hold your opponent under water until he is drowned.

lage against village, school against school, one part of a town against the rest, etc. That the process started in nineteenth century England is understandable up to a point, though how far the specifically Anglo-Saxon bent of mind can be deemed an efficient cause is less certain. But it cannot be doubted that the structure of English social life had much to do with it. Local self-government encouraged the spirit of association and solidarity. The absence of obligatory military training favoured the occasion for, and the need of, physical exercise. The peculiar form of education tended to work in the same direction, and finally the geography of the country and the nature of the terrain, on the whole flat and, in the ubiquitous commons, offering the most perfect playing-fields that could be desired, were of the greatest importance. Thus England became the cradle and focus of modern sporting life.

Ever since the last quarter of the nineteenth century games, in the guise of sport,[2] have been taken more and more seriously. The rules have become increasingly strict and elaborate. Records are established at a higher, or faster, or longer level than was ever conceivable before. Everybody knows the delightful prints from the first half of the nineteenth century, showing the cricketers in tophats. This speaks for itself.

Now, with the increasing systematization and regimentation of sport, something of the pure play-quality is inevitably lost. We see this very clearly in the official distinction between amateurs and professionals (or "gentlemen and players" as used pointedly to be said). It means that the play-group marks out those for whom playing is no longer play, ranking them inferior to the true players in standing but superior in capacity. The spirit of the professional is no longer the true play-spirit; it is lacking in spontaneity and carelessness.[3] This affects the amateur too, who begins to suffer from an inferiority complex. Between them they push sport further and further away from the play-sphere proper until it becomes a thing *sui generis*: neither play nor earnest. In modern social life sport occupies a place alongside and apart from the cultural process. The great competitions in archaic cultures had always formed part of the sacred festivals and were indispensable as health and happiness-bringing activities. This ritual tie has now been completely severed; sport has become profane, "unholy" in every way and has no organic connection whatever with the structure of society,

---

2. It is probably significant that we no longer speak of "games" but of "sport." Our author may not have been sufficiently familiar with the development of "sport" in the last ten or twenty years, here and in America, to stress the all-important point that sport has become a business, or, to put it bluntly, a commercial racket. Trans.
3. Note G. K. Chesterton's dictum: If a thing is worth doing at all it is worth doing badly! Trans.

least of all when prescribed by the government. The ability of modern social techniques to stage mass demonstrations with the maximum of outward show in the field of athletics does not alter the fact that neither the Olympiads nor the organized sports of American Universities nor the loudly trumpeted international contests have, in the smallest degree, raised sport to the level of a culture-creating activity. However important it may be for the players or spectators, it remains sterile. The old play-factor has undergone almost complete atrophy.

This view will probably run counter to the popular feeling of to-day, according to which sport is the apotheosis of the play-element in our civilization. Nevertheless popular feeling is wrong. By way of emphasizing the fatal shift towards over-seriousness we would point out that it has also infected the non-athletic games where calculation is everything, such as chess and some card-games.

A great many board-games have been known since the earliest times, some even in primitive society, which attached great importance to them largely on account of their chanceful character. Whether they are games of chance or skill they all contain an element of seriousness. The merry play-mood has little scope here, particularly where chance is at a minimum as in chess, draughts, backgammon, halma, etc. Even so all these games remain within the definition of play as given in our first chapter. Only recently has publicity seized on them and annexed them to athletics by means of public championships, world tournaments, registered records and press reportage in a literary style of its own, highly ridiculous to the innocent outsider.

Card-games differ from board-games in that they never succeed in eliminating chance completely. To the extent that chance predominates they fall into the category of gambling and, as such, are little suited to club life and public competition. The more intellectual card-games, on the other hand, leave plenty of room for associative tendencies. It is in this field that the shift towards seriousness and over-seriousness is so striking. From the days of *ombre* and *quadrille* to whist and bridge, card-games have undergone a process of increasing refinement, but only with bridge have the modern social techniques made themselves master of the game. The paraphernalia of handbooks and systems and professional training has made bridge a deadly earnest business. A recent newspaper article estimated the yearly winnings of the Culbertson couple at more than two hundred thousand dollars. An enormous amount of mental energy is expended in this universal craze for bridge with no more tangible result than the exchange of relatively unimportant sums of money. Society as a whole is neither benefited nor damaged by this futile activity. It seems difficult to speak of it as an elevating recreation in the sense of Aristotle's *diagoge*. Proficiency at bridge is a sterile excellence, sharpening the mental faculties very one-sidedly without enriching the soul in any way, fixing and consuming a quantity of intellectual energy that might have been better applied. The most we can say, I think, is that it might have been applied worse. The status of bridge in modern society would indicate, to all appearances, an immense increase in the play-element to-day. But appearances are deceptive. Really to play, a man must play like a child. Can we assert that this is so in the case of such an ingenious game as bridge? If not, the virtue has gone out of the game.

The attempt to assess the play-content in the confusion of modern life is bound to lead us to contradictory conclusions. In the case of sport we have an activity nominally known as play but raised to such a pitch of technical organization and scientific thoroughness that the real play-spirit is threatened with extinction. Over against this tendency to over-seriousness, however, there are other phenomena pointing in the opposite direction. Certain activities whose whole *raison d'être* lies in the field of material interest, and which had nothing of play about them in their initial stages, develop what we can only call play-forms as a secondary characteristic. Sport and athletics showed us play stiffening into seriousness but still being felt as play; now we come to serious business degenerating into play but still being called serious. The two phenomena are linked by the strong agonistic habit which still holds universal sway, though in other forms than before.

The impetus given to this agonistic principle which seems to be carrying the world back in the direction of play derives, in the main, from external factors independent of culture proper—in a word, communications, which have made intercourse of every sort so extraordinarily easy for mankind as a whole. Technology, publicity and propaganda everywhere promote the competitive spirit and afford means of satisfying it on an unprecedented scale. Commercial competition does not, of course, belong to the immemorial sacred play-forms. It only appears when trade begins to create fields of activity within which each must try to surpass and outwit his neighbour. Commercial rivalry soon makes limiting rules imperative, namely the trading customs. It remained primitive in essence until quite late, only becoming really intensive with the advent of modern communications, propaganda and statistics. Naturally a certain play-element had entered into business competition at an early stage. Statistics stimulated it with an idea that had originally arisen in sporting life, the idea, namely, of trading records. A record, as the word shows, was once simply a memorandum, a note which the inn-keeper scrawled on the walls of his inn to say that such and such

a rider or traveller had been the first to arrive after covering so and
so many miles. The statistics of trade and production could not fail to
introduce a sporting element into economic life. In consequence, there
is now a sporting side to almost every triumph of commerce or technology: the highest turnover, the biggest tonnage, the fastest crossing,
the greatest altitude, etc. Here a purely ludic element has, for once, got
the better of utilitarian considerations, since the experts inform us that
smaller units—less monstrous steamers and aircraft, etc.—are more efficient in the long run. Business becomes play. This process goes so far
that some of the great business concerns deliberately instil the play-
spirit into their workers so as to step up production. The trend is now
reversed: play becomes business. A captain of industry, on whom the
Rotterdam Academy of Commerce had conferred an honorary degree,
spoke as follows:

> "Ever since I first entered the business it has been a race between
> the technicians and the sales department. One tried to produce so much
> that the sales department would never be able to sell it, while the other
> tried to sell so much that the technicians would never be able to keep
> pace. This race has always continued: sometimes one is ahead, sometimes
> the other. Neither my brother nor myself has regarded the business as a
> task, but always as a game, the spirit of which it has been our constant
> endeavour to implant into the younger staff."

These words must, of course, be taken with a grain of salt. Nevertheless there are numerous instances of big concerns forming their own
Sports Societies and even engaging workers with a view not so much to
their professional capacities as to their fitness for the football eleven.
Once more the wheel turns.

It is less simple to fix the play-element in contemporary art than
in contemporary trade. As we tried to make clear in our tenth chapter,
a certain playfulness is by no means lacking in the process of creating
and "producing" a work of art. This was obvious enough in the arts of
the Muses or "music" arts, where a strong play-element may be called
fundamental, indeed, essential to them. In the plastic arts we found that
a play-sense was bound up with all forms of decoration; in other words,
that the play-function is especially operative where mind and hand move
most freely. Over and above this it asserted itself in the master-piece
or show-piece expressly commissioned, *the tour de force,* the wager in
skill or ability. The question that now arises is whether the play-element
in art has grown stronger or weaker since the end of the eighteenth
century.

A gradual process extending over many centuries has succeeded
in de-functionalizing art and making it more and more a free and

independent occupation for individuals called artists. One of the land-marks of this emancipation was the victory of framed canvases over panels and murals, likewise of prints over miniatures and illuminations. A similar shift from the social to the individual took place when the Renaissance saw the main task of the architect no longer in the build-ing of churches and palaces but of dwelling-houses; not in splendid galleries but in drawing-rooms and bed-rooms. Art became more inti-mate, but also more isolated; it became an affair of the individual and his taste. In the same way chamber music and songs expressly designed for the satisfaction of personal aestheticisms began to surpass the more public forms of art both in importance and often in intensity of expression.

Along with these changes in form there went another, even more profound, in the function and appreciation of art. More and more it was recognized as an independent and extremely high cultural value. Right into the eighteenth century art had occupied a subordinate place in the scale of such values. Art was a superior ornament in the lives of the privileged. Aesthetic enjoyment may have been as high as now, but it was interpreted in terms of religious exaltation or as a sort of curiosity whose purpose was to divert and distract. The artist was an artisan and in many cases a menial, whereas the scientist or scholar had the status at least of a member of the leisured classes.

The great shift began in the middle of the eighteenth century as a result of new aesthetic impulses which took both romantic and classical form, though the romantic current was the more powerful. Together they brought about an unparalleled rise in aesthetic enjoyment all the more fervent for having to act as a substitute for religion. This is one of the most important phases in the history of civilization. We must leap over the full story of this apotheosis of art and can only point out that the line of art-hierophants runs unbroken from Winckelmann to Ruskin and beyond. All the time, art-worship and connoisseurship remained the privilege of the few. Only towards the end of the nineteenth century did the appreciation of art, thanks largely to photographic reproduction, reach the broad mass of the simply educated. Art becomes public property, love of art *bon ton*. The idea of the artist as a superior species of being gains acceptance, and the public at large is washed by the mighty waves of snobbery. At the same time a convulsive craving for originality distorts the creative impulse. This constant striving after new and unheard-of forms impels art down the steep slope of Impressionism into the turgidities and excrescences of the twentieth century. Art is far more susceptible to the deleterious influences of modern techniques of production than is science. Mechanization, advertising, sensation-mongering have a much greater hold upon art because as a rule it works directly for a market and has a free choice of all the techniques available.

None of these conditions entitles us to speak of a play-element in contemporary art. Since the eighteenth century art, precisely because recognized as a cultural factor, has to all appearances lost rather than gained in playfulness. But is the net result a gain or loss? One is tempted to feel, as we felt about music, that it was a blessing for art to be largely unconscious of its high purport and the beauty it creates. When art becomes self-conscious, that is, conscious of its own grace, it is apt to lose something of its eternal child-like innocence.

From another angle, of course, we might say that the play-element in art has been fortified by the very fact that the artist is held to be above the common run of mortals. As a superior being he claims a certain amount of veneration for his due. In order to savour his superiority to the full he will require a reverential public or a circle of kindred spirits, who will pour forth the requisite veneration more understandingly than the public at large with its empty phrases. A certain esotericism is as necessary for art to-day as it was of old. Now all esoterics presuppose a convention: we, the initiates, agree to take such and such a thing thus and thus, so we will understand it, so admire it. In other words, esoterics requires a play-community which shall steep itself in its own mystery. Wherever there is a catch-word ending in -ism we are hot on the tracks of a play-community. The modern apparatus of publicity with its puffy art-criticism, exhibitions and lectures is calculated to heighten the play-character of art.

It is a very different thing to try to determine the play-content of modern science, for it brings us up against a fundamental difficulty. In the case of art we took play as a primary datum of experience, a generally accepted quantity; but when it comes to science we are constantly being driven back on our definition of that quantity and having to question it afresh. If we apply to science our definition of play as an activity occurring within certain limits of space, time and meaning, according to fixed rules, we might arrive at the amazing and horrifying conclusion that all the branches of science and learning are so many forms of play because each of them is isolated within its own field and bounded by the strict rules of its own methodology. But if we stick to the full terms of our definition we can see at once that, for an activity to be called play, more is needed than limitations and rules. A game is time-bound, we said; it has no contact with any reality outside itself, and its performance is its own end. Further, it is sustained by the consciousness of being a pleasurable, even mirthful, relaxation from the strains of ordinary life. None of this is applicable to science. Science is not only perpetually seeking contact with reality by its usefulness, i.e. in the sense that it is *applied,* it is perpetually trying to establish a universally valid pattern of reality, i.e. as *pure* science. Its rules, unlike those of play, are not unchallengeable for all time. They are constantly being belied by experience and undergoing modification, whereas the rules of a game cannot be altered without spoiling the game itself.

The conclusion, therefore, that all science is merely a game can be discarded as a piece of wisdom too easily come by. But it is legitimate to enquire whether a science is not liable to indulge in play within the closed precincts of its own method. Thus, for instance, the scientist's continued penchant for systems tends in the direction of play. Ancient science, lacking adequate foundation in empiricism, lost itself in a sterile systematization of all conceivable concepts and properties. Though observation and calculation act as a brake in this respect they do not altogether exclude a certain capriciousness in scientific activities. Even the most delicate experimental analysis can be, not indeed manipulated while actually in progress, but played in the interests of subsequent theory. True, the margin of play is always detected in the end, but this detection proves that it exists. Jurists have of old been reproached with similar manoeuvres. Philologists too are not altogether blameless in this respect, seeing that ever since the Old Testament and the Vedas they have delighted in perilous etymologies, a favourite game to this day for those whose curiosity outstrips their knowledge. And is it so certain that the new schools of psychology are not being led astray by the frivolous and facile use of Freudian terminology at the hands of competents and incompetents alike?

Apart from the possibility of the scientific worker or amateur juggling with his own method he may also be seduced into the paths of play by the competitive impulse proper. Though competition in science is less directly conditioned by economic factors than in art, the logical development of civilization which we call science is more inextricably bound up with dialectics than is the aesthetic. In an earlier chapter we discussed the origins of science and philosophy and found that they lay in the agonistic sphere. Science, as some one has not unjustly said, is polemical. But it is a bad sign when the urge to forestall the other fellow in discovery or to annihilate him with a demonstration, looms too large in the work done. The genuine seeker after truth sets little store by triumphing over a rival.

By way of tentative conclusion we might say that modern science, so long as it adheres to the strict demands of accuracy and veracity, is far less liable to fall into play as we have defined it, than was the case in earlier times and right up to the Renaissance, when scientific thought and method showed unmistakable play-characteristics.

These few observations on the play-factor in modern art and science must suffice here, though much has been left unsaid. We are hastening to an end, and it only remains to consider the play-element in contemporary social life at large and especially in politics. But let us be on our guard against two misunderstandings from the start. Firstly, certain play-forms may be used consciously or unconsciously to cover up some social or political design. In this case we are not dealing with the eternal play-element that has been the theme of this book, but with false play. Secondly, and quite independently of this, it is always possible to come upon phenomena which, to a superficial eye, have all the appearance of play and might be taken for permanent play-tendencies, but are, in point of fact, nothing of the sort. Modern social life is being dominated to an ever-increasing extent by a quality that has something in common with play and yields the illusion of a strongly developed play-factor. This quality I have ventured to call by the name of Puerilism,[4] as being the most appropriate appellation for that blend of adolescence and barbarity which has been rampant all over the world for the last two or three decades.

It would seem as if the mentality and conduct of the adolescent now reigned supreme over large areas of civilized life which had formerly been the province of responsible adults. The habits I have in mind are, in themselves, as old as the world; the difference lies in the place they now occupy in our civilization and the brutality with which they manifest themselves. Of these habits that of gregariousness is perhaps the strongest and most alarming. It results in puerilism of the lowest order: yells or other signs of greeting, the wearing of badges and sundry items of political haberdashery, walking in marching order or at a special pace and the whole rigmarole of collective voodoo and mumbo-jumbo. Closely akin to this, if at a slightly deeper psychological level, is the insatiable thirst for trivial recreation and crude sensationalism, the delight in mass-meetings, mass-demonstrations, parades, etc. The club is a very ancient institution, but it is a disaster when whole nations turn into clubs, for these, besides promoting the precious qualities of friendship and loyalty, are also hotbeds of sectarianism, intolerance, suspicion, superciliousness and quick to defend any illusion that flatters self-love or group-consciousness. We have seen great nations losing every shred of honour, all sense of humour, the very idea of decency and fair play.

4. Cf. *In the Shadow of To-morrow*, Heinemann, 1936, chapter 16.

This is not the place to investigate the causes, growth and extent of this world-wide bastardization of culture; the entry of half-educated masses into the international traffic of the mind, the relaxation of morals and the hypertrophy of technics undoubtedly play a large part.

One example of official puerilism must suffice here. It is, as we know from history, a sign of revolutionary enthusiasm when governments play at nine-pins with names, the venerable names of cities, persons, institutions, the calendar, etc. *Pravda*[5] reported that as a result of their arrears in grain deliveries three *kolkhozy* in the district of Kursk, already christened Budenny, Krupskaya and the equivalent of Red Cornfield, has been re-christened Sluggard, Saboteur and Do-Nothing by the local soviet. Though this *trop de zèle* received an official rebuff from the Central Committee and the offensive soubriquets were withdrawn, the puerilistic attitude could not have been more clearly expressed.

Very different is the great innovation of the late Lord Baden-Powell. His aim was to organize the social force of boyhood as such and turn it to good account. This is not puerilism, for it rests on a deep understanding of the mind and aptitudes of the immature; also the Scout Movement expressly styles itself a game. Here, if anywhere, we have an example of a game that comes as close to the culture-creating play of archaic times as our age allows. But when Boy-Scoutism in degraded form seeps through into politics we may well ask whether the puerilism that flourishes in present-day society is a play-function or not. At first sight the answer appears to be a definite yes, and such has been my interpretation of the phenomenon in other studies.[6] I have now come to a different conclusion. According to our definition of play, puerilism is to be distinguished from playfulness. A child playing is not puerile in the pejorative sense we mean here. And if our modern puerilism were genuine play we ought to see civilization returning to the great archaic forms of recreation where ritual, style and dignity are in perfect unison. The spectacle of a society rapidly goose-stepping into helotry is, for some, the dawn of the millennium. We believe them to be in error.

More and more the sad conclusion forces itself upon us that the play-element in culture has been on the wane ever since the eighteenth century, when it was in full flower. Civilization to-day is no longer played, and even where it still seems to play it is false play—I had almost said, it plays false, so that it becomes increasingly difficult to tell where play ends and non-play begins. This is particularly true of politics. Not very long ago political life in parliamentary democratic form was full

5. January 9th, 1935.
6. *Over de grenzen van spel en ernst in de cultuur*, p. 25, and *In the Shadow of To-morrow*, ch. 16.

of unmistakable play-features. One of my pupils has recently worked up my observations on this subject into a thesis on parliamentary eloquence in France and England, showing how, ever since the end of the eighteenth century, debates in the House of Commons have been conducted according to the rules of a game and in the true play-spirit. Personal rivalries are always at work, keeping up a continual match between the players whose object is to checkmate one another, but without prejudice to the interests of the country which they serve with all seriousness. The mood and manners of parliamentary democracy were, until recently, those of fair play both in England and in the countries that had adopted the English model with some felicity. The spirit of fellowship would allow the bitterest opponents a friendly chat even after the most virulent debate. It was in this style that the "Gentleman's Agreement" arose. Unhappily certain parties to it were not always aware of the duties implicit in the word gentleman. There can be no doubt that it is just this play-element that keeps parliamentary life healthy, at least in Great Britain, despite the abuse that has lately been heaped upon it. The elasticity of human relationships underlying the political machinery permits it to "play," thus easing tensions which would otherwise be unendurable or dangerous—for it is the decay of humour that kills. We need hardly add that this play-factor is present in the whole apparatus of elections.

In American politics it is even more evident. Long before the two-party system had reduced itself to two gigantic teams whose political differences were hardly discernible to an outsider, electioneering in America had developed into a kind of national sport. The presidential election of 1840 set the pace for all subsequent elections. The party then calling itself Whig had an excellent candidate, General Harrison of 1812 fame, but not platform. Fortune gave them something infinitely better, a symbol on which they rode to triumph: the log cabin which was the old warrior's modest abode during his retirement. Nomination by majority vote, i.e., by the loudest clamour, was inaugurated in the election of 1860 which brought Lincoln to power. The emotionality of American politics lies deep in the origins of the American nation itself: Americans have ever remained true to the rough and tumble of pioneer life. There is a great deal that is endearing in American politics, something naïve and spontaneous for which we look in vain in the dragoonings and drillings, or worse, of the contemporary European scene.

Though there may be abundant traces of play in domestic politics there would seem, at first sight, to be little opportunity for it in the field of international relationships. The fact, however, that these have touched the nadir of violence and precariousness does not in itself exclude the possibility of play. As we have seen from numerous examples, play can be cruel and bloody and, in addition, can often be false play. Any law-abiding community or community of States will have characteristics linking it in one way or another to a play-community. International law between States is maintained by the mutual recognition of certain principles which, in effect, operate like play-rules despite the fact that they may be founded in metaphysics. Were it otherwise there would be no need to lay down the *pacta sunt servanda* principle, which explicitly recognizes that the integrity of the system rests on a general willingness to keep to the rules. The moment that one or the other party withdraws from this tacit agreement the whole system of international law must, if only temporarily, collapse unless the remaining parties are strong enough to outlaw the "spoilsport."

The maintenance of international law has, at all stages, depended very largely on principles lying outside the strict domain of law, such as honour, decency, and good form. It is not altogether in vain that the European rules of warfare developed out of the code of honour proper to chivalry. International law tacitly assumed that a beaten Power would behave like a gentleman and a good loser, which unhappily it seldom did. It was a point of international decorum to declare your war officially before entering upon it, though the aggressor often neglected to comply with this awkward convention and began by seizing some outlying colony or the like. But it is true to say that until quite recently war was conceived as a noble game—the sport of kings—and that the absolutely binding character of its rules rested on, and still retained, some of the formal play-elements we found in full flower in archaic warfare.

A cant phrase in current German political literature speaks of the change from peace to war as "das Eintreten des Ernstfalles"—roughly, "the serious development of an emergency." In strictly military parlance, of course, the term is correct. Compared with the sham fighting of manoeuvres and drilling and training, real war is undoubtedly what seriousness is to play. But German political theorists mean something more. The term "Ernstfall" avows quite openly that foreign policy has not attained its full degree of seriousness, has not achieved its object or proved its efficiency, until the stage of actual hostilities is reached. The true relation betwen States is one of war. All diplomatic intercourse, insofar as it moves in the paths of negotation and agreement, is only a prelude to war or an interlude between two wars. This horrible creed is accepted and indeed professed by many. It is only logical that its adherents, who regard war and the preparations for it as the sole form of serious politics, should deny that war has any connection with the contest and hence with play. The agonistic factor, they tell us, may have been operative in the primitive stages of civilization, it was all very well then, but war nowadays is far above the competitiveness of mere savages. It is based on the "friend-foe principle." All "real" relationships between nations and States, so they say, are dominated by this ineluctable principle.[7] Any "other" group is always either your friend or your enemy. Enemy, of course, is not to be understood as *inimicus* or ἐχθρός, i.e., a person you hate, let alone a wicked person, but purely and simply as *hostis* or πολεμιος, i.e., the stranger or foreigner who is in your group's way. The theory refuses to regard the enemy even as a rival or adversary. He is merely in your way and is thus to be made away with. If ever anything in history has corresponded to this gross over-simplification of the idea of enmity, which reduces it to an almost mechanical relationship, it is precisely that primitive antagonism between phratries, clans or tribes where, as we saw, the play-element was hypertrophied and distorted. Civilization is supposed to have carried us beyond this stage. I know of no sadder or deeper fall from human reason than Schmitt's barbarous and pathetic delusion about the friend-foe principle. His inhuman cerebrations do not even hold water as a piece of formal logic. For it is not war that is serious, but peace. War and everything to do with it remains fast in the daemonic and magical bonds of play. Only by transcending that pitiable friend-foe relationship will mankind enter into the dignity of man's estate. Schmitt's brand of "seriousness" merely takes us back to the savage level.

Here the bewildering antithesis of play and seriousness presents itself once more. We have gradually become convinced that civilization is rooted in noble play and that, if it is to unfold in full dignity and style, it cannot afford to neglect the play-element. The observance of play-rules is nowhere more imperative than in the relations between countries and States. Once they are broken, society falls into barbarism and chaos. On the other hand we cannot deny that modern warfare has lapsed into the old agonistic attitude of playing at war for the sake of prestige and glory.

Now this is our difficulty: modern warfare has, on the face of it, lost all contact with play. States of the highest cultural pretensions withdraw from the comity of nations and shamelessly announce that "pacta non sunt servanda." By so doing they break the play-rules inherent in any system of international law. To that extent their playing at war, as we have called it, for the sake of prestige is not true play; it, so to speak, plays the play-concept of war false. In contemporary poli-

7. Carl Schmitt, *Der Begriff des Politischen*, Hamburg, 1933.

tics, based as they are on the utmost preparedness if not actual preparation for war, there would seem to be hardly any trace of the old play-attitude. The code of honour is flouted, the rules of the game are set aside, international law is broken, and all the ancient associations of war with ritual and religion are gone. Nevertheless the methods by which war-policies are conducted and war-preparations carried out still show abundant traces of the agonistic attitude as found in primitive society. Politics are and have always been something of a game of chance; we have only to think of the challenges, the provocations, the threats and denunciations to realize that war and the policies leading up to it are always, in the nature of things, a gamble, as Neville Chamberlain said in the first days of September 1939. Despite appearances to the contrary, therefore, war has not freed itself from the magic circle of play.

Does this mean that war is still a game, even for the aggressed, the persecuted, those who fight for their rights and their liberty? Here our gnawing doubt whether war is really play or earnest finds unequivocal answer. It is the *moral* content of an action that makes it serious. When the combat has an ethical value it ceases to be play. The way out of this vexing dilemma is only closed to those who deny the objective value and validity of ethical standards. Carl Schmitt's acceptance of the formula that war is the "serious development of an emergency" is therefore correct—but in a very different sense from that which he intended. His point of view is that of the aggressor who is not bound by ethical considerations. The fact remains that politics and war are deeply rooted in the primitive soil of culture played in and as contest. Only through an ethos that transcends the friend-foe relationship and recognizes a higher goal than the gratification of the self, the group or the nation will a political society pass beyond the "play" of war to true seriousness.

So that by a devious route we have reached the following conclusion: real civilization cannot exist in the absence of a certain play-element, for civilization presupposes limitation and mastery of the self, the ability not to confuse its own tendencies with the ultimate and highest goal, but to understand that it is enclosed within certain bounds freely accepted. Civilization will, in a sense, always be played according to certain rules, and true civilization will always demand fair play. Fair play is nothing less than good faith expressed in play terms. Hence the cheat or the spoil-sport shatters civilization itself. To be a sound culture-creating force this play-element must be pure. It must not consist in the darkening or debasing of standards set up by reason, faith or humanity.

It must not be a false seeming, a masking of political purposes behind the illusion of genuine play-forms. True play knows no propaganda; its aim is in itself, and its familiar spirit is happy inspiration.

In treating of our theme so far we have tried to keep to a play-concept which starts from the positive and generally recognized characteristics of play. We took play in its immediate everyday sense and tried to avoid the philosophical short-circuit that would assert all human action to be play. Now, at the end of our argument, this point of view awaits us and demands to be taken into account.

"Child's play was what he called all human opinions," says late Greek tradition of Heraclitus.[8] As a pendant to this lapidary saying let us quote at greater length the profound words of Plato which we introduced into our first chapter: "Though human affairs are not worthy of great seriousness it is yet necessary to be serious; happiness is another thing. . . . I say that a man must be serious with the serious, and not the other way about. God alone is worthy of supreme seriousness, but man is made God's plaything, and that is the best part of him. Therefore every man and woman should live life accordingly, and play the noblest games, and be of another mind from what they are at present. For they deem war a serious thing, though in war there is neither play nor culture worthy the name, which are the things *we* deem most serious. Hence all must live in peace as well as they possibly can. What, then, is the right way of living? Life must be lived as play, playing certain games, making sacrifices, singing and dancing, and then a man will be able to propitiate the gods, and defend himself against his enemies, and win in the contest." Thus "men will live according to Nature since in most respects they are puppets, yet having a small part in truth." To which Plato's companion rejoins: "You make humanity wholly bad for us, friend, if you say that." And Plato answers: "Forgive me. It was with my eyes on God and moved by Him that I spoke so. If you like, then, humanity is not wholly bad, but worthy of some consideration."[9]

The human mind can only disengage itself from the magic circle of play by turning towards the ultimate. Logical thinking does not go far enough. Surveying all the treasures of the mind and all the splendours of its achievements we shall still find, at the bottom of every serious judgement, something problematical left. In our heart of hearts we know that none of our pronouncements is absolutely conclusive. At that point, where our judgement begins to waver, the feeling that the

---

8. *Fragments,* 70.
9. *Laws,* 803-4; cf. also 685. Plato's words echo sombrely in Luther's mouth when he says: "All creatures are God's masks and mummeries" (Erlanger Ausgabe, xi, p. 115).

world is serious after all wavers with it. Instead of the old saw: "All is vanity," the more positive conclusion forces itself upon us that "all is play." A cheap metaphor, no doubt, mere impotence of the mind; yet it is the wisdom Plato arrived at when he called man the plaything of the gods. In singular imagery the thought comes back again in the *Book of Proverbs,* where Wisdom says: "The Lord possessed me in the beginning of his ways, before he made any thing from the beginning. I was set up from eternity, and of old before the earth was made . . . I was with him forming all things: and was delighted every day, playing before him at all times; playing in the world. And my delights were to be with children of men."[10]

Whenever we are seized with vertigo at the ceaseless shuttlings and spinnings in our mind of the thought: What is play? What is serious? we shall find the fixed, unmoving point that logic denies us, once more in the sphere of ethics. Play, we began by saying, lies outside morals. In itself it is neither good nor bad. But if we have to decide whether an action to which our will impels us is a serious duty or is licit as play, our moral conscience will at once provide the touchstone. As soon as truth and justice, compassion and forgiveness have part in our resolve to act, our anxious question loses all meaning. One drop of pity is enough to lift our doing beyond intellectual distinctions. Springing as it does from a belief in justice and divine grace, conscience, which is moral awareness, will always whelm the question that eludes and deludes us to the end, in a lasting silence.

10. viii, 22-3, 30-1. This is the Douay translation, based on the Vulgate. The text of the English A.V. and R.V. does not bring out the idea of "play."

THE INTERDEPENDENCE OF SPORT
AND CULTURE

GÜNTHER LÜSCHEN

INTRODUCTION

Sport is a rational, playful activity in interaction, which is extrinsically rewarded. The more it is rewarded, the more it tends to be work; the less, the more it tends to be play. If we describe it in an action system frame of reference, this activity depends on the organic, personality, social, and cultural systems. By tradition, physical education has tried to explain this action system largely on the grounds of the organic system, and sometimes making reference to the personality system. Only on rare occasions has it been approached systematically from the social and cultural systems as well. Yet it seems obvious that any action going on in this system ought to be explained with reference to all of the subsystems of the action system.

Even such a simple motor activity as walking is more than a matter of organic processes initiated by the personality system. It is determined by the social and cultural systems as well, as is most evident in the way the Israelians from the Yemen walk. Since in their former society in the Yemen, the Jews were the outcasts, and every Yemenite could feel free to hit a Jew (whenever he could get hold of one), the Yemenitic Jew would always run in order to escape this oppression. This way of walking finally became an integrated pattern of his culture. And though the environment in Israel no longer is hostile to him, the Yemenitic Israelite still carries this pattern with him as part of his culture and walks in a shy and hasty way. This example shows in addition that the different

Gunther Luschen, "The Interdependence of Sport and Culture," *International Review of Sport Sociology* 2 (1967): 27-141. Reprinted by permission.

subsystems of action are not independent from one another; they are structurally related. Thus, in dealing with the cultural system of sport and its interdependence with general culture, we will not always be able to explain the culture of sport and that of its environment in terms of the cultural system, and therefore should refer as well to the social and personality system to describe and explain what we call culture. It was Radcliffe-Brown who stressed the point that culture should be explained through its social structure. Furthermore, one should discuss the function of a unit within general culture, as well as cultural process and change (1952).

CONCEPTS OF CULTURE AND REVIEW OF RESULTS

Culture as a concept does not refer to behavior itself. It deals with those patterns and abstractions that underlie behavior or are the result of it. Thus culture exists of cognitive elements which grow out of everyday or scientific experience. It consists of beliefs, values, norms, and of signs that include symbols of verbal as well as non-verbal communication (cf., Johnson, 1960).

Anthropologists have sometimes held a broader view of culture and given more attention to the material results of human behavior. Leslie White in a critique of the above-stated concept of culture has called for more attention to "acts, thoughts and things dependent upon symboling." These would include not only the study of the above-mentioned elements, but also those of art, tools, machines, fetishes, etc. (1959). As attractive as White's critique may be, especially for cultural anthropology as an independent science, this approach as related to the cultural study of sport has led more to mere curiosity about things than to theoretical insights. This methodological approach has also dealt more with the cultural diffusion of sport and games than with the social structure of which they are a part. For decades we have learned about all types of games in all types of societies (especially primitive ones), which may well lead to the conclusion that we know more about the games and sports displayed by some Polynesian tribe than those of our own children and ancestors. For an understanding of sport it is less important to find the same games in different cultures as Tylor did (1896). It is more important to analyze, for example, the different meaning of baseball in the United States and Lybia, which in the one culture has at least latent ritualistic functions, while it has also economic functions in the other (Gini, 1939).

Another concept of culture, mainly held in Central Europe, has almost led to the same results for sport. In this concept "higher" culture was separated from civilization and expressed itself significantly in the arts and sciences. On the basis of values attributed to sport *a priori*, it was related either to "Zivilisation" or to Kultur. Physical educationalists through Huizinga's theory on the origin of culture in play saw in the latter approach their main support (1955). Thus defining sport as a special form of play, physical educationalists felt safe in their implicit attempt to justify sport for educational purposes. Yet Huizinga's theory has not only been criticized on the basis of ethnological findings, (c.f., Jensen, 1942), but he himself was very critical about the play element in sport. Those that believed in the role of sport within higher culture were hardly able to prove their hypothesis. So, as recently as Rene Maheu (1962), they often expressed their hope that sport in the future would contribute to "Kultur."

One can hardly deny that sport has indeed some impact on "higher" culture, as may be shown by symbolic elements from sport to be found in script and language. In an analysis of the cultural meaning of the ballgame of the Aztecs and Maya, Krickeberg found that in their script there were elements related to this game. The symbol for movement, for example, was identical with the I-shape of the ball court (1948). "To get (take) a rain check" refers to baseball, but has now become in American English symbolic for any situation where you get another chance. "That's not cricket" refers to a dishonest procedure in everyday life. And though German is not as idiomatic as English, it contains elements which originated in sport and games as well. "Katzbalgerei," and the phrase "sich gegenseitig die Bälle zuspielen," refer to a game which today is still known in the Netherlands as "Kaatsen" and perhaps appears in the New York children's game of one-o-cat. As did football in Shakespeare's "King Lear," so appeared this game and its terminology in the 16th century poetry of J. G. Fischart.

How weak these relationships of sport indeed are to "higher" culture may be shown by the relatively unsuccessful attempts to establish through special contests in modern Olympics, a relationship between sport and the arts. Sport only rarely expresses itself in the material aspects of culture. It is what I would like to call a momentary activity. Just from a certain level on, an event may have its appearance on such a short range cultural element as the sports page of the next day's newspaper. This appearance of sport in the media of mass communication, in language, poetry, and the arts is significant for the overall meaning of sport within society, but these manifestations tell us little about sport itself and its interdependence with general culture as we define it.

It may also be interesting to discuss cognitive elements such as scientific insight coming out of sport. Also religious beliefs and ritual found in sport would be an interesting point of analysis. Yet after showing how sport is indeed bound to society and structured by general culture, we will mainly discuss our problem on the level of cultural values and their related social structure.

SPORT AS PART OF CULTURE AND SOCIETY

That sport is structurally related to culture and society has sometimes been questioned. Yet it is quite easy to show how strong this relationship is. Sport is indeed an expression of that socio-cultural system in which it occurs. David Riesman and Reuel Denney describe how American football was changed through the American culture from rugby to a completely different game. It is now well integrated and quite obviously shows in its vigor, hard contact and a greater centrality on the individual the basic traits of the culture of American society (1954).

On the level of the so-called primitive societies we see the same dependence of sport and games on culture and its underlying social structure. The Hopi Indians had 16 different terms for foot races which nearly all referred to one aspect of the social organization of that tribe (Culin, 1907). A recent socio-historical study on three Illinois subcultures finds the same close relationship between socio-cultural system and sport (Hill, 1966). And Käte Hye-Kerkdal outlines the tight structural relation between the log-races of the tribe of the Timbira in Brazil and their socio-cultural system. This ritualistic competition between two teams has symbolic meaning for nearly every aspect of the dual organization of this tribe. It refers to all kinds of religious and social polarities and is so strongly imbedded in this religious-dominated system that winning or losing does not have any effect on the status of the team or individual, nor are there any other extrinsic rewards. Yet these races are performed vigorously and with effort (1956).

Now that we have proven that there is a structural relationship between sport and culture, the first question is that of sport's dependency on culture. What factors make for the appearance of sport? Or more specifically, what are the underlying cultural values?

CULTURE VALUES AND SPORT

By values we mean those general orientations in a socio-cultural system that are not always obvious to its members, but are implicit in actual behavior. On the level of the personality system they are expressed partly in attitudes. Values should be separated from norms which are derived from values and are actual rules for behavior. For instance, health is a high value in the American culture, as it seems to be in all young cultures, while death is higher in the hierarchy of values in old cultures like India (Parsons, 1960). On this continuum we may explain why sport as an expression of the evaluation of health is more important in American than in Indian society. The whole emphasis on physical fitness in the United States may well be explained by this background, and the norm "run for your life" is directly related to it.

Sport, Industrialization and Technology

In comparing the uneven distribution and performance level of sport all over the world, one widely accepted hypothesis is that sport is an offspring of technology and industrialization. The strong emphasis on sport in industrialized societies seems to show that industrialization and technology are indeed a basis for sport. This would be a late confirmation of Ogburn's theory of social change, as well as of Marxian theory that society and its structure depend on its economic basis. However, there are quite a number of inconsistencies. Not all sport-oriented societies or societal subsystems show a relation to technology and industrialization, and historically games and sport have been shown to have existence prior to industrialization. Yet it can hardly be denied that certain conditions in the later process of industrialization have promoted sport, and technology has at least its parallels in modern sport. The above-stated hypothesis may, despite its obvious limitations, lead us to the independent variables.

Sport, A Protestant Subculture?

In an investigation that because of its methodological procedure turned out to be a profound critique of Marxian materialism, Max Weber studied the interrelationship of what he called "The Protestant Ethic and the Spirit of Capitalism." (1920). This investigation about the underlying values of capitalism in Western societies quoted data on the over-representation of Protestants in institutions of higher learning, their preference for industrial and commercial occupations and professions and the stronger trend towards capitalism in Protestant-dominated countries (most obvious in the United States). Weber found not the material basis but Protestant culture, with achievement of worldly success and asceticism held as the basic values, caused industrialization and capitalism. In accordance with the Calvinistic belief in predestination, the Protestant felt that he was blessed by God once he had achieved success. Thus, need for achievement became an integrated part of his personality and a basic value in Protestantism. Together with the value of asceticism this led to the accumulation of wealth and to Western capitalism. If we turn to sport, we find the same values of achievement and asceticism. Even the puritans, generally opposed to a leisurely life, could therefore justify sport as physical activity that contributed to health (cf., McIntosh, 1963). Today we find significance for this relationship in the YMCA, in a group like the American Fellowship of Christian Athletes, and also in the Protestant minister who in Helsinki became an Olympic medal winner in the pole vault. He showed the consistency between Protestantism and sport in his prayer right after his Olympic winning vault. Max Weber's findings about the relationship between the Protestant ethic and the spirit of capitalism may thus well be extended to the "spirit" of sport. Not only Weber was aware of this relationship, but also Thorstein Veblen who described the parallels in religious and sport ritual (1899).

The relationship between sport and Protestantism is not only to be observed in the emphasis on sport in the Scandinavian and other Protestant countries. A rough compilation of the probable religious preference of Olympic medal winners on the basis of the percentage of different religious groups in their countries also shows the dominance of Protestantism up to 1960. Protestantism accounted for more than 50 per cent of the medal winners, while its ratio among the world population is less than 8 per cent (Lüschen, 1962). Furthermore, in 1958 a survey of young athletes in West Germany by Lüschen showed the following distribution according to religious preference:

	Whole Population West Germany	Sport Club Members 15-25	Track Swimming	High Achievers Track/ Swimming
Protestants	52%	60%	67%	73%
Catholics	44%	37%	31%	26%
Others	4%	3%	2%	1%
n =	universe	1,880	366	111

These figures indicate the overrepresentation of Protestants in German sport. Moreover, they indicate a higher percentage in individual sports, and an even higher percentage of Protestants among those that have achieved a higher level of performance. Thus it may be concluded that there is a correlation between Protestantism and sport and the culture of both. This was obvious for individual sports, but less for team sports where in the German sample Catholics appeared quite often. Since in Catholicism collectivity is highly regarded, this inconsistency is to be explained by the value of collectivity in team sports. It is consistent with this hypothesis that Catholic Notre Dame University has been one of the innovators of football in America. At present, it is a leading institution in this discipline. And internationally Catholic-dominated South America is overall rather poor in individual sports, but outstanding in team sports like soccer and basketball.

This result on the overall, strong relationship between sport and Protestantism is, despite support by data, theoretically insufficient. As was the case with sport in its relationship to industrialization, there are many exceptions. The high achievement in sport of the Russians, the Poles, the Japanese, the Mandan Indians, the Sikhs in India, or the Watusi in Africa cannot be related to Protestantism though in Japanese Zen-Buddhism there are parallels.

The Centrality of the Achievement-Value

Since again Protestantism cannot be specifically identified as being the independent variable, we may hypothesize that there is a more general system of values as the basis for Protestantism, capitalism and sport. In his critique of Max Weber, McClelland has considered the ethic of Protestantism as a special case of the general achievement orientation of a system, this being the independent variable. Achievement orientation (or, as he puts it on the personality-system-level, need-achievement) precedes all periods of high cultural achievement in ancient Greece, in the Protestant Reformation, in modern industrialism and, as we may conclude, in modern sport. He referred in his analysis also to the related social structure of the achievement value (such as family organization), which should also be studied in relationship to sport.

If we turn again to the cross-cultural comparison of those systems that participate and perform strongly in sport, we find that in all of these societies achievement-orientation is basic. In Russia this value is expressed in the norm that social status should depend only on achievement. The Sikhs and the Watusi are both minority groups in their environment. In order to keep their position, they have to achieve more than the other members of the societies they live in. The Japanese (Bellah, 1957) and the Mandan Indians (McClelland, 1961) also place a heavy emphasis on achievement.

Similar results appear in cross-cultural investigations of different types of games as related to basic orientations in the process of socialization. Roberts and Sutton-Smith find in a secondary analysis of the Human Relation Area Files of G. P. Murdock that games of chance are related to societies that emphasize routine responsibility in the socialization process. Games of strategy are found in societies where obedience, games of physical skill in those where achievement is stressed (1963). Individual sports would mainly qualify as games of physical skill and again show achievement as their basic cultural value. Team sports as well are games of strategy. Their relation to training of obedience would support exactly what we called earlier the value of collectivity.

It remains an open question, for further research into the value structure of sport, as to which other values are related to this system. It is to be expected that the structure of values will be more complex than it appears on the basis of our limited insight now. Roberts and Sutton-Smith briefly remark that games of physical skill are related to occupational groups that exert power over others (1963). Thus, power orientation may be another value supporting sport. This would cross-culturally be consistent with power-oriented political systems that strongly emphasize sport. Here we could refer to countries like Russia or the United States, as well as to a tribe like the Mandan Indians.

The Culture of Societal Subsystems and Its Relation to Sport

Within a society we find subsystems that have their own subculture, which will be another condition for sport. The female role in modern societies still depends on a culture that stresses obedience as the main value-orientation, while the male culture is strongly oriented towards achievement. Thus we find a disproportionately high participation of men in sport which in most of the disciplines is a male culture. One of the most male-oriented sports, however, is pool, a game supported mainly by the subculture of the bachelor. This has, with the general change in the number of people marrying, lost its main supporting culture (Polsky, 1967).

Another subsystem which in its culture shows a strong relationship to sport is that of the adolescent age group (cf. Coleman, 1961). Sport is dependent more on the culture of the adolescent than on that of any other age group. Helanko raises the point, referring to his studies of boys' gangs in Turku, that sport has its origin in the gang-age and in boys' gangs. The fact that there are no rules for early sports to be found is seen as one of the supporting factors (1957). Generally speaking, achievement is again more central as a value in adolescence and early adulthood than later, where the main response to sport goes not so much towards achievement but towards values of health and fitness.

The different social classes have a culture of their own. The greatest emphasis on achievement, and thus the highest sport participation, is to be found in the upper-middle class. It is considerably less important in the lower class where routine responsibility is valued. The notion that there is no way to gain higher status accounts for the high regard for games of chance or those sports where one may just have a lucky punch, as in boxing (Weinberg and Arond, 1952). Loy has related the different types of games and the passive and active participation in sport to different modes of adaptation and to the members of social classes (1966). His theoretical analysis as to "innovation" found in the lower class, ritualism in the lower-middle class and conformity in the upper-middle class is supported by data (cf. Lüschen, 1963; Loy, 1969) that show the same ways of adaptation in sport. However, in responding to the social class system and its culture as related to sport one should have in mind that class determined behavior may not follow the traditional class lines in sport. Sport may indeed show or promote new orientations in the class system (Kunz and Lüschen, 1966).

Finally, sport is organized within, or relates to different associations whose cultures sometime have a profound influence on sport itself. This is especially true for physical education in schools where, with the same skills and rules, we may find a completely different culture as compared to sport in the military establishment. And while intercollegiate and interscholastic athletics are overall a surprisingly well integrated subculture within American schools and universities, the different values held by an educational (the school or university) and a solely success-oriented unit (the team) may well lead to strong value conflicts. This could result in a complete separation of school and athletics.

FUNCTIONS AND DYSFUNCTIONS

After we have found achievement, asceticism in individual sports, obedience (collectivity) in team sports, and exertion of power, the basic value orientations that give structure to this activity, we may then proceed to the second question: How does sport influence the socio-cultural system at large? Though we have little evidence through research, we may on the basis of structural-functional methodology be able to outline the basic functions of sport for pattern maintenance, integration, adaptation and goal attainment.

The Functions of Sport Within Culture and Society

As in the case of the Timbria, Hye-Kerkdal states that the basic values of that culture were learned through the log-race. Furthermore, the participants were functionally integrated into the social system (1956). Thus, we may hypothesize that the main functions of sport are pattern maintenance and integration.

Since sport implies (as we saw) basic cultural values, it has the potential to pass these values on to its participants. We know from studies of the process of socialization that the exposure of children to competitive sport will cause these children to become achievement-motivated; the earlier this exposure occurs, the more achievement-motivated they become (Winterbottom, 1953). And the child's moral judgment may, for instance, be influenced through games such as marbles. Again, according to Piaget, the child not only becomes socialized to the rules but at a later age he also gets an insight into the underlying structure and function of the rules of a game, and thus into the structure and function of social norms and values as such (1965). Overall, from the level of primitive societies to modern societies, sport not only socializes to the system of values and norms but in primitive societies it socializes towards adult and warfare skills as well.

Since we mentioned that sport is also structured along such societal subsystems as different classes, males, urban areas, schools and communities, we should say it functions for integration of these systems as well as for the society at large. This is most obvious in spectator sports where the whole country or community identifies with its representatives in a contest. Thus, sport functions as a means of integration, not only for the actual participants, but also for the represented members of such a system.

Sport in modern societies may function for goal-attainment on the national polity level. In primitive societies, sport functions for adaptation as well as goal-attainment since the sport skills of swimming, hunting and fishing are used to supply food and mere survival.

Possible Dysfunctions of Sport and Social Control

A question should be raised at this point asking whether sport is dysfunctional for culture and society as well. Th. W. Adorno called sport an area of unfreedom ("ein Bereich der Unfreiheit"), (1957) in which he obviously referred to the differentiated code of rules which earlier led Huizinga to his statement that excluded sport from play (1955). Both seem to overlook what Piaget called the reciprocity and mutual agreement on which such rules rest (1965). And they may also be considered as an expression of a highly structured system.

Another dysfunctional element for culture and for the sport system itself could be the centrality of achievement. It has such a high rank in the hierarchy of values of sport that, by definition, the actual objective performance of a member of this system will decide the status he gets. In the core of sport, in the contest on the sports field, there is only achieved status. It seems that there is no other system or any societal subsystem, with the exception of combat, where achievement ranks that high. It may create conflict once this value-orientation is imposed on the whole culture, and it may create conflict within the system of sport itself since its members bring other values into this system as well. M. Mead in an investigation of competition and cooperation (the first concept of which is related to achievement) of primitive peoples, however, finds that there seems to be no society where one of these principles existed alone (1946). And on the micro-sociological level, small groups seem to control this value by discriminating against those that deviate from the group norm of a fair performance (Roethlisberger and Dickson, 1939). Thus, one would notice some kind of a mechanism built into a social system like a group that keeps it in a state of balance. Exactly this seems to happen within sport where the sporting groups themselves and their differentiated organizational and institutional environment exert social control on those participants achieving beyond a certain level.

In a survey of sport club members in Germany, it was found that the norms expressed for an athlete's behavior referred surprisingly less to the achievement value but more often to a value of affiliation, which is to be defined as a positive orientation towards other group members or opponents. Fair play was the one mentioned most frequently. The value of affiliation expressed by the respondents was found more in normative statements the higher their level of performance. On the basis of the hypothesized mechanism of social control, they are under stronger pressure to affiliate with others (Lüschen, 1963). This may explain (on the basis of this structural relationship) why in the culture of sport we find not only the value of achievement but also that of fair play and other affiliative orientations.

However, achievement and affiliation may not necessarily be related. It depends on the amount of social control imposed on sport from the internal as well as external system, whether this relationship will be strong or weak. In professional boxing these controls are very weak; while in golf with the handicap rule, they seem to be comparatively strong (Lüschen, 1970).

How much this pattern would influence the culture as such is an open question. Yet it seems not so mis-oriented as often thought when Oetinger stated that sport would provide a good model for political partnership (1954). We may on the basis of our findings hypothesize that also on the political level the amount of social control will decide whether two or more systems will coexist or not.

Sport and Socio-Cultural Change

After we have discussed the culture and underlying social structure of sport and its function, we are left with Radcliffe-Brown's third programmatic point—that of social and cultural change. We know little about the role of sport in socio-cultural change, though we hypothesized earlier that it may have a function of innovation, or at least structural relationship to changes in the system of social classes. Sport has also functioned as an initiator for the diffusion of technical inventions, such as the bicycle or the automobile (Kroeber, 1963). The same holds true to a degree for conduct in regard to fashion and a healthy life. Typically, this question of change has been highly neglected so far.

Sport and Cultural Evolution

If we finally try to explain the different cross-cultural appearance of sport on the basis of an evolutionary theory, it is hard to justify on the basis of our present knowledge about the appearance of sport that there are such things as primitive and developed cultures of sport. The Mandan Indians had a highly developed sport culture, the Australian aboriginals, as perhaps the most primitive people known to us today, know quite a variety of recreational activities and physical skills, and the variety of competitive games in Europe and America in the past was perhaps richer than today.

An evolution can only be seen on a vertical level which on the one hand shows in a state of mechanic solidarity rather simple rules in sport and games, while in a state of organic solidarity, as in modern industrialized societies, the code of rules and the structure of games get more differentiated.

What we may furthermore state is that, on the level of primitive cultures, sport's function is universal, often religious, collectively oriented, and in the training of skills, representative and related to adult and warfare skills; while modern sport's function may be called specific for pattern maintenance and integration, is individual oriented and non-representative in the training of skills. The rewards are more intrinsic in primitive cultures, while they are more extrinsic in the sport of modern cultures. Thus, referring to our definition at the beginning, one may well differentiate between physical and recreational activities of primitive cultures and sport in modern cultures (c.f. Damm, 1960).

SUMMARY AND CONCLUSION

The interdependence of sport and culture, up to now mainly outlined on the basis of sport's contribution to higher culture (Kultur), was discussed on sport's relation to culture with the emphasis on values, sport's function for the socio-cultural system and its relation to change and evolution.

The system of sport, an integrated part of the socio-cultural system, seems to depend on the industrialized, technological or Protestant religious system. Yet cross-culturally it appears that these systems as intermediate variables are just special cases of a more general system. This is determined for sport by the achievement-value, a value of collectivity and supposedly power orientation. On the basis of these cultural value orientations one may explain the uneven distribution of sport as such, and of team sports versus individual sports in certain socio-cultural systems.

Sport's function for a socio-cultural system can mainly be seen for pattern maintenance and integration, in modern polity dominated societies as well for goal attainment. In primitive cultures it is universal and thus functions for adaptation as well.

Though a relation of sport to social change is obvious (sport fulfills a certain role for innovation), this neglected question of social change needs more careful investigation. Evolutionary theories applied to sport need more study as well; this might contribute to evolutionary theories as such. It appears that physical activity on the level of "primitive" cultures should be kept apart from sport in modern cultures since meaning and manifest functions are as universal on the one level as they are specific and segmentary on the other.

RELATED LITERATURE

Adorno, T. W. *Prismen*. Frankfurt, 1957.
Bellah, R. N. *Tokugawa Religion: The Values of Pre-Industrial Japan*. Glencoe, Ill., 1957.
Coleman, J. S. *The Adolescent Society*. Glencoe, Ill., 1961.
Culin, S. *Games of the North American Indians*. 24th Report, Bureau of American Ethnology, Washington, D. C., 1907.
Damm, H. "Vom Wesen sogenannter Leibesübungen bei Naturvölkern." *Studium Generale* 13 (1960): 3-10.
Gini, C. "Rural ritual games in Lybia." *Rural Sociology* 4 (1939): 283-299.
Helanko, R. "Sports and socialization." *Acta Sociologica* 2 (1957): 229-240.
Hill, P. J. A cultural history of frontier sport in Illinois 1673-1820. Unpub. Ph.D. Dissertation, University of Illinois, 1966.
Huizinga, J. *Homo Ludens*. Boston, 1955.
Hye-Kerkdal, K. Wettkampfspiel und Dualorganisation bei den Timbira Brasiliens. J. Haekel, ed. *Die Wiener Schule der Völkerkunde*. Wein, 1956: 504-533.
Jensen, A. E. "Spiel und Ergriffenheit." *Paideuma* 2 (1942): 124-139.
Krickeberg, W. "Das mittelamerikanische Ballspiel und seine teligiöse Symbolik." *Paideuma* 3 (1948): 118-190.
Kroeber, A. L. *Anthropology*. New York, 1963.
Kunz, G. and Lüschen, G. Leisure and social stratification. Paper at *International Congress for Sociology*. Evian, France, 1966.

Loy, J. W. Sport and social structure. Paper at the *AAHPER Convention*. Chicago, 1966.

Lüschen, G. "Der Leistungssport in seiner Abhangigkeit vom sozio-kulturellen System." *Zentralblatt für Arbeitswissenschaft* 16 (1962): 186-190.

———. "Soziale Schichtung und soziale Mobilität." *Kölner Zeitschrift für Soziologie und Sozialpsychologie* 15 (1963): 74-93.

———. Leistungsorientierung und ihr Finfluss auf das soziale und personale System. In Lüschen, G. ed., *Kleingruppenforschung und Gruppe im Sport*. Köln, 1966: 209-223.

———. "Cooperation, association and contest." *Journal of Conflict Resolution*, 14, 1970 (forthcoming).

Maheu, R. "Sport and culture." *International Journal of Adult and Youth Education* 14 (1962): 169-178.

McClelland, D. C. *The Achieving Society*. New York, 1961.

McIntosh, P. C. *Sport and Society*. London, 1963.

Mead, M. *Competition and Cooperation Among Primitive Peoples*. Berkeley, 1946.

Oetinger, F. *Partnerschaft*. Stuttgart, 1954.

Parsons, T. *Societies*. Englewood-Cliffs, N.Y., 1966.

———. "Toward a healthy maturity." *Journal of Health and Human Behavior* 1 (1960): 163-173.

Piaget, J. *The Moral Judgment of the Child*. New York, 1965.

Polsky, N. "Poolrooms and poolplayers." *Trans-action* 4 (1967): 32-40.

Radcliffe-Brown, A. R. *Structure and Function in Primitive Society*. Glencoe, Ill., 1952.

Riesman, D. and Denney, R. Football in America. Riesman, D., ed. *Individualism Reconsidered*. Glencoe, Ill., 1954: 242-251.

Roberts, J. M. and Sutton-Smith, B. "Child training and game involvement." *Ethnology* 1 (1962): 166-185.

Roethlisberger, F. J. and Dickson, W. J. *Management and the Worker*. Cambridge, Mass., 1939.

Stumpf, F. and Cozens, F. W. "Some aspects of the role of games, sports and recreational activities in the culture of primitive peoples." *Research Quarterly* 18 (1947): 198-218, and 20 (1949): 2-30.

Sutton-Smith, B. Roberts, J. M. and Kozelka, R. M. "Game involvement in adults." *Journal of Social Psychology* 60 (1963): 15-30.

Tylor, F. B. "On American lot-games." *Internationales Archiv für Ethnographie* 9 (1896 supplement): 55-67.

Veblen, T. *The Theory of the Leisure Class*. Chicago, 1899.

Weber, M. *Gesammelte Aufsätze zur Religionssoziologie*. Tübingen, 1920, I.

Weinberg, S. K. and Arond, R. "The occupational culture of the boxer." *American Journal of Sociology* 57 (1952): 460-463.

White, L. "The concept of culture." *American Anthropologist* 61 (1959): 227-251.

Winterbottom, M. R. The relation of childhood training in independence to achievement motivation. Unpub. Ph.D. Dissertation, Univ. of Michigan, 1953.

THEORIES OF WHY AND HOW

PETER C. MCINTOSH

Sport has always flourished in civilized societies even when the environment has not been favourable. Under the Roman Empire the professional athletes, tightly organized in their guilds and unions, converted the great stadia from Nîmes to Antioch into "closed shops," yet informal play and sport still persisted at a lower level. When monasticism thrust a repressive asceticism upon Christendom sport remained a solace and a joy to villagers and townsmen and even, on occasion, to monks. Calvinism and Puritanism in their extreme forms were unable to prevent ordinary people from committing the sin of indulging in sport. While the people played, philosophers and educationists examined the contribution that physical activities and training might make to the development of society and of the individual. Until the twentieth century, however, few attempts were made to examine why people played or how sportsmen achieved their results. Only recently has the phenomenon of sport and sporting performance been analysed by social scientists, physiologists, psychologists, physicists and mathematicians.

Some of the first investigations were concerned with play itself. The fact that animals, children and grown-ups all play excited the interest of researchers. Numerous and various attempts were made to define or describe the biological function of play. The discharge of superfluous vital energy, abreaction—an outlet for harmful impulses—wish-fulfillment, satisfaction of the imitative instinct, a form of training for the more serious side of life, satisfaction of an innate urge to dominate, these roles were ascribed to play as a feature of human existence.

In so far as sport is playful the roles could also be transferred to it as an individual and social phenomenon. All these psychological or biological theories of play made a fundamental assumption that play was a means to an end, that it had some biological purpose, and was ultimately determined by something that was not play. In the past, many, indeed most, philosophers and educationists had justified sport as a means to an end and few had seen it as self-justified, so now biologists and psychologists were making a similar assumption about play. J. Huizinga in the 1930s pointed to the fact that all such theories could only offer partial solutions to the problems which they set out to solve, because they left almost untouched the questions what play was in itself and what it meant for the player. In a book entitled *Homo Ludens* he set out to answer these questions and "to show that genuine, pure play is one of the main bases of civilization."[1]

Huizinga's concept of play was succinct. He recognized that not every language could have hit on the same concept and found a single word for it. He took, therefore, the concept corresponding to the English word *play* and defined it as follows—

> play is a voluntary activity or occupation executed within fixed limits of time and place according to rules freely accepted but absolutely binding, having its aim in itself and accompanied by a feeling of tension, joy and the consciousness that it is "different" from "ordinary life."

Huizinga claimed that this definition embraced play in animals, children and grown-ups, games of strength and skill, inventing-games, guessing-games, games of chance as well as exhibitions and performances of all kinds. It would also embrace dancing, even in its free forms and such non-competitive sports as hunting, and sports of adventure such as climbing, and crossing the Atlantic alone in a thirteen-ton yacht. When the etymology of the English word play is considered its relevance to adventure sports is even more obvious. *Play* comes from the Anglo-Saxon *plega*, or verb *plegan*. The oldest meaning of these words is "to vouch or stand guarantee for, to take a risk, to expose oneself to danger for someone or something." The words *pledge* and *plight* are both etymologically connected with *play*.

Huizinga did not identify play with sport nor did he say that play was an essential element in sport by definition. He did maintain that play was a valuable ingredient in sport, so valuable that when sport lost this particular element it became divorced from culture and had little dignity or worth for mankind. The precise relationship of play to sport is a matter for argument but a closer examination of Huizinga's definition of play shows how much is lost from sport if play is extinguished or obscured.

Huizinga's definition lays down three conditions which apply to play. First is freedom. The player cannot be forced to participate without the activity changing its nature. To run round a track by command of military or civil authority in order to prove a certain degree of attainment of fitness causes the act of running to be no longer play. Compulsory games at school are only play when the intrinsic interest and challenge so dominate the players that the original obligation is forgotten. For a number of boys and girls this never happens. The particular activity may then be valuable as a form of physical education, but it is not play. The contempt of some adults for sport has undoubtedly orginated in the extinction of the play element in their physical education in childhood and adolescence.

The second condition is separateness. According to Huizinga the activity must be circumscribed with boundaries of time and space that are precise and fixed in advance. Such circumscription certainly applies to all competitive games and sports. The running track, the cricket pitch, the fencing piste, the slalom course, the chess-board all prescribe the area of play. The time factor is known to the competitors in advance. But what of some of the non-competitive sports, angling, mountaineering, hunting? The prescription of time and space is very indefinite and may be changed by those who take part during the course of their activity. In these sports the physical environment itself, the river or loch, the peak, the habitat of the quarry provide the limitations which in other sports have to be imposed by definitions of time and space.

The third condition is regulation, and this is more fundamental than the other two conditions. Conventions and rules of a sport suspend the ordinary rules of life and for the duration of the sport the new law is the only one which counts. Even the play of animals appears to be regulated by certain self-imposed regulations eliminating serious injury or death. In the sports of human beings the degree and complexity of regulation varies. It might be thought to be least complex in the play and the sports of children and most complex in the sports of adults. This is not necessarily so. Hopscotch is much more carefully regulated than mob football, which has been played for centuries by adults. However, the purpose of the regulations is to define the sphere in which the ordinary rules of life are suspended, to define the unreality of the sport. They also help to define the nature of the skill to be employed or the way in which chance may operate. Limitation to provide scope for skill is very well exemplified in the off-side laws of team ball-games. There is no rule which has done more to transform violent and brutish sports into games of grace and skill. As recently as 1829 it was recorded that a Frenchman passing through Derby and seeing a game of football remarked that if Englishmen called this playing it would be impossible to say what they would call fighting. Football and other games have undergone some refinement since then and there is now hardly one team ball-game which does not work under an off-side regulation. Even basket-ball, which for many years was played without such a rule, now has the so-called "three-second" rule which prevents a player waiting under the opponents' basket to receive a pass and put the ball in. In games of skill the regulations strictly limit the areas for the operation of chance, strength and skill. They also provide artificial obstacles for the exercise of skill and thereby enable players to obtain an utterly useless but definite result. In a sport such as mountaineering the environment provides the regulation, yet artificial regulation is sometimes wanted in addition in order to preserve the play element. In the 1930s in Britain there were sharp differences of opinion on the justification for using pitons on English rock cliffs, and again in the 1950s disputes arose whether it would be legitimate to use mortars to dislodge snow and ice during an ascent of Mount Everest. Even in mountaineering, then, regulation or convention is necessary for the separation and differentiation of sport from ordinary life.

In amplification of his definition of play Huizinga notes that society is more lenient to the cheat than to the spoil-sports for the spoil-sport shatters the play world itself. He robs play of its illusion, i.e. *in-lusio*.

Modern pharmaceutical research has led to a problem of cheating which is only superficially scientific but in reality philosophical. In the Olympic Games of 1960 the Danish cyclist Knud Jensen collapsed during the one-hundred-kilometer race and died later. It was established that he had taken a drug, Ronicol, which has the general effect of stimulating the circulation by dilating the blood-vessels. The effect of the drug, the exertion of a big race and the heat of the day combined to kill him. In the next year Toni Hiebeler and his three companions made the first ascent of the North Face of the Eiger. Hiebeler and his companions also used Ronicol to stave off frost-bite. The use of the drug may well have saved their lives as well as enabled them to reach the summit. Death or glory has always been the ultimate alternative in mountaineering and in some other sports and is not incompatible with the fundamental concept of sport or with the play element in sport. Death, of course, immediately shatters the illusion of unreality and if death or glory is the inevitable as it was in many gladiatorial combats in ancient Rome then indeed the combat is neither play nor sport.

The use of drugs in sport can be questioned philosophically but not medically. It would only destroy the basis of sport if it broke the conventions or regulations defining the area of unreality, and to decide such an issue is difficult. Regulations are deliberately framed and specific; conventions, which are sometimes more important than the rules, are often unconsciously accepted and are non-specific. Malice, anger and loss of temper are generally thought to destroy sport, but where mechanical aids are concerned convention is capricious. In athletics starting-blocks and spiked shoes have been accepted, but built-up heels for high jumpers have been rejected. In lacrosse the use of body protection in Canada and the United States and the rejection of it in England have led to the development of two essentially different games, neither one being less nor more a sport than the other.

Drugs have hitherto been thought of as unsporting because their effect was to impair performance and the only way to use them was to administer them to an opponent. Poor Abraham Wood inadvertently drank liquid laudanum received from pretended friends while he was contesting a pedestrian contest with Captain Barclay Allardice in 1807 and shortly afterwards had to resign the match. More recent products have been found to have positive rather than negative effects on performance and a different situation has, therefore, arisen. No serious attempt has yet been made to regulate the use of drugs for positive assistance. Already caffeine is widely used by professional cyclists and Varidase was used by boxers in the Olympic Games in 1960 to minimize the effects of bruising. Other sportsmen take other drugs, some to stimulate, and some to relax or induce sleep between two strenuous efforts. Pharmaceutical research has been rapid and spectacular. The American Medical Association has estimated on the basis of research at Harvard that amphetamine alone could improve the performance of runners by one and a half per cent and swimmers by one per cent. As the use of drugs becomes more and more a part of daily life so the governing bodies of sport will need to decide how to regulate their use and still maintain a satisfactory and acceptable area of competition or play where the ordinary rules of life are suspended. Until that is done it is impossible to decide whether, in Huizinga's terminology, the taker of drugs is a cheat, a spoil-sport or neither.

The second part of Huizinga's book sheds light upon the manifestation of play in culture as a whole, in law, in literature, poetry and drama, in art and in war. This does not concern us here, but consideration of Huizinga's definition of play has already led us towards differentiating sports in order to understand their essence more fully. Three problems of relationship present themselves: the first lies between unorganized play and organized sport, the second between games of skill and games of chance, and the third between competitive and non-competitive sport. These problems arising from Huizinga's work have been tackled by Roger Caillois.[2] In order to clarify the problems and offer solutions to them he devised his own classification which is presented schematically in Table I.

The table shows a horizontal classification to deal with the problem of relationship between unorganized play and organized sport and a vertical classification to deal with the other two problems, that is to say the relationship between games of skill and games of chance and between competitive and non-competitive sport.

TABLE 1
Caillois' Classification of Play

	AGON Competitions		ALEA Chance	MIMICRY Pretence	ILINI Vertigo
PAIDIA Noise Agitation Laughter Dance Hoop Solitaire Games of patience Crossword puzzles LUDUS	Races } not reg- Combats } ulated Athletics Boxing Fencing Football Checkers Chess		Comptines Heads or tails Betting Roulette Lotteries	Childish imitation Masks Costumes Theatre	Children's swings Merry-go- round Tetter- totter Waltz Outdoor sports Skiing Mountain- climbing

The horizontal classification attempts to deal with a problem which was left unsolved by Huizinga, namely how to account for the variation of the play element in different games and sports, and its variation within a single sport performed at different levels of competence. Huizinga ended his book with a sweeping condemnation of sport which is difficult to support. He maintained that in modern sport the old play factor had undergone almost complete atrophy. Increasing systematization and regimentation had led to the loss of the play quality and the neglect of playing for fun. The division between professional and amateur had led to a situation where the professionals were marked off as inferior in standing to true players but superior in capacity, a situation which had produced an inferiority complex in amateurs. "Between them they push sport further and further away from the play sphere proper until it becomes a thing *sui generis*: neither play nor earnest. In modern social life sport occupies a place alongside and apart from cultural process." Huizinga even added that sport no longer had any organic cultural process.

It might have been easier to accept Huizinga's analysis in 1938 than it is in 1963. It is easy to see the encroachment of the principle of commercial entertainment upon the sphere of playing for fun in professional sport at the highest level and even in some so-called amateur sport at the same level. The price which the best performers pay for success is the sacrifice of almost all, but not quite all, the spontaneity and play element. The winner of the British Open Golf Championship in 1961 and 1962, Arnold Palmer, claimed that in the final days of preparation for a big competition he must have complete freedom from care; that he must be free to play a round or not, and even abandon a round if he felt a lack of enthusiasm for it. Part of his recipe for success was to maintain a vestige of the play element right into the big competition.

Whatever may be said of the divorce of professional and commercial sport as entertainment from the concept of sport as play, it would be difficult to maintain in the 1960s that the part-timers in sport suffer an inferiority complex because of the superiority of the professionals any more than amateur dramatic performers or amateur musicians suffer from a psychological complex because of the existence of professional actors and musicians performing in commercial theatres or municipal concert halls. In the public parks, on the commons and village greens, in halls, squash courts and swimming-baths the play element is very much a feature of sport. Systematization and organization by themselves do not appear to destroy or undermine sport.

Caillois' graduation from *paidia* to *ludus* is an attempt to show a progressive formalization of play from the spontaneous activities of children to the organized play of adults. He does not thereby answer Huizinga's strictures on modern sport but he does suggest that formalization is not incompatible with playing for fun.

In his vertical classification Caillois distinguishes competitive sport (*agon*) from games of chance (*alea*), from play which is dramatic (*mimicry*) and from activities which seek the sensations of falling or centrifugal force, games in which "people have deliberately sought out the confusion that a slight giddiness provokes."

The distinction between games of skill and of chance is illuminating. The former "implies discipline and perseverance. It makes the champion rely solely on his own resources, encourages him to make the best possible use of them, and forces him to utilize them fairly and within fixed limits which, being the same for everyone, result in rendering the superiority of the winner indisputable." The latter, on the contrary, is "based on an inequality external to the player, over which he has not the slightest control . . . fate is the sole agent of victory, and where rivalry exists, victory means only that the winner was luckier than the loser." In short, a game of skill is a vindication of personal responsibility in an artificially contrived situation, a game of chance is a resignation of the will, a surrender to destiny also in an artificially contrived situation. This is true only of the two types of game in their extreme form. In bridge or poker reason and psychological insight are allowed to the player as a means of defence against the lot assigned to him by fate.

A comparable distinction can be seen within that group of activities which seek satisfaction in speed, giddiness, vertigo, or the subjection of the being to the risk of loss of equilibrium or to its actual loss. In the fairground switchback the abandonment is complete, but in the downhill ski run the exhiliration of speed and hazard is heightened by the awareness of skill and of power to control the forces of nature to a safe and successful completion of the run. In such a sport there is acceptance rather than abandonment of responsibility. Caillois' category of vertigo is thus seen not to be fundamental but to subdivide within his classification of competition and chance depending on whether resourcefulness or resignation is the dominant factor.

The vertical classification is least satisfactory in dealing with non-competitive sport. The predatory sports, hunting, shooting and fishing, are not mentioned at all, nor is swimming in its non-competitive form. Mountaineering and other similar outdoor sports appear in the category of "vertigo" as if the climber derived his satisfaction from a feeling of giddiness rather than from the exercise of skill. But vertigo may never be experienced during a climb which may still be intensely satisfying to the climber. Dancing, too, is unhappily divided between vertigo, which includes the waltz, and mimicry, which presumably includes various forms of expressive dance.

Close consideration of Caillois' category of competition (*agon*) shows that it is not wide enough. The essential feature of sport, as distinct from other realms in which the element of play is to be found—games of chance and dramatic or mimetic play—is the striving for superiority and this may take a personal or an impersonal form. The playful element in this striving means that victory is never complete and for all time and that defeat is never irreparable. The effort to conquer an opponent, the self or an environment in play and only in play gives to sport its peculiar satisfaction and its especial virtue in human life.

The desire for superiority in play is itself subdivisible. To prove oneself or one's team better than an opponent or an opposing team within prescribed limits is the aim and object of all competitive sport. The areas for the exercise of skill for the sportsman to prove himself or herself "better than" are many and variable. The running-track, the cricket field, the tennis court, the billiard table, the football pitch, the swimming-bath, the river estuary and many other locations allow sportsmen with different aptitudes and abilities either singly or in pairs or in larger groups or teams to strive for superiority in their chosen sphere of useless contest. These activities comprise a broad category of sport.

A second category comprises combat sports. Here again the aim of the contestant is to prove himself "better than" an opponent. The special feature of personal contact with the opponent either directly through limb and body or indirectly through foil, blade or single stick deserves a special category.

A third category might be called conquest sports. In these the challenge is provided not by an individual or group of opponents but by an environment or a situation. Mountaineering is the purest example of a conquest sport although on occasion even here the environment may be personified. It was reported that the comment of one of the party which made the first successful ascent of Mount Everest was "we knocked the bastard off." A more sensitive reaction to a successful climb was that of Mallory many years earlier. He lost his life on Everest in 1924. "Have we vanquished an enemy? None but ourselves. Have we gained success? That word means nothing here . . . We have achieved an ultimate satisfaction." For most of those who take up conquest sports the appeal is just the impersonal nature of the challenge. Swimming, cycling, hiking, camping and many other activities offer opportunities for conquest sports. Much educational gymnastics, which is non-competitive, makes its appeal as a conquest sport.

There is a fourth category of physical activity which is not sport but which needs to be considered here because of affinity with it. In this type of activity the object is not to be "better than" but to express or communicate ideas and feelings using and enjoying the movements and sensations of the body in the process. Dance, dance drama, eurhythmics and some systems of gymnastics such as those developed by Medau or Idla fall into this category.

The classification of sport here given depends on the motive and the nature of the satisfaction which the sport gives, not upon the activity itself. Swimming when it is not competitive may well be a conquest nature of the satisfaction which the sport gives, not upon the activity sport. The environment of water has to be conquered by the would-be swimmer. It may even become an expressive activity when it takes the form of synchronized swimming and is done to a musical accompaniment. On the other hand mountaineering on occasions becomes competitive and the first ascent of the Matterhorn by Whymper and his party with its tragic ending became just that. Even dancing may become a competitive sport when prizes are given for the best troupe or group in a dance festival. Some sports, even while remaining competitive, may make their appeal to a particular individual for aesthetic rather than competitive reasons but such an individual is unlikely to be successful in the toughest contests. An American high jumper once said to his inferior English opponent: "Sure I like your style but I prefer my height." Many players feel in the midst of their vigorous activity that they are expressing their personality. Indeed, all sport is expressive in this sense, yet in competitive sport it is nevertheless true that the dominant object is to be "better than." In sport and in dance human motives are never simple but it seems justifiable to postulate dominant desires and corresponding satisfactions.

There may well be a sex link with the classification given above, with women being attracted more by the fourth category of expressive activities and men more often deriving satisfaction from sports in the first two categories. There are many good women games players and many men who are excellent dancers, yet the vast following of women for "keep fit" classes in Britain and for other similar systems of movement in other countries suggests that they find particular satisfaction in release of tensions and expression of feeling through rhythmical movement. Men on the other hand clearly dominate numerically the playing fields of the world, and more often derive satisfaction from proving their superiority in a chosen sport.

An "adolescent growth study" carried out in California in 1947 shows just such a sexually divergent pattern of interest. The study was carried out on adolescents by adolescents and was designed to find out what qualities were most admired in boys and girls of different ages. The most admired qualities among boys of eleven to thirteen years of age were skill in organized games, aggressiveness, boisterousness and unkemptness. At the age of sixteen admiration for physical skills, courage, strength and aggressiveness was retained, and even later at the age of nineteen skill in competitive sport still had prestige value.

On the other hand among girls success in games was tolerated but not imitated. At the age of sixteen good sportsmanship with the implication of active participation in sport was admired. At the age of nineteen athletic prowess carried little prestige by itself but skill in dancing and swimming was considered an advantage, so was skill in tennis, the competitive game above all others in which boys and girls can meet each other on common ground.[3]

Any society which is to provide a pattern of sport where all its members may satisfy their natural desires must afford opportunities in all categories. A feature of development in Europe and America and Australasia since the end of the war in 1945 has been the great increase of participation in conquest sports, such as camping, canoeing, sailing, skiing. For some the conquest sports become competitive after the basic skills have been mastered, but for very many the appeal of these sports remains impersonal for most of the time. The social significance of this growth of conquest sports is still obscure but some of its implications national and international will be examined in later chapters. There has also been a great increase in competitive sport both domestic and international at all levels from mediocre schoolboy football to first-class competition in the World Cup and the Olympic Games. This feature, too, will be examined in later chapters.

The "how" of sport has been investigated by so many researchers during the present century that it is only possible to notice in general terms two opposite approaches. In the first an interest in the problems of performance has shed light upon problems outside sport and has led to further investigations in other realms. The second approach, which is more common, has been from the opposite direction. Investigation of sport has been secondary to a primary interest in some other topic, such as disease or industrial techniques. An example of the first approach is the classical paper on "The Theory of Games of Strategy" presented by John von Neumann in 1928 to a mathematical congress. The paper was concerned with the following question—

> n players S_1, S_2 . . . S_n are playing a given game of strategy G. How must one of the participants S_m play in order to achieve the most advantageous results?

A game of strategy, roulette, chess, baccarat, bridge, consists of a certain series of events each of which may have a finite number of distinct results. In some the outcome depends on chance, i.e., the probabilities with which each of the possible results will occur are known, but nobody can influence them. All other events depend on the free decision of the players. Von Neumann worked out a theorem on a system of constants which always satisfied three conditions expressed in the form of three equations. The theorem could only apply, however, to games of strategy where the free decisions of players could be implemented with precision as in draughts, bridge or chess. In games of strategy involving physical skill free decisions are but imperfectly implemented even by the most skillful players and the theorem is for them also imperfect.

In his final sentence von Neumann says: "In conclusion I would like to add that a later publication will contain numerical calculations of some well-known two-person games (poker, though with certain schematical simplifications and baccarat). The agreement of the results with the well-known rules of thumb of the games (e.g., proof of the necessity to bluff in poker) may be regarded as an empirical corroboration of the results of our theory." Von Neumann had at least satisfied himself that birds could fly.

Von Neumann's work stimulated a large number of mathematicians to analyse games of strategy. In 1959 the University of Princeton published four large volumes of such papers. The publication was sponsored by the Government's Office of Naval Research, not, presumably, because of the analysis of games of strategy was seen to have an important bearing upon the conduct of warfare.

The movement of investigators in the opposite direction, from military to sporting activities, is exemplified by the programme of the Division of Human Physiology within the Medical Research Council of Great Britain. The Division was set up in 1949 under Dr. Edholm and within two years was investigating two paramilitary problems—the physical development of cadets at the Royal Military College, Sandhurst, and survival at sea. The first problem led to an examination of the sporting activities of the cadets as well as their military training. The second problem led to experiments on channel swimmers. Experience during the war had suggested that maximum time for survival in water at the temperature of the English channel was five to six hours, yet channel swimmers were known to be in the water for any time from twelve to twenty hours.

The next investigations had less connexion with military problems although they were relevant to a parapolitical problem of national prestige. They concerned problems of climbing at high altitude first on Eric Shipton's expedition in 1951-2 to explore the Southern approaches to Everest, then on the expedition which went to Cho Oyu and finally on the ascent of Everest itself in 1953.

In 1955 the Division began work on the study of whole-body-training using brief daily training sessions. It became interested in peak performance in sport and has had research workers at the Olympic and Commonwealth Games. There have been other research teams from other countries investigating the physiological problems of sport and the general trend in the west is an increasing interest in the intrinsic problem and a fading interest in military, political, or other utilitarian considerations. At the same time in the communist countries research into sport is tightly harnessed to political purposes. Perusal of the research reports of, for instance, the High School for Physical Education at Leipzig in Eastern Germany shows that many, if not all, of the research projects are chosen with political considerations in mind. In the

United States a proportion of the thousands of research projects on physical performance have had little purpose other than to secure a higher degree for the research worker. Undoubtedly, however, the sum of research has made coaching sport more intelligent and more systematic. There is a risk that concentration on techniques and technical knowledge may obscure the element of play in sport, but the majority of those who play are not noticebly corrupted by being informed why and how they do what they do.

BIBLIOGRAPHY

1. Huizinga, Johan. *Homo Ludens: A Study of the Play Element in Society.* 1938, p. 5. (English ed., London, 1949).
2. Caillois, Roger. "The Structure and Classification of Games," in *Diogenes,* No. 12 (Winter, 1955).
3. Fleming, C. M. *Adolescence.* London, 1948.

SEE ALSO

Cozens, F. W., and F. Stumpf. *Sports in American Life.* Chicago, 1953.
Henderson, R. *Bat, Ball and Bishop.* New York, 1947.
Neuman, J. von. *Theory of Games.* London, 1930.
Riesman, D., Glazier, N. and Denney, R. *The Lonely Crowd.* Princeton, 1950.
Stokes, A. "Psycho-Analytic Reflections on the Development of Ball Games." *International Journal of Psychoanalysis* 36, (1956).

SECTION

B

SPORT AND SOCIAL
ORGANIZATION

The task of defining the nature of sport is done by Loy in a clear and logical presentation. He takes sport from the game occurrence level to that of an institutional pattern. The kind and degree of involvement is analyzed by Loy in a section of his article called "Sport as a Social Situation."

Another step in acquiring a basic format for the analysis of sport is presented in the article "Small Group Research and the Group in Sport" by Lüschen. The author asks and deals with the questions, "What is the structure of the sport group and what is its functional problem?" The discussion which follows the article centers around the value of "highly abstract categories" and ways of getting one's thinking organized in the study of sport. It may be enlightening to others to see the experts struggling with these problems.

THE NATURE OF SPORT:
A DEFINITIONAL EFFORT

JOHN W. LOY, JR.

Sport is a highly ambiguous term having different meanings for various people. Its ambiguity is attested to by the range of topics treated in the sport sections of daily newspapers. Here one can find accounts of various sport competitions, advertisements for the latest sport fashions, advice on how to improve one's skills in certain games, and essays on the state of given organized sports, including such matters as recruitment, financial success, and scandal. The broad yet loose encompass of sport reflected in the mass media suggests that sport can and perhaps should be dealt with on different planes of discourse if a better understanding of its nature is to be acquired. As a step in this direction we shall discuss sport as a game occurrence, as an institutional game, as a social institution, and as a social situation or social system.

I. SPORT AS A GAME OCCURRENCE

Perhaps most often when we think of the meaning of sport, we think of sports. In our perspective sports are considered as a specialized type of game. That is, a sport as one of the many "sports" is viewed as an actual game occurrence or event. Thus in succeeding paragraphs we shall briefly outline what we consider to be the basic characteristics of games in general. In describing these characteristics we shall continually make reference to sports in particular as a special type of game. A game

From *Quest,* Monograph X (May, 1968): 1-15 Copyright © 1968 *Quest* Board (The National Association for Physical Education of College Women and The National College Physical Education Association for Men). College Park, Maryland.

we define as any form of playful competition whose outcome is determined by physical skill, strategy, or chance employed singly or in combination.[1]

IA. "Playful." By "playful competition" we mean that any given contest has one or more elements of play. We purposely have not considered game as a subclass of play,[2] for if we had done so, sport would logically become a subset of play and thus preclude the subsumption of professional forms of sport under our definition of the term. However, we wish to recognize that one or more aspects of play constitute basic components of games and that even the most highly organized forms of sport are not completely devoid of play characteristics.

The Dutch historian Johan Huizinga has made probably the most thorough effort to delineate the fundamental qualities of play. He defines play as follows:

> Summing up the formal characteristics of play we might call it a free activity standing quite consciously outside "ordinary" life as being "not serious," but at the same time absorbing the player intensely and utterly. It is an activity connected with no material interest, and no profit can be gained by it. It proceeds within its own proper boundaries of time and space according to fixed rules and in an orderly manner. It promotes the formation of social groupings which tend to surround themselves with secrecy and to stress their differences from the common world by disguise or other means (Huizinga, 1955, p. 13).

Caillois has subjected Huizinga's definition to critical analysis (Caillois, 1961, pp. 3-10) and has redefined play as an activity which is free, separate, uncertain, unproductive, and governed by rules and make-believe (*Ibid.*, pp. 9-10). We shall briefly discuss these qualities ascribed to play by Huizinga and Caillois and suggest how they relate to games in general and to sports in particular.

IA1. "Free." By free is meant that play is a voluntary activity. That is, no one is ever strictly forced to play, playing is done in one's free time, and playing can be initiated and terminated at will. This characteristic of play is no doubt common to many games, including some forms of amateur sport. It is not, however, a distinguishing feature of all games, especially those classified as professional sport.

IA2. "Separate." By separate Huizinga and Caillois mean that play is spatially and temporally limited. This feature of play is certainly relevant to sports. For many, if not most, forms of sport are conducted in

---

1. This definition is based largely on the work of Caillois (1961) and Roberts and others (1959). Other definitions and classifications of games having social import are given in Berne (1964) and Piaget (1951).
2. As have done Huizinga (1955), Stone (1955), and Caillois (1961).

spatially circumscribed environments, examples being the bullring, football stadium, golf course, race track, and swimming pool. And with few exceptions every form of sport has rules which precisely determine the duration of a given contest.

IA3. "Uncertain." The course or end result of play cannot be determined beforehand. Similarly, a chief characteristic of all games is that they are marked by an uncertain outcome. Perhaps it is this factor more than any other which lends excitement and tension to any contest. Strikingly uneven competition is routine for the contestants and boring for the spectators; hence efforts to insure a semblance of equality between opposing sides are a notable feature of sport. These efforts typically focus on the matters of size, skill, and experience. Examples of attempts to establish equality based on size are the formation of athletic leagues and conferences composed of social organizations of similar size and the designation of weight class for boxers and wrestlers. Illustrations of efforts to insure equality among contestants on the basis of skill and experience are the establishment of handicaps for bowlers and golfers, the designation of various levels of competition within a given organization as evidenced by freshman, junior varsity, and varsity teams in scholastic athletics, and the drafting of players from established teams when adding a new team to a league as done in professional football and basketball.

IA4. "Unproductive." Playing does not in itself result in the creation of new material goods. It is true that in certain games such as poker there may occur an exchange of money or property among players. And it is a truism that in professional sports victory may result in substantial increases of wealth for given individuals. But the case can be made, nevertheless, that a game *per se* is non-utilitarian.[3] For what is produced during any sport competition is a game, and the production of the game is generally carried out in a prescribed setting and conducted according to specific rules.

IA5. "Governed by rules." All types of games have agreed-upon rules, be they formal or informal. It is suggested that sports can be distinguished from games in general by the fact that they usually have a greater variety of norms and a larger absolute number of formal norms (i.e., written prescribed and proscribed rules.[4] Similarly, there is a larger number of sanctions and more stringent ones in sports than in games. For example, a basketball player must leave the game after he has com-

3. Cf. Goffman's discussion of "rules of irrelevance" as applied to games and social encounters in general (1961), pp. 19-26).
4. E.g., compare the rules given for games in any edition of Hoyle's *Book of Games* with the NCAA rule books for various collegiate sports.

mitted a fixed number of fouls; a hockey player must spend a certain amount of time in the penalty box after committing a foul; and a football player may be asked to leave the game if he shows unsportsmanlike conduct.

With respect to the normative order of games and sports, one explicit feature is that they usually have definite criteria for determining the winner. Although it is true that some end in a tie, most contests do not permit such an ambivalent termination by providing a means of breaking a deadlock and ascertaining the "final" victor. The various means of determining the winner in sportive endeavors are too numerous to enumerate. But it is relevant to observe that in many sport competitions were "stakes are high," a series of contests are held between opponents in an effort to rule out the element of chance and decide the winner on the basis of merit. A team may be called "lucky" if it beats an opponent once by a narrow margin; but if it does so repeatedly, then the appelations of "better" or "superior" are generally applied.

IA6. "Make-believe." By the term make-believe Huizinga and Caillois wish to signify that play stands outside "ordinary" or "real" life and is distinguished by an "only pretending quality." While some would deny this characteristic of play as being applicable to sport, it is interesting to note that Veblen at the turn of the century stated:

> Sports share this characteristic of make-believe with the games and exploits to which children, especially boys, are habitually inclined. Make-believe does not enter in the same proportion into all sports, but it is present in a very appreciable degree in all (Veblen, 1934, p. 256).

Huizinga observes that the " 'only pretending' quality of play betrays a consciousness of the inferiority of play compared with 'seriousness'" (Huizinga, 1955, p. 8). We note here that occasionally one reads of a retiring professional athlete who remarks that he is "giving up the game to take a real job"[5] and that several writers have commented on the essential shallowness of sport.[6] Roger Kahn, for example, has written that:

> The most fascinating and least reported aspect of American sports is the silent and enduring search for a rationale. Stacked against the atomic bomb or even against a patrol in Algeria, the most exciting rally in history may not seem very important, and for the serious and semi-serious people who make their living through sports, triviality is a nagging, damnable thing. Their drive for self-justification has contributed much to the development of sports (Kahn, 1957, p. 10).

5. There is, of course, the amateur who gives up the "game" to become a professional.
6. For an early discussion of the problem of legitimation in sport, see Veblen, 1934, pp. 268-270.

On the other hand, Huizinga is careful to point out that "the consciousness of play being 'only pretend' does not by any means prevent it from proceeding with the utmost seriousness" (Huizinga, 1955, p. 8). As examples, need we mention the seriousness with which duffers treat their game of golf, the seriousness which fans accord discussions of their home team, or the seriousness that national governments give to Olympic Games and university alumni to collegiate football?[7,8]

Accepting the fact that the make-believe quality of play has some relevance for sport, it nevertheless remains difficult to empirically ground the "not-ordinary-or-real-life" characteristic of play. However, the "outside-of-real-life" dimension of a game is perhaps best seen in its "as-if" quality, its artificial obstacles, and its potential resources for actualization or production.

IA6(a). In a game the contestants act as if all were equal, and numerous aspects of "external reality" such as race, education, occupation, and financial status are excluded as relevant attributes for the duration of a given contest.[9]

IA6(b). The obstacles individuals encounter in their workaday lives are not usually predetermined by them and are "real" in the sense that they must be adequately coped with if certain inherent and socially conditioned needs are to be met; on the other hand, in games obstacles are artificially created to be overcome. Although these predetermined obstacles set up to be conquered can sometimes attain "life-and-death" significance, as in a difficult Alpine climb, they are not usually essentially related to an individual's daily toil for existence.[10]

IA6(c). Similarly, it is observed that in many "real" life situations the structures and processes needed to cope with a given obstacle are often not at hand; however, in a play or game situation all the structures and processes necessary to deal with any deliberately created obstacle and to realize any possible alternative in course of action are potentially available.[11]

7. An excellent philosophical account of play and seriousness is given by Kurt Riezler (1941, pp. 505-517).

8. A sociological treatment of how an individual engaged in an activity can become "caught up" in it is given by Goffman in his analysis of the concept of "spontaneous involvement" (1961, pp. 37-45).

9. For a discussion of how certain aspects of "reality" are excluded from a game situation, see Goffman's treatment of "rules of irrelevance." Contrawise see his treatment of "rules of transformation" for a discussion of how certain aspects of "reality" are permitted to enter a game situation (1961, pp. 29-34).

10. Professional sports provide an exception, of course, especially such a sport as professional bullfighting.

11. Our use of the term "structures and processes" at this point is similar to Goffman's concept of "realized resources" (1961, pp. 16-19).

In sum, then, games are playful in that they typically have one or more elements of play: freedom, separateness, uncertainty, unproductiveness, order, and make-believe. In addition to having elements of play, games have components of competition.

IB. "Competition." Competition is defined as a struggle for supremacy between two or more opposing sides. We interpret the phrase "between two or more opposing sides" rather broadly to encompass the competitive relationships between man and other objects of nature, both animate and inanimate. Thus competitive relationships include:

1. competition between one individual and another, e.g., a boxing match or a 100-yard dash;

2. competition between one team and another, e.g., a hockey game or a yacht race;

3. competition between an individual or a team and an animate object of nature, e.g., a bullfight or a deer-hunting party;

4. competition between an individual or a team and an inanimate object of nature, e.g., a canoeist running a set of rapids or a mountain climbing expedition; and finally,

5. competition between an individual or team and an "ideal" standard, e.g., an individual attempting to establish a world land-speed record on the Bonneville salt flats or a basketball team trying to set an all-time scoring record. Competition against an "ideal" standard might also be conceptualized as man against time or space, or as man against himself.[12]

The preceding classification has been set forth to illustrate what we understand by the phrase "two or more opposing sides" and is not intended to be a classification of competition *per se*. While the scheme may have some relevance for such a purpose, its value is limited by the fact that its categories are neither mutually exclusive nor inclusive. For instance, an athlete competing in a cross-country race may be competitively involved in all of the following ways: as an individual against another individual; as a team member against members of an opposing team; and as an individual or team member against an "ideal" standard (e.g., an attempt to set an individual and/or team record for the course).[13]

---

12. Other possible categories of competition are, of course, animals against animals as seen in horse racing or animals against an artificial animal as seen in dog racing. As noted by Weiss: "When animals or machines race, the speed offers indirect testimony to men's excellence as trainers, coaches, riders, drivers and the like—and thus primarily to an excellence in human leadership, judgment, strategy, and tactics" (1967, p. 22).

13. The interested reader can find examples of sport classifications in Schiffer (1965), McIntosh (1963), and Sapora and Mitchell (1961).

IC. "Physical skill, strategy, and chance." Roberts and Sutton-Smith suggest that the various games of the world can be classified:

> . . . on the basis of outcome attributes: (1) games of *physical skill*, in which the outcome is determined by the players' motor activities; (2) games of *strategy*, in which the outcome is determined by rational choices among possible courses of action; and (3) games of *chance*, in which the outcome is determined by guesses or by some uncontrolled artifact such as a die or wheel (Roberts and Sutton-Smith, 1962, p. 166).

Examples of relatively pure forms of competitive activities in each of these categories are weight-lifting contests, chess matches, and crap games, respectively. Many, if not most, games are, however, of a mixed nature. Card and board games, for instance, generally illustrate a combination of strategy and chance. Whereas most sports reflect a combination of strategy and physical skill. Although chance is also associated with sport, its role in determining the outcome of a contest is generally held to a minimum in order that the winning side can attribute its victory to merit rather than to a fluke of nature. Rather interestingly it appears that a major role of chance in sport is to insure equality. For example, the official's flip of a coin before the start of a football game randomly determines what team will receive the kickoff and from what respective side of the field; and similarly the drawing of numbers by competitors in track and swimming is an attempt to assure them equal opportunity of getting assigned a given lane.

ID. "Physical prowess." Having discussed the characteristics which sports share in common with games in general, let us turn to an account of the major attribute which distinguishes sports in particular from games in general. We observe that sports can be distinguished from games by the fact that they demand the demonstration of physical prowess. By the phrase "the demonstration of physical prowess" we mean the employment of developed physical skills and abilities within the context of gross physical activity to conquer an opposing object of nature. Although many games require a minimum of physical skill, they do not usually demand the degree of physical skill required by sports. The idea of "developed physical skills" implies much practice and learning and suggests the attainment of a high level of proficiency in one or more general physical abilities relevant to sport competition, e.g., strength, speed, endurance, or accuracy.

Although the concept of physical prowess permits sports to be generally differentiated from games, numerous borderline areas exist. For example, can a dart game among friends, a horseshoe pitching contest between husband and wife, or a fishing contest between father and son be considered sport? One way to arrive at an answer to these questions is to define a sport as any highly organized game requiring physical prowess. Thus a dart game with friends, a horseshoe pitching contest between spouses, or a fishing contest between a father and son would not be considered sport; but formally sponsored dart, horseshoe, or fishing tournaments would be legitimately labelled sport. An alternative approach to answering the aforementioned questions, however, is to define a sport as an institutionalized game demanding the demonstration of physical prowess. If one accepts the latter approach, then he will arrive at a different set of answers to the above questions. For this approach views a game as a unique event and sport as an institutional pattern. As Weiss has rather nicely put it:

> A game is an occurrence; a sport is a pattern. The one is in the present, the other primarily past, but instantiated in the present. A sport defines the conditions to which the participants must submit if there is to be a game; a game gives rootage to a set of rules and thereby enables a sport to be exhibited (1967, p. 82).

II. SPORT AS AN INSTITUTIONALIZED GAME

To treat sport as an institutionalized game is to consider sport as an abstract entity. For example, the organization of a football team as described in a rule book can be discussed without reference to the members of any particular team; and the relationships among team members can be characterized without reference to unique personalities or to particular times and places. In treating sport as an institutionalized game we conceive of it as distinctive, enduring patterns of culture and social structure combined into a single complex, the elements of which include values, norms, sanctions, knowledge, and social positions (i.e., roles and statuses).[14] A firm grasp of the meaning of "institutionalization" is necessary for understanding the idea of sport as an institutional pattern, or blueprint if you will, guiding the organization and conduct of given games and sportive endeavors.

The formulation of a set of rules for a game or even their enactment on a particular occasion does not constitute a sport as we have conceptualized it here. The institutionalization of a game implies that it has a tradition of past exemplifications and definite guidelines for future realizations. Moreover, in a concrete game situation the form of a particular sport need not reflect all the characteristics represented in its institutional pattern. The more organized a sport contest in a concrete setting, however, the more likely it will illustrate the institutionalized

14. This definition is patterned after one given by Smelser (1963, p. 28).

nature of a given sport. A professional baseball game, for example, is a better illustration of the institutionalized nature of baseball than is a sandlot baseball game; but both games are based on the same institutional pattern and thus may both be considered forms of sport. In brief, a sport may be treated analytically in terms of its degree of institutionalization and dealt with empirically in terms of its degree of organization. The latter is an empirical instance of the former.

In order to illustrate the institutionalized nature of sport more adequately, we contrast the organizational, technological, symbolic, and educational spheres of sports with those of games. In doing so we consider both games and sports in their most formalized and organized state. We are aware that there are institutionalized games other than sports which possess characteristics similar to the ones we ascribe to sports, as for example chess and bridge; but we contend that such games are in the minority and in any case are excluded as sports because they do not demand the demonstration of physical prowess.

IIA. "Organizational sphere." For present purposes we rather arbitrarily discuss the organizational aspects of sports in terms of teams, sponsorship, and government.

IIAI. "Teams." Competing sides for most games are usually selected rather spontaneously and typically disband following a given contest. In sports, however, competing groups are generally selected with care and, once membership is established, maintain a stable social organization. Although individual persons may withdraw from such organizations after they are developed, their social positions are taken up by others, and the group endures.[15]

Another differentiating feature is that as a rule sports show a greater degree of role differentiation than games do. Although games often involve several contestants (e.g., poker), the contestants often perform identical activities and thus may be considered to have the same roles and statuses. By contrast, in sports involving a similar number of participants (e.g., basketball), each individual or combination of just a few individuals performs specialized activities within the group and may be said to possess a distinct role. Moreover, to the extent that such specialized and differentiated activities can be ranked in terms of some criteria, they also possess different statuses.

IIA2. "Sponsorship." In addition to there being permanent social groups established for purposes of sport competition, there is usually found in the sport realm social groups which act as sponsoring bodies for sport teams. These sponsoring bodies may be characterized as being

15. Huizinga states that the existence of permanent teams is, in fact, the starting-point of modern sport (1955, p. 196).

direct or indirect. Direct sponsoring groups include municipalities which sponsor Little League baseball teams, universities which support collegiate teams, and business corporations which sponsor AAU teams. Indirect sponsoring groups include sporting goods manufacturers, booster clubs, and sport magazines.

IIA3. "Government." While all types of games have at least a modicum of norms and sanctions associated with them, the various forms of sport are set apart from any games by the fact that they have more— and more formal and more institutionalized—sets of these cultural elements. In games rules are often passed down by oral tradition or spontaneously established for a given contest and forgotten afterwards; or, even where codified, they are often simple and few. In sports rules are usually many, and they are formally codified and typically enforced by a regulatory body. There are international organizations governing most sports, and in America there are relatively large social organizations governing both amateur and professional sports. For example, amateur sports in America are controlled by such groups as the NCAA, AAU, and NAIA; and the major professional sports have national commissioners with enforcing officials to police competition.

IIB. "Technological sphere." In a sport, technology denotes the material equipment, physical skills, and body of knowledge which are necessary for the conduct of competition and potentially available for technical improvements in competition. While all types of games require a minimum of knowledge and often a minimum of physical skill and material equipment, the various sports are set apart from many games by the fact that they typically require greater knowledge and involve higher levels of physical skill and necessitate more material equipment. The technological aspects of a sport may be dichotomized into those which are intrinsic and those which are extrinsic. Intrinsic technological aspects of a sport consist of the physical skills, knowledge, and equipment which are required for the conduct of a given contest *per se.* For example, the intrinsic technology of football includes: (a) the equipment necessary for the game—field, ball, uniform, etc.; (b) the repertoire of physical skills necesary for the game—running, passing, kicking, blocking, tackling, etc.; and (c) the knowledge necessary for the game —rules, strategy, etc. Examples of extrinsic technological elements associated with football include: (a) physical equipment such as stadium, press facilities, dressing rooms, etc.; (b) physical skills such as possessed by coaches, cheer leaders, and ground crews; and (c) knowledge such as possessed by coaches, team physicians, and spectators.

IIC. "Symbolic sphere." The symbolic dimension of a sport includes elements of secrecy, display, and ritual. Huizinga contends that play "promotes the formation of social groupings which tend to surround themselves with secrecy and to stress their difference from the common world by disguise or other means" (1955, p. 13). Caillois criticizes his contention and states to the contrary that "play tends to remove the very nature of the mysterious." He further observes that "when the secret, the mask or the costume fulfills a sacramental function one can be sure that not play, but an institution is involved" (1961, p. 4).

Somewhat ambivalently we agree with both writers. On the one hand, to the extent that Huizinga means by "secrecy" the act of making distinctions between "play life" and "ordinary life," we accept his proposition that groups engaged in playful competition surround themselves with secrecy. On the other hand, to the extent that he means by "secrecy" something hidden from others, we accept Caillois's edict that an institution and not play is involved.

IIC1. The latter type of secrecy might well be called "sanctioned secrecy" in sports, for there is associated with many forms of sport competition rather clear norms regarding approved clandestine behavior. For example, football teams are permitted to set up enclosed practice fields, send out scouts to spy on opposing teams, and exchange a limited number of game films revealing the strategies of future opponents. Other kinds of clandestine action such as slush funds established for coaches and gambling on games by players are not always looked upon with such favor.[16]

IIC2. A thorough reading of Huizinga leads one to conclude that what he means by secrecy is best discussed in terms of display and ritual. He points out, for example, that "the 'differentness' and secrecy of play are most vividly expressed in 'dressing up'" and states that the higher forms of play are "a contest *for* something or a representation *of* something"—adding that "representation means display" (1955, p. 13). The "dressing-up" element of play noted by Huizinga is certainly characteristic of most sports. Perhaps it is carried to its greatest height in bullfighting, but it is not absent in some of the less overt forms of sport. Veblen writes:

> It is noticeable, for instance, that even very mild-mannered and matter-of-fact men who go out shooting are apt to carry an excess of arms and accoutrements in order to impress upon their own imagination the seriousness of their undertaking. These huntsmen are also prone to a histrionic, prancing gait and to an elaborate exaggeration of the motions, whether of stealth or of onslaught, involved in their deeds of exploit (1934, p. 256).

16. Our discussion of "sanctioned secrecy" closely parallels Johnson's discussion of "official secrecy" in bureaucracies (1960, pp. 295-296).

A more recent account of "dressing-up" and display in sports has been given by Stone (1955), who treats display as spectacle and as a counter-force to play. Stone asserts that the tension between the forces of play and display constitute an essential component of sport. The following quotation gives the essence of his account:

> Play and dis-play are precariously balanced in sport, and, once that balance is upset, the whole character of sport in society may be affected. Furthermore, the spectacular element of sport, may, as in the case of American professional wrestling, destroy the game. The rules cease to apply, and the "cheat" and the "spoilsport" replace the players.
>
> The point may be made in another way. The spectacle is predictable and certain; the game, unpredictable and uncertain. Thus spectacular display may be reckoned from the outset of the performance. It is announced by the appearance of the performers—their physiques, costumes, and gestures. On the other hand, the spectacular play is solely a function of the uncertainty of the game (pp. 261-62 in Larrabee and Meyershon). (Stone, 1955, p. 98).

In a somewhat different manner another sociologist, Erving Goffman, has analyzed the factors of the uncertainty of a game and display. Concerning the basis of "fun in games" he states that "mere uncertainty of outcome is not enough to engross the players" (1961, p. 68) and suggests that a successful game must combine "sanctioned display" with problematic outcome. By display Goffman means that "games give the players an opportunity to exhibit attributes valued in the wider social world, such as dexterity, strength, knowledge, intelligence, courage, and self-control" (*Ibid.*). Thus for Goffman display represents spectacular play involving externally relevant attributes, while for Stone display signifies spectacular exhibition involving externally non-relevant attributes with respect to the game situation.

IIC3. Another concept related to display and spectacle and relevant to sports is that of ritual. According to Leach, "ritual denotes those aspects of prescribed formal behavior which have no direct technological consequences" (1964, p. 607). Ritual may be distinguished from spectacle by the fact that it generally has a greater element of drama and is less ostentatious and more serious. "Ritual actions are 'symbolic' in that they assert something about the state of affairs, but they are not necessarily purposive: i.e., the performer of ritual does not necessarily seek to alter the state of affairs" (*Ibid.*). Empirically ritual can be distinguished from spectacle by the fact that those engaged in ritual express an attitude of solemnity toward it, an attitude which they do not direct toward spectacle.

Examples of rituals in sport are the shaking of hands between team captains before a game, the shaking of hands between coaches after a game, the singing of the national anthem before a game, and the singing of the school song at the conclusion of a game.[17]

IID. "Educational sphere." The educational sphere focuses on those activities related to the transmission of skills and knowledge to those who lack them. Many if not most people learn to play the majority of socially preferred games in an informal manner. That is, they acquire the required skills and knowledge associated with a given game through the casual instruction of friends or associates. On the other hand, in sports, skills and knowledge are often obtained by means of formal instruction. In short, the educational sphere of sports is institutionalized, whereas in most games it is not. One reason for this situation is the fact that sports require highly developed physical skills which games often do not; to achieve proficiency requires long hours of practice and qualified instruction, i.e., systematized training. Finally, it should be pointed out that associated with the instructional personnel of sport programs are a number of auxiliary personnel such as managers, physicians, and trainers—a situation not commonly found in games.

III. SPORT AS A SOCIAL INSTITUTION

Extending our notion of sport as an institutional pattern still further, we note that in its broadest sense, the term sport supposes a social institution. Schneider writes that the term institution:

> . . . denotes an aspect of social life in which distinctive value-orientations and interests, centering upon large and important social concern . . . generate or are accompanied by distinctive modes of social interaction. Its use emphasizes "important" social phenomena; relationships of "strategic structural significance" (1964, p. 338).

We argue that the magnitude of sport in the Western world justifies its consideration as a social institution. As Boyle succinctly states:

> Sport permeates any number of levels of contemporary society, and it touches upon and deeply influences such disparate elements as status, race relations, business life, automotive design, clothing styles, the concept of the hero, language, and ethical values. For better or worse it gives form and substance to much in American life (1963, pp. 3-4).

17. For an early sociological treatment of sport, spectacle, exhibition, and drama, see Sumner (1960, pp. 467-501). We note in passing that some writers consider the totality of sport as a ritual; see especially Fromm (1955, p. 132) and Beisser (1967, pp. 148-151 and pp. 214-225).

When speaking of sport as a social institution, we refer to the sport order. The sport order is composed of all organizations in society which organize, facilitate, and regulate human action in sport situations. Hence, such organizations as sporting goods manufacturers, sport clubs, athletic teams, national governing bodies for amateur and professional sports, publishers of sport magazines, etc., are part of the sport order. For analytical purposes four levels of social organization within the sport order may be distinguished: namely, the primary, technical, managerial, and corporate levels.[18] Organizations at the primary level permit face-to-face relationships among all members and are characterized by the fact that administrative leadership is not formally delegated to one or more persons or positions. An example of a social organization associated with sport at the primary level is an informally organized team in a sandlot baseball game.

Organizations at the technical level are too large to permit simultaneous face-to-face relationships among their members but small enough so that every member knows of every other member. Moreover, unlike organizations at the primary level, organizations at the technical level officially designate administrative leadership positions and allocate individuals to them. Most scholastic and collegiate athletic teams, for example, would be classified as technical organizations with coaches and athletic directors functioning as administrative leaders.

At the managerial level organizations are too large for every member to know every other member but small enough so that all members know one or more of the administrative leaders of the organization. Some of the large professional ball clubs represent social organizations related to sport at the managerial level.

Organizations at the corporate level are characterized by bureaucracy: they have centralized authority, a hierarchy of personnel, and protocol and procedural emphases; and they stress the rationalization of operations and impersonal relationships. A number of the major governing bodies of amateur and professional sport at the national and international levels illustrate sport organizations of the corporate type.

In summary, the sport order is composed of the congeries of primary, technical, managerial, and corporate social organizations which arrange, facilitate, and regulate human action in sport situations. The value of the concept lies in its use in macro-analyses of the social significance of sport. We can make reference to the sport order in a historical and/or

---

18. Our discussion of these four levels is similar to Caplow's treatment of small, medium, large, and giant organizations (Caplow, 1964, pp. 26-27).

comparative perspective. For example, we can speak of the sport order of nineteenth-century America or contrast the sport order of Russia with that of England.

IV. SPORT AS A SOCIAL SITUATION

As was just noted, the sport order is composed of all social organizations which organize, facilitate, and regulate human action in sport situations. Human "action consists of the structures and processes by which human beings form meaningful intentions and, more or less successfully, implement them in concrete situations" (Parsons, 1966, p. 5). A sport situation consists of any social context wherein individuals are involved with sport. And the term situation denotes "the total set of objects, whether persons, collectivities, culture objects, or himself to which an actor responds" (Friedsam, 1964, p. 667). The set of objects related to a specific sport situation may be quite diverse, ranging from the elements of the social and physical environments of a football game to those associated with two sportniks[19] in a neighborhood bar arguing the pros and cons of the manager of their local baseball team.

Although there are many kinds of sport situations, most if not all may be conceptualized as social systems. A social system may be simply defined as "a set of persons with an identifying characteristic plus a set of relationships established among these persons by interaction" (Caplow, 1964, p. 1). Thus the situation represented by two teams contesting within the confines of a football field, the situation presented by father and son fishing from a boat, and the situation created by a golf pro giving a lesson to a novice each constitutes a social system.

Social systems of prime concern to the sport sociologist are those which directly or indirectly relate to a game occurrence. That is to say, a sport sociologist is often concerned with why man gets involved in sport and what effect his involvement has on other aspects of his social environment. Involvement in a social system related to a game occurence can be analyzed in terms of degree and kind of involvement.

Degree of involvement can be assessed in terms of frequency, duration, and intensity of involvement. The combination of frequency and duration of involvement may be taken as an index of an individual's "investment" in a sport situation, while intensity of involvement may be considered an index of an individual's "personal commitment" to a given sport situation.[20]

19. The term sportnik refers to an avid fan or sport addict.
20. Cf. McCall and Simmons (1966, pp. 171-172).

Kind of involvement can be assessed in terms of an individual's relationship to the "means of production" of a game. Those having direct or indirect access to the means of production are considered "actually involved" and are categorized as "producers." Those lacking access to the means of production are considered "vicariously involved" and are categorized as "consumers." We have tentatively identified three categories of producers and three classes of consumers.

Producers may be characterized as being primary, secondary, or tertiary with respect to the production of a game. "Primary producers" are the contestants who play the primary roles in the production of a game, not unlike the roles of actors in the production of a play. "Secondary producers" consist of those individuals, who while not actually competing in a sport contest, perform tasks which have direct technological consequences for the outcome of a game. Secondary producers include club owners, coaches, officials, trainers, and the like. It may be possible to categorize secondary producers as entrepreneurs, managers, and technicians. "Tertiary producers" consist of those who are actively involved in a sport situation but whose activities have no direct technological consequences for the outcome of a game. Examples of tertiary producers are cheerleaders, band members, and concession workers. Tertiary producers may be classified as service personnel.

Consumers, like producers, are designated as being primary, secondary, or tertiary. "Primary consumers" are those individuals who become vicariously involved in a sport through "live" attendance at a sport competition. Primary consumers may be thought of as "active spectators." "Secondary consumers" consist of those who vicariously involve themselves in a sport as spectators via some form of the mass media, such as radio or television. Secondary consumers may be thought of as "passive spectators." "Tertiary consumers" are those who become vicariously involved with sport other than as spectators. Thus an individual who engages in conversation related to sport or a person who reads the sport section of the newspaper would be classified as a tertiary consumer.

In concluding our discussion of the nature of sport we note that a special type of consumer is the *fan.* A fan is defined as an individual who has both a high personal investment in and a high personal commitment to a given sport.

REFERENCES

Berne, Eric. *Games People Play.* New York: Grove Press, 1964.
Beisser, Arnold R. *The Madness in Sports.* New York: Appleton-Century-Crofts, 1967.

Boyle, Robert H. *Sport—Mirror of American Life*. Boston: Little, Brown, 1963.

Caillois, Roger. *Man, Play and Games*, tr. Meyer Barash. New York: Free Press, 1961.

Caplow, Theodore. *Principles of Organization*. New York: Harcourt, Brace and World, 1964.

Friedsam. H. J. "Social Situation." in *A Dictionary of the Social Sciences*, edited by Julius Gould and William L. Kolb, p. 667. New York: Free Press. 1964.

Fromm, Eric. *The Sane Society*. New York: Fawcett, 1955.

Goffman, Erving. *Encounters*. Indianapolis: Bobbs-Merrill, 1961.

Huizinga, Johan. *Homo Ludens—A Study of the Play-Element in Culture*. Boston: Beacon Press, 1955.

Johnson, Harry M. *Sociology: A Systematic Introduction*. New York: Harcourt, Brace, 1960.

Kahn, Roger. "Money, Muscles—and Myths," *Nation*, CLXXXV (July 6, 1957), 9-11.

Leach, E. R. "Ritual," in *A Dictionary of the Social Sciences*, ed. Julius Gould and William L. Kolb. New York: Free Press, 1964.

Lüschen, Günther. "The Interdependence of Sport and Culture." Paper presented at the National Convention of the American Association for Health, Physical Education and Recreation, Las Vegas, 1967.

McCall, George J., and J. L. Simmons, *Identities and Interactions*. New York: Free Press, 1966.

McIntosh, Peter C. *Sports in Society*. London: C. A. Watts, 1963.

Piaget, Jean. *Play, Dreams and Imitation in Childhood*, tr. C. Gattegno and F. M. Hodgson. New York: W. W. Norton, 1951.

Riezler, Kurt. "Play and Seriousness," *The Journal of Philosophy*, XXXVIII (1941), 505-517.

Roberts, John M., and others. "Games in Culture," *American Anthropologist*, LXI (1959), 597-605.

———, and Brian Sutton-Smith. "Child Training and Game Involvement," *Ethnology*, I (1962), 166-185.

Sapora, Allen V., and Elmer D. Mitchell. *The Theory of Play and Recreation*. New York: Ronald Press, 1961.

Schiffer, Donald. "Sports," *Colliers Encyclopedia* 21 (1965): 449-460.

Schneider, Louis. "Institution," in *A Dictionary of the Social Sciences*, ed. Julius Gould and William L. Kolb. New York: Free Press, 1964.

Smelser, Neil J. *The Sociology of Economic Life*. Englewood Cliffs, N. J.: Prentice-Hall, 1963.

Stone, Gregory P. "American Sports: Play and Display," *Chicago Review*, IX (Fall 1955), 83-100.

Sumner, William Graham. *Folkways*. New York: Mentor, 1960.

Torkildsen, George E. "Sport and Culture." M. S. thesis, University of Wisconsin, 1957.

Veblen, Thorstein. *The Theory of the Leisure Class*. New York: Modern Library, 1934.

Weiss, Paul. "Sport: A Philosophical Study." Unpublished manuscript, 1967.

SMALL GROUP RESEARCH
AND THE GROUP IN SPORT

GÜNTHER LÜSCHEN

The topic I wish to discuss today has been chosen for a number of reasons. First, I think the area should be included in the sociology of sport, and second, I think there's a certain neglect of it in the field of physical education. You could, of course, expect that psychologists in the field of physical education work with aspects of small groups, but they are mainly concerned with motor learning and motor performance.

The field of study, which by R. F. Bales has been labeled Small Group Research, originated at the end of the last century in a study on sport. Triplett (1898), in observing the performance of cyclists, noticed the differences in the level of records of individually racing cyclists, of those cycling with a pacer and those with a pacer competing against others. A number of theories to explain the superior performance of the paced competitors over the non-competing paced cyclists and even more over the non-paced cyclists, caused him to design an experiment with fishing reels, in which he was able to control the different factors, from suction to automatic stimulation, that had supposedly an effect on cycling performance. He found bodily presence of a competitor to be one of the stimulating factors to release energy not ordinarily available. A number of questions remained unanswered, yet his study is still a classic example of experimental design in social psychology.

After Triplett, a number of schools may be listed as originators of the small group approach. Mayo and his co-workers (cf. Roethlisberger and Dickson, 1939) explored productivity in industry and more or less

From *Aspects of Contemporary Sport Sociology: Proceedings of C.I.C. Symposium on the Sociology of Sport,* edited by Gerald S. Kenyon, pp. 52-75. Chicago, Illinois: The Athletic Institute, 1969. Copyright © 1969 by The Athletic Institute.

accidentally discovered the standards of production of the small work group a determining factor in productivity. K. Lewin promoted experimental psychology, studied the influence of groups on the individual, and among others inaugurated the influence of leadership styles on group morale and the performance of group functions. (White and Lippitt, 1960). In World War II combat groups and their structure were the target of sociologists and social psychologists (cf. Stouffer, 1950). And finally, the promotion of two specific techniques for the study of groups, sociometry and sociodrama, by J. L. Moreno (1953) should be mentioned.

Small group research has, since the beginning of this century, established itself rather solidly. At annual meetings in sociology and psychology one will definitely run into reports dealing with this approach. Even in administration, psychotherapy and education, research techniques and results of small group research are well accepted. The number of relevant studies has cumulated in the last decade. Already in 1954 Strodtbeck and Hare listed almost 1500 titles. Topics investigated range from the effect of audiences on performance, and the situational determination of leadership, to sympathy structures in school class and the equilibrium of discussion groups. There is almost no question in social psychology, group sociology and their related fields that could not be studied in the realm of the small group. What integrates the field is method of research and a *physical* object of study, a number of people from two to two dozen, who are called a small group—although they may not be a group at all.

The objective in theory and research is for a number of scientists the *group as a system* (Bales, 1950; Mills, 1967). For others the group has only relevance as a place of study where the *individual's response* to social factors, often in an experimental setup, or the *individual personality as a basis* for social structure, are studied. As Homans in partial retreat from his earlier efforts put it, "The group is not what we study, but where we study it" (1959). This "it" for him contained every aspect of social interaction of individuals which should give insight not only into micro- but into macro-structures as well. In his later publications, he denounced part of his earlier systems-approach and in an address to the American Sociological Association, "Bringing Man Back In," argued for building sociological theories on psychological propositions only and thus making the individual personality the basis of study (1954). Yet one can not deny that Homans still deals with individuals in a group context, more explicitly with interaction. The problem is here more one of quality of theory or denial of explanatory power of system variables. The points of interest are still questions of power, status or exchange mechanisms in social settings. The ultimate goal is definitely the development of theoretical insights from limited structural units into complex macrostructures, this being quite evident in Blau's work *Exchange and Power in Social Life*, (1964). Yet the small group seems to appear only accidentally. As far as Blau is concerned quite intentionally so, since he wants to focus on dynamics, on what he calls the structure of social associations. In the approach of many psychologists in this field the small group or even interaction as a focus have even less interest. Under study is the individual's behavior in a social situation, but social structure itself is of no particular interest and provides only certain single variables. Many of the laboratory studies are of this type. This has of course led to valuable results for individual behavior. Also the rigor of research designs and the superior formal validity over many sociological studies are quite impressive. Yet for interaction or small group theory these studies have not given much insight. As a psychologist one perhaps couldn't care less. As a sociologist I do care.

The magnitude in the number of studies has also produced quite conflicting results. Not that the tests implied were wrong or the designs were poor. What appears to be one major problem is the negligence of socio-cultural factors involved in many of these research setups. Most prominently, there is first the neglect of cultural factors, which indeed exert the strongest control over social behavior. There is second, the neglect of groups as parts of larger systems and organizations. There is third, a problem which has not sufficiently been recognized: the difference between what Stone called interpersonal and structural relations (1966). The neglect of these properties may be partly due to a psychologist's wish to study interactions between controlled factors only. Very often the problem will be due to the structural poverty of the lab situation. In putting two to five persons (most "groups" of this type do not go beyond that number) into a lab in order to test, e.g., anxiety, one has not created a group at all. Only gradually will this collection of persons develop a group structure—and often against the actual planning of the experimenter. The neglect of the distinction between interpersonal and structural relations is also a problem in the more recent work of Homans (1961). His concept of distributive justice, e.g., depends not only on investment by individuals but on a distinct normative structure and other qualities of a social system. The critique of Parsons (1964) that Homans did neglect the levels of organization in dealing with interactions is essentially the same as that of Stone. After the psychological approach has dominated the field in the last decade, and after Homans has gone to a pure psychological reductionism in explaining interaction and interaction systems, one may now well reverse the title of his address to the ASA and ask for efforts in "Bringing the Group Back In." Precisely at this point I see the potentialities of the study of sport groups for the small group approach. In the following I will thus deal with groups and interaction systems only and consider the behavior of individuals only insofar as they are performing social roles.

Sport has not only the potentialities to bring the group back in—and for developing theoretical propositions concerning the magnitude of social aggregates, sport will also lead us again out of the laboratory. Not only does sport provide the clearly defined structure of groups and roles, and the ultimate definition of values like achievement in group culture, the clear outcome of winning and losing provide for controlled variable. It is also in this realm quite easy to create experimental conditions with a minimum side effect. Newcomers on a team, backward referees, reinforcement of achievement, and odd rules are all very natural conditions in sport, but could well be used for experimental controls. Moreover, the very structure of sport will be a barrier to dealing with isolated groups only, since the determination of their structure through systems at large and the continuous interaction with other groups in sport's contest can hardly be overlooked.

What we face in sport is on the one hand the spontaneously formed casual play group of children or adults. They engage in play primarily determined by interpersonal relations, out of which a form of game may emerge, yet only for the length of the gathering. The play will show a certain order, yet the frequent interruptions of such games through arguing over rules and the meaning of the game situation (cf. Piaget, 1965) reveal the structural instability of these relations and thus a low degree of system organization. Indeed the social system is always threatening to break down. What integrates this type of play group is mainly interpersonal exchange, and possibly rewards are intrinsic.

On the other hand, the team of top competitors, like a national squad, is defined in its behavior primarily by the social system. The interpersonal structure is of little importance. What we find here is a highly differentiated code of rules determining the activity that this group engages in. There are not only formula rules of a specific sport but other norms as well, which in general will restrict the action of the individual considerably. The extension of all types of social control on this level is strong and determined by system and subsystem structures. What we face here is almost a complete loss of individual freedom in role performance. Interpersonal relations are of low importance. Rewards are extrinsic in this situation.

The argument over interpersonal versus structural (system) relationships is quite easily to be resolved referring to the spontaneous play group and the highly competitive team. Both levels are of importance. The magnitude of structural differentiation, e.g., determined by the amount of extrinsic rewards, will decide where on a continuum between play and top athletics a sport group will be located.

A question which for the clarification of our topic sport group should be answered is: What is the structure of the sport group and what are its functional problems? In Chart I, following Parsons, a sport group is outlined as a social system, which as any other social system has four levels of structure: values, norms, the normative structure of subcollectivities, and the structure of roles. The chart states under each of the

CHART I
The Sport Group as a Social System*

Structural Levels	Functional Problems
Values (achievement, fair play)	Pattern maintenance
Norms (defining amateur, foul; rules of a game; defining "good" team member)	Integration
Subcollectivities (offense or defense; "braintrusts" of a team; cliques, friendships)	Goal attainment
Roles (unique clusters of recognized formal or informal rights and obligations of individual members; specific quarterback, peacemaker, scapegoat on a team)	Adaptation

*In regard to the section on Parsonian theory I owe much to a discussion with my friend and colleague Harry M. Johnson. For further readings cf.:

T. Parsons. An outline of the social system. In: T. Parsons et al., *Theories of Society.* Vol. I. Glencoe, III. 1961:30-84.
T. Parsons. An approach to psychological theory in terms of the theory of action. In: S. Koch, *Psychology: A Study of a Science.* Vol. III. New York, 1959:612-711.

structural levels specific examples that could be identified in a sport team. Of course in very small groups like that of tennis partners in a doubles match there may be no subcollectivities. It should also be mentioned that a social system in sport may well be identified as a contest of two sport groups.

In regard to the functional problems that such a system of a sport group has to meet the value and general norm levels are roughly focused on the "internal" problems of the system, having to do with maintenance of basic patterns and with the interrelations between "units" of the system (subcollectivities and roles), while the levels of subcollectivities and norms have to do primarily with "external" problems of goal attainment and adaptation. The "internal" problem of relations between units covers all aspects of solidarity, including not only positive incentives for participation but also the terms of competition and the forestalling, channeling or settling of conflict.

Any social system—and also a small sport group—is intimately part of a more general action system, consisting of culture, the social system (including all types of sport groups and associations), the personality system and the behavioral organism as outlined in Chart II. In turn the general action system is related to the physical-organic environment, most directly through the behavioral organism. According to the theory, the

CHART II
Sport in the Action System

Subsystems	
Culture	
(including the culture of sport in general and of particular sport disciplines)	
Social System	Outlined in Chart I
(including many types of sport "groups," such as sport federations, associations, clubs, teams, a contest of teams)	for the example of a small sport group, such as a team
Personality System	
(including the specific personality system of participants in sport)	
Behavioral Organism	
* * * *	
Physical-organic Environment	

four systems composing the action system are arranged in a hierarchy of control ranging from culture to behavioral organism, and a hierarchy of conditioning in the reverse direction.

As Chart II suggests any sport group is part of a much larger set of social systems and is "controlled" by the general culture, which itself may be thought of as having many subsystems. Factors such as age, sex, social class, and skill are partly environmental, but they may be the focuses of rules of the sport group, arising in part from the overall concern for such broad values as competitive achievement and fair play.

A role such as that of coach is a role in a social system larger than the "team" narrowly defined, as in a different direction the football "squad" is larger than the "team." Again, a referee is obviously a role-specialized participant in a social system having still different boundaries.

The complex interrelations roughly indicated in the charts raise many problems for research and will help clarify many open questions in persisting results. Many of the distinctions made are also treated in other theoretical schemes, but some point to particularly neglected areas in small group research. This theory applies well to systems as large as a society and as small as a game of tennis singles. Indeed the small group studies of Bales (1950, 1953) had, at one period, considerable influence on the development of Parsons' theory, including the discussion on functional problems. Moreover this theory provides a framework for systematically relating cultural, social-system, personality variables and even those of the behavioral organism. In the field of sport we have hardly begun to analyze the problems connected with these fundamental distinctions.

We might mention that the common allegation that this theory implies too much concern for the static, rests on rather fundamental misunderstanding of the theory itself. Conflict, exchange, and structural change all find a place in the theory. This does not mean, of course, that many problems in the study of small groups may not be well handled by other theoretical approaches, such as those of Bales, Blau, Homans, the field-theorists or the newly emerging mathematical theorists. Yet not all of these approaches lend themselves easily to the study of sport groups since they have been partially designed for the study of discussion groups, therapeutic groups, or groups in laboratory settings.

We have been talking so far about the sport group in regard to its analysis from the point of view of sociology. This question may now well be: Is there no hope for physical education and social practice in sport? This is a legitimate question. And as far as the area of small group research is concerned, a question that can easily be answered. Yes, there is hope and not only on the basis of more theoretical insight into this area. Results, whether they are obtained on the level of psychological studies of individuals in social situations or on the level of an approach that we have emphasized, namely sociological studies concerned with groups, will very often have an immediate payoff for teaching of physical education or coaching of athletics. A review of the main results obtained so far in the area of small group research will make that quite explicit.

There have been a number of studies focused on conditions of individual and group performance in sport or physical skill. Effects of audiences on performance which earlier did not lead to significant results in a number of studies (cf. Kenyon and Loy, 1966) have shown recently, when separating the phase of learning and performance, a facilitative effect of audiences in a motor task (Martens, 1968). Competition with other groups seems to result in an increase in performance only when competing against potentially similar groups, while the performance of potentially weaker groups matched against stronger ones decreases (Start, 1966). Positive interpersonal relations in rifle teams showed an effect on performance (McGrath, 1962), yet a sociometric and participant observation study of rowing teams did not confirm, that harmony of team members was a condition of high team efficiency. Quite to the contrary strong internal conflict correlated with a consistent increase in level of performance (Lenk, 1965). Investigations of basketball teams seem to indicate that the formal organization of the team is a crucial variable. Moreover, the very general result concerning conflict and efficiency seems to need more qualifications. In the study of Klein and Christiansen, the strength of the opponent was found to have an influence on relations between liking and efficiency. Moreover, interactions were observed to occur more with the most liked and disliked (1966).

The motivation of a group of mountain climbers was found to be inversely related to certainty of outcome. In case of optimistic prospects communication between team members carried pessimistic statement and vice versa (Emerson, 1966). Achievement as an independent variable was set in field experiments with physical education classes. The reinforcement of the achievement value showed less effect in highly structural classes (Hammerich, 1966) and resulted in changes of ranks, yet opposite to the hypothesized changes, since the groups under study seemed to balance the experimentally created imbalances out (Lüschen, 1966).

The surrendering of defensive layers in situations of high pressure was studied in a sociodramatic experiment and showed in a baseball team loyalty to the team the most important layer, which was surrendered last (Charnofsky, 1966). A more recent study with rowing teams confines the result, and in general, shows, however, in the sequence of surrendering layers the determination of groups by situational factors. In a potential championship team winning over rivals was given up later than in the college baseball team (Lenk, 1968).

Following the general interest in leadership studies since the early work by the Lewin school, Fiedler found psychological distance of leaders positively correlated with team effectiveness (1960). More recently leadership was found to be curvilinearly dependent on a number of situational variables: relation between leader and followers, task structure and the power of a leadership position. As a general result of a number of studies one may state that leadership is more determined by situational factors than was anticipated earlier. Thus, good leaders may well turn out to be bad in different situations. A recommendation to adjust the situation to the leader and not vice versa may thus be well based (Myers and Fiedler, 1966). Field managers in baseball were, in another study, found to have less effectiveness on teams than is generally believed (Grusky, 1963). In situations of crisis, however, they are functioning as scapegoats (Gamson and Scotch, 1964).

The studies cited so far, are concerned primarily with structural properties of single groups, often only individuals in social situations. Only in a few cases have systems of two interacting, competing teams been analyzed. Yet, these units seem to be of primary importance and small group studies in sport should definitely expand to these systems of interaction of small units, which are joined by a third party, the referee. The two studies that could be mentioned in this regard are first, the Sherifs' *Groups in Harmony and Tension* (1953) in which the increase of hostility of competing groups of boys in a camp is analyzed. The second one, is that by Elias and Dunning on the dynamics of sport groups in which they try to explain the configuration of two opposing football teams (1966). The problem brought up by them is of quite some prominence for the theory of conflict. Whereas, cooperation and competition had so far been studied e.g., in their separate influence on group structure, the problem occurs now as one, where the structural relationships between both orientations in groups have to be studied. Gumpert, Deutsch and Epstein (1969) report on findings with the prisoner's dilemma game. Cooperation in a competitive situation occurred more likely under conditions of symbolic rewards, where one was rewarded for good performance by points. Cooperation was absent under conditions of reward with money. Results of one of our earlier studies (Lüschen, 1961) showed a high prominence of values of affiliation in sport. The higher the level of performance among athletes, the more values of affiliation were expressed. One may thus state the hypothesis, that the more symbolic the rewards, the more likely cooperation will be displayed in a competitive situation; one of the reasons being, that the system of interaction and the conditioning rules for reward have meaning only for those involved and depend on mutual consent (cf. Homans, 1961; Anderson and Moore, 1960). This is an old problem (Simmel, 1923). Yet the theoretical explanation is open. The study of sport groups in contest could make a definite contribution to that needed insight and into the study of conflict in general (cf. Lüschen, 1968).

The discussion of results in the study of small sport groups has made the casualness of research findings quite obvious. Yet, even these casual results have shown potentialities for the study and theoretical insight of groups and interaction systems in general, and moreover, the applicability of those results for theory and social practice in physical education and athletics.

RELATED LITERATURE

Anderson, A. R. and Moore, O. K. "Autotelic folk models," *Sociological Quarterly* 1 (1960): 203-216.

Back, K. W., Hood, T. C. and Brehm, M. L. "The subject role in small group experiments," *Social Forces* 2 (1964): 181-187.

Bales, R. F. *Interaction Process Analysis*. Reading, Mass., 1950.

Bales, R. F. "The equilibrium problem in small groups," In *Working Papers in the Theory of Action*, T. Parsons, R. F. Bales and E. A. Shils, Glencoe, Ill., 1953. pp. 111-161.

Blau, P. M. *Exchange and Power in Social Life*. New York, 1964.

Cartwright, D. and A. Zander. *Group Dynamics*. New York, 1968.

Charnofsky, H. "Die Aufgabe von Verteidigungsschichten in Drucksituationen," In G. Lüschen, 1966, 237-250.

Deutsch, M. and R. M. Krauss. *Theories in Social Psychology*. New York, 1965.

Elias, N. and E. Dunning. "Dynamics of sport groups with special reference to football," *British Journal of Sociology* 4 (1966): 388-402.

Emerson, R. M. "Mount Everest," In G. Lüschen, 1966. Also in: *Sociometry* 3 (1966): 213-227.

Fiedler, F. E. "The leader's psychological distance and group effectiveness," In Cartwright and Zander, 1960.

Goffman, E. *Encounters*. Indianapolis, 1961.

Gumpert, P., Deutsch, M. and Epstein, Y. "Effect of incentive magnitude in the prisoner's dilemma game," *Journal of Personality and Social Psychology* 1 (January 1969) 66-69.

Hammerich, K. "Leistungsforcierung im Sportunterricht," In G. Lüschen, 1966, 224-236.

Hare, A. P. *Handbook of Small Group Research*. New York, 1962.

Homans, G. C. *The Human Group*. New York, 1950.

Homans, G. C. *Social Behavior: Its Elementary Forms*. New York, 1961.

Homans, G. C. "Bringing man back in," *American Sociological Review*, 1964.

Kenyon, G. and Loy, J. W. "Soziale Beeinflussung der Leistung bei vier psychomotorischen Aufgaben," In G. Lüschen, 1966, 192-202.

Klein, M. and Christiansen, G. "Gruppenkomposition, Gruppenstruktur und Effektivitat von Basketballmannschaften," In G. Lüschen, 1966, 180-191.

Kozman, H. C. *Group Process in Physical Education*. New York, 1951.

Lenk, H. "Konflikt und Leistung in Spitzensportmannschaften," *Soziale Welt* 1965: 4.

Lenk, H. "Aufgabe von Wertbindungen bei Hockleistungsruderern," *Soziale Welt* 1 (1968): 67-73.

Lüschen, G. "Leistungsorientierung und ihr Einfluss auf das soziale und personale System," In G. Luschen, 1966.

Lüschen, G. *Kleingruppenforschung und Gruppe im Sport*. Koln, 1966.

Lüschen, G. "Cooperation, association and contest," paper at AAAS meeting, Dallas, Texas, 1968.

Lüschen, G. "The Sociology of Sport. Trend-report with annotated bibliography", *Current Sociology*, The Hague and Paris, 1968.

Malewski, A. *Interaction and Behavior* (in Polish). Warsaw, 1964.

Martens, R. "The Effects of an Audience . . . A Complex Motor Skill," Ph.D. Thesis, University of Illinois, 1968.

McGrath, J. E. "The influence of positive interpersonal relations on adjustment effectiveness in rifle teams," *Journal Abnormal and Social Psychology* 6 (1962): 365-375.

Mills, T. M. *The Sociology of Small Groups*. Englewood Cliffs, N. J.: Prentice-Hall, 1967.

Moede, W. "Der Wetteifer, scine Struktur and swin Ausmass," *Zeitschrift fur Paedagogische Psychologic* 15 (1914): 353-368.

Moede, W. *Experimentelle Massenpsychologie*. Leipzig, 1927.

Moreno, J. L. *Who Shall Survive?* Beacon Press, Boston, Mass.: 1953.

Myers, A. "Team competition, success and the adjustment of group members," *Journal Abnormal and Social Psychology* 5 (1962): 325-332.

Myers, A. E. and Fiedler, F. E. "Theorie und Probleme der Fuhrung," In G. Lüschen, 1966: 92-106.

Olmsted, M. S. *The Small Group*. New York: 1959.

Parsons, T. "Levels of organization and the mediation of social interaction," *Sociological Inquiry*, Spring, 1964.

Piaget, J. *The Moral Inducement of the Child*. New York, 1965.

Schafer, W. E. "Die Soziale Struktur von Sportgruppen," In G. Lüschen, 1966, 107-117.

Sherif, M. and Sherif, C. W. *Groups in Harmony and Tension*. New York, 1953.

Sherif, M. *Intergroup Conflict and Cooperation: The Robbers Cave Experiment*. Norman, Okla.: University of Oklahoma Press, 1961.

Simmel, G. "The number of members as determining the sociological form of the group," *Amercian Journal of Sociology*, 1902, July: 1-46, September: 158-196.

Simmel, G. "Der Streit," In Simmel, *Soziologie*, Berlin, 1923.

Start, K. B. "Wettbewerb und Geschicklichkeit im Sport," In G. Lüschen, 1966, 203-208.

Stogdill, R. M. "Team achievement under high motivation," *Business Research Monograph*. Ohio State University, 1963, 113.

Stone, G. P. "Bergriffliche Probleme in der Kleingruppenforschung," In G. Lüschen, 1966, 44-65.

Stouffer, S. A., et al. *The American Soldier*. Vol. I, Princeton, N. J.: University of Princeton Press, 1950.

Triplett, M. "The dynamogenic factors in pacemaking and competition," *American Journal of Psychology* 4 (1898): 507-533.

Whyte, W. F. *Street Corner Society*. Chicago, 1943.

REACTION TO LÜSCHEN PAPER

John W. Loy, Jr.

As the hour is late, and since I know that several of you have questions which you wish to address to Professor Lüschen, I will dispense with the sheaf of notes in my hand and confine myself to making a few very broad remarks.

First, I would like to congratulate Dr. Lüschen for his excellent job of outlining the problems and prospects of small group research in the sport situation. He covered a lot of territory in a short space of time.

In large measure I find myself in nearly full agreement with the various positions Professor Lüschen took in his paper. I especially support his statement that although several hundred small group studies have been conducted, there has been correspondingly relatively little development of micro-social theory and the empirical findings themselves have not always been the most conclusive. My special fear is that things are likely to get worse before they get better. Since the study of small groups is such a highly developed subfield in sociology; and as physical education students prefer the concrete to the abstract; and since quantitative theses rather than qualitative theses are currently the norm, I expect to see as many white sophomores and white rats in small group laboratories as are now found in exercise physiology and motor learning laboratories. It is evident in physical education that the several thousand empirical investigations in exercise physiology and motor learning have not produced a very large body of theoretical knowledge. Hopefully, students pursuing small group research in the sport context will produce profound as well as profuse studies.

I suggest that one way of assuring better research is for the interested student to pay careful heed to the insightful admonitions given by Professor Lüschen. Specifically, I make reference to Dr. Lüschen's discussion of the neglect of socio-cultural variables in past small group work. He states, and I think rightly so, that studies are needed: (1) which place greater emphasis on culture and social structure rather than personality; (2) which examine small groups as micro-social systems or subsystems or larger and more encompassing macro-social systems; and (3) which consider "real" rather than "contrived" groups.

As somewhat of an aside I note that one manner of getting sport out of the laboratory and to correct the three oversights pointed out by Dr. Lüschen is to study sport groups as subcultures. Although experimental control may be admittedly lost, many theoretical insights might be gained regarding sport involvement when sport groups are studied from this suggested perspective. Two analyses of "deviant" sport subcultures have recently been made which could provide useful models for the interested student. Marvin Scott has examined behavior at the race track from a dramaturgical perspective and presents his findings in a book just out, titled *The Racing Game*. Similarly, Ned Polsky, by means of participant observation has studied the subculture of the pool room and records his observations in a recent text titled *Hustlers, Beats and Others*.

Professor Lüschen's call to "bring the group back in" leads me to make a counter call to "bring sport back in." For it seems to me that Dr. Lüschen stresses the potential importance of sport situations for testing sociological theories; whereas I wish to argue for the importance of studying sport as a social phenomenon. In short, I think there is a fundamental difference between the individual who is trying to explain a phenomenon and draws upon sociological theory to do so, and the individual who has a theory in hand and seeks a situation in which he can test its implications.

However, I believe both Professor Lüschen and myself concur in the importance of using the sport context as a medium for developing social theory. It strikes me as surprising that social psychologists and sociologists have virtually ignored sport teams in their analyses of small groups. I think that they have missed the boat because sport teams as small social systems can be viewed as microcosms of larger social systems, including society itself. They present in miniature such societal features as a division of labor, a code of ethics, a government, means of communication, prestige rankings, ideologies, myths, and even religious practices.

Some of these features of sport teams as social systems were presented by Dr. Lüschen in his interesting Parsonian paradigm of the sport group. His taxonomy is an effort to delineate the overall structure of the sport group and to suggest the functional problems a given group must resolve in order to maintain itself as an ongoing social entity. I am not clear as to how Dr. Lüschen proposes to use his paradigm in the development of social theory, but believe that his taxonomy may have some merit as a didactic service. In fact, I employ a similar Parsonian paradigm in my undergraduate class when discussing the possible implications of Bales' small group research in the analysis of leadership roles among athletic teams. I specifically use my taxonomy to illustrate the fact that in sport groups one may often find the two complementary leaders, i.e., a task leader and a social-emotional leader, that Bales found emergent in his laboratory analysis of small discussion groups.

Since my own paradigm is similar to that of Professor Lüschen's I'll present it for those who wish to compare the two. Although my paradigm lacks some of the teutonic characteristics of Professor Lüschen's it features the same functional problems and similarly stresses the external and internal dimensions of a sport group as a social system. In addition, however, I emphasize the instrumental and expressive dimensions of a sport group and am solely concerned with the question of leadership roles. Thus, I indicate that one may find Bales' two types of leaders both within the collectivity of players and the collectivity of coaches. In my class I typically make reference to the Green Bay Packers of "old" with Bart Starr at quarterback as the task leader of the team, and Paul Hornung at halfback as the team's social-emotional leader.

| External | Internal | |
Cultural Dimension	Social Structural Dimension	
Adaptive Problem—winning games from other teams	*Decision-Making Problems*— relating of team members to each other to reach and carry out group decisions	**Members as Means**
Leader role—coach as technical expert and executive leader	*Leader role*—team member as task leader	**Instrumental Dimension**
Pattern maintenance and Member Recruitment and Retention Problem—acquisition, training and control of group members	*Integrative Problem*— relating members to each other to "get along" with each other	**Members as Ends**
Leader role: coach as educator and morale leader	*Leader role:* team member as social-emotional leader	**Expressive Dimension**

Well, since we have gotten somewhat removed from Dr. Lüschen's paper I'll conclude my own remarks at this point and throw things open for questions from the floor for Professor Lüschen.

DISCUSSION

CHARLES H. PAGE: I'm very much tempted to make a speech. I've been talking too much today, but every time I'm confronted with an effort to use Parson's social systems scheme which Dr. Lüschen used in order to make more sense out of a concrete area, an area of reality, I get increasingly confused and sometimes furious. I think the utilization of highly abstract categories, to use a technical word, which are analytical and not at all concrete categories, to bring order—and this is the presumed purpose of such a scheme of categories—to bring order and to make more sense and to learn more about the reality itself, I think it's extremely difficult when we try to apply the system of Parsons to any concrete small group area such as certain kinds of sport teams or sport organizations and so on. Therefore, I was very pleased when John Loy flashed on the screen essentially the same scheme so far as the categories are concerned but in a much more simplified manner. I'm not sure, however, that any of us can learn more about the world of sports by applying a scheme which has been designed in my judgment not for the purpose of learning about reality but for developing sociology. Parsons, who incidentally is an old friend of mine, is a man who is deeply concerned with sociology, but, I don't know how concerned he is with society. His schemes are of use in the chess-like ratiocinational, theoretical activities of people who are interested in the development of abstract sociological theory. Similarly, people who are interested in applying theory to sport are apt to be less interested in sport—I was glad to hear Mr. Loy's call for bringing sport back in—than in seeing whether or not their highly theoretical schemes can be applicable. And, of course, they can be if you go through certain verbal exercises, and thus we have the sociology of everything, the Parsonian sociology of everything, if you want to make the application. But I'd call for looking at this thing in a reverse fashion. Look at sports as a concrete area of activity and then, as I think Mr. Loy was beginning to suggest when he all too briefly described his paradigm, see what more we can learn about reality by applying certain distinctions, such as Bales' distinction between task and morale leadership and perhaps even Parson's basic functional problems of all social systems, which are the four categories that Dr. Lüschen outlined and also appear in Loy's paradigm; but I'm really disturbed by this effort unless I see it done in black and white where I can struggle with it for about ten hours. I don't know how the rest of you feel, but I thought I'd say that as a sociologist, which I am, who is interested I think in sport more than I am in sociology.

LÜSCHEN: I would completely agree with you that my primary interest was in developing sociology, exactly that. I see the merits of the Parsonian approach in this way. Although you may not want to buy the theoretical insights provided by this rather abstract systems approach, I would say it will at least get your thinking organized. I know, of course, quite well the opposite point of view; that as of today, I think is held by Andre Malewski. He couldn't care less about Parsons, and thinks that theory should be developed within the realm of small testable hypotheses. You may hold this point of view, but still fail to come up with the anticipated results. As a case in point, the theory of which recently he has claimed, has led him into all types of difficulties although at the first glance it seemed to be quite easy.

PAGE: I should qualify my own comments, and then I'll be quiet, and that is, I certainly agree with you, Dr. Lüschen, that one of the merits of this system, or a less complex system, is that it does call the attention of people who are seriously interested in a field such as this, to all of its possible aspects; that is, it calls for an inclusive kind of search. With a theoretical scheme of this sort you are guarded to some extent against missing things that you might otherwise miss. That I agree with. I think this is one of the advantages. But I'm not sure how helpful it will be when actually analyzing what goes on in fact.

GREGORY STONE: I just want to make a brief comment. This sort of "taxonomics game" may not facilitate our vision, for another reason. If we look through lenses or maybe a better word would be prism, there may be certain types of light filtered out. I think that we are being overly generous to talk of Parsons and others of that ilk. I'm not sure this is the way to develop any science—to sit down and build elaborate boxes and then find out where the world fits into them. For me the important part of science is the problem, the question. I think that this kind of taxonomy avoids the matter of problems. The history of science, I think, is typically a graveyard of theory. It's the problems that live in the science and the least interesting part of the science, I think, are the answers. Once you have an answer, that's it, for a while anyway, until somebody comes up with another question that throws the earlier answer into doubt. For example, one of the schemes of Parsons is essentially a static scheme. The emphasis is upon integration and upon equilibrium; consequently, matters of historical change in this case, in sport, don't fit anywhere in the box. The whole matter of rules, or, for example, Riesman's very beautiful little essay on the emergence of American football out of British rugby primarily because Americans have problems in knowing what a scrimmage was. This kind of problem was stated so well by Riesman that I don't see where it fits in the scheme at all. I kept wondering where the water buckets were in the box or the sports equipment, which are very important parts, I should think, of performance in sport. I wondered what a non-symbolic reward was as opposed to a symbolic reward in terms of Dr. Lüschen's hypothesis. In other words, I think such a scheme blinds us and buries questions. I think in any kind of a scientific endeavor the important matter is the matter of the question; so if I were going to pull the gown off the sociology of sport, I think I would lay out a set of problems trying to be as concrete as possible, and then having these questions, begin looking for the sorts of hypotheses that might be incorporated into carefully designed research, although I'm beginning to worry also about carefully designed research. It seems to me the more tightly designed the research, the more trivial the results of the research and this bothers me very much in sociology generally. So I share Professor Page's concern with this particular approach in sociology of sport. I could go on, but I become overly emotional.

LOY: Do you wish to respond, Professor Lüschen?

LÜSCHEN: Problems of, for instance, change of the rugby into the American football game would perhaps be treated only as functional problems in this scheme. I am well aware of the problems of change. However, Parsons would claim that you can do it this way and has worked on that considerably in the last five or six years.

STONE: Supposing you take changes in basketball. What's the matter with basketball now? It's boring—this parade up and down the court. The concern in changing the rules has to do with speeding it up, much as wrestling has been speeded up in college and high school, to make it more appealing to the spectator. I don't see the explanation of this kind of change in that diagram. And that's a very important part of the sociology of sports—to know how the rules change.

LÜSCHEN: Well, you know of the work in this area by Elias and Dunning who could, in a way, explain this situation based upon the problems of integration and equilibrium. In this way they concluded that since there was disequilibrium, the system or the rules had to be adjusted again.

STONE: You can say that basketball has achieved such a monotonous state of equilibrium and integration that something has got to be done to shake it up.

LÜSCHEN: Yes. But you are thinking now in terms of the team. The overall system must, of course, also consist of the spectators and thus there may be quite a bit of disequilibrium insofar as, for instance, the interest of the audience fades completely.

STONE: Or because of the box office.

HARRY WEBB: Why does it? I feel like Charles does, if I don't like it, I get mad as hell. What seems to be involved really is the question of how best to get at the social information, information about social process. So, I want to make two points. First of all, there is some variation on the so-called structural-functional approach, which isn't that bad I suppose, in sociology. With some alterations in it, it is possible to produce some beautiful kinds of information. On the other hand, I think you can demonstrate fairly clearly that the structural-functional approach leads not only to an inability to deal with change, but leads to a real conservative attitude towards everything proper and so the change is not going to get you anywhere. Of course in sport, as sport develops in our kind of society, the change is very much in the operation. You cannot examine sport from that kind of an approach.

The most ambitious example of the application of this kind of approach to real phenomena is Smelser's theory of collective behavior. Smelser takes the baggage and dispenses with a good deal of it conservatively by setting up a hierarchy of those four components: values, norms, the way in which people are rewarded as they operate in interaction, and the facilities which they employ, and he attempts to rank these in order from highest to lowest. He attempts to explain social change, revolutions, this kind of thing, down to and including panics. In other words you reorganize the way a component itself is organized. Once he has started that, he sets up these components and values and norms and down to facilities. In the change of facilities process he says you explain the relationship that exists between these different kinds of components—for example, revolution includes panics. This points to a beautiful model. It's very, very interesting. It says, strain appears at these lowest levels where social action is actually going on and it reorganizes some things; it organizes the aspects of these things at the very top which are abstract. Now an interesting thing occurs here, because you get a direct line between what is abstract and what is concrete. Recall for a minute, this business about the difference between the real and the ideal. The real thing is this thing that we do in real life. We talk about this in terms of the terms that we use. For example, the way in which terms get meaning is that the first cycle that is read and the second cycle that is read refer to some abstract assigned time. Now the nature of this relationship is never identified but it is by participating in that assigned time that they retain similarity of meaning. This problem goes on for a very long time. What is the relationship between the abstract and the ideal? Finally, philosophers throw it out entirely. The sociologists don't know because they don't even know the problem exists. They certainly don't recognize it as a philosophical one. But what you get in Smelser, an otherwise brilliant theorist, is an attempt to show a relationship between what is not real and what is real on a step by step basis. In other words operating across a continuum. That simply cannot occur. The abstract and the real are qualities and there is no connection between them. So at that point Smelser runs into a lot of trouble, but what does he do with the internal organization of his component? He throws it out and does not use it, in the rest of the book which is a brilliant attack on social problems. He has to get rid of the very theoretical framework which he introduces at the beginning to get to the problem. What kind of lesson does that provide? It provides the problem, the kind of thing which Charles mentioned earlier and that is by taking the large view you control things that you otherwise might miss. But until the stone floats out and you get down to the concrete, the nitty-gritty, if you like, you haven't got anything that's worth listening to or looking at. The acceptance of such problems cannot provide that kind of insight, concrete insight, into the way in which people interact. They are absolutely useless.

I'm not sure, and I agree with Page. There is a very little difference between the small group studies that are reported and the format that is identified at the beginning. I mention this and feel strongly about it because there is a drive in sociology today to force the large group—the hedgehog thinkers—that's the way he puts it—out of the world and to introduce the fox. Once you introduce the fox, the small minded myopic kind of thinker, the possibility of ever getting to the big problem is enormously diminished, as you can see. The value again of that approach is that larger concerns remain and the things that you finally develop are worth looking at and maybe employable.

I'm now going to give you an example of how this thing can operate. If you get rid of the baggage and take the structural forms alone and ignore the business about constitution and function, boundary making, this kind of thing, you can examine the way structures in society are organized. You can then take a look at the more dominant ones and watch the way their values and their system of operating filter over into others and this comes back to the basketball example that you just gave. Over a long period of time it finally develops and it's a sufficient labor process because of the increasing sophistication in the measurement of time. You can always correlate the development or the measurement of units to the increasing rationalization of the production process itself. What goes on in sport? Sport develops as an alternative way of providing tensioned release in a system which is closing it off in other areas, the community type kinds of things. The time then comes in in the economy where sport develops only in industrial life of the large scale merging societies. It does not occur anywhere else but in sport. It then comes to be a popular kind of development to the extent that it reflects kinds of structural organization and the values that occur in that dominant situation in the economy. Time is one of those elements. You can then go back and examine those activities most popular. What are they? Those that are most crucially limited by time factors—for example, football in which each play is set up on a time basis. It's interesting to note that the excitement of the game increases at the end of both halves where the competition with time as a major factor is always greater. The same thing happens in a basketball game. Everybody is apathetic as hell but at the last moments, or the last moment, of each half it becomes an interesting game as production of units constantly competes with time. You can see this process, you can also read the paper about the subject. You can see this process in piecework units and shots. The same thing operates there. To the extent these activities themselves are more or less greatly rationalized, they are more or less popular. So you take the two components, rationalization of activity on the one hand and time dimension on the other. Those activities emphasizing most of both are the ones that are most popular, as in football. The extreme rationalization of the fact that a kid starting at any position at fourteen, winds up as a guy who runs back and punts exclusively on a professional team. Introduce the time unit as well and you've got the popular activity. In that sense you can demonstrate what kinds of activity for example become popular in terms of structural elements existing in the larger and more dominating institution and the ones in which more people participate as they get older. This is essentially true.

The point, finally, to get this thing out of the way—I'm sorry that I got wound up—but the point finally is that we must avoid destruction of the hedgehog because he's got a good deal to say, where the fox is capable only of analyzing the kinds of things that the hedgehog produces. If you lose one-half, you lose it all. That's why it's important to protect this kind of approach and at the same time it is also important to very much learn of the difficulties.

CYRIL WHITE: The sociologists are talking all about sports, something that the sociologists are not supposed to be doing, whereas the sports men are arguing about sociological theory, something that they know nothing about, and so we have a type of conflict at the moment.

We should look to what Doctor Lüschen is saying, something that he's said to me many times. I'll try to do this in my own way. Deal with the social realities that you know, like sport, and use what methods of understanding, and use what tools of understanding, seem to give the best result. I think this is what he's saying. Instead, we have been taking the view that Parsons is the answer to the maiden's prayer as far as sport is concerned, or any other prayer. I am interested in sociological theory, but in my work, which I mentioned this morning, Smelser's theory seemed to be the best for my purposes. I think this is what we must try and do if we want to make progress and not get back at the rather absurd situation where the sociologists argue about "Let's have more sport" and the sportsmen argue "Let's have more sociology."

BRIAN SUTTON-SMITH: I can draw an analogy as to what is happening—perhaps it may be out of order—but there are certain things happening in the field of education, not only in the sociology of sport, like people who are trying to dream up schemes about what is inclusive and what is exclusive, what you can fit it in, and where certain parts of the whole business ought to be replaced; and then we come up with a big taxonomy something like sociology. Oftentimes in an effort to make the things fit we tortuously try and shove things closely together but in so doing we distort. The danger is that we should not be trapped by system, and I think that is what our two sociologists were trying to tell us in essence and we have to be quite careful about that. Let's utilize system but don't let's be trapped by it, and I think we have to be careful in our instruction about that.

LÜSCHEN: Well, I would like to mention that, of course, I knew what I would get into here, since I knew my colleagues, and the reason why I applied this system is that it is for the time being the most conclusive system that we have, the most conclusive theoretical system I think there is. I don't think anybody would disagree.

On the point brought up by Mr. Webb, that it does not meet reality and that indeed it can be compared with a kind of Platonic approach, people who strongly oppose Parsons very often would, however, make the remark that it very well fits reality. I may just mention Mr. Homans who says Parsons doesn't know anything about theory, but he is a very good empiricist, and indeed for a number of instances his taxonomic system fits reality. I would claim that. However, I am well aware of certain things I cannot explain and can't get out of, and I think Parsons himself couldn't get out of. Certain boxes have not a very strong explanatory power. The problem is, of course, always a conflict, whether you want to explain certain problems in a particular frame of reference on the one hand, or whether, on the other hand, you would just like to study the plain facts which, of course, would have meaning only if you apply certain models from the very beginning. So there is no way of avoiding certain theoretical systems in any type of research. The distance here between reality and the theoretical system may be quite high, I give you that, and I think it is definitely a problem here.

One more point, the problem of equilibrium, for which Parsons has, of course, been quite strongly criticized and most strongly by my fellow countryman Ralf Dahrendorf, who even earned a prize with an article he wrote for the *American Journal*; the thing is, if you read Parsons as far as I understand him, he will always claim that this is some kind of an assisting model, a model that would help you to organize your data, but that you should, of course, always be aware that it actually is a consistent problem, a consistent stage of disequilibrium. Blau, of course, stating it more strongly, has said "I had better do away with the equilibrium problem and start with the disequilibrium problem," but implicit in that is some kind of equilibrium notion. So I think that Parsons himself would not die for the equilibrium model, but as you may have observed many of his followers would. Thank you.

TECHNOLOGY—
A PERSPECTIVE

Much of our knowledge of technology as related to sport has been from a normative position. We have accepted both technology and sport as having positive value, with only the benefits of each presented and without an analysis of all the consequences. Technology is such a pervasive aspect of the American environment that this brief section is included to introduce technology into one's thinking as background for "Sport American Style."

What Roszak has to say is significant in this time of search for one's humanity in a technological society, a society which has little or no precedent in the history of humankind. That technology itself has become a game with competitive goals of growth, maximizing profit, expansion and control, creating "industrial productivity which is ceaselessly elaborated," is of major concern to him. Has our whole culture been caught up in the competitive ethic measured only by winning, quantitative measures and efficiency? Roszak suggests that we have developed efficiency to the level of "idiot efficiency." One might do well at this point to reflect back to the last paragraph in the article by McIntosh (Section A), and consider again the direction in which a focus on the technical in sport has led us.

In the second article Lahr sees sport as the theatre of a highly industrialized state and further as a reaction to industry. He states, "But as the opportunity for physical prowess and uncomplicated, noble victory is denied mechanized man, the spectacle of sport has assumed a potency and ritual importance that most theatre has lost."

Lahr also takes a look at the "space game" in relation to sport. The connections are described in his statement, "Baseball and football make reality out of a game. The space race makes a game out of reality. Technology extends the demand, fed by sport, for continued, easy victory with no sacrifice from the community of observers."

It is impossible to separate into neat categories games, work, theatre and technology when we consider them within the organically functioning and dynamically reacting force of human society as presented by Roszak and Lahr. We have often studied these entities as if they operated in a laboratory situation. The extrinsic motivation of technology and sport, in the form of quotas, scores and rewards, has caused us to lose sight of the personal process and the value of intrinsic motivation.

The last author represented in this section, Betts, has much to offer in historical information about technological developments pertinent to sport. In his article he states that, "The technological revolution is not the sole determining factor in the rise of sport, but to ignore its influence would result only in a more or less superficial understanding of the history of one of the prominent social institutions of modern America."

FORBIDDEN GAMES

THEODORE ROSZAK

Those of us who find ourselves distressed or even horrified at the shape that the technological society is forcing upon our lives find ourselves again and again brought up short by the familiar cliché that technology—in both its mechanical and its organizational aspects—is, after all, a neutral force that can be wielded for man's well-being as well as for his harm. It is a cliché that is bound to leave us unsatisfied as a final verdict on the nature of technological development. For suppose one followed its suggestion and surrendered analysis in favor of a simple-minded act of double-entry tabulation (balancing off "good things" against "bad things"). Surely, sooner or later, any reasonably curious mind would begin to wonder why the technological account finishes with a liability column of such significant size. Or, indeed, those with a utopian bent to their curiosity might wonder why there is a liability column at all. Why haven't *all* of man's inventiveness and organizational skill worked out for the best, as an unmixed blessing?

Unless we insist upon an examination of the human perversity that has again and again cheated us of the full promise of technology, we will have to settle down to the grotesque complacency of the prominent American physicist who found a strange consolation in the fate that would befall mankind in the radioactive environment following World War III. The fall-out would, he concluded, only shorten man's life span by about the same amount that modern medicine had lengthened it in

Theodore Roszak, "Forbidden Games," *An Occasional Paper on the Role of Technology in a Free Society*, 1966. Copyright © 1966, The Fund for the Republic, Inc. Reprinted by permission, from the Center Occasional Paper #147, 1966, a publication of the Center for the Study of Democratic Institutions in Santa Barbara, California.

the last sixty years. Science giveth and science taketh away: blessed be the name of science.

In such an attitude may lie the key to technology's indiscriminate scattering of goods and evils. What is it that offends us so much in this easy casting-up of life and death accounts but the technician's implicit denial that technology in all its manifold works has anything to do, *essentially,* with promoting human welfare? Sometimes it does, and sometimes it doesn't: technology produces penicillin *and* the H-bomb . . . and lets the chips fall where they may. It is the same attitude that is reflected in the consoling conclusion of another technician that a thermonuclear disaster, while producing untold devastation to human life and culture, might at the same time lead the way to a renaissance of the arts by clearing away the dead hand of the cultural past.

What the technicians seem to be saying (and they seem very content to be saying it) is that technology is some manner of chance force that has as its main object the unfolding of its own inherent capacities. Its benefits and its destructive features are mere by-products. But, meanwhile, what goes without question is the assertion that the technology *must* be elaborated; it *must* go on "progressing." The technicians leave it to others to put their achievemnts to good use . . . or to pick up the pieces: a task that becomes increasingly more difficult as technology rapidly proliferates effects beyond anyone's anticipation or full understanding.

But if the technician's exclusive and often compulsive pursuit of progress is taken to have no inherent responsibility for the social results of that progress, then how are we to understand what the technician is about? What is the psychology of his project?

From the humanistic critic's viewpoint, the technician's lack of a clear, moral purpose may make technology seem a monstrosity, a chaos, a blind, erratic force throwing up unaccountable effects without reason or purpose. But what such a characterization overlooks is the fact that the technological project, for all the harm it does, has a very definite structure and discipline to it, an order that ought to be familiar to us all. The scientists, economists, engineers, entrepreneurs, managers, systems analysts, and bureaucrats who contribute to technological excellence are behaving far from blindly and erratically; their lives and careers are not lacking in purpose. They are seeking to do whatever they lay their hands to faster, more economically, and on a larger scale with less friction and with better control over more and more variable factors. And for all of these usually competitive objectives they can produce definitive quantitative measures that are often ingeniously refined and marvelously discriminating. Moreover, each technician is pursuing a career within an established and articulated hierarchy which has a well-developed scale of rewards and honors and some critical public to enforce legal or professional rules and standards. These are, of course, arbitrary—in the sense that the question "why" cannot be sensibly applied to them any more than it can be applied to, say, the standards of dress or the rules of courtship in our society.

We have a name for the sort of human activity that absorbs people in the orderly pursuit of arbitrary—usually competitive—goals according to arbitrary rules. We call it a "game." *Why* must an economy grow, *why* must profit be maximized, *why* must every bureaucracy expand and concentrate control, *why* must scientific truth and organizational efficiency and industrial productivity be ceaselessly elaborated? As soon as we grasp the fact that the expansion of technology is, for those who participate in the project, a game, these questions have the same logical status as the question: "Why is first base 90 feet from home plate?" or "Why is climbing a difficult mountain better than climbing an easy mountain?" And, of course, there is no answer to such questions other than to reassert the rule.

The elaboration of the technological society is, then, a game played by its own rules and for its own well-established goals. To be sure, because the players manipulate people and resources, their game is bound to have effects "beyond" itself—in the "real" world outside its perimeters. But whether those effects are good or harmful is as irrelevant to the game as what happens to a baseball once it has been hit outside the ball park: perhaps a father catches it for his son and makes the boy happy; perhaps it hits a bystander in the head and kills him. "Wonderful," we may say, or "too bad" . . . but the game goes on.

One objects, of course: an activity embracing so many people and resources should not be merely a game. Nonetheless, technological progress *is* a game, and those who participate in making the technological society work, and in perfecting its techniques, possess the psychology of people playing games. It is the structure and discipline of game-playing that bound their understanding of themselves and their work. The important questions, then, are: How did technological progress become a game? And how can that game be stopped . . . or, at least, its rules altered?

None of this will sound new to those familiar with the work of the mathematicians Von Neumann and Morgenstern and of the school of game theorists that follows from them. Since the end of World War II their work has made clear that both war and business—the two greatest technological projects—have all the characteristics of games. But the purpose of the game theorists has emphatically *not* been to develop a radical critique of military and economic activity. They do not, for example, ask the question whether such activities ought properly to be games, or how their rules ought to be "moralized." In game theory there is no such category as "forbidden games." Rather, game theory has only reinforced the game structure and practice of war and business by elaborating more elegant strategic principles for their pursuit. Its effect has been to estrange business and war further from their flesh-and-blood implications by imposing a rarefied and intriguingly playful set of mathematical abstractions upon the real world in which men work and live and die.

What we want to know here is not how to play, more cunningly and self-consciously, games that should perhaps not be played at all, but rather how technological progress ever became a game in the first place and so lost its contact with the reality it molds . . . and too often torments.

For answers to these questions, it is not the game theorists we want to turn to, but rather to the work of the Dutch historian Johan Huizinga. In 1938 Huizinga published a book which, although it has since been widely read and cited, has never really been assimilated into the mainstream of contemporary thought. *Homo Ludens* compares in scope, originality, and profundity with the seminal works of Freud and Marx: a superb effort to create a comprehensive theory of human behavior and social life.

In exploring the "play element in culture," Huizinga wished to avoid the conclusion that the need to play is instinctual, recognizing that to call anything an "instinct" is a bad (and dull) way to begin or end a study. And yet, when one tries to summarize Huizinga's theory, there seems no way to avoid the word. Whatever we consider to be an inborn and irreducible animal need—"an absolutely primary category of life," as Huizinga put it—is bound to fall under the classification "instinct." Any one who has ever observed the pointless, just-for-fun antics and romping of a baby or a puppy would grant that playfulness *is* an inherent, spontaneous animal activity—and so qualifies as being one of those mysterious things called "instincts." But what do we gain by adding still another item to the ever lengthening list of instincts psychologists and physiologists have drawn up and squabble over?

It was Huizinga's ingenious thesis that play is a supremely important instinct (or "function" as he preferred to call it) because, in contrast to the other drives—hunger, thirst, sex, etc., which serve to guard, comfort, and propagate the physical being of the species—play is superfluous to survival, safety, physical well-being. Play is what we do just for the fun of it—and, as Huizinga insists, it reaches beyond all moral, biological, and aesthetic considerations. His purpose in *Homo Ludens* was to show how this essential playfulness is elaborated into our repertory of cultural games: ritual, law, art, philosophy, science, war—none of which is simply "game-like," but actually arises from the same mode of human behavior that generates sports and contests.

Homo Ludens is a pioneer effort, and like the work of all intellectual trail-blazers, it is flawed with shortcomings and inconsistencies. There is a great deal more Huizinga might have done with the "gamesmanship" of our social manners, which the humorists Stephen Potter and Jules Feiffer have done so much to popularize. And the grasp contemporary psychiatrists now have of those involuted psychic strategies we call neurosis and psychosis completely eluded him. His interest was in the healthy and productive play of people, not in the secret and diseased games we invent to defend ourselves against the demands of culture. Of business life and technological organization Huizinga says little, beyond recognizing the agonistic drive that underlies capitalist competition. It escaped him wholly that the bureaucracy-building and social engineering of the "organization man"—whether latter-day capitalist or socialist—can have all the game-playing instinct about it that once motivated the robber barons in their drive for monopoly and empire.

But deeper than these lacks is Huizinga's facile identification of "play" and "games." "Play," he decided at the very outset of his study, "demands order absolute and supreme." Play "creates order, *is* order." And because the study rapidly sweeps us along into an analysis of various cultural games that do, indeed, possess a strict orderliness, we tend to accept his statement. Every game must have its rules, its official players, its delimited area, its defined objective. We know this is the case with cocktail parties and presidential conventions, just as it is with golf and bowling.

But, then, think again. "Game" is the word we reserve for this kind of *organized* play. All games draw upon the instinct to play. But it is not always to the regularity and orderliness of a game that play gives itself. Playing is clearly a much more generalized and lawless form of activity. Babies and animals "play" in a perfectly chaotic fashion. In fact, playful babies have very little patience with rules and regulations. They play quite naturally, but they must be taught their *games*.

Playfulness is an animal passion, not a cultural exercise. Indeed, it would not be too much to say that play is antagonistic to order. It satisfies itself in the immediate experience, not in the strategic pursuit of a goal or a score. "Playing around" is what we do when we are clowning, goofing off, being silly, acting spontaneously and randomly, and often so perversely as to subvert all order.

In what is certainly one of the most thorough investigations of the psychology of play in children, *Play, Dreams and Imitation in Childhood,* Jean Piaget clearly recognizes, as we do here, that play at the infantile level—motor-sensory play "purely for functional pleasure"—must be set apart from games with rules. Piaget's classification of play, which he examines entirely from the structural aspects of the child's behavior and not from its content or purpose, is three-fold. At the earliest stage of life, the child indulges in what Piaget calls "practice games," by which he means the reproduction of "behaviors merely for pleasure, accompanied by smiles and even laughter, and without the expectation of results. . . ." This is what I myself would call, simply, "play," as the word is most commonly used in our language. Then, somewhere toward the end of the second year, Piaget discovers that the child's repertory of play broadens to include the manipulation of symbols, a kind of play that increases as the child's mastery of language progresses. At this point, Piaget creates his second category of play: "symbolic games."

The important distinction Piaget's research has discovered is that which divides the young child's free play of body and mind from the older child's interest in games with rules—an interest that develops between the ages of 4 and 7 and that will then usually take over his sense of play for the remainder of his life. Piaget's "games with rules" (which I would simply call "games") are almost the only ones that persist at the adult stage. Somewhere after the first four or five years of life, the free manipulation of body and thought gives way to the pattern of the game with its orientation toward a specific goal and its structured rules.

So, in fact, there would seem to be a profound difference between the orderliness of a game and the chaotic fun of playing. They almost seem to be radically divergent modes of behavior. And yet we also sense that they are essentially related: that our many highly structured social and athletic games somehow absorb the impish spirit of play.

In his study of the "play-element in culture" Huizinga was really investigating the "game-element in culture." Play, being pre-cultural, indeed pre-human in character, escaped his attention. But let us give it our attention now. For if it is the case that technological "progress," with all its attendant, apparently inescapable liabilities of totalitarian politics and ever more efficient methods of genocidal warfare, is a game that strategists, bureaucrats, and social engineers play with the people and resources of the world, then we will want to understand how this compulsively organized game relates to the freedom of play.

The pleasure of infants, Norman Brown reminds us in his study of Freud, *Life Against Death,* "is in the active life of the body." And, he continues, "what is the pattern of activity, free from work, the serious business of life, and the reality-principle, which is adumbrated in the life of children? The answer is that children play." The ground of play, then, lies in that free and all-pervasive eroticism of the infant human being that Freud called "polymorphous perversity." The "*fun* of playing," which Huizinga felt "resists all logical interpretation," yields, I think, to Freud's *psycho*-logical interpretation. Play begins with the child's (and the animal's) sensuous manipulation of his body and all that comes in contact with it, and the *fun* of it all is a very fleshly satisfaction—the satisfaction most of us tend to know in later life only in its abbreviated genital form. But for the infant, stimulation anywhere upon the entire surface of the flesh, the work of the internal organs, the operation of the senses—in and of themselves, without any purpose or goal—is erotically satisfying. There is a simple and immediate joyousness in the functions and capacities of the body simply for what they are: the body's knowledge and enjoyment of itself *is* the act of play.

It is wonderful to imagine that there once glowed in all of us the sensuous satisfaction a painter discovers in the sheer act of seeing, or a muscian in the sheer act of hearing, or a dancer in the sheer act of manipulating his muscles. Wonderful, and also tragic, when we realize how little of this sensual capacity survives even in gifted people. For, of course, this erotic tenor of life with all its richness of feeling and imagination is the victim of those life-long denials and repressions "growing-up" demands of us. But it is precisely "the play-element in culture," Norman Brown observes, which "provides a prima facie justification for the psychoanalytical doctrine of sublimation which views 'higher' cultural activities as substitutes for lost infantile pleasures." Games, then, are the hardened, disciplined remnants the forces of repression have left us of infantile play.

Freud arrived at two markedly different explanations of repression in the course of his life's work. In his early writings repression of erotic joy was simply the price reality exacted for survival: survival demands work, and work demands sexual restraint. But in his later writings he modified the dire opposition of culture to sexual joy, and decided, instead, that repression was the product of an internal struggle between Eros, the life principle, and Thanatos, the death principle: man represses himself in attempting to defend his organism against the inevitable advance of death.

Both of these theories have their philosophical charm and both have proved therapeutically useful in one degree or another. But it may not be the psychiatrists who have said the last word on the subject of repression. Just as many of Freud's basic psychic insights arose out of his early training and study as a physician, so the work of A. T. W. Simeons in problems of physical medicine has brought a new approach to repression by calling our attention to the physiology of the brain and the evolutionary development of intelligence.

Since repression is a uniquely human experience, it is only logical to seek its explanation in that faculty which most distinguishes man from other animals: his highly elaborated intelligence. Intelligence, Dr. Simeons reminds us in his book, *Man's Presumptuous Brain,* arose from a very humble origin. It began as a neural complication in the olfactory lobes of man's reptilian ancestors, a kind of loop or hitch in the nervous network that began to behave as a "censor" between incoming stimuli and those more primitive parts of the brain which reacted automatically to such stimuli. The more complicated this neural "trap" became, the more efficiently it could intervene to discriminate among raw experiences and, on the basis of stored-up learning, allow for a choice of responses.

The intervention of this complex "censorial" intelligence between sensory stimuli and the automatic animal reactions to them has placed man in a privileged position among all animals. It has permitted him to make ingenious and novel choices where other animals are bound to the fixed pattern of instinctive behavior. Moreover, in man it has led to the creation of culture, of an artificial and controlled environment within which many of the primordial reactions of rage, fear, sexual excitement, etc., are either unnecessary or disruptive.

But, as Dr. Simeons points out, the advantage of cortical intelligence has had its liabilities. So rapidly have the cerebral hemispheres grown along the course of mammalian evolution that their censorial function has grown significantly out of balance with the primitive brain-stem and its instinctual repertory. He suggests that the development has been "freakish"—a specialization which, like so many successful specializations, has elaborated itself "faster and faster and may even develop of its own accord beyond the limits of usefulness." It is this impaired communication between cortex and diencephalon which Dr. Simeons holds responsible for the phenomenon of psychosomatic disease. Sexual frigidity and impotence, insomnia, arteriosclerosis, the digestive disorders —perhaps even diabetes and lumbago—all may result from the imperfect or even perverse cortical interpretation of organic reactions that have served as beneficial evolutionary responses and that remain locked in the brain-stem below the level of consciousness.

Dr. Simeons' contribution to the study of repression calls special attention to the adverse effects that have followed from the cortical repression, not simply of sex and aggression, but of fear and flight reflexes—extremely useful forms of behavior for the rather timid line of mammals from which we descend but now rendered largely unnecessary by the artificial protection of the cultural environment. In contrast to Freud, who identified the aggressive-destructive aspect of the death instinct as a basic human attribute, Dr. Simeons believes that timidity is the essential attribute of the human animal, and that aggressiveness has actually developed out of a latter-day cortical perversion of man's animal fearfulness. In turn, it is from this aggressive failure to be true to human nature that many of the psychosomatic ailments follow:

". . . when biologically timid man started to arm himself with inorganic armour to which the diencephalon had no functional relationship, he suddenly grew bold. His body and his brain-stem, having spent eons specializing in timidity, could not adjust themselves to the new courage. Their once normal responses became ever more inappropriate as culture and civilization swept onwards. . . . Ferocity was quite contrary to [man's] evolutionary nature, which was pusillanimous and non-violent. He learned to make up for his lack of natural weapons by impatiently creating an invincible armoury of artificial defenses . . . and to act as if he were the most aggressive creature on earth."

I have spent this much time on Dr. Simeon's work because I want to draw on his observations concerning the structure and evolution of the brain, especially on his conception of repression as being essentially an evolutionary breakdown in communication between complex intelligence and the body it presumes to govern. In choosing the word "intelligence" to summarize the activity of the cortical brain, I realize I am entering into one of the more troubled battlegrounds of professional psychology. But I believe that most of the problems psychologists ever since Binet have had with the "meaning of intelligence" stems from their preoccupation with the task of providing efficient screening tests for various social projects and, in turn, with the historical confusion of this task with the highly prestigious label "intelligence." This has led to what is often for the layman the perplexing but nonetheless professionally utilitarian conclusion that intelligence is what various tests measure.

To approach intelligence as a thing to be measured for immediate social needs may be legitimate enough for some purposes. But it leaves out of consideration the question we are concerned with here, which is the place of intelligence in the total organism. This was the question Henri Bergson raised sixty years ago when he asked in *Creative Evolution* that we reflect on the evolutionary function of intelligent behavior.

Much as we value human intelligence for its capacity to generate a high culture, we are really guilty of the sort of teleological fallacy Bergson himself is often accused of, when we fall into the habit of assuming that intelligence came into existence to create mathematics, philosophy, theoretical physics, etc., and that it is in terms of these highly sophisticated activities that intelligence is best understood. Bergson reminded us that intelligence probed and groped its way into existence long before high culture appeared and that, in its earliest manifestations, it possessed a rather humble character. It was then an instrument of survival, successful enough in its activity to be chosen and strengthened by the process of natural selection. Its orientation was toward "practical action." As a result, the tool remains for the anthropologist the single most concrete evidence of intelligence.

Within the context of evolution Bergson sought to do away with the notion that intelligence is a "thing" or static faculty. He wished, rather, to know what the dynamic relationship was between the intelligent animal and the world in which it had to act and move and survive. As Bergson portrayed intelligence, it was the capacity to rigidify, to quick-freeze, portions of the flow of experience so that these portions could then be acted upon with discretion. This process of solidifying and shaping the ceaseless flow of experience is the way in which intelligence seeks to adjust and orient experience with respect to selected goals: "useful ends," as Bergson called them. Within this provisional field of frozen experience, intelligence seeks constantly to routinize behavior and choice, to eliminate novelty and the unpredictable, to find similarities at the expense of uniqueness so that "a definite end calls forth definite means." In short, intelligence seeks constantly to find dependable rules of behavior that will achieve the same postulated results. From Bergson's point of view, science and technology progress by constantly reformulating or rearranging the field of experience, thus reassessing and generalizing the rules of successful (predictable) action.

Intelligence, then, as Bergson understood it, is that activity of the mind which makes experience "orderly" by isolating fields of attention within which the rules of successful action can be adjusted to selected goals. As he pointed out, intelligent "order" has so usurped our very conception of orderliness that everything which lies outside of it—the whole vast flow of vital experience—is perceived only as "disorder." But "disorder," he contended, is a nonsense concept, for it comes down ultimately to designating a different kind of order that one is unused to or did not expect to discover.

If we can accept Bergson's morphology of intelligence, we recognize at once what it is that intelligence essentially does. The isolation of a field of attention, the postulating of goals, the formation of rules: these are the three essential characteristics of what we call games. Intelligence plays games with reality. Its natural response to experience will always be the same: to define a field, fix a goal, apply rules.

Such is the life of the intelligent animal. He moves from arbitrary field to arbitrary field of activity: business, war, philosophy, politics, law, friendship, courtship, marriage. In each field he adopts the arbitrary goals and arbitrary rules appropriate to that field. And then he "plays the game"—the game being a social projection of the structure of his intelligence. Four hundred years ago Erasmus, perceiving the arbitrariness of man's earthly conduct, could smile good-naturedly at our human follies. But Erasmus was a religious man and could not bring himself to doubt that ultimately man's religious calling transcends the absurdity of his worldly pursuits. In our own time, when even the divine goal of salvation with its cosmic playing field and moral or theological rules has come to seem as arbitrary as any other human activity, nothing but absurdity seems to remain at the foundations of human life. So it is human absurdity that provides the basis for Ionesco's comedy, and for Kierkegaard's spiritual agony, and for the dour heroism of our existentialist philosophers. Indeed, in his *Myth of Sisyphus*, Albert Camus goes so far as to ask if human survival itself is not an arbitrary rule of the human game. Why survival? Why not suicide, he asks; and finishes by simply reasserting the rule . . . in all its naked absurdity. His essay is an excellent example of how impossible it is for the human intellect to get beyond its game-making habits, even when it deals with "ultimate questions."

Now, if we insist once again, with Bergson, that this game-making capacity grows out of an evolutionary background as a tool of survival, we can see what its relationship is to the spirit of play. Play, for all its joyousness, is chaotic and spontaneous. It reaches out toward experience without purpose and without discipline. It moves impractically with the stream of experience, rather than immobilizing and dividing that stream. It gives no power. It manipulates whatever it happens upon not for the sake of controlling, but for the sake of enjoying. Although we have a need to play, play possesses no survival value. Playfulness is, I suggest, what the game-making power of intelligence must discipline—and, in fact, has very effectively disciplined, substituting its own world of goals, symbols, rules, and rigidly defined fields for the fluidity and immediacy of play.

In describing the situation as I have here I have not, of course, identified the social forces, vested professional and economic interests, and historical circumstances that have brought about the apotheosis and dominance of the game-making intelligence. It is not something that

has come about automatically or inevitably. Works like Roderick Seiden-
berg's *Post-historic Man,* which interprets the advance of technical organization as an impersonal and irreversible conquest of "instinct" by
"intellect," or Jacques Ellul's *The Technological Society,* which suggests
that the progress of *la technique* is a matter of inexorable destiny, contribute a grim urgency to our thinking, but little enlightenment. At least
since the time William Blake hurled his visionary verse at England's
"Dark Satanic Mills," men have been aware of what technological progress can cost the human spirit. One thinks of the two memorable images
Chaplin captured in his film, *Modern Times.* On the one hand, we
remember the shabby little operator imprisoned in an automatic feeding
machine which was designed to diminish the time and motion required
for the lunch hour, a device that batters a scientifically balanced diet
into a recalcitrant and therefore probably obsolete human mouth and
digestive system. On the other hand, we remember the little operator
on roller skates, careening gaily about a department store, symbolically
reducing the compulsive orderliness of the modern world to slaphappy
chaos. It is a gesture of happy rebellion, of irreverent play, that amounts
to more than the vision of a single artist. It is an act of sabotage that an
audience of millions has understood, applauded, and, probably in a million secret ways, emulated.

It is at this point that I part company with the technological pessimists. While one would have to be a fool to believe that all is bound
to turn out for the best, it may nevertheless be the case that (for better
or worse, and usually for the better) the world is really a great deal less
organized and under control than its official leadership would have us
believe. In his play, *An Angel Comes to Babylon,* Frederick Dürenmatt
has dramatized a truth most historians are aware of: there is apt to be
an immense difference between the way a society really works and the
way in which its domineering élite believes it works and wants it to
work.

Once upon a time the reigning monarchs of the world, as a matter
of course, kept jesters at their courts to remind them of this discrepancy
and of their own presumptuous folly. In our contemporary governments,
the commissars and social engineers no longer keep jesters, but they
have not necessarily eliminated their own folly along with the jester.
In the many back rooms, pool halls, pubs, bedrooms—the secret places
that elude discovery and frustrate analysis—a mass life of sarcasm, cyni-
cal good sense, and incorrigible resistance to organization continues,
mixed with as much superstition and crude incomprehension as ever.

The most critical charge I would level at Jacques Ellul and those
other technological pessimists centers on their systematic ignorance of

this factor. For them "technique" is that one *efficient* way of doing things which leads, irresistibly and finally, to a single technical solution. Efficiency is thus a purely quantitative and unambiguous measure. But I would call such efficiency by a different name: "idiot efficiency." It is the conception of efficiency that led nineteenth century capitalists to conclude that an army of docile automatons toiling a sixteen-hour work-day at starvation wages and under bestial conditions was the secret of high productivity and industrial wealth. It is the conception of efficiency that led to Stalin's brutal collectivization of Russian agriculture. It is the conception of efficiency that first conceives of the body as a mechanism that must be *made* to run by the brain, and then, in the familiar image of the body politic, conceives of society as a collection of members and organs that must be similarly *made* to function by specialized decision-makers. But the ultimate result of such jealous centralization of "control" is always paralysis and malfunction—to the extent that the whole system collapses as the "head" eventually drives the "members" into intolerable despair or rebellion.

In economics and social engineering, efficiency is a weasel-word which tends to obscure a multitude of human values. When is any social or economic system "efficient"? No doubt the idiot technician will answer: when every factor is organized according to an expert plan and implemented by an omniscient command and control center. But as working men have recognized for generations, "working to rule" is one of the best ways to gum up an economy. When everybody works to rule —no more, no less, and no differently—the system falls apart. So, in the West, we have learned the value of seeking efficiency by way of consensus, by way of encouraging a sense of participation, initiative, and high morale among citizens, as producers, consumers, or voters. To be sure, governing élites, by and large, still seek to engineer consensus and, in a variety of clever ways, to render freedom and initiative illusory. But why bother with the whole intricate hypocrisy of manipulated consensus unless one recognizes that the illusions meet real human needs and that it is actually more "efficient" to cater to those needs than to crush them?

A truly efficient social system—one that is stable, enduring, secure, productive—works *with* the grain of human needs and not against it. Thus, efficiency is not a purely quantitative measure, but a profoundly qualitative one. An efficient technological society, like an efficient machine shop or office, is ultimately one that cares for the quality of life, for the freedom, initiative, and playfulness of the human animal that participates in the enterprise. The fact that idiot efficiency crushes these qualities is undeniable and tragic. But there is also the fact—perhaps the only fact from which one can take consolation and inspiration—that idiot efficiency stagnates and frustrates, subverts and destroys, the systems it creates. Ultimately, those who play forbidden games lose them, and the ruins their loss frequently leaves us with invariably offer an opportunity to rebuild a more natural and livable society.

THE THEATRE OF SPORTS

John Lahr

The human being is delivered helpless, in respect to life's most impor-
tant and trivial affairs, to a power (technology) which is in no sense
under his control. For there can be no question today of man's control-
ling the milk he drinks or the bread he eats, any more than of his con-
trolling his government.

—Jacques Ellul,
The Technological Society

Take me out to the ball game,
Take me out to the park.
Buy me some peanuts and Cracker Jack,
I don't care if I never get back . . .
—Old baseball song

Games are a means, through make-believe, of coping with the world.
So is theatre. But as the opportunity for physical prowess and uncomplicated, noble victory is denied mechanized man, the spectacle of sport
has assumed a potency and ritual importance in America that most
theatre has lost. Sports have become a twentieth-century obsession.
Sports are the nation's grand distraction, incorporating a tableau of
affluence once reserved for the Broadway musical into the larger am-
bitions of a highly industrial state. Formal, controlled, efficiently organized, the modern spectacles reflect the technological thrust of this
century. They offer not only escape but confirmation, adjusting the
public to the violence and inequities of the system. Theatre, emphasizing
immediacy, emotional depth, psychic and social change, is reminiscent

John Lahr, "The Theatre of Sports," *Evergreen Review* 13 (November, 1969): 39-76.
Reprinted by permission.

of a humanity eroded by urban living. Spectacle is more comfortable and reassuring. It asks no questions of the viewer but provides the thrill of external action.

The sports spectacle has become America's right-wing theatre, affirming the status quo by making those processes which emasculate man palatable in "play." Spectacle is an important barometer of an age. Each type of spectacle has evolved with the demands of contemporary society, reflecting and influencing its view of the world.

I

Medieval pageants were a concrete expression of the living faith. They brought the teachings of the Church off the cathedral walls and into the town square. The floats which squeaked under the weight of peasant angels, devils, and biblical heroes were preceded at each station by the blare of trumpets and the hoots of an obstreperous crowd. The spectacles were an escape and an educational device, as well as a means of keeping the feudal population obedient to the Church. Spectacle was a local community activity. In the town of Wakefield, which produced the memorable cycle of mystery plays, records show that two hundred and forty parts were filled from a town of approximately five hundred and sixty people. The guilds competed in building floats. The actors, miming the drama of Heaven and Hell which surrounded their lives, often played roles parallel to their position in the town pecking order.

Although the pageants were referred to as "mystery" plays, there was no mystery for the medieval audience for whom the stories were a familiar affirmation of the Church's truth. With pulleys to suspend angels and trapdoors to dispatch devils, the medieval multiple set reinforced the hierarchical view of man's place in the Divine scheme. The process of man's life was not as important as the reassuring iconography which surrounded it. The groupings, gestures, symbols in spectacle had an orthodoxy that the words did not. The spectacle incarnated the medieval mentality, communicating in sculptural, vivid images to nonliterate medieval minds. The simple images made profound sense of a confusing world. The people witnessing the spectacle were intimately involved with those performing it. They were seeing the Divine in themselves and themselves in the Divine. The effect was to create a political as well as spiritual unity. "The crowd assembled for the great festivals felt itself to be a living whole, and became the mystical body of Christ, its soul passing into his Soul."[1]

---

1. J. Huizinga. *The Waning of the Middle Ages* (New York: Doubleday and Company, 1934), p. 147.

While spoken sermons were few in the Middle Ages (a thirteenth-century papal decree commanded at least four a year), spectacle was used by radical priests like St. Francis of Assisi (who went among the people and made a "spectacle of himself") to dramatize the necessity of a saintly life and the onus of sin. St. Francis' attempt to embrace the mythic formula of spectacle for individual drama is described by Erich Auerbach in *Mimesis*:

> He forced his inner impulse into outer forms; his being and his life became public events; from the day when, to signify his relinquishment of things of the world, he gave back his clothes to his upbraiding father, down to the day when, dying, he had himself laid naked on the naked earth so that in his last hour, when the archfiend might still rage, he could fight naked with the naked enemy.[2]

St. Francis confronted his audience with immediate images. After a night of gluttony he had himself dragged through town with a rope around his neck while he confessed. The spectacle matched the pageants in clarity and scenic force. It demanded imitation and participation by the community. St. Francis used the contemporary sense of the world to captivate an audience.

In Elizabethan England spectacle was also a means of community control. The seasonal celebrations were organized anarchy intended to take the head off the frustration and violence of a stratified society. The Lord and Lady of Misrule mocked the Lords and Ladies of the Manor by mimicking and exaggerating their power. A Puritan observer described a typical May game:

> They have twenty or forty yolk of oxen, every ox having a sweet nosegay of flowers on the tip of his horns, and these oxen draw home this Maypole which is covered all over with flowers and herbs, bound round about with strings, from the top to the bottom . . . with two or three hundred men, women and children following it with great devotion. And thus being reared up with handkerchiefs and flags . . . they strew the ground about, bind green boughs about it, set up summer halls, bowers and arbors hard by it. And then they fall to dance about it, like as the heathen people did at the dedication of Idols . . .[3]

Trespassing beyond the allotted festival period could bring severe penalties. But, once begun, the momentum of spectacle was sometimes hard to stop. In *Henry IV* (Part 1) Prince Hal criticizes Falstaff, the archetypal Lord of Misrule who forgets the boundaries of spectacle:

2. Erich Auerbach. *Mimesis* (New York: Doubleday Anchor Books, 1957), p. 141.
3. C. L. Barber, *Shakespeare's Festive Comedy* (Cleveland: Meridian Books, 1963), p. 21.

If all the year were playing holidays
To sport would be as tedious as work;
But when they seldom come, they wished-for come . . .

(1, ii, 228-230)

As C. L. Barber writes in *Shakespeare's Festive Comedy*, the anarchy
allowed the mock lord to enjoy "building up his dignity, and also
exploding it by exaggeration, while his followers both relish his bom-
bast as a fleer at proper authority and also enjoy turning on him and
insulting his majesty . . . the game at once appropriates and annihilates
the mana of authority."[4] These popular spectacles fed theatre, especially
Shakespeare's comedies. Shakespeare transported this "midsummer madness" to the stage, not merely by adopting its sights and sounds, but by
applying the festival process of release and clarification through playing.
In Shakespeare's comedies the characters move into a safe, festival
world (Arden, Oberson's Wood, Olivia's house) where identities are
tested and explored. Shakespeare's characters often *game* at the world in
order to discover it, while remaining outside its passions. Viola says of
Feste in *Twelfth Night*:

This fellow is wise enough to play the fool
And to do that craves a kind of wit.
He must observe the mood on whom he jests
The quality of persons and the time . . .

(111, i, 66-70)

Festivals dramatized identity; people found out about the world
by playing at it. In *As You Like It* Rosalynd escapes the chaos of the
court, discovers the "liberty" of Arden, and finally returns to the real
world. She is now socially and psychically whole. The play parallels
the process of Elizabethan spectacle, a game which clarifies the actual
experience.

Feste's final song in *Twelfth Night* emphasizes the illusion of spectacle: that man is not responsible for his actions. "The rain that raineth
every day" is the stark reality which makes it necessary to play but also
to realize the limitation of the spectacle. The paradox is built into the
sadness of Feste's chronicle of his life:

But when I came to man's estate,
    With a hey, ho, the wind and the rain
'Gainst knaves and thieves men shut their gate,
    For the rain it raineth every day . . .

(V, i, 402-405)

Twelfth Night's popularity rests with Shakespeare's ability to harness
the frenzy of folk spectacle to more responsible ends.

4. *Ibid.*, p. 9.

II

The pressure of technology molds the form of modern spectacle. Games admit a mechanized sense of time; they stress a system of rules and moves. The spectacle, before the development of technique, was eccentric. The modern spectacle has become national through the television set. In previous centuries a large portion of the society participated in the event, but the most popular modern spectator sports (baseball, football) are not the ones which Americans play most (golf, bowling). Football and baseball can be enjoyed in statistics as well as on the field. They have a fictional appeal in a society whose organization fractures work and puts a premium on efficiency rather than imagination. Sports recast man in an heroic mold. They are important for creating a sense of well-being in troubled times.

As the primal sources of man's identity are strangled by technology, as his primacy and his relation to the land are minimized, his fanaticism toward sports spectacle increases. Technology is both an oppressor and a reason for hope. The modern American games try to palliate this paradox. But the spectacles which set out to be diversion end up as cultural anesthesia. From childhood, the American male is steeped in the rules and lore of the games which imbue control, team play, and moral value. Life is equated with sport; the body (especially in football) aspires to become the machine which has replaced it in the real world. The spectacles institutionalize conformity and obedience, laying the groundwork for totalitarian response. The stress on toughness and violent victory ("slaughter," "kill," "pound," "ream," "cream," "mutilate") indicate a more primitive militarism:

> . . . . Technicized sport was first developed in the United States, the most conformist of all countries, and . . . it was then developed as a matter of course by the dictatorships. Fascist, Nazi, and Communist, to the point that it became an indispensable constituent element of totalitarian regimes.[5]

Sports spectacle also feeds a larger psychic yearning: the illusion of primitive power, now lost to the machine. As Lionel Tiger points out in *Men In Groups* (Random House, 1969) sports allow the spectator to rediscover his identity through "hunter-aggressive endeavors." The team names dramatize the spectators' wish-fulfillment; animals in the chase (Falcons, Tigers, Cubs, Bears, Hawks, Broncos) or mythic figures of power and bravery (Buffalo Bill, Giants, Vikings, Warriors, Braves).

Baseball is a spectacle of America's early industrialization. Football is the daydream of a passive, computerized society, melding violence

5. Jacques Ellul, *The Technological Society* (New York: Vintage Books, 1967), p. 383.

with elaborate efficiency. They are both epic struggles which have their real-life consummation in the astronauts, the game of the technological present. The space game takes its place as a popular spectacle, exhibiting the national fascination with teamwork and hardware which rationalizes and sublimates the social ulcer. With astronautics, the machine becomes the hero of the spectacle, assuming the mythic power once invested in man. The space program is named "Apollo"; the moonship has the imperial, predatory title of "Eagle"; and even the NASA satellites are called "Mariner," an image reminiscent of Viking journeys into uncharted waters, also a test of selfhood.

All these spectacles emphasize the American articles of faith: accomplishment, production, bravery, and goodness. In breaking in an audience to its technological environment, modern spectacle answers to the demands of the people. As individuality decreases in America, sports turn human beings into ritual objects, elevating the Mantles, Namaths, and Aldrins beyond public scrutiny. Spectacle becomes imaginative balm for new wounds.

III

Sport is tied to industry because it represents a reaction to industry.[6] Baseball became the nation's favorite game during violent, squalid industrialization. The game melded field with factory, incorporating the techniques of an emerging capitalism with a pastoral panorama. The sward of green turf still exists amidst the bleakness of surrounding industrial tenements it was meant to deny. The pace, now too slow for an electronic age, promised long outdoor hours as an antidote to the boredom of industry:

> He jeers the officials and indulges in hot arguments with his neighbors, stamping and ranting . . . All the time his vital organs are summoned into strenuous sympathy and he draws deep breaths of pure air. He may be weary when the game is over but for it he will eat and sleep better, his step will be more determined, his eyes will cease resembling those of a dead fish . . . He goes back to his desk or bench next day with a smiling face.[7]

Baseball was not only an escape; it reinforced capitalist values. The game treated people as property. "Trading" and "bonuses" were a means of improving efficiency and sharpening competition. Baseball also incorporated "stealing"— risk proportional to an individual's ability and his

6. *Ibid.*, p. 382.
7. Douglass Wallop, *Baseball: An Informal History* (New York: W. W. Norton & Company, 1969), p. 109.

luck. Industry increased production through standardization; so did baseball. Each player is a specialist; the team (with its "manager" and "front office") became a proto-corporation where the spectator could measure the output (of runs). Batting averages, earned-run averages were comfort percentiles: simple calculations in a world of outrageous figures and complicated equations. Medieval pageants attested to the Church's accuracy; baseball affirmed the new world of accounting and double-entry bookkeeping. "It is good to care in any dimension," William Saroyan said about the national pastime. "More Americans put their spare (and purest?) caring into baseball."[8] Seymour Siwoff, the accountant who keeps the statistics for the National League, has a sign above his door. ETERNAL VIGILANCE IS THE PRICE OF ACCURACY IN STATISTICS. If baseball reduces people to numbers the figures have, at least, a continuity and a relationship to the past. The faith in statistics prevents baseball from changing its rules because the hitting and pitching averages of the future would have no relationship to those of the past. The sentimental attachment to statistics is expressed by Siwoff in *Sports Illustrated* (August 18, 1969):

> What I enjoy most about statistics is the chance they give you to relive the past. When Ernie Banks gets seven RBIs in a game or when Reggie Jackson gets ten, it brings back memories of when Jim Bottomley drove in twelve or Tony Lazzeri drove in eleven. In looking up those things, I can see those guys as clearly as if they were playing again.

Invoking an uncomplicated past, statistics and the umpire's rule book bring the authority of "science" and "law" onto the field. The spectators and players respect both forces; they abide by a trained, "objective" decision. The game allows the illusion of freedom, but violent disagreement is not tolerated. Eccentricity, like Richie Allen's scribbling of words to the spectators in front of first base, is carefully patrolled. (The Commissioner of Baseball told Allen to stop writing "Boo," "No," "Why" in the dirt. No one balked when he wrote "Mom.") Allen is a renegade within a system that cannot tolerate friction. Baseball dramatizes acquiescence to system, law, and the mathematics of productivity.

IV

Technology creates its own demand. As America becomes increasingly systematized, unified, and efficient, the public wants more technique in its spectacles. Football offers a picture of the "gorgeousness"

---

8. A. Lawrence Holmes, *More Than a Game* (New York: The Macmillan Company, 1967), p. 11.

of enforced specialization of human effort. In the game, technique is concomitant with victory. Talking of coach Vince Lombardi, veteran guard Jerry Kramer stresses the importance of superhuman performance and accuracy:

> He makes us execute the same plays over and over, a hundred times, two hundred times, until we do every little thing right *automatically*. He works to make the kickoff return team perfect. He ignores nothing. Technique, technique, technique, over and over and over, until we feel like we're going crazy. But we win.[9]

The football player's ability to make a machine of his body sustains the spectator's faith in technology. The drama of football pits man-and-technique against man-and-technique. Films, training devices, medical equipment, special diets reflect the game's reliance on scientific discovery for *protection, defense,* and *victory.* When a Miami Dolphin end received a second concussion, a special helmet was devised to protect him. Joe Namath's million-dollar knees are guarded by a specially constructed brace. Scientific innovation is part of the team's efficiency.

Football's appeal rests with the intricacy of its system. The game emphasizes a mechanized, industrial sense of time. The players "watch the clock"; seconds become dramatic divisions. Even the vocabulary of play is in pseudo-mathematical language in which the offensive runner and his destination on the line of scrimmage are identified by number. Jerry Kramer mentions a "forty-nine sweep," which means that the number four back will take the ball into the "nine" hole, the area outside the right end.

Graceful, strong, fierce—the football player is an automation in the world of action. Jerry Kramer describes the fatigue of training:

> All I know is that when everyone else moves, I move, and when everyone files on the bus, I get on the bus . . . I really don't know what time it is, what day it is . . . I don't know anything at all.[10]

Joe Namath recounts the programming of new data ("automatics") on the line of scrimmage during the Super Bowl:

> When I change a play . . . they've got to drive the play they've been thinking about from their minds and they've got to replace it with a new one, and in a few seconds they've got to be ready for a different assignment, maybe on a different snap count, maybe in a whole different direction.[11]

9. Jerry Kramer, *Instant Replay* (New York: World Publishing Company, 1968), p. 41.
10. *Ibid.,* p. 35.
11. Joe Namath, "I Can't Wait Until Tomorrow . . . Cause I Get Better Looking Every Day," *True Magazine* (September, 1969), p. 54.

The implications of football are hidden by the excitement. The game confirms America's abiding faith in technology as a means of progress. Football is a spectacle of superhuman effort attesting to the value of research, training, discipline, and refinement. Although the players battle for money and publicize their off-season businesses, the contest on the field is beyond pecuniary consideration. There is a messianic atmosphere to football—the lockerroom talks, the bravado of the spectators which brings them to their feet or sends them out into the field after a game to rip down the goalposts. Football is a triumph of technique and community. The spectacle offers an image of athletic unity and creates an *emotional consensus*:

> Technique provides a justification to everybody and gives all men the conviction that their actions are just, good, and in the spirit of truth. The individual finds the same conviction in his fellow workers and feels himself strengthened.[12]

V

Baseball and football make reality out of a game. The space race makes a game out of reality. Technology extends the demand, fed by sport, for continued, easy victory with no sacrifice from the community of observers. The Apollo 11 was described in terms of a game. The familiar features of sport facilitate public acquiescence to the awesome specter of the machine being willed to power over man. The astronauts are the golddust twins of the galaxies; their training is an athlete's regimen of diet, study, and drills. Neil Armstrong's statement in *Life* (August 22, 1969) illustrates how the vocabulary becomes propaganda:

> This nation was depending on the NASA-industry *team* to do the job and that team was staking its reputation on Apollo 11. A lot of necks had been put voluntarily on the chopping block, and as more and more attention focussed on the flight it became evident that any failure would bring certain tarnish to the U. S. image.

The moonshot is an instant image of progress in a society where social reform is thought to involve sacrifice: "Landing men on the moon has proven easier than unraveling problems such as public welfare." (*Life*, August 22, 1969) Trained to witness gargantuan athletic feats, the American spectator accepts scientific hardware as matter-of-factly as a batting machine. The space program is its own justification:

> Modern men are so enthusiastic about technique, so assured of its superiority, so immersed in the technical milieu, that without exception they are oriented toward technical progress.[13]

12. Ellul, *op. cit.*, p. 369.
13. *Ibid.*, p. 431-32.

The moonshot is the triumph of system. Aficionados of the moon spectacle can only applaud and succumb. Yet a new world has been spawned which will affect the way man works and how he relates to his environment. As a chauvinistic article in the July, 1969 *Fortune* testified:

> The really significant fallout from the strains, traumas, and endless experiment of Project Apollo has been . . . techniques for directing the massed endeavors of scores of thousands of minds in a close-knit mutually enhancive combination of government, university, and private industry.

The space game makes man wetnurse to machinery. Armstrong, Aldrin, and Collins manipulate dials. They were first on the moon, but there are dozens waiting in the wings who can do the same thing as efficiently. They do not fit the conventional heroic mold; their function is not total. They are not free, lone men grappling with a recalcitrant universe. Thousands of others, behind dials and levers, are keeping them aloft. The hero is the machine, not man. As Michael Collins said, "The computer, of course, had been telling me that everything was going well. . . ." In the space game, as with all sports spectacles, man is the master of external details which have no bearing on his inner life. The technician's freedom is a slavery to machinery and the system that organizes it. Human value is compromised, the inner life devalued in the performance of tasks. Aldrin, discussing the content of his prayers during the moon trip, told *Life*:

> I was not so selfish as to include my family in those prayers, nor so spacious as to include the fate of the world. *I was thinking of our particular task* and the challenge and opportunity that had been given us.

The drama of teamwork, the tension of statistics and physical accuracy, are now firmly established in the real world as well as on the playing field. Spectacle overwhelms the senses. The astronauts are praised for characteristics which warp the human fiber. They represent in life the process that Americans cheer in the stadium: "a new dismembering and a complete reconstruction of the human being so that he can at last become the objective (and also total object) of technique. He is also completely despoiled of everything that traditionally constitutes his essence. Man becomes pure appearance, a kaleidoscope of external shapes, an abstraction in a milieu that is frighteningly concrete . . ."[14]

VI

Spectacle reinforces the illusion of objectivity. Events are paraded before the eye and the spectator feels imaginatively in control of both

14. *Ibid.*, p. 85.

the game and its rules. Spectacle's clarity, its system, deny mystery:

> Technique worships nothing, respects nothing. It has a single role: to strip off externals, to bring everything to light, and by rational use to transform everything to means.[15]

The nonrational, the non-law-abiding, the emotionally unpalatable must be dismissed and ultimately eliminated.

Theatre cannot compete with the ritual experience of spectacle, but it can learn from it. As a handicraft industry in a technological age, theatre has lost its sense of ritual and forgotten how to deal with primal impulses. Too often our theatre is overly polite and self-conscious. It rarely understands the spectacle it offers and how to capitalize on the *forms* of pleasure which feed its audience's mythology. The fact of theatre being a game is often forgotten in the attempt to make a serious statement. Yet the process of "gaming" can have a more profound effect on an audience than a narrative plot. Theatre pieces like John Ford's Noonan's *The Year Boston Won the Pennant*. Peter Terson's *Zigger Zagger* (soccer), and Arthur Kopit's *Indians* have a radical stage potential because they invoke memories of comfortable spectacle and mythic appeal, only to work against those assumptions. The spectator subsequently becomes aware of his two faces: the dreamer and the diminished man.

By understanding the force of spectacle, American threatre can redefine itself more vigorously. It can forge an island of humanity and freedom in a sea of banal uniformity and data. The axioms of a technological society cannot be answered by an equally pat denial. But the forms which make them acceptable to the public can be imaginatively exploded. Technology and the forces which promote it are too large to be reversed, but a countervailing theatre may have an heroic destiny and a liberty the rest of America has lost.

15. *Ibid.*, p. 142.

THE TECHNOLOGICAL REVOLUTION AND THE
RISE OF SPORT, 1850-1900

JOHN RICKARDS BETTS

The roots of our sporting heritage lie in the horse racing and fox hunting of the colonial era, but the main features of modern sport appeared only in the middle years of the nineteenth century.[1] Organization, journalistic exploitation, commercialization, intercommunity competition, and sundry other developments increased rapidly after 1850 as the agrarian nature of sport gave way gradually to the influences of urbanization and industrialization. Just as the Industrial Revolution was to alter the interests, habits, and pursuits of all classes of society, it was to leave a distinct impress on the development of sport.

Many other factors were responsible for the directions taken by sport in the half century from 1850 to 1900. Continuing rural influences, the decline of Puritan orthodoxy, the English athletic movement, the immigrant, frontier traditions of manliness and strength, and the contributions of energetic sportsmen were to have a significant effect on the sporting scene. Industrialization and urbanization, however, were more fundamentally responsible for the changes and developments in sport during the next generation than any other cause. Manufacturers,

John Rickards Betts, "The Technological Revolution and the Rise of Sports, 1850-1900," *The Mississippi Valley Historical Review* 40 (September, 1953): 231-256. Copyright © 1953 by the Organization of American Historians.

1. Among the most useful works to be consulted on early American sport are John A. Krout, *Annals of American Sport* (New Haven, 1929); Jennie Holliman, *American Sports, 1785-1835* (Durham, 1931); Foster R. Dulles, *America Learns To Play: A History of Popular Recreation, 1607-1940* (New York, 1940); Robert B. Weaver, *Amusements and Sports in American Life* (Chicago, 1939); and Herbert Manchester, *Four Centuries of Sport in America, 1490-1890* (New York, 1931). For certain aspects of ante-bellum sport, see Arthur M. Schlesinger and Dixon R. Fox (eds.), *A History of American Life*, 13 vols. (New York, 1927-1948).

seeking cheap labor, encouraged immigration; factories were most efficiently run in larger towns and cities; urban masses, missing the rustic pleasures of hunting and fishing, were won to the support of commercialized entertainment and spectator sports; the emergence of a commercial aristocracy and a laboring class resulted in distinctions every bit as strong in sport as in other social matters; and the urgency of physical exercise as life became more sedentary was readily recognized.

The revolution in manufacturing methods, which had such profound social consequences for the American way of life, derived from a powerful inventive spirit which flourished throughout the nineteenth century. From England and western Europe we borrowed many mechanical innovations and most of our scientific theory, but Americans demonstrated a native ability soon recognized everywhere as "Yankee ingenuity." These inventions were to revolutionize transportation, communication, manufacturing, finance, and all the many facets of economic life. Although the tendency in narrating the history of sport has been to emphasize the role of individuals, the changing social scene was of equal importance in directing sport into the channels it eventually took in modern society. The impact of invention had a decisive influence on the rise of sport in the latter half of the century. By 1900 sport had attained an unprecedented prominence in the daily lives of millions of Americans, and this remarkable development had been achieved in great part through the steamboat, the railroad, the telegraph, the penny press, the electric light, the streetcar, the camera, the bicycle, the automobile, and the mass production of sporting goods.

The transformation of the United States from a rural-agrarian to an urban-industrial society, of course, affected the development of sport in other ways. Urbanization brought forth the need for commercialized spectator sports, while industrialization gradually provided the standard of living and leisure time so vital to the support of all forms of recreation. But it is the relationship of invention to sport, and that alone, which constitutes the theme of this study.

Early American interest in outdoor exercise was largely confined to hunting, fishing, horse racing, field sports, and the informal games of the local schoolyard. As the nation became more commercially minded in the decades after the War of 1812, many of those who lived in rapidly growing cities became concerned over the sedentary habits of clerks, office workers, and businessmen. In the years before 1850 there emerged a limited interest in rowing, running, prize fighting, cricket, fencing, and similar activities, but the only organized sport which excited the minds of most Americans was the turf. A more general interest in horse racing appeared in the 1820's and 1830's, and many jockey clubs held meetings attended by throngs of spectators in their carriages and barouches.[2]

From the early years of the century steamboat captains engaged in racing on the Hudson, Ohio, Mississippi, and other rivers, and the steamboat served as a common carrier of sports crowds. By the 1850's it became an indispensable means of transport to the races along the eastern seaboard and in the Mississippi Valley. As one of the first products of the age of steam it played a significant role in the rise of the turf and outdoor games.[3]

In the years preceding the Civil War the turf was also encouraged by the development of a railroad network. As early as 1838 Wade Hampton was transporting race horses to Charleston by rail;[4] in 1839 the Nashville Railroad was carrying New Orleans crowds to the Metairie Course;[5] in 1842 the Long Island Railroad was already suffering the abuse of irate passengers swarming to the races; and three years later it carried some 30,000 passengers to the Fashion-Peytona race at more than fifty cents each.[6] Kentucky became the leading breeding center for thoroughbreds and Louisville could announce in 1851: "Lexington, Georgetown, Frankfort, Paris and other towns in this State, are now but a short ride from our city by railroad conveyance. Horses can come from Lexington here in five hours."[7] The famous trotter Flora Temple began barnstorming tours; racing and trotting benefited from the cooperation of railroad lines; and "speed trials" at agricultural fairs during the 1850's were at-

---

2. See the New York *American*, May 27, 1823; New Orleans *Daily Picayune*, March 27, 1839; New York *Weekly Herald*, May 17, 1845, July 11, 1849; and accounts of many races in the *Spirit of the Times* (New York) for prewar years. In an era when bridges were more the exception than the rule the ferry was an indispensable means of transportation. See, for example, Kenneth Roberts and Anna M. Roberts (eds.), *Moreau de St. Méry's American Journey, 1793-1798* (Garden City, 1947), 173; New York *American*, May 27, 1823.

3. For examples of the steamboat in early sport, see the New York *Herald*, June 17, 1849; *Wilkes' Spirit of the Times* (New York), XII (August 5, 1865), 380; New Orleans *Daily Picayune*, December 1, 1855, December 10, 1859; *Spirit of the Times*, XX (June 19, 1869), 276; New York *World*, June 19, 1869. When the passenger lines began converting to steam in the Civil War era, the development of international sport was facilitated to a considerable degree. In the latter decades of the century the steam yacht became the vogue among American millionaires.

4. John Hervey, *Racing in America, 1665-1865*, 2 vols. (New York, 1944), II, 101.

5. New Orleans *Daily Picayune*, March 27, 1839.

6. *American Turf Register and Sporting Magazine* (Baltimore), XIII (July, 1843), 367; New York *Daily Tribune*, May 14, 1845.

7. *Spirit of the Times*, XXI (July 12, 1851), 246.

tended by excursionists.[8] Other outdoor sports also profited from the interest shown by certain lines. When excitement over rowing began to catch on in the late 1830's the first boat shipped west of the Appalachians went by way of the Erie Canal.[9] It was a railroad, however, which encouraged the holding of the first intercollegiate rowing race between Harvard and Yale in 1852.[10] Baseball clubs were organized throughout the East and Midwest during the decade and the National Association of Base Ball Players was formed in 1857, soon after both sections had been connected by rail. Chicago had its first baseball team in 1856, two years after it was linked by rail to Baltimore, Maryland, and Portland, Maine. In 1860 the Excelsior Club of Brooklyn made a tour of upper New York state. Most of the early prize fights were held along the rivers served by steamboats; the Harlem Railroad carried fight crowds in the early 1850's to the Awful Gardiner-William Hastings (*alias* Dublin Tricks) match sixty miles north of New York City and to a highly publicized championship fight at Boston Four Corners, New York;[11] and the John Morrissey-John Heanan match on the Canadian shore near Niagara Falls in 1858 was advertised by the Erie Railroad.[12]

The Civil War failed to halt turf meetings and outdoor recreation in the North. It was, however, only with the return of peace that the nation felt a new sporting impulse and began to give enthusiastic support to the turf, the diamond, the ring, and other outdoor activities. The game of baseball, spreading from cities to towns and villages, became a national fad, and matches were scheduled with distant communities. A tournament at Rockford, Illinois, in 1866 was attended by teams from

---

8. Albert L. Demaree, *The American Agricultural Press, 1819-1860* (New York, 1941), 203-204. Specific instances of such aid can be found in the *Cultivator* (Albany), IX (March, 1842), 50; *American Agriculturist* (New York), II (October 16, 1843), 258; New York *Daily Tribune*, September 18, 1851; *Transactions of the Illinois State Agricultural Society* (Springfield), I, 1853-54 (1855), 6; II 1856-57 (1857), 24-32; *Report and Proceedings of the Iowa State Agricultural Society . . . October, 1855* (Fairfield, 1856), 24; *Fifth Report of the Indiana State Board of Agriculture . . . For the Year 1856* (Indianapolis, 1858), 34, 482-83; *Kentucky Farmer* (Frankfort), I (July, 1858), 12; *Wisconsin Farmer and North-Western Cultivator* (Madison), IX (October, 1857), 873; XI (October, 1859), 386-87; Springfield *Weekly Illinois State Journal*, September 5, 19, 1860. The "ploughing matches" of the ante-bellum era attracted large crowds seeking both entertainment and the latest improvements in agricultural implements.

9. Samuel Crowther and Arthur Ruhl, *Rowing and Track Athletics* (New York, 1905), 11.

10. James N. Elkins, superintendent of the Boston, Concord and Montreal Railroad, agreed to pay all transportation costs for the crews and their equipment to the New Hampshire lake where the race was to be held. Robert F. Kelley, *American Rowing: Its Background and Traditions* (New York, 1932), 100-101.

11. New York *Daily Times*, October 13, 1853; Boston *Advertiser*, October 14, 1853.

12. New York *Herald*, October 23, 1858.

Detroit, Milwaukee, Dubuque, and Chicago.[13] In 1869 Harry Wright's Cincinnati Red Stockings were able to make a memorable transcontinental tour from Maine to California; a New Orleans club visited Memphis, St. Louis, and Cincinnati; and eastern teams condescended to travel as far west as the Queen City. The Erie line offered to convey a New Orleans club, then visiting Cincinnati, to New York and return at half-fare rates. When the Cincinnati Red Stockings made their tour by boat, local lines, and the Union Pacific in 1869 it was reported: "The boys have received every attention from the officers of the different roads. . . . At all the stations groups stare us almost out of countenance, having heard of the successful exploits of the Club through telegrams of the Western Associated Press."[14]

Baseball clubs made use of the rapidly expanding network of the 1870's, and the organization of the National League in 1876 was only possible with the continued development of connecting lines. In the 1886 edition of *Spalding's Official Base Ball Guide* the Michigan Central advertised: "The cities that have representative clubs contesting for the championship pennant this year are—Chicago, Boston, New York, Washington, Kansas City, Detroit, St. Louis and Philadelphia. All of these cities are joined together by the Michigan Central Railroad. This road has enjoyed almost a monopoly of Base Ball travel in former years." Throughout the 1870's and 1880's the expanding railroad network played an indispensable role in the popularization of the "national game."[15]

A widespread interest in thoroughbred trotting races also was in great part sustained by railroad expansion. In 1866 the Harlem, Rensselaer and Saratoga Railroad Company, realizing the advantage of encouraging the racing public, arranged to convey race horses at cost by express train from New York to Saratoga. *Turf, Field and Farm* pointed to the need for better transportation arrangements and predicted, "The completion of the Pacific Railroad will not be without effect upon the

---

13. *Wilkes' Spirit of the Times,* XIV (July 7, 1866), 294. More rural areas felt the impact somewhat later, Warrenton, Mississippi, holding a tourney in 1885 to which special trains were sent. New Orleans *Daily Picayune,* July 19, 1885.

14. New York *World,* August 21, 1869; Cincinnati *Commercial,* September 22, 1869; San Francisco *Evening Bulletin,* October 5, 1869. Their use of Pullman cars set a precedent in sports circles. Advertising by local lines for an approaching game appeared in the Cincinnati *Commercial,* August 24, 1869.

15. See *Spalding's Official Base Ball Guide* (New York, 1886), appendix. The Memphis Reds Base Ball Association sent a printed circular to Harry Wright of the Boston team in 1877 in which it stressed the reduced rates to any club visiting St. Louis or Louisville. Harry Wright Correspondence, 7 vols., I (1865-1877), 40, Spalding Baseball Collection (New York Public Library). In the 1880's enthusiastic crowds turned out to the railroad station to welcome home the victorious nines. *Frank Leslie's Boys' and Girls' Weekly* (New York), XXXV (October 6, 1883), 174; New York *Sun,* September 7, 1886.

blood stock interests of the great West."[16] Jerome Park, Long Branch, and Gravesend catered to New York crowds, Baltimore attracted huge throngs of sportsmen, and in California racing was encouraged by the building of lines into the interior of the state. In the 1870's western turfmen began sending their horses by rail to eastern tracks, the Grand Circuit linked Hartford, Springfield, Poughkeepsie, and Utica with Rochester, Buffalo and Cleveland, and racing associations formed in virtually every section. When Mollie McCarthy and Ten Broeck raced at Louisville in 1877, "Masses of strangers arrived by train, extra trains and steamboats." People from "all over the land" attended the Kentucky Derby in 1885, the City Council declared a holiday, and sixteen carloads of horses were sent from Nashville to Louisville.[17] Agricultural fairs, with the cooperation of numerous companies, drew thousands to their fairground tracks, and the railroads encouraged intersectional meetings by introducing special horse cars in the middle eighties.[18]

In the decades after the Civil War an apologetic but curious public acquired a "deplorable" interest in prize fighting, and railroad officials were not slow to capitalize on the crowd appeal of pugilism despite its illegality. When Mike McCoole met Aaron Jones in 1867 at Busenbark Station, Ohio, "Tickets were openly sold for excursion trains to the bout" and sporting men from the East were in attendance, while another McCoole fight in 1869 encouraged the lines to run specials from Cincinnati and other nearby cities.[19] After 1881 John L. Sullivan, the notorious "Boston Strong Boy," went on grand tours of the athletic clubs, opera houses, and theaters of the country, his fights in the New Orleans area with Paddy Ryan, Jake Kilrain, and James J. Corbett luring fans who jammed the passenger coaches. When the Great John L. met Kilrain near Richburg, Mississippi, in 1889, the Northeastern Railroad carried a tumultous crowd from New Orleans to the site, even though Governor Robert Lowry of Mississippi issued a proclamation against the affair and called out armed guards to prevent any invasion of the state. After the brawl the Governor requested the attorney general "to begin proceedings to forfeit the charter of the Northeastern railroad."[20]

16. *Turf, Field and Farm* (New York), I (September 2, 1865), 69; VIII (May 28, 1869), 344.

17. *Wilkes' Spirit of the Times,* XIV (May 19, 1866), 185; San Francisco *Evening Bulletin,* October 15, 1869; Baltimore *American and Commercial Advertiser,* October 25, 1877; New Orleans *Daily Picayune,* April 20, 1884, May 9, 15, 1885; Charles E. Trevathan, *The American Thoroughbred* (New York, 1905), 371.

18. New York *World,* April 29, 1884.

19. Alexander Johnston, *Ten—And Out! The Complete Story of the Prize Ring in America* (New York, 1947), 42-43.

20. Dunbar Rowland (ed.), *Encyclopedia of Mississippi History,* 2 vols. (Madison, 1907), II, 142; St. Paul and Minneapolis *Pioneer Press,* February 8, 1882; New Orleans *Daily Picayune,* August 6, 1885; New York *Sun,* May 12, 1886.

Railroad companies expressed only a minor concern for such sporadic events, it is true, but the prize ring was greatly aided by their cooperation.[21]

Poor connections, uncomfortable cars, and the absence of lines in rural sections remained a problem for some years.[22] Many of the difficulties and inconveniences of travel remained throughout these expansive years of railroading, but all sports were encouraged by the improved transportation of the post-bellum era. Immediately after the war a New York crew visited Pittsburgh to participate in a regatta held on the Monongahela River.[23] The first intercollegiate football game between Rutgers and Princeton was attended by a group of students riding the train pulled by "the jerky little engine that steamed out of Princeton on that memorable morning of November 6, 1869."[24] Intercollegiate athletics depended on railroad service for carrying teams and supporters to football, baseball, and rowing, as well as track and field contests.

Harvard's crack baseball team made the first grand tour in 1870, "the most brilliant in the history of college baseball," according to Henry Chadwick almost two decades later. Playing both amateur and professional clubs, Harvard won a majority of the games played in New Haven, Troy, Utica, Syracuse, Oswego (Canada), Buffalo, Cleveland, Cincinnati, Louisville, Chicago, Milwaukee, Indianapolis, Washington, Baltimore, Philadelphia, New York, and Brooklyn.[25] Amateur and professional cycling races were held throughout the country,[26] while rod and gun enthusiasts relied on branch lines into rural preserves.[27] By the closing years of the century virtually every realm of sport had shared in the powerful impact of the railroad on American life.

21. Railroad interest in sport was illustrated by the *New York Railroad Gazette*: "Horse-racing tracks of the violest [sic] character are encouraged (indirectly, it may be) in more than one case by railroads normally law-abiding. Sunday excursions patronized chiefly by roughs who conduct baseball games of a character condemned by all decent people are morally the same as prize fights in kind though not in degree." Quoted in the New Orleans *Daily Picayune*, August 6, 1885.

22. For illustrations of the difficulties of railroad travel, see the Walter Camp Correspondence, Box 64 (Yale University Library, New Haven).

23. *Wilkes' Spirit of the Times*, XIII (October 14, 1865), 102.

24. Parke H. Davis, *Football, The American Intercollegiate Game* (New York, 1911), 45.

25. *Outing* (New York), XII (August, 1888), 407-408.

26. By the 1890's many railroads carried bicycles as free freight and professional cyclists could tour their National Circuit in luxury cars. New York *Journal*, September 18, 1897.

27. Scores of railroads in every section of the country served those seeking to hunt or fish in the rustic countryside. See, particularly, Charles Hallock (ed.), *The Sportsman's Gazetter and General Guide* (New York, 1877), Pt. II, 1-182. See also the Chicago and Northwestern Railroad advertisement in the *Spirit of the Times*, XCII (August 19, 1876), 53.

Almost contemporaneous with the development of a continental railroad system came the diffusion of telegraph lines throughout the nation. From its invention in 1844 the electric telegraph rapidly assumed a significant role in the dissemination of news.[28] When the Magnetic Telegraph Company's lines reached New York, James Gordon Bennett's *Herald* and Horace Greeley's *Tribune* installed apparatus in 1846. Direct contact was made between the East and New Orleans two years later, largely to meet the urgent demand for quicker news from the Mexican War front. By 1861 San Francisco was connected by wire with the Atlantic coast, and throughout the war years use of the telegraph was extended in military operations.

During the pioneer years telegraphic messages were both costly and brief, and sports events were reported on a limited scale. One of the first reports by wire was that of the Tom Hyer-Yankee Sullivan brawl at Rock Point, Maryland, in 1849. A New York dispatch read, "We hope never to have to record a similar case of brutality in this country," and even Greeley, an inveterate foe of the prize ring, permitted the printing of dispatches of this brutal encounter. Interest was not confined to Baltimore, Philadelphia, and New York, for some newspapers in the West noticed it. In the next decade several fights were widely reported by telegraph. When Morrissey and Heanan fought for the American championship in Canada in 1858, anxious crowds waited at Western Union offices for the news; when Heanan met Tom Sayers in England two years later the news was spread by wire after it was brought to America by the *Vanderbilt*.[29] Horse racing and yachting news was less novel and less sensational, but Lady Suffolk's appearance on the course at the Rochester, New York, fair in 1851, the victory of Commodore John Cox Stevens' yacht *America* at Cowes in the same year, and the exciting trotting races of the decade were given extensive wire coverage.[30] When Lexington met Lecomte at New Orleans in 1855, however, there seems to have been little reporting of the race in the North. Newspapers of that section were primarily concerned in that year with the trouble in Kansas, the rise of the Republican party, the heat of the

28. For the early development of the telegraph, see James D. Reid, *The Telegraph in America and Morse Memorial* (New York, 1887); Waldemar Kaempffert (ed.), *A Popular History of American Invention*, 2 vols. (New York, 1924); and Robert L. Thompson, *Wiring a Continent: The History of the Telegraph Industry in the United States, 1832-1866* (Princeton, 1947).

29. Boston *Daily Journal*, February 7, 8, 9, 1849; New York *Daily Tribune*, February 8, 9, 1849; Milwaukee *Sentinel and Gazette*, February 10, 1849; Boston *Daily Courier*, October 21, 1858; New York *Times*, October 21, 1858; New Orleans *Daily Picayune*, May 6, 7, June 29, 1860; Nashville *Daily News*, April 29, 1860.

30. New York *Daily Tribune*, September 19, 1851; Natchez *Courier*, September 19, 1851.

abolitionist crusade, and the public furor over the murder of pugilist William Poole.

The expansion of sporting news in ensuing years was directly related to the more general usage of telegraphy, which made possible instantaneous reporting of ball games, horse races, prize fights, yachting regattas, and other events. Box scores, betting odds, and all kinds of messages were relayed from one city to another, and by 1870 daily reports were published in many metropolitan papers. In that year the steamboat race of the *Natchez* and the *Robert E. Lee* was reported throughout the country in one of the most extensive telegraphic accounts of any nonpolitical event prior to that time.[31] Not only did the newspapers make a practice of publishing daily messages from all corners of the sporting world, but crowds formed around Western Union offices during any important contest.[32] When the Associated Press sent its representatives in 1889 to the Sullivan-Kilrain fight in New Orleans, reporters appeared from "every prominent journal in the Union," and Western Union was said to have employed 50 operators to handle 208,000 words of specials following the fight. Poolrooms and saloons were often equipped with receiving sets to keep customers and bettors posted on baseball scores and track results, while newspapers set up bulletin boards for the crowds to linger around.[33] And the business transactions of sporting clubs and associations were often carried on by wire.

Sport had emerged into such a popular topic of conversation that newspapers rapidly expanded their coverage in the 1880's and 1890's, relying in great part on messages sent over the lines from distant points. Among the leaders in this field during these formative years of "yellow journalism" were such New York papers as Bennett's *Herald,* Charles Dana's *Sun,* and Joseph Pulitzer's *World.* The sports pages was not solely the result of improvements in telegraphy, however, for popular interest had encouraged the employment of specialists who were extremely quick, as were the publishers, to capitalize on the news value of sporting events. Chicago produced the pioneers in baseball writing

31. New Orleans *Daily Picayune,* July 6, 1870.
32. *Ibid.* See also New York *Times,* October 21, 1858; Harper's Weekly (New York), XXVII (October 13, 1883), 654.
33. Oliver Gramling, *AP; The Story of News* (New York, 1940), 232; New Orleans *Daily Picayune,* July 10, 1889. For poolrooms, saloons, and bulletin boards, see the New York *Sun,* October 6, 1878; New York *Herald,* February 7, 1882; New Orleans *Daily Picayune,* May 17, 1884, July 6, 1885; New York *World,* September 8, 1892. Also see *Harper's Weekly,* XXVII (October 13, 1883), 654; XXXVI (April 2, December 17, 1892), 319, 324, 1210. Henry L. Mencken, in *Happy Days, 1880-1892* (New York, 1940), 225, nostalgically recalled how, since there were few sporting "extras" in Baltimore in the 1880's, "the high-toned saloons of the town catered to the [baseball] fans by putting in telegraph operators who wrote the scores on blackboards."

in such masters of breezy slang and grotesque humor as Leonard Washburne, Charles Seymour, and Finley Peter Dunne. Cincinnati newspapers, staffed by experts like Harry Weldon, O. P. Caylor, and Byron (Ban) Johnson, were among the most authoritative journals in the diamond world. In 1895, when William Randolph Hearst invaded the New York field and bought the *Journal*, he immediately brought in western writers and, within a few years, developed the first sports section.[34] The telegraph retained its functional importance in recording daily box scores and racing statistics, but it was no longer the one indispensable factor it had been in earlier decades.

The Atlantic cable, successfully laid in 1866 by Cyrus Field, had overcome the mid-century handicap of reporting two- or three-weeks-old English sporting news. At the end of that year James Gordon Bennet, Jr., with the aid of the Associated Press, featured cable dispatches of the great ocean race. When the Harvard crew rowed against Oxford in a highly publicized race in 1869, "the result was flashed through the Atlantic cable as to reach New York about a quarter past one, while the news reached the Pacific Coast about nine o'clock, enabling many of the San Franciscans to discuss the subject at their breakfast-tables, and swallow the defeat with their coffee!"[35] The combination of cable and telegraph aroused a deeper interest in international sport. Nor must we ignore that forerunner of the modern radio, the wireless which was demonstrated publicly in America for the first time in the yacht races of 1899. From Samuel F. B. Morse to Guglielmo Marconi the revolution in communication had encouraged the rise of sport.

Public interest in sport was also aroused by the enlarged format and greater circulation achieved by numerous inventions which revolutionized the printing process. By 1830 the Napier double-cylinder press was imported from England and developed by R. Hoe and Company,

34. The New York *Transcript* and the *Sun* sensationalized the news as early as the 1830's and began reporting prize fights. James Gordon Bennett's *Herald* exploited sporting interest in pre-Civil War years and his son continued to do so in the period following the war. Magazines which capitalized on sport included the *American Turf Register and Sporting Magazine*, the *Spirit of the Times*, the *New York Clipper*, and the *National Police Gazette* (New York), as well as a host of fishing and hunting journals. Through the 1880's and 1890's the New York *Sun* and the *World* competed for the sporting public, only to be outdone by the *Journal* at the end of the century. Among the prominent writers of the era were Henry Chadwick, Timothy Murnane, Harry Weldon, Harry C. Palmer, Al Spink, Sam Crane, Walter Camp, Caspar Whitney, and Charles Dryden. See William H. Nugent, "The Sports Section," *American Mercury* (New York), XVI (February, 1929), 329-38; and Hugh Fullerton, "The Fellows Who Made the Game," *Saturday Evening Post* (Philadelphia), CC (April 21, 1928), 18 ff.

35. New York *Herald*, December 30, 31, 1866; Cincinnati *Commercial*, August 24, 28, 1869; *Frank Leslie's Illustrated Newspaper* (New York), XXIX (September 28, 1869), 2.

printing those cheap and sensational papers which were the first to
feature horse races, prize fights, and foot races—the New York *Sun*, the
New York *Transcript*, and the Philadelphia *Public Ledger*.[36] James Gordon Bennett, Sr., recognized the value of catering to the whims of the
masses and occasionally featured turf reporting in the *Herald* of the
1840's.[37] In 1846 the Hoe type-revolving cylinder press was introduced
by the *Public Ledger*, enabling newspaper publishers, after improvements were made in the machine, to print 20,000 sheets an hour.[38]
Other inventions facilitated the mass publication of the daily paper,
making possible the sensationalized editions of Bennett, Pulitzer, and
Hearst.[39] With the arrival of the new journalism of the 1880's, sporting
news rapidly became a featured part of the metropolitan press.[40]

Publishers also aided in the popularization of outdoor sport throughout this whole era. From the 1830's onward sporting books appeared,
the most famous of prewar authors being Henry William Herbert, whose
illustrious pseudonym was Frank Forester. After the Civil War cheap
methods of publication gave a great stimulus to the dime novel and
the athletic almanac. While the vast majority of the thrillers and shock-
ers concerned the Wild West or city crime, athletic stories and manuals
were put out by Beadle & Adams, the leading publisher of the paper-
backed dime novel.[41] After the establishment of A. G. Spalding & Brothers the *Spalding Guide* developed into the leading authority on rules of
play, and all sorts of handbooks were included in the *Spalding Library
of Athletic Sports*. The *New York Clipper* began publishing a theatrical
and sporting *Clipper Almanac* in the 1870's, while newspapers like the
New York *World*, the New York *Tribune*, the Chicago *Daily News*, the
Washington *Post*, and the Brooklyn *Daily Eagle* issued almanacs listing
athletic and racing records and sporting news. Richard Kyle Fox of the
National Police Gazette published *Fox's Athletic Library* and sporting
annuals. By the end of the century book publication had grown to

36. The origins of the penny press are ably discussed in Willard G. Bleyer, *Main
Currents in the History of American Journalism* (Boston, 1927), 154-84; and in
Frank L. Mott, *American Journalism, A History* (New York, 1941), 228-52.
37. Bleyer, *History of American Journalism*, 197, 209; Alfred M. Lee, *The Daily
Newspaper in America* (New York, 1937), 611; New York *Weekly Herald*, May 15,
17, 1845, and *Herald* files for the 1840's.
38. Bleyer, *History of American Journalism*, 394.
39. *Ibid.*, 394-98.
40. Joseph Pulitzer's New York *World* began an intensive exploitation of sport as
a front-page attraction almost immediately after its purchase in 1883, and by the
following year first-page accounts of pedestrian matches, dog shows, and similar
topics became regular features.
41. Albert Johannsen, *The House of Beadle and Adams and its Dime and Nickel
Novel: The Story of a Vanished Literature*, 2 vols. (Norman, 1950), I, 260, 377-79.

astronomic proportions when compared to the Civil War era, and the Outing Publishing Company issued more than a hundred titles on angling, canoeing, yachting, mountain climbing, hunting, shooting, trapping, camping, cycling, and athletics.

A few dime novels had taken up the athletic theme in the 1870's, but more mature stories like Mark Sibley Severance's *Hammersmith: His Harvard Days* (1878), Noah Brook's *Our Baseball Club* (1884), and, of course, Thomas Hughes's English classics, *Tom Brown at Rugby* and *Tom Brown at Oxford*, were responsible for the rising desire for sports fiction. By the 1890's a demand for boys' athletic stories was met in the voluminous outpouring of the heroic sporting achievements of Gilbert Patten's "Frank Merriwell."[42] Along with the newspaper and the sporting journal the field of publishing, with its improved techniques and expanded output, did much to attract attention to athletics at the turn of the century.

Much of the angling and hunting equipment and horseman's supplies came from England in the colonial era, but in the years before and after the American Revolution several dealers in sporting wares appeared in Philadelphia, New York, and Boston. From the early years of the nineteenth century merchants and gunsmiths in Kentucky supplied the settlers west of the Appalachian range.[43] Field sports were still enjoyed mainly by schoolboys and sportsmen with their simple rods in the 1840's and 1850's, but from the 1830's onward fishing and hunting purely for recreation developed into a sporting fad, the end of which is not in sight. Charles Hallock, noted sportsman, conservationist, and journalist of the post-Civil War era recalled how the rural folk of Hampshire County, Massachusetts, responded to a visiting sportsman of the 1840's who brought with him a set of highly finished rods, reels, and fly-fishing equipment.

> Ah! those were halcyon days. No railroads disturbed the quiet seclusion of that mountain nook. . . . Twice a week an oldfashioned coach dragged heavily up the hill into the hamlet and halted in front of the house which was at once post-office, tavern, and miscellaneous store. . . . One day it brought a passenger. . . . He carried a leather hand-bag and a handful of rods in a case. The village *quidnuncs* said he was a surveyor. He allowed he was from Troy and had "come to go a-fishing." From that stranger I took my first lesson in fly-fishing.[44]

42. John L. Cutler, *Gilbert Patten and His Frank Merriwell Saga*, University of Maine *Studies* (Orono), Ser. II, No. 31 (1934).

43. Charles E. Goodspeed, *Angling in America: Its Early History and Literature* (Boston, 1939), 285 ff.

44. Charles Hallock, *The Fishing Tourist: Angler's Guide and Reference Book* (New York, 1873), 18.

By the 1850's the manufacture of cricket bats and stumps, billiard tables, archery equipment, guns, fishing tackle, and other sporting accessories was carried on by a host of individual craftsmen and by such concerns as J. W. Brunswick & Brothers of Cincinnati, Bassler of Boston, Conroy's of New York, and John Krider's "Sportsmen's Depot" in Philadelphia.

Mass-production methods of manufacture were still in their infancy in post-Civil War decades, but the factory system became ever more deeply entrenched. While the sporting goods business never attained any great economic importance in the nineteenth century,[45] much of the popularity for athletic games and outdoor recreation was due to standardized manufacturing of baseball equipment, bicycles, billiard tables, sporting rifles, fishing rods, and various other items.[46] Although most American youths played with restitched balls and a minimum of paraphernalia, college athletes, cycling enthusiasts, and professional ballplayers popularized the products of George B. Ellard of Cincinnati, Peck & Snyder of New York, and other concerns.[47]

By the end of the century A. G. Spalding & Brothers was the nationally recognized leader in this field. As a renowned pitcher for the Boston and Chicago clubs and then as the promoter of the latter, Albert Spalding had turned to the merchandizing of athletic goods in 1876.[48] One of the most avid sponsors of the national game, he branched out

45. In 1900 the value of sporting goods manufactured was only $3,628,496. United States Bureau of the Census, *Statistical Abstract of the United States* (Washington, 1909), 188.

46. See the *Spirit of the Times,* XX (May 4, 1850), 130; Natchez *Courier,* November 26, 1850; Madison *Daily State Journal,* March 26, 1855; New Orleans *Daily Picayune,* April 4, 1856. As midwestern merchants began to purchase large stocks from the East, John Krider advertised widely. Madison *Daily State Journal,* April 13, 1855. Michael Phelan, who in 1854 developed an indiarubber cushion permitting sharp edges on billiard tables, joined with Hugh W. Collender in forming Phelan and Collender, the leading billiards manufacturer until the organization of the Brunswick-Balke Collender Company in 1884. Gymnastic apparatus, created by Dudley A. Sargent and other physical educators, was featured by many dealers, while the readers of *American Angler* (New York), *Forest and Stream* (New York), and other sporting journals were kept informed of the latest models of rifles, shotguns, and fishing rods and reels.

47. George B. Ellard, who sponsored the Red Stockings, advertised his store as "Base Ball Headquarters" and "Base Ball Depot," with the "Best Stock in the West." Cincinnati *Commercial,* August 24, 1869. Other merchandisers included Horsman's Base Ball and Croquet Emporium in New York and John H. Mann of the same city. Peck & Snyder began dealing in baseball equipment in 1865 and by the 1880's claimed to be the largest seller of sporting goods.

48. Moses King (ed.), *King's Handbook of the United States* (Buffalo, 1891), 232; Arthur Bartlett, *Baseball and Mr. Spalding: The History and Romance of Baseball* (New York, 1951), *passim; Fortune* (New York), II (August, 1930), 62 ff.; Arthur Bartlett, "They're Just Wild About Sports," *Saturday Evening Post,* CCXXII (December 24, 1949), 31 ff.; *Spalding's Official Base Ball Guide for 1887* (New York and Chicago, 1887), *passim.*

into varied sports in the 1880's, and acquired a virtual monopoly over athletic goods by absorbing A. J. Reach Company in 1885, Wright & Ditson in 1892, as well as Peck & Snyder and other firms. By 1887 the Spalding "Official League" baseball had been adopted by the National League, the Western League, the New England League, the International League, and various college conferences, and balls were offered to the public ranging in price from 5 cents to $1.50. To gain an even greater ascendancy over his rivals A. G. Spalding published a wide range of guides in *Spalding's Library of Athletic Sports,* in which his wares were not only advertised but those of rivals were derided as inferior.

The sewing machine was one of many inventions which made possible the more uniform equipment of the last decades of the century when local leagues and national associations took shape throughout the United States. Canoeing and camping were other diversions which gave rise to the manufacture of sporting goods on an ever larger scale. In the latter years of the century the mail-order house and the department store began to feature sporting goods. Macy's of New York began with ice skates, velocipedes, bathing suits, and beach equipment in 1872, although all sporting goods were sold by the toy department. By 1902, with the addition of numerous other items, a separate department was established. Sears, Roebuck and Company, meanwhile, devoted more than eighty pages of its 1895 catalogue to weapons and fishing equipment, and within a decade not only hunting and fishing equipment but also bicycles, boxing gloves, baseball paraphernalia, and sleds were featured.[49]

When Thomas A. Edison developed the incandescent bulb in 1879 he inaugurated a new era in the social life of our cities. Although the first dynamo was built within two years, gas lighting did not give way immediately, and the crowds which jammed the old Madison Square Garden in New York in 1883 to see John L. Sullivan fight Herbert Slade still had to cope not only with the smoke-filled air but also with the blue gas fumes. The Garden had already installed some electric lights, however. At a six-day professional walking match in 1882 the cloud of tobacco smoke was so thick that "even the electric lights" had "a hard

---

49. It was on mass manufacture of baseballs and uniforms that Spalding gained such a leading position in the sporting goods field. Since the business was restricted in these early years certain difficulties had to be overcome. To make the most out of manufacturing bats Spalding bought his own lumber mill in Michigan, while Albert Pope received little sympathy from the rolling mills in his first years of manufacturing bicycles. *Wheelman* (Boston), I (October, 1882), 71. For department and mail-order stores, see Ralph M. Hower, *History of Macy's of New York, 1858-1919* (Cambridge, 1946), 103, 162, 234-35, 239; Boris Emmet and John C. Jeuck, *Catalogues and Counters: A History of Sears, Roebuck and Company* (Chicago, 1950), 38; David L. Cohn, *The Good Old Days* (New York, 1940), 443-60.

struggle to assert their superior brilliancy" over the gas jets. Even "the noisy yell of programme, candy, fruit and peanut venders who filled the air with the vilest discord" failed to discourage the crowd, according to a philosophically minded reporter who wondered what Herbert Spencer would think of "the peculiar phase of idiocy in the American character" which drew thousands of men and women to midnight pedestrian contests.[50]

Within a few years electric lighting and more comfortable accomodations helped lure players and spectators alike to Y.M.C.A.s, athletic clubs, regimental armories, school and college gymnasiums, as well as sports arenas. In 1885, at the third annual Horse Show in Madison Square Garden, handsomely dressed sportswomen reveled in the arena, "gaudy with festoons of racing flags and brilliant streamers, lighted at night by hundreds of electric lights," while visitors to the brilliantly lighted New York Athletic Club agreed that "fine surroundings will not do an athlete any harm."[51] The indoor prize fight, walking contest, wrestling match, and horse show were a far cry from the crude atmosphere of early indoor sport. In 1890 carnivals were held at the Massachusetts Mechanics' Association by the Boston Athletic Association and at the new Madison Square Garden in New York by the Staten Island Athletic Club; the horse show attracted fashionable New Yorkers to the Garden; and indoor baseball, already popular in Chicago, was taken up in New York's regimental armories.[52] A decade of electrification, paralleling improvements in transportation and communication, had elevated and purified the atmosphere of sport. The saloon brawls of pugilists in the 1850's and 1860's were gradually abandoned for the organized matches of 1880's and 1890's. At the time of the Sullivan-Corbett fight in the New Orleans Olympic Club in 1892, an observer wrote in the Chicago *Daily Tribune*, September 8, 1892: "Now men travel to great boxing contests in vestibule limited trains; they sleep at the best hotels . . . and when the time for the contest arrives they find themselves in a grand, brilliantly lighted arena."

50. New York *Herald*, October 23, 1882; New York *Sun*, August 7, 1883. The introduction of electric lighting in theaters was discussed, while the opposition of gas companies was recognized. *Scientific American*, Supplement (New York), XVI (November 10, 1883), 6535-36.
51. *Harper's Weekly*, XXIX (February 14, November 14, 1885), 109, 743.
52. See *ibid.*, XXXIV (March 1, 8, 1890), 169, 171, 179. A new Madison Square Garden with the most modern facilities was built in the years 1887-1890; the California Athletic Club in San Francisco featured a "powerful electric arc light" over its ring; and electric lights in the Manhattan Athletic Club's new gymnasium in 1890 "shed a dazzling whiteness." *Ibid.*, XXXIV (April 5, 1890), 263-64; New York *Daily Tribune*, November 2, 30, 1890.

Basketball and volleyball, originating in the Y.M.C.A. in 1892 and 1895, were both developed to meet the need for indoor sport on winter evenings. The rapid construction of college gymnasiums and the building of more luxurious clubhouses after the middle eighties stemmed in great part from the superior appointments and more brilliant lighting available for athletic games, and much of the urban appeal of indoor sport was directly attributable to the revolution which electric lighting made in the night life of the metropolis.

Electrification, which transformed everything from home gadgets and domestic lighting to power machinery and launches, exerted an influence on the course of sport through the development of rapid transit systems in cities from coast to coast. Horse-drawn cars had carried the burden of traffic since the 1850's, but the electric streetcar assumed an entirely new role in opening up suburban areas and the countryside to the pent-up city populace. Soon after the Richmond, Virginia, experiment of 1888, the streetcar began to acquaint large numbers of city dwellers with the race track and the ball diamond.[53] Experimental lines had been laid even earlier in the decade, and Chicago crowds going to the races at Washington Park in 1887 were jammed on "the grip," one reporter noting the "perpetual stream of track slang," the prodding and pushing, and the annoying delay when it was announced that "the cable has busted."[54] Trolley parks, many of which included baseball diamonds, were promoted by the transit companies; ball teams were encouraged by these same concerns through gifts of land or grandstands; and the crowds flocked to week-end games on the cars.[55] At the turn of the century the popular interest in athletic games in thousands of towns and cities was stimulated to a high degree by the extension of rapid transit systems, a development which may possibly have been as significant in the growth of local sport as the automobile was to be in the development of intercommunity rivalries.

Numerous inventions and improvements applied to sport were of varying importance: the stop watch, the percussion cap, the streamlined

53. After the completion of the Richmond line rapid transit spread throughout the country. Although in 1890 there were only 144 electric railways in a national total of 789 street lines, by 1899 there were 50,600 electric cars in operation as contrasted to only 1,500 horse cars. Gilson Willets et al., Workers of the Nation, 2 vols. (New York, 1903), I, 498. For the suburban influence, see the Street Railway Journal (New York), XVIII (November 23, 1901), 760-61.
54. Chicago Tribune, July 5, 1887.
55. Street Railway Journal, XI (April, 1895), 232; XII (May, November, 1896), 317, 319, 708; Cosmopolitan (New York), XXXIII (July, 1902), 266; Collier's (New York), CXXV (May, 1950), 85; Oscar Handlin, This Was America (Cambridge, 1949), 374; New Orleans Daily Picayune, February 27, 1899.

sulky, barbed wire, the safety cycle, ball bearings, and artificial ice for skating rinks, among others. Improved implements often popularized and revolutionized the style of a sport, as in the invention of the sliding seat of the rowing shell, the introduction of the rubber-wound gutta-percha ball which necessitated the lengthening of golf courses, and the universal acceptance of the catcher's mask.

Vulcanization of rubber by Charles Goodyear in the 1830's led to the development of elastic and resilient rubber balls in the following decade, and eventually influenced the development of golf and tennis balls as well as other sporting apparel and equipment. The pneumatic tire, developed by Dr. John Boyd Dunlop of Belfast, Ireland, in 1888, revolutionized cycling and harness racing in the next decade. Equipped with pneumatic tires, the sulky abandoned its old highwheeler style, and the trotter and pacer found it made for smoother movement on the track. Sulky drivers reduced the mile record of 2:08 3/4 by Maud S. with an old highwheeler to 1:58 1/2 by Lou Dillon in 1903 with a "bicycle sulky." According to W. H. Gocher, a racing authority, the innovation of pneumatic tires and the streamlining of the sulky cut five to seven seconds from former records, which was "more than the breeding had done in a dozen years."[56] The pneumatic tire, introduced by racing cyclists and sulky drivers, went on to play a much more vital role in the rise of the automobile industry and the spectacular appeal of auto racing.

The camera also came to the aid of sport in the decades following the Civil War. Professional photography had developed rapidly in the middle period of the century, but nature lovers became devotees of the camera only when its bulkiness and weight were eliminated in the closing years of the century. Development of the Eastman Kodak after 1888 found a mass market as thousands of Americans put it to personal and commercial use. Pictorial and sporting magazines which had been printing woodcuts since the prewar era began to introduce many pictures taken from photographs, and in the late 1880's and early 1890's actual photographic prints of athletes and outdoor sportsmen came into common usage. *Harper's Weekly, Leslie's Illustrated Weekly, Illustrated American,* and the *National Police Gazette* featured photography, and by the end of the century the vast majority of their pictures were camera studies.[57] Newspapers recognized the circulation value of half-tone prints, but because of paper and technical problems they were used sparsely

---

56. W. H. Gocher, *Trotalong* (Hartford, 1928), 190.
57. Robert Taft, *Photography and the American Scene: A Social History, 1839-1889* (New York, 1938), 441.

until the New York *Times* published an illustrated Sunday supplement in 1896, soon to be imitated by the New York *Tribune* and the Chicago *Tribune*. The year 1897 saw the half-tone illustration become a regular feature of metropolitan newspapers, rapidly eliminating the age-old reliance on woodcuts. At the turn of the century sport was available in visual form to millions who heretofore had little knowledge of athletics and outdoor games.[58]

It was in 1872 that Eadweard Muybridge made the first successful attempt "to secure an illusion of motion by photography." With the help of Leland Stanford, already a noted turfman, he set out to prove whether "a trotting horse at one point in its gait left the ground entirely."[59] By establishing a battery of cameras the movements of the horse were successively photographed, and Muybridge later turned his technique to "the gallop of dogs, the flight of birds, and the performances of athletes." In his monumental study entitled *Animal Locomotion* (1887) he included thousands of pictures of horses, athletes, and other living subjects, demonstrating "the work and play of men, women and children of all ages; how pitchers throw the baseball, how batters hit it, and how athletes move their bodies in record-breaking contests."[60] Muybridge is considered only one among a number of the pioneers of the motion picture, but his pictures had presented possibly the best illusion of motion prior to the development of flexible celluloid film. A host of experimenters gradually evolved principles and techniques in the late 1880's which gave birth to the true motion picture. Woodville Latham and his two sons made a four-minute film of the prize fight between Young Griffo and Battling Barnett in 1895, showing it on a large screen for an audience, an event which has been called "the first flickering, commercial motion picture."[61] When Bob Fitzsimmons won the heavyweight championship from James J. Corbett at Carson City, Nevada, in 1897, the fight was photographed for public distribution. With the increasing popularity in succeeding years of the newsreel, the short sub-

58. Photography developed throughout the nineteenth century as an adjunct of the science of chemistry. Chemical and mechanical innovations were also responsible for the improvements of prints and all kinds of reproductions. Woodcuts were featured in the press, engravings were sold widely, and lithographs were found in the most rural home. Nathaniel Currier (later Currier & Ives) published hunting, fishing, pugilistic, baseball, rowing, yachting, sleighing, skating, trotting, and racing scenes for more than half a century. Cheap prints, calendars, and varied reproductions of sporting scenes did much to popularize the famous turf champions and sporting heroes of the era. See Harry T. Peters, *Currier & Ives: Printmakers to the American People* (Garden City, 1942).
59. Frank L. Dyer and Thomas C. Martin, *Edison: His Life and Inventions*, 2 vols. (New York, 1910), II, 534-35.
60. Kaempffert, *Popular History of American Inventions*, I, 425.
61. Lloyd Morris, *Not So Long Ago* (New York, 1949), 24.

ject, and an occasional feature film, the motion picture came to rival the photograph in spreading the gospel of sport.[62]

When sport began to mature into a business of some importance and thousands of organizations throughout the country joined leagues, associations, racing circuits, and national administrative bodies, it became necessary to utilize on a large scale the telephone, the typewriter, and all the other instruments so vital to the commercial world. Even the phonograph, at first considered a business device but soon devoted to popular music, came to have an indirect influence, recording for public entertainment such songs as "Daisy Bell," "Casey at the Bat," "Slide, Kelly, Slide," and, early in the present century, the theme song of the national pastime, "Take Me Out to the Ball Game." All of these instruments created a great revolution in communication, and they contributed significantly to the expansion of sport on a national scale.

The bicycle, still an important means of transport in Europe but something of a casualty of the machine age in the United States, also had an important role. After its demonstration at the Philadelphia Centennial, an interest was ignited which grew rapidly in the 1880's and flamed into an obsession in the 1890's.[63] Clubs, cycling associations, and racing meets were sponsored everywhere in these years, and the League of American Wheelmen served as a spearhead for many of the reforms in fashions, good roads, and outdoor exercise. Albert H. Pope was merely the foremost among many manufacturers of the "velocipede" which became so popular among women's clubs, temperance groups, professional men, and, at the turn of the century, in the business world and among the trades. Contemporary observers speculated on the social benefits to be derived from the cycle, especially in enticing women to the pleasures of outdoor exercise. Bicycling was discussed by ministers and physicians, it was considered as a weapon in future wars, police

62. The pioneer years of the motion picture industry are described by numerous other works, among them Deems Taylor, *A Pictorial History of the Movies* (New York, 1943), 1-6; Leslie Wood, *The Miracle of the Movies* (London, 1947), 66 ff.; George S. Bryan, *Edison: The Man and His Work* (Garden City, 1926), 184-94; Josef M. Eder, *History of Photography*, trans. by Edward Epstean (New York, 1945), 495 ff.; Taft, *Photography and the American Scene*, 405-12; Morris, *Not So Long Ago*, 1-35.

63. There was a brief craze in 1869, during which year, according to Albert H. Pope, "more than a thousand inventions were patented for the perfection and improvement of the velocipede." *Wheelman*, I (October, 1882), 70. Interest declined, however, until the Philadelphia celebration of 1876. Although race meetings and cycling clubs were widely reported in the 1880's, there were only 83 repair establishments in 1890 and the value of products in bicycle and tricycle repairs was only about $300,000. By 1900 there were 6,378 repair shops and the value in repairs exceeded $13,000,000. United States Bureau of the Census, *Statistical Abstract of the United States* (Washington, 1904), 516.

squads in some cities were mounted on wheels, mail carriers utilized it, and many thought it would revolutionize society.[64]

As a branch of American industry the bicycle was reputed to have developed into a $100,000,000 business in the 1890's. Mass-production techniques were introduced, Iver Johnson's Arms and Cycle Works advertising "Every part interchangeable and exact." The Indiana Bicycle Company, home of the Waverley cycle, maintained a huge factory in Indianapolis and claimed to be the most perfect and complete plant in the world: "We employ the highest mechanical skill and the best labor-saving machinery that ample capital can provide. Our methods of construction are along the latest and most approved lines of mechanical work."[65]

Much of the publicity given to competing manufacturers centered around the mechanical improvements and the speed records of their products. Between 1878 and 1896 the mile record was lowered from 3:57 to 1:55 1/5. While recognizing the effect of better riding styles, methodical training, improved tracks, and the art of pacemaking, one critic contended, "The prime factor . . . is the improvement in the vehicle itself. The racing machine of 1878 was a heavy, crude, cumbersome affair, while the modern bicycle, less than one-sixth its weight, equipped with scientifically calculated gearing, pneumatic tires, and friction an-

---

64. For summaries of the impact of the bicycle, see E. Benjamin Andrews, *History of the Last Quarter-Century in the United States, 1870-1895*, 2 vols. (New York, 1896), II, 289-90; Arthur M. Schlesinger, *The Rise of the City, 1878-1898* (New York, 1933), 312-14; Roger Burlingame, *Engines of Democracy: Inventions and Society in Mature America* (New York, 1940), 369-74.

65. *Harper's Weekly*, XL (April 11, 1896), 365. It is interesting that the "father of scientific management," Frederick W. Taylor, a tennis champion and golf devotee, was said to have learned through sport "the value of the minute analysis of motions, the importance of methodical selection and training, the worth of time study and of standards based on rigorously exact observation." Charles De Fréminville, "How Taylor Introduced the Scientific Method Into Management of the Shop," *Critical Essays on Scientific Management*, Taylor Society *Bulletin* (New York), X (February, 1925), Pt. II, 32. Mass-production techniques, however, were only partially responsible for the outpouring of athletic goods which began to win wider markets at the turn of the century. The manufacture of baseball bats remained a highly specialized trade, while Scotch artisans who came to the United States maintained the personalized nature of their craft as makers of golf clubs. Despite the great improvements in gun manufacture, Elisha J. Lewis asserted in 1871 that there were thousands of miserable guns on the market: "The reason of this is that our mechanics have so many tastes and fancies to please, owing principally to the ignorance of those who order fowling-pieces, that they have adopted no generally-acknowledged standard of style to guide them in the getting up of guns suitable for certain kinds of sport." Elisha J. Lewis, *The American Sportsman* (Philadelphia, 1871), 435. Although numerous industries had taken up the principle of interchangeable parts, mass-production techniques were to come to the fore only with the assembly lines of Henry Ford and the automobile industry in the years before World War I.

nihilators, represents much of the difference."[66] Roger Burlingame has pointed out the impact of the bicycle on the health, recreation, business, and the social life of the American people, and on the manufacture of the cycle he claimed that "it introduced certain technical principles which were carried on into the motor car, notably ball bearings, hub-breaking and the tangential spoke."[67] Little did cycling enthusiasts realize that in these same years a much more revolutionary vehicle, destined to transform our way of life, was about to make its dramatic appearance on the national scene.

One of the last inventions which the nineteenth century brought forth for the conquest of time and distance was the automobile. During the 1890's the Haynes, Duryea, Ford, Stanley Steamer, Packard, and Locomobile came out in quick succession, and the Pierce Arrow, Cadillac, and Buick were to follow in the next several years.[68] Manufacturers of bicycles had already turned to the construction of the motor car in a number of instances. As early as 1895 Herman H. Kohlsaat, publisher of the Chicago *Times-Herald,* sponsored the first automobile race on American soil. One of the featuers of this contest, run through a snow-storm and won by Charles Duryea, was the enhanced reputation achieved for the gasoline motor, which had not yet been recognized as the proper source of motor power. A number of European races inspired American drivers to take to the racecourse, and the experimental value of endurance or speed contests was immediately recognized by pioneer manufacturers. Nor were they slow to see the publicity value of races featured by the newspapers.[69]

Henry Ford "was bewitched by Duryea's feat," and he "devoured reports on the subject which appeared in the newspapers and magazines of the day." When other leading carbuilders sought financial backing for their racers, Ford determined to win supremacy on the track. After defeating Alexander Winton in a race at Detroit in 1902, "Ford's prowess as a 'speed demon' began to appear in the columns of the widely circulated trade journal *Horseless Age.*"[70] In later years he was to contend, "I never thought anything of racing, but the public refused to consider

66. *Harper's Weekly,* XL (April 11, 1896), 366.
67. Burlingame, *Engines of Democracy: Inventions and Society in Mature America,* 3.
68. Herbert O. Duncan, *World on Wheels,* 2 vols. (Paris, 1927), II, 919 ff.
69.Lawrence H. Seltzer, *A Financial History of the American Automobile Industry* (Boston, 1928), 91; Pierre Sauvestre, *Histoire de L'Automobile* (Paris, 1907), *Passim;* Ralph C. Epstein, *The Automobile Industry, Its Economic and Commercial Development* (Chicago, 1928), 154; Reginald M. Cleveland and S. T. Williamson, *The Road Is Yours* (New York, 1951), 175-76, 194-97.
70. Keith Sward, *The Legend of Henry Ford* (New York, 1948), 14.

the automobile in any light other than as a fast toy. Therefore later we had to race. The industry was held back by this initial racing slant, for the attention of the makers was diverted to making fast rather than good cars." The victory over Winton was his first race, "and it brought advertising of the only kind that people cared to read." Bowing to public opinion, he was determined "to make an automobile that would be known wherever speed was known," and he set to work installing four cylinders in his famous "999." Developing 80 horse power, this machine was so frightening, even to its builders, that the fearless Barney Oldfield was hired for the race. Oldfield had only a tiller with which to drive, since there were no steering wheels, but this professional cyclist who had never driven a car established a new record and helped put Ford back on his feet. The financial support of Alex Y. Malcomson, an admirer of "999," gave him a new start: "A week after the race I formed the Ford Motor Company."[71]

The next few years witnessed the establishment of Automobile Club of America races, sport clubs in the American Automobile Association, the Vanderbilt Cup, and the Glidden Tour. Reporting on the third annual Glidden Tour in 1906, *Scientific American* defended American cars, heretofore considered inferior to European models: "Above all else, the tour has demonstrated that American machines will stand fast driving on rough forest roads without serious damage to the cars or their mechanism. Engine and gear troubles have practically disappeared, and the only things that are to be feared are the breakage of springs and axles and the giving out of tires. Numerous shock-absorbers were tried out and found wanting in this test; and were it not for the pneumatic tires, which have been greatly improved during the past two years, such a tour would be impossible of accomplishment."[72]

The Newport social season featured racing, Daytona Beach soon became a center for speed trials, and tracks were built in various parts of the nation, the first of which may have been at Narragansett Park in 1896.[73] Not until the years just prior to World War I did auto racing attain a truly national popularity with the establishment of the Indianapolis Speedway, but the emphasis on speed and endurance in these early years spurred manufacturers to build ever faster models and advertisers to feature the record performances of each car. Henry Ford had long since lost interest, while the Buick racing team was discontinued

71. Henry Ford and Samuel Crowther, *My Life and Work* (Garden City, 1927), 36-37, 50-51.
72. *Scientific American*, XCV (August 11, 1906), 95.
73. G. F. Baright, "Automobiles and Automobile Races at Newport," *Independent* (New York), LIV (June 5, 1902), 1368.

in 1915. By then mass production had turned the emphasis toward design, comfort, and economy. Racing was not abandoned and manufacturers still featured endurance tests in later years, but the heated rivalry between pioneer builders had become a thing of the past.[74]

Technological developments in the latter half of the nineteenth century transformed the social habits of the Western World, and sport was but one of many institutions which felt their full impact. Fashions, foods, journalism, home appliances, commercialized entertainment, architecture, and city planning were only a few of the facets of life which underwent rapid change as transportation and communication were revolutionized and as new materials were made available. There are those who stress the thesis that sport is a direct reaction against the mechanization, the division of labor, and the standardization of life in a machine civilization,[75] and this may in part be true, but sport in nineteenth-century America was as much a product of industrialization as it was an antidote to it. While athletics and outdoor recreation were sought as a release from the confinements of city life, industrialization and the urban movement were the basic causes for the rise of organized sport. And the urban movement was, of course, greatly enhanced by the revolutionary transformation in communication, transportation, agriculture, and industrialization.[76]

74. In these years the motorcycle and the motorboat also created interest, Sir Alfred Harmsworth (later Lord Northcliffe) establishing the Harmsworth Trophy for international competition in 1903. Air races also won widespread publicity in the press from 1910 onward. Glenn H. Curtiss achieved an enviable reputation as an aviator, newspapers sponsored air meets, and considerable attention was given to the "new sport of the air." *Ibid.*, LXIX (November 3, 1910), 999.

75. Lewis Mumford, *Technics and Civilization* (New York, 1934), 303-305; Arnold J. Toynbee, *A Study of History*, 6 vols. (London, 1934-1939), IV, 242-43.

76. Technological developments throughout the business world transformed the pattern of city life. The electric elevator and improvements in the manufacture of steel made possible the skyscrapers of Chicago and New York in the late 1880's. Concentration of the business community in the central part of the city was increased also by the telephone switchboard and other instruments of communication. Less and less open land remained for the youth living in the heart of the metropolis, and it was to meet this challenge that the Y.M.C.A., the settlement house, the institutional church, the boys' club, and other agencies expanded their athletic facilities. The playground movement and the public park grew out of the necessity for recreational areas for city dwellers, and public authorities early in the twentieth century began to rope off streets for children at play. The subway, the streetcar, and the automobile made possible the accelerated trend toward suburban development, where the open lot or planned play area offered better opportunities to participate in sport. The more general implications of the impact of the technological revolution on society, already considered by several outstanding scholars, are not discussed here, the principal aim of this study being to describe the interrelationship of sport and invention in the latter half of the nineteenth century. Although the account of the auto slightly transgressed the limits of this study, it was felt necessary to give it an abbreviated treatment. The twentieth century, and the role of improved sporting equipment, racing and training devices, the radio, television, improved highways, and bus and air transport, would require an equally extensive study.

The first symptoms of the impact of invention on nineteenth-century sports are to be found in the steamboat of the ante-bellum era. An intensification of interest in horse racing during the 1820's and 1830's was only a prelude to the sporting excitement over yachting, prize fighting, rowing, running, cricket, and baseball of the 1840's and 1850's. By this time the railroad was opening up new opportunities for hunters, anglers, and athletic teams, and it was the railroad, of all the inventions of the century, which gave the greatest impetus to the intercommunity rivalries in sport. The telegraph and the penny press opened the gates to a rising tide of sporting journalism; the sewing machine and the factory system revolutionized the manufacturing of sporting goods; the electric light and rapid transit further demonstrated the impact of electrification; inventions like the Kodak camera, the motion picture, and the pneumatic tire stimulated various fields of sport; and the bicycle and automobile gave additional evidence to the effect of the transportation revolution on the sporting impulse of the latter half of the century. Toward the end of the century the rapidity with which one invention followed another demonstrated the increasingly close relationship of technology and social change. No one can deny the significance of sportsmen, athletes, journalists, and pioneers in many organizations, and no one can disregard the multiple forces transforming the social scene. The technological revolution is not the sole determining factor in the rise of sport, but to ignore its influence would result only in a more or less superficial understanding of the history of one of the prominent social institutions of modern America.

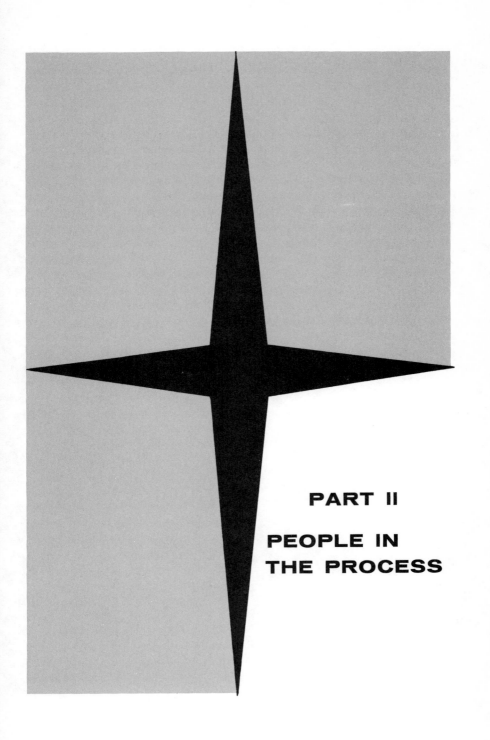

PART II

**PEOPLE IN
THE PROCESS**

SECTION

A

SPORT AND GAMES:
AMERICAN STYLE

The articles in the previous sections have defined and described the cultural phenomenon of sport as it functions within the social system. The influence of the technological environment and resulting effect on work and theatre were presented. Now we turn more specifically to the meaning and experience of sport in America.

In the first article of this section, McLuhan considers games as information and communication media that are extensions "not of our private selves but as our social selves." He concludes that "Games are situations contrived to permit simultaneous participation of many people in some significant pattern of their own corporate lives."

How to get at meaning is a complex task. Stone pursues meaning by "exploring social relationships that are mobilized by sport and sport activities." He pursues the study of the social relationships in sport largely within the variables of sex and socio-economic strata. (If the reader desires to continue the consideration of meaning from a more philosophical point of view, Metheny's book, *Movement and Meaning*, will be of interest.)

Friedenberg, in his two books, *The Vanishing Adolescent* and *Coming of Age in America*, takes a penetrating look at the youth of America. Athletic prowess, status and experience are an integral part of his description of the life style of those in high school. In the selection included here, his writing cuts deeply into some of the protected areas of sport. How revealing of a society is its choice of sport forms? Friedenberg believes that, "Societies reveal much of themselves, and of their differences from other societies, in their preferences among sports. Basketball, for example, seems to me to provide an abstract parody of American middle-class life."

In "The City Game," Axthelm contends that "every American sport directs itself in a general way toward certain segments of American life." He continues, "basketball belongs to the cities" and especially to

143

New York, the most "dedicated basketball city of all." In his writing, Axthelm catches the style, rhythm and drama of the game. Most of all he describes school yard basketball in Harlem as a "rite of passage" and a way of transcending life in the ghetto. The sad ending for most of the brilliant young players is that they never pass into manhood but drift off into the drug scene or meet other tragic ends.

The article by Riesman and Denney is a classic in the analysis of the relationship of sport to culture. These authors take football from its earliest stages in America (as a cultural inheritance from England) to modern day football. The process of diffusion is clearly exemplified.

GAMES:
THE EXTENSIONS OF MAN

Marshall McLuhan

Alcohol and gambling have very different meanings in different cultures. In our intensely individualist and fragmented Western world, "booze" is a social bond and a means of festive involvement. By contrast, in closely knit tribal society, "booze" is destructive of all social pattern and is even used as a means to mystical experience.

In tribal societies, gambling, on the other hand, is a welcome avenue of entrepreneurial effort and individual initiative. Carried into an individualist society, the same gambling games and sweepstakes seem to threaten the whole social order. Gambling pushes individual initiative to the point of mocking the individualist social structure. The tribal virtue is the capitalist vice.

When the boys came home from the mud and blood baths of the Western Front in 1918 and 1919, they encountered the Volstead Prohibition Act. It was the social and political recognition that the war had fraternalized and tribalized us to the point where alcohol was a threat to an individualist society. When we too are prepared to legalize gambling, we shall, like the English, announce to the world the end of individualist society and the trek back to tribal ways.

We think of humor as a mark of sanity for a good reason: in fun and play we recover the integral person, who in the workaday world or in professional life can use only a small sector of his being. Philip Deane, in *Captive in Korea,* tells a story about games in the midst of successive brainwashing that is to the point.

From *Understanding Media: The Extensions of Man* by Marshall McLuhan, pp. 234-245. Copyright © 1964 by Marshall McLuhan. Used with permission of McGraw-Hill Book Company.

There came a time when I had to stop reading those books, to stop practising Russian because with the study of language the absurd and constant assertion began to leave its mark, began to find an echo, and I felt my thinking processes getting tangled, my critical faculties getting blunted. . . . Then they made a mistake. They gave us Robert Louis Stevenson's *Treasure Island* in English. . . . I could read Marx again, and question myself honestly without fear. Robert Louis Stevenson made us lighthearted, so we started dancing lessons.

Games are popular art, collective, social *reactions* to the main drive or action of any culture. Games, like institutions, are extensions of social man and of the body politic, as technologies are extensions of the animal organism. Both games and technologies are counter-irritants or ways of adjusting to the stress of the specialized actions that occur in any social group. As extensions of the popular response to the workaday stress, games become faithful models of a culture. They incorporate both the action and the reaction of whose populations in a single dynamic image.

A Reuters dispatch for December 13, 1962, reported from Tokyo:

BUSINESS IS A BATTLEFIELD

Latest fashion among Japanese businessmen is the study of classical military strategy and tactics in order to apply them to business operations. . . . It has been reported that one of the largest advertising companies in Japan has even made these books compulsory reading for all its employees.

Long centuries of tight tribal organization now stand the Japanese in very good stead in the trade and commerce of the electric age. A few decades ago they underwent enough literacy and industrial fragmentation to release aggressive individual energies. The close teamwork and tribal loyalty now demanded by electrical intercom again puts the Japanese in positive relation to their ancient traditions. Our own tribal ways are much too remote to be of any social avail. We have begun retribalizing with the same painful groping with which a preliterate society begins to read and write, and to organize its life visually in three-dimensional space.

The search for Michael Rockefeller brought the life of a New Guinea tribe into prominent attention in *Life* a year ago. The editors explained the war games of these people:

The traditional enemies of the Willigiman-Wallalua are the Wittaia, a people exactly like themselves in language, dress and custom. . . . Every week or two the Willigiman-Wallalua and their enemies arrange a formal battle at one of the traditional fighting grounds. In comparison with the catastrophic conflicts of "civilized" nations, these frays seem more like a dangerous field sport than true war. Each battle lasts but a single day, always stops before nightfall (because of the danger of ghosts) or if it begins to rain (no one wants to get his hair or ornaments wet). The men are very accurate with their weapons—they have all played war games since they were small boys—but they are equally adept at dodging, hence are rarely hit by anything.

The truly lethal part of this primitive warfare is not the formal battle but the sneak raid or stealthy ambush in which not only men but women and children are mercilessly slaughtered. . . .

This perpetual bloodshed is carried on for none of the usual reasons for waging war. No territory is won or lost; no goods or prisoners seized. . . . They fight because they enthusiastically enjoy it, because it is to them a vital function of the complete man, and because they feel they must satisfy the ghosts of slain companions.

These people, in short, detect in these games a kind of model of the universe, in whose deadly gavotte they can participate through the ritual of war games.

Games are dramatic models of our psychological lives providing release of particular tensions. They are collective and popular art forms with strict conventions. Ancient and nonliterate societies naturally regarded games as live dramatic models of the universe or of the outer cosmic drama. The Olympic games were direct enactments of the *agon*, or struggle of the Sun god. The runners moved around a track adorned with the zodiacal signs in imitation of the daily circuit of the sun chariot. With games and plays that were dramatic enactments of a cosmic struggle, the spectator role was plainly religious. The participation in these rituals kept the cosmos on the right track, as well as providing a booster shot for the tribe. The tribe or the city was a dim replica of that cosmos, as much as were the games, the dances, and the icons. How art became a sort of civilized substitute for magical games and rituals is the story of the detribalization which came with literacy. Art, like games, became a mimetic echo of, and relief from, the old magic of total involvement. As the audience for the magic games and plays became more individualistic, the role of art and ritual shifted from the cosmic to the humanly psychological, as in Greek drama. Even the ritual became more verbal and less mimetic or dancelike. Finally, the verbal narrative from Homer and Ovid became a romantic literary substitute for the corporate liturgy and group participation. Much of the scholarly effort of the past century in many fields has been devoted to a minute reconstruction of the conditions of primitive art and ritual, for it has been felt that this course offers the key to understanding the mind of primitive man. The key to this understanding, however, is also available in our new electric technology that is so swiftly and profoundly re-creating the conditions and attitudes of primitive tribal man in ourselves.

The wide appeal of the games of recent times—the popular sports of baseball and football and ice hockey—seen as outer models of inner psychological life, become understandable. As models, they are collective rather than private dramatizations of inner life. Like our vernacular tongues, all games are media of interpersonal communication, and they could have neither existence nor meaning except as extensions of our immediate inner lives. If we take a tennis racket in hand, or thirteen playing cards, we consent to being a part of a dynamic mechanism in an artificially contrived situation. Is this not the reason we enjoy those games most that mimic other situations in our work and social lives? Do not our favorite games provide a release from the monopolistic tyranny of the social machine? In a word, does not Aristotle's idea of drama as a mimetic reenactment and relief from our besetting pressures apply perfectly to all kinds of games and dance and fun? For fun or games to be welcome, they must convey an echo of workaday life. On the other hand, a man or society without games is one sunk in the zombie trance of the automation. Art and games enable us to stand aside from the material pressures of routine and convention, observing and questioning. Games as popular art forms offer to all an immediate means of participation in the full life of a society, such as no single role or job can offer to any man. Hence the contradiction in "professional" sport. When the games door opening into the free life leads into a merely specialist job, everybody senses an incongruity.

The games of a people reveal a great deal about them. Games are a sort of artificial paradise like Disneyland, or some Utopian vision by which we interpret and complete the meaning of our daily lives. In games we devise means of nonspecialized participation in the larger drama of our time. But for civilized man the idea of participation is strictly limited. Not for him the depth participation that erases the boundaries of individual awareness as in the Indian cult of *darshan,* the mystic experience of the physical presence of vast numbers of people.

A game is a machine that can get into action only if the players consent to become puppets for a time. For individualist Western man, much of his "adjustment" to society has the character of a personal surrender to the collective demands. Our games help both to teach us this kind of adjustment and also to provide a release from it. The uncertainty of the outcomes of our contests makes a rational excuse for the mechanical rigor of the rules and procedures of the game.

When the social rules change suddenly, then previously accepted social manners and rituals may suddenly assume the stark outlines and the arbitrary patterns of a game. The *Gamesmanship* of Stephen Potter speaks of a social revolution in England. The English are moving toward social equality and the intense personal competition that goes with equality. The older rituals of long-accepted class behavior now begin to appear comic and irrational, gimmicks in a game. Dale Carnegie's *How to Win Friends and Influence People* first appeared as a solemn manual of social wisdom, but it seemed quite ludicrous to sophisticates. What Carnegie offered as serious discoveries already seemed like a naïve mechanical ritual to those beginning to move in a milieu of Freudian awareness charged with the psychopathology of everyday life. Already the Freudian patterns of perception have become an outworn code that begins to provide the cathartic amusement of a game, rather than a guide to living.

The social practices of one generation tend to get codified into the "game" of the next. Finally, the game is passed on as a joke, like a skeleton stripped of its flesh. This is especially true of periods of suddenly altered attitudes, resulting from some radically new technology. It is the inclusive mesh of the TV image, in particular, that spells for a while, at least, the doom of baseball. For baseball is a game of one-thing-at-a-time, fixed positions and visibly delegated specialist jobs such as belonged to the now passing mechanical age, with its fragmented tasks and its staff and line in management organization. TV, as the very image of the new corporate and participant ways of electric living, fosters habits of unified awareness and social interdependence that alienate us from the peculiar style of baseball, with its specialist and positional stress. When cultures change, so do games. Baseball, that had become the elegant abstract image of an industrial society living by split-second timing, has in the new TV decade lost its psychic and social relevance for our new ways of life. The ball game has been dislodged from the social center and and been conveyed to the periphery of American life.

In contrast, American football is nonpositional, and any or all of the players can switch to any role during play. It is, therefore, a game that at the present is supplanting baseball in general acceptance. It agrees very well with the new needs of decentralized team play in the electric age. Offhand, it might be supposed that the tight tribal unity of football would make it a game that the Russians would cultivate. Their devotion to ice hockey and soccer, two very individualist forms of game, would seem little suited to the psychic needs of a collectivist society. But Russia is still in the main an oral, tribal world that is undergoing detribalization and just now discovering individualism as a novelty. Soccer and ice hockey have for them, therefore, an exotic and Utopian quality of promise that they do not convey to the West. This is the quality that we tend to call "snob value," and *we* might derive some similar "value" from owning race horses, polo ponies, or twelve-meter yachts.

Games, therefore, can provide many varieties of satisfaction. Here we are looking at their role as media of communication in society as a whole. Thus, poker is a game that has often been cited as the expression of all the complex attitudes and unspoken values of a competitive society. It calls for shrewdness, aggression, trickery, and unflattering appraisals of character. It is said women cannot play poker well because it stimulates their curiosity, and curiosity is fatal in poker. Poker is intensely individualist, allowing no place for kindness or consideration, but only for the greatest good of the greatest number—the number one. It is in this perspective that it is easy to see why war has been called the sport of kings. For kingdoms are to monarchs what patrimonies and private income are to the private citizen. Kings can play poker with kingdoms, as the generals of their armies do with troops. They can bluff and deceive the opponent about their resources and their intentions. What disqualifies war from being a true game is probably what also disqualifies the stock market and business—the rules are not fully known nor accepted by all the players. Furthermore, the audience is too fully participant in war and business, just as in a native society there is no true art because *everybody* is engaged in making art. Art and games need rules, conventions, and spectators. They must stand forth from the overall situation as models of it in order for the quality of play to persist. For "play," whether in life or in a wheel, implies *interplay*. There must be give and take, or dialogue, as between two or more persons and groups. This quality can, however, be diminished or lost in any kind of situation. Great teams often play practice games without any audience at all. This is not sport in our sense, because much of the quality of interplay, the very medium of interplay, as it were, is the feeling of the audience. Rocket Richard, the Canadian hockey player, used to comment on the poor acoustics of some arenas. He felt that the puck off his stick rode on the roar of the crowd. Sport, as a popular art form, is not just self-expression but is deeply and necessarily a means of interplay within an entire culture.

Art is not just play but an extension of human awareness in contrived and conventional patterns. Sport as popular art is a deep reaction to the typical action of the society. But high art, on the other hand, is not a reaction but a profound reappraisal of a complex cultural state. Jean Genet's *The Balcony* appeals to some people as a shatteringly logical appraisal of mankind's madness in its orgy of self-destruction. Genet offers a brothel enveloped by the holocaust of war and revolution as an inclusive image of human life. It would be easy to argue that Genet is hysterical, and that football offers a more serious criticism of life than he does. Seen as live models of complex social situations, games may lack moral earnestness, it has to be admitted. Perhaps there is, just for this reason, a desperate need for games in a highly specialized industrial culture, since they are the only form of art accessible to many minds. Real interplay is reduced to nothing in a specialist world of delegated tasks and fragmented jobs. Some backward or tribal societies suddenly translated into industrial and specialist forms of mechanization cannot easily devise the antidote of sports and games to create countervailing force. They bog down into grim earnest. Men without art, and men without the popular arts of games, tend toward automatism.

A comment on the different kinds of games played in the British Parliament and the French Chamber of Deputies will rally the political experience of many readers. The British had the luck to get the two-team pattern into the House benches, whereas the French, trying for centralism by seating the deputies in a semicircle facing the chair, got instead a multiplicity of teams playing a great variety of games. By trying for unity, the French got anarchy. The British, by setting up diversity, achieved, if anything, too much unity. The British representative, by playing his "side," is not tempted into private mental effort, nor does he have to follow the debates until the ball is passed to him. As one critic said, if the benches did not face each other the British could not tell truth from falsehood, nor wisdom from folly, unless they listened to it *all*. And since most of the debate must be nonsense, it would be stupid to listen to all.

The form of any game is of first importance. Game theory, like information theory, has ignored this aspect of game and information movement. Both theories have dealt with the information content of systems, and have observed the "noise" and "deception" factors that divert data. This is like approaching a painting or a musical composition from the point of view of its content. In other words, it is guaranteed to miss the central structural core of the experience. For as it is the *pattern* of a game that gives it relevance to our inner lives, and not who is playing nor the outcome of the game, so it is with information movement. The selection of our human senses employed makes all the difference say between photo and telegraph. In the arts the particular mix of our senses in the medium employed is all-important. The ostensible program content is a lulling distraction needed to enable the structural form to get through the barriers of conscious attention.

Any game, like any medium of information, is an extension of the individual or the group. Its effect on the group or individual is a reconfiguring of the parts of the group or individual that are *not* so extended. A work of art has no existence or function apart from its *effects* on human observers. And art, like games or popular arts, and like media of communication, has the power to impose its own assumptions by setting the human community into new relationships and postures.

Art, like games, is a translator of experience. What we have already felt or seen in one situation we are suddenly given in a new kind of material. Games, likewise, shift familiar experience into new forms, giving the bleak and the blear side of things sudden luminosity. The telephone companies make tapes of the blither of boors, who inundate defenseless telephone operators with various kinds of revolting expressions. When played back this becomes salutary fun and play, and helps the operators to maintain equilibrium.

The world of science has become quite self-conscious about the play element in its endless experiments with models of situations otherwise unobservable. Management training centers have long used games as a means of developing new business perception. John Kenneth Galbraith argues that business must now study art, for the artist makes models of problems and situations that have not yet emerged in the larger matrix of society, giving the artistically perceptive businessman a decade of leeway in his planning.

In the electric age, the closing of the gaps between art and business, or between campus and community, are part of the overall implosion that closes the ranks of specialists at all levels. Flaubert, the French novelist of the nineteenth century felt that the Franco-Prussian War could have been avoided if people had heeded his *Sentimental Education*. A similar feeling has since come to be widely held by artists. They know that they are engaged in making live models of situations that have not yet matured in the society at large. In their artistic play, they discovered what is actually happening, and thus they appear to be "ahead of their time." Non-artists always look at the present through the spectacles of the preceding age. General staffs are always magnificently prepared to fight the previous war.

Games, then, are contrived and controlled situations, extensions of group awareness that permit a respite from customary patterns. They are a kind of talking to itself on the part of society as a whole. And talking to oneself is a recognized form of play that is indispensable to any growth of self-confidence. The British and Americans have enjoyed during recent times an enormous self-confidence born of the playful spirit of fun and games. When they sense the absence of this spirit in their rivals, it causes embarrassment. To take mere worldly things in dead earnest betokens a defect of awareness that is pitiable. From the first days of Christianity there grew a habit, in some quarters, of spiritual clowning, of "playing the fool in Christ," as St. Paul put it. Paul also associated this sense of spiritual confidence and Christianity play with the games and sports of his time. Play goes with an awareness of huge disproportion between the ostensible situation and the real stakes. A similar sense hovers over the game situation, as such. Since the game, like any art form, is a mere tangible model of another situation that is less accessible, there is always a tingling sense of oddity and fun in play or games that renders the very earnest and very serious person or society laughable. When the Victorian Englishman began to lean toward the pole of seriousness, Oscar Wilde and Bernard Shaw and G. K. Chesterton moved in swiftly as countervailing force. Scholars have often pointed out that Plato conceived of play dedicated to the Deity, as the loftiest reach of man's religious impulse.

Bergson's famous treatise on laughter sets forth the idea of mechanism taking over life-values as the key to the ludicrous. To see a man slip on a banana skin is to see a rationally structured system suddenly translated into a whirling machine. Since industrialism had created a similar situation in the society of his time, Bergson's idea was readily accepted. He seems not to have noticed that he had mechanically turned up a mechanical metaphor in a mechanical age in order to explain the very unmechanical thing, laughter, or "the mind sneezing," as Wyndham Lewis described it.

The game spirit suffered a defeat a few years ago over the rigged TV quiz shows. For one thing, the big prize seemed to make fun of money. Money as store of power and skill, and expediter of exchange, still has for many people the ability to induce a trance of great earnestness. Movies, in a sense, are also rigged shows. Any play or poem or novel is, also, rigged *to produce an effect.* So was the TV quiz show. But with the TV effect there is deep audience *participation.* Movie and drama do not permit as much participation as that afforded by the mosaic mesh of the TV image. So great was the audience participation in the quiz shows that the directors of the show were prosecuted as con men. Moreover press and radio and interests, bitter about the success of the new TV medium, were delighted to lacerate the flesh of their rivals. Of course, the riggers had been blithely unaware of the nature of their medium, and had given it the movie treatment of intense realism, instead of the softer mythic focus proper to TV. Charles Van Doren merely got clobbered as an innocent bystander, and the whole investigation elicited no insight into the nature or effects of the TV medium.

Regrettably, it simply provided a field day for the earnest moralizers. A moral point of view too often serves as a substitute for understanding in technological matters.

That games are extensions, not of our private but of our social selves, and that they are media of communication, should now be plain. If, finally, we ask, "Are games mass media?" the answer has to be "Yes." Games are situations contrived to permit simultaneous participation of many people in some significant pattern of their own corporate lives.

SOME MEANINGS OF AMERICAN SPORT:
AN EXTENDED VIEW

GREGORY P. STONE

What this paper represents is an extension of an earlier preliminary paper that I gave at Ohio State University a little more than a decade ago. At that time I had collected just under 200 interviews. The final sample consists of 566 interviews and for all intents and purposes that study is done.

First, a word about meaning—when I talk about meaning I use it in the sense of George Herbert Mead as the responses that are mobilized by a particular event. Consequently, the first matter of meaning has to do precisely with what kind of response people make when they are confronted with the symbol *sport*. It is this with which I am concerned and thus will get into it substantially.

To explore this problem I developed what probably is best called a proposive quota sample. I was interested not so much in making estimates of what's out there in the world or in the parameters of the problem if you like, as I was exploring social relationships that are mobilized by sport and sport activities. Consequently, I developed a box with three, six, twelve, with twenty-four cells. I was concerned in the first place with adults, married adults, with men and women, with older people and younger people, with urban and suburban residents and finally, with upper, middle, and lower socio-economic strata. Within each cell I selected relatively the same number of respondents, because I was concerned with getting at age, sex, residential and socio-economic differences. In selecting the urban sample I employed census tracts, and

From *Aspects of Contemporary Sport Sociology: Proceedings of C.I.C. Symposium on the Sociology of Sport*, edited by Gerald S. Kenyon, pp. 5-27. Chicago, Ill.: The Athletic Institute, 1969. Copyright © 1969 by The Athletic Institute.

using about seventeen different socio-economic variables, which I won't enumerate, picked out the top three tracts and told my students to go into those tracts, make a kind of reconnaissance and select only the best residences in their view within those tracts, for their sample. Then I took three tracts in the dead center of the distribution, again asking students to reconnoiter the tract areas in the city and try to reach some agreement among themselves on the model residents in those tracts. Next I took the three lowest ranking tracts and told the students to pick out the worst residences. So, I was trying to get socio-economic extremes, plus the dead center of the middle mass.

With suburbs it was more difficult because at that time, in terms of the tract data available, the suburban tracts were quite large and quite heterogeneous. So, I had to go pretty much on local reputation of the suburbs and thus we picked two of the high status suburbs, Edina and some parts of Minnetonka, two reputedly middle-class suburbs, and two working class suburbs, and then followed the same procedures in gathering interviews. One interesting point, I think, is that it was very difficult to find young, upper urban people who were married. The young upper-class seems to have abandoned the central city.

Now to begin with, all I did was ask these people what activities they thought of when they heard the word "sport." The number of activities that they reported are provided in Table 1.[1] Over 2,600 activities were mentioned so that each person on the average mentioned between four and five activities. There is a status relationship or socio-economic relationship between the number of activities that were reported or mentioned by these people. In general, the higher the status the greater the number of activities mentioned. This, I think, should be taken with a grain of salt because it may indicate merely a difference in verbalization among the strata and I may be reporting that rather than the fact that sport thas a greater saliency for upper status people than for lower status people. But the consistency between the middle and the lower socio-economic strata suggests that this may only be partially true, since there is no great difference between the middle strata and the lower strata. By the way, as is indicated in the footnote of the table, there are only 6 people of the 562 who answered the question who could not come up with any activities relating to sport, so certainly this underscores Dr. Lüschen's observations to the effect that sport has a profound saliency in our entire society.

1. For all tables only significant associations are presented. If age is not presented, there is no signficant association. I might say that because sport is still pretty much a male world, there are always significant sex differences, and thus I have only reported the ones that seem particularly interesting.

TABLE 1
Socio-Economic Differences in the Range of Activities
Interpreted as Sport by Metropolitan Residents

Number of Activities Interpreted as Sport	Socio-Economic Strata			Totals* (Per Cent)
	Upper (Per Cent)	Middle (Per Cent)	Lower (Per Cent)	
0-2‡	9.0	18.1	13.1	13.3
3	15.3	13.2	25.7	18.1
4	16.9	19.8	17.8	18.1
5	18.5	20.3	21.5	20.1
or more	40.2	28.6	22.0	30.2
Totals*	99.9 (n = 189)	100.0 (n = 182)	100.1 (n = 191)	99.8 (n = 562)

Chi square = 26.41   .05 > p > .001

*Four respondents, three in the upper stratum and one in the middle stratum, did not respond to the question.

‡Six respondents, two in the middle stratum and four in the lower stratum, mentioned no activities.

Some of the activities mentioned are quite interesting. Included as sport were such activities as relaxing, dancing, television, movies, woodworking and sex. Perhaps the inclusion of sex as sport is kind of apt testimony to the inappropriateness of the Freudian perspective for the interpretation of contemporary American sport David Riesman wrote about some time ago in a collection of very good essays on Freud. Freud viewed work as an inescapable and tragic necessity; and sex, too, was for Freud, a realm of necessity. He saw it not as presenting man with a problem to be solved nor with a game to be played nor coupled with love as a road to human closeness and intimacy, but rather as a teleological prime mover charged with the task of socializing and civilizing man and thus preserving the species. Sex could fulfill this task because of its ability to bribe with an elemental release. Work was then the means by which the species maintains itself while performing its endless procreative mission. Although, of course, in Freud's time sex was

purchasable in the sporting houses of the day, the purchasers were probably not called athletes as some of them are called these days.

In spite of the mention of these rather unusual activities associated
with the term sport, Table 2 indicates that the responses were, by and
large, conventional. Spectator sports received the most frequent mention
—football, baseball, and basketball; and that the mentioning of partici-

TABLE 2
The Differential Saliency of Various Sports
for Metropolitan Residents

Activities	Selected Social Characteristics*				Per Cent of Respondents Mentioning at Least One Sport (N = 556)
	Age	Sex	Residence	Socio-Economic Strata	
Football	——	——	——	——	72.7
Baseball	O-Y	M-F	——	L-M-U	66.9
Basketball	——	——	——	——	42.6
Hockey	——	M-F	——	——	21.0
Boxing	——	M-F	——	L-M-U	16.4
Wrestling	O-Y	——	——	L-U-M	10.2
Golf	——	——	——	U-M-L	35.2
Tennis	——	F-M	——	U-M-L	21.6
Bowling	——	——	——	L-M-U	19.4
Swimming	Y-O	F-M	——	U-M-L	30.6
Skiing	——	F-M	——	U-M-L	11.3
Fishing	——	M-F	——	——	29.0
Hunting	——	M-F	——	——	18.7

*Only significant associations as determined by the Chi-square Test are presented in
the body of the table. The level of significance has been set at .05. Categories of
informants making most mentions of any specified activity are listed first, those
making fewest mentions are listed last, reading from left to right. In the age category,
those less than forty years of age are designated "Y," those forty years of age or
more are designated "O." In the sex category, men are designated "M" and women,
"F." In the residence category, "U" designates respondents living in the Minneapolis
city limits; "S," those living in the suburbs. In the socio-economic category, those in
the highest category are designated "U," those in the middle, "M," and those in the
lowest, "L."

pant sports is somewhat less. In short it seems that in the public mind, sport is still primarily a spectator or a spectatorial affair, a spectacle, if you like.

Again these are just words that people mentioned when they were presented with the symbol "sport" and I suppose that what is measured here is a kind of saliency of these different activities, but because the question is open-ended, again I would like to have you view these data with a kind of grain of salt. But saliency indicates what is salient. In other words I think we can say from these data that these particular sports are salient, are in the minds of people when we hear this term, but it doesn't indicate what is not salient. In other words, the fact that only 11 per cent of the people mentioned skiing does not indicate that skiing is not salient. The fact that 73 per cent mentioned football indicates that football is salient. Or that 10 per cent of the people mentioned wrestling does not indicate that wrestling is not salient as a sport in their minds. So some sports not mentioned or receiving very, very infrequent mentions may be much more salient than this table suggests. There may also be a seasonal kind of censure operating here. The fact that the interviews are taken in the fall may also affect these results. There certainly, I'm sure, is a status bias operating. I'm quite sure that people are loathe to confess to a higher status interviewer, a college student, that, in fact, wrestling is their bag.[2] So there are biases operating to distort those figures.

The two primary differentiating variables seems to be sex and status and some age differences which you would expect, particularly in the case of swimming. So that the sport audience, if you like, is "chopped up." As a sociologist might conceive it, it is differentiated. It is differentiated along the primary axes of sex and status.

The thing that I found also very interesting is the absence of any residential differences in these saliencies. I seriously had expected to see suburban-urban differences in conceptions of sport. Of course, there has been a vast literature on the leisure time of suburbia, but I uncovered no differences at all in terms of the saliency of these sports. This may indicate that, as another sociologist, Berger, has indicated, that of the sociological literature on suburbia is as biased as some of my own data

2. They are somewhat ashamed of being caught up in that marvelously curious spectacle which manages to outdraw professional basketball in Minneapolis. It will easily outdraw it. I'd say it gets about twice or three times the attendance of professional basketball, and that's only in the city and, of course, the wrestlers are working a circuit four or five nights a week. People probably don't know either that wrestling is probably the most lucrative professional sport. By and large, on the average, a third rate wrestler can count on about $18,000 a year.

are here, namely, dealing primarily with middle status suburban areas, not concerned with working class suburbs as I'm concerned with here or with high status suburbs.

I then asked people "what is your favorite sport?" Now, here we get into less difficulty in terms of saliencies and you can see that in terms of favorites, the people are about evenly divided between the selection of a spectator sport and a participant sport. The one point I think I'd like to make in terms of Table 3, is that we tend to think of spectatorship as being somehow low status or lower class in character.[3] So that we tend to look at spectatorship as being lower class. Now you will see a slight tendency—I don't think it's enough really to warrant a great deal of emphasis—for participation as a favorite sport to be somewhat greater in the lower strata than in the middle strata, which I think is rather interesting. There was one study done some time ago by Clarke on Leisure and Levels of Occupational Prestige in the *American Sociological Review*, in June of 1956, (Vol. 21, pp. 301-307) where he

TABLE 3

Socio-Economic Differences in the Designation of Spectator or Participant Sports as Favorites by Metropolitan Residents

Favorite Sport	Socio-Economic Strata			Totals (Per Cent)
	Upper (Per Cent)	Middle (Per Cent)	Lower (Per Cent)	
Spectator	35.6	57.1	54.7	48.8
Participant	64.4	42.9	45.3	51.2
Totals	100.0 (N = 188)	100.0 (N = 175)	100.0 (N = 172)	100.0 (N = 535)

Chi square = 20.25   .05 > p > .001

3. I think sociologists themselves are pretty snobbish about sport. I think this is one reason that there has been so little done by sociologists in this country in sport. If you look at the two main journals, *The American Sociological Review* and *The American Journal of Sociology*, you will find that you can count the number of articles dealing with sport on one hand and on the fingers of one hand. I forget what the number actually is; I think it's only about four or five in the two journals. I have a friend who has been doing research on camping, for example. He sent his article first to the *American Sociological Review*, and received a letter back from the editor suggesting that he really should submit this article to Outdoor Life because it didn't belong in sociology. On the other hand, the editor seldom suggests that we submit articles on industrial sociology to Chamber of Commerce publications. However, through some mediation the paper was eventually published in the *American Journal of Sociology*.

did find in terms of leisure time activities a kind of U curve with more participation, more active forms of leisure occurring at the extremes of status rather than in the middle, and these data somewhat follow this. He was concerned with leisure activities; I'm concerned with sport, which is different, but there is a tendency to follow the U type of distribution which Clarke uncovered.

In Table 4 you will find the concrete activities designated as "favorites" and you will notice that there were some 26 respondents who

TABLE 4
Social Differences in Sports Designated as Favorites by Metropolitan Residents

Favorite Sports	Selected Social Characteristics*				Per Cent of Respondents Selecting a Favorite Sport (N = 540)
	Age	Sex	Residence	Socio-Economic Strata	
Football	―――	―――	U-S	M-U-L	24.4
Baseball	―――	M-F	―――	L-M-U	15.4
Basketball	―――	―――	―――	M-L-U	6.8
Boxing	―――	M-F	―――	L-M-U	3.3
Golf	―――	―――	―――	U-M-L	11.3
Tennis	―――	―――	―――	U-M-L	3.7
Bowling	―――	F-M	―――	L-M-U	6.3
Swimming	Y-O	F-M	U-S	M-U-L	7.6
Hunting	―――	M-F	―――	―――	3.7
Fishing	―――	M-F	―――	―――	9.6
Others too diverse to analyze	―――	―――	―――	―――	7.8

*Only significant associations as determined by the Chi-square Test are presented in the body of the table. The level of significance has been set at .05. Categories of informants making most mentions of any specified activity are listed first, those making fewest mentions are listed last, reading from left to right. In the age category, those less than forty years of age are designated "Y," those forty years of age or more are designated "O." In the sex category, men are designated "M" and women, "F." In the residence category, "U" designates respondents living in the Minneapolis city limits; "S" those living in the suburbs. In the socio economic category, those in the highest category are designated "U," those in the middle, "M," and those in the lowest, "L."

did not designate a favorite sport. Again you get the primary differentiation here of sex and status and although there are some differences
in the relationships reported in Table 4 as compared with Table 2, I
think that the relative presence of similarity in those two tables indicates something, some kind of argument for the validity of the data in
the second table.

I'm not primarily interested, of course, in what sports have saliency
in the population, because what a sociologist is concerned with is the
activities that are mobilized by sport itself and one very important activity is, of course, conversation. I mentioned earlier, for example, if a
man in our society does not have at least some conversational knowledge
of sport he's viewed as suspect, and I know of at least one psychiatrist,
who I mentioned in the earlier article, who used knowledge of sports as
a diagnostic device for recruits into the Army during World War II. If
the recruit didn't know, for example, who had won the last World Series
then perhaps it's better to give him a rather careful test in terms of his
maleness or homosexuality.

As to what is important in terms of conversation, it is that in the
presumed anonymity of the city a conversational knowledge of sports
gives strangers access to one another, so that if they meet in the bar or

TABLE 5

**Sex Differences in Frequency of Sport Conversations
Carried on by Metropolitan Residents**

Frequency of Sport Conversation	Sex		Totals* (Per Cent)
	Male (Per Cent)	Female (Per Cent)	
Rarely, Almost Never, or Never‡	10.6	28.5	19.8
Occasionally	25.9	32.0	29.0
Frequently	31.8	24.4	27.9
Very Frequently	31.8	15.1	23.2
Totals*	100.1 (n = 274)	100.0 (n = 291)	99.9 (n = 565)
Chi square = 44.45		.05 > p > .001	

*One female respondent did not reply to the question.

‡Three males and seven females never discussed sports.

in other public places or on a plane or a train or a bus, one can immediately start up a conversation with a total stranger and gain access and penetrate the barriers or the insulations of anonymity that presumably we find in the city. So, Table 5 shows that in the first place it is a man's world; that the conversation about sports is quite frequent for men. About two-thirds of them say that they talk about sports frequently or very frequently, compared to somewhat more than a third of the women. Women, by the way, resent this, although I don't have time to go into it, but some of them are avid sports fans and they have a difficult time in finding anybody to talk about sport because the men refuse to discuss it with them. Imputing female interest in sports is probably somewhat on the order of an invasion of their world, and women then become indignant, and frequently you will find letters to the editors in the paper with women complaining that they are avid Twins fans, for example, but nobody will talk to them about sport. So, the fact that it is a man's world acts to seal off the sexual world, and particularly in the middle and lower strata, to set men and women a little bit further apart than perhaps they should be.

Table 6 shows the socio-economic differences and frequency of conversations. The most interesting datum is the polarization in the lower

TABLE 6

Socio-Economic Differences in Frequency of Sport Conversations
Carried on by Metropolitan Residents

Frequency of Sport Conversation	Socio-Economic Strata			Totals* (Per Cent)
	Upper (Per Cent)	Middle (Per Cent)	Lower (Per Cent)	
Rarely, Almost Never, or Never‡	10.4	17.5	31.6	19.8
Occasionally	33.3	32.8	21.1	29.0
Frequently	32.3	27.3	24.2	27.9
Very Frequently	24.0	22.4	23.2	23.2
Totals*	100.0 (n = 192)	100.0 (n = 183)	100.1 (n = 190)	99.9 (n = 565)

Chi square = 30.96   .05 > p > .001

*One lower stratum respondent did not reply to the question.

‡Two middle and eight lower stratum respondents never discussed sports.

strata between a third or almost a third who rarely or never talk about sports, and about a fourth of those who talk very frequently about sports. You will notice that in terms of frequent conversations the differences among the strata are so slight as to be negligible. I think what this means is that many lower strata people are left outside the world of sport. Based upon other data, I have found that there is a general alienation of the lower stratum when using such measures as integration with the neighborhood, and a sense of belonging to the larger city. There is a general alienation and perhaps this lack of involvement as measured by frequency of sport conversation on the part of the lower stratum indicates a larger alienation than being simply alienation from the sport world. But, once people in the lower stratum do get involved as are other people and the differences more or less disappear so that the association in Table 6 is primarily due to the relatively large number of lower strata people who simply are not involved in the sports world through their conversations.

Next, I asked in what situations did they discuss sport and here again we see the same shortcoming of open ended questions because the people answered this question spontaneously without being probed. Again, as shown in Table 7, you find it's a man's world, that most women

TABLE 7
Sex Differences in Situational Range of Sport Conversations
Carried on by Metropolitan Residents

Number of Situations Mentioned	Sex		Totals* (Per Cent)
	Male (Per Cent)	Female (Per Cent)	
0-1‡	18.5	32.1	25.5
2	30.7	29.3	30.0
3	30.4	23.4	27.0
4 or more	20.4	15.2	17.7
Totals*	100.0 (n = 270)	100.0 (n = 290)	100.2 (n = 560)
Chi square = 14.75 .05 > p > .01			

*Five respondents, three males and two females did not respond to the question. One male respondent gave a "Don't know" reply.

‡Fifteen respondents, four males and eleven females, did not converse about sports in any specific social situation.

talk about sports in relatively few situations. Most men identify a rela-tively large number of situations, three or more, so that sport, then, is not only more salient to men and involves them more, but also carries over into a larger number of the situations of their daily life. Table 8 shows largely the same status differences in terms of the situations as is found in the frequency of the conversation.

TABLE 8
Socio-Economic Differences in Situational Range of Sport Conversations Carried on by Metropolitan Residents

Number of Situations Mentioned	Socio-Economic Strata			Totals* (Per Cent)
	Upper (Per Cent)	Middle (Per Cent)	Lower (Per Cent)	
0-1‡	15.8	26.2	34.8	25.5
2	30.0	31.7	28.3	30.0
3	32.6	26.8	20.9	27.0
4 or more	21.6	15.3	16.0	17.7
Totals*	100.0 (n = 190)	100.0 (n = 183)	100.0 (n = 187)	100.2 (n = 560)
Chi square = 21.85	.05 > p > .01			

*Five respondents, one upper and four lower stratum, did not respond to the question. One upper stratum respondent gave a "Don't know" reply.

‡Fifteen respondents, one upper stratum, four middle, and ten lower stratum, did not converse about sports in any specified social situation.

Turning to what situations are used for discussion in the mobiliza-tion of involvement in sports, there are several comments I can make about the data in Table 9. In the first place, there is the problem of the open-ended question. Some people would say neighbors and some say friends, and I was very literal in my code. Of course, I know not all neighbors are friends. Anybody knows that who has a neighbor. But some neighbors are friends and thus there is some overlap between these categories. Nevertheless, there are some interesting differences here. In terms of the family of procreation, that is, the immediate family, I did get a residential difference which may testify somewhat to the socio-logical contention that familism is enhanced in the suburban environ-

TABLE 9

Social Differences in Situational Contexts of Sport
Conversation Carried on by Metropolitan Residents

Situational Contexts	Selected Social Characteristics *				Per Cent of Respondents Mentioning at Least One Situational Context (n = 945)
	Age	Sex	Residence	Socio-Economic Strata	
Family of Procreation	O-Y	F-M	S-U	U-M-L	63.4
Other Family	——	——	——	M-L-U	14.5
Neighbors	——	——	——	L-M-U	8.8
Friends	——	F-M	——	U-M-L	38.6
Parties and Other Social Gatherings	——	——	——	U-M-L	17.2
Work	——	M-F	——	L-M-U	40.3
Clubs and Voluntary Associations without Sports Facilities	——	——	——	——	6.4
Public Places (Bars, Taverns, Stores)	——	M-F	——	L-M-U	7.5
Sport Scene	——	——	——	U-M-L	22.2

*Only significant associations as determined by the Chi-square Test are presented in the body of the table. The level of significance has been set at .05. Categories of informants making most mentions of any specific activity are listed first, those making fewest mentions are listed last, reading from left to right. In the age category, those less than forty years of age are designated "Y," those forty years of age or more are designated "O." In the sex category, men are designated "M" and women, "F." In the residence category, "U" designates respondents living in the Minneapolis city limits; "S," those living in the suburbs. In the socioeconomic category, those in the highest category are designated "U," those in the middle, "M," and those in the lowest, "L."

ment as opposed to the environment of the central city. The interesting difference, I think, between the status differentiation of neighbors and friends may reflect the fact that in the lower strata there is a greater reliance upon neighboring as a source of friendship than is the case in the upper strata. I have some other materials on that. I would then point out that the prime situations then for the discussion of sports in the lower strata aside from neighbors, are at work. This is a very important activity at the work scene and in public places such as bars, taverns and the like. For the upper stratum it is in the family, with friends, on parties and on the sports scene itself. One of the consequences of this is that sport involvement may operate to increase family cohesion in the upper stratum. Although differences are not reported here, this may well be because membership in associations dealing with sport or peripheral to sport, like country clubs and so forth, are often family memberships in those strata; that sport may further set apart men and women in the lower strata; and in the middle strata simply from the data I have the same impression I had a number of years ago, that the middle class wife has possibly taken a course in famliy sociology where she has learned that it's important to have a companion in marriage, while the husband, who is a sports fan or sports follower anyway, then goes to the break-fast table, picks up the morning paper and begins reading the sports page. This is very threatening to the middle class wife who has had this course in family sociology because it's hardly companionable. I have the notion that she may be grasping at sport among several other straws as a way to build some companionship into the marriage, that it's a kind of frantic quest for companionship on her part as opposed to the upper class wife. In the lower stratum the sexual worlds are quite different and extend into leisure and work activities. For example, it would be un-likely, I think, in the middle strata of our society to follow a pattern that I've observed where the working class husband will take his wife to a dance hall and order her some beer, etc. and then leave here there to dance and go out with her friend's husband to some other bar to drink beer with a man and perhaps talk about sports with him. So that the insulation of the sexes is extensive in the lower stratum and perhaps sport functions to further insulate the sexes in that stratum. I, of course, have a number of other materials. The analysis is quite extensive but this is about all the time that I have to report today. Thank you.

REACTION TO STONE PAPER

Charles H. Page

I should explain first a major delinquency of Gregory Stone concerning his very interesting paper about which I will have some things to say in a moment. The delinquency, of course, is that so far as I was concerned there was no paper and I am as new to this material as all of you are except that I did have the advantage about two minutes before we began this morning of being passed the nine tables you've heard discussed.

Let me say first that I think the most interesting things about Mr. Stone's presentation are his asides all along, his comments about some of the possible implications of his data, and to three, four, or five of those comments I'd like to speak briefly in the next few minutes. I should also say in a preliminary way that there is no need for me (even if I had the expertise, which I do not have) to comment on his data as data or the possible limitations of those data or his methods because he's done that for us as he's gone along. He has exercised an extraordinary judiciousness, I think, in this respect. Some of you may wish to talk about those limitations, but I'll avoid that. And finally, by way of an introductory comment, I'd like to correct a canard that he has committed, namely, his reference to that sacred journal, perhaps the dullest of all printed publications in the United States, the *American Sociological Review,* which I happened to edit for one term, and indeed preceded the editor to whom Stone referred, who in my judgment was the best editor that the ASR has ever had. At least one editor of that journal, namely myself, tried to find good material in the sociology of sport, solicited articles without success in this area—which is out of keeping or was out of keeping with the editorial policies of that magazine. He's right that very little has been published in the two leading sociology journals in

168

the United States, the ASR and the AJS. I think the figure is six rather than four or five if one includes a piece by a then obscure sociologist that was published before World War II. I think that's the total number plus about three book reviews. I was interested recently to count up the number of books on sports that have actually been reviewed in the *American Sociological Review*. Well, I can say that I've reviewed the great majority of them—three. There have been I think, four such reviews published during the last quarter of a century or thereabouts.

Turning to the paper itself, I'm simply going to make some running comments on the basis of notes I have made during the presentation itself. First of all, early on in Gregory's presentation he emphasized, when he began to talk about the tables, that in general they show that the higher the social status of the respondents or the people interviewed, the more they had to say about sports, the more activities they identified, and so on. I would be pretty strongly convinced until the opposite was proven that he's absolutely right when he suggests that this is pretty much a reflection of more highly developed verbal skills and perhaps a larger range of exposure of people of higher status. They simply read more, for example; they talk more in general, they are more verbal in general. I certainly wouldn't suggest a greater "saliency" (to use his term) in any affective or emotional or psychologically significant sense. At least I would throw that out as something we might discuss.

At two or three different points in the paper there is a discussion of spectatorship and participation. That is something we are all interested in, of course, particularly, I suppose, people in physical education. One of the things I've been interested in discovering from reading papers, mostly unpublished, at Columbia University—I think that Stone mentioned the fairly recent work of Clarke on leisure—is that there is some positive correlation between the growth of spectatorship and participation, so far as sport is concerned in the United States during the 30 years or so, whether the spectatorship is in the arenas of our large cities or, as is the case more frequently, looking at the boob box. While there seems to be a positive correlation between spectatorship and participation in sport, I'm not suggesting that there is any causal relationship between the two. There may or may not be, but it is something that's well worth finding out. (This is even more the case, I would judge, from reading a recent volume on leisure in France by Dumazedier, in Western European countries or at least in France itself. There the amount of participation in sport is even more closely associated with spectatorship.)

My next point also has something to do with spectatorship with respect to lower status people. I think Greogry is correct when he suggests that many sociologists, at least, who do talk about or speculate about—that is what most of them do in fact—about the world of sport, have a biased image with regard to the activity, participation, knowledge, and so on, of lower status people.

STONE: Even the lower status families.

PAGE: Yes, I think this is possibly true. And in this connection, turning to his concluding remarks, I might say that I have occupied from time to time, and for fairly prolonged periods, a strategic listening post, so far as lower status people are concerned—in the saloons, bars, and taverns, talking with and playing the role of an espionage agent in lower status groups. I've been struck over and over again in these fairly informal exercises about the tremendous amounts of expertise with respect to this or that sport or sometimes sport in general, including some of the sports one would not normally or conventionally associate with lower status people. I have heard people discussing the new black polo team that developed on Long Island 10 to 12 years ago, and the skills of that fellow from Texas—Smith—back in the late 1930's who had a ten-goal polo rating. One might ask, why are these people interested in polo? Well, some of them are. I've also heard some very interesting discussions in recent years of tennis matches—a sport which, as you know, historically was associated with private clubs and upper status groups in our society. So, I think there is much to learn, if we are interested in class differences with respect to not only sport activity, but to sport expertise, sport knowledge, the psychological role and the psychological functions that sport play for people of different strata. I believe that this is the kind of factual, if you like, or at least suggestive information, the kinds of "data," that we need to play with.

I was interested in Gregory's comment about one of the functions of sport. This is both its psychological and social function in helping to break down the impersonality, the anonymity, of what is conventionally called our increasingly cold world, our increasingly urbanized world. I certainly would fully agree that this is one of its functions, an important function. It shares it along with some other elements of our popular culture, so-called, and it certainly shares it—again I'm thinking primarily of that strategic post I referred to a moment ago—with the even more ubiquitous and in some respects, but certainly not in all, interesting of sex—which Gregory talked about in passing in a very interesting and I think highly suggestive way.

Which takes me to women. Well, starting out in the 1920's, when I belonged to a barnstorming swimming and water polo playing group (which had as its chief attraction a man named Weismueller), we traveled around the country with about six women. We thought of them as women. They ranged in age between 12 and 15 or 16, but they were women, not only as athletes but as sexually attractive objects. I'm not so sure that Gregory this morning (I'm certain that he doesn't do this normally) didn't engage a little in something that might be called sexnocentrism. I think that more and more—I'll put this point every cautiously—women are involved psychologically as well as actively in the sport world, and I'd be curious to know how many middle-class wives you portrayed a few minutes ago actually get annoyed in any serious sense when their husbands turn, at the breakfast table, to the sporting page; indeed, I'd like to know how many middle class wives quarrel with their husbands about getting that page. Women not only participate in sport, they are interested in sport. The reason they are interested in sport is because sport is an important part of the world, as we all know. It's a culturally very important part and therefore is a psychologically important part—and I don't think that the shutting off of women from the sport world to the extent suggested by the data, to be sure, is something I'd buy without some more convincing evidence. (I'm sorry that I'm addressing at the moment—only one, two, three, or four, so far as I can tell, women in the audience.)

I have another point, which takes me back to a point I raised earlier, in connection with Table 6 and Mr. Stone's discussion to the data when he was speaking about class or status differences with respect to "conversation." He noted, I think quite correctly, that generally speaking or comparatively speaking, I should say, that lower class people (I used the word "lower" here deliberately) tend to be "left out of the world of sport." I am sure this is correct, that this deprivation is related to what Stone referred to as their general alienation from many if not all aspects of conventional "middle class" life, presumably the modal type of life in American society. As one now reads the increasing number of studies on the so-called "culture of poverty" (as you know, we've rediscovered the fact of poverty with a distinctive culture in the United States in the last dozen years) one is struck by the reportedly large amount of "alienation." I'm not sure that's the correct word (alienation is a term for several concepts), but there is a real separation of the very poor from almost all of the more or less conventional facets of life including sport, which is such an important part of life today.

I was interested in the reference to the psychiatrist that Gregory had made in his earlier (and now famous) article on sport—the psychiatrist who used knowledge of or participation in sport as an index of masculinity and their absence as a possible indication of homosexuality. When I first read the paper I was surprised, and when I heard this idea repeated I was also surprised. I think that most of the psychiatrists I know would turn the idea around and suggest that a great preoccupation with sport may be a possible indicator of not heterosexuality but homosexuality. Indeed, as we all know, this is one of the ways that men often "prove" their musculinity when they suspect otherwise. This is the hypothesis I would entertain, and I think the psychiatrist in question may have known little about the masculinity-proovers among athletes.

Let me conclude by saying that as usual Gregory Stone has proven himself to be the intellectual virtuoso in this all too little worked field in this country. The rest of us who are marginal members of the sociology of sport world are greatly indebted to him.

DISCUSSION

SEYMOUR KLEINMAN: I thought it might be interesting and helpful perhaps if we clearly distinguished in our studies the categories which are involved, which sometimes tend to become muddled in a way. Thus, I would like to ask whether there is a category of the sport of spectating in which we act as spectators, as opposed to the category of the sport of engagement, active engagement in sport. I'm not really clear in your presentation of the data whether there was this kind of flow of one into another when you asked people what they regarded as sport. Were they considering themselves as spectators or as participants or as both? Or where does one leave off and the other begin in the eyes of your question or the responses to it?

STONE: In terms of the saliency thing I didn't make these distinctions. I just listed the most frequently mentioned activities in terms of favorite sport. I asked, first of all, what was their favorite sport. If they had mentioned a spectator sport, then I asked them what was their favorite patricipant sport, and vice versa, so I got both you see. But first of all I meant the favorite sport. So it's, I think, quite reliable.

KLEINMAN: I have a further comment to make on what I might want to call the sport of spectating itself. The sport of spectating, it appears to me, might involve a lot more than just observing sports. I think within our contemporary kind of existence, we become a kind of society oriented toward observing things. We just watch things and we get caught up in a watching or observing kind of business. It almost doesn't make any difference what you watch, you are just engaged in a kind of sport of observation. Whether it happens to be observation of a sport, a variety show, a dance, or drama, the act of observation becomes an end in itself, regardless of what you're watching. This is the kind of activity in which we are engaged over and above what we generally consider to be within the framework of sport itself.

PAGE: I'd like to briefly respond to one statement you made about that subject. I fully agree, myself, that spectatorship or what you nicely referred to as the sport of spectatorship or something like that, today involves much more than watching. It involves (to use fancy terms in true sociological fashion as Gregory would say) a great deal of cognitive activity on the part of spectators. It involves knowledge, an increasing knowledge. It involves expertise. Probably, however, the audience studies that are being made at Columbia and elsewhere today show that audiences break down into various types of spectators. I suppose I have a misleading image of the women who watch Gregory Stone's professional wrestlers because I have seen a few of them. I can't stand that interesting exercise myself, but I've seen some matches and I have a stereotypical view of kindly old ladies with knitting needles screaming "Kill the so-and-so" and so on at these matches. So this might be one type that doesn't involve any great knowledge or expertise. On the other hand, people who watch a great deal starting at about the age of 9 or 10 on their television sets at home not only develop knowledge, but in order to see the things they increasingly want to see on the field or in the arena they develop more and more knowledge. Their internal psychology becomes adjusted to this sort of thing. You have all had the experience of 10 year olds, for example, or 11 year olds, who psychologically and in terms of knowledge are better prepared to watch, say, a basketball game or a football game on television than many adults who don't have the child's knowledge. I wish that we had some—I don't care whether we call it sociology, it's the field that's important, not the disciplines—good studies of spectatorship, as such. Some are underway at the present time.

STONE: It isn't only a cognitive participation, but a vicarious and empathic participation. It's not unusual to come away from a football game or from a boxing match with your shoulders aching. But I didn't mean to imply that spectatorship was merely a passive kind of thing just because I used the word. I think, however, that most of the snobs writing about sports do make this implication. I suggest that sport functions in a very positive way in terms of urban identification. I'd like to comment also on the work I've done in wrestling, which is fascinating. Women certainly participate very actively. One of my wrestler friends still has scars on his back which he received when a little lady came in not with knitting needles, but with a bagful of broken glass in her handbag and threw it at him as he was going down the aisle. Probably the major occupational hazard for the wrestler, second to heart attack, is precisely the spectators. A list of injuries suffered by wrestlers at the hands of spectators is much greater in number than the injuries they suffered at the hands of other wrestlers.

On this business of women in sport, although Page may not agree with the data, the only exception that I can think of in terms of spectatorship, or in terms of the act of participation of women, is in wrestling.

The most frequent incidence of spectators in wrestling are older lower status women, when you combine these three factors. Now I can explain to some extent the age and the status relationships particularly in terms of wrestling being a con game with the older people and lower status people more or less accepting appearances as they are, and not probing behind the mask. But, I can't explain women being interested in this, although I have tried. Since wrestling is kind of a great passion play or morality play, I thought perhaps it was because women are the custodians of morality in society and they consequently get much more involved in the struggle between good and evil that is depicted in the wrestling arenas. I actually had data to test this out, but it didn't work, so I still don't know what's bringing these ladies into this very active observation of the wrestling pageant in the arenas. I seriously think that it's still pretty much a man's world. Now it's changing. One of the obvious research projects that I asked for years ago which nobody has taken up—nobody ever acts on my suggestions— would be to do a content analysis of advertisements in outdoor magazines, over a considerable period of time and notice when women began to appear in the ads in these magazines. I think it would be fascinating to pin it down historically and see what historical processes are operating. Obviously women are increasingly coming into some sports, but I think it's still by and large a male world. The people who complain about the New Year's football binge—which now lasts almost a week, and God knows how long it's going to last now that we have this expansion of conferences and we can play off games until Easter—are the housewives. Maybe they will come in and watch a particular game, but they cannot be part of this binge. I can think of no other word for it than binge. And they wonder how the husband can sit there, and I wonder how I can sit there sometimes day after day and on into the evening, watching these various pageants. I think that's probably the best term for it. I do think it's a differential thing, but we need more data on it. We need more data rather than thought.

PAGE: I don't want this to be a discourse between the two of us. I'm keen to answer him, but I will restrain.

NANCY BALDWIN: I don't want to belabor the participation of women, but I would like to ask you, do you not think that many times the verbalized or expressed interest in sports by women is so much governed by what she perceives the man to expect her to be?

STONE: That's right. That's why I'm talking about the middle-class housewife.

PAGE: I'm so glad you asked that question.

BALDWIN: Do you not think as men perceive woman to become more and more a participating or at least a knowledgeable individual in these areas, that she would feel more free in becoming involved or interested?

PAGE: Offhand, I'd have two answers. Clearly, and in keeping with basic differences in character structure between the sexes, one of the strong bents of many, many women is to be attractive to men, whereas one of the basic bents among men is to prove themselves, as we all know, whether it's in sports or business or anything else, to demonstrate our capacity to do things. So this, I think, is a sort of constant in the picture and I think your point is well taken. I might say this in connection with your question and also a comment that Gregory made—and I say this lightheartedly, but with some degree of seriousness—that increasingly I think that women are less and less the custodians of morality in our society and more and more such types as college and high school coaches are the custodians of morality.

STONE: Things are coming to a terrible pass.

PAGE: And I think there is a great deal of evidence of this.

GÜNTHER LÜSCHEN: May I comment on the social class problem. Although I believe as you do, Professor Page, that just to elicit a response is more likely from the upper class, I think there is by and large enough evidence that there is some, although not linear, correlation between social class and participation in sport. I said this is not completely linear since what we have observed for instance in Germany is that particular groups in the lower class, which I would call more the progressive group—those who are employed as industrialized labor —participate quite strongly in sport where, as Mr. Stone mentioned, the very lower class almost does not participate at all. In a paper given at the International Sociological Association meetings, we proposed the hypothesis that this signalizes a redefinition of the social class system. I don't know how much there is in it, but what we saw was, for instance, that the traditionally lower middle-class people were not participating in sport but that they were, in their leisure time, participating in activities that were traditionally lower lower-class activities, so there seemed to be some switch, and we in our hypothesis felt that this would signalize a redefinition of the class system. As far as the relationship between passive and active participation is concerned, I agree that this is a very bad distinction in general. It's also that in general there is—

STONE: Not a term by the way that was used, I don't think. I don't think this distinction was made either in my paper or—

PAGE: Mr. Kleinman made the conceptual distinction. He didn't use that terminology.

LÜSCHEN: The situation is that you have here a somewhat positive correlation between both, so that those who participate also view sports. But if you compare, for instance, this along the social class dimension, then you will find that there is a certain inverse relationship between active participation and call it passive or spectatorship, which is much higher in the lower class, which I would think in a way signalizes high interest. On the other hand, considering a certain deprivation that the lower class faces, as suggested by James Coleman in his high school studies, interestingly enough, if there was not enough sports participation supplied for the adolescents then they would turn to viewing sports on TV. The TV viewing was much higher among those that weren't able to participate that much.

One point that may also be studied in the future is the change of social class affiliation with the same or different sport disciplines. I think there is some evidence that you have something like what a rather old German sociologist by the name of Naumann has once called *Sinkendes Kulturgut*—thinking is cultural material, which somewhere it starts in the upper class and then moves down all the way and you have the same hypothesis inverted. It would be interesting to see for instance, whether the upper class gives up certain sports, or whether sport that they have formerly engaged in moved down to a lower class. Also, what new types of sport do the upper classes now create, or whether they do it at all.

PAGE: Just one comment: I hope that we will have an opportunity later in the conference to pursue this theme. There is good historical evidence that the development of specific sports to a point of popularity, general cultural popularity, can be a development that has either upper class origins, lower class origins or middle class origins. My own study of sport illustrates these different class origins.

STONE: May I make some observations here. I think that in the first place it's very difficult to talk about sport in an all-inclusive manner. So I think that some of the things that Dr. Lüschen says will be true for some sports and not for other sports, and this is the implication of your comment. There are also very important variables that are left out of this discussion. One is age, which is certainly quite important in terms of explaining sport participation, and then, of course, the whole process of urbanization. In terms of these two we have little decent material. Probably the best material that I know of in terms of data was gathered by the Outdoor Recreation Resources Review Commission, but this refers only to outdoor sports. In terms of urbanization, at least as far as outdoor sport is concerned, I have gathered some data which indicate that as suburbia becomes urbanized, as our suburbs become more and more similar to cities, participation in outdoor recreation tends to decline in proportion.

WALTER GREGG: I wonder if you could go back and clarify your ideas about participation as related to heterosexuality and homosexuality. I'm not sure right now whether I should reexamine my boy or not!

PAGE: Well, I would be very glad to speak with you privately about this or alternatively to discuss this matter. I gather that we are aproaching closing hour, aren't we?

GREGG: Well, I wasn't clear what you said in contrast to what Mr. Stone had said.

PAGE: I'm sorry I goofed up the illustration. Gregory referred in passing to a psychiatrist, in this case in the Army, who was apparently using knowledge of sport as a possible indicator of masculinity. I suggested that the opposite hypothesis might be more in keeping with at least traditional Freudian views, that intensive knowledge of and capacity in sport, or at least certain sports, might be just the opposite. That's all I was suggesting.

HARRY WEBB: I'd like to address a question to Dr. Stone. I'm wondering, did you take into consideration race in your particular sample?

STONE: I specifically did not include Negroes in the sample. It would have simply complicated the cells. You see this would have added two more and I would have then had 48 cells in terms of sampling. I might say that we do have some data which I haven't really had a chance to look at yet, gathered in St. Paul a couple of years ago in the Negro area, with a few questions pertaining to sport and particularly favorite players and sports heroes and this sort of thing. So that if I ever get around to it, the data are available and if anybody would like to look at it I could probably make it available to them.

CYRIL WHITE: May I address this question to Dr. Stone? You mentioned the concept of the culture of poverty in relationship to sports. I'm particularly interested in the unusual happenings at sport contests, particularly the hostile outbursts. From the investigations I have been involved in over the past two or three years now, I feel that one of the structural strains is a cultural one. In fact it's a sub-cultural one. And in these investigations which have gone into the hostile outbursts taking place not only in the United States but in Britain and South America, it is very clear that the two competing elements which act as predisposing factors toward hostile outbursts, that one of them is certainly sub-cultural strain. We see this if we look at one that I am particularly interested in which took place at a high school football game in Washington, D. C. in 1962. I read very extensively about Washington, D. C. and the background of one particular team and it's very obvious that the cultural poverty here is a very worthwhile concept in identifying the value systems. It's very different from the value system of the other team. Now when those teams come in conflict in violent exercise like American football for example, the results can be on certain occasions not only explosive but a catastrophe. In some cases over 500 people can be seriously injured, in other cases over 300 people can be killed. And this is not something that is just happening now and again. We are now seeing this happen about twice a year in sport, so your mention of the cultural poverty is something I'm particularly interested in, and I think very apropos to this when we talk about social class. Thus, I would like to ask Dr. Stone what type of lower class respondents was he dealing with? Was it people who could be identified as impoverished people?

STONE: You remember I mentioned that I picked the areas, three tracts that were furthest down the scale and within those tracts I told the students to go to the lousiest places of residence that they could to pick the sample. The sample was then reclassified in terms of perhaps more sophisticated techniques. That was just the way of getting these people, but I would say probably half of the 190 people classified as lower here are really lower.

WHITE: Then you would say that they would be in the culture of poverty rather than just being impoverished, being poor?

STONE: I don't know what the culture of poverty is, but they are very poor. Whether they are in the culture of poverty, it's difficult. The culture of poverty can be Puerto Rican and a number of other things.

PAGE: I was very interested in your comments and I would like to respond to one of them. You were discussing the possible relationship between distinctive sub-cultures and violence or potentiality for violence. I'm sure this is a relationship that we should know a great deal more about (however, I'm sure that you know more about this than I do because you are obviously studying it and interested in it). When one examines comparative studies, a look at the Latin American develop- ments, for example, at football games and soccer games where you some- times, as we all know, have really violent outbursts resulting in all sorts of things, it is very questionable to me whether a distinctive sub-culture is involved in that kind of episode as contrasted, say with the incident in Washington, D. C. you were referring to. I just don't know.

WHITE: I could answer you here and now: yes, it is. It is even more so than Washington, D. C. This has been clearly identified. Dr. Stone, I would like to suggest that it would be useful if some type of partitioning system be used to see which of the cells in your tables con- tributes most to your overall Chi squares. As it stands now it's difficult to see what the difference is between upper, lower or middle classes, or whether it's part of your rating system.

STONE: In general I cannot tell you. As I recall from the file of data that I have, the directions were fairly unilinear, but I'll have to look and see.

VERDELLE PARKER: I would like an elaboration on the part of the panel on the subject of cohesion and insulation as you mention it as they fit these two stratas, the lower and the upper. This would be of real interest to me and it might be for the group.

STONE: That would take some time. What I was concerned about in that step, and I really wish I had some tables that are interesting on this, was whether people under objective conditions of low integration would develop a subjective identification with a larger community by virtue of relatively active spectatorship measured by their designating themselves as sport fans. In other words, a fan, certainly a self-designated fan, would be a more active spectator than one who said, "No, I'm not a fan." In general, I found out that spectatorship or active spectatorship as designated by being a fan, or fanatic if you like, did not have this effect, unless it was combined with active participation in sport. Once active spectatorship was combined with active participation, then the sense of subjective identification was developed, at all levels irrespective of status. But, again there was much less active spectatorship and active participation in the lower levels. But, when those who were active combined their spectatorship with participation, this did have a cohesive influence. I hope I didn't make that too complicated.

FOREWORD TO MAN, SPORT AND EXISTENCE

EDGAR Z. FRIEDENBERG

Man, Sport and Existence is a unique work. So far as I know, it is the only book yet written that raises and explores serious philosophical questions about the role of conventional, organized sport in individual life experience of contemporary American participants, from surfers to football players. Countless authors have dealt with the social psychology of sport; and some, like Reuel Denney, have written perceptively about the involvement of spectators in terms that are philosophical as well as sociological. But only Professor Slusher has explored the state of being of the athlete in the course of his participation in American sport today, attending, with faint irony, to the continuous contrast between the sense of authenticity that athletic competence affords and the sense of instrumentality—of using oneself or being used as a thing—imposed on the player by the way sport is institutionalized in America and even by the rules and purpose of the game itself.

Philosophically, Slusher represents a pure existential position; he is nowhere concerned with establishing that athletics have a pragmatic function for the athlete, though he is, of course, interested in their value to the athlete as a form of self-realization. Nor is he interested in the social or psychological functions of athletics except insofar as these affect the athlete's sense of self. In fact, he does rather less with this aspect of the matter than might have been useful. So much of what a player experiences depends precisely on the way society uses sport and on the way players use it to establish or alter their position in society that even a strictly existential critique of sport requires a more concrete description of the athlete's life than Slusher gives. The book would be enriched by the kind of anecdotal detail found in such a work as George Plimpton's *The Paper Lion,* for example, which, at one level, depicts what it *is to be* a professional football player.

But experience of sporting life at the level described by Plimpton has been fully and vividly discussed by many other authors, while Slusher is the first to extend to the world of sport the kinds of questions about being and relationship that Buber, Heidegger, Kierkegaard and Sartre—to name only the most familiar of Slusher's rather technical array of sources—have raised. He extends these questions without being either pompous or patronizing about sport; he does not exaggerate the role of sport in the life of man in order to justify taking sport seriously; he does not deride sport in order to establish his philosophical gravity. He never sentimentalizes sport either through nostalgia for the lost Hellenic ideal of youthful physical perfection or, as has been more common since Victorian times, by attributing to it unusual power to build character or even sportsmanship. Sportsmanship is, no doubt, properly so called; but most sportsmen, as Slusher notes, play to win.

Since Slusher assumes, I think correctly, that existential philosophy deals with the key issues that affect central aspects of the athlete's experience, he has no occasion to be pretentious. The most important of these issues is *authenticity.* The terms, and even the idea, have become cliché, but few modern writers who have dealt with sport have considered how one's sense of one's own body contributes to one's sense of self, except in social-psychological terms, *e.g.,* whether one feels inadequate, or inferior, and compensates by psuedomasculine aggression, or whether athletes who are admired for their prowess tend to become alienated from their bodies and regard them as equipment that they own, polish, and display. Both these processes are common enough and, sometimes, important, but Slusher is more interested in how the athlete's sense of the peculiar grace that he brings to his life-space becomes a part of his consciousness and identity. In George Herbert Mead's terms, this book is almost totally concerned with how being an athlete affects the "I" rather than the "me."

Sport is a kind of applied art. Aesthetically, it resembles ballet in that the human body is the medium, but the limitations that the athlete must accept are more like those that are binding the sculptor whose work is to become part of a public building of traditional design. The expressive function of the athlete is subordinate to spectacle and profitability, while his performance must fit completely within a framework of rigid convention if it is to have any meaning at all. If the athlete insists on presenting a virtuoso performance without regard for its place in the total structure, he mars the whole work. Athletics, therefore, is among the most formal of the arts; and team-sports are more convention-bound than are athletic activities such as track-and-field or surfing in which the rules that govern what may be done, like those that govern classical ballet, grow out of the function of the human body in relation to the task rather than out of the need to create and regulate a contest. In German, track-meets are termed *Leichtathletik,* in the sense in which Mozart's music is light and easy.

Formality, however, does not make sport inexpressive; by limiting and channeling expression into previously established modes it makes expression more forceful. "Art is not a plaything, but a necessity," Rebecca West observed in *Black Lamb and Gray Falcon,* "and its essence, form, is not a decorative adjustment but a cup into which life can be poured, and lifted to the lips, and be tasted." Sport provides a rather shallow cup, but one which nevertheless tells us a great deal about the people who designed it and choose to drink from it. Societies reveal much of themselves, and of their differences from other societies, in their preferences among sports. Basketball, for example, seems to me to provide an abstract parody of American middle-class life. I have written elsewhere about what I think it reveals concerning the quality of adolescence itself, through its tempo and vividness; but it also mirrors the society we live in. How else could one dramatize so effectively our legalism and the intricate web of regulations among which we live and on which we climb? Who but contemporary Americans could have designed a sport in which status changes so swiftly that no lead can be considered commanding until the last few seconds of play, and in which the officials run back and forth like agitated ferrets looking for breaches of regulations? Basketball rules in fact affect the game quite differently from the way in which the rules of most other sports do. In football, for example, the actions defined as illegal, such as being offside or holding, generally either disrupt the game or are dangerous to the players, such as clipping or unnecessary roughness, and the penalities assessed are genuinely intended to discourage illegal play. But the basketball player—or, certainly, the coach—must respond to the rules of his game as a business executive does to the Internal Revenue and Fair Labor Practice codes. He wins, not by obeying them, but by cannily balancing the penalties risked by each violation against the strategic advantage that might be gained by, say, a back-court foul committed so as to interrupt a probable scoring drive by the team in possession, thus giving his opponents a chance to win one point instead of two, and gaining possession of the ball afterward on more favorable terms. Slusher quotes one of the early pioneers of basketball as having been dismayed that the present-day sport should have become the kind of game it has, with The Man blowing the whistle at every turn and the play so harrassed by interruption that it becomes all tactics and no strategy, as has become our life. A more leisurely sport would make us envious of the players and get on our nerves.

Perhaps the most peculiar thing about basketball is the way it reflects the anxiety about homosexuality that pervades our society. Is there any other sport in which bodily contact between opposing players is *itself* an offense? Certain kinds of body contact, which might be dangerous or which impede play, are forbidden in all sports in which such contact might occur. But to design a game in such a way that provides its "thinclads" with continuous occasion for physical encounter, but must be stopped the instant an encounter occurs, so that the boy judged more aggressive may be punished surely is a dramatic acting-out of a widespread anxiety in our society which could never, I think, accept high school or college wrestling as a genuinely popular sport. Among Americans, wrestlers must be ugly clowns who seek no real victory and yield no real submission.

Man, Sport and Existence has in it many valid and original observations about the silences—true moments of truth—in sports, and their relation to the players' occasional ecstasy. But it touches only by implication, and then gingerly, on the erotic function of athletics, which seems to me a regrettable omission from a book that includes a brilliant chapter on the related question of "Sport and the Religious." Athletic events occur, and always have occurred, in an atmosphere of erotic tension and excitement that enriches their contribution either to sacred or secular occasions. Our conception of physical beauty is still primarily that of the athlete, while the epithet "jock" applied to a young man expresses as much envy as scorn even now, in a bureaucratic, technically developed, utilitarian society in which physical prowess has little practical utility. Our religious tradition puts the athlete down; a beautiful body is regarded as either sinful in itself or a temptation to sin in others—to be valued only as evidenced of physical fitness. Still, there it is; the pupils dilate, along with certain of the smaller blood vessels, and the heart sings on beholding it—but not so loudly as it once did, for many young people have become aware that the heart of the athlete is less likely to sing back than is that of a wilder, hippier creature, who is less comely but more comforting, if you want somebody to love. So, the concept of beauty is changing its emphasis and becoming more various; Allen Ginsberg, people say, is a beautiful man—and it is true.

But the athlete is losing his status and part of his charisma in the course of the same reappraisal; much of this loss is attributable to the way sports have become institutionalized in this country. By experiencing himself as an athlete, a young man learns what it can mean to live fully in his body joyfully and exuberantly, though under self-imposed discipline. I cannot myself express how this feels nearly as well as a fifteen-year-old high-school athlete whom I interviewed a few years ago in the course of a research study:

> Well, I think there's no feeling quite like running down the track or something and winning. Or going out on the football field and suddenly deciding you liked this, and you do it and you feel kinda crazy. Like I was in a fall game last year that we lost by a very bad score but in the midst of it I was, seemed to be, having a fairly good day. And I just felt light-headed, and I just didn't play—I played for the heck of it, for the fun of it, because I just wanted to. And I was very, I mean, I'd be schmeared a couple of times—I'd get up and laugh my head off and I wouldn't know why I was laughing, and I certainly shouldn't have been laughing because I really got schmeared. And I'd go back to the huddle and I'd be dying laughing, and they'd think I was crazy, but I enjoyed it. And it was just, I couldn't stop it and I, I mean, after the game was over I felt terrible because we lost so bad. But during the game it was just this feeling of exuberance; I was having fun and nothing much could do anything about it, you know? And I was having fun because I was just—I was able to have fun; I was doing something that, at the time, I was doing reasonably well. And I just enjoyed it. During that time I was happy. But after the game I was not so happy, because we lost so badly. And that's the thing, I think that it's a temporary thing, when you're not realizing it, you're not really trying to think about it; you just know that you're enjoying what you're doing right now. . . . I just enjoyed it. And I don't see how, I mean we were getting schmeared all over the field. I was going out there; I was doing a fairly good job. It seems the fellow in front of me that was supposed to be first string wasn't doing so good; so I played. And I did a pretty good job; but I just enjoyed it, and I couldn't help it, and I'd get hit and bounced all over the ground and I'd get up laughing and the guys would think I was crazy . . . but I enjoyed it; it's a release. And you feel as if you don't have to worry about anything, it's too—I don't know, it's just exuberance. As if there's something that really can touch you. And you're running toward this . . . you're doing it because right then and there you're enjoying it. . . . You're not geting rid of anything, it's just *now*, and you're hoping that two seconds from now will be just like that. And that's the thing.

The inner glow from this experience is an important part of erotic attractiveness but to say this is to say little more than that being a good athlete contributes to animal, and therefore human, vitality. It is precisely this vitality, however, which the institutions that socialize youth are designed to stifle. Where, as in America, exuberant youth are regarded as a threat to good order and good adjustment, athletic activity will be channeled into organized sport; and organized sport will be dominated by authorities—usually school authorities—who will administer it in such a way as to deprive their students of the sense of themselves as beautifully coordinated aggressive young animals—the sense that they might otherwise have gained from participation.

The same thing happens outside of school also. In our society, it occurs wherever athletics are controlled by business-like—not necessarily puritanical—adults. Some of Slusher's most penetrating comments pertain to Little League sports, which he sees as frequently alienating the children who take part in them from any sporting sense they might develop: the children do not feel that they are doing their own *thing* and either go about the game as if driven or develop a slick professional approach inappropriate to their age and actual level of competence. Compared to the influence of the schools, however, Little League is peanuts.

Judging from the behavior of many high-school athletic coaches, and even the way the plant is designed, the characteristic attitude of physical education instruction toward the body, and the joy it may yield, is not merely repressive—it is truly counterphobic. It is the "phys ed" men, typically, who are the school disciplinarians—who snarl at "wise guys" and put down "troublemakers." It is they among teachers who show the most hostility to boys with long hair or odd, mod dress, and who encourage the members of their teams to harass these youths; if the "gung-ho" young athletes are provoked into assaulting the "longhairs" verbally or physically, school authorities then use the incidents as a pretext for forbidding long hair or mod clothes on the basis that they are conducive to violence. School authorities, moreover, are increasingly recruited from former "phys ed" personnel; a large proportion of vice-principals and principals formerly were coaches. These men bring to school administration the spirit of the informal martinet, superficially jolly but intollerant of spirit in young people and of poetry in anything—especially in athletics itself. Generally speaking, sport as a social institution is hostile to precisely the existential values that Professor Slusher stresses in this book and that provide the occasion for writing it.

This is a paradox, for the athlete and the flower-children ought to be allies. It is only possible to be a first-rate athlete if you can allow yourself to feel sport in your blood and open up to what it means. As Slusher makes clear, you have to "dig" the experience. The best athletes, in short, are "hippy" about sport; they hang loose but tough—relax and let it "turn them on." This implies, perhaps, that athletics is to the world of organized sport what creative scholarship is to the university. Great universities need real scholars, and great teams need real athletes, but the universities' deans and coaches will never admit without regret that this is so; they will continue to try to use substitutes instead, thus permitting excellence to be more widely shared, and widely feared.

THE CITY GAME

Pete Axthelm

Basketball is the city game. Its battlegrounds are strips of asphalt between tattered wire fences or crumbling buildings; its rhythms grow from the uneven thump of a ball against hard surfaces. It demands no open spaces or lush backyards or elaborate equipment. It doesn't even require specified numbers of players; a one-on-one confrontation in a playground can be as memorable as a full-scale organized game. Basketball is the game for young athletes without cars or allowances—the game in which the drama and action are intensified by its confined spaces and chaotic surroundings.

Every American sport directs itself in a general way toward certain segments of American life. Baseball is basically a slow, pastoral experience, offering a tableau of athletes against a green background, providing moments of action amid longer periods allowed for contemplation of the spectacle. In its relaxed, unhurried way, it is exactly what it claims to be—the national "pastime" rather than an intense, sustained game crammed with action. Born in a rural age, its appeal still lies largely in its offer of an untroubled island where, for a few hours, a pitcher tugging at his pants leg can seem to be the most important thing in a fan's life.

Football's attraction is more contemporary. Its violence is in tune with the times, and its well-mapped strategic war games invite fans to become generals, plotting and second-guessing along with their warriors on the fields. With its action compressed in a fairly small area and its formations and patterns relatively easy to interpret, football is the ideal

Abridged from Introduction, Chapters 1, 10 and 11 in *The City Game* by Pete Axthelm. Copyright © 1970 by Pete Axthelm. Reprinted by permission of Harper & Row, Publishers, Inc.

television spectacle. Other sports have similar, if smaller, primary audiences. Golf and tennis belong first to country-club members, horse racing to an enduring breed of gamblers, auto racing to Middle Americans who thrive on its violent roaring machines and death-defying risks. But basketball belongs to the cities—and New York, from its asphalt playgrounds to the huge modern arena that houses the professional basketball champions of the world, is the most active, dedicated basketball city of all.

The game is simple, an act of one man challenging another, twisting, feinting, then perhaps breaking free to leap upward, directing a ball toward a target, a metal hoop ten feet above the ground. But its simple motions swirl into intricate patterns, its variations become almost endless, its brief soaring moments merge into a fascinating dance. To the uninitiated, the patterns may seem fleeting, elusive, even confusing; but on a city playground, a classic play is frozen in the minds of those who see it—a moment of order and achievement in a turbulent, frustrating existence. Basketball is more than a sport or diversion in the cities. It is a part, often a major part, of the fabric of life. Kids in small towns— particularly in the Midwest—often become superb basketball players. But they do so by developing accurate shots and precise skills; in the cities, kids simply develop "moves." Other athletes may learn basketball, but city kids live it.

The New York Knickerbockers, champions of the National Basketball Association, are not direct products of the city's playgrounds. Like all professional teams, they have been assembled by drafting and trading to amass the best available athletes from across the country. Geographically and socially, they could hardly have more diverse backgrounds. The coach, Red Holzman, was a pure New York ballplayer; the captain, Willis Reed, is from the black rural South. The other stars include black products of city streets and the white son of a bank president. Yet as they rose to the summit of basketball, the Knicks became inextricably identified with the city they represented.

The media, based largely in New York, have fallen in love with the Knicks and with basketball, giving the sport its first taste of heavy television coverage, national-magazine cover stories, and all forms of advertising and promotion. New York's rich citizens also joined the love affair, and the traditionally scruffy pro basketball audiences were replaced by a chic new breed in Madison Square Garden. And in the playgrounds, the kids too responded to the Knicks acknowledging that a New York team was at last bringing a rare playground art to new levels of perfection. The Knicks seemed ideal symbols of the traditions of New York basketball, and if the media portrayed the Knick stars as larger than life, the playground kids understood that too.

The first week of May, when the Knicks won the championship, had been a brutalizing, feverish ordeal for most New Yorkers. United States armies were marching into Cambodia and a shocked young girl was screaming silently from the front pages of newspapers and magazines, in terrible, haunting testimony to the four murders at Kent State University. Demonstrators were assembling near the United Nations and in the Wall Street area, pleading almost hopelessly to a government they knew wasn't listening. Then the city's darkest fears took shape, as mobs of Wall Street construction workers unleashed the small hatreds and resentments that had been building within them for years, and descended on the young people who their President had reassured them were merely bums. On the afternoon before the final Knicks game against Los Angeles Lakers, the workers came down to bully the kids at close range. Aided by Wall Street clerks, they went on a spree, ganging up on the kids, kicking them when they were on the pavement, and leaving scores of bloody victims while policemen stood placidly by.

The politics of hate and polarization had thrust deep into New York's consciousness, and few people on either side could relish the sight of open war between Nixon's newly unleashed Silent Majority and opponents of the war. Some of the spectators who came to watch the Knicks that night may have wondered just how much they could still care about a game. Then the Knicks showed them. They didn't solve the world's problems, any more than playground games cure the ills of the ghetto. But the Knicks and Lakers did offer a moment of high drama, a brief and necessary escape from reality—a transcendent experience that, in the end, is all anyone can ask of a great sporting event.

Basketball has always had this special quality for the boys of New York's streets. Two decades ago, it fed the dreams of the Irish athletes on famous playgrounds like the one on 108th Street in Rockaway, Queens. Those playgrounds produced Bob Cousy and Dick McGuire and other superb playmakers and brilliant passers; they also spawned countless athletes who were almost as accomplished but never made it to college and did not achieve public recognition. On Kingsbridge Road in the Bronx, tough, aggressive Jewish youths grew into defense-minded, set-shooting stars; some led the colleges of the city to national prominence in the late 1940s, but still others faded before the public ever learned their names. With money available for cars and stereos and surfboards, the hunger vanished from many white playgrounds, and so did top-caliber basketball. But the blacks of Harlem and Bedford-Stuyvesant more than filled the void. Some made it to colleges and into the pros, helping to reshape the game with their flamboyant moves. Still others failed to find a niche in college or the pros, but endured as playground heroes, facing the challenges of the best of each new generation of players, occasionally proving themselves against pro players who return to the parks for summer games.

Each ethnic group and each generation of street ballplayers produced its special styles and legends, and each left its colorful brand on the sport. But more than that, each built a distinctive kind of pride —partly ethnic or racial, partly athletic, but much more than the sum of those parts. Veterans of playground ball describe it in terms of individuality, status, manhood; they also talk of the way it brings kids together. If the Knicks brought a special pride to all New York, they were only multiplying the feeling that the playground kids have always understood.

Occasionally the two distinct worlds of New York basketball converge. A playground idol such as Connie Hawkins joins the Phoenix Suns and comes into the Garden to challenge the Knicks; Knick stars like Bill Bradley and Willis Reed appear at 155th Street and Eighth Avenue to enter Harlem's most prestigious summer competition, the Rucker Pro Tournament. These confrontations are always electric. Hawkins may pack the Garden, while a Reed or Bradley will add hundreds to the overflowing crowds at a Rucker game. And if a playground star like Herman ("Helicopter") Knowings or Harold ("Funny") Kitt goes up to block a pro's shot or stuff a basket over a pro defender, he creates myths that endure long after the score of the game is forgotten.

A morning rain had left wide shallow puddles in the asphalt, and some of Saturday night's litter had washed down from the corners of the small park, giving the basketball court a grimy and abandoned look. The green- and red-tinted glass of discarded wine and whiskey bottles glinted in the sunlight that was just breaking through; the surrounding wire fence was scarred every few yards by unrepaired holes. Within hours the court would be fairly dry, the debris would be kicked aside, and the games—raucous, exuberant pickup affairs or perhaps even full-scale epic battles featuring local titans—would fill the Sunday afternoon with excitement. But for the moment the playground, set back from Seventh Avenue near 130th Street, seemed silently evocative of its illustrious past. Walking across it, Pat Smith was lost in thought.

Smith, who played for several seasons at Marquette University in Milwaukee, is twenty-four now, and years of studying in a less basketball-oriented city have rendered him out of shape for the highest caliber of playground competition back in Harlem. Yet he remains a cultural hero on the streets. He was a classic Harlem product, a 6-foot 3-inch center who spent his college career outleaping and outfighting 6-foot 10-inch rivals. He never had any illusions about his basketball future: very weak eyesight made him a terrible outside shooter and limited him to center, and 6-foot 3-inch centers—regardless of their jumping ability —are not sought after by the pros. But at Benjamin Franklin High School in Harlem and then at Marquette, Smith had used moves and muscle and a fierce instinct for domination to delight his Harlem followers.

The second reason for Smith's prestige was equally important: he had "made it." Like most ghetto youths, he had faced tremendous adjustment problems when he arrived on a predominantly white campus. In his first months at Marquette, he had fought everyone who seemed unable to understand his ghetto jargon, his racial pride, or his competitive fury. He was so combative that teammates and friends nicknamed him "The Evil Doctor Blackheart." The name stayed with him, but the attitudes that produced it began to change. He became extremely popular on campus, did well scholastically, and developed a deep bond with his coach, Al McGuire. In Smith's senior year, that bond faced its ultimate test. For reasons that neither man has ever confided, McGuire suspended Smith for most of that season—and, incredibly, the two men grew closer than ever. Most black athletes who encounter such crises and find their basketball eligibility running out drift back home, feeling lost and exploited, and lacking a college degree. Smith stayed at Marquette through the suspension, then remained two more years before earning his degree in 1970. The reasons for his remarkable determination are as shadowy as the man himself sometimes seems, but it made the Evil Doctor a figure to be respected back home. And though he is intent on building a future outside Harlem, Smith returns home often, to be troubled once again by friends who have succumbed to drugs, to be enraged by conditions, and to remember some of the good things about growing up:

"The old Rucker tournament was held in this park," Smith said, gesturing to one of the trees alongside the court. "When I was a kid I'd climb up into that tree. I'd stake out one of the branches early in the morning and just sit up there all day. A guy with a cart would come by and I'd yell for him to hand me up some lemon ices, and I'd eat one after another. There was no way anyone could get me to come down while the games were going on. I was in a world of my own, sitting up above the crowd and watching the great ones come in and do their thing. . . ."

The Rucker tournament is actually not a tournament but a summer league in which teams play one another through the weekends of July and August. Established in 1946 by a remarkable young teacher named Holcombe Rucker, it was originally intended mainly to keep kids off the streets and in school by encouraging them in both studies and basketball. Rucker's idea was to give dignity and meaning to pickup games by adding referees, local publicity, and larger audiences; it worked, and gradually the Rucker tournament expanded to include divisions for young athletes from junior high school through the pro level. A project that had begun with four teams and one referee began to offer basketball from morning until dark in various Harlem parks, before crowds estimated as high as five thousand. It remains the pinnacle of playground ball in New York, attracting stars from both pro leagues, members of touring teams like the Harlem Globetrotters, as well as the best players of the regular pickup games of the city.

The pro section of the Rucker tournament had long since been moved to another storied playground on 155th Street and Eighth Avenue, but the lure of a decade-old game remained in that Seventh Avenue park for Pat Smith. Near the knots of women engaged in Sunday conversation on church steps, grown men in boys' uniforms joined small children in formation for one of the minor parades that still serve some Harlemites as straggly symbols of unity and pride. Young, educated, and militant, Pat Smith had very different ideas about black dignity; moments earlier he had been depressed by what he felt to be the Sunday delusions of some of his people. But now under the tree that had once been his reserved seat, he recalled a game of street basketball at its best:

"It was the kind of game that established citywide reputations. Clinton Robinson was playing. Jackie Jackson was there. So was Wilt Chamberlain, who was in his first or second year of pro ball at the time. . . ." He savored each name as he spoke it; this was a very special honor roll. Some of the names, like Robinson's and Jackson's, would be familiar only to the ghetto kids who once worshiped them; others, like Chamberlain's would be recognized by every basketball fan. But to Smith and many others they were all gods, and their best games were Olympian clashes.

"Chamberlain and Robinson were on the same team along with some other greats, and they were ahead by about fifteen points. They looked like easy winners. Then, up in the tree, I heard a strange noise. There were maybe four, five thousand people watching the game, and all of a sudden a hush came over them. All you could hear was a whisper: 'The Hawk, the Hawk, the Hawk is here.' Then the crowd parted. And the Hawk walked onto the court."

"The Hawk" was Connie Hawkins. When you ask ghetto basketball fans to cite the very best players ever to come out of New York, you find much disagreement; but a few names are invariably included, and one of them is the Hawk. Yet for years he seemed fated to become one of those virtually forgotten playground stars. Connie made his reputation at Brooklyn's Boys High in the late 1950s, but when he was a freshman at Iowa in 1961, he was linked to a gambling scandal. His chief crime had been naïveté in talking to glad-handing gamblers, and he had never been indicted or even accused of trying to shave points or fix games. But his college career was shattered and for almost a decade he was an outcast, barred from the NBA, laboring in the short-lived American Basketball League and then in the American Basketball Association as it struggled for survival.

In 1969, after a prolonged legal battle, Hawkins won a million-dollar lawsuit and readmission to the NBA as a member of the Phoenix Suns. He quickly justified everything the playground kids had been saying about him for years. At the time of the game Smith described, Hawkins was a year or two out of Boys High, a man without a team. Yet he was the most magnetic star in Harlem.

"The crowd was still hushed as they called time out," Smith remembered. "They surrounded the man. They undressed the man. And finally he finished lacing up his sneakers and walked out into the backcourt. He got the ball, picked up speed, and started his first move. Chamberlain came right out to stop him. The Hawk went up—he was still way out beyond the foul line—and started floating toward the basket. Wilt, taller and stronger, stayed right with him—but then the Hawk hook-dunked the ball right over Chamberlain. He *hook*-dunked! Nobody had ever done anything like that to Wilt. The crowd went so crazy that they had to stop the game for five minutes. I almost fell out of the tree.

"But you didn't get away with just one spectacular move in those games. So the other guys came right back at the Hawk. Clinton Robinson charged in, drove around him and laid one up so high that it hit the top of the backboard. The Hawk went way up, but he couldn't quite reach it, and it went down into the basket. Clinton Robinson was about six feet tall and the Hawk was six feet eight, so the crowd went wild again. In fact, Clinton had thrown some of the greatest moves I'd ever seen, shaking guys left and right before he even reached the Hawk.

"Then it was Chamberlain's turn to get back. Wilt usually took it pretty easy in summer games, walking up and down the court and doing just enough to intimidate his opponents with his seven-foot body. But now his pride was hurt, his manhood was wounded. And you can't let that happen in a tough street game. So he came down, drove directly at the hoop and went up over the Hawk. Wilt stuffed the ball with two hands, and he did it so hard that he almost ripped the backboard off the pole.

"By then everybody on the court was fired up—and it was time for the Hawk to take charge again. Clinton Robinson came toward him with the ball, throwing those crazy moves on anyone who tried to stop him, and then he tried to loft a lay-up way up onto the board, the way he had done before. Only this time the Hawk was up there waiting for it. He was up so high that he blocked the shot with his *chest*. Still in midair, he kind of swept his hands down across his chest as if he were wiping his shirt—and slammed the ball down at Robinson's feet. The play seemed to turn the whole game around, and the Hawk's team came from behind to win. That was the Hawk. Just beautiful. I don't think anybody who was in that crowd could ever forget that game."

In March of 1964, Boys High of Brooklyn faced Benjamin Franklin High of Harlem in the old Madison Square Garden, on Eighth Avenue and 50th Street, for the public-high-school championship of New York. Boys won the title; but the result was quickly overshadowed by a seat-slashing, bottle-throwing melee that resulted in the end of high-school ball in the Garden and established a negative landmark in city basketball. The riot occurred against the backdrop of the city's first black school boycott; and it happened on St. Patrick's Day, when many patrolmen who might have handled the crowd were out parading. But administrators were not much interested in the details or causes of the disturbance. It was much easier to run from the problem than to solve it. So the Public School Athletic League moved its tournaments into small neutral gyms, and the black stars who dominate high-school ball in the city were swept quietly out of sight.

Since that time, the Garden has promoted a series of fights featuring Latin-American boxers with their bottle-throwing followers. It has had rallies for such public figures as George Wallace. But the young black ballplayers have not reappeared. While the Knicks turn on the city, its most talented young stars play in virtual secrecy in musty gyms and youth centers and playgrounds, before only their peers and a handful of college scouts. While the media fall in love with the Knicks, a top high-school star searches in vain for a paragraph or two in the *Times* on his team's victories. A year ago, the Boys High team went to New Haven, Connecticut, to face Hillhouse High for the informal championship of the East. Boys won by a point. It was the team's forty-sixth consecutive victory. And it drew more attention in New Haven in one day than Boys had gathered in New York with the forty-five wins that preceded it. The irony was not lost on the athletes. The struggle to establish an identity is basic to city basketball, but many black kids in New York have learned that their identity is a well-kept secret to the general public.

The bitterness was not readily apparent at the playground on 135th Street near Lenox Avenue. The June afternoon was warm and the basketball was very good. The games were just pickup affairs, with five-man teams being assembled on the spot to challenge the winners of whatever game was in progress. But a few pro players dropped by, as well as several Globetrotters and the established stars of the neighborhood, and somebody said that it was the best ball you would find in Harlem short of the Rucker tournament itself. The cars were double-parked all the way down the block, and the crowd was three deep alongside the high fences.

Then one athlete, who didn't want to give his name, began talking about it all, and there was an edge on his voice: "Sure there are good players here, and good ones who have made it in college and the pros. But don't try to write this up as a beautiful breeding ground for future stars, because for every star you hear about, there are many more who never escaped. I mean, I can look back on the group that I grew up with down on 111th Street, and I can tell you all about the one or two who are playing college ball, and it will make a great story. But there were twenty of us. And now maybe fifteen are on drugs and three are dead or just gone, who knows where? So how much do the two lucky ones count?" The kid sounded very old. He said he was twenty-one.

The less fortunate grow old even faster, leaving the bright moments behind them on the courts as the real world drags them down to earth. There is a sustaining power to basketball in the playgrounds: a young athlete walks into a bar or luncheonette and hears people say, "That's the dude that dunked on Lew up at Rucker." The admirers want to talk to him, to ask advice, to be near the star, and maybe that sense of importance and identity will keep a kid going for weeks. But if he is a dropout and he is broke, and the hustlers and pushers are around him with their cars and fancy clothes, the magic of his game can begin to wear off. Sooner or later, stuffing a basketball through a hoop is not quite enough to transcend the reality of his life.

"At one point in most guys' lives," said Keith Edwards, a Harlem ballplayer and youth worker, "basketball is the top priority, because it is the one escape valve from the ghetto. But once the paths toward college or pro ball are closed to an athlete, merely playing the game is not as much of an escape. Then the kids get offered a much easier escape, an escape to within themselves, in drugs. A few years ago, I would have said that the athletes I knew looked ninety per cent to ball, ten per cent to drugs. Now, the ratio is reversed. The kids are looking to drugs ninety per cent of the time. And they are destroying themselves."

Everyone in Harlem has watched the process of destruction, but no one feels it more acutely than the ballplayers. "You see somebody who can do everything on the court," said Pat Smith. "You know that his playing can open up a whole new world to him. It gives you a feeling of excitement. It makes you build high hopes. And when you watch him start to deteriorate, it tears you apart." Smith paused, shying momentarily from the subject. Two of Smith's nine brothers have died on the Harlem streets; another was a dope pusher at the age of fourteen. Six years away at school in Milwaukee have not erased the streets from Smith's life. "There's such great waste of humanity," he said slowly. "Such tragic waste." And then the memories came pouring out, a remarkable testament to the darkest side of basketball in the city:

"I remember when I was just developing as a ballplayer, early in high school. I played a lot with a guy named Artie. I never knew his last name, just Artie. He played often at Millbank Center, and his team was known for winning a lot of local tournaments. Artie was capable of scoring every way: jump shots, hooks, lay-ups, set shots. His scoring totals were forty to fifty points every game. When I knew him, Artie was about twenty-eight, and he was trying to make a comeback. From alcohol. He was a wine drinker. That shows you how far back it was—people still ruined themselves the slow way with wine, instead of drugs.

"Anyway, Artie had been in a hospital, trying to dry out and recuperate. When he started playing again, he was probably a step slower than he once was, but he still had those fantastic shots. He took an interest in me for some reason, and he picked me to play with him in pickup games whenever he could. When we played together, he would teach me, and he would also get so many good passes to me that I was sure of getting twenty-five or thirty points—while he still got his fifty.

"But after a few months he began showing up less at the playgrounds. Then he didn't come at all. And one day I was on the street and somebody asked if I'd heard about Artie. Then the guy told me. They'd found Artie dead in a hallway. He drank himself to death.

"There was another guy we knew only by his first name, Frank," Smith said. "He came from uptown, around 155th Street, but he would come down to our neighborhood around 128th Street to play. He was a strong guy, very good-looking, with a great build. I didn't know him well, I didn't know what high school he was from, but I always assumed that he had the potential to go on and start for some college team.

"Then we heard the news. Frank had tried to rob a drugstore. The storekeeper had a gun, and Frank got shot in the back. He was paralyzed from the waist down. He was maybe nineteen years old, and it was all over for him.

"People still see him, in his wheelchair. When anyone goes up in that neighborhood they look for him. He's about twenty-four now, and he tries to take the thing very well. Talking to him, you can hardly realize that he knows he'll never walk again. But the way he hides his pain only makes it hurt more to look at him and think of what he could have been.

"Dexter Westbrook was one of the few big men that ever came from the uptown playgrounds," said Smith. "For some reason, most of the taller guys happened to play downtown around 135th Street or 128th Street, while the players up at 155th were known more for quickness and ball-handling. But Dexter was about six feet eight, and he was a super big man. Playing with so many fast little guys, he developed the quickness and moves of a guard. He had a beautiful left-handed jump shot, and could do everything with the ball.

"Dexter went to Providence College for a while. Then he failed out and came home and worked in a few jobs in the poverty program. But with his size and talent, everybody insisted that he could still make the pros, and two or three years ago he tried out. I forget which team it was, but word got back to Harlem that Dexter was doing great. He was the high scorer and the best rebounder in rookie camp; nobody could touch him. Then it came time for the routine physical examination, and he couldn't pass it. There were needle tracks on his arms.

"Now this was a man who could have made it big. But he just couldn't seem to adjust his mind to bigger things than what's here in Harlem. The last time I heard of Dexter was in the summer of 1969. There was a robbery on Riverside Drive, and he was arrested for taking somebody's wallet. His drug habit had gotten beyond his means. Like it always does."

If it hurt Smith to talk of his contemporaries, it seemed to wrench him more to turn to younger kids. "I saw guys I played with get ruined, and it was bad, but it wasn't always unexpected," he said. "You go to school or play a lot of ball with a guy and you get an idea whether he can make it. But watching kids come up, you lose that perspective. You somehow hope they'll all make it. And you forget that the drug thing is much worse now than it was when you were in school yourself. You forget that escaping the streets is harder than ever. And then you see what happens to a kid like Kenny Bellinger.

"Kenny earned a city-wide basketball reputation when he was still in junior high school. I was a senior in high school when I played against him, and he was still in ninth grade. But he couldn't go on playing against kids his own age, because he was too good. He was always looking for older guys to challenge, and he always held his own. A lot of high-school players waited to see where he would decide to go, and we were glad when he chose Franklin. He was a cinch to make all-city, and he had a great future ahead of him.

"Then one day, I was walking on 111th Street between Seventh and Eighth Avenues, and I saw four or five squad cars. I asked somebody what was going on, and people said that a lady's purse had been snatched, and someone had run into one of the buildings with it. The next thing we knew, there was a helicopter over the buildings. The purse-snatcher was on the roofs, and they were trying to spot him. Nobody had ever seen the police use a helicopter before, but somebody said that the purse belonged to a white lady with some influence. Anyway, it looked like they were fighting the whole Vietcong instead of looking for a purse.

"Suddenly all the cops rushed into an alley, and in a few minutes the word spread: the thief had tried to hurdle a six-foot gap between the buildings, and he hadn't made it. I went home, and I didn't find out until the next day that the kid who had plunged into the alley had been Kenny.

"I couldn't believe it. I thought there must have been a mistake. Kenny couldn't have risked so much . . . and anyway, he could have leaped a six-foot gap with no problem at all. So I went up onto the building and checked out the gap, and it was more like fifteen feet. Then it began to sink in. All that potential was gone. Whether it was drugs or despair or what, Kenny hadn't been able to stay straight. One more victim. Kenny was sixteen years old when he died.

"Boobie Tucker was also in junior high when he first came around to play with us older guys," Smith said. "He was about six feet nine, but he wasn't as advanced as Kenny Bellinger. He was still clumsy and uncoordinated. He didn't know how to take advantage of his size. But while I was at Franklin and he was in junior high, he would come to our gym and try to learn, and we watched him develop into a really good ballplayer. He learned to get position under the boards for rebounds, and he practiced a short jump shot until he could make it regularly. Here was a kid only about sixteen, and he was six feet nine, and still growing: he might have had the world in front of him. The year I went away to college, he started playing for Franklin.

"Every so often I'd ask somebody about Boobie. First I heard that he was coming along fine, scoring nicely. But gradually the other rumors reached me: 'Yeah, Tucker's on stuff. . . . Yeah, he's snorting pretty heavy. . . . Yeah, Tucker's strung out.' Boobie stopped playing altogether and went out onto the streets. And finally I learned that he had died of an overdose. It was a shock, because he hadn't been strung out for that long. He probably hadn't even developed an expensive habit yet. But of course when times get hard, pushers will put anything into that white bag and sell it. Some guys have shot up rat poison and died instantly.

"It was a terrible, frustrating thing to imagine Boobie dead. I felt very close to his career, because I'd watch him develop from a clumsy kid into a ballplayer. Day to day, I'd seen the improvements. I'd watch him work at the game, and I couldn't help thinking he would be repaid for all that work.

"But the one thing I wasn't thinking about, the one thing you never think about, I guess, until it's too late, was that the pusher was watching him develop, too."

In the litany of quiet misfortunes, it may seem almost impossible to select one man and give him special importance. Yet in the stories and traditions that are recounted in the Harlem parks, one figure does emerge above the rest. Asked about the finest athletes they have seen, scores of ballplayers in a dozen parks mention Connie Hawkins and Lew Alcindor and similar celebrities. But almost without exception, they speak first of one star who didn't go on: Earl Manigault.

No official scorers tabulate the results of pickup games; there are no composite box scores to prove that Manigault ranked highest among playground athletes. But in its own way, a reputation in the parks is as definable as a scoring average in the NBA. Street ballplayers develop their own elaborate word-of-mouth system. One spectacular perfor-mance or one backwards, twisting stuff shot may be the seed of an athlete's reputation. If he can repeat it a few times in a park where the competition is tough, the word goes out that he may be something special. Then there will be challenges from more established players, and a man who can withstand them may earn a "neighborhood rep." The process continues in an expanding series of confrontations, until the best athletes have emerged. Perhaps a dozen men at a given time may enjoy "city-wide reps," guaranteeing them attention and respect in any playground they may visit. And of those, one or two will stand alone.

A few years ago, Earl Manigault stood among the loftiest. But his reign was brief, and in order to capture some feeling of what his stature meant in the playground world, one must turn to two athletes who enjoy similar positions today. Herman ("Helicopter") Knowings, now in his late twenties, is among the most remarkable playground players; he was a demigod before Manigault, and he remains one after Earl's departure. Uneducated and unable to break into pro ball, the Helicopter has managed to retain the spring in his legs and the willpower to remain at the summit after many of his contemporaries have faded from the basketball scene. Joe Hammond, not yet twenty, is generally recognized as the best of the young crop. He has not finished school or vaulted into the public spotlight but, like Knowings, he picks up money playing in a minor league, the Eastern League—and returns home between games to continue domination of the parks.

The Helicopter got his name for obvious reasons. When he goes up to block a shot, he seems to hover endlessly in midair above his prey, daring him to shoot—and then blocking whatever shot his hapless foe attempts. Like most memorable playground moves, it is not only effective but magnetic. As Knowings goes up, the crowd shouts, "Fly, Copter, fly," and seems to share his heady trip. When he shoves a ball down the throat of a visiting NBA star, as he often does in the Rucker tournament, the Helicopter inflates the pride of a whole neighborhood.

Like Connie Hawkins, Knowings can send waves of electricity through a park with his mere presence. Standing by a court, watching a game in progress, the Helicopter doesn't have to ask to play. People quickly spot his dark, chiseled, ageless face and 6-foot 4-inch frame, and they make room for him. Joe Hammond is less imposing. A shade over 6 feet, he is a skinny, sleepy-eyed kid who looks slow and tired, the way backcourt star Clinton Robinson appeared during his reign. But like Robinson, Hammond has proved himself, and now he stands as the descendant of Pablo Robertson and James Barlow and the other backcourt heroes of the streets.

The kings of playground ball are not expected to defend their titles every weekend, proving themselves again and again the way less exalted players must. But when a new athlete begins winning a large following, when the rumors spread that he is truly someone special, the call goes out: if he is a forward, get the Helicopter; if he's a guard, let's try him against Joe Hammond. A crowd will gather before the star arrives. It is time for a supreme test.

Jay Vaughn has been in such confrontations several times. He saw the Helicopter defend his reign, and he watched Joe Hammond win his own way to the top. He described the ritual:

"When I first met the Helicopter, I was only about seventeen, and I was playing with a lot of kids my age at Wagner Center. I was better than the guys I was playing with and I knew it, so I didn't feel I had anything to prove. I was playing lazy, lackadaisical. And one of the youth workers saw how cocky I was and decided to show me just how good I really was. He sent for the Helicopter.

"One day I was just shooting baskets, trying all kinds of wild shots, not thinking about fundamentals, and I saw this older dude come in. He had sneakers and shorts on and he was ready to play. I said, 'Who's this guy? He's too old for our games. Is he supposed to be good?' 'The coach sent for him,' somebody told me. 'He's gonna play you.'

"I said to myself, well fine, I'll try him, and I went out there one-on-one with Herman Knowings. Well, it was a disastrous thing. I tried lay-ups, jump shots, hooks. And everything I threw up, he blocked. The word had gone out that Herman was there, and a crowd was gathering, and I said to myself, 'You got to do something. You're getting humiliated.' But the harder I tried, the more he shoved the ball down into my face. I went home and thought about that game for a long time. Like a lot of young athletes, I had been put in my place.

"I worked out like crazy after that. I was determined to get back. After about a month, I challenged him again. I found myself jumping higher, feeling stronger, and playing better than ever before. I wasn't humiliated again. But I was beaten. Since that time, I've played against Herman many times. He took an interest in me and gave me a lot of good advice. And now, when I see he's going to block a shot, I may be able to fake and go around him and score, and people will yell, 'The pupil showed the master.'

"Then, of course, he'll usually come back and stuff one on me. . . .

"Joe Hammond was playing in the junior division games in the youth centers when I was in the senior games," Vaughn said. "He was three years younger than me, and sometimes after I'd played, I'd stay and watch his game. He wasn't that exceptional. Just another young boy who was gonna play ball. In fact, at that time, I didn't even know his last name.

"Then I came home from school in the summer of 1969, and one name was on everyone's lips: Joe Hammond. I thought it must have been somebody new from out of town, but people said, no, he'd been around Harlem all the time. They described him and it sounded like the young kid I'd watched around the centers, but I couldn't believe it was the same guy. Then I saw him, and it was the same Joe, and he was killing a bunch of guys his own age. He was much improved, but I still said to myself, 'He's young. He won't do much against the older brothers. They've been in business too long.'

"But then I heard, 'Joe's up at 135th Street beating the pros. . . . Joe's doing everything to those guys.' I still didn't take it too seriously. In fact, when Joe came out to Mount Morris Park for a game against a good team I was on, I said, 'Now we'll see how you do. You won't do anything today.'

"Now I believe in him. Joe Hammond left that game with seven minutes to go. He had forty points. Like everybody had said, Joe was the one."

Earl Manigault played at Benjamin Franklin High School in 1962 and 1963, then spent a season at Laurinburg Institute, the North Carolina prep school that has steered so many ghetto stars toward colleges.

Earl never reached college, but when he returned to Harlem he was the king of his own generation of ballplayers, the idol for the generation that followed. He was a 6-foot 2-inch forward who could outleap men 8 inches taller.

But he was also a very human ghetto youth, with weaknesses and doubts that left him vulnerable. Lacking education and motivation, looking toward an empty future, he found that basketball could take him only so far. Then he became the image of the hellish side of ghetto existence. Earl is now in his mid-twenties, a dope addict, in prison. On the playgrounds Earl was a powerful magnetic figure who carried the dreams and ideals of every kid around him as he spun and twisted and sailed over all obstacles. When he fell, he carried those aspirations down with him.

"You think of him on the court and you think of so many incredible things that it's hard to sort them out," Bob Spivey, who played briefly with Earl at Franklin, said. "But I particularly recall one all-star game in the gym at PS 113, in about 1964. Most of the best high-school players in the city were there: Charlie Scott, who went on to North Carolina; Vaughn Harper, who went to Syracuse, and a lot more. But the people who were there will hardly remember the others. Earl was the whole show.

"For a few minutes, Earl seemed to move slowly, feeling his way, getting himself ready. Then he got the ball on a fast break. Harper, who was six feet six, and Val Reed, who was six feet eight, got back quickly to defend. You wouldn't have given Earl a chance to score. Then he accelerated, changing his step suddenly. And at the foul line he went into the air. Harper and Reed went up, too, and, between them, the two big men completely surrounded the rim. But Earl just kept going higher, and finally he two-hand dunked the ball over both of them. For a split second there was complete silence, and then the crowd exploded. They were cheering so loud that they stopped the game for five minutes. Five minutes. That was Earl Manigault."

Faces light up when Harlem veterans reminisce about Manigault. Many street players won reputations with elaborate innovations and tricks: Jackie Jackson was among the first to warm up for games by picking quarters off the top of the backboard. Willie Hall, the former St. John's leader, apparently originated the custom of jumping to the top of the board and, instead of merely blocking a shot, slamming a hand with tremendous force against the board; the fixture would vibrate for several seconds after the blow, causing an easy lay-up to bounce crazily off the rim. Other noted leapers were famous for "pinning"— blocking a lay-up then simply holding it momentarily against the backboard in gesture of triumph. Some players seemed to hold it for seconds, suspended in air, multiplying the humiliation of the man who had tried the futile shot. Then they could slam the ball back down at the shooter or, for special emphasis, flip it into the crowd.

Earl Manigault did all those things and more, borrowing, innovating, and forming one of the most exciting styles Harlem crowds ever watched. Occasionally, he would drive past a few defenders, dunk the ball with one hand, catch it with the other—and raise it and stuff it through the hoop a second time before returning to earth.

"I was in the eighth grade when Earl was in the eleventh," Charley Yelverton, now a star at Fordham, recalled. "I was just another young kid at the time. Like everybody else on the streets, I played some ball. But I just did it for something to do. I wasn't that excited about it. Then there happened to be a game around my block, down at 112th Street, and a lot of the top players were in it—and Earl came down to play. Well, I had never believed things like that could go on. I had never known what basketball could be like. Everybody in the game was doing something, stuffing or blocking shots or making great passes. There's only one game I've ever seen in my life to compare to it—the Knicks' last game against the Lakers.

"But among all the stars, there was no doubt who was the greatest. Passing, shooting, going up in the air, Earl just left everybody behind. No one could turn it on like he could."

Keith Edwards, who lived with Earl during the great days of the Young Life team, agreed: "I guess he had about the most natural ability that I've ever seen. Talent for talent, inch for inch, you'd have to put him on a par with Alcindor and the other superstars. To watch him was like poetry. To play with him or against him—just to be on the same court with him—was a deep experience.

"You can't really project him against an Alcindor, though, because you could never picture Earl going to UCLA or any place like that. He was never the type to really face his responsibilities and his future. He didn't want to think ahead. There was very little discipline about the man. . . ."

And so the decline began. "I lived with the man for about two or three years," Edwards said, "from his pre-drug period into the beginning of his drug period. There were six of us there, and maybe some of us would have liked to help him out. But we were all just young guys finding themselves, and when Earl and another cat named Onion started to get into the drug thing, nobody really had a right, or was in a position, to say much about it."

It didn't happen suddenly. On the weekends, people would still find Earl Manigault at the parks, and flashes of the magnetic ability were there. Young athletes would ask his advice, and he would still be helpful; even among the ones who knew he was sinking deeper into his drug habit, he remained respected and popular. But by early 1968 he seldom came to the parks, and his old friends would find him on street corners along Eighth Avenue, nodding.

In the summer of 1968, Bob Hunter was working on a drug-rehabilitation program. He looked up Earl. They became close, building a friendship that went deeper than their mutual respect on a basketball court. "Earl was an unusual type of addict," Hunter said. "He understood that he was a hard addict, and he faced it very honestly. He wanted to help me in the drug program, and he gave me a lot of hints on how to handle younger addicts. He knew different tricks that would appeal to them and win their trust. And he also knew all the tricks they would use, to deceive me into thinking they were getting cured. Earl had used the tricks himself, and he helped me see through them, and maybe we managed to save a few young kids who might have gotten hooked much worse.

"But it's the most frustrating thing in the world, working with addicts. It's hard to accept the fact that a man who has been burned will go back and touch fire. But they do it. I have countless friends on drugs, and I had many more who have died from drugs. And somehow it's hard to just give up on them and forget that they ever existed. Maybe you would think that only the less talented types would let themselves get hooked—but then you'd see a guy like Earl and you couldn't understand. . . ."

Some people hoped that Earl would be cured that summer. He did so much to help Hunter work with others that people felt he could help himself. Hunter was not as optimistic. "The truth is that nobody is ever going to cure Earl," he said. 'The only way he'll be cured is by himself. A lot of people come off drugs only after they've been faced with an extreme crisis. For example, if they come very close to dying and somehow escape, then they might be able to stay away from the fire. But it takes something like that, most of the time."

Earl was not cured, and as the months went on the habit grew more expensive. He broke into a store, and he is now in prison. "Maybe that will be the crisis he needs," Hunter said. "Maybe, just possibly. . . . But when you're talking about addicts, it's very hard to get your hopes too high."

Harold ("Funny") Kitt went to Franklin three years behind Earl Manigault. When Funny finished in 1967, he was rated the best high-school player in the city, largely because he had modeled himself so closely after Earl. "We all idolized Earl in those days," Kitt said. "And when you idolize somebody, you think of the good things, not the bad. As we watched Earl play ball, we had visions of him going on to different places, visiting the whole world, becoming a great star, and then maybe coming back here to see us and talk to us about it all.

"But he didn't do any of those things. He just went into his own strange world, a world I hope I'll never see. I guess there were reasons. I guess there were frustrations that only Earl knew about, and I feel sorry for what happened. But when Earl went into that world, it had an effect on all of us, all the young ballplayers. I idolized the man. And he hurt me."

Beyond the hurt, though, Earl left something more. If his career was a small dramatization of the world of Harlem basketball, then he was a fitting protagonist, in his magnitude and his frailty, a hero for his time. "Earl was quiet, he was honest," Jay Vaughn said, "and he handled the pressures of being the star very well. When you're on top, everybody is out to challenge you, to make their own reps by doing something against you. One guy after another wants to take a shot, and some stars react to all that by bragging, or by being aloof from the crowd.

"Earl was different. The game I'll never forget was in the G-Dub (George Washington High) tournament one summer, when the team that Earl's group was scheduled to play didn't show. The game was forfeited, and some guys were just looking for some kind of pickup game, when one fellow on the team that forfeited came in and said, 'Where's Manigault? I want to play Manigault.'

"Well, this guy was an unknown and he really had no right to talk like that. If he really wanted to challenge a guy like Earl, he should have been out in the parks, building up a rep of his own. But he kept yelling and bragging, and Earl quietly agreed to play him one-on-one. The word went out within minutes, and immediately there was a big crowd gathered for the drama.

"Then they started playing. Earl went over the guy and dunked. Then he blocked the guy's first shot. It was obvious that the man had nothing to offer against Earl. But he was really determined to win himself a rep. So he started pushing and shoving and fouling. Earl didn't say a word. He just kept making his moves and beating the guy, and the guy kept grabbing and jostling him to try to stop him. It got to the point where it wasn't really basketball, And suddenly Earl put down the ball and said, 'I don't need this. You're the best.' Then he just walked away.

"Well, if Earl had gone on and whipped the guy thirty to nothing, he couldn't have proved any more than he did. The other cat just stood there, not knowing what to say. The crowd surrounded Earl, and some of us said things about the fouling and the shoving. But he didn't say anything about it. He didn't feel any need to argue or complain. He had everyone's respect and he knew it. The role he played that day never left anyone who saw it. This was a beautiful man."

FOOTBALL IN AMERICA:
A STUDY IN CULTURE DIFFUSION

DAVID RIESMAN AND REUEL DENNEY

I

On October 9, 1951, Assistant Attorney General Graham Morrison instituted an anti-trust action against a number of universities on account of their efforts to limit TV broadcasts of their games—efforts dictated by the terrible burdens of what we might speak of as "industrialized football." This action occurred only a few weeks after the scandal of the West Point student firings, which, along with the William and Mary palace revolution, indicated that football was indeed reaching another crisis in its adaptation to the ever-changing American environment. Small colleges such as Milligan—a church-supported school in the mountains of Eastern Tennessee—were discovering that football was now so mechanized that they could no longer afford the necessary entry fee for machinery and personnel. Last year, Milligan spent $17,000, or two-thirds of its whole athletic budget—and did not get it all back in the box-office net. Football had come to resemble other industries or mechanized farms, into which a new firm could not move by relying on an institutional lifetime of patient saving and plowing back of profits, but only by large corporate investment. The production of a team involves the heavy overhead and staff personnel characteristic of high-capital,

David Riesman and Reuel Denney. "Football in America: A Study in Culture Diffusion," *American Quarterly*, 3: 309-319. Reprinted by permission.

functionally rationalized industries, as the result of successive changes in the game since its post-Civil-War diffusion from England.[1]

It would be wrong, however, to assert that football has become an impersonal market phenomenon. Rather, its rationalization as a sport and as a spectacle has served to bring out more openly the part it plays in the ethnic, class, and characterological struggles of our time— meaning, by "characterological struggle," the conflict between different styles of life. The ethnic significance of football is immediately suggested by the shift in the typical origins of player-names on the All-American Football Teams since 1889. In 1889, all but one of the names (Heffelfinger) suggested Anglo-Saxon origins. The first name after that of Heffelfinger to suggest non-Anglo-Saxon recruitment was that of Murphy, at Yale, in 1895. After 1895, it was a rare All-American team that did not include at least one Irishman (Daly, Hogan, Rafferty, Shevlin); and the years before the turn of the century saw entrance of the Jew. On the 1904 team appeared Pierkarski, of Pennsylvania. By 1927, names like Casey, Kipke, Oosterbaan, Koppisch, Garbisch, and Friedman were appearing on the All-American lists with as much frequency as names like Channing, Adams, and Ames in the 1890's.

While such a tally does little more than document a shift that most observers have already recognized in American football, it raises questions that are probably not answerable merely in terms of ethnic origins of players. There is an element of class identification running through American football since its earliest days, and the ethnic origins of players contain ample invitations to the making of theory about the class dimensions of football. Most observers would be inclined to agree that the arrival of names like Kelley and Kipke on the annual All-American list was taken by the Flanagans and the Webers as the achievement of a lower-class aspiration to be among the best at an upper-class sport. The question remains: what did the achievement mean? What did it mean at different stages in the development of the game? Hasn't the meaning worn off in the fifty-odd years, the roughly two generations since Heffelfinger and Murphy made the grade?

1. The growing scale of college football is indicated by its dollar place in the American leisure economy. In 1929, out of $4.3 billion recreation expenditures by Americans, the college football gate accounted for $22 million. In 1950, out of $11.2 billion in such expenditures, it accounted for $103 million. While something less than 1% of the total United States recreation account, college football had ten times the gross income of professional football. The 1950 gate of $103 million suggests that a total capital of perhaps $250 million is invested in the college football industry. The revenue figures, above, of course, do not include the invisible subsidization of football, nor do they hint at the place that football pools occupy in the American betting economy.

There are many ways to begin an answer to such questions, and here we can open only a few lines of investigation. Our method is to study the interrelations between changes in the rules of the game (since the first intercollegiate contest: Rutgers, 6 goals—Princeton, 4 goals, in 1869) and to analyze the parallel changes in football strategy and ethos. All these developments are to be seen as part of a configuration that includes changes in coaching, in the training of players, and in the no less essential training of the mass audience.

Since football is a cultural inheritance from England, such an analysis may be made in the perspective of other studies in cultural diffusion and variation. Just as the French have transformed American telephone etiquette while retaining some of its recognizable physical features, so Americans have transformed the games of Europe even when, as in track or tennis, the formalities appear to be unaltered. Even within the Western industrial culture, there are great varieties on a class and national basis, in the games, rules, strategy, etiquette, and audience structures of sport. In the case of college football—we shall leave aside the symbolically less important professional game—the documentation of sportswriters (themselves a potent factor in change) allows us to trace the stages of development.

II

A study of Anatolian peasants now under way at the Bureau of Applied Social Research indicates that these highly tradition-bound people cannot grasp the abstractness of modern sports. They lack the enterprise, in their fatalistic village cultures, to see why people want to knock themselves out for sportsmanship's remote ideals; they cannot link such rituals, even by remote analogy, with their own. These peasants are similarly unable to be caught up in modern politics, or to find anything meaningful in the Voice of America. Nevertheless, football itself, like so many other games with balls and goals, originated in a peasant culture.

Football, in its earliest English form, was called the Dane's Head and it was played in the tenth and eleventh centuries as a contest in kicking a ball between towns. The legend is that the first ball was a skull, and only later a cow's bladder. In some cases, the goals were the towns themselves, so that a team entering a village might have pushed the ball several miles en route. King Henry II (1154-89) proscribed the game, on the ground that it interferred with archery practice. Played in Dublin even after the ban, football did not become respectable or legal until an edict of James I reinstated it. The reason was perhaps less ideological than practical: firearms had made the art of bowmanship obsolete.

During the following century, football as played by British schoolboys became formalized, but did not change its fundamental pattern of forceful kicking. In 1823, Ellis of Rugby made the mistake of picking up the ball and running with it towards the goal. All concerned thought it a mistake: Ellis was sheepish, his captain apologetic. The mistake turned into innovation when it was decided that a running rule might make for an interesting game. The localism, pluralism, and studied casualness of English sports made it possible to try it out without securing universal assent—three or four purely local variants of football, football-hazing and "wall games" are still played in various English schools. Rugby adopted "Rugby" in 1841, several years after Cambridge had helped to popularize it.[2]

This establishment of the running or Rugby game, as contrasted with the earlier, kicking game, had several important results. One was that the old-style players banded themselves together for the defense of their game, and formed the London Football Association (1863). This name, abbreviated to "Assoc," appears to have been the starting point for the neologism, "Soccer," the name that the kicking game now goes by in many parts of the English-speaking world. A second result was that the English, having found a new game, continued to play it without tight rules until the Rugby Union of 1871. As we shall see, this had its effects on the American game. The third and most important result of Ellis' "mistake," of course, was that he laid the foundations for everything fundamental about the American game between about 1869 and the introduction of the forward pass. (The forward pass is still illegal in Rugby and closely related football games.)

III

In the Colonial period and right down to the Civil War, Americans played variants on the kicking football game on their town greens and

---

2. A commemorative stone at Rugby reads as follows:

THIS STONE
COMMEMORATES THE EXPLOIT OF
WILLIAM WEBB ELLIS
WHO WITH A FINE DISREGARD FOR THE RULES OF
FOOTBALL, AS PLAYED IN HIS TIME,
FIRST TOOK THE BALL IN HIS ARMS AND RAN WITH IT,
THUS ORIGINATING THE DISTINCTIVE FEATURE OF
THE RUGBY GAME
A. D. 1823

schoolyards. After the war, Yale and Harvard served as the culturally receptive importers of the English game. Harvard, meeting McGill in a game of Rugby football in 1874, brought the sport to the attention of collegiate circles and the press—two identifications important for the whole future development of the game. But if Harvard was an opinion leader, Yale was a technological one. A Yale student who had studied at Rugby was instrumental in persuading Yale men to play the Rugby game and was, therefore, responsible for some of Yale's early leadership in the sport.

It happened in the following way, according to Walter Camp and Lorin F. Deland.[3] The faculty in 1860, for reasons unknown, put a stop to interclass matches of the pre-Rugby variety. "During the following years, until 1870, football was practically dead at Yale. The class of '72, however, was very fond of athletic sports, and participated especially in long hare and hound runs. The revival of football was due in a large measure to Mr. D. S. Schaft, formerly of Rugby School, who entered the class of '73 and succeeded in making the sport popular among his classmates, and eventually formed an association which sent challenges to the other classes."

Soon after the period described by Camp, it became clear that American players, having tasted the "running" game, were willing to give up the soccer form. It became equally clear that they either did not want to, or could not, play Rugby according to the British rules. "The American players found in this code [English Rugby Rules] many uncertain and knotty points which caused much trouble in their game, especially as they had no traditions, or older and more experienced players, to whom they could turn for the necessary explanations," says Camp. An example of such a problem was English rule number nine:

"A touchdown is when a player, putting his hand on the ball in touch or in goal, stops it so that it remains dead, or fairly so."

The ambiguity of the phrase "fairly so" was increased by the statement in rule number eight that the ball is dead "when it rests absolutely motionless on the ground."

Camp's description of these early difficulties is intensely interesting to the student of cultural diffusion not only because of what Camp observed about the situation, but also because of what he neglected to observe. Consider the fact that the development of Rugby rules in England was accomplished by admitting into the rules something that we could call a legal fiction. While an offensive runner was permitted to carry the ball, the condition of his doing so was that he should *happen*

3. Walter Camp and Lorin F. Deland, *Football.*

to be standing behind the swaying "scrum" (the tangled players) at the moment the ball popped back out to him. An intentional "heel out" of the ball was not permitted; and the British rules of the mid-nineteenth century appear to take it for granted that the difference between an intentional and an unintentional heel-out would be clear to everyone. Ellis' mistake became institutionalized—but still as a mistake. This aspect of Rugby rule-making had important implications for the American game.

British players, according to tradition as well as according to rules, could be expected to tolerate such ambiguity as that of the heel-out rule just as they tolerated the ambiguity of the "dead" ball. They could be expected to tolerate it not only because of their personal part in developing new rules but also (a point we shall return to) because they had an audience with specific knowledge of the traditions to assist them. In America it was quite another matter to solve such problems. No Muzafer Sherif was present[4] to solidify the perceptions of "nearly so," and the emotional tone for resolving such questions without recurrent dispute could not be improvised. Rather, however, than dropping the Rugby game at that point, because of intolerance for the ambiguities involved, an effort was undertaken, at once systematic and gradual, to fill in by formal procedures the vacuum of etiquette and, in general, to adapt the game to its new cultural home.

The upshot of American procedure was to assign players to the legalized task of picking up and tossing back out of scrimmage. This in turn created the rôle of the center, and the centering operation. This in turn led to a variety of problems in defining the situation as one of "scrimmage" or "non-scrimmage," and the whole question of the legality of passing the ball back to intended runners. American football never really solved these problems until it turned its attention, in 1880, to a definition of the scrimmage itself. The unpredictable English "scrum" or scramble for a free ball was abandoned, and a crude line of scrimmage was constructed across the field. Play was set in motion by snapping the ball. Meanwhile Americans became impatient with long retention of the ball by one side. It was possible for a team that was ahead in score to adopt tactics that would insure its retention of the ball until the end of the period. By the introduction of a minimum yardage-gain rule in 1882, the rulemakers assured the frequent interchange of the ball between sides.

The effect of this change was to dramatize the offensive-defensive symmetry of the scrimmage line, to locate it sharply in time ("downs"),

4. Cf. his *An Outline of Social Psychology*, pp. 93-182.

and to focus attention not only on the snapping of the ball, but also on the problem of "offside" players. In the English game, with no spatially and temporally delimited "line of scrimmage," the offside player was penalized only by making him neutral in action until he could move to a position back of the position of the ball. In the American game, the new focus on centering, on a scrimmage line, and on yardage and downs, created the need for a better offside rule. From that need developed offside rules that even in the early years resembled the rules of today. American rulemakers were logically extending a native development when they decided to draw an imaginary line through the ball before it had been centered, to call this the "line of scrimmage," and to make this line, rather than the moving ball itself, the offside limit in the goalward motion of offensive players. At first, lined-up players of the two sides were allowed to stand and wrestle with each other while waiting for the ball to be centered; only later was a neutral zone introduced between the opposing lines.

Even with such a brief summary of the rule changes, we are in a position to see the operation of certain recurrent modes or patterns of adaptation. The adaptation begins with the acceptance of a single pivotal innovation (running with the ball). The problems of adaptation begin with the realization that this single innovation has been uprooted from a rich context of meaningful rules and traditions, and does not work well in their absence. Still more complex problems of adaptation develop when it is realized that the incompleteness of the adaptation will not be solved by a reference to the pristine rules. In the first place, the rules are not pristine (the English rules were in the process of development themselves). In the second place, the tradition of interpreting them is not present in experienced players. In the third place, even if it were, it might not be adaptable to the social character and mood of the adapters.

Let us put it this way. The Americans, in order to solve the heel-out problem, set in motion a redesign of the game that led ultimately to timed centering from a temporarily fixed line of scrimmage. Emphasis completely shifted from the kicking game; it also shifted away from the combined kicking and running possible under Rugby rules; it shifted almost entirely in the direction of an emphasis on ballcarrying. Meanwhile, to achieve this emphasis, the game made itself vulnerable to slowdowns caused by one team's retention of the ball. It not only lost the fluidity of the original game, but ran up against a pronounced American taste for action in sports, visible action. There is evidence that even if players had not objected to such slowdowns, the spectators would have raised a shout. The yardage rule was the way this crisis was met. This, in turn, led to an emphasis on mass play, and helped to create the early twentieth-century problems of football. But before we consider this step in the game's development we must turn to examine certain factors in the sport's audience reception.

IV

A problem posed for the student of cultural diffusion at this point can be stated as follows: What factor or factors appear to have been most influential in creating an American game possessing not only nationally distinct rules, but also rules having a specific flavor of intense legality about many a point of procedure left more or less up in the air by the British game?

We can now go beyond the rule-making aspect of the game and assert that the chief factor was the importance of the need to stand-ardize rules to supply an ever-widening collegiate field of competition, along with the audience this implied. The English rulemakers, it appears, dealt with a situation in which amateur play was restricted to a fairly limited number of collegians and institutions. The power of local-ism was such that many an informality was tolerated, and intended to be tolerated, in the rules and their interpertation. American football appeared on the American campus at the beginning of a long period in which intercollegiate and interclass sportsmanship was a problem of ever-widening social participation and concern. Football etiquette itself was in the making. Thus, it appears that when early American teams met, differences of opinion could not be resolved between captains in rapid-fire agreement or penny-tossing as was the case in Britain. Ameri-can teams did not delegate to their captains the rôle of powerful com-rade-in-antagonism with opposing captains, or, if they did, they felt that such responsibilities were too grave.[5]

Into just such situations football players thrust all of the force of their democratic social ideologies, all their prejudice in favor of equali-tarian and codified inter-player attitudes. Undoubtedly, similar con-siderations also influenced the audience. Mark Benney, a British sociol-ogist who is familiar with the games played on both sides of the Atlantic, points out that, whereas the American game was developed in and for a student group, the English game was played before quite large crowds

---

5. "Fifty years ago arguments followed almost every decision the referee made. The whole team took part, so that half the time the officials scarcely knew who was captain. The player who was a good linguist was always a priceless asset." John W. Heisman, who played for both Brown and Penn in the 1890's, quoted in Frank G. Menke, *Encyclopedia of Sports*, p. 293.

who, from a class standpoint, were less homogeneous than the players themselves, though they were as well informed as the latter in the "law of the game. Rugby football was seldom played by the proletariat; it was simply enjoyed as a spectacle.

Held by the critical fascination the British upper strata had for the lower strata, the audience was often hardly more interested in the result of the game than in judging the players as "gentlemen in action." "The players," Mr. Benney writes, "had to demonstrate that they were sportsmen, that they could 'take it'; and above all they had to inculcate the (politically important) ideology that legality was more important than power." The audience was, then, analogous to the skilled English jury at law, ready to be impressed by obedience to traditional legal ritual and form, and intolerant of "bad form" in their "betters." The early Yale games, played before a tiny, nonpaying audience, lacked any equivalent incentive to agree on a class-based ritual of "good form," and when the audiences came later on, their attitude towards upper-class sportsmanship was much more ambivalent—they had played the game too, and they were unwilling to subordinate themselves to a collegiate aristocracy who would thereby have been held to norms of correctness. The apparent legalism of many American arguments over the rules would strike British observers as simply a verbal power-play.

Such differences in the relation of the game to the audience, on this side of the Atlantic, undoubtedly speeded the development of the specifically American variant. Native, too, are the visual and temporal properties of the game as it developed even before 1900: its choreography could be enjoyed, if not always understood, by nonexperts, and its atomistic pattern in time and space could seem natural to audiences accustomed to such patterns in other foci of the national life. The midfield dramatization of line against line, the recurrent starting and stopping of field action around the timed snapping of a ball, the trend to a formalized division of labor between backfield and line, above all, perhaps, the increasingly precise synchronization of men in motion—these developments make it seem plausible to suggest that the whole procedural rationalization of the game which we have described was not unwelcome to Americans, and that it fitted in with other aspects of their industrial folkways.

Spurred by interest in the analysis of the athletic motions of men and animals, Eadweard Muybridge was setting out his movie-like action shorts of the body motion (more preoccupied even than Vesalius or da Vinci with the detailed anatomy of movement)[6] at about the same time

6. Sigfried Giedion, *Mechanization Takes Command,* pp. 21-27.

that Coach Woodruff at Pennsylvania (1894) was exploring the possibilities for momentum play: linemen swinging into motion before the
ball is snapped, with the offensive team, forming a wedge, charging
toward an opposition held waiting by the offside rule. In Philadelphia,
the painter Eakins, self-consciously following the tenets of Naturalism
and his own literal American tradition, was painting the oarsmen of the
Schuylkill. Nearby, at the Midvale plant of the American Steel Company,
efficiency expert Frederick Winslow Taylor was experimenting with
motion study and incentive pay geared to small measurable changes in
output—pay that would spur but never soften the workman.[7]

Since we do not believe in historical inevitability, nor in the necessary homogeneity of a culture, we do not suggest that the American
game of football developed as it did out of cultural compulsion and
could not have gone off in quite different directions. Indeed, the very
effectiveness of momentum play, as a mode of bulldozing the defense,
led eventually to the rule that the line must refrain from motion before the ball is snapped. For the bulldozing led, or was thought to lead,
to a great increase in injuries. And while these were first coped with
by Walter Camp's training table (his men had their choice of beefsteak
or mutton for dinner, to be washed down with milk, ale, or sherry), the
public outcry soon forced further rule changes designed to soften the
game. After a particular bloody battle between Pennsylvania and Swarthmore in 1905, President Roosevelt himself took a hand and insisted on
reform.[8]

Camp's colleague at Yale, William Graham Sumner, may well have
smiled wryly at this. Sumner was exhorting his students to "get capital,"

7. In view of the prejudice against "Taylorism" today, shared by men and management as well as the intellectuals, let us record our admiration for Taylor's achievement, our belief that he was less insensitive to psychological factors than is often
claimed, and more "humane" in many ways than his no less manipulative, self-
consciously psychological successors.
8. "In a 1905 game between Pennsylvania and Swarthmore, the Pennsy slogan was
'Stop Bob Maxwell,' one of the greatest linesmen of all time. He was a mighty man,
with the amazing ability to roll back enemy plunges. The Penn players, realizing
that Maxwell was a menace to their chances of victory, took 'dead aim' at him
throughout the furious play.
"Maxwell stuck it out, but when he tottered off the field, his face was a bloody
wreck. Some photographer snapped him, and the photo of the mangled Maxwell,
appearing in a newspaper, caught the attention of the then President Roosevelt. It
so angered him, that he issued an ultimatum that if rough play in football was
not immediately ruled out, he would abolish it by executive edict." Frank G.
Menke, *Encyclopedia of Sports.*
Notice here the influence of two historical factors on football development: one,
the occupancy of the White House in 1905 by the first President of the United
States who was a self-conscious patron of youth, sport, and the arts; two, the relative newness in 1905 of photographic sports coverage. Widespread increased photographic coverage of popular culture was the direct result of the newspaper policies
of William Randolph Hearst, beginning about 1895.

and cautioning them against the vices of sympathy and reformism—a theme which has given innumerable American academes a good living since—while Camp was exhorting his to harden themselves, to be stern and unafraid. In spite of them both, the reformers won out; but the end of momentum play was not the end of momentum. Rather, with an ingenuity that still dazzles, the game was gentled and at the same time speeded by a new rule favoring the forward pass. But before going on to see what changes this introduced, let us note the differences between the subjects of Sumner's and Camp's exhortations on the one hand, and Taylor's on the other.

Frederick Taylor, as his writings show, was already coming up against a work force increasingly drawn from non-Protestant lands, and seeking to engender in them a YMCA-morality, whereas Camp was inculcating the same morality into young men of undiluted Anglo-Saxon stock and middle- to upper-class origins. Not for another fifty years would the sons of Midvale prove harder, though fed on kale or spaghetti, and only intermittently, than the sons of Yale. Meanwhile, the sons of Yale had learned to spend summers as tracklayers or wheat harvesters in an effort to enlarge their stamina, moral toughness, and cross-class adventures.

Nevertheless, certain basic resemblances between the purposes of Taylor and those of Sumner and Camp are clearly present. In contrast with the British, the Americans demonstrated a high degree of interest in winning games and winning one's way to high production goals. The Americans, as in so many other matters, were clearly concerned with the competitive spirit that new rules might provoke and control. (British sports, like British industry, seemed to take it more for granted that competition will exist even if one does not set up an ideology for it.) Much of this seems to rest in the paradoxical belief of Americans that competition is natural—but only if it is constantly recreated by artificial systems of social rules that direct energies into it.

Back of the attitudes expressed in Taylor, Sumner, and Camp we can feel the pressure not only of a theory of competition, but also a theory of the emotional tones that ought to go along with competition. It is apparent from the brutality scandals of 1905 that President Roosevelt reacted against roughhouse not so much because it was physical violence, but for two related reasons. The first and openly implied reason was that it was connected with an unsportsmanlike attitude. The second, unacknowledged, reason was that Americans fear and enjoy their aggression at the same time, and thus have difficulty in pinning down the inner meanings of external violence. The game of Rugby as now played in England is probably as physically injurious as American football was at the turn of the century. By contrast, American attitudes toward football demonstrates a forceful need to define, limit, and conventionalize the symbolism of violence in sports.

If we look back now at England, we see a game in which shouted signals and silent counting of timed movements are unknown—a game that seems to Americans to wander in an amorphous and disorderly roughhouse. Rugby, in the very home of the industrial revolution, seems pre-industrial, seems like one of the many feudal survivals that urbanization and industrialization have altered but not destroyed. The English game, moreover, seems not to have developed anyone like Camp, the Judge Gary of football (as Rockne was to be its Henry Ford): Camp was a sparkplug in efforts to codify inter-collegiate rules; he was often the head of the important committees. His training table, furthermore, was one of the signs of the slow rise in "overhead" expense—a rise which, rather like the water in United States Steel Stock, assumed that abundance was forthcoming and bailing out probable, as against the British need for parsimony. But at the same time the rise in costs undoubtedly made American football more vulnerable than ever to public-relations considerations: the "gate" could not be damned.

V

This public relations issue in the game first appears in the actions of the rules committee of 1906—the introduction of the legalized forward pass in order to open up the game and reduce brutal power play. Between 1906 and 1913 the issue was generally treated as a problem centered about players and their coaches, and thus took the form of an appeal to principles rather than to audiences. However, the development of the high audience appeal that we shall show unfolding after 1913 was not autonomous and unheralded. If public relations became a dominant factor by 1915, when the University of Pittsburgh introduced numbers for players in order to spur the sale of programs, it had its roots in the 1905-13 period. The rules committee of 1906, by its defensive action on roughhouse rules had already implicitly acknowledged a broad public vested interest in the ethos of the game. Let us turn to look at the speed with which football was soon permeated by broad social meanings unanticipated by the founders of the sport.

By 1913, the eve of the First World War, innovation in American industry had ceased to be the prerogative of Baptist, Calvinist, and North of Ireland tycoons. Giannini was starting his Bank of America; the Jews were entering the movies and the garment hegemonies. Yet these were exceptions, and the second generation of immigrants, taught in America to be dissatisfied with the manual work their fathers did, were seldom finding the easy paths of ascent promised in success literature. Where, for one thing, were they to go to college? If they sought to enter the older eastern institutions, would they face a social struggle? Such anxieties probably contributed to the fact that the game of boyish and spirited brawn played at the eastern centers of intellect and cultivation was to be overthrown by the new game of craft and field maneuver that got its first rehearsal at the hands of two second-generation poor boys attending little-known Notre Dame.

The more significant of the two boys, Knute Rockne, was, to be sure, of Danish Protestant descent and only later became a Catholic.[9] During their summer vacation jobs as lifeguards on Lake Michigan, Rockne and Gus Dorais decided to work as a passing team. Playing West Point early in the season of 1913, they put on the first demonstration of the spiral pass that makes scientific use of the difference in shape between the round ball used in the kicking game and the oval that gradually replaced it when ball-carrying began. As the first players to exploit the legal pass, they rolled up a surprise victory over Army. One of the effects of the national change in rules was to bring the second-generation boys of the early twentieth century to the front, with a craft innovation that added new elements of surprise, "system" and skull-session to a game that had once revolved about an ethos of brawn plus character-building.

With the ethnic shift, appears to have come a shift in type of hero. The work-minded glamor of an all-'round craftsman like Jim Thorpe gave way to the people-minded glamor of backfield generals organizing deceptive forays into enemy territory—of course, the older martial virtues are not so much ruled out as partially incorporated in the new image. In saying this, it must not be forgotten, as sports columnist Red Smith has pointed out, that the fictional Yale hero, Dick Merriwell, is openly and shamelessly represented as a dirty player in the first chapters of his career. But the difference is that his deviation from standard sportsmanship consisted largely of slugging, not of premeditated wiliness. In fact, the Yale Era, even into Camp's reign, was characterized by a game played youthfully, with little attention to the players' prestige outside college circles. Again, the second-generationers mark a change. A variety of sources, including letters to the sports page, indicate that a Notre Dame victory became representational in a way a Yale or Harvard victory never was, and no Irish or Polish boy on the team could escape the symbolism. And by the self-confirming process, the Yale or

9. "After the church, football is the best thing we have," Rockne.

Harvard showing became symbolic in turn, and the game could never be returned, short of intramuralization, to the players themselves and their earlier age of innocent dirtiness.[10] The heterogeneity of America which had made it impossible to play the Rugby game at Yale had finally had its effect in transforming the meaning of the game to a point where Arnold of Rugby might have difficulty in drawing the right moral or any moral from it. Its "ideal types" had undergone a deep and widespread characterological change.

For the second-generation boy, with his father's muscles but not his father's motives, football soon became a means to career ascent. So was racketeering, but football gave acceptance, too—acceptance into the democratic fraternity of the entertainment world where performance counts and ethnic origin is hardly a handicap. Moreover, Americans as onlookers welcomed the anti-traditional innovations of a Rockne, and admired the trick that worked, whatever the opposing team and alumni may have thought about the effort involved. One wonders whether Rockne and Dorais may not have forgotten a particular pleasure from their craftiness by thinking of it as a counter-image to the stereotype of muscle-men applied to their fathers.

It was in 1915, at about the same time that the newcomers perfected their passing game, that the recruitment of players began in earnest. Without such recruitment, the game could not have served as a career route for many of the second generation who would not have had the cash or impetus to make the class jump that college involved.[11]

The development of the open and rationalized game has led step by step not only to the T formation, but also to the two-platoon system. These innovations call for a very different relationship among the players than was the case under the older star system. For the game is now a coöperative enterprise in which mistakes are too costly—to the head coach, the budget, even the college itself—to be left to individual initiative. At least at one institution, an anthropologist has been called in to

---

10. One of us, while a Harvard undergraduate, sought with several friends to heal the breach between Harvard and Princeton—a breach whose bitterness could hardly be credited today. The Harvards believed Princeton played dirty—it certainly won handily in those years of the 20s—while Princetonians believed themselves snubbed by Harvard as crude parvenus trying to make a trio out of the Harvard-Yale duo. The diplomatic problems involved in seeking to repair these status slights and scars were a microcosm of the Congress of Westphalia or Vienna—whether the Harvard or Princeton athletic directors should enter the room first was an issue. A leak to the Hearst press destroyed our efforts, as alumni pressure forced denials of any attempt to resume relations, but the compromise formulas worked out were eventually accepted, about the time that the University of Chicago "solved" the problem of the intellectual school by withdrawing from the game altogether.

11. See George Saxon, "Immigrant Culture in a Stratified Society," *Modern Review*, II, No. 2, February 1948.

study the morale problems of the home team, and to help in the scouting of opposing teams. To the learning of Taylor, there has been added that of Mayo, and coaches are conscious of the need to be group-dynamics leaders rather than old-line straw bosses.

Today, the semi-professionalized player, fully conscious of how many people's living depends on him, cannot be exhorted by Frank Merriwell appeals, but needs to be "handled." And the signals are no longer the barks of the first Camp-trained quarterback—hardly more differentiated than a folkdance caller's—but are cues of great subtlety and mathematical precision for situations planned in advance with camera shots and character fill-ins of the opposing team. James Worthy and other advocates of a span of control beyond the usual half-dozen of the older military and executive manuals might find support for their views in the way an eleven is managed. Industrial, military, and football teamwork have all a common cultural frame.

Yet it would be too simple to say that football has ceased to be a game for its players, and has become an industry, or a training for industry. In the American culture as a whole, no sharp line exists between work and play, and in some respects the more work-like an activtiy becomes, the more it can successfully conceal elements of playfulness.[12] Just because the sophisticated "amateur" of today does *not* have his manhood at stake in the antique do-or-die fashion (though his manhood may be involved, in very ambivalent ways, in his more generalized rôle as athlete and teammate), there can be a relaxation of certain older demands and a more detached enjoyment of perfection of play irrespective of partisanship.

The rôle of football tutor to the audience has been pushed heavily onto radio and TV announcers (some of whom will doubtless be mobile into the higher-status rôle of commentators on politics or symphony broadcasts). The managerial coalescence of local betting pools into several big oceans has also contributed to the audience stake in the game. Yet all that has so far been said does not wholly explain alumnus and subway-alumnus loyalties. It may be that we have to read into this interest of the older age groups a much more general aspect of American behavior: the pious and near-compulsory devotion of the older folks to whatever the younger folks are alleged to find important. The tension between the generations doubtless contributes to the hysterical note of solemnity in the efforts of some older age groups to control the ethics of the game, partly perhaps as a displacement of their efforts to control youthful sexuality.

12. Compare the discussion of Freud's playful work, pp. 331-333, below.

And this problem in turn leads to questions about the high percentage of women in the American football audience, compared with that of any other country, and the high salience of women in football as compared with baseball imagery (in recent American football films, girls have been singled out as the most influential section of the spectators). The presence of these women heightens the sexual impact of everything in and around the game, from shoulderpads to the star system, as the popular folklore of the game recognizes. Although women are not expected to attend baseball games, when they do attend they are expected to understand them and to acquire, if not a "male" attitude, at least something approaching companionship on a basis of equality with their male escorts.[13]

For all its involvement with such elemental themes in American life, it may be that football has reached the apex of its audience appeal. With bigness comes vulnerability: "inter-industry" competition is invited, and so are rising costs—the players, though not yet unionized, learn early in high school of their market value and, like Jim in Huckleberry Finn, take pride in it.[14] The educators' counter-reformation cannot be laughed off. With the lack of ethnic worlds to conquer, we may soon find the now-decorous Irish of the Midwest embarrassed by Notre Dame's unbroken victories. Perhaps the period of innovation which began in 1823 at Rugby has about come to an end in the United States, with large changes likely to result only if the game is used as a device for acculturation to America, not by the vanishing stream of immigrants to that country, but by the rest of the world that will seek the secret of American victories on the playing fields of South Bend.

13. Anthropologist Ray Birdwhistell convincingly argues that football players play with an eye to their prestige among teammates, other football players, and other men.

14. Their pride varies to some extent with their place on the team. Linemen, with the exception of ends, have lower status than backfield men. Many players believe that backfields are consciously and unconsciously recruited from higher social strata than linemen.

RITES OF PASSAGE AND
SEXUAL IDENTITY

Sport serves different purposes for different age groups. It seems to be part of the symbolic formulation of the various coming of age stages. The articles in this next section were chosen to illuminate the social process from childhood through the adult male and female roles in sport.

The first selection looks at the socializing experiences of children in games. Iona and Peter Opie consider the reasons why children play: Is it for reasons of their own or of adult imposition? They have also inquired: Do children play differently in space of their own choosing than in space designated for play by adults? Their concern for the child in play is revealed by the statement: "Participation in sport has become a prestige activity. And when we apply our adult criteria to our children, we are liable to rob them of the chief pleasure of being young, let alone impair valuable and natural instincts."[1]

Maleness and femaleness become important considerations for the maturing individual. Several of the authors in this section clearly formulate theories on sexual identification in sport, as well as the variation in sexual roles and expectations within different socio-economic classes. Coming of age in American society occurs many times through sport, especially for the male child. Fiske considers the male adolescent and football in this light. In an anthropological study, she presents the criteria for rites of passage from adolescence to adulthood and looks at American college football in relation to these criteria. The aim of the study was "first to show that the formal outlines of American college football can be considered an initiation ceremony, occurring on the threshhold of the status change from adolescence to adulthood; secondly, to see what might be addended to a theory of initiation upon consideration of the cultural data in our own culture." She proceeds to carefully outline the

1. Personal correspondence.

roles of the elders (coaches) and novices (players) and the basic format of the ceremony.

In the next article, Beisser contends that though changes in technology and family have occurred, the cultural expectations of masculinity have remained fixed. He takes a different point of view from other authors in emphasizing the comparison of male and female athletic performance, in which man is consistently superior. Beisser concludes that man "has learned that this is one area where there is no doubt about sexual differences and where his biology is not obsolete. Athletics help assure his difference from women in a world where his functions have come to resemble hers." We now seem to be in the midst of redefinition of cultural values and sexual roles in American society. How will this redefinition relate to or cause change in roles in sport? As Beisser contends, it may well reinforce them.

The next article by Metheny stresses man's sports competition as symbolic of "some more significant conception of man's interaction with the universe of his existence" than with any effect produced by his physical effort. What does man's sport competition symbolize? Is it closely associated with his work and with his maleness among other men? Metheny asks some relevant questions and provides theories in answer to them.

The second presentation by Metheny is a thorough analysis of women in sport. It deals with the roles "appropriate" to women, and with the "socially sanctioned image of feminine sport competition." The author in broad terms looks at what either sex may do in sports competition "without impairing their opportunities for finding a mate within their own social classification."

In the final selection Hart is concerned with the problems that women face as athletes in the American culture. These problems differ somewhat from those faced by women in other Western cultures. A consideration of why this is so leads one into a very complex situation, difficult to untangle. Additionally, the author examines the reasons for having arrived at this present situation in sport.

INTRODUCTION TO CHILDREN'S GAMES IN STREET AND PLAYGROUND

IONA AND PETER OPIE

When children play in the street they not only avail themselves of one of the oldest play-places in the world, they engage in some of the oldest and most interesting of games, for they are games tested and confirmed by centuries of children, who have played them and passed them on, as children continue to do, without reference to print, parliament, or adult propriety. Indeed these street games are probably the most played, least recorded, most natural games that there are. Certainly they are the most spontaneous, for the little group of boys under the lamp-post may not know, until a minute before, whether they are to play "Bish Bash" or "Poison" or "Cockarusha," or even know that they are going to play.

A true game is one that frees the spirit. It allows of no cares but those fictitious ones engendered by the game itself. When the players commit themselves to the rhythm and incident of "Underground Tig" or "Witches in the Gluepots" they opt out of the ordinary world, the boundary of their existence becomes the two pavements this side of a pillar-box, their only reality the excitement of avoiding the chaser's touch. Yet it is not only the nature of the game that frees the spirit, it is the circumstances in which it is played. The true game, as Locke recognized years ago, is the one that arises from the players themselves.

> Because there can be no *Recreation* without Delight, which depends not always on Reason, but oftener on Fancy, it must be permitted Children not only to divert themselves, but to do it after their own Fashion; provided it be innocently, and without Prejudice to their Health.

"Introduction," in its entirety from *Children's Games in Street and Playground* by Iona and Peter Opie, pp. 1-16, 1969. Reprinted by permission.

It may even be argued that the value of a game as recreation depends on its inconsequence to daily life. In the games which adults organize for children, or even merely oversee in a playground, the outside world is ever present. Individual performances tend to become a matter for congratulation or shame; and in a team game, paradoxically, individual responsibility presses hardest. The player who "lets down his side" can cheer himself only with the sad reflection that those who speak loudest about the virtues of organized sport are the people who excel in it themselves, never the duffers. He is not likely to have been told that such a man as Robert Louis Stevenson felt that cricket and football were colourless pastimes, scarcely play at all, compared with the romance of Hide and Seek.

THE APPEAL OF THE GAMES

Play is unrestricted, games have rules. Play may merely be the enactment of a dream, but in each game there is a contest. Yet it will be noticed that when children play a game in the street they are often extraordinarily naïve or, according to viewpoint, highly civilized. They seldom need an umpire, they rarely trouble to keep scores, little significance is attached to who wins or loses, they do not require the stimulus of prizes, it does not seem to worry them if a game is not finished. Indeed children like games in which there is a sizeable element of luck, so that individual abilities cannot be directly compared. They like games which restart almost automatically, so that everybody is given a new chance. They like games which move in stages, in which each stage, the choosing of leaders, the picking-up of sides, the determining of which side shall start, is almost a game in itself. In fact children's games often seem laborious to adults who, if invited to join in, may find themselves becoming impatient, and wanting to speed them up. Adults do not always see, when subjected to lengthy preliminaries, that many of the games, particularly those of young children, are more akin to ceremonies than competitions. In these games children gain the reassurance that comes with repetition, and the feeling of fellowship that comes from doing the same as everyone else. Children may choose a particular game merely because of some petty dialogue which precedes the chase:

> "Sheep, sheep, come home."
> "We're afraid."
> "What of?"
> "The wolf."

"Wolf has gone to Devonshire
Won't be here for seven years,
Sheep, sheep, come home."

As Spencer remarked, it is not only the amount of physical exercise that is taken that gives recreation, "an agreeable mental excitement has a highly invigorating influence." Thus children's "interest" in a game may well be the incident in it that least appeals to the adult: the opportunity it affords to thump a player on the back, as in "Strokey Back," to behave stupidly and be applauded for the stupidity, as in "Johnny Green," to say aloud the colour of someone's panties, as in "Farmer, Farmer, may we cross your Golden River?" and in a number of games, for instance "Chinese Puzzle," there may be little purpose other than the ridiculousness of the experiment itself:

> Someone as to be on. The one who is on as to turn round while the others hold hands and make a round circul. Then you get in a muddle, one persun could clime over your arms or under your legs or anything ales that you could make a muddle, then when they have finished they say "Chinese Puzzle we are all in a muddle," then the persun turns around and goes up to them and gets them out of the muddle without breaking their hands, and then the persun who was on choose someone ales, and then it goes on like that. It is fun to play Chinese Puzzle.

Here, indeed, is a British game where little attempt is made to establish the superiority of one player over another. In fact the function of such a game is largely social. Just as the shy man reveals himself by his formalities, so does the child disclose his unsureness of his place in the world by welcoming games with set procedures, in which his relationships with his fellows are clearly established. In games a child can exert himself without having to explain himself, he can be a good player without having to think whether he is a popular person, he can find himself being a useful partner to someone of whom he is ordinarily afraid. He can be confident, too, in particular games, that it is his place to issue commands, to inflict pain, to steal people's possessions, to pretend to be dead, to hurl a ball actually at someone, to pounce on someone, or to kiss someone he has caught. In ordinary life either he never knows these experiences or, by attempting them, makes himself an outcast.

It appears to us that when a child plays a game he creates a situation which is under his control, and yet it is one of which he does not know the outcome. In the confines of a game there can be all the excitement and uncertainty of an adventure, yet the young player can comprehend the whole, can recognize his place in the scheme, and, in contrast to the confusion of real life, can tell what is right action. He can, too, extend his environment, or feel that he is doing so, and gain knowledge of sensations beyond ordinary experience. When children are small, writes Bertrand Russell, "it is biologically natural that they should, in imagination, live through the life of remote savage ancestors." As long as the action of the game is of a child's own making he is ready, even anxious, to sample the perils of which this world has such plentiful supply. In the security of a game he makes acquaintance with insecurity, he is able to rationalize absurdities, reconcile himself to not getting his own way, "assimilate reality" (Piaget), act heroically without being in danger. The thrill of a chase is accentuated by viewing the chaser not as a boy in short trousers, but as a bull. It is not a classmate's back he rides upon but a knight's fine charger. It is not a party of other boys his side skirmishes with but Indians, Robbers, "Men from Mars." And, always provided that the environment is of his own choosing, he—or she—is even prepared to meet the "things that happen in the dark," playing games that would seem strange amusement if it was thought they were being taken literally: "Murder in the Dark," "Ghosties in the Garrett," "Moonlight, Starlight, Bogey won't come out Tonight." And yet, within the context of the game, these alarms *are* taken literally.

THE AGE OF THE PLAYERS

When generalizing about children's play it is easy to forget that each child's attitude to each game, and his way of playing it, is constantly changing as he himself matures; his preferences moving from the fanciful to the ritualistic, from the ritualistic to the romantic (i.e. the free-ranging games, "Hide and Seek," "Cowboys and Indians"), and from the romantic to the severely competitive. The infants, five to seven years old, may play some of the same games in their playground that the juniors do across the way, but in a more personal, less formalized style. Their chasing game, in which they clutch the railings to be safe, is called, perhaps, "Naughty Boys." "We're playing naughty boys, we've run away from home." ("Touch Iron" or "Touch Green" is only emerging from make-believe.) The boys who are moving on hands and feet, stomachs upward, in another part of the playground, say they are being Creatures, "horrible creatures in the woods." The juniors, in the next playground, would not play like this, not move about publicly on hands and feet, unless, that is, it was part of a "proper" game, one in which they were *chasing* each other.

Today, in an increasingly integrated society, children become self-conscious about the games they play on their own more quickly than they used to do. They discard them two, and even three years earlier than they did in the days before the introduction of organized sport.

When Lord John Russell, aged eleven, started his school-days at West-minister in 1803, he recorded in his diary that "the boys play at hoops, peg-tops, and pea-shooters." At Eton in 1766 the sports in vogue included Hopscotch, Headimy, Peg in the Ring, Conquering Lobs (marbles), Trap-ball, Chuck, Steal Baggage, and Puss in the Corner. At Sedgley Park School in Staffordshire, about 1805, the boys were content with Kites, Marloes (marbles), Peg-tops, Hoops, Backs (leap-frog), Beds (hopscotch), Cat, Rounders, Skipping, and even with "playing horses." Today few boys at grammar school would contemplate such sports. The experts are aged eight, nine, and ten. Even girls, who it might be thought would hold out against being organized, now look down upon informal games once they have a chance of taking part in the recognized sports:

> When I was five I played at Beddies. At seven I learned to play E.I.O. At nine I played "Alla Baba who's got the ball-a." Now I am fourteen I play tennis and netball, not the games I used to play when I was smaller.

Indeed, a game which at one time was the breath of life to child a short while later may be cast aside and become an embarrassment to remember. Thus a ten-year-old's description of "Queeny" starts as follows:

> My favourite game is a game that lots and lots of children can play at once. It is a lovely game, children of two years old can play it right up to the age of twelve. It is very enjoyable. It has also a rhyme to it. It goes like this:
>> Queeny, Queeny, who's got the ball,
>> Is she fat or is she small,
>> Is she big or is she thin,
>> Does she play the violin,
>> Yes or no?

But a fourteen-year-old girl says of the game:

> When I was smaller I used to play with my friends games which seem very silly and babyish to me now . . . for example Queeny Ball. Now that was babyish! Today I would never dream of standing out in the street chanting "Queeny ball, ball, ball" but then I simply wallowed in such fun as I called it.

Thus one child's attitude to a game may vary from another's to a greater extent than does either of them from that of the adult spectator. In fact when a child enters his teens (earlier if in the "A" stream) a curious but genuine disability may overtake him. He may, as part of the process of growing up, actually lose his recollection of the sports that used to mean so much to him. As a thirteen-year-old wrote when describing "Aunts and Uncles," "King Ball," "Kick the Can," "Hide and Seek," and " I Draw a Snake":

> All these games are quite common round Glenzier, that is how I can remember them. There are other games played once in a while but these I cannot remember. The games I can remember are a little too young for me to play, although I play King Ball sometimes.

Older children can thus be remarkably poor informants about the games. Twelve-year-olds may be heard talking like old men and women ("Our street used to be very lively but children don't play the games like we used to do"). A fifteen-year-old in Liverpool, where "Queeny" is popular, was certain the game was no longer known. Fourteen-year-olds, re-met in the street, from whom we wanted further information about a game they had showed us proudly a year before, have listened to our queries with blank incomprehension. Paradoxical as it may appear, a five-year-old in his first term at school may well be aware of more self-organized games than a fifteen-year-old about to leave school.

THE AGE OF THE GAMES

These games that "children find out for themselves when they meet," as Plato put it, seem to them as new and surprising when they learn them as the jokes in this week's comic. Parties of schoolchildren, at the entrance to the British Museum, secretly playing "Fivestones" behind one of the columns as they wait to go in, little think that their pursuits may be as great antiquities as the exhibits they have been brought to see. Yet, in their everyday games, when they draw straws to see who shall take a disliked role, they show how Chaucer's Canterbury pilgrims determined which of them should tell the first tale. When they strike at each other's plantains, trying to decapitate them, they play the game a medieval chronicler says King Stephen played with his boy-prisoner William Marshal to humour him. When they jump on a player's back, and make him guess which finger they hold up ("Husky-bum, Finger or Thumb?") they perpetuate an amusement of ancient Rome. When they hit a player from behind, in the game "Stroke the Baby," and challenge him to name who did it, they unwittingly illuminate a passage in the life of Our Lord. And when they enter the British Museum they can see Eros, clearly depicted on a vase of 400 B.C., playing the game they have just been told to abandon.

There was no need for Plato to urge that boys be forbidden to make alterations in their games, lest they be led to disobey the laws of the

State in later life. Boys are such sticklers for tradition that after 2,000
years they have not yet given up Epostrakismos ("Ducks and Drakes").
Schoenophilinda ("Whackem"), Apodidraskinda (running-home "Hide
and Seek"), Ostrakinda (a form of "Crusts and Crumbs"), Chytrinda
("Frog in the Middle"), Strombos ("Whipping top"), Dielkustinda
("Tug of War"), and at least two forms of Muinda ("Blind Man's Buff"
and "How Far to London"). Even the limping witch Empusa seems to
have survived to this day in the guise of Limpety Lil.

If a present-day schoolchild was wafted back to any previous century he would probably find himself more at home with the games
being played than with any other social custom. If he met his counterparts in the Middle Ages he might enjoy games of Prisoners' Base, Twos
and Threes, street-football, Fox and Chickens, Hunt the Hare, Pitch and
Toss, and marbles, as well as any of the games from classical times; and
judging by the illuminations in the margins of manuscripts, he would
be a prince among his fellows if he was good at piggyback fighting.

The Elizabethans played Bowls (one of their most common games),
Barley-break, Stoolball, "King by your Leaue" (a form of running-home
Hide and Seek), "Sunne and Moone" (Tug of War), and "Crosse and
Pile" (Heads and Tails). Shakespeare himself mentions "All hid, all hid,"
"Cherrie-pit," "Fast and Loose," "Handy-dandy" (see *Oxford Dictionary
of Nursery Rhymes*, pp. 197-8), "Hide Fox and all after," "Hoodman-
blinde," "Leape-frogge," "Push-pin" (a game now played with pen-nibs),
and "Spancounter."

Amongst games "used by our countrey Boys and Girls," named by
the Cheshire antiquary Randle Holme in 1688, were "Battle-dore or
Shuttle cock," "Bob Apple" (see *Lore and Language of Schoolchildren*,
pp. 272-3), "Chase Fire," "Drop Glove," "Hare and Hound," "Hide and
seech," "Hop skotches," "Hornes Hornes," "Fives," "Jack stones," "King
I am," "Long Larrance," "Pi[t]ch and Hussle," and "Puss in the corner."
And the "innocent Games that Good Boys and Girls" diverted themselves
with in *A Little Pretty Pocket-Book*, 1744, one of the first books to be
published for juvenile amusement, included: Cricket, Base-Ball, "Chuck-
Farthing," "Peg-Farthing," "Taw" (marbles), "Knock out and Span,"
"Hop-Hat," "Thread the Needle," "All the Birds in the Air," and "I sent
a Letter to my Love."

Even more revealing, perhaps, than the age of the games, is the
persistence of certain practices during the games. The custom of turning
round a blindfold player *three times* before allowing him to begin
chasing seems already to have been standard practice in the seventeenth
century. The quaint notion that a player becomes "warm" when nearing
the object he is seeking was doubtless old when Silas Wegg adopted it

(*Our Mutual Friend*, III. vi). The strategem of making players choose
one of two objects, such as an "orange" or a "lemon," to decide which
side they shall take in a pulling match, was almost certainly employed
by the Elizabethans. The rule that a special word and finger-sign shall
give a player respite in a game appears to be a legacy of the age of
chivalry. The convention that the player who does worst in a game shall
be punished, rather than that he who does best shall be rewarded, has
an almost continuous history stretching from classical antiquity. And the
ritual confirmation that a player has been caught, by crowning him or
by tapping him three times, prevalent today even in such sophisticated
places as Ilford and Enfield, was mentioned by Cromek in his *Remains
of Nithsdale and Galloway Song* in 1810 ("If the intruder be caught
on the hostile ground he is *taend*, that is, clapped three times on the
head, which makes him a prisoner"), and is also the rule—as are other
of these conventions—amongst children in France, Germany, Austria,
Italy, and the United States.

VARIATION IN THE GAMES

If children played their games invariably in the way the previous
generation played them, the study of youthful recreation could be a
matter merely of antiquarian scholarship. But they do not. Despite the
motherly influence of tradition, of which we have seen examples, children's play is like every other social activity, it is subject to continual
change. The fact that the games are played slightly differently in different
places, and may even vary in name, is itself evidence that mutation takes
place. ("Chinese Puzzle," for instance, is also known as "Chinese Muddle,"
"Chinese Puddle," "Jigsaw Puzzle," "Chinese Knots," "French Knots,"
"Chain Man," "Tangle Man," "Policeman," and "Cups and Saucers.") In
addition, as is well known, new sports emerge that may or may not in the
course of time become traditional. (During the past decade there has
been the "Hula Hoop," "Scoobeedoo," "Split the Kipper," "American
Skipping," and "Ippyop" or "Belgian Skipping.") And for reasons that
are usually social or environmental, some games become impracticable
(e.g. games played with caps are fast disappearing), while others are
overlaid or replaced by new versions that are found to be more satisfactory. ("Conkers," played with horse chestnuts, which became possible
with the introduction of the horse-chestnut tree, *Aesculus hippocasta-
num*, has now displaced the centuries-old contest with cobnuts.)

Yet the most fundamental kind of change that takes place is less
obvious, although continual. This is the variation that occurs over the
years in the relative popularity of individual games. At any one time

some games are gaining in popularity; some, presumably, are at their peak; and others are in marked decline; and this variation affects not only the frequency with which each game is played but its actual composition. Thus games that are approaching their peak of popularity are easily recognizable, just as are customs and institutions that are nearing their zenith and about to decay. A game enjoying absolute favour fatally attracts additional rules and formalities; the sport becomes progressively more elaborate, the playing of it demands further finesse, and the length of time required for its completion markedly increases. (In our day "Statues" was a simple amusement of seeing who, after a sharp pull, could be the best statue; today it is a procedure-ridden pastime incorporating at least four additional operations.) Indeed, as a game grows in popularity its very name may grow. (Thirty years ago in Liss the old game known as "Stoop" was already being called "Three Stoops and Run for Your Life;" today, still more popular, it is "Three Stoops, Three Pokers, and Run for Your Life.") On the other hand, games which are in a decline lose their trimmings; the players become disdainful of all but the actual contest; the time-taking preliminaries and poetic formulas which gave the name its quality are discarded; and fragments of the game may even be taken over by another game that is on the up-grade (part of the introductory formula of "Hickety Bickety," for instance, is now repeated in the seeking game, "North, South, East, West").

The identification and listing of games that have been declining in popularity over the past fifty years, and those that have been most noticeably gaining in popularity, may help to show the factors that currently affect children's choice of games.

Games diminishing in popularity	Games growing in popularity
Anything under the Sun	Bad Eggs (a ball game)
Baste the Bear (virtually obsolete)	Bar the Door
Blind Man's Buff	Block
Bull in the Ring	British Bulldog
Cat and Mouse	Budge He
Crust and Crumbs	Donkey (a ball-bouncing game)
Duckstone (an aiming game)	Fairies and Witches
Finger or Thumb?	Farmer, Farmer, may we cross your Golden River?
Fool, Fool, Come to School	Film Stars
French and English	Hi Jimmy Knacker
Hide and Seek (the simple form)	I Draw a Snake upon your Back
Honey Pots	Jack, Jack, Shine a Light
I Sent My Son John	Kerb or Wall
King of the Castle	

Kiss in the Ring

Knifie (Mumbletypeg)

Leapfrog

Odd and Even (a gambling game)

Old Man in the Well

Prisoners' Base

Sardines

Stag

Stroke the Baby (Hot Cockles)

Territories

Tipcat

Tom Tiddler's Ground

Touch Iron and Touchwood

Tug of War

Twos and Threes

Warning

Kingy

Kiss Chase

May I?

Off-Ground He

Peep Behind the Curtain

Poison

Queenie (in its new form)

Relievo

Split the Kipper

Statues

Stuck in the Mud

Three Stoops and Run For Ever

Tin Can Tommy

Touch Colour

Truth, Dare, Promise, or Opinion

What's the time, Mr. Wolf?

There has been a marked decrease in the playing of games in which one player is repeatedly buffeted by the rest. (It is apparently not now felt as amusing as it used to be that one player should remain at a disadvantage indefinitely.) There has been an increase (possibly a corresponding increase) in the playing of games in which children fight each other on roughly equal terms. Above all, we feel it is no coincidence that the games whose decline is most pronounced are those which are best known to adults, and therefore the most often promoted by them; while the games and amusements that flourish are those that adults find most difficulty in encouraging (e.g. knife-throwing games and chases in the dark), or are those sports, such as ball-bouncing and long-rope skipping, in which adults are ordinarily least able to show proficiency.

WHERE CHILDREN PLAY: PLAYING IN THE STREET

Where children are is where they play. They are impatient to be started, the street is no further than their front door, and they are within call when tea is ready. Indeed the street in front of their home is seemingly theirs, more theirs sometimes than the family living-room; and of more significance to them, very often, than any amenity provided by the local council. When a young coloured boy from Notting Hill was being given a week's holiday in a Wiltshire village, and was asked how he liked the country, he promptly replied, "I like it—but you can't play in the road as you can in London."

Yet, as we know, Zechariah's vision of the new Jerusalem is not as splendid in practice as he makes it appear. Windows are liable to be broken, caretakers appear from blocks of flats telling the children to keep off the grass, obstinate car-drivers insist on making their way down the street, and, nightly, little dramas are enacted between ten-year-olds and the tendentious:

> We were having a lovely game of Relievo when a man across the the road came out and moved us. My friend Ann said, "Oh shut up you're always moaning." Then the man said, "I will see your father about this it is going too far. Someone is trying to have a sleep." Then my other friend said "So is my dad." Then the man shouted for his dog Flash and sent him after us.

What is curious about these embroilments is that children always do seem to have been in trouble about the places where they played. In the nineteenth century there were repeated complaints that the pavements of London were made impassable by children's shuttlecock and tipcat.[1] In Stuart times, Richard Steele reported, the vicinity of the Royal Exchange was infested with uninvited sportsmen, and a beadle was employed to whip away the "unlucky Boys with Toys and Balls." Even in the Middle Ages, when it might be supposed a meadow was within reach of every Jack and Jill in Britain, the young had a way of gravitating to unsuitable places. In 1332 it was found necessary to prohibit boys and others from playing in the precincts of the Palace at Westminster while Parliament was sitting. In 1385 the Bishop of London was forced to declaim against the ball-play about St. Paul's; and in 1447, away in Devonshire, the Bishop of Exeter was complaining of "yung peple" playing in the cloister, even during divine service, such games as "the toppe, queke, penny prykke, and most atte tenys, by the which the walles of the saide Cloistre have be defowled and the glas wyndowes all to brost."

Should such persistant choice of busy and provocative play-places alert us that all is not as appears in the ghettos of childhood? Children's deepest pleasure, as we shall see, is to be away in the wastelands, yet they do not care to separate themselves altogether from the adult world. In some forms of their play (or in certain moods), they seem deliberately to attract attention to themselves, screaming, scribbling on the pavements, smashing milk bottles, banging on doors, and getting in people's way. A single group of children were able to name twenty games they played

---

1. "This mania for playing at cat," commented *Punch*, 23 April 1853, "is no less absurd than dangerous, for it is a game at which nobody seems to win, and which, apparently, has no other aim than the windows of the houses, and the heads of the passengers."

which involved running across the road. Are children, in some of their games, expressing something more than high spirits, something of which not even they, perhaps, are aware? No section of the community is more rooted to where it lives than the young. When children engage in "Last Across" in front of a car is it just devilment that prompts the sport, or may it be some impulse of protest in the tribe? Perhaps those people will appreciate this question most who have asked themselves whether the convenience of motorists thrusting through a town or village is really as important as the well-being of the people whose settlement it is, and who are attempting to live their lives in it.

PLAY IN RESTRICTED ENVIRONMENT

It is a pleasant sight to see the young play with those of their own age at tick, puss in the corner, hop-scotch, ring-taw, and hot beans ready buttered; and in these boyish amusements much self-denial and good nature may be practised. This, however, is not always the case . . .
The Boy's Week-Day Book, 1834

The places specially made for children's play are also the places where children can most easily be watched playing: the asphalt expanses of school playgrounds, the cage-like enclosures filled with junk by a local authority, the corners of recreation grounds stocked with swings and slides. In a playground children are, or are not, allowed to make chalk diagrams on the ground for hopscotch, to bounce balls against a wall, to bring marbles or skipping ropes, to play "Conkers," "Split the Kipper," "Hi Jimmy Knacker." Children of different ages may or may not be kept apart; boys may or may not be separated from girls. And according to the closeness of the supervision they organize gangs, carry out vendettas, place people in Coventry, gamble, bribe, blackmail, squabble, bully, and fight. The real nature of young boys has long been apparent to us, or so it has seemed. We have only to travel in a crowded school bus to be conscious of their belligerency, the extraordinary way they have of assailing each other, verbally and physically, each child feeling—perhaps with reason—that it is necessary to keep his end up against the rest. We know from accounts of previous generations with what good reason the great boarding schools, and other schools following, limited boys' free time, and made supervised games a compulsory part of the curriculum. As Sydney Smith wrote in 1810, it had become an "immemorial custom" in the public schools that every boy should be alternately tyrant and slave. The tyranny of the monitors at Christ's Hospital, wrote Lamb, was "heart-sickening to call to recollection." Southey's friend who went to Charterhouse was nearly killed by the cruelty of the other boys who "used to lay him before the fire till he was scorched, and shut him in a trunk with sawdust till he had nearly expired with suffocation." Even at Marlborough, not founded until 1843, a new boy might be branded with an anchor by means of a red-hot poker. And at so tranquil-seeming an establishment as Harnish Rectory, run by the Revd. Robert Kilvert, some of the boys were "a set of little monsters" in their depravity. "The first evening I was there," recalled Augustus Hare, "at nine years old, I was compelled to eat Eve's apple quite up—indeed, the Tree of Knowledge of Good and Evil was stripped absolutely bare: there was no fruit left to gather."

Such accounts, which can usually be reinforced by personal experience of school life, have increasingly influenced educational practice over the past hundred years, leading us to believe that a *Lord of the Flies* mentality is inherent in the young. Yet there is no certainty that this judgment is well founded. In one respect we remain as perverse as we were in Spencer's day, devoting more time to observing the ways of animals than of our own young. Thus recent extensive studies of apes and monkeys have shown, perhaps not unexpectedly, that animal behaviour in captivity is not the same as in the wild. In the natural habitat the welfare of the troop as a whole is paramount, the authority of the experienced animal is accepted, the idiosyncrasies of members of the troop are respected. But when the same species is confined and over-crowded the toughest and least-sensitive animal comes to the top, a pecking order develops, bullying and debauchery become common, and each creature when abused takes his revenge on the creature next weakest to himself. In brief, it appears that when lower primates are in the wild, and fending for themselves, their behaviour is "civilized," certainly in comparison with their behaviour when they are confined and cared for, which is when they most behave "like animals."

Our observations of children lead us to believe that much the same is true of our species. We have noticed that when children are herded together in the playground, which is where the educationalists and the psychologists and the social scientists gather to observe them, their play is markedly more aggressive than when they are in the street or in the wild places. At school they play "Ball He," "Dodge Ball," "Chain Swing," and "Bull in the Ring." They indulge in duels such as "Slappies," "Knuckles," and "Stinging," in which the pleasure, if not the purpose, of the game is to dominate another player and inflict pain. In a playground it is impracticable to play the free-ranging games like "Hide and Seek" and "Relievo" and "Kick the Can," that are, as Stevenson said, the "well-spring of romance," and are natural to children in the wastelands.

Often, when we have asked children what games they played in the playground we have been told "We just go round aggravating people." Nine-year-old boys make-believe they are Black Riders and in a mob charge on the girls. They play "Coshes" with knotted handkerchiefs, they snatch the girls' ties or hair ribbons and call it "Strip Tease," they join hands in a line and rush round the playground shouting "Anyone who gets in our way will get knocked over," they play "Tweaking," running behind a person and tweaking the lobe of his ear as they run off. One teacher, who asked her own six-year-old what game he really enjoyed at school, was surprised to find it was "getting gangs on to people." He said, "We get in a line and slap our sides as we run, and push down or bump a child."

Such behaviour would not be tolerated amongst the players in the street or the wasteland; and for a long time we had difficulty reconciling these accounts with the thoughtfulness and respect for the juvenile code that we had noticed in the quiet places. Then we recollected how, in our own day, children who had seemed unpleasant at school (whose term-time behaviour at boarding school had indeed been barbarous), turned out to be surprisingly civilized when we met them in the holidays. We remembered hearing how certain inmates of institutions, and even people in concentration camps during the war, far from having a feeling of cama-raderie, were liable to seek their pleasure in making life still more intol-erable for those who were confined with them (see, for instance, Pierre d'Harcourt, *The Real Enemy*). It seems to us that something is lacking in our understanding of the child community, that we have forgotten Cowper's dictum that "Great schools suit best the sturdy and the rough," and that in our continual search for efficient units of educational admin-istration we have overlooked that the most precious gift we can give the young is social space: the necessary space—or privacy—in which to be-come human beings.

THE WASTELANDS

There is no doubt that the first world war and the coming of the motor car killed, I suppose for ever, the playing of street games in this country.
                                                                        H. E. Bates

Children are all about us, living in our own homes, eating at our tables, and it might be wondered how we ever supposed (along with H. E. Bates, J. B. Priestley, Richard Church, Howard Spring, and other professional observers of the social scene) that they had stopped play-ing in the way we ourselves used to play. Yet the belief that traditional games are dying out is itself traditional; it was received opinion even when those who now regret the passing of the games were themselves vigorously playing them. We overlook the fact that as we have grown older our interests have changed, we have given up haunting the places where children play, we no longer have eyes for the games, and not noticing them suppose them to have vanished. We forget that children's amusements are not always ones that attract attention. They are not prearranged rituals for which the players wear distinctive uniforms, freshly laundered. Unlike the obtrusive sports of grown men, for which ground has to be permanently set aside and perpetually tended, children's games are ones which the players adapt to their surroundings and the time available. In fact most street games are as happily played in the dark as in the light. To a child "sport is sweetest when there be no spectators." The places they like best for play are the secret places "where no one else goes."

The literature of childhood abounds with evidence that the peaks of a child's experience are not visits to a cinema, or even family outings to the sea, but occasions when he escapes into places that are discussed and overgrown and silent. To a child there is more joy in a rubbish tip than a flowering rockery, in a fallen tree than a piece of statuary, in a muddy track than a gravel path. Like Stanley Spencer he may "see more in a dustbin in his village than in a cathedral abroad." Yet the cult amongst his elders is to trim, to pave, to smooth out, to clean-up to prettify, to convert to economic advantage—as if "the maximum utilisation of surrounding amenities" had become a line of poetry.

Ironically the bombing of London was a blessing to the youthful generations that followed. "We live facing a bombsite where boys throw stones, light fires, make camps and roast potatoes," writes an eleven-year-old: "In my neighborhood," wrote a Peckham child in 1955, "the sites of Hitler's bombs are many, and the bigger sites with a certain amount of rubble provide very good grounds for Hide and Seek and Tin Can Tommy." To a child the best parts of a park are the parts that are the least maintained. It is his nature to be attracted to the slopes, the bushes, the long grass, the waterside. "Ours is a good park there are still places in it that are wild," observed a ten-year-old. But what do the authorities do? They exploit our wealth to make improvements for the worse. They invade the parks, erecting kiosks and tea gardens, and side-shows for those who require their entertainments ready-made. It is not only Battersea Park (the enchanted garden of our childhood) that has been turned into a honky-tonk. The trend is universal. In one small town we know there are some municipal gardens, the only place where children can play, and on the largest lawn they have laid-out and fenced off an immense bowling green for the summer pleasure of the middle-aged. The centre of our own home town possessed, miraculously, until two years ago, a small dark wood adjoining a car park. If an adult entered its shade he might imagine he was alone, unless he became aware that the trees above his head were a playground for Lilliputians. Now the trees have been cut down, the ground levelled, a stream canalized, and the area flooded with asphalt to make an extension to the car park. Should we be surprised if children play around the cars, if cars get damaged, if sometimes boys are tempted to more serious offenses? Having cleared away the places that are naturally wild it is becoming the fashion to set aside other places, deposit junk in them, and create "Adventure Playgrounds," so called, the equivalent of creating Whipsnades for wild life instead of erecting actual cages. The next need is to advertise in *The Times Educational Supplement* (for example 8 February 1963) for Play Leaders at 32s for 2 1/2 hours: apply Chief Officer (A/B/197/2) L.C.C. Parks Department, County Hall, S.E. I. (WAT 5000 Ext. 7621) P.K. A2. Or, more recently (24 January 1969) for "Senior Play Leader" at 40s. 6d. for 2 1/2 hours: apply Parks Department, Cavell House, 2a Charing Cross Rd., W.C. 2, 836 5464, Ext. 144. The provision of playmates for the young has become an item of public expenditure.

In the past, traditional games were thought to be dying out, few people cared, and the games continued to flourish. In the present day we assume children to have lost the ability to entertain themselves, we become concerned, and are liable, by our concern, to make what is not true a reality. In the long run, nothing extinguishes self-organized play more effectively than does action to promote it. It is not only natural but beneficial that there should be a gulf between the generations in their choice of recreation. Those people are happiest who can most rely on their own resources; and it is to be wondered whether middle-class children in the United States will ever reach maturity "whose playtime has become almost as completely organized and supervised as their study" (Carl Withers). If children's games are tamed and made part of school curricula, if wastelands are turned into playing-fields for the benefit of those who conform and ape their elders, if children are given the idea that they cannot enjoy themselves without being provided with the "proper" equipment, we need blame only ourselves when we produce a generation who have lost their dignity, who are ever dissatisfied, and who descend for their sport to the easy excitement of rioting, or pilfering, or vandalism. But to say that children should be allowed this last freedom, to play their own games in their own way, is scarcely to say more than John Locke said almost three centuries ago:

Children have as much a Mind to shew that they are free, that their own good Actions come from themselves, that they are absolute and independent, as any of the proudest of your grown Men.

And speaking of their recreation he observed how it was freedom "they extreamly affect"; it was "that Liberty alone which gives the true Relish and Delight to their ordinary Play Games."

PIGSKIN REVIEW: AN AMERICAN INITIATION

SHIRLEY FISKE

INTRODUCTION

> We anthropologists treat a familiar culture as though it were a
> strange one . . . we consciously choose this approach so that we may
> view the culture from a new angle and throw into relief features obscured
> by other forms of study. (Nadel 1951:7)

This statement succinctly sums the prime impetus for writing this
paper: it is imperative to adopt the analytic framework of anthropology
in order to explain in proper perspective events which occur in our own
culture. Let us consider what we Americans think to be a harmless athletic contest: when closely inspected through the Truth-Lens of anthropology, it is actually a stealthy type of ritual behavior escaped from
"primitive" camps. American traditions are ethnologically cubby-holed
curiosities paralleling those found in pre-literate cultures throughout the
world. Basic cultural processes which produce behavioral similarities
across technological gulfs may manifest themselves in forms somewhat
sheltered from the awareness of the natives, but they do not cease to
operate.

Having direct contact with several football players and the coaches
of a well-known university, I observed many of their quaint customs
and beliefs; as the season progressed, my Anthropology-Eyes brightened,
for the various ritual behaviors closely resembled that which in other
cultures is labeled "puberty rites," or "initiation ceremonies." Further
investigation along these lines has supported my hypothesis—this study
is an effort to demonstrate that the actual nature of a football season

Printed with permission of the author.

is an initiation into adulthood. The format for the body of this paper
is first, a brief review of the theoretical background of initiation ceremonies, the presentation of the data gathered, and the analysis and
interpretation of it. Finally, perhaps some alteration may be made in
the models as a result of studying the rite in our own culture.

Before embarking on the major discussion of this paper, it might
be well to justify the relevance of *collegiate* football to initiation ceremonies, and also the choice of the University of Southern California as
the subject of analysis. Football events range in ritual content on a continuum from the football of high school to that of college and then professional ball. A cross-cutting dimension is that of athletic entertainment,
an economic criterion relating to the outside society. High school football
and professional football are at the extremes of these axes: high school
football does not have the elaborate ritual of collegiate football, and
furthermore it is primarily an athletic contest, without important economic ramifications. Professional football is on the other end of the

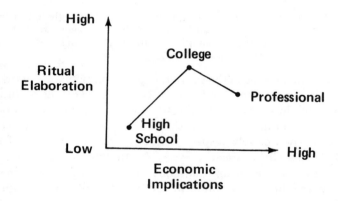

economic extreme—its very existence is determined by the economic
conditions it creates. It rates lower on ritual concomitants than college,
but higher than high school; it is not a a temporary status during one's
lifetime, but is a mode of living for the players, so it has not the symbolic content of initiation ceremonies. Professional football is a specialized type of entertainment of a very different nature than collegiate
football, where team members are competing among themselves for a
livelihood.

The justification for the choice of schools from among many colleges
is twofold: first, the proximity of location, and the accessibility of data;
secondly, and more importantly, the University of Southern California

is the epitome of a college enmeshed in football tradition. The fervor and pride generated by the football team are evident to an extreme degree. USC represents college life and the football centrifuge at its peak development, approximately as it was across the nation previous to the current trend to de-emphasize athletics in favor of intellectualism. *Middletown,* although published in 1929, illustrates the strength of the American pride even in the choice of a college: " 'My daughter plans to go to the University of ....,' said one mother, 'because, she says, 'Mother, I just *couldn't* go to a college whose athletics I couldn't be proud of' " (Lynd 1929:214). A successful football team brings honor and develops pride in the social, academic, and economic attitudes of individuals at SC; these attitudes represent the reverence and the un-questioning importance of the role of football in college life which was once the norm on all college campuses. This exposé, then, revolves around showing that American college football can be considered an initiation ceremony, occurring on the threshhold of the status change from adolescence to adulthood.

THEORETICAL BACKGROUND

The occurrence of ritual at puberty has posed a rather complex problem for anthropologists. It reflects both the physical aspect of reproductive maturity; as well, it is at this point that the individual has attained the socio-emotional responsibility of adulthood. In most socie-ties, there is some association in peoples' minds between the notion of sexual maturity and that of social maturity: for this reason, the puberty ritual is described by anthropologists as an "initiation ceremony," or "rite of passage" from one role to another. Puberty is a sign of the final and completed difference between the man's body and the woman's—a time when both sexes must assume their respective masculine and femi-nine roles.

The flexibility of these rites in marking both a cultural and physical change in the individual has shown amazing variability in the types of ritual of the event. The adaptability of the initiation ritual is one of its foremost features, for it is found in some form, however sublimated, in all societies. One group may stress the aspects of proper training for parenthood and emphasize appropriate role assumption. All primitive societies have some method of marking this dual change; the same pro-cess is at work in familiar institutions within our own society.

A consideration of initiation rites reveals many types, for each society marks the initiations of the individual throughout his life cycle without recognition of the modes of transition—e.g., baptism, confirmation, graduation, puberty, marriage. Most of these examples indicate a transition from one social role to another to be adopted. In our American society, a frequent, and one of the most obvious, types of initiation, is that into a closed group, club, or fraternity—often, interestingly, with a sex-linked membership requirement[1]—where there is some form of testing or hazing connected with entering the group. Naturally, sororities and fraternities stand as good examples of this type of initiation, as well as Shriners, Elks, and secret societies. These initiation ceremonies share much in common with the transition into adulthood, *viz.*, the individual is given new duties, rights, and responsibilities, and a new set of people with which to interact in a new role; nonetheless, they differ fundamentally from puberty rites, with which we are concerned, for they do not apply equally over the vast majority of men or women in that particular age-grade. The ceremony and the adoption of the new role has no wider significance than the small sub-group of the society to which it pertains, and would not be understood by the wider audience.

Hence the passage from one social situation to another is often accompanied by some form of *rite de passage*. However, the most important transition for any society is the transition from adolescence to adulthood, because it is here that the cognitive-emotional training for adult roles is condensed, and this is the most crucial period for transmission. The childhood bonds, especially with parents, are broken and adult values are instilled in both young men and young women. Each society must have a way of dramatizing the importance of adopting these values which will perpetuate the society; for if there were no importance attached to the way to become a proper adult person—if there were no values inculcated in growing citizens—then that society would function less than economically.[2]

Due to a desire for brevity, I will summarize only three of the authors who have written definitively on the anthropology of initiation into adulthood; Van Gennep (1909), Whiting (1958, 1960, 1964), and Young (1962, 1965).

Since the first major treatise elucidating the subject in 1909, Van Gennep's comprehensive *Les Rites de Passage*, no one has seriously shaken his basic postulates concerning the generic category of rites of passage. Throughout an initiation ceremony, Van Gennep emphasized

---

1. The sexes are also segregated in most preliterate societies' initiation ceremonies into adulthood.
2. Since values are usually (historically and in some contemporary societies) passed on from elders to younger generations with little or no questioning allowed, it will be interesting to see what comes out of the current situation where we are questioning the very validity of accepting without questioning the basic assumptions of our social systems that our elders hand down to us.

the importance of the transition from the profane world to that of the sacred. The person who enters a new status at variance with one formerly held becomes "sacred" to the others who remain in the "profane" world.

The rites have a common function, in easing the individual in transition from one social role to another, and they also have common stages. There is a separation or death from the old state of being, a transition between the two states, and an incorporation or rebirth into the new one. An important feature is often that of symbolic dramatization of the stages: separation or death is often symbolized in physical seclusion (a bush camp, or a separate building or corporal punishment (whipping, beating, etc.) of the initiates; "the purpose is to make the novice 'die,' to make him forget his former personality and his former world" (Van Gennep 1909:81, n. 2). The transition period allows the initiates to interact with the other members of the society, but often on a markedly different level—i.e., with special favors, compensations, etc., from others, for the novices are still in the "sacred" sphere relative to the rest of the society. Rebirth or incorporation is a phase which occurs variably in different societies. During this period, initiates may act as though they are newly born, and must relearn all the gestures of ordinary life. The individual is symbolically reintegrated into the ways of the society, only this time with a new social role—adulthood.[3]

While Van Gennep considers initiation to be a dramatization of role change through the opposition of profane and sacred worlds, the two authors who we will consider next felt that initiation emphasizes *sex* role adoption in adulthood. In three consecutive articles (Whiting, Kluckhohn, and Anthony 1958, Burton and Whiting 1960, and Whiting 1964), Whiting, through thorough cross-cultural research, upheld what has become known as his "cross sex identity" hypothesis. This hypothesis maintains that in those societies where it is necessary to switch the child or adolescent abruptly from an identification with his mother to that of the father, then this will be marked by a severe initiation ritual. That is, where children grow up emotionally very close to their mothers, then,

3. Although the influence of Durkheim's previous work is evident in Van Gennep's theory (in the primacy of the social nature of phenomena, and the division of the world into sacred and profane spheres), Durkheim in his works subsequent to Van Gennep's perceived initiation ceremonies as essentially religious events. In his *Elementary Forms of Religious Life* he states that initiation ceremonies are, foremost, instruments which emphasize the "essential duality of the two kingdoms sacred and profane" (Durkheim 1913:39). It implies a "veritable metamorphosis" for Durkheim, who sees the ceremony as indicative of a transformation of the whole being. The individual leaves the purely profane world and enters the sacred world.

See also James Bossard and Eleanor Boll (1948), who analyzed the debutantes' presentation to society as a contemporary rite of passage using Van Gennep's criteria.

if they are a male, in order to insure proper adult behavior, the former bonds must be broken in favor of male role assumption.[4] The dimensions of a ceremony necessary to call that event an adolescent initiation are the presence of one of the following: (1) painful hazing by adult males; (2) genital operations; (3) seclusion from women; (4) tests of manliness (Whiting, Kluckhohn, and Anthony 1958:360).

Frank Young also looks at initiation ceremonies via cross-cultural methodology, and concludes somewhat similarly that initiation ceremonies serve to dramatize sex role recognition and reinforce social solidarity of adult males. Young removes the causation from the realm of infantile fixations and places it on a societal level.

Sex role dramatization is necessary where there is a high degree of male solidarity, defined as the consensus among the men regarding the purpose and activities of males (Young 1962:387).[5] Young notes that this situation usually occurs in societies where resources are exploited by cooperation, and where intergroup hostilities are conducive to male solidarity.

The social meaning of male solidarity must be dramatized in a memorable way; the candidate must participate intensely. Young offers a scale of degrees of dramatization of initiation rites, from the lowest step of customary minimal social recognition (gifts, party, change of names), to the next step, social seclusion (physical or social separation), then personal dramatization (initiate is ceremoniously dressed and/or gives a public performance), organized social response (group dresses ceremonially and/or performs), and finally the most dramatic step— emotionalized social response (beating or hazing) (Young 1962:385).

Whiting and Young led a spirited controversy over their respective interpretations of initiation ceremonies. Using the techniques available through their methodology, they come to a close agreement on the ultimate value of initiation as a technique of male sex identification: their main disagreement resides in the interpretation of systems of causation —Whiting emphasizes childhood patterns of behavior and emotions and the necessity of breaking them, and Young chooses to place causation on the societal level in the form of male solidarity.

---

4. Two conditions which might lead to this situation where there is maximum conflict in sexual identity—where a boy has initial exclusive sleeping arrangements with his mother, but where the domestic unit is patrilocal and controlled by men.

5. The degrees of male solidarity are indicated on the following scale from low to high: (1) informal solidarity that does not attain the behavioral expression; (2) exclusive male activity for adult males, protected by physical or normative perception barriers; (3) ritualization of male activity, at least in part; (4) definite ranking of men within the activity; (5) training for war a part of the activity (Young 1965:67).

CEREMONIAL DATA

I would like to demonstrate that the "athletic" phenomenon of American collegiate football may be considered an initiation ceremony celebrating the status change from adolescence to adulthood.

The data is of two kinds: first, the actual descriptions of the formal content of the ceremony itself. This data is derived from interviews with the players and coaches, and from my own observation. To clarify, the actual strategy employed in the defensive-offensive maneuvers on field during a game does not concern us except symbolically; the many plays and formations are relatively unimportant except inasfar as they demonstrate the elaborate and highly ritualized nature of the ceremony. I have interviewed four players, consulted manuals, and observed behavior. There is little or no disagreement among the sources about the formal characteristics of the program—these are explicit, clear-cut events.

The second type of data is what is generally referred to as the "native's viewpoint" of the reasons for and the effects of the ceremony. This aspect necessarily involves interpretation on the part of both informant and the anthropologist, so I spoke to many more individuals to get a representative view. As well as the four initiates, I spoke to three of their coaches, the head yell leader, and engaged innumerable individuals in informal discussion about the importance of the football festivals.

The duration of the ceremony is eight months, each year, with the activity concentrated in the first four months. During the four weeks of intense ritual activity, there are discrete weekly festivals. Membership in the novice group is a desirable goal for all young males, although only the most fit are allowed to participate. A boy may enter the activities for one year or up to four years, but not more; and once he has begun the yearly cycle, quitting it is accompanied by a heavy stigma both among the initiates and in the society at large.

The Setting: The sacred ground upon which the public part of the ceremony occurs (weekly for eleven weeks) is a rectangular field, 100 yds. long. The spectators gather on all sides to watch the ceremony. Public rites occur in this setting.

The Personnel: These people of the ceremony can be classified into the actual participant, the affiliates, and the spectators; each of these is removed one degree further from emotional identification with the novice group, respectively. The first group is the most important, obviously. It is composed of a set of seven directors (elders), one of which is the head co-ordinator who is oldest and who has accumulated vast wisdom. He is revered and respected. The other participants are the initiates themselves—usually about seventy—who are ranked internally according to ability to perform properly and according to senority. The hierarchy, from the top down, is composed of groups referred to as the "varsity," the "red shirts," and the "j.v.s."

The affiliated personnel travel with the novices when ceremonies occur at fields other than their own. They do not participate in the ceremony directly, nor are they admitted to the secret meetings or secluded areas. The affiliated personnel are of two kinds: there are specialized individuals hired to care for certain needs of the novices (team "trainers" and "managers"), and there are individuals whose goal is the interpretation of the novices' actions to the audience during public performances. These virginous dancers and their male counterparts ("yell leaders," and "song girls") lead organized chants and incite emotionalized responses from the crowd during the performance.

The last group is the audience, which is composed of multitudes of people, both kin and non-kin. They must remain off the sacred ground whenever the novices occupy it, but are encouraged to react vocally and with gestures to the movements of the novices on the field.

Various phases of the ceremony emerge from the data, and are given below along with a brief synopsis of their import.

Yearly Ceremonial Cycle
Phase I: "Double Days"

The official schedule starts in early September, for a period of two weeks before the first public ceremony. This period is termed "Double Days" (because the novices practice two times a day, and is designed to promote unity among the group through hard work, fatigue, and practice. There is a set number of gatherings which can occur, ruled by higher authorities in the nation. The novices are confined to a strict daily schedule. They are secluded from women, and their diet is controlled—the initiated eat all meals together in an institution known as "Training Table"—and certain foods with a high concentration of starch and carbohydrates are taboo. This period is characterized by the initiates as a very trying, tiring time, and very tense because all the novices are living in such close quarters. The daily schedule is reproduced below. There is a four-day break before the first public ceremony.

7:00 A.M.	Awakened
7:30	Eat first meal of the day together
9:00	On a secret field, dressed in costumes, participate in rigorous physical activity for two hours
11:00	Off field

12:00 P.M.	Eat second meal together
2:00	On field again, repeat same physical punishment as earlier
4:00	End punishment
5:30	Eat third meal together; the meals have been planned by the elders according to specific regulations
6:00	Meeting of all novices, presided over by elders, to discuss the inadequacies of the novices; psychologically harassed.
8:00	End of gathering; the novices are now free to mingle with each other, but they cannot leave the building.
10:30	Bed check by the elders to see if all novices are in bed.

Phase II: "The Season"

The cycle now enters a period lasting through December 7, characterized by weekly confrontations between the initiates of this group and those of the same age-group, but of a different locality. Traditionally, these are considered hostile encounters, varying in degree of hostility between the groups. Open hostility is precluded by the set ritual of the game in which the two groups engage.

This period, where the initiates are once again interacting with society, is still characterized by numerous taboos, such as sex on the nights preceding the contest, and on diet, and even implicitly on their personal appearance. There are secret meetings daily for two hours, during which time there is continued physical punishment. On the evenings and mornings before each public ceremony, the novices are secluded. In addition, they are also exempt from many of the requirements of their peers. Within their living groups (most noticeably, frats) they are excused from duties, both physical and mental. In interaction with their peers, they are given great deference and respect. Even in interaction with their superiors such as administrators of the educational institution and their instructors of formal education, they are excused from duties which others must execute, such as tests, papers, etc. On an even higher plane, the novices are exempt from induction (armed service) while they maintain their ability to participate (through mediation of the elders).

There are two variants of the weekly schedule; one is adapted for ceremonies which will occur on the sacred field of another institution, and the other is adapted for events which will occur on the home field. The major difference in the schedules is that the rally is usually moved up to Thursday, and the novices fly to the other field and back again. The generalized schedule is reproduced here:

| Mon: | 3:00 | Meeting of all novices |
| | 3:30 | On field in secret session; wear "sweats" |

	5:30	Off field
	6:00	Eat dinner together
Tues:	3:00	Meeting
	3:30	On field, with more elaborate dress than Mon., called "full dress"
	5:30	Watch films
Wed:		Same as Tues.
Thurs:	3:00	Meeting
	3:30	On field, work on entire ceremony together
	5:30	Off field
	6:00	Eat together
Fri:	3:00	Meeting
	3:30	Brief practice
	4:00	Off field—Nearing the culmination of the weekly routine, the peers of the initiates express their appreciation and devotion, loyalty and admiration, to the novices. The affiliates organize a crowd around the players as they exit from the secret practice and pass through their admirers, always showing extreme modesty, into another sacrosanct area called the "Locker Room." At this time, the elders take little part in the ceremony; they call upon the weekly leader ("team captain") of the novices, who speaks to the crowd. The crowd responds with traditional chants of encouragement to the novices, urging them to honorable victory in the forthcoming contest.
	6:00	Eat dinner together
	7:00	Seclusion (in the "Sheraton Wilshire Hotel")
	7:30	Entertainment (motion picture) viewed by the novices as a group, and apart from the rest of society. The lodging and entertainment are of the finest quality available.
	10:30	Elders "bed check" to make sure the novices are in bed
Sat:	8:00	Orange juice served in bed
	9:00	Last meal served before the contest: steak and eggs
	11:00	Meeting of the entire group; the *chief elder* (in a rare appearance) talks to the team
	12:00	Novices go to the sacred field, where they are dressed in colorful costumes and protective padding of debatable protectiveness. At this time the "trainer" lovingly massages, tapes, and wraps the bodies of the participants. The costumes are symbolic in that the whole team is identified by a particular color of the costumes, but each individual is given specific recognition by his identifying number.

    1:00   The novices warm up, doing various gymnastics

    1:30   The novices emerge as if by magic from the bowels of the stadium, and are greeted by the cheers of the crowd; there is much that is symbolic in the actual maneuvers, the setup of the players on the bench, the hierarchy of coaches, the acceptance of authority by the novices, the actions of the affiliates (especially the virgins and their male counterparts), and the reaction of the crowd, but space does not permit its analysis here.

    4:00   End of contest—the novices are free.

Sun: 6:00   Novices assemble to watch "films," a magical method which can recreate the events of the last contest, and put the individuals' actions up for scrutiny and ridicule by the elders.

Ritual Elaboration: The novice group being victorious in all its confrontations, (USC was National Collegiate Champions in this year of 1967) was invited to perform publicly in opposition to another champion group. Since this is a *very* desirable goal (i.e., to play in a "Bowl" game), the novices were further honored and lauded, and there was further ritual elaboration of their initiation.

The daily schedule is the same as the one during "Double Days," and it continues for two weeks previous to the celebrated game. The novices are again secluded in an all-male residence, they eat their meals together, and are subjected to two brutal practices daily. During the first week, they are free to leave the building in the evenings (until 10:00 P.M.); during the second week, they must remain with the elders at all times.

The second week marks the highest degree of seclusion in the entire ceremonial cycle: the novices change their residence from the first week (dorms) and are secluded in the luxury accommodations formerly reserved for the night before the event. They are to speak only to their elders or another novice, they may not receive messages, or send them, or speak to anyone in the outside society.

The entertainment which is provided the novices is symbolically important. Two events are of special interest, although others occurred; there is no attempt to analyze them here. On the first Tuesday there is held a gigantic feast, specifically for the novices, and hosted free by a local merchant (Lawry's Prime Rib). The object of the feast is to consume as much beef as possible; for there is a myth accompanying the feast which states the prophecy that the group of novices which consumes the greatest quantity of beef will triumph in the contest. The feast is termed the "Beef Bowl," and the two groups of novices compete on different nights. (USC consumed 349 lbs.: Indiana consumed 280 lbs.)

An evening festival (closed party) was hosted for the novices, with various performers entertaining them. The highlight of the evening was the presentation of gifts to the novices, from representative groups in the outside society. Each novice received a silver platter (Chrysler Corp.), a transistor radio (RCA), a watch (Jurgenson), a pair of binoculars.

Phase III: Latency

After the final public ceremony, the novices are released from their authoritarian submission, and re-enter the social network, ostensibly free from the restrictions once imposed. However, they are in effective communication with the elders at all times, and constantly under their surveillance. The coaches are omniscient: they know the families, the girls the players date, the brawls, and the problems of all the players.

The novices now enter a latency period, with no formal structure intervening between the novices and their directors; the taboos, though implicit, are no longer agents of direct punishment. There is still much contact between the novices and directors, but its nature has changed —the novices are now entrusted to help with jobs which the coaches would ordinarily do themselves (recruiting); and there are scheduled conferences between the novices and his coach every two weeks.

Phase IV: "Spring Ball"

This is the final phase of the yearly cycle, and involves an emphasis on the role played by the *individual* novice and his skills, in contrast to the unity emphasis during Double Days. There are few restrictions placed on him in the form of seclusion or taboos. The main object is the competition between individuals, to beat out the other person who is competing for the same position.

The two-week phase is culminated on May 5 by a public ceremony, which is intra-novice; the top-ranked novices are pitted against the second-ranked. There is little ritual elaboration associated with this ceremony. After this event the novices are freed of all formal restrictions, taboos, etc.; they are on their own to use their best judgment in all situations. The summer may be a period of trial of the effectiveness of the indoctrination and internalization of the precepts passed on by the elders.

INTERPRETATION AND CONCLUSIONS

Having presented the data on the formal mechanics of the ceremony, I would like to show that football, as expressed by USC, may be considered an initation ceremony, according to the criteria of Van Gennep, Whiting et al., and Young. Ultimately, all these analyses involve a re-identification with the adult role, so it is necessary first to show this transition.

The period of adolescence in the U.S. has long been known as a turbulent transition period. The teen-age period reaches a culmination toward the end, from ages seventeen to twenty, and a symbolic rite is necessary to focus attention of the adult dogma to be assimilated . . . this is the role of football.

Ralph Linton makes an important observation when he states that the puberty ceremony in the U. S. depends to a great extent on the social class of the individual. For the lower levels, the parents ask children to extend down the bottom level of adulthood and become wage-earners early. Conversely, professional groups and people who send their children to college treat adolescence as a continuum of childhood, with economic dependence on parents perpetuating the submissive role of childhood. "For males in the higher social levels, a similar transition comes when the individual leaves the sheltered environment of college and embarks in the cut-throat competition of modern business" (Linton 1942:602).

Or, as Talcott Parsons notes, values of the young male must change rather abruptly from the youth culture with its emphasis on fun to a "prosaic business executive or lawyer" (Parsons 1942:8). The young man is expected to assume the mundane responsibilities of adult status, and football prepares him for this.

In terms of Van Gennep's scheme, the three phases which occur in rites of passage are evident. During Double Days the novice is separated from his previous environment, in relation to which he is "lost from the world," according to Coach Marv Goux. The comments of the novices also emphasize the death state: "It kills you," "You have to eat, sleep, think football," i.e., the novice is dead to the rest of society (Oliver, McConnell). There is grueling physical and mental punishment. The object of this period is the separation (mentally and psysically) of the initiates from society, and to create among the novices a sense of working as a *unit* for a desired goal. The behavior stressed during Double Days is opposed to the normal individually-oriented goal behavior, and hence symbolizes the death of the novice as an isolated individual, and entrance into a cooperative unit (*viz.* society).

The rites of transition are saliently marked by the increased inter-action of the novice in the society. No longer is he secluded, except for about three hours daily, and for the night before the public ceremony. The novices still eat together one meal daily, and the restrictions are more implicit than forced on them; the elders determine the right to dismiss any boy who by their judgment has not adhered to the taboos and whose behavior shows it. The transition period, then, swings from short periods of seclusion and ceremonial action to semi-normal inter-action within the society.

Rites of reintegration are accomplished during the third phase of the yearly cycle—Spring Ball. The reintegration does not utilize such drastic behavior as the novices pretending not to know how to walk, eat, etc. The rites are composed of the same elements of which the other phases are composed, but the emphasis is on the *individual,* and lends a contrasting atmosphere to that of Double Days of The Season. Spring Ball prepares the novice for action once again in the society, by con-centrating on the skills and performance of the individual player; com-petition within the group is high—this is a relearning process to prepare for reintegration within a competitive society.

Now let us turn to the dimensions of initiation as outlined by Whit-ing. Initiation is characterized by *one* or more of the following features according to Whiting's 1958 article: (1) painful hazing by adult males; (2) genital operations; (3) seclusion from women; (4) tests of endur-ance and manliness (Whiting, Kluckholn, and Anthony 1958:360). Foot-ball has all but the second element, and thus qualifies as an initiation ceremony.

Turning to Young's discussion of initiation ceremonies, we find that his solidarity hypothesis defines initiation ceremonies as dramatic forms of sex role recognition. On his scale of degree of dramatization of male initiation, football rates as one of the most dramatic of all possible rites. In addition, there are three criteria of the ceremonies: (1) it must be periodic in the same general form and supervised by adults. (2) it must apply to all adolescents of one sex only, and (3) of a series of initiation events only the most elaborate are to be considered. Football meets the demands of all three criteria, although the second deserves justification: the performance of football is a symbolic act of initiation for the entire male adolescent group. The college residence of each particular novice is conceived as his local tribal affiliation, although a pan-tribal identity with the age-grades of all adolescents exists above the provincial loyalty. The participation in the actual ceremony where the initiatory principles are displayed publically is limited to the few who are most capable and who represent most obviously the specifications of adult status. Although precipitation is limited to the fittest, the *principles* which are taught the novices apply to *all* adolescents of the tribe. And since the novices are objects of admiration and respect, the values which they represent are emulated by their male peers. The general precepts apply to all males;

football is a symbolic rite of transformation for the total adolescent group.

The previous analyses by Whiting, Van Gennep, and Young of the initiation event by a unidimensional model, i.e., in terms of the import on one conceptual level, bypasses much of the important ramifications of the ceremony. To understand the ceremony adequately it is necessary to view it through the cross-cutting levels of the individual, the peer age-grade, and the society. There is a different significance in the ritual for each subgroup of society, and it is inaccurate to interpret initiation as having an immutable or constant meaning for all members of the society. This tripartite view is more profitable to elucidate initiation, for it allows for the interplay of more variables in the explanation of it. The relation of the *individual* to the ceremony: The elders were much more adept and explicit in their answers to this question, having formulated the aims and hopes previously; the novices were more unsure about what it meant to participate in the event, and one novice refused to tell me, saying, "Do you think I'd tell *you*?" (McConnell). It emerged later that this was not a sexual taboo against telling me, but that the novice felt extremely moved by the ceremony and did not feel at ease in expressing his feelings.

There is, obviously, a physical aspect to the ceremony, and bodily fitness must be relevant to the novices. However, this element was rarely stressed when asked to relate their conceptions of the importance of football to their own lives. Instead, the importance of the ceremony to the novice is due to the development of personal qualities, all of which are deemed virtuous in adult society. The compiled list herein covers the most salient reasons why it is felt that the initiation cycle is significant in the lives of the novices.

1. Merlin Olsen, a celebrated post-novice, feels football allows men to concentrate on *work*, and develops a dedication which is carried on through one's life; he stresses that work is the greatest aid to creating *men*.
2. Closely related to this is the view that football forces an individual to become somewhat self-sacrificing for the good of a cooperative effort; it shows how to "sacrifice for the good of the whole organization and not just play for your own sake," as Coach Fertig puts it.
3. Within the general pattern of conformity, football teaches individuality (Kreuger). A player must conform to the training rules, and behavioral standards, but he is encouraged to express himself in

his playing formation. The second and third points together constitute a unitary quality: there is a contribution to the group effort
wholeheartedly, and yet allowance for the development of individuality *within the norms*.

4. The football ceremonies develop the ability to think quickly and
   clearly under pressure; the novice must mobilize all his knowledge
   and physical resources in split-second decisions (Fertig).
5. Leadership is developed, e.g., each weekly team captain represents
   the group in all public appearances.
6. The equality of individuals is taught, for the novices are judged on
   ability and performance.[6]
7. Football allows individuals to focus their socially unacceptable
   drives into something worthwhile (Krueger).
8. The experience of traveling with the group, exposure to public performance, being on display, develops in the novices a sense of social
   competence. "They are able to meet people in any circle and can
   handle themselves socially" (Fertig).
9. Football heightens the competitive desire "to win."
10. Of course there are the obvious attributes which are implicitly in-
    culcated and so explicitly demonstrated every Saturday afternoon:
    the sexual identification provided through the demonstration of
    manliness, aggressiveness, and prowess on the field. The traditional
    image of the "All-American male," and the "clean-cut football hero,"
    is emphasized and re-emphasized as a model.

Ideally, then, football has the facility to turn out perfect ideal-types,
according to the specifications of the older generation. The elders feel
that an individual will become a different person through playing the
game; the transformation will create adult members of a social organization. Phil Krueger cites the great number of football players who have
achieved successful transformation and become leading businessmen. He
emphasizes the point that football as a means to an end is all right; but
if it represents the high point in a player's life, then he's in trouble. In
effect, football should represent a transition phase through which one
develops the qualities necessary for successful adult orientation. "You
put yourself in a dangerous, yet controlled situation; and you become a
better man for having faced the danger" (Krueger).

---

6. Perhaps football teaches as well the racial hypocrisy which often permeates the
white world—although the black players are treated with all the respect due a white
player, and are accepted as equals among the white players, the elders segregate
along racial lines during the periods of seclusion: rarely does a white player room
with a black player.

Relation of the *peer age-group* to the ceremony: Being a symbolic ceremony, the relationships between the novices and their peers is a unique one, a dimension not yet explored in initiation ceremonies. Yet the relation is obvious, and is consonant with the expectations: the behavior and values of the novices serve as a model for males to emulate; they are desirable sexual objects for females, and this fact reinforces the behavior of the age-group in adopting the values.

Interestingly, part of the male image (which the peers also identify with) is the cultivating of the ability "to get away with" as much as possible without being caught. It is considered manly to flaunt authority, but only *up to a point*; and the novices know exactly where that threshold is which will invoke supernatural punishment—expulsion from ceremonial participation.

The relation of the society to the ceremony: One aspect is particularly outstanding when the ceremony is analyzed on this plane—the economic benefits circulated by the occurrence of the event. The ceremonies act as an attraction for financial backing of the university, as well as supporting activities from the profits gained from admission, concessions, etc. The money made in net profit alone from the football season at USC supports all the other athletic programs in the university (Krueger). The economic ramifications of the football season is amazingly intricate, affecting the welfare of the players (through the sale of their tickets), producers of sports equipment, contractors, and even the city council of Pasadena.

People like to identify with a group which shows successful application of the discipline and qualities admired by them; the alumni will support the institution if it can be proud of its accomplishments, and they judge the quality of its accomplishments through the performance of its football team. The primary importance of the ceremony differs for each group—for the individual, it is foremost a program of personal development; for the peer age-grade, it is a model to emulate; for the society, the economic factor looms most important.

The foremost task faced by each society is to perpetuate its ethnocentricity—its values and traditions. It must fashion a sense of *identity* for each adult which will incorporate those elements that must be passed to future generations.

In a culture as heterogeneous as America, this task is not easily accomplished. The diversity of role choice open to the adolescent necessites a centripetal force, to focus on a coherent and perceivable bundle of adult values with which to identify. Initiation, in the football ceremony, is a symbolic process whereby a confluence of the desired roles of adult life is achieved; and it is expedient to unify the diverse models of identification in order that transformation occur *effectively*.

REFERENCES

Bossard, James H. S. and Eleanor D. Boll. 1948. Rite of passage—a contemporary study. *Social Forces* 26:247-255.

Burton, Roger V. and John M. Whiting. 1960. The absent father and cross-sex identity. *Merrill-Palmer Quarterly* 7:85-95.

Durkheim, Emile. 1913. *Les formes elementaires de le vide religieuse*. Paris, Alcan. Trans. by Joseph Swain. *Elementary forms of religious life*. Glencoe, Ill.: The Free Press, 1947.

Fertig, Craig. 1968. Interview February 9, at USC; quarterback coach.

Goux, Marv. 1968. Interview Feb. 23, at USC; defensive linemen coach.

Krueger, Phil. 1968. Interview Feb. 9, at USC; coach of defensive ends and linebackers.

Linton, Ralph. 1942. Age and sex categories. *American Sociological Review* 7:589-603.

Lynd, Robert S. and Helen Merrell Lynd. 1929. *Middletown*. New York: Harcourt, Brace, and Co.

McConnell, Steve. 1968. Interview February 10, at USC; middle guard.

Nadel, S. F. 1951. Foundations of social anthropology. Quoted from Honigmann, John J., *Theory of Ritual*, Chapel Hill, U. of N. Carolina.

Oliver, Ralph. 1968. Interview Feb. 10, at USC; middle guard.

Olsen, Merlin. 1968. Speech delivered to Sigma Chi fraternity at USC, Feb. 7.

Van Gennep, Arnold. 1909. *Rites de passage*. Paris. Emile Nourry. Trans. by Monika B. Vizedom and Gabrielle L. Caffee. *The Rites of Passage*. Routledge & Kegan Paul, 1960.

Whiting, John M. and Richard Kluckholn and Albert Anthony. 1958. "The function of male initiation ceremonies at puberty," In *Readings in social psychology*. Eleanor E. Maccoby, Theodore M. Newcomb, and Eugene Hartley, eds. New York: Holt, Rinehart and Winston.

Whiting, John M. 1964. "Effects of climate on certain cultural practices," *In Explorations in cultural anthropology*. Ward H. Goodenough, ed. New York: McGraw-Hill.

Young, Frank W. 1962. "The function of male initiation ceremonies: a cross-cultural test of an alternative hypothesis." *The American Journal of Sociology* 67:379-91.

————. 1965. *Initiation ceremonies*. New York: Bobbs-Merrill Co., Inc.

THE AMERICAN SEASONAL
MASCULINITY RITES

Arnold R. Beisser

Not all of the characteristics which are attributed to being male or female are to the same degree biologically determined. Some, considered to be basic to masculinity or femininity, are determined by the culture in which one lives rather than by obvious physical differences. In our culture athletics are considered the most masculine of activities. Let us turn now to a consideration of what part sexual orientation plays in the intense interest in sports in America.

Before puberty, boys can be distinguished from girls mainly on the basis of primary sexual characteristics. When puberty is reached, biological distinctions become more apparent. At that time, with the differences in hormonal balance, the distinct secondary sexual characteristics begin to develop. Boys begin to have hair on their faces, and their bodies and become more muscular and angular. Girls become more curvaceous and develop breasts. Primary and secondary characteristics are predictable and universal: girls' hips broaden; boys' shoulders grow wider.

Beyond these physical characteristics are others which are largely, if not exclusively, determined by the society in which one lives. These can be termed tertiary characteristics and are transmitted from generation to generation by the examples of the men and women in the culture. To suggest, as Margaret Mead does, that the nature of maleness and femaleness, outside the physical characteristics, is culturally

From Arnold Beisser, *The Madness in Sports* (New York: Appleton-Century-Crofts, 1967), Chapter 16. Copyright © 1967, Appleton-Century-Crofts. Reprinted by permission of Appleton-Century-Crofts, Division of Meredith Corporation.

determined, may be an extreme point of view. For differences must develop just from living in a male body which has greater physical strength compared to living in a female body which experiences menstruation and pregnancy. Nevertheless, it is true that many of the male or female characteristics which are taken for granted in our society are determined by social custom rather than genetics. For example, up to very recently in this country, boys wore short hair and girls wore long hair, but in other parts of the world the reverse is true.[1] Similarly, an American boy would hide in shame if he had to wear a skirt, but in Greece it is the attire worn by a particularly virile and courageous group of soldiers.

There is a story which, although of doubtful validity, nevertheless illustrates the importance of these tertiary sexual characteristics: "Two children were playing outside a nudist camp. One of them discovered a hole through which he could look in the wall surrounding the camp. While he peeked through the hole, the other child excitedly inquired, 'What do you see, are they men or women?' The peeper responded in dismay, 'I don't know, they don't have any clothes on'!"

Tertiary sexual characteristics, such as dominance, mannerisms, dress, and speech, are often considered unalterable, yet studies of different cultures reveal quite different ideas about what constitutes male and female behavior. Each culture assumes that it "knows" how a man or woman should act. The folklore is justified by a self-fulfilling prophecy, as parents transmit to children their cultural expectations.

To be considered feminine in Victorian society women had to be frail, passive, and the potential victims of aggressive, lecherous males. Yet, according to the stories of Greek mythology, women were as urgently sexed as men. In our own age primitive tribes differ grossly in what we consider basic masculinity and femininity. Among the Arapesh tribes of New Guinea, for example, studies in the early twentieth century found that men as well as women showed such characteristics as concern, giving, protectiveness, which we in America associate with mothering. Their neighbors, the Mundugumor, living only a short distance away, had quite opposite attitudes, with both men and women

---

1. Since the above comments were first written, a remarkable change has taken place in the dress and hair styles of American teenagers and young people. Boys often now wear long hair and bright attention-getting clothing making their dress more similar to the traditional feminine attire. Girls frequently wear trousers and male-style shirts. These changes are consistent with the reduction of difference between the sexes in our society as discussed in previous chapters. For the purposes of of this chapter it is sufficient to note that standards of dress can change depending on taste and are not inherently either male or female.

being strong, tough, and aggressive, like the idealized pioneer male in the United States.[2]

Another tribe in New Guinea, the Tchambuli, showed a reversal of conceptions about masculinity-femininity in another way. The male job was head-hunting, war making, and war preparation. To carry out their plans the men congregated daily in the "men's house." The women on the other hand were charged with all of the economic responsibilities in the village, such as fishing, food preparation, pottery, basket weaving. When the British banned head-hunting and imposed a peace upon these people, the men became essentially unemployed, while the women continued their traditional activities. These women were temperamentally stable, secure, and cooperative with others, but the men, having lost their important function, became insecure, capricious, and aesthetic. Although men could no longer make war, the preparation rituals were continued. Their interest in the cosmetic arts and in creating suitable costumes, previously an important part of war, was now used instead to make themselves sexually attractive in competing through charm for the favors of the "important sex," the women. The women were tolerant of their men whom they viewed as gossipy, self-centered playthings.

Among the Manus it is the father who is endowed with what in America are considered maternal characteristics. While the women are occupied with the economy and have little time for children, the father cares for and raises them. When Dr. Mead brought dolls to the children of the Manus, she found that it was the boys who eagerly played with them, while the girls were disinterested. The boys in their play were emulating their fathers' activities.

Largely, then, the tertiary sexual characteristics of people, the ones which are most visible and apparent, are socially determined and subject to considerable change from one generation to another and from one culture to another. Sometimes, however, the roles assigned to certain members of a society are intolerable, and in order for such a society to survive and maintain stability there have to be safety valves through which those who are placed in ambiguous or deprecated positions can gain some satisfaction or status.

The Iatmul are a tribe of New Guinea natives who had such a culture. The men despised women, considered them unimportant, worth-

2. The information in this paragraph and the following paragraphs about New Guinea is from Margaret Mead, *Sex and Temperament in Three Primitive Societies: Manus, Mundugumor, and Tchambuli* (New York: William Morrow & Co., Inc., 1939), 2, pp. 1-384, 3, pp. 164-244, 237-322; and from a lecture by the noted anthropologist, Weston LaBarre.

less, almost subhuman, allocating to them only the most menial and routine of tasks. Men, in contrast, were considered to be the "real human beings," strong, brave, and courageous; they, too, were head hunters. The men were expected to be proud, the women self-effacing. Everything in this culture was either all black or all white, all good or all bad. There were no shades of gray. To be a man was to approach perfection; women epitomized all that was to be avoided. If a man showed the slightest feminine interests or characteristics, he was considered to be sliding toward the subhuman. Such rigid standards of human behavior placed each man in constant jeopardy of losing his humanity. This dichotomy was hard on the women, but it was equally difficult for the men. Adjustment in the Iatmul society was precarious: men walked a tight rope and women were scorned.

A society like the Iatmul has doubtful durability, for the tensions and resentment engendered are at an explosive pitch. This tribe's "safety valve" was the ceremony of Naven,[3] an annual occasion in which bitterness and tensions were discharged in a convulsive reversal of the year's pressures. Naven was a ceremony of cultural transvestism, during which men and women exchanged not only their clothes but also their roles. Boys who had been rigorously taught the shamefulness of femininity were now contemptuously called "wife" by their maternal uncles. They were bullied in the same way that women had been bullied throughout the year. The women, during Naven, were given a vacation from their despised roles and identified themselves dramatically as men, wearing their clothes and assuming their actions, strutting and swaggering. They could enter the "men's house" and could even beat certain designated men. They could engage in a theatrical simulation of the war games that men played. The men, who had spent the year taking elaborate ritualized precautions to avoid anything feminine could relax during the ceremony. It was a great relief actually to assume, in deliberate fashion, the female role.

By the end of the ceremony the tensions and resentments accumulated during the year were dissipated. The women felt better about their position in the community and the men admired the women for having been able to assume the masculine position. For a short time the women had become human and the men could love them. Over the next year the tensions built up again and hatred pervaded community life until the next Naven.

3. Gregory Bateson, "The Naven Ceremony in New Guinea," *Primitive Heritage: An Anthropological Anthology*, eds. Margaret Mead and Nicholas Calas (New York: Random House, 1953), pp. 186-202.

The Naven ceremony of the Iatmul is not unique, for other cultures have similar festivals. Rome's ancient feast of Saturnalia served a related function in discharging the year's accumulated tensions between masters and slaves. In this ceremony, slaves were waited upon by their masters and enjoyed all the privileges which they were denied during the year. It is easy to understand the necessity for such rites and their vital function in preserving a culture. Beyond a certain point, tensions and resentment would destroy any community life.

The Iatmul looked forward throughout the year to their ceremony of Naven. The Romans, both slaves and masters, eagerly awaited the festival of Saturnalia. In fact, in these cultures and others with similar rites, the populace lived from festival to festival. These were the most important events in their lives. Similarly Americans, particularly many American males, mark time by their own seasonal rites: football season, basketball season, baseball season, and so on. Many men live from one sports season to the next, with sports representing the most vital part of their lives.

Iatmul men and women were in a precarious psychological position as a result of the extreme demands which their culture placed upon them. The Naven rite offered an opportunity for the expression of strong feelings which had to be disowned throughout the year preceding the ceremony. For the women it was denial of self-assertion and aggression; for the men it was denial of passivity, with no opportunities for relaxation of their facade of superstrength. Naven saved the Iatmul people from the otherwise impossible demands of their culture and thereby saved the culture from extinction.

American men, as we have seen, are also on shaky cultural ground. Their position is precarious as a result of the contradictions in their lives. To an ever-increasing degree, American male children early in their lives have close physical and emotional experiences with their fathers. Fathers share almost equally with mothers in the maternal activities: feeding, bathing, cuddling, and comforting, which were once the exclusive domain of the American female. American parents are apt to take turns in getting up with the baby when he cries at night. When either parent has a "night out" the other serves as baby sitter. If the egalitarianism is disrupted it is likely for bitterness to develop.

"Togetherness" has largely meant the diminution of the uniqueness of the female position as well as the male position in the family. Father is no longer the ultimate authority; he has become a "pal"; he is now not a teacher but a co-learner. He has an equal, but not a greater voice in the collective activities of the household than have the children and his wife. The wife, who may have a job outside the home and may make as much as or even more money than her husband, quite naturally expects him to share the housecleaning, dishwashing, and caring for the children. The roles are diffused and the differences between male and female, between adult and child are diminished.

Like the Tchambuli, American men have had a change in status. The Tchambuli men lost their principal function, head hunting; American men have had to share with their wives their economic productivity as bread winners. Tchambuli men became superfluous; the authority and uniqueness of the American man has diminished. Previously, the main way men were superior to women was in their physical strength. Now, development of machines has caused male strength to be less important, almost obsolete. Machines are stronger than men, and the sexes are equally competent in running most machines. Dexterity has become more important than power, and women are at least as competent as men in this respect. The serious consequence is, that in their work, the new breed of factory and office workers are essentially neuter in gender.

While these changes in technology and in the family have taken place, the cultural expectations of masculinity have remained fixed as they were in pioneer days. Physical strength and agility were the qualities by which a man was measured, for then only the strong were able to survive. Obviously, such values are more appropriate to the frontier than to the office. Now, in order to fit this already obsolete image, men and boys must engage in artificial, nonproductive displays of strength.

As the real demands for what was considered traditional male strength have decreased, the expectation of show of strength has grown. Parents have a special concern that their boys are not aggressively masculine enough. Mothers are more apt to be concerned about passive, compliant behavior in male children than about their destructiveness. Often they are even relieved by, and subtly encourage, overt displays of aggression, for in that way, they are reassured that their sons are not "sissies." This is quite different from the concept of several decades ago that the quiet child was the "good" child.

As fathers and sons have grown closer together, an obsessive cultural concern with homosexuality has grown. In a counter move to avoid such taint, as already noted, children are pushed earlier and earlier into heterosexual relationships. The tragedy of this parental encouragement is that it is self-defeating, since the child in latency has other more important business to learn than sex appeal. In addition, his premature explorations in heterosexuality promote a sense of inadequacy within him as he recognizes his inability to perform as expected. This inadequacy, in turn, is interpreted as the "taint" and the parental efforts and encouragement towards aggression and heterosexuality are redoubled, the situation becoming a vicious circle.

Just as Naven helps to relieve the Iatmul tensions, American sports have a similar function. The first man outside the home that a boy encounters is usually a coach. In school he meets a series of female teachers who are the purveyors of morality, knowledge, and competence. The coach is not only a man among men but, more important, a man among women teachers. Boys try to model themselves after the coach and find security in imitating him. Their roles are clearer on the diamond than in the classroom, for it is on the athletic field in those seasonal masculinity rites that males become the kind of men their grandfathers were and their mothers want them to be. Strength is king; men are separated from boys, and boys, in turn, from girls. In the best tradition of the frontier, an athlete overpowers his opponent, and the sexual roles are re-established to conform with the expectancies of the culture. Male and female are relieved of their discrepancy just as they are following the Naven ceremony. Fortunately, this can be accomplished, not only by participation, but by observation as a spectator who identifies with the players. They can both then return to the office and the home with renewed respect for the uniqueness of the sexes and the re-establishment of their own identities, until the distinction gradually diminishes and another masculinity rite is necessary.

In a subtle way, these supermasculine "frontier rites" also allow for the expression of warmth and closeness among men which society compels them to disown. In sports, players huddle together; they caress, pat "fannies," shout affectionate phrases, and engage in activities which are scorned elsewhere but condoned in sports. In a recent heavyweight boxing match, the victor was embraced and kissed by his manager before several thousand fans in the sports arena and perhaps several million more on television. Such behavior anywhere but in the context of sports would be highly suspect. But here, with full cultural approval and without detracting from the supermasculine atmosphere, men can satisfy either physically or vicariously their needs for close male companionship like that which they experienced in childhood. In this context, physical contact, either aggressive or friendly, is applauded rather than condemned, and in the frenzy of American sports, males are purged of their femininity, and at the same time provided with an outlet for close contact.

Among the Iatmul, Naven takes place annually, and a single festival appears to take care of a year's accumulated tensions between the sexes. Fifty years ago a single sports season, namely baseball, sufficed for Americans. Today each season of the year is occupied with a different sport. Sport seasons now fuse with one another into a continuous succession of ceremonial demonstrations. The fall rite, football, now overlaps with the spring rite of baseball and track. The vacant moments are filled with transitional rites: basketball, hockey, tennis, and golf, to mention a few.

Although the potential for wild celebration is always present, the pitch of these ceremonies is somewhat lower than the yearly Naven in New Guinea. This is consistent with the lower pitch of all activities in our sophisticated country. Very little can be termed a "special event," since we are bombarded daily with the spectacular and the overwhelming. Just as the differences between sexes have diminished, the difference between holiday and weekday has also. Activities converge into a more integrated (for the hopeful) or amorphous (for the pessimistic) mass of ongoing activities. The Fourth of July, once fraught with danger and excitement, is now closely controlled and tame. Similarly, other holidays such as Armistice Day, Flag Day, St. Patrick's Day have lost their appeal except to the most enthusiastic. Since the range of the pitch is lower, the exposure time must be increased. Thus, sports go on continuously from the beginning to the end of the year.

Among primitives, the transition from boyhood to manhood is accomplished in a single, brief ceremony—the puberty rite. A symbolic gesture, such as circumcision or knocking out a tooth, bears witness to the cliché, "Today I am a man." For American men the transition is quite different. Puberty, the time of traditional manhood when the secondary sexual characteristics appear, is now only the signal for the prolonged period of suspension between boyhood and manhood called adolescence. Biologically and sexually, manhood has been reached, but the technical complexity of our society requires an extension of many years of education and preparation before the productive work of life can begin. The preparation extends temporally toward mandatory early retirement, which advances from the other side, allowing only a relatively brief period for the adult work career.

The adolescent is thus in a state of moratorium, suspended in his choices of occupation and a wife, prohibited from sexual activity, prevented from making any firm commitment.[4] No true identity can be achieved in the face of such a moratorium. In the medical profession this problem is well exemplified. A boy who decides that he wants to be a doctor must make this decision at least a score of years before his goal is

---

4. In the past decade young people have revolted against this state of suspension. They have adopted new and more permissive sexual mores and have often shown an unwillingness to delay gratification. They often choose not to wait the required period of time to achieve an occupational identity or traditionally defined marriage.

achieved. If, for example, he wishes to be a surgeon he may not complete his training until he is past thirty. Failure at any stage of this process would force him to seek a new occupation and a new direction for his life. With the endless series of what can be likened to initiation rites—high school, college for four years, medical school for four years, residency—it is as senescence approaches that the moratorium is over and the man can say with some degree of finality, "I have an identity, I am a doctor."

Because of the nature of this moratorium, adolescence is a period of turmoil. Rebellion and confusion can be expected from the man who has not yet found a place for himself, who is suspended, seemingly for an infinite length of time, between his family of origin and his family of procreation.

But as we have seen, a culture with contradictions and ambiguities, if it is to survive, must have some way of relieving and integrating its tensions. Sports form an elongated bridge across childhood, adolescence, and adulthood for American males. Although the adolescent boy may have to suspend decision and commitment on most of his affairs until many years hence, he can enter athletics with full exuberance and play and work at sports with a dedication which satisfies his personality and his society.

Among my patients has been a successful attorney who came to treatment because his marriage was on the point of dissolution. The bone of contention between him and his wife was that in her eyes he was not "man enough." She was bitterly disappointed that he was not handy around the house, that he did not make the family decisions, and was not more assertive—all qualities she had admired in her father. Her husband's competence in a learned profession seemed unimportant, while her father's physical strength resulting from his being an unskilled laborer was important. She feared that their son would develop into a "passive man" like her husband. The husband, too, doubted his own masculinity, shared her fears, and so sought therapy in order to try to conform to her expectations of him. The bickering that went on between them always subsided when they engaged in sports or jointly watched sports events. This seemed to adjust the perspective and after such activity each respected the other for his or her distinctiveness.

This is not an unusual case. Wives are worried about their husbands not being aggressively masculine enough; mothers are worried about their sons being too passive; men fear that they will be dominated or thought to be effeminate.

In reality, men are larger and weigh more than women, they do have more powerful muscles, they do have bigger lung and heart capacities, and they do have a sexual organ which makes them different. They are built for physical combat, for hunting, as well as for a unique sexual role. In the work and social world, however, this combat strength is largely obsolete. A 200-pound man can easily lose a business encounter (symbolic combat) to a 130-pound man or to a 90-pound woman. Slender feminine fingers can push the buttons on a computer as well as can thick, strong, male fingers, perhaps better. Machines are stronger than either men or women, and to the machine it makes no difference if its buttons are pushed hard or lightly. Male strength has, at least in part, lost its function and its value in society.

In sports, male and female are placed in their historical biological roles. In sports, strength and speed do count, for they determine the winner. As in premechanized combat, women can never be more than second place to men in sports. They can cheer their men on, but a quick review of the record books comparing achievements in sports of men and women confirms the distinctness of the sexes here.

It is small wonder that the American male has a strong affinity for sports. He has learned that this is one area where there is no doubt about sexual differences and where his biology is not obsolete. Athletics help assure his difference from women in a world where his functions have come to resemble theirs.

SYMBOLIC FORMS OF MOVEMENT:
THE OLYMPIC GAMES

Eleanor Metheny

Today it is commonly conceded that men interpret their perceptions of reality in three ways. They may attempt to describe a perceivable form in terms of the composition of its substantial elements. They may recognize it as a representative of a general category of forms, as denoted by the name commonly assigned to it. And they may interpret it as a symbol or symbolic form that represents some meaningful conception of human interaction with the universe, other than that denoted by the common name of the form. The present analysis of sports competition is patterned along these lines.

For the purposes of this analysis, *human behavior* is construed in terms of interaction between a person and the universe. The term *personal behavior* is reserved for those forms of interaction that occur when a person knowingly makes an attempt to organize his own behavior in some self-chosen way. The concept denoted by the term *sports competition* is largely defined as participation in the Olympic Games.

I—THE CHARACTERISTICS OF SPORT COMPETITION

In general terms, the characteristics common to all forms of *sports competition* may be described with reference to four principles: a per-

Eleanor Metheny, "Symbolic Forms of Movement: The Olympic Games," *Connotations of Movement in Sport and Dance* (Dubuque, Iowa: Wm. C. Brown Company Publishers, 1965), pp. 35-42. Reprinted by permission. Adapted from a paper presented at the Fourth Session of the International Olympic Academy, Olympia, Greece, August, 1964. Original text published in *Report of The Fourth Summer Session of The International Olympic Academy*, Athens, Greece, 1964.

sonal attempt to overcome inertia, finite limits, nonconsequential effect, and human control.

The Principle of Overcoming Inertia: All forms of sports competition are structured by a personal attempt to overcome the inertia of some specific organization of mass. The human objective is stated in terms of causing the mass to move through space and time in some way determined by the person. Within this general structure, the contest may be organized in three different ways:

1. *The person attempts to overcome the inertia of his own body mass.*

In all forms of foot-racing, broad jumping, swimming, platform diving, and free exercise, the contestant organizes his personal forces into an attempt to move his own body about within his milieu. In the hurdle races, high jump, and gymnastic events, he introduces certain man-made obstacles into the situation. In the pole vault, he erects a man-made barrier, and then increases his own mechanical advantage by applying his personal forces through a man-made device. Similarly, in springboard diving, skiing, ice skating, cycling, canoeing and sculling, he utilizes man-made devices to support his body and to amplify his own propelling powers. The team forms of this type of contest are represented by the relays and the two-or-more-man aquatic events. In all of these events, however, the outcome of the contest is measured in units that describe the displacement of his own body in space and time.

2. *The person attempts to overcome the inertia of some external unit of mass.*

In the shot put, the discuss throw, javelin throw, hammer throw, and weight-lifting, the person attempts to overcome the inertia of some external form of mass by direct application of force with his own body. In golf and bowling, which are not included in the Olympic list of events, the application of force is effected through a man-made implement. In the shooting events, including archery, the effective forces inhere in the man-made device, and the contest is structured as an attempt to utilize these man-made organizations of energy to overcome the inertia of another object. The team forms of this type of contest are represented by golf and bowling, in which teams of two or more persons make sequential attempts to achieve the objective, with each man performing individually within the sequence. However, in all of these events the outcome of the contest is measured in units that describe the displacement of the specified mass in space and time.

The equestrian events employ a nonhuman form of life as the inertial object, the outcome of the contest being determined by the extent to which the horse is induced to move in accordance with the rider's intent.

3. *Two persons, or two teams, designated as opponents, attempt to overcome the inertia in some external form of mass while opposing the efforts of the other.*

In wrestling, boxing, and judo, the specified mass is the body of the opponent, and the outcome is determined by the relative displacement of his body in space. In fencing, the specified mass is still the body of the opponent, but a spatial barrier is maintained between the opponents; an arm-extending device is used to bridge this barrier; and the outcome is determined by a physically inconsequential touch on some presumably vulnerable spot on the opponent's body. There are no team forms of these events in which the objective is to physically or symbolically subdue the opponent.

In handball, squash, badminton, and tennis, which are not included in the Olympic list, the inertial mass is a small object. The spatial barrier between the opponents is extended, and neither person intentionally touches the other's body or weapon. In handball, force is applied through the person's hand; in squash, badminton, and tennis, the force is applied through a light implement; and in badminton and tennis, the spatial barrier is maintained by a restraining net that serves to divide the playing area into two equal parts. The team forms of these events are organized as doubles, with the partners cooperating in the attempt to cause the inertial object to move through space in some specified way.

No new principles are introduced in the team sports, but the conception of cooperative effort is extended to teams of five or more persons. In all of these sports the team attempts to direct the movement of some relatively small and light object in space, either by applying force to it with some part of the player's body—as in basketball, soccer, water polo, and volleyball—or with the aid of a man-man device, as in field hockey and ice hockey. In all of these games, intentional body contact between players is prohibited by the rules. In volleyball, such contact is prevented by a restraining net. In American football, both body contact and an attempt to subdue the opponent physically are permitted and encouraged by the rules.

The Principle of Finite Limits: Within the infinite reaches of the universe, sports competition is intentionally confined to a small segment of reality, the limits of which are defined in finite terms, as follows:

Time: The circumstances which will determine the beginning and end of the sports competition, as such, are specified.

Space: The spatial boundaries of the area within which the sports competition, as such, may occur are clearly established, and other persons are excluded from this space during the appointed time.

Mass: The dimensions and substantial characteristics of all material objects utilized in the competition are specified.

Objective: The objective of the competition is defined in terms of the displacement of finite units of mass within the limits of time and space.

Outcome: Some way of quantifying relative degrees of achievement of this objective is designated.

The Principle of Nonconsequential Effect: When the sports competition is terminated by the finite limitations imposed on time, space, and mass, the contest area and all material objects in it are immediately restored to their precompetition state. The competitors leave the area. The contested inertial objects and all man-made devices used in the competition are taken away to be stored or discarded. The area is then made available for use by other persons. Thus, except for incidental deformation of the masses involved, no tangible evidence of the competitive effort remains, and the contest has no substantial continuing effect on the competitors, the spectators, or their environmental milieu.

The Principle of Human Control: The man-made rules that establish the finite limits of time, space, mass, objective, and outcome also impose certain limitations on the personal conduct of the competitors. Within the Olympic Games, the conditions imposed by these rules include:

Public Statement of Intent: Each competitor must publicly identify his personal intention to enter the sports competition. Additionally he must testify that he has systematically prepared himself by practice, that he is entering the contest voluntarily and without coercion from other persons, and that he has no expectation of receiving any material reward for his efforts within the competition.

Personal Behavior within the Competition: Forms of personal conduct deemed appropriate within the limits of the competition are defined, and penalties for inappropriate behavior are designated.

Personification of Authority: Authority to enforce the man-made rules, to judge the appropriateness of personal behavior, and to penalize or punish personal transgression is vested in some person not involved in the contest, as such.

II—SPORTS COMPETITION AS A SYMBOLIC FORM

The category of personal behavior called *sports competition* has been characterized as an intentional personal effort to overcome the inertia of mass, conducted under man-made rules that serve to govern personal behavior within a finite segment of reality. This elaborately constructed form of personal interaction with the forces of the universe is essentially futile, in that no tangible or seemingly consequential effect is produced by it. Nonetheless, men attach great value to this seemingly futile effort. It would seem, therefore, that this behavioral form must symbolize some more significant conception of man's interaction with the universe of his existence.

One symbolic interpretation is suggested by the central theme of a contest between man and inertia. In its larger outlines, this contest must be waged continuously by all living organisms within the infinite dimensions of the universe.

Living organisms are brought into being by the action of universal forces. In order to survive within this life-giving universe, the organism must continuously organize its own lesser forces into an attempt to overcome the inertia of the organism's own body masses and the inertia of other forms of mass in its immediate milieu. The penalty for failure to overcome these forms of inertia is death. Thus, life may be construed as a contest between the forces *of* or *in* the living organism and the forces that act *on* it. Human life, as distinguished from animal life, is characterized by full awareness of the inevitability of eventually being destroyed by the forces that brought it into being. Thus the human question is: Why was I born? What is the significance of my life as a man? What consequential effect does my life have on the continuing structure of the universe?

In sports competition, men seem to be answering that question by staging a dramatic demonstration of the effect they *can* have on the universe, as denoted by their ability to overcome the inertial forces of its masses in accord with some human plan. This demonstration is planned on a stage set apart for this purpose, and the finite limits imposed on this time-space area clearly set it apart from the limitless reaches of space and time within which men must attempt to accomplish their significant human purposes. Every act performed within this finite area is ritualized by the imposition of man-made rules. The events enacted in this ritualistic situation resemble the actions men perform within their ongoing attempts to survive within the universe, but there is no expectation that the usual consequences will ensue from them.

It may be noted, however, that the performers are not play-acting. In drama, the performer assumes the role of a person other than himself, and hides his own identity within the illusion he is attempting to create. In sports, the performer calls attention to his own identity as a person as he, literally or figuratively, stands naked before his gods and other men to testify to the extent of his own personal powers. Then, within the ritualized context of the dramatic event, he makes a wholly realistic attempt to actually overcome the inertia of his own body and other real forms of mass.

All drama serves to call attention to some idea about the relationships between man and man within the context of their common relationship to the forces that structure the universe. In sports, this idea deals specifically with some conception of man's personal ability to "move the earth"—or, by extension, with some more comprehensive conception of the performer's power to cope with the physical forces that structure his own earthly existence, within the finite limits of his personal life.

This interpretation is suggested in Homer's description of the funeral games that were held to honor the fallen warrior Patroclus. His comrades had been wrestling with the Trojans for many years; they had thrown spears beyond counting and repeatedly performed every action represented by the games many times over. Nonetheless, in the truce that was called to honor Patroclus, they asked their gods to witness a demonstration of how the warrior had proved his manhood by mastering the forces of mass, space, and time during his all-too-brief life.

This interpretation is re-enforced by the parallels between a man's conception of "my work" and the sports forms he chooses. In Homeric Greece, no man was exempt from heavy manual labor. Even the master of many slaves worked the earth with his own muscular powers, and he used those powers directly in overcoming the forces in other men as he warred against them. These strength-oriented conceptions of human power are represented in all of the oldest events on the Olympic list: wrestling, boxing, the now-discarded pancratium, the foot races, the jumps, shot put, and the discus, javelin, and hammer throws. It may be noted, too, that the right to rule was centered in the strength of one powerful man—as suggested by the fact that none of the team sports were developed during this era.

The earliest forms of the team sports were developed by the peasants of feudal Europe, perhaps as an indication of some emerging sense of the power represented by a group of men, each of whom might be individually at the mercy of a strong ruler. These early team forms involved the inertia of large and heavy objects, and intentional body contact used to physically subdue the opponent. But as the concept of the team was adapted to suit the needs of the emerging class called gentlemen, the fact that these priviliged persons did not labor with their strong muscles is suggested by their preference for smaller and lighter objects that might be manipulated with skillfully-designed implements. Thus, the elements of brute force and bodily contact with the opponent were eliminated from the gentlemanly team sports, and the objective of the contest was focussed on moving symbolic objects with skill rather than with strength.

Similarly, games like tennis, badminton, handball, and squash were developed by gentlemen who prided themselves on their intellectual powers rather than on their muscular strength. This sense of class distinction is associated with these sports as they are played today.

Turning now to the significance attached to the code of personal conduct, as prescribed by man-made rules and judged, rewarded, or punished by some personification of authority. Perhaps the earliest formulation of this code is represented by Hesiod's concept of "the good strife," in which men strive together in mutual respect as they attempt to improve their common human situation. In contrast, Hesiod identified "the bad strife" in which men strike against each other, attempting to establish mastery over the lives of other men even as they might establish personal mastery over the life of an animal. Thus, in "the good strife" men treat each other as partners in a common enterprise; in "the bad strife" they treat each other as animals or things.

The concept of "the good strife" is implicit in the word *competition*, as derived from *cum* and *petere*—literally, *to strive with* rather than *against*. The word *contest* has similar implications, being derived from *con* and *testare—to testify with another* rather than *against* him. The concept of "the bad strife" is implicit in the idea of "beating the opponent" as distinguished from "winning the contest."

In the larger context of Greek thought, the code that governs "the good strife" is denoted in the concept of *aidos*. In the English language, it is represented by the term *sportsmanship* or *sportsmanlike behavior*.

These interpretations suggest that sports competition may well symbolize some conception of a self-imposed code of behavior that marks the distinction between men and animals. It seems significant, too, that the earthly power to judge and punish men who violate that code is not vested in the gods, but in man, himself. Thus, men seem to be identifying their own sense of kinship with the gods, who have the ultimate power to judge, reward, and punish men and animals for their earthly behavior.

The concept of the athlete as a god-like being is well represented in the sculptured marble forms that have come down to us from ancient

Greece. It is also expressed in the poetry of the period, as in Pindar's ode to the winner of a boys' wrestling match: "Thing of a day! such is man; a shadow in a dream. Yet when god-given splendor visits him, a bright radiance plays over him, and how sweet is life." The modern athlete's sense of kinship with his gods may be less explicit, but he may still be accorded well-nigh worshipful adoration as an exemplar of superhuman or extraordinary powers.

Thus it would seem that the forms of sports competition embodied in the modern Olympic Games may well symbolize man's conception of himself as a consequential force within the grand design of the universe, as well as each man's conception of his own ability to perform those functions that identify him as a man among men.

SYMBOLIC FORMS OF MOVEMENT:
THE FEMININE IMAGE IN SPORTS

Eleanor Metheny

The issues debated in this paper have a very long history. They were raised as early as 776 B.C. by the custom of excluding women from the sacred precincts of Olympia. They were raised in 1896 when women were admitted to competition in some events in the modern Olympic Games, but excluded from others. They are being argued around the world today as every national Olympic Committee makes its own decisions about the inclusion of women in the lists of competitors. This paper is not an attempt to resolve all of these long-standing issues; rather it is an attempt to inquire into the underlying nature of these controversies.

In an earlier paper—"Symbolic Forms of Movement: The Olympic Games"—I have interpreted the Olympic events as symbolic formulations of man's conception of himself as a consequential force within the universe of space, time, mass, and energy. In the present paper I shall pursue that interpretation with reference to some conceptions of roles appropriate for women.

I. THE BIOLOGICAL BASIS OF THE FEMALE ROLE

At the biological level, arguments about appropriate roles for men and women must be pursued in terms of differences in anatomical

Eleanor Metheny, "Symbolic Forms of Movement: The Feminine Image in Sports," *Connotations of Movement in Sport and Dance* (Dubuque, Iowa: Wm. C. Brown Company Publishers, 1965), pp. 43-56. Reprinted by permission. Adapted from a paper presented at the Fourth Session of the International Olympic Academy, Olympia, Greece, August, 1964. Original text published in *Report of The Fourth Summer Session of The International Olympic Academy*, Athens, Greece, 1964.

277

structure and function. These sexually significant differences are too well known to need explication here. With reference to sports competition, the important question is: How are these differences related to the ability to overcome the inertia of mass?

In terms of averages, it is a truism that men are larger and stronger than women; but this generalization does not hold for individual representatives of the two sexes. Some women may be very large and strong, and their ability to overcome the inertia of mass may be far greater than that of the majority of men. Similarly, some men may be smaller and less muscular than many women, and in any contest with the inertia of mass they may make a very poor showing—and may, in fact, be bested by the majority of the opposite sex.

To some extent these relationships may be modified by pregnancy, the demands of infant care, and possibly menstruation; and all of these episodes may serve to limit a woman's interest in the kind of training men may undergo in preparation for international competition. But they do not vitiate the biological fact that women appear to be fully competent to engage in a contest with the inertia of mass. In terms of averages, women's achievements may be less spectacular than those of men; in terms of individual achievement, some women may well excel most of the male competitors in any athletic event.

It would seem then that the age-old arguments about whether or not women should be admitted to competition in the Olympic events cannot be pursued in meaningful terms at the strictly biological level of anatomical structure and function.

II. THE MYTHICAL IMAGE OF THE FEMALE ROLE

In every culture, men and women play different roles within the social organization. In part, these roles are defined by the relative contribution each sex makes to the reproduction of the species—a biologically-determined contribution which is the same in all cultures. But in larger terms, these roles are established by some less well-defined set of factors not directly related to these biological differences, as evidenced by the fact that they differ from culture to culture. This complex of factors serves to determine the *masculine image* of behaviors appropriate to males and the corresponding *feminine image* of behaviors appropriate to females in each social group.

At the time of the early Olympic Festivals, which date back beyond the first recorded games of 776 B.C., the images of masculinity and femininity within the emerging culture of ancient Greece were clearly delineated. These early Greeks envisioned their gods as persons very like themselves, differing from human beings only in the extent of their personal powers over the natural forces of the universe. Thus, they assigned to their male gods all of the behaviors appropriate to their own image of supermasculinity, while the behaviors of superfemininity were assigned to the female goddesses. A brief review of the characteristics of these gods and goddesses may give us some insight into the fact that women were excluded from the sacred precincts of Olympia.

Among the male gods, Zeus, the hurler of thunderbolts, had dominion over all the forces of earth; and his messenger, Hermes, could overcome both space and time with winged feet. Poseidon, the earth-shaker, had similar dominion over the forces of the sea. Ares, the god of war, was a powerful destructive force; and Hephaestus, the god of the metal workers, could subdue the materials of earth with one powerful blow of his hammer and shape them into forms of his own choosing. Even Apollo, who epitomized the intellectual powers of reason and logic, was pictured as an athlete, well able to overcome the forces of earth by skilful use of his bodily strength as well as by his intellectual prowess.

What an Olympic team the gods would have been! How they would have excelled in every contest in the early Olympic Festivals! And it may be noted that the Olympic Games in which men strove to overcome the forces of the earth in symbolic contests were held in honor of Zeus, the all-powerful father of the gods.

In contrast, the image projected by the female goddesses is almost totally devoid of any suggestion of physical strength that might be used to overcome the forces of earth—or of men.

Demeter, the Earth Mother, is envisioned as the ground in which all life is bred and nurtured. Hera, the wife of Zeus, is pictured as his helpmate, whose own will must ever be subordinated to the desires of her husband. (It may be noted, however, that Hera is never wholly resigned to this role and at times she uses her own female resources to seduce Zeus into doing her will rather than his.) Aphrodite, born of the foam of the sea, has none of these homely virtues. She is the goddess of beauty, infinitely desirable to all men. But if she delights in arousing their sexual desires, she can also be cruel and treacherous. In return for her favors, she demands tribute from her admirers, and men may well be fearful of her vengeance when her need for adoration is not satisfied. We are told that she was an accomplished swimmer, but she appears to have used this skill largely to display her lovely body in attractive poses that lured men to their own destruction.

The fact that these early Greeks could not reconcile feminine desirability with athletic prowess is underlined in the legends of Artemis and Athena. Artemis, the beautiful goddess of the hunt, was fleet of foot, and none excelled her in the use of bow and arrow—but men did not find her lovely body desirable. Or perhaps it was the other way around. At at any rate, legend relates that Artemis and her followers rejected the love of men and found delight in the companionship of women. Athena, goddess of wisdom, and of all goddesses the most respected, carried her own spear as she led men into battle, and her most famous statue shows her in full fighting array. But, alas, she too was denied the love of men, her perpetual virginity being commemorated in the Temple of the Maiden called the Parthenon.

Perhaps Artemis might have entered the foot races in the earliest games at Olympia; perhaps Athena might have thrown the javelin as well as the spear—and in fact there were some limited competition of this type for maidens in some of the festivals attended by women. But even in Sparta, where young girls were encouraged to develop both strength and skill, marriage put an end to such competitive endeavours. For adult women, the virtues demanded were those of Demeter, Hera, and Aphrodite—and the strength, skill and intellect of Athena and Artemis did not fit in this image of feminine desirability.

These are the elements out of which the prototypes of masculinity and femininity were compounded by the early ancestors of Western civilization. But these images were never wholly static. As men learned increasingly to control the stuff of their universe with skill and intellect, rather than with sheer strength of muscle, the masculine image reflected this evolving interpretation of man's role as a consequential force within the grand design. So, too, the feminine image began to change—albeit much more slowly.

The shift from muscle to skill and intellect may be seen in the contrast between Heracles, the legendary hero of pre-Homeric Greece, and Theseus, the later hero who made Athens into the most powerful of all Greek cities.

Heracles, who is sometimes credited with founding the earliest form of the Olympic Games, was a man of incredible strength. Certainly he would have been a formidable competitor in all of the early Olympic events, for no man could excel him in size or in strength of muscle. In all truth, however, he was not very bright, and his great strength led him into all sorts of trouble. He suffered great pangs of remorse for the damage caused by his own ineptitude, but he did not seem to learn much from these destructive episodes.

Theseus, who comes along much later in the story of Greece, presents quite a different picture. He is smaller than Heracles, and he has less strength, but he uses that strength with far greater skill—and is more disposed to forethought than to remorse and vain regret. He is the first king to establish and maintain his right to rule largely by force of intellect, and in his story we find the first recognition of the virtues of cooperation among men and cities. Heracles might well have bested Theseus in the pancratium and other weight events in the Olympic arena, but Theseus would have excelled in any contest demanding skill and strategy in the use of the lighter implements, and probably in the team games—which were later to demand cooperation as well as competition.

In the time of Heracles, the feminine image projected by Demeter, Hera and Aphrodite was embodied in the legendary first woman, Pandora. She was lovely to behold, her name means "all joys," and she was welcomed as a helpmate—but, alas, she was really very stupid. Allowing her curiosity to overcome her caution, she opened the box that contained all the evils and sorrows of mankind, and let them loose in the world— where they plague men to this very day. But in her one display of good sense, she did slam the lid down just in time to preserve woman's greatest gift to man—the gift of hope.

In the picture of Pandora, there is little to suggest an interest in overcoming the inertia of mass. But Hippolyta, Queen of the Amazons, who won the enduring love of Theseus many centuries later, presents quite a different image.

As ruler of her own kingdom, Hippolyta was the equal of Theseus in intelligence and skill, although smaller in size and of lesser strength. As they confronted each other in mortal combat at their first meeting, her courage matched his, and she fought bravely and well, neither asking nor offering advantage. In the eyes of Theseus she was both beautiful and desirable, and when he had won her he found new joy in the sexual embrace, for her ardor and skill matched his own. In marriage, she was a faithful helpmate and a devoted mother, and equally she was a good companion, both at home and in the hunt. In the end, she proved her love for Theseus by offering up her own life to save his—and it is said that he mourned her unceasingly for the rest of his days.

The legendary Hippolyta seems to have combined in her own person the skill and intellect of Artemis and Athena, the homely virtues of Demeter and Hera, and the beauty and desirability of Aphrodite. Surely, to Theseus, she was everything a man might hope to find in a woman. Had she been admitted to the lists of the Olympic Games, it seems likely that she would have earned her laurels proudly—not in the pancratium or weight-events, perhaps, but surely in the foot races and the javelin throw. And it seems likely that Theseus would have found pride in her achievements. But for the citizens of Athens, the time for recognition of such womanly feats had not yet come.

Hippolyta was cruelly rejected by the Athenians, both male and female. They could not reconcile intellect, skill and strength with their image of adult female sexuality. In her own life, however, Hippolyta proved them wrong—and they never forgave her for this. To this day, her name evokes suspicion in the minds of many men and women. Nonetheless, she left her own bright legend for future generations— the legend of a woman who delighted in using *all* of her own personal powers, a woman far ahead of her own time who won and held the love of the most eminent and farseeing man among the citizens of early Athens.

The gods and goddesses of ancient Greek myth have long departed from their old home on Mt. Olympus, but their images are still reflected in the connotations of the words *masculine* and *feminine* as we use them today. Historically, as men have moved forward on the path of skill and intellect pointed out by Theseus, they have tended to devalue the virtues of sheer muscular power—but the term *masculine* still suggests the image of Heracles. So, too, it is Pandora's image that is suggested by the term *feminine*. And many of the arguments about the appropriateness of sports competition for women hinge on those connotations.

However, when the modern Olympic Games were established in 1896, the image of Hippolyta was partially cleansed of the slurs that have tarnished it through the years, and women were at long last permitted to seek their own laurels in some events. Today the image of the feminine athlete is still somewhat blurred, but its modern outlines now seem to be emerging in currently sanctioned patterns of sports competition for women.

III. THE SOCIALLY SANCTIONED IMAGE OF FEMININE SPORT COMPETITION

The socially sanctioned images of femininity and masculinity are always relative. They differ from era to era, from culture to culture, and from group to group within a given social organization. In broadest general terms, these socially sanctioned images may be described as a composite interpretation of what the members of either sex may be or do without impairing their opportunities for finding a mate within their own social classification.

The social sanctions indicated below were derived from attitudes expressed by college women in the United States. I am indebted to Dr. Laura Huelster of the University of Illinois and Miss Mabel (Marie) Hart of the University of Southern California for many of the data used here. They must not, however, be held responsible for my interpretation of their findings nor for the extension of these data to international level or Olympic competition.

1. At the international level, some forms of competition appear to be *categorically unacceptable,* as indicated by the fact that women are excluded from Olympic competition in these events.

These forms include: Wrestling, judo, boxing, weight-lifting, hammer throw, pole vault, the longer foot races, high hurdles, and all forms of team games—with the recent exception of volleyball.

These forms appear to be characterized by one or more of the following principles:

An attempt to physically subdue the opponent by bodily contact
Direct application of bodily force to some heavy object
Attempt to project the body into or through space over long distances
Cooperative face-to-face opposition in situations in which some body contact may occur

It may be noted that the excluded team games are generally acceptable to college women in the United States at the level of intramural competition, and these games are popular during the years of adolescence. Some extramural competition is sponsored at the high school level, but this decreases in the college age group, and only a very limited number of college women continue their interest in team games during their adult years.

2. Some forms of competition are generally *not acceptable* to college women in the United States, although they *may be acceptable to a minority group* within the college population.

These forms include: Shot put, discus throw, javelin throw, the shorter foot races, low hurdles, long jump, gymnastics events, and free exercise.

These forms appear to be characterized by one or more of the following principles:

Direct application of bodily force to a moderately heavy object
Attempt to project the body into or through space over moderate distances
Display of strength in controlling bodily movements

Very few college women show any sustained interest in performance in these events, although some may have found them challenging during the early years of adolescence. Among the Olympic competitors from the United States, Negro women are disproportionately represented in the track and field events. In the gymnastic events, there is a preponderance of women of Germanic and Slavic ancestry, most of whom have developed their interests and abilities in ethnically-defined social and athletic clubs rather than in the college setting.

3. Some forms of individual competition are *generally acceptable* to the college women of the United States, and competence in these events does not appear to militate against social acceptance by males within the college population.

These forms include: Swimming, diving, skiing, and figure skating, and such non-Olympic events as golf, archery, and bowling.

These forms appear to be characterized by one or more of the following principles:

Attempts to project the body into or through space in aesthetically pleasing patterns

Utilization of a manufactured device to facilitate bodily movement

Application of force through a light implement

Overcoming the resistance of a light object

In one way or another, all of these sports involve a considerable expenditure of time, money, or both; and participation is accordingly limited to women in the economically-favored groups. Bowling, which is the least expensive insofar as time is concerned, and in which a moderately heavy ball is used, finds greatest favor with middle-class groups. Success in the other events may contribute to upward social mobility in some instances.

4. Some forms of face-to-face competition are also *generally acceptable* to college women of the United States, with no implication of limited social acceptance for successful competitors.

These forms include: Fencing, such non-Olympic sports as squash, badminton, and tennis, and the team-game of volleyball.

These forms appear to be characterized by one or more of the following principles:

Application of force through a light implement

Overcoming the resistance of an essentially weightless object

Maintenance of a spatial barrier that prevents body contact with opponent

Fencing is not acceptable to certain religiously-defined groups, presumably because it symbolizes the destruction of human life. Adult competition in squash and badminton is largely limited to members of private clubs, but these groups include women from the middle as well as the higher socioeconomic levels. Tennis, which was once a private club game, is now commonly played by all groups having access to public facilities, but as yet only a few women from the darker-skinned minorities have reached the level of national competition. Volleyball is commonly played as a recreational game with mixed teams including both sexes.

It is of interest to note the difference between squash, which is socially acceptable for women in the upper economic levels, and handball, which is not. Here the distinction seems to rest on the use of a light implement to apply force in the one game and the use of the hand in the other. However, such resistance to hitting an object with the hand seems to be overcome in the growing popularity of volleyball.

Summarizing this analysis, it appears that the socially sanctioned image of feminine sports competition for college women in the United States may be derived from a few general principles:

1. It is *not appropriate* for women to engage in contests in which:
   the resistance of the *opponent* is overcome by bodily contact
   the resistance of a *heavy object* is overcome by direct application of bodily force
   the body is projected into or through space over long distances or for extended periods of time

2. It *may be appropriate* for women identified in the lower levels of socioeconomic status to engage in contests in which:
   the resistance of an *object of moderate weight* is overcome by direct application of bodily force
   the body is projected into or through space over moderate distances or for relatively short periods of time

3. It is *wholly appropriate* for women identified with the more favored levels of socioeconomic status to engage in contests in which:
   the resistance of a *light object* is overcome with a *light implement*
   the body is projected into or through space in aesthetically pleasing patterns
   the velocity and maneuverability of the body is increased by the use of some manufactured device

a spatial barrier prevents bodily contact with the opponent in face-to-face forms of competition

IV. SPORT AS A SYMBOLIC FORMULATION OF SOCIALLY SANCTIONED FEMALE ROLES

Within the context of the biological, mythological, and social interpretations of the nature of females, we may now examine the theory that the sports in which women compete serve to formulate some conception of the female's role as a consequential force within the universe of space, time, mass and energy.

At the international level, as represented by the Olympic Games women are categorically prohibited from any attempt to overcome an opponent by direct application of bodily force. Since this prohibition cuts across all cultural lines, it would seem to be traceable to some biologically-defined difference common to the men and women of all social groups. The clue may lie in the differences between the ways in which males and females may use their own bodily forces in the mutual act of procreation.

For the male, the procreative act may be construed in terms of direct application of bodily forces subject to the male's control. Conversely, the female role must be construed in passive terms as the act of receiving and nurturing new life rather than creating it by personal intent expressed in terms of bodily force. Thus, the male may use his own muscular powers to coerce the female and force her to submit to his will, but the female cannot similarly coerce the male. By extension, then, it may well seem biologically appropriate for the male to force another person to submit to his will by direct application of muscular powers through bodily contact; conversely, it would be biologically inappropriate for the female to coerce or subdue another person by use of the muscular powers of her own body.

This interpretation may be further extended in the roles assigned to men and women in the mortal combat of war. Here, men have long found it possible to justify their own attempts to coerce other men into submission by threat of death; but men have seldom permitted their women to engage in such direct forms of mortal combat. Athena may have carried her spear as she led men into battle, but, insofar as legend relates, she did not personally use her own body to wrestle with the enemy. Hippolyta and her Amazons did, on occasion, engage in hand-to-hand combat—but the most severe charge made against Hippolyta by the Athenians was that she had "fought like a man."

When the resistance to be overcome in a contest is centered in an *object,* rather than in the body of another *person,* the prohibitions against use of bodily force by women are stated in relative, rather than in categorical, terms. Here the issue seems to be: *How much force* may a woman appropriately apply to an object?

At the Olympic level, women are not permitted to lift heavy weights or to throw the hammer. They are, however, permitted to put the shot, hurl the discus, and throw the javelin. Similarly, they are barred from the pole vault, the high jump,* the high hurdles, and the longer foot races, but they are permitted to compete in the long jump, the low hurdles, and the shorter races. They are also barred from the more strenuous team games, but in 1964 they were permitted to compete in the milder game of volleyball—the only team game in which there is no possibility of direct body contact between opponents.

The facets of biology provide no logical basis of support for these relative destinctions. The number of women competent to perform in the excluded events may be small—but so is the comparable number of men; and this is generally true for all of the events included on the women's list, with the numbers increasing as the events become less physically demanding.

Socially, however, there appears to be a relationship between participation in such strenuous events and the kinds of work commonly done by the performer's parents. Women from homes in which both the father and mother are commonly employed in some form of manual labor may seemingly use their own muscular forces in athletics without impairing their own marriageability. Here the old fallacy of associating displays of strength with sexual inadequacy seems to be greatly weakened—although it still cannot be wholly dismissed as a factor in the determination of social approval. It must also be noted that even within the manual laborer group social approval tends to decrease as the muscular forces demanded by the events increase.

Within the category of fully-approved events in which the contestant attempts to overcome the resistance of an object, strength is generally far less important than skill. The contested objects in such games as golf, archery, tennis, badminton, and squash are essentially weightless, and the objective of the contest is to move these objects through space by manipulating a light instrument with skill and speed. (The heaviest such instrument is probably the bowling ball, which even very small women can lift without difficulty.) This emphasis on in-

---

*(It may be noted that women are now involved in this event. M. Hart)

strumental manipulation is further emphasized in the face-to-face games by either nets or rules that prohibit bodily contact. (Even in fencing, in which the body of the opponent is touched by the instrument, the touch is symbolic rather than forceful.)

All of these games were developed in the later years of human history by men called "gentle"—men whose personal status rested on the presumption of superiority in intellect and skill rather than on their muscular powers. But women did not participate in the early forms of these games. Not until the Industrial Revolution had created new forms of employment for women in industry, and not until women in the more socially-favored classes had begun to claim some measure of personal equality with their husbands, did women begin to participate in these sports reserved for gentlemen.

Significantly, these sports pioneers seldom competed with men directly in any of these games, and there is still strong aversion to this form of competition. Today, the socially-approved forms of competition in tennis, for example, are still man-man, woman-woman, and mixed doubles—in which the marriage relationship is symbolized by a partnership in which a man and woman combine their forces in a contest with another partnership team. Today, styles in double play are changing—but the most common strategy still emphasizes the man's strength of arm, while the woman uses her skill to support his efforts within a smaller part of their common court area.

Thus, in mixed doubles the woman still tends to play the role appropriate to Hera, the helpmate, as she uses the skills of Artemis and Athena and Hippolyta to support the efforts of her male partner, reinforcing his attempts to win the contest rather than threatening his mastery over their common environment. However, it must be noted that side-by-side play is now frequently seen in mixed doubles, particularly when both of the partners are superior players. So it would seem that men who are sure of their own strength and skill are not offended by displays of strength and skill in their mates—particularly when these female forces are combined with their own male forces to their mutual advantage.

Within the category of socially approved events in which the contestant attempts to project her body into or through space, women display a high degree of muscular strength as well as great skill and daring. In swimming they propel themselves through the water with great speed, but they seldom compete in the longer distances. As Aphrodite noted, however, the water-supported movements of swimming display the female body to advantage, and it is noteworthy that the aesthetically pleasing patterns of synchronized swimming were developed by women, rather than by men. Similarly, women in gymnastics and free exercise have developed their own movement patterns, which emphasize grace and beauty to a far greater extent than do the standard events of men.

Diving, figure-skating, and skiing are also classed graceful forms of movement, and in these sports personal velocity is greatly facilitated by the use of such manufactured devices as springboards, skates, and skis. The management of the high velocities produced by these devices requires both strength and skill, but it is skill that is emphasized rather than strength.

Today, in the United States, the image of femininity projected by college women and endorsed by their potential mates is a "double image" —with one aspect identified as "woman at work" and the other identified as "woman at home."

As workers, these college women see themselves dealing with the forces of the universe in consequential ways, even as their men do. But neither the men nor the women picture themselves overcoming the resistance of mass, or of other persons, by sheer muscular force of bodily contact. Rather, they are prepared to use their wits in the realm of ideas, and they are adept in the use of lightweight equipment and manufactured devices that call for detexerity and skill rather than strength. On occasion, the men may still feel called upon to demonstrate the age-old conception of masculinity by performing feats of strength; but few college women seek this expression of their own human powers.

As potential wives and mothers, the college women are concerned with expressing their femininity in quite different ways. Recognizing their own biologically-based need for dependence on the male wage-earner, they modify their behavior in ways designed to enhance their own sexual desirability. They may also, on occasion, conceal their own abilities as workers lest the man of their choice might feel belittled by their competence.

Both sides of the image are evidenced in the socially approved list of sports for women. Strength and bodily contact are de-emphasized in favor of skill and grace; force is applied to weightless objects with lightweight implements; and velocity is attained by use of manufactured devices. And there is no serious competition in which women are matched against men. Rather, in those sports in which men and women participate together, they play as partners, with women generally accepting the supporting rather than the dominant role.

Thus, in our own time, it would seem that the college women of the United States have found it possible to combine the sexually-based image of Aphrodite, Hera, and Demeter with the personal powers of Athena, Artemis, and Hippolyta, without doing violence to either, within the realm of sports competition. Thus, too, the forms of competition they have chosen may be construed as a dramatic formulation of their conception of the complex roles females may play as consequential forces within the grand design of the universe. Perhaps Heracles and Pandora might have been dismayed by this interpretation of what a woman is and what she can do—but let it be said to the credit of Theseus that he foresaw this picture some three thousand years ago when he described Hippolyta as everything a man might hope to find in a woman—and let us remember, too, that the legend of his love for her has endured, time without end, through the long years of human history.

ON BEING FEMALE IN SPORT

M. MARIE HART*

The topic of social and sexual roles in sport is a complicated one about which Americans seem particularly sensitive. The sexually separated facilities and organizations that often accompany sport and physical education activities may be an extension of certain problems in this area. There is an urgent need to consider these questions if we are concerned about the quality of the experience for all those who engage in sport. Many times it seems that people find it difficult to consider such problems with any degree of objectivity. To remove the personal self from the social process being examined requires a thorough grounding in knowledge of self and a deep understanding of one's own personal sport involvement.

This article is particularly concerned with being a woman and being in sport. Although we have isolated and studied "Women in Sport," we have not so separated "Men in Sport" as a special topic. This is because the latter is the accepted, rather than the exception, in sport discussions. It seems well established that sport is male territory; therefore participation of female newcomers is studied as a peripheral, non-central aspect of sport. If one aspect of sport is social experience, it seems appropriate to study it in total context and to note the differences of role and reaction in the variety of people taking part. The separation and alienation of women in sport is not the healthiest of situations. It is only through interaction that we can gain awareness and acceptance of differences. Why is it that in most of the rest of the Western world women co-exist with men in sport with less stigma and more as accepted and respected partners?

*Another version of this material appeared in *Psychology Today* Magazine, October, 1971. Copyright © Communication/Research/Machines, Inc.

Being female in this culture does not necessarily mean that one is perceived or accepted as "feminine." Each culture has its social norm and sex roles within which one must live, but in the United States this definition seems especially rigid and narrow. For longer than one can remember, women in sport have known and experienced rejection due to their failure to live up to a particular concept of "feminine." It has been an unpleasant and painful memory for many.

Why has it been difficult for women to stay "woman" and be an athlete, especially in games emphasizing physical skill? Games of physical skill are associated with achievement and aggressiveness which seem to make them an expressive model for males rather than females. Women are more traditionally associated with high obedience training and routine responsibility training, and with games of strategy and games of chance which empasize those qualities supposedly desirable in women (9)(11)(12). This all begins so early that the young girl in elementary school already begins feeling the pressure to select some games and avoid others if she is to be a "real" girl. If she is told often enough at eleven or twelve that sports are not ladylike, she may at that point make a choice between being a lady and being an athlete. Having to make this choice has potential for setting up deep conflict in female children, which continues later into adulthood.

The concept of conflict-enculturation theory of games is developed in an essay by Sutton-Smith, Roberts and Kozelka. They maintain that "conflicts induced by social learning in childhood and later (such as those related to obedience, achievement, and responsibility) lead to involvement in expressive models, such as games . . . (12:15). This process can be applied also to the game involvement of adults. Cultural values and competencies are acquired in games. It would appear that games operate on various levels as expressive models to ease conflict, with the exception of the case of the woman athlete. As girls become more and more proficient in sport, the level of personal investment increases which may, due to the long hours of practice and limited associations, isolate her socially. Personal conflict and stress increase as it becomes necessary for her to assure others of her femininity, sometimes requiring evidence. This level of tension and conflict may increase dramatically if a girl makes the choice to be intensely involved in a sport which is thought of as male territory.

In an interview Chi Cheng, who holds several world track records, was quoted as saying, "The public sees women competing and immediately thinks that they must be manly—but at night, we're just like other women" (14:15). Why does a woman need to comment about herself in this way and how does this awareness of stigma affect her daily life? Chi goes on to say: "I'm gone so much of the day and on weekends. I give a lot of public appearances—where I can show off my femininity" (14:16).

Numerous occasions have occurred in college discussion groups over the past few years that convince one that we have imposed a great burden on women who are committed to performing or teaching sport. As an example, several married women students majoring in physical education confided to a discussion group that they had wanted to cut their hair but felt they couldn't. Members of the group asked why this was so, if their husbands objected, if they would feel less feminine, if they were in doubt about their own femaleness. In every case they responded that they simply didn't want the usual stereotype image and comments from friends and family in their social lives. Even when hair styles are short women in sport are judged by a standard other than fashion. If the married sportswoman experiences anxiety over such things, one can imagine the struggle of the single woman. Unfortunately, this often results in a defensive attitude developed as a shield against those who poke and probe.

When young women do enjoy sport what activities are really open to them? A study done in 1963 (4) shows recommendations made on sports participation by 200 freshman and sophomore college women from four Southern California schools. Although their own background had been strong in the team sports of basketball, softball and volleyball (Chart I), they did not recommend that a girl, even though highly skilled, pursue these activities at a professional level. They strongly discouraged participation in track and field activities. The sports they did recommend for a talented young woman were those that they had not necessarily experienced personally. They were ranked as follows: tennis, swimming, ice skating, diving, bowling, skiing and golf (Chart II). All of these recommended sports are identified with aesthetic considerations, social implications, and fashions for women. Physical strength and skill may be components of some but are not their primary identifications. The study included two church schools which had sanctions against dance, a factor which caused a lower than usual ranking for this activity.

In contrast to the findings of this study is the situation of the black woman athlete. In the black community, the woman can be strong and achieving in sport and still not deny her womanness. She may actually gain respect and status as evidenced by the reception of women like Wilma Rudolph and other great performers. The black woman seems also to have more freedom to mix her involvement in sport and dance without the conflict expressed by many white women athletes. This in itself could be the subject for research study.

CHART I

Participation in Sports and Dance

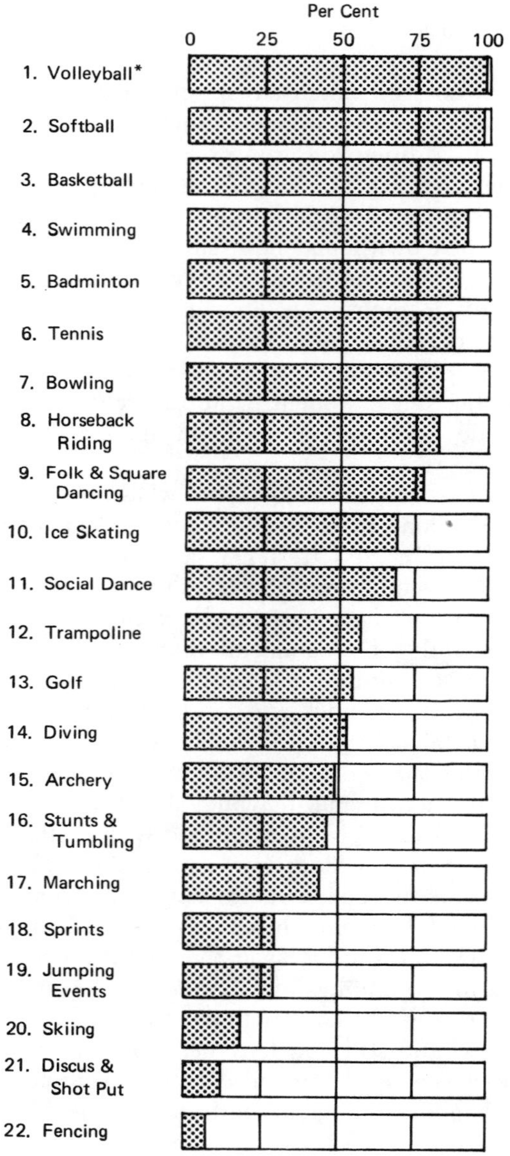

Per Cent

0   25   50   75   100

1. Volleyball*
2. Softball
3. Basketball
4. Swimming
5. Badminton
6. Tennis
7. Bowling
8. Horseback Riding
9. Folk & Square Dancing
10. Ice Skating
11. Social Dance
12. Trampoline
13. Golf
14. Diving
15. Archery
16. Stunts & Tumbling
17. Marching
18. Sprints
19. Jumping Events
20. Skiing
21. Discus & Shot Put
22. Fencing

*This graph should be read as follows: 99 per cent of the respondents reported participation in volleyball.

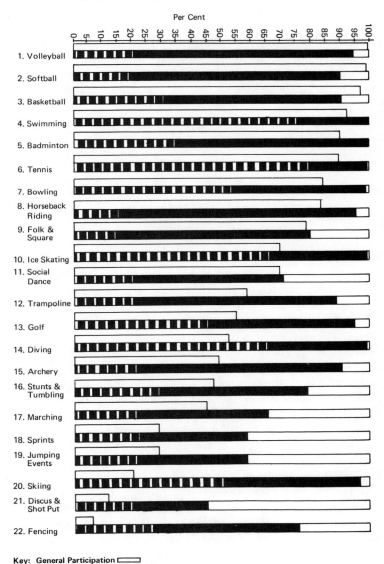

CHART II

Comparison Between General Participation and Recommendations

Per Cent

1. Volleyball
2. Softball
3. Basketball
4. Swimming
5. Badminton
6. Tennis
7. Bowling
8. Horseback Riding
9. Folk & Square
10. Ice Skating
11. Social Dance
12. Trampoline
13. Golf
14. Diving
15. Archery
16. Stunts & Tumbling
17. Marching
18. Sprints
19. Jumping Events
20. Skiing
21. Discus & Shot Put
22. Fencing

Key: General Participation
      Level of Recommendation
                              Prof.   Rec.   Disc.

This graph should be read as follows: 99 per cent of the respondents reported participation in volleyball, 20 per cent would recommend it for professional or competitive level, 74 per cent for recreation and 6 per cent would discourage participation in volleyball.

The limitations on sport choices for women have been instituted largely by social attitudes about women in sport as previously discussed. These attitudes have a long history which is revealed in the sport literature. Early sport magazines reinforced the idea of women being physically inferior to men in sport and furthermore inferred that their female emotionality rendered them incompetent. As an example, in response to a strong desire of women to be involved in the new and exciting sport of flying in 1912, the editor of *Outing Magazine* was outspoken in his bias:

> Other things being equal, the man who has had the most experience in outdoor sports should be the best aviator. By the same token, women should be barred. . . . Women have not the background of games of strength and skill that most men have. Their powers of correlation are correspondingly limited and their ability to cope with sudden emergencies inadequate. (10:253)

The social process by which women had arrived at this helpless state of being was never mentioned or discussed.

In 1936 the editor of *Sportsman,* a magazine for the wealthy, commented about the Olympic Games that he was ". . . . fed up to the ears with women as track and field competitors." He continued, "her charms shrink to something less than zero" and urged the organizers to "keep them where they are competent. As swimmers and divers girls are beautiful and adroit as they are ineffective and unpleasing on the track" (13:18).

More recent publications such as *Sports Illustrated* have not been openly negative, but the implication is sustained by the limitation in their coverage of women in sport. Content is small and consists mostly of a discussion of fashions and of women in traditionally approved activities such as swimming, diving, ice skating, tennis and golf. The emphasis in periodicals is still largely on women as attractive objects rather than as skilled and effective athletes.

Attitudes toward women in sport have been slow to change because of misunderstandings like the muscle myth. It has been difficult to allay the fear that sport activity will produce bulging muscles which imply masculinity. Young girls are frightened away from sport by "caring" adults who perpetuate this false idea. The fact, well documented by exercise physiologists, is that "excessive development (muscles) is not a concomitant of athletic competition "(6:130). Klafs and Arnheim further affirm this situation, reporting: "Contrary to lay opinion, participation in sports does not masculinize women. Within a sex, the secretion of testosterone, androgen, and estrogen varies considerably, accounting for marked variation in terms of muscularity and general morphology among males and females "(6:128). Participation in sport cannot make changes in the potential of hereditary and structural factors of any individual.

Perhaps what occasionally gives observers the impression that the muscle myth is true is the reality that some girl athletes are indeed muscular. However, it is due to their muscularity that they enter sport; it is the reason why they participate in sport rather than the result of their participation. This is further explained by Klafs and Arnheim:

> Girls whose physiques reflect considerable masculinity are stronger per unit of weight than girls who are low in maculinity and boys who display considerable femininity of build. Those who are of masculine type often do enter sports and are usually quite successful because of the mechanical advantages possessed by the masculine structure. However, such types are the exception, and by far the greater majority of participants possess a feminine body build. (6:128)

Some of the most important considerations of women have been written by Simone de Beauvoir. In her book, *The Second Sex,* she discusses sport as a way of experiencing oneself in the world and of asserting one's sovereignty. She says that outside of participation in sport, a girl must experience most of her physical self in a passive manner (2). De Beauvoir makes one point that is worth the serious consideration of all who are concerned about the dilemma of the woman athlete. She states:

> And in sports the end in view is not success independent of physcial equipment; it is rather the attainment of perfection within the limitations of each physical type; the featherweight boxing champion is as much of a champion as is the heavyweight; the woman skiing champion is not the inferior of the faster male champion; they belong to two different classes. It is precisely the female athletes who, being positively interested in their own game, feel themselves least handicappd in comparison wtih the male. (2:311)

Americans seem not to be able to apply this view of "attainment of perfection within the limitations of each" to the woman in sport. Women have been continually compared to males and have had male performance and style set as model and goal for them. Repeatedly young girls and women athletes listen to, "Wow, what a beautiful throw. You've got an arm like a guy." "Look at that girl run, she could beat lots of boys." Father comments, "Yes, she loves sports. She's our little tomboy." It would seem strange to say of a young boy, "Oh, yes, he is our little marygirl." We have ways of getting messages to boys who don't fit the role, but we haven't integrated it into our language terminology so securely.

These kinds of comments carry with them the message of expected cultural behavior. When well learned it results in girls loosing games to boys purposely, avoiding dates which show her sports talent or risking never dating the boy again if she performs better than he does.

The male performance standards and the attending social behavior have extended into even more serious problems. In the early international competitions of the 1920's, women were not subjected to medical examinations. After doubt arose over one or two competitors, each country was asked to conduct medical examinations to determine if indeed the performer was female. Countries did not trust the honesty of non-supervised tests so additional tests began to be employed. In international events a woman must now pass the "Barr Sex Test" perfected by a Canadian doctor. The test consists of scraping cells from the inside of the cheek and then analyzing them for "Barr bodies." The number fluctuates normally during a month but all women have a minimum percentage of Barr bodies all the time. In the test, if the percentage drops below the minimum for females then the femaleness of the performer is suspect and she is dropped from the competition.

In 1968, the "Barr Sex Test" was administered for the first time at an Olympic Game, causing quite a stir. The scene was described by Marion Lay, a Canadian swimmer performing in both the 1964 and 1968 Olympics. The line-up awaiting the test in Mexico erupted in reactions ranging from tension-releasing jokes to severe stress and upset. Some performers suggested that if the doctor were good looking enough, one might skip the test and prove their femininity by seducing him. At the end of the test the women received a certificate verifying their femaleness and approving their participation in the Games. Many were quite baffled by the necessity of the test, feeling that their honesty as much as their femininity was in question. Most could not imagine anyone wanting to win so badly that they would create a disguise or take drugs that might jeopardize their female identity.

In addition to the concern over proof of sexual identity, there has been much discussion about the use of "steroid" drugs by some women performers, particularly those from Russia and Eastern block nations. These drugs are derived from male sex horomones and tend to increase muscle size. The subject of the use of these drugs by women has been somewhat muted with the result that there is not much literature describing the effects of this drug on women performers. There have been strong and continued warnings against its use by men because of its dangerous effects but there is very little published about the effects of the "steroid drug" on women. It is known to increase body size and also to produce secondary male characteristics such as increasing of facial hair and lowering of the voice (1:135). Why would a woman take such a drug? Because the values are on male records and performance, and she will attempt to come as close to this goal as possible. This kind of performance and attending social behavior have caused serious problems for women athletes. If the performance of women could be recognized on its own merit wihout comparison to male records and scores, many painful social and "medical" experiences for women would be avoided.

If women in sport feel outside of the mainstream of social life in this country, perhaps another question could be posed to representatives of the new movements. Where has the Women's Lib platform been in relation to women athletes? When the role of women is no longer limited to mother, secretary, or Miss America, isn't it about time that women were given not only freedom to be but respect for being success-ful in sport?

It seems apparent that the female athlete in general has much, if not more, to contend with than any other women in the American way of life. To entertain doubts about one's sexual identity and role results in more than a little stress. An editorial in *Women: A Journal of Liberation* states: "In America, dance is a field for women and male homosexuals. There is the dancer's cult of starving and punishing one's body "(15:65). In contrast, one might think of sport as a field for men and female homo-sexuals, or so the image seems often to be interpreted. The need of women athletes to be out from under and free of such stereotypes and fears is long overdue in its fulfillment.

The aforementioned editorial goes on to say: "My dream is that dance will not have to be an escape from America's sick sexuality but a celebration of all of our bodies, dancing "(15:65). What else could one wish for both men and women in sport? Why could not sport be a cele-bration, both personal and mutual, of the body-self? A celebration— rather than a conflict over best scores and most points, over who is most masculine and who is least feminine—a celebration of one's body-self whoever he or she is. The jokes, stories and oppression are old and far too heavy to be carried along further. The present-day women athlete may soon demand her female space and identity in sport.

Today women *have* begun to enter sport with more social accep-tance and individual pride. After World War II the increase in women athletes and their success became more apparent and better received. In 1952 researchers from the Finnish Institute of Occupational Health conducted an intensive study of the athletes participating in the Olym-pics in Helsinki. Their findings were of major importance in the study of women athletes. After studying their athletic achievements, physio-logical and clinical data, age, fitness and social status, the researchers stated that "women are about to shake off civic disabilities which millennia of prejudice and ignorance have imposed upon them "(5:84). The researchers concluded that the participation of women was a significant indication of positive health and living standards of a country.

In addition to the physiological and clinical data, the researchers observed other factors apparent in the performance of women athletes. Criteria for describing the performances expanded to include aesthetic considerations because it "added itself" to the researchers data. They stated:

> A third criterion for the evaluation of women's athletics is an aesthetic one. Parallel with the growth of athletic performance standards there has taken place during the past fifty years or so a display of new dynamic patterns of motion and form which contain elements of artistic value and of creative beauty. The great woman hurdlers and discus throwers, fencers, and divers, gymnasts and canoeists have introduced, unwittingly, of course, features of elegance and of power, of force and of competence such as had previously not been known. That sports and athletics should be able to elicit in women categorical values of this kind and that performance and beauty should thus be correlated is a surprising and highly relevant experience. (5:84-85)

In the same vein, Ogilvie, a professor of psychology, stated:

> The review of the data upon San Jose State College women swimmers presents evidence that there has been no loss of the feminine traits most valued within our culture. There was strong evidence that at least this small sample of women had outstanding traits of personality in the presence of outstanding success as competitors. I must reject the prejudiced view that would deny women the joys and rewards of high level athletic competition. It appears to this investigator that you would have to search the whole world over before you could find twenty women who measure up to these in both personality and natural physical beauty. (8:7)

"Natural physical beauty" and personal fulfillment as expressed by a young woman in the following description of her sports experience must not be denied to anyone in the name of last century's image of "femininity," a binding, limiting, belittling one. This is the age of the woman in space.

> The storm has ended and the sky is a clear and brilliant blue. The air is clean, brisk and invigorating. The snow sparkles as if millions of diamonds are imbedded within it. There is a presence in the air that is both one of calmness and of excitement. I'm eager to investigate and experience this phenomenon. I kick at the snow and it rises lightly, airily and floats back sparkling to the ground—some of it seems to hang suspended and still sparkles in the air.
>
> Let's go! Quick, to the top of the hill. I can't wait to fall and just lie in it, be covered by it, be part of it.

The top. Check boots, poles, bindings. Begin! But wait! I just have to fill myself with the beauty of it first. Is it right to scar such beauty with sitz marks and ski tracks? Keep it virgin and untouched just a little longer.

The majesty of the trees whose limbs are drooping from their burden, the expanse of the snow-peaked mountains, the clear blue of the sky and that beautiful deep sparkling powder white snow—God, it's beautiful!

I go! Can I handle this? Can I ski this powder? Will I fall? So what? Falling into this lovely soft, feathery light bed will be fun too.

I treat the snow gingerly. I'm cautious. I tell myself—sit back, keep knees together, ankles locked and pressed forward against the boots, down, plant pole, up and release, sink—I'm doing it!! I feel the tension begin to ease. I can. I am. I ski.

I feel myself relaxing and feeling the movement. It's a relaxed tension! I feel my whole body functioning as a unit, the muscles are working yet there is no antagonism, no effort. Everything is working smoothly and efficiently. I feel the effortless synchronization of pure movement—I'm alive. I'm living and God, it is good.

I feel the snow—I feel it. My skis are part of me, an extension of myself. I feel the snow. I ski on it, through it and out of it. I soar, I'm flying. I am free.

I can do what I want. I can pick my turns—it's steep but I am not afraid. There is no fear. Let's try a steeper hill. It makes no difference. I am with this white world—united!

I'll try the trees—the slope is steep and the trees are close together. I am alone and it is peaceful. I'm not lonely but filled with a presence all about me and it is good.

I'm hesitant. The trees seem awfully close together. So what? Go to it. It's like a slalom course—turn right, turn left, shuss, head right between those big firs, go—fly—soar. I become the Universe! (3)

BIBLIOGRAPHY

1. Blythe, Myrna. "Girl Athletes: What Makes Them Skate, Fence, Swim, Jump, Run?" *Cosmopolitan,* (October, 1969), pp. 110-114.
2. de Beauvoir, Simone. *The Second Sex.* New York: Bantam Books, 1952.
3. Hambric, Lois. "To Ski." Unpublished paper. California State College at Hayward, June, 1971.
4. Hart, M. Marie. "Factors Influencing College Women's Attitudes Toward Sport and Dance," Master's Thesis, University of Southern California, 1963.
5. Jokl, Ernst. *Medical Sociology and Cultural Anthropology of Sport and Physical Education.* Springfield, Ill.: Charles C. Thomas, Publisher, 1964, pp. 73-85.
6. Klafs, Carl E. and Arnheim, Daniel D. *Modern Principles of Athletic Training.* St. Louis, Mo.: C. V. Mosby Company, 1969, pp. 127-134.

7. Novich, Max M. and Taylor, Buddy. *Training and Conditioning of Athletes.* Philadelphia, Penn.: Lea and Febiger, 1970.
8. Ogilvie, Bruce. "The Unanswered Question: Competition, Its Effect Upon Feminity." Address given to the Olympic Development Committee, Santa Barbara, California, June 30, 1967.
9. Roberts, J. M. and Sutton-Smith, B. "Child-Training and Game Involvement," *Ethnology* 1 (1962): 66-185.
10. "Still They Fall," *Outing* 67 (November, 1912): 253.
11. Sutton-Smith, B., Rosenberg, B. G. and Morgan, E. F., Jr. "Development of Sex Differences in Play Choices During Preadolescence," *Child Development* 34 (1963): 119-126.
12. Sutton-Smith, B., Roberts, J. M. and Kozelka, R. M. "Game Involvement in Adults," *The Journal of Social Psychology* 60 (1963): 15-30.
13. "Things Seen and Heard." *Sportsman* 20 (October, 1936): 17-20.
14. Winner, Karin. "At Night We're Just Like Other Women," *Amateur Athlete.* (April, 1971), pp. 15-17.
15. *Women: A Journal of Liberation* 2 (Fall, 1970): 1+.

RELATED LITERATURE

Harres, Bea. "Attitudes of Students Toward Women's Athletic Competition," *Research Quarterly* 39 (May, 1968): 278-284.
Higdon, Rose and Higdon, Hal. "What Sports for Girls?" *Today's Health* 45 (October, 1967): 21-23, 74.
Krotz, L. E. " A Study of Sports and Implications for Women's Participation in Them in Modern Society," Ph.D. Dissertation, Ohio State University, 1958.
McGree, Rosemary. "Comparisons of Attitudes Toward Intensive Competition for High School Girls," *Research Quarterly* 27 (1956): 60-73.
Metheny, Eleanor. "Symbolic Forms of Movement: The Feminine Image in Sport," *Connotations of Movement in Sport and Dance.* Dubuque, Iowa: Wm. C. Brown Company Publishers, 1965, pp. 43-56.
Trekell, M. "The Effect of Some Cultural Changes Upon the Sports and Physical Education Activities of American Women—1860-1960," Paper presented at the History and Philosophy Section of the National Convention of the American Association of Health, Physical Education and Recreation, Dallas, Texas, March 18, 1965.
Watts, D. P. "Changing Conceptions of Competitive Sports for Girls and Women in the United States from 1880 to 1960," Ed.D. Dissertation, University of California, Los Angeles, 1960.

ETHNIC GROUP
PATTERNS

The first author gives the reader a quick and potent look into the "roots of the revolt of the black athlete." Edwards was involved in organizing the efforts and energy of the black athletes prior to the 1968 Olympics. In his article he suggests that this athlete's revolt relates to the black liberation movement. Edwards makes the reader aware that the protest of athletes was in reaction to the same iniquities that caused other protests and rebellions in the United States.

The plight of the black athlete is expanded in the second article. "Racial Segregation in American Sport," by Loy and McElvogue, is a thorough analysis of segregation and discrimination in professional baseball and football. The research pursues the relationship between discrimination and centrality. Are Negroes excluded from central positions on the teams and, if so, how does this reflect possibilities for advancement in the sports world?

In a study of ethnic soccer clubs in Milwaukee, Pooley analyzes the aspect of cultural assimilation. Do these clubs exist within ethnic subcultures and thereby inhibit assimilation of the ethnic group into "the standard setting" core culture? Or, one might ask, is it a way of maintaining ethnic identity? Pooley looks at ten different soccer clubs and their activities during club meetings, playing soccer and at social occasions, to discern answers to these questions.

Smith presents the rich tradition of games and sport as integral to the ways of life of early Native Americans. He has brought together a variety of anthropological studies on Indian games. With a heritage so rich, he asks, where is the Native American in American sport today?

PREFACE TO THE REVOLT OF THE BLACK ATHLETE

Harry Edwards

It's beyond me why these people would allow themselves to be misled by fanatics like Harry Edwards and H. Rap Brown. These athletes are seen by millions of people on nation-wide and world-wide television, they have first-string-starting assignments at white schools, and they are invited to all the big athletic events. Why our Niggers right here at the University have never had it so good.

This statement was made by the Director of Intercollegiate Athletics at one of America's major universities, later to be "white-listed" by the Olympic Committee for Human Rights during the Spring, 1968, track and field season. He was speaking to the sports editor of one of America's leading weekly news magazines. His remarks are typical of the sentiment of many of the athletic administrations that determine policy in the world of intercollegiate, amateur, and professional athletics in America. Equally typical was the response of the sports editor. He merely shook his head, indicating that he, too, could not understand such ingratitude, and then went on about the business of obtaining a *publishable* story for next week's issue. All too often too many of these self-proclaimed guardians of the morals and ethics of the sports world lend tacit approval to such racially corrupt and hypocritical attitudes, thus further degrading and violating the basic human dignity and intelligence of black athletes.

Recreation and athletics have traditionally been billed as essentially therapeutic measures—measures that cure faulty or deteriorating charcter, that weaken prejudice, and that bind men of all races and nationalities closer together. The evidence does not support the theory. Athletic and recreational centers set up in high-crime or delinquency areas have become merely convenient meeting places for criminals and delinquents.[1] Recreational and athletic activities, far from inhibiting crime, actually have spawned it in both the amateur and professional areas. As for eliminating prejudice, whites may grudgingly admit a black man's prowess as an athlete, but will not acknowledge his equality as a human being. In athletics, where the stakes are position, prestige, and money, where intense competition prevails and a loser is anathema, a white racist does not change his attitude toward blacks; he merely alters his inclination to abuse him or discriminate against him overtly.

Recreational patterns in America widen and perpetuate racial separation. Recreation is exclusive, compounded of all sorts of considerations, not the least of which are racial and economic. There is, therefore, usually little opportunity for recreation to narrow the gap between white and black Americans. Moreover, there is absolutely nothing inherent in recreation that would change attitudes. Recreation simply refreshes the mind and body and gives old attitudes a new start and a fresh impetus.

At an athletic event, by no means are all the bigots and racists sitting in the stands. They also are on the field of play.

The roots of the revolt of the black athlete spring from the same seed that produced the sit-ins, the freedom rides, and the rebellions in Watts, Detroit, and Newark. The athletic revolt springs from a disgust and dissatisfaction with the same racist germ that infected the warped minds responsible for the bomb murders of four black girls as they prayed in a Birmingham, Alabama, church and that conceived and carried out the murders of Malcolm X, Martin Luther King, and Medgar Evers, among a multitude of others. The revolt of the black athlete arises also from his new awarenes of his responsibilities in an increasingly more desperate, violent, and unstable America. He is for the first time reacting in a human and masculine fashion to the disparities between the heady artificial world of newspaper clippings, photographers, and screaming spectators and the real world of degradation, humiliation, and horror that confronts the overwhelming majority of Afro-Americans. An even more immediate call to arms for many black athletes has been their realization that once their athletic abilities are impaired by age or injury, only the ghetto beckons and they are doomed once again to that faceless, hopeless, ignominious existence they had supposedly forever left

---

1. For a brief discussion of value, delinquency, and organized recreation and athletics, see A. W. Green, *Recreation, Leisure, and Politics,* McGraw-Hill Book Company, New York, pp. 98-105.

behind them. At the end of their athletic career, black athletes do not become congressmen, as did Bob Mathias, the white former Olympic decathlon champion, or Wilmer Mizell, ex-Pittsburgh Pirate pitcher. Neither does the black athlete cash in on the thousands of dollars to be had from endorsements, either during his professional career or after he retires. And all his clippings, records, and photographs will not qualify him for a good job, even in any of the industries that supposedly produce the breakfast foods that champions feed on. These are only the most obvious of the inequities faced by the black athlete. Others are less obvious but no less humiliating and they have no less a devastating effect on the black athlete's psyche. Like other blacks, black athletes find housing, recreational facilities, clubs, and off-season jobs closed to them (unless the coach passes the word to a prospective employer or renter that the candidate is a "good" Negro, the implication of course being that most black people are in some mysterious fashion not "good").

In essence then, the black revolution in America has not been carried into the locker room, as one sportswriter has stated. What has happened is that the black athlete has left the facade of locker room equality and justice to take his long vacant place as a primary partici-pant in the black revolution. Underlining the importance and significance of the political and social status of this new generation of black athletes is the fact that candidates for political offices at the local and national levels in both major political parties worked vigorously in 1968 to secure the endorsements and active support of black athletes. Where the ath-letes' amateur status would have been jeopardized by such public com-mitment, statements were sought from them regarding their approval of some particular candidate's program (for instance, that of Hubert H. Humphrey) to establish equality in amateur athletics or to give the athlete more say in settling disputes between such competing athletic organizations as the National Collegiate Athletic Association and the Amateur Athletic Union. Robert Kennedy with Rosey Grier and Rafer Johnson, Hubert H. Humphrey with Ralph Metcalf, Richard Nixon with Wilt Chamberlain, and Nelson Rockefeller with Jackie Robinson attest that the stupid, plow-jack stereotype of the black athlete is no more. Whether they made a truly significant contribution to black progress or merely prostituted their athletic ability for the sake of other aims is a matter of keen debate among politically conscious blacks.

In this book we will analyze the newest phase of the black libera-tion movement in America. Within the context of that movement we will define the goals that underlie the athletes' protests and clarify what has been portrayed as the substantially elusive and irrational tactics and direction of their efforts. The statements we will make are not the rantings of some sideline journalist, but the documentary facts of the movement from the perspective of a man who himself was victimized by the American athletic structure, who helped plan, direct, and implement the revolt, and who intends to continue the fight until the goals of that revolt have been achieved.

The exploitation and suffering of the black athlete in America is no more a recent development than is the inhumanity and deprivation suffered by Afro-American non-athletes. Nor do these recent athletic protests mark the first instances of black athletes speaking out. The difference in this instance is that they are speaking out not only on their own behalf, but on behalf of their downtrodden race, and the world and the nation are listening. America's response to what the black athlete is saying and doing will undoubtedly not only determine the future course and direction of American athletics, but also will affect all racial and social relations between blacks and whites in this country.

Hopefully this book will be read and understood by many people, but particularly by those who control athletics and exert political and economic power in America. For it is the latter who have the power to correct the injustices that beset the American sports scene before they spawn conflict. And by some means, somewhere along the line, these injustices shall be corrected.

RACIAL SEGREGATION IN
AMERICAN SPORT*

JOHN W. LOY AND JOSEPH F. McELVOGUE

INTRODUCTION

Numerous journalists have commented on the social functions which sport fulfills for minority groups in American society. Boyle, for example, forcefully writes:

> Sport has often served minority groups as the first rung on the social ladder. As such, it has helped further their assimilation into American life. It would not be too far-fetched to say that it has done more in this regard than any other agency, including church and school (1963, p. 100).

Recently, journalists have placed special emphasis on the many contributions sport has made for the Negro. As Olsen observes:

> Every morning the world of sport wakes up and congratulates itself on its contributions to race relations. The litany has been so often repeated that it is believed almost universally. It goes: "Look what sports has done for the Negro" (1968, p. 7).

In view of the many journalistic accounts of the contributions of sport to the social success of minority groups, it is somewhat surprising that sociologists and physical educators have largely ignored the issue of minority group integration in American sport. The purpose of this paper is to direct the attention of sport sociologists to the issue by presenting a theoretical and empirical examination of racial segregation in America's major professional baseball and football teams.

*Appreciation is accorded to Mr. Schroeder, director, and Mr. Dyer, assistant director of Helms Hall for assistance in the collection of data for this paper.
From the *International Review of Sport Sociology* 5 (1970) 5-23. Copyright © 1970 ARS Polona, Krakowskie Przedmiescie 7, Warsaw, Poland. Reprinted with permission.

THEORETICAL OVERVIEW

Theoretically considered, our examination largely draws upon Grusky's (1963) theory of formal structure of organizations and Blalock's (1962) set of theoretical propositions regarding occupational discrimination.

Grusky's Theory of Formal Structure

According to Grusky, "the formal structure of an organization consists of a set of norms which define the system's official objectives, its major offices or positions, and the primary responsibilities of the position occupants" (p. 345). The formal structure ". . . patterns the behavior of its constituent positions along three interdependent dimensions: (1) spatial location, (2) nature of task, and (3) frequency of interaction" (p. 345). The theoretical import of Grusky's model is contained in his statement that:

> All else being equal, the more central one's spatial location: (1) the greater likelihood dependent or coordinative tasks will be performed and (2) the greater the rate of interaction with the occupants of other positions. Also, the performance of dependent tasks is positively related to frequency of interaction (p. 346).

Combining these three criteria, Grusky distinguishes positions of high interaction potential and position of low interaction potential within the social structure of organizations. He defines the occupants of these two types of positions as high and low interactors, respectively.

For our purposes, we prefer to use the concept of "centrality" in dealing with Grusky's three interdependent dimensions of organizational positions. With an extension to permit us to embrace all three of Grusky's criteria, we accepted Hopkins' (1964) definition of this concept:

> Centrality designates how close a member is to the "center" of the group's interaction network and thus refers simultaneously to the frequency with which a member participates in interaction with other members and the number or range of other members with whom he interacts (p. 28) [and the degree to which he must coordinate his tasks and activities with other members].

Blalock's Theoretical Propositions

Several years ago, Blalock (1962) made a very astute analysis of why "professionial baseball has provided Negroes with one of the relatively few avenues for escape from blue-collar occupations." From his analysis, Blalock developed thirteen theoretical propositions concerning occupational discrimination which can be empirically tested in other occupational settings. His analysis is an excellent example of how the critical examination of a sport situation can enhance the development of sociological theory in an area of central concern. Blalock was, however, perhaps naive in assuming that professional baseball is ". . . an occupation which is remarkably free of racial discrimination" (p. 242).

We sought to test Blalock's assumption that professional baseball is relatively free of racial discrimination by drawing upon three of his propositions to predict where racial segregation is most likely to occur on the baseball diamond. The three particular propositions which we considered were:

> 1. The lower the degree of purely social interaction on the job . . . ,the lower the degree of discrimination" (p. 246).
> 2. "To the extent that performance level is relatively independent of skill in interpersonal relations, the lower the degree of discrimination" (p. 246).
> 3. "To the extent that an individual's success depends primarily on his own performance, rather than on limiting or restricting the performance of specific other individuals, the lower the degree of discrimination by group members" (p. 245).

On the one hand, the consideration of proposition 1 in conjunction with proposition 2 suggested that discrimination is directly related to level and type of interaction. On the other hand, the combined consideration of propositions 2 and 3 suggested that there will be less discrimination where performance of independent tasks are largely involved; because such tasks do not have to be coordinated with the activities of other persons, and therefore do not hinder the performance of others, nor require a great deal of skill in interpersonal relations.

Since the dimensions of interaction and task dependency treated by Blalock are included in our concept of centrality, we subsumed his three propositions under a more general one, stating that: "discrimination is positively related to centrality."

STATEMENT OF THEORETICAL HYPOTHESIS

Broadly conceived, discrimination ". . . denotes the unfavourable treatment of categories of persons on arbitrary grounds" (Moore, 1964, p. 203). Discrimination takes many forms, but a major mode is that of segregation. Segregation denotes the exclusion of certain categories of persons from specific social organizations or particular positions within organizations on arbitrary grounds, i.e., grounds which have no objective relation to individual skill and talent.

Since we were chiefly concerned with the matter of racial segregation in professional sports, we took as our specific theoretical hypothesis
the proposition that: *racial segregation in professional team sports is
positively related to centrality.* In order to test this hypothesis, we empirically examined the extent of racial segregation within major league
baseball and major league football.

THE CASE OF PROFESSIONAL BASEBALL

Baseball teams have a well defined social structure consisting of the
repetitive and regulated interaction among a set of nine positions combined into three major substructures or interaction units: (1) the battery,
consisting of pitcher and catcher; (2) the infield, consisting of first
base, second base, shortstop and third base; and (3) the outfield, consisting of leftfield, centerfield and rightfield positions.

Empirical Hypothesis

As is evident from Figure 1, one can readily see that the outfield
contains the most peripheral and socially isolated positions in the organizational structure of a baseball team. Therefore, on the basis of our theoretical hypothesis, we predicted that Negro players in comparison to
white players on major league teams are more likely to occupy outfield
positions and less likely to occupy infield positions.

Methods

Data. On the basis of the *1968 Baseball Register* all professional players
in the American and National Leagues who played at least fifty games
during the 1967 season were categorized according to race and playing
position.[1]

1. The criterion of fifty games was established in order to eliminate the partial
participant, such as the pinch hitter or runner, the player brought up from the
minor leagues on a part-time basis, the occasional utility man, and the unestablished
rookie trying to make the team at any position.
Players were ethnically classified as Caucasians, Negroes or Latin Americans. The
latter group was excluded from most analyses, however, as it was impossible in terms
of the sources available to determine which Latin American athletes were Negroes.
Players at all positions were considered except for pitchers. They were excluded for
purposes of analysis because: (1) data comparable to that collected for other players
was not available, (2) the high rate of interchangeability among pitchers precluded
accurate recording of data, and (3) pitchers are in a sense only part-time players,
in that they typically play in only one game out of four, or if relief pitchers, play
only a few innings in any given game. In order that the reader may make certain
comparisons later in the paper, we note at this point that "only 13 of 207 pitchers
in 1968 major league rosters were Negroes" (Olsen, 1968, p. 170).

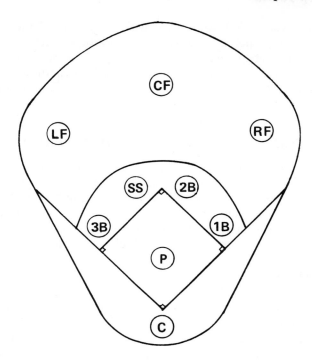

Treatment. The X^2 test for two independent samples was used to test the null hypothesis that there is no difference between white and black ballplayers in terms of the proportion who occupy infield and outfield positions. The .01 level of significance, using a one-tailed test, was selected as being sufficient to warrant the rejection of the null hypothesis.

Findings

Table 1 presents the number of white and black athletes occupying specific positions in the major leagues in 1967. It is clearly evident from the table that Negro players are predominantly found in the outfield. The highly significant X^2, resulting from the test of our null hypothesis, gives strong support to our empirical hypothesis and provides some confirmation of our theoretical hypothesis that racial segregation in professional sports is related to centrality. As a further test of our hypothesis we examined the extent of racial segregation in professional football.

THE CASE OF PROFESSIONAL FOOTBALL

Like baseball teams, football teams have well defined organizational structures. However, whereas the positions in baseball organization are

TABLE 1

**A Comparison of Race and Position Occupancy
in Major League Baseball in 1967**

Playing Position	American League		National League		Both Leagues	
	White	Black	White	Black	White	Black
Catcher	13	0	14	1	27	1
Shortstop	7	0	10	1	17	1
1st Base	11	2	7	5	18	7
2nd Base	10	3	6	1	16	4
3rd Base	9	2	7	4	16	6
Outfield	26	14	12	22	38	36
N =	76	21	56	34	132	55

Race

Position	White	Black	Total
Infield	94	19	113
Outfield	38	36	74
	132	55	187

$X^2 = 20.32; p < .0005$ (df = 1)

determined by defensive alignment, there exists both a distinctive offensive and a distinctive defensive team within modern professional football organization. Figure 2 shows the constituent positions of the offensive and defensive teams of any given professional football organization.

Empirical Hypothesis

It is clear from Figure 2 that the most central positions on the offensive team consist of center, right guard, left guard and quarterback; while the most central position on the defensive team are the three linebacker positions. Therefore, on the basis of our theoretical hypothesis, we predicted that Negro football players in comparison to white players are more likely to occupy non-central positions than central positions on both offensive and defensive teams.

Methods

Data. Using the *Official 1968 Autographed Yearbooks* of the American and National Football Leagues in conjunction with Zanger's *Pro Football 1968* we classified all starting offensive and defensive players according to race (black or white) and playing position (central or non-central).[2] *Treatment.* The X^2 test for two independent samples was used to test the null hypothesis that there is no difference between white and black occupancy of centrally located positions on either offensive or defensive teams. The .01 level of significance, using a one-tailed test, was selected as being sufficient to warrant the rejection of the null hypothesis.

2. The major difficulties we experienced in data collection were associated with the problems of determining the race of the players and in determining who were the first string or starting players. In the case of major league football, we used the "official yearbooks" to ascertain the race of given players as these sources contained photographs of the members of every team in a given league. Zanger's text was used as a means of determining the first string or starting lineup for each team. However, Zanger's lineups were preseason forecasts based upon the players' performance the previous season. A more accurate means of recording would have been to determine the players having the most playing time at each position for every team during the 1968 season.

An indication, however, that the data which we present in Tables 2 and 3 is reasonably accurate are the following facts cited from a study made independently of our own:

"On on typical weekend in the 1967 NFL season, no Negro center started a game. Of the 32 offensive guards in the starting lineups of NFL teams, 29 were white" (Olsen, 1963, p. 171).

". . . (on that same typical weekend in the 1967 season, 48 linebackers lumbered out on the field to start NFL games, and 45 of them, or 94 per cent, were white)" (Olsen, 1968, p. 172).

Findings

Tables 2 and 3 present the number of white and black athletes occupying central and non-central offensive and defensive positions, respectively, in the major professional football leagues in 1968. It is evident from the tables that very few Negro players occupy central positions,

TABLE 2
A Comparison of Race and Position Occupancy within Offensive Teams in Major League Football in 1968

Playing Position	American League		National League		Both Leagues	
	White	Black	White	Black	White	Black
Center	10	0	16	0	26	0
Quarterback	9	1	16	0	25	1
Right Guard	9	1	15	1	24	2
Left Guard	10	0	15	1	25	1
Right Tackle	10	0	11	5	21	5
Left Tackle	8	2	11	5	19	7
Tight End	7	3	13	3	20	6
Split End	8	2	10	6	18	8
Fullback	4	6	11	5	15	11
Halfback	3	7	7	9	10	16
Flankerback	7	3	10	6	17	9
$N =$	85	25	135	41	220	66

Race

Position	White	Black	Total
Central	100	4	104
Noncentral	120	62	182
	220	66	286

$$X^2 = 32.37; p < .0005 \text{ (df = 1)}$$

either defensively or offensively. The significant X^2 tests of our null hypothesis give strong support to our empirical hypothesis and provide further confirmation of our theoretical hypothesis.

DISCUSSION

The preceding findings leave little doubt that only a very small proportion of black athletes occupy central positions in America's pro-

TABLE 3

**A Comparison of Race and Position Occupancy within Defensive
Teams in Major League Football in 1968**

Playing Position	American League		National League		Both Leagues	
	White	Black	White	Black	White	Black
Middle Linebacker	8	2	16	0	24	2
Right Linebacker	10	0	15	1	25	1
Left Linebacker	8	2	15	1	23	3
Right End	6	4	12	4	18	8
Right Tackle	7	3	13	3	20	6
Left Tackle	7	3	10	6	17	9
Left End	8	2	11	5	19	7
Right Safety	7	3	10	6	17	9
Left Safety	7	3	10	6	17	9
Right Cornerback	2	8	6	10	8	18
Left Cornerback	1	9	3	13	4	22
N =	71	39	121	55	192	94

Race

Position	White	Black	Total
Central	72	6	78
Noncentral	120	88	208
	192	94	286

$$X^2 = 29.26; p < .0005 \text{ (df = 1)}$$

fessional baseball and football organizations. However, notwithstanding
our theoretical buttress, a number of telling questions can be raised
regarding the revealed relationships between race and position occupancy. Three such questions are: (1) Does the discovered relationship
between race and position occupancy indicate the actual presence of
racial segregation? (2) If racial segregation is actually present, what
are the "social mechanisms" linking it to centrality? (3) If racial segregation does exist in professional sports, what are its social consequences?
Let us briefly consider each of these questions in turn.

DOES RACIAL SEGREGATION ACTUALLY
EXIST IN SPORT?

One can argue that showing that Negro athletes infrequently occupy central positions does not confirm that they are racially segregated. They may be excluded from central positions for objective rather than arbitrary reasons. On the one hand, Negroes may not have as great a talent or skill for certain tasks as white players, and are thus excluded from selected positions for that reason. On the other hand, Negroes may possess greater athletic ability than whites for certain activities, and are accordingly found proportionately more often in some positions than others. A third alternative, of course, is that Negro athletes exclude themselves from selected positions by personal preference.

Although we are not presently prepared to fully assess the validity of each of these three perspectives, we must frankly state we find them tenuous. For example, we have found no evidence which would lead us to believe that Negro athletes have inferior ability in comparison to white athletes for any role assignment in professional baseball or football. We observe that time and again in the world of sport athletic stereotypes of Negroes have been refuted. It will be recalled that, not too long ago, there existed the myth among track authorities that Negroes were racially suited for the sprints and perhaps the shorter distance races, but did not possess the capabilities for the endurance events. The success of black athletes in long distance running events, including the Olympic marathon, in recent years has dispelled the notion that Negro trackmen are speed merchants without stamina.

Similarly, we have discovered little support for the view that Negro athletes possess certain abilities in greater abundance than white athletes. We have, however, encountered some findings which indicate that a black athlete must be superior to his white counterpart before he is permitted to occupy a given position. For example, a recent study shows that the cumulative major league batting averages in 1968 were higher for Negroes at every position as follows: catcher-whites .238, blacks .279; first and third bases-whites .265, blacks .277; second and shortstop-whites .246, blacks .258; outfield-whites .253, blacks .266 (Los Angeles Time, May 15, 1969, part 3, p. 3).[3]

Finally, we find it difficult to believe that Negro athletes are largely selecting the positions which they occupy in baseball and football on the

---

3. For a more complete account of how Negro athletes must be superior to white athletes in professional baseball in order to maintain their positions, see Rosenblatt, 1967. Finally, we note that the three outfield positions were considered as a single category since data were not available for each of the three outfield positions taken separately.

basis of personal preference. What seems to be operating is a self-fulfilling belief. A black athlete assumes that he doesn't have much chance at being accepted at certain positions and thus tries out for other positions where his estimate of success is much higher. As Olsen succinctly states: "He *anticipates* the white man's categorization of him, and acts accordingly" (1968, p. 170). An interesting study, we suggest, would be to compare the playing positions of white and black athletes in professional football with those they filled in college football. Our prediction is that a greater proportion of black than white athletes will be discovered to have acquired new role assignments.

Some would perhaps contend that we are overstating our case regarding racial segregation in professional sports; because:

> The degree to which Negroes have moved into pro sports is astonishing. More than half the players in the National Basketball Association are Negroes—as were eight of the ten starters in the last NBA All-Star Game. A quarter of the players in the National Football League are Negroes, and the 1967 NFL team was 40 per cent black. Nearly 25 per cent of all players in major league baseball are American Negroes, and here too a disproportionate number of the stars are not white. For example, of the top ten hitters in the National League for the 1967 season, only one was a Caucasian (Olsen, 1968, p. 170).

Nevertheless, we point out that sport seems to mirror American life at large, in that, integration has been very slow, and where it has been rather fully achieved there remain many forms of discrimination other than that of segregation.

Professional baseball is a good example of how slowly the process of integration takes place. Many herald 1947 as the year "the color line was broken" with the entrance of Jackie Robinson into major league baseball. But, as illustrated in Table 4, ten years later there were only a dozen Negro players in the National League and as late as 1960 there were only a half dozen black athletes in the American League. Table 4 does reveal, however, that there has been a substantial increase in the number of Latin American players in recent years and indicates that there exists an intermediate "brown zone" between the "white and black belts" of major league baseball.[4]

4. It would be interesting to find out whether or not "darker" Latin American athletes are more often found in the outfield than the "lighter" Latin players. There are some small indications that "quota systems" are operating for American Negro players and Latin American players, in that, if members of one group are prominent occupants of a given field position within a league, then the members of the other group tend to be predominant at another playing position. For a discussion of the social relations between American Negro and Latin American players, see Boyle, 1963, pp. 108-113.

WHAT ARE THE SOCIAL MECHANISMS
OF SEGREGATION?

Assuming that there is racial segregation in professional baseball and football, one is led to inquire as to what are the underlying causes of this form of discrimination. We have argued that segregation is a function of centrality and its associated interdependent dimensions of spatial location, rate of interaction and task dependency. Sociologically viewed, our theoretical rationale is probably a fairly satisfactory one; but those of a more social psychological orientation would likely want to know what sort of personal qualities and behavioral dispositions are associated with centrality which influence segregation.

There are no doubt many kinds of normative beliefs and attitudes which act as antecedent and/or intervening variables in the relationship between segregation and centrality. We specifically speculate that there is a relationship between interaction and attitudes regarding persona intimacy; and a relationship between tasks dependency and beliefs concerning the qualities of judgment and decision-making ability.

A major generalization of discrimination research states that: "there is a range within discriminatory practice such that there is most discrimination and most prejudice as the practice comes closer to intimate personal contact" (Berelson and Steiner, 1964, p. 511). Thus, we reason that Negroes may be excluded from central positions because these positions involve high rates of interaction which lead to greater personal contact among players than do peripheral positions in an organization.

We conject, in passing, that there may even be normative beliefs regarding the interaction of Negro athletes among themselves. In the case of professional football, for instance, black athletes are most often found at the two cornerback positions. Similarly, in the case of professional baseball, we point out that in the infield Negroes are most often found at first and third bases. While the relationship may be a spurious one, it is interesting that Negroes are placed in the extreme corners of the field in both baseball and football. A related observation is that seldom does one find two Negroes playing side-by-side in either major league baseball or football.

In treating interaction, one should, of course, distinguish between task interaction and social interaction since there is probably only a moderate correlation between the two. Although we expect that there may be a substantial degree of prejudice regarding the intermixing of white and black players off the field, we are not sure that there is

TABLE 4
Distribution of White, Black and Latin American Players by Position in Major League Baseball 1956-1967

National League

Year	Catcher	Short-stop	2nd Base	3rd Base	1st Base	Outfield	Total No.
1967	14	10	6	7	7	12	56
	1	1	1	4	5	22	34
	0	1	4	1	3	7	16
1966	13	9	8	8	5	15	58
	2	2	2	3	4	21	34
	0	2	4	2	3	8	19
1965	15	10	10	8	7	13	63
	1	1	1	3	5	19	30
	1	3	3	0	5	8	19
1964	13	8	11	8	8	18	66
	2	2	1	3	5	20	33
	0	3	2	2	2	8	16
1963	14	8	8	14	10	22	76
	1	2	2	2	4	18	29
	0	3	2	0	1	3	9
1962	Data not available						
1961	11	5	8	8	6	18	56
	1	2	2	2	2	11	20
	0	3	2	0	2	5	12
1960	12	6	7	9	9	21	64
	1	2	2	1	2	11	19
	0	1	2	0	2	4	9
1959	Data not available						
1958	12	7	8	9	10	18	64
	2	1	1	0	2	8	14
	2	1	1	0	1	2	5
1957	11	6	8	8	11	25	69
	1	2	1	2	1	5	12
	1	1	0	1	0	2	5
1956	11	9	8	9	9	20	66
	1	1	3	1	1	5	12
	0	0	2	0	0	2	2

320

TABLE 4 (cont.)

Distribution of White, Black and Latin American Players
by Position in Major League Baseball 1956-1967

American League

Ethnic Group	Catcher	Short-stop	2nd Base	3rd Base	1st Base	Outfield	Total No.
White	13	7	10	9	11	26	76
Black	0	0	3	2	2	14	21
Latin	2	4	1	1	1	6	15
White Black Latin				Data not available			
White	12	12	10	10	14	29	87
Black	2	0	1	1	1	12	17
Latin	1	3	2	2	1	6	13
White	12	9	13	10	12	29	85
Black	2	0	1	1	2	10	16
Latin	1	2	0	1	1	7	12
White	14	10	11	6	13	31	87
Black	2	0	2	1	1	7	13
Latin	2	2	0	1	1	5	1
White	13	11	11	9	11	34	85
Black	2	0	1	2	0	3	8
Latin	2	3	0	1	1	2	9
White	13	9	13	12	12	29	89
Black	2	1	1	1	0	9	14
Latin	1	3	0	0	1	3	8
White	10	6	9	11	11	27	74
Black	2	0	1	0	0	3	6
Latin	0	3	0	0	2	2	7
White	13	12	12	9	10	28	84
Black	0	0	0	0	2	3	5
Latin	0	2	0	1	2	2	7
White Black Latin				Data not available			
White Black Latin				Data not available			
White Black Latin				Data not available			

marked prejudice among players concerning racial interpersonal contact on the field.[5]

We speculate that segregation in professional sports is more a function of management than playing personnel. For example, there appears to be a myth among coaches that Negro players lack judgment and decision-making ability. This myth results in black athletes being excluded from positions requiring dependent or coordinative tasks as such activities generally require greater judgment than independent tasks. In short, the central positions in major league baseball and football are typically the most responsible or so-called "brains positions." The following quotations from Olsen with respect to central and peripheral defensive positions within football organization well illustrate the matter:

> "Most defensive football players have a single job to do, with little variation, but the linebacker has to exercise judgment" says a thoughtful NFL player. "He may wind up tackling the quarterback fifteen yards behind the line of scrimmage, and he may wind up knocking down a pass twenty-yards up the field. He has to be able to read plays-well, everybody knows all the things the linebacker has to do. It's one of the most responsible defensive positions. Therefore, he can't be a Negro" (p. 172).
>
> "Cornerback is not a brains position" says Bill Koman, retired St. Louis Cardinal linebacker. "You pick up the split end or the flanker and you stay with him all the way. That's it (p. 173).
>
> "Yassuh, white man, boss," says one NFL cornerback derisively when asked about the situation, "We ain't got the brains to play center, 'cause we can't count, but we can follow that flanker's ass all the way down the field, *yuck, yuck*" (p. 173).

In our discussion herein we have emphasized the interaction and task dependency dimensions of centrality; whereas in our empirical examination of racial segregation we stressed the dimension of spatial location. Additional limitations of our empirical analysis include the fact that our measure of spatial location was dichotomous rather than continuous in nature; and the fact that we only looked at major league baseball and football for specific one-year periods. In an effort to overcome these limitations, we extend our analysis of the racial composition of professional baseball to cover a twelve year period; and we developed

5. Charnofsky (1967), for example, presents evidence which suggests that while there exists a degree of racial prejudice among a number of players, the majority of athletes in professional baseball hold favorable attitudes toward minority group members on their teams. We note, however, that off the field the problem of discrimination may be a horse of a different color. For example, the 1969 season is the first where several teams have set forth explicit policies assuring the racial integration of teammates on the road via mixed room assignments.

an operational index of centrality which is continuous in nature and which reflects the interaction and task dependency dimensions of centrality.

Table 5 shows the approximate number of individual white and black athletes at each field position in the major leagues over a twelve year period.[6] The table also shows the rank order of playing positions in terms of the proportion of Negro players at each position. This rank order is nearly identical to that given in Table 1.

TABLE 5

Distribution of Individual White and Black Players
by Position in Major League Baseball 1956-1967

Playing Position	White Players	Black Players	Total No. of Players	% of Black Players	Rank Order % White Players
Catcher	85	5	90	.0555	1
Shortstop	39	4	43	.0930	2
2nd Base	61	7	68	.1029	3
3rd Base	41	9	50	.1800	4
1st Base	54	13	67	.1940	5
Outfield	129	61	190	.3210	6
N =	409	99	508	.1948	

Having reaffirmed the relationship between segregation and spatial location, we turned our attention to the interaction and task dependency dimensions of centrality. We decided that the total number of "assists" made by occupants of given field positions during a season would serve as an adequate operational indicator of centrality.[7] On the one hand, assists are an indicator of the rate of interaction and the number and range of other group members with whom a position occupant interacts.

6. As is evident from Table 4, we were unable to obtain relevant data for a number of seasons for the two major leagues between 1956 and 1967. However, there does not appear to be much change in playing personnel from one year to the next. Moreover, our figures provide a conservative estimate of the racial composition of professional baseball, in that the missing data includes more white players.

It was not difficult to keep track of a small number of players switching leagues over the period sampled, but a small number of players switching playing positions over the period covered did pose a bit of a problem. We arbitrarily assigned them the position where they had played the most games in their major league career.

7. An assist is the official credit awarded in the scoring of a game to a player who throws a ball in such a way that it results in a putout. Data regarding assists were obtained from the *American League Red Book* and the *National League Green Books*. These are annual publications of the two major leagues which report vital statistics about all players, teams and games each season.

On the other hand, assists are an index of the degree to which dependent tasks are associated with given positions.

We discovered that the rank order of field positions with respect to number of annual assists remained the same for both leagues for every year covered.[8] More strikingly, however, we found a perfect rank order correlation between our measures of segregation and centrality (see

TABLE 6
Ranks for Position Occupancy and Annual Assists in Professional Baseball

Field Position	Rank Order		d_i	d_i^2
	% of Whites*	Annual Assists**		
Catcher	1	1	0	0
Shortstop	2	2	0	0
2nd Base	3	3	0	0
3rd Base	4	4	0	0
1st Base	5	5	0	0
Outfield	6	6	0	0

$$r_s = 1 - \frac{6 \sum\limits_{i=1}^{n} d_i^2}{N^3 - N} = 1 - \frac{6(0)}{6(3) - 6} \; ; \text{rho} = 1.00$$

*See Table 5.   **See Footnote 8.   (Siegel, 1956, pp. 202-213)

8. In the scoring of a game, the strikeouts made by the pitcher which are caught by the catcher are recorded as putouts for the catcher. For purposes of analysis we considered such putouts as assists. We reasoned that the catcher calls the pitch and assists in making the strikeouts by receiving the thrown ball from the pitcher. We note that a strikeout is recorded regardless of whether the ball is caught or not. An example of the consistency of the number of annual assists by position for both leagues is the following data for the 1963, 1964 and 1965 seasons:

Year	American League	Position	National League
1963	10,508	C	9,946
	4,724	SS	4,749
	4,427	2nd	4,253
	3,176	3rd	3,029
	1,119	1st	1,002
	325	Out	323
1964	10,713	C	10,112
	4,775	SS	4,939
	4,425	2nd	4,404
	3,225	3rd	3,096
	1,059	1st	1,018
	308	Out	322
1965	10,461	C	10,454
	4,696	SS	4,886
	4,274	2nd	4,831
	3,341	3rd	3,093
	1,050	1st	1,045
	274	Out	292

Table 6). Thus, we concluded that we had obtained substantial support for our theoretical hypothesis that racial segregation in professional team sports is positively related to centrality.

WHAT ARE THE SOCIAL CONSEQUENCES OF SEGREGATION?

It is exceedingly difficult to assess the social consequences of racial segregation in professional baseball and football because data is limited; and because the consequences are both manifest and latent, acute and chronic. It would appear, however, that one of the major disadvantageous consequences of segregation is the retardation of upward career mobility in professional sports. Grusky (1963) has shown that approximately three-fourths of all major league baseball managers are recruited from infield positions.[9] Therefore, to the degree that Negro athletes are denied access to central positions, they are also limited in obtaining positions of leadership in professional baseball.[10]

Grusky assumes that the position which an individual occupies influences his development of varying kinds of role skills; and further assumes that the occupancy of central positions enhances the obtainment of key role skills related to upward career mobility. These rather broad assumptions are likely related to Hopkins' (1964) set of fifteen theoretical propositions regarding small groups. For example, Hopkins states that: "For any member of a small group, the greater his centrality:

1. the greater his observability;
2. the greater his conformity;
3. the greater his influence; and,
4. the higher his rank" (1964, p. 51).

Another related proposition is that centrality is positively related to liking (Grusky, 1963, p. 347; Homans, 1950, p. 133).[11]

This latter proposition suggests that there may be a "vicious cycle" operating in professional sports. Negroes, because they are not liked by the white establishment, are placed in peripheral positions; and, as a result of this placement, do not have the opportunity of high rates of

---

9. In Grusky's study about twenty-five per cent of the managers were found to be ex-catchers. Recent investigations by Loy and Sage concerning collegiate baseball show that college coaches and college team captains are most often recruited from infield positions; especially that of catcher. Moreover, their findings indicate that, although there are relatively few Negroes playing college baseball, there are proportionately more Negroes in outfield than infield positions.

10. It is only recently that a token number of former Negro athletes have been hired as coaches in professional sports; and to date there are no Negro head coaches in major league football or Negro managers in major league baseball.

11. See Hopkins, 1964, pp. 112-117 for a critique of this proposition.

interaction with teammates, and do not receive the potential positive sentiment which might accrue from such interaction. In view of the nature of our problem, our discussion is likely too brief and superficial. However, we hope that we have been successful in directing the attention of sport sociologists to the matter of integration in American sport, and in providing stimulation for further theoretical and empirical analyses of the subject.[12]

REFERENCES CITED

American Football League Official Autographed Yearbook 1968. Dallas: Sports Underwriters, Inc., 1968.
American League Red Book. Boston: American League Publicity Department.
Baseball Register. St. Louis: Sporting News.
Berelson B. and Steiner G. A., *Human Behavior—an Inventory of Scientific Findings.* New York: Harcourt, Brace World, Inc., 1964.
Blalock H. M. Jr., "Occupational Discrimination: Some Theoretical Propositions," *Social Problems* 9 (1962): 240-247.
Boyle H. H., *Sport—Mirror of American Life.* Boston: Little, Brown Co., 1963.
Charnofsky H., "The Major League Professional Baseball Player: Self-Conception Versus The Popular Image," *International Review of Sport Sociology* 3 (1968): 39-55. Polish Scientific Publishers, Warsaw.
Grusky O., "The Effects of Formal Structure on Managerial Recruitment: A Study of Baseball Organization," *Sociometry* 26 (1963): 345-353.
Homans G. C., *The Human Group.* New York: Harcourt, Brace World, Inc., 1950.
Hopkins T. K., *The Exercise of Influence in Small Groups.* Totowa, N. J.: Bedminster Press, 1964.
Loy J. W. and Sage J. N., "The Effects of Formal Structure on Organizational Leadership: An Investigation of Interscholastic Baseball Teams." Paper presented at the second International Congress of Sport Psychology, November 1, 1968 in Washington, D. C.
Moore H. E., "Discrimination," pp. 203-204 in Julius Gould and William L. Kolb (eds.), *A Dictionary of the Social Sciences.* New York: The Free Press of Glencoe, 1964.
Olsen J., *The Black Athlete—a shameful story.* New York: Time, Inc., 1968.
National Football League Official Autographed Yearbook 1968. Dallas: Sports Underwriters, Inc., 1968.

12. This article is based solely on an unrevised paper presented at the International Seminar on the Sociology of Sport, organized by the Research Institute of the Swiss Federal School of Gymnastics and Sports and the University of Bern on behalf of the International Committee for the Sociology of Sport, September 7-13, 1969 at Macolin, Switzerland. Since the presentation of this paper there has appeared two reports which treat the topic in much greater depth and which offer selected findings somewhat different from those given above; see: Anthony H. Pascal and Leonard A. Rapping, "Racial Discrimination in Organized Baseball," (Report for the RAND Corporation, Santa Monica, California, May 1969); and, Garry Smith and Carl F. Grindstaff, "Race and Sport in Canada," (University of Western Ontario, October 1970).

National League Green Book. Cincinnati: National League Public Relations Department.

Rosenblatt A., "Negroes in Baseball: The Failure of Success," *Trans-Action* 4 (September, 1967): 51-53, with a reply by Whitehead 4 (October, 1967): 63-64.

Siegel S., *Nonparametrics Statistics*. New York: McGraw-Hill Book Co., Inc., 1956.

"Study Indicates Cracking Majors Harder for Blacks." Los Angeles: Times, May 15, 1969, Part III, p. 3.

Zanger J., *Pro Football 1968*. New York: Pocket Books, 1968.

ETHNIC SOCCER CLUBS IN MILWAUKEE: A STUDY IN ASSIMILATION*

JOHN C. POOLEY

INTRODUCTION

Sport has shown itself to be a factor in forming a point of contact between ethnic groups who find themselves living in close proximity. Expatriate groups in African countries, missionaries and traders in isolated communities and military forces representing different nations[1] are good examples of this. Immigrants who become lodged in already established "advanced" societies are equally affected. For example, West Indians who emigrate to Britain, Southern Europeans who emigrate to Australia and diverse ethnic groups immigrating to the United States would fall into this category. Whenever members of an ethnic group move to another society, some degree of assimilation occurs and their survival depends upon it.

The primary purpose of this study was to determine the role of sport in assimilation. More specifically, the study endeavored to deter-

*Part of this paper was read at the AAHPER Annual Convention, Boston, April 11, 1969. The author wishes to acknowledge the valuable assistance of Gerald S. Kenyon, University of Waterloo, who acted as advisor for the study which formed part of a Masters Degree at the University of Wisconsin, Madison, completed in 1968. Printed with permission of the author.

1. The point of contact made possible through sport, can lead to discord as Reid found. In his book which tells the story of an Allied prisoner of war camp in Germany, he relates how arguments developed as a result of a "wall game" competition *between* different nationalities, where as in games played by prisoners from within a single group (in this case Britain), arguments never occurred. P. R. Reid, *Escape from Colditz* (New York: Berkeley Publishing Corporation, 1952), p. 64.

mine the significance of the structure and function of ethnic soccer clubs in the assimilation of their members.

The terms used in this study are defined below:

Assimilation
Assimilation is a process of interpenetration and fusion in which persons and groups acquire the memories, sentiments, and attitudes of other persons or groups, and, by sharing their experiences and history, are incorporated with them in a common cultural life.[2]

From the definition, it is clear that "acculturation" is included. As Gordon[3] has commented, the phrases "sharing their experiences" and "incorporating with them in a common cultural life" suggest the added criterion of social structure relationships.

Ethnic group. An ethnic group[4] is a group with a shared feeling of peoplehood.[5] According to Tumin,

The term is most frequently applied to any group which differs in one or several aspects of its patterned, socially-transmitted way of life from other groups, or in the totality of that way of life or culture. Frequently, the group in question formerly enjoyed or still enjoys a separate political-national identity as well. Thus, various national-ethnic stocks in the United States would be considered as ethnic groups, e.g., Greeks, Poles, Hatians, Swedes, etc.[6]

Core Society. This term refers to "the dominant subsociety which provides the standard to which other groups adjust or measure their relative degree of adjustment."[7] According to Fishman,[8] the culture of this society is that "into which immigrants are assimilated, and it forms the one accepted set of standards, expectations, and aspirations, whether they pertain to clothing, household furnishings, personal beauty, entertainment or child rearing."

2. Robert E. Park and Ernest W. Burgess, *Introduction to the Science of Sociology* (Chicago: University of Chicago Press, 1921), p. 735.
3. Milton M. Gordon, *Assimilation in American Life* (New York: Oxford University Press, 1964), p. 62.
4. From the Greek word "ethnos" meaning "people" or "nation."
5. Gordon, *op. cit.,* p. 24.
6. Melvin M. Tumin, "Ethnic Group" in Julius Gould and William L. Kolb, *A Dictionary of the Social Sciences* (Free Press of Glencoe, 1965), p. 243.
7. Gordon, *op. cit.,* p. 72. Gordon prefers the term "core group," which used by A. B. Hollingshead to describe the old Yankee families of colonial, largely Anglo-Saxon ancestry who have traditionally dominated the power and status system of the community. See August B. Hollingshead, "Trends in Social Stratification: A Case Study," *American Sociological Review* 17 (December, 1952): p. 686.
8. Joshua A. Fishman, "Childhood Indoctrination for Minority-Group Membership," in "Ethnic Groups in American Life," *Daedalus: The Journal of the American Academy of Arts and Sciences* (Spring, 1961): 329.

SCOPE AND SIGNIFICANCE

In this study and attempt was made to assess the factors which accelerate or retard the rate of assimilation. Saxon[9] and Warner Srole[10] have recognized that the recreational habits of a group have considerable import in the degree to which such a group may identify themselves with, or be isolated from, the core society. This point has greater relevance in an age when increased leisure time is available to the majority of the population.[11]

The existence of a sport club provides varying degrees of social intercourse between active and non-active members of the same club and between different clubs. The amount and type of social interaction practiced depends upon the size of the club, makeup of its members, arrangement of social events, and type of club accommodation.

More specifically, this study was concerned with determining the factors which influence assimilation. Questions asked were as follows:

1. To what degree does participation in ethnic soccer influence assimilation?
   a. Positively
   b. Negatively
2. What forces within ethnic soccer explain this influence?

9. George Saxon, "Immigrant Culture in a Sratified Society," *Modern Review* 11 (February, 1948): 122.

10. W. Lloyd Warner and Leo Srole, *The Social Systems of American Ethnic Groups* (New Haven: Yale University Press, 1945), pp. 254-282.

11. This point is taken up by Martin when he says, "At present, we are participating in an extremely drastic and rapid cultural change, affecting our entire Western society. The rapid advance of technological science, spear-headed by automation, is causing a steady shrinkage of the workaday world. Plans now underfoot for a six-week vaction and a three-day weekend indicate that before long our work force will have 200 free days in the year." He goes on to qualify this as follows: "These changes do not apply, to the same extent, to professional executive and management groups. However, the fact remains that, coincidental with a rising standard of living, higher employment, and a steadily increasing national product, the American people are finding themselves with more and more time off the job. In other words, we have already acquired, in large measure, the latest and the greatest freedom of all —free time, unstructured time, discretionary time, time for leisure." (Alexander Reid Martin, "Man's Leisure and His Health," *Quest* 5 (December, 1965): 26.)

Three publications by Brightbill, Miller and Robinson, and Dumazedier, which discuss societal problems and current theories related to leisure, either directly or indirectly, point to the increase in leisure time during the current era. "It seems curious that at a time when many people have more leisure than ever before . . ." (Charles K. Brightbill, *Man and Leisure* (Englewood Cliffs, N. J.: Prentice-Hall, 1961), p. v. "The twentieth century finds man turning more and more to his increasing free time, to fulfill himself." (Norman P. Miller and Duane M. Robinson, *The Leisure Age* (Belmont, Calif.: Wadsworth Publishing Co., 1963), p. v. "Leisure today is a familiar reality in our advanced societies." (Joffre Dumazedier, *Toward a Society of Leisure* (New York: The Free Press, 1967), p. 1.)

a. Structural factors

b. Functional factors

While other studies have focused attention on the significance of religion,[12] color, [13] occupation,[14] and concentration,[15] on the acculturation or assimilation of ethnic groups, little has been written on the use of sport as a vehicle in this process. Participation in a single sport, albeit from a professional standpoint, as a means to assimilate, has been discussed by Andreano,[16] Handlin,[17] Saxon,[18] Boyle,[19] Shibutani,[20] and Weinberg.[21] These studies have been directed toward the individual's motives and attitude, whereas the present study was a departure from this approach in that it examined the role of the sport club as exemplified by the constitution of the club through the voice of the committee. Also, researchers have invariably confined themselves to a single ethnic

12. For example, Erich Rosenthal, "Acculturation without Assimilation: The Jewish Community of Chicago, Illinois," *American Journal of Sociology* 66 (1960): 275-288. Yaroslav Chyz and Read Lewis, "Agencies Organized by Nationality Groups in the United States," *The Annals of the American Academy of Political and Social Science* 262 (March, 1949). Harold L. Wilensky and Jack Ladinsky, "From Religious Community to Occupational Group: Structural Assimilation Among Professors, Lawyers and Engineers," *American Sociological Review* 32 (August, 1967): 541-542.

13. For example, Harry J. Walker, "Changes in the Structure of Race Relations in the South," *American Sociological Review* 14 (1949): 377-383. Clarence Senior, "Race Relations and Labor Supply in Great Britain," *Social Problems* 4 (1957): 302-312. Michael P. Banton, *White and Colored* (New Brunswick, N. J.: Rutgers University Press, 1960). J. A. Neprash, "Minority Group Contacts and Social Distance," *Phylon* 14, 19 (June, 1953), pp. 207-212. R. B. Davison, *Black British: Immigrants in Britain* (London: Oxford University Press, 1966), p. 170. Martin Luther King, Jr., *Where Do We Go From Here: Chaos or Community?* (New York: Harper and Row), p. 269.

14. For example, Raymond Breton and Maurice Pinard, "Group Formation among Immigrants: Criteria and Process," *Canadian Journal of Economics and Political Science* 26 (August, 1960): 465-477. Alexander S. Weinstock, "Role Elements: A Link Between Acculturation and Occupational Status," *British Journal of Sociology* 14 (1963): 144-149. Wilensky, *loc. cit.*

15. For example, Otis Dudley Duncan and Stanley Lieberson, "Ethnic Segregation and Assimilation," *American Journal of Sociology* 64 (January, 1959): 364-374. Stanley Lieberson, *Ethnic Patterns in American Cities* (New York: Free Press of Glencoe, 1963).

16. Ralph Andreano, *No Joy in Mudville* (Cambridge, Massachusetts: Schenkman Publishing Co., 1965), p. 133.

17. Oscar Handlin, "The Family in Old World and New," in *Social Perspectives on Behavior,* Herman D. Stein and Richard A. Cloward, p. 103. (New York: The Free Press, 1958).

18. Saxon, *loc. cit.*

19. Robert H. Boyle, *Sport-Mirror of American Life* (Boston: Little, Brown and Company, 1963), p. 97.

20. Tamotsu Shibutani and Kian M. Kwan, *Ethnic Stratification* (New York: The MacMillan Company, 1965), pp. 543-544.

21. S. Kirson Weinberg and Henry Arond, "The Occupational Culture of the Boxer," *American Journal of Sociology* 57 (1951): 462.

group[22] or they have analyzed the many factors which have contributed to the acculturation or assimilation process of an ethnic group or groups in a city or rural community.[23]

This study was concerned with the role of the sport club (soccer), in a culturally heterogeneous setting; it sought to uncover club policy rather than individual attitude; it incorporated six ethnic groups in a confined area.

Milwaukee was chosen as the location for the study. Soccer was introduced in the city in 1913; the Wisconsin State Football Association was organized in 1914, and the Wisconsin State Soccer Football League was initiated in 1924.[24] With a population of 1,149,977 in Milwaukee, 326,666, or 28.4 percent comprised the element of foreign stock.[25] It was they who originally were responsible for the introduction of soccer into the area.

The choice of soccer allowed the study to pay some attention to the "foreign game" element. Soccer is a world game, being played on all five continents.[26] Of the larger countries, it is probably played least in

22. For example, Pauline V. Young, *The Pilgrims of Russian Town* (Chicago: University of Chicago Press, 1932); Joseph S. Roucek, "The Yugoslav Immigrants in America," *American Journal of Sociology* 40 (March, 1935): 602-11; John S. Hawgood, *The Tragedy of German-America* (New York: G. P. Putnam's Sons, 1940); S. N. Eisenstadt, "The Place of Elites and Primary Groups in the Absorption of New Immigrants in Israel," *American Journal of Sociology* 57 (1951): 222-231; Alan Richardson, "The Assimilation of British Immigrants in Australia," *Human Relations* 10 (1957): 157-165; S. Alexander Weinstock, *The Acculturation of Hungarian Immigrants: A Social-Psychological Analysis.* Columbia University, Ph.D. (1962), *University of Microfilms, Inc.,* Ann Arbor, Michigan; R. Talf, "The Assimilation of Dutch Male Immigrants in a Western Australian Community," *Human Relations* 14 (1961): 265-281; Leonard Broom and E. Shevky, "Mexicans in the United States: A Problem in Social Differentiation," *Sociology and Social Research* 36 (1952): 150-158. In some instances, two ethnic groups have been studied allowing some comparative analysis. For example, Wilfred D. Borrie, *Italians and Germans in Australia: A Study of Assimilation* (Melbourns: Published for the Australian National University by F. W. Cheshire, 1954), pp. 217-231.

23. For example, Stanley Lieberson, *loc. cit.*

24. Wisconsin State Football Association, *Soccer Souvenir Book,* issued on the occasion of the United States Football Association Convention, June 30-July 1 (Milwaukee: Wisconsin State Football Association, 1928). Pages not numbered.

25. U. S. Bureau of the Census, *U. S. Census of Population:1960.* Vol. 1. Characteristics of the Population, Part 51: Wisconsin. (Washington, D. C.: U. S. Government Printing Office, 1963), p. 309.

26. "In May 1904 in Paris, five nations got together to found the F.I.F.A. (Federation Internationale de Football Association) . . . . Those five nations—France, Holland, Belgium, Switzerland, and Denmark . . . have increased and multiplied." There were eighty-one countries controlled by F.I.F.A. in 1954. Dengil Batchelor, *Soccer—A History of Association Football* (London: Batsford Ltd., 1954), p. 139. In 1963, there were ". . . 119 National Associations affiliated to it (F.I.F.A.) . . . ." A. G. Doggart (Chairman of the English Football Association), in *Fiftieth Anniversary Golden Jubilee Journal* (New York: 1963 U.S.S.F.A. Convention Committee, July, 1963). Hackensmith makes explicit reference to soccer on the five continents, C. W. Hackensmith, *History of Physical Education* (New York: Harper and Row, 1966), pp. 59, 89, 159, 233, 235, 258, 266, 280, 292, 303, 368.

America. By contrast, the countries of origin of the ethnic groups, represented by the sport clubs in Milwaukee, all have soccer as their major national outdoor game.

Since the sport of soccer is alien to the core society; and since soccer is the major national game of the countries of origin of the ethnic groups; and since members of the ethnic groups in question were involved in the activities of soccer clubs, either in the role of player, club official, manager, coach, spectator or social member; it is, therefore, hypothesized that ethnic soccer clubs in Milwaukee inhibit structural assimilation.

POPULATION

The population used for this investigation was the ten soccer clubs located within the City of Milwaukee. Some statistical information relating to the ten clubs is included in Tables I, II, and III. It will be seen from Table I that only three clubs were founded in the 1920's. Five clubs came into being within a span of seven years from 1947 to 1953 inclusive. The remaining two clubs, founded in 1961 and 1964, respectively, were formed from members of two existing clubs. Club I was originally the second team Club C. When friction developed between

TABLE I
Dates of Foundation and Ethnic Orientation[a] of
the Soccer Clubs in Milwaukee

Club	Date When Founded	Ethnic Orientation
A	1922	Croatian
B	1926	Hungarian
C	1929	German
D	1947	German
E	1950	Polish
F	1950	Serbian
G	1952	Italian
H	1953	German
I	1961	German
J	1964	Serbian

[a]Demonstrated by ethnicity of committee members, players, ordinary members, original members, or a combination of these.

the first and the second teams, three men contacted members of the second team and invited them to form a new club.[27]

Club J was founded as the result of a split in the Eastern Orthodox Church which served the Serbian community. Club F represented the original community; the splinter group formed Club J because a sufficient number of players wished to play soccer.[28] Therefore, the last occasion when an entirely new club was formed was in 1953.

The ethnic orientation of the soccer clubs is seen in Table I. Four ethnic groups are represented by one club as follows: Croatian, Hungarian, Polish and Italian. One ethnic group is represented by two clubs: Serbian. Another ethnic group is represented by four clubs: German. This does not mean that a club represented exclusively a single ethnic group. It does mean that each club in question was predominantly repre-

TABLE II
Details of Club Membership[a]

Club	Total Membership	Membership According to Age				
		Under 18	18-25 Years	25-35 Years	35-45 Years	Over 45
A	84	14	10	10	10	40
B	71	16	0	40	15	0
C	540	150	100	100	100	90
D	300	50	60	50	40	100
E	160	50	20	45	35	10
F	410	100	30	120	60	100
G	135	25	30	35	30	15
H	240	40	45	75	60	20
I	25	0	12	12	1	0
J	200	20	50	50	40	40

[a]Membership figures are an approximation. Several clubs did not have membership lists.

27. Personal interview with the committee of Club I, April 11, 1967.
28. Personal interview with the committee of Club J. April 20, 1967.

sented by a single ethnic group, according to the criteria indicated in Table I.

Details of club membership are indicated in Table II. These figures are approximate only because it was difficult to obtain precise figures. Normally the payment of dues provides an exact indication of membership. However, in the case of some of the clubs, committee members indicated that dues were not demanded because clubs did not wish to restrict the use of the term "member" to those who had become paid members. In most instances, therefore, the figures were agreed upon following a consultation between the clubs' committee members. To be classed as a member, a person was required to demonstrate continuous interest in the club through support of club games or social functions, or through payment of dues.

A total of thirty-five teams were sponsored by the ten soccer clubs in 1967. These included eighteen adult teams and seventeen boys' teams. Details are indicated in Table III.

TABLE III
Details of the Number of Teams Sponsored by Each Club and the Leagues[a] in Which They Play

Club	Number of Teams Sponsored	Major Division	Major Reserve	First Division	Junior	Intermediate	Midget
A	3	1	1				1
B	3	1	1				1
C	5	1	1		1	1	1
D	5	1	1		1	1	1
E	4	1	1			1	1
F	4			1	1		2
G	3	1	1				1
H	5	1	1		1	1	1
I	1			1			
J	2			2			

[a]The most senior division is the Major Division. At the end of each season, the last placed club is relegated to the First Division. The team which wins the First Division is promoted to the Major Division. Each Major Division team is required to sponsor a reserve team.

NATURE OF THE BASIC VARIABLES

The nature of the dependent variable and the independent variable, and the procedures used for operationalizing them, are given below.

Dependent Variable: Structural Assimilation

The concept of "structural assimilation" was defined for this study as follows: entrance of an ethnic group into primary group relations with the core society.

In his model of the seven assimilation variables, Gordon demonstrates the key role of structural assimilation in the total process of assimilation.[29] He reiterates: "Once structural assimilation has occurred, . . . all of the other types of assimilation will follow."[30] The implication of this is that the price of such assimilation is the disappearance of the ethnic group as a separate entity and the evaporation of its distinctive values.[31]

The level of assimilation of club members was sought by directly questioning the club committees. The committees were asked to state whether the other six stages of assimilation has occurred. These variables, together with a brief definition of each, are listed below. They are taken from Gordon's model.[32]

Cultural assimilation (acculturation): Change of cultural pattern to those of the core society.

Marital assimilation (amalgamation): Large scale intermarriage between club members and members of the core society.

Identificational assimilation: Development of a sense of peoplehood based exclusively on the core society.

Attitude receptional assimilation: An absence of prejudice by the core society.

Behavior receptional assimilation: An absence of discrimination by the core society.

Civic assimilation: An absence of value and power conflict between club members and the core society.

Independent Variable: Club Policy

The concept of "club policy" was defined for this study as follows: Courses or actions of a club, either explicit or implicit, in matters per-

29. Milton M. Gordon, *Assimilation in American Life* (New York: Oxford University Press, 1964), p. 81.
30. *Ibid.*
31. *Ibid.*
32. See Table IV.

TABLE IV
The Assimilation Variables

Subprocess or Condition	Type or Stage of Assimilation	Special Term
Change of cultural patterns to those of host society	Cultural or behavioral	Acculturation
Large scale entrance into cliques, clubs, and institutions of host society, on primary group level.	Structural assimilation	None
Large scale intermarriage	Marital assimilation	Amalgamation
Development of sense of peoplehood based exclusively on host society	Identificational assimilation	None
Absence of prejudice	Attitude receptional assimilation	None
Absence of discrimination	Behavioral receptional assimilation	None
Absence of value and power conflict	Civic assimilation	None

taining to its organization and activities, demonstrated by the actions it has taken in the past and the opinions held by its present committee.

It was found desirable to divide the concept into two aspects. These were operationalized by utilizing a number of elements in each case, as follows:

A. Characteristics of and Policies Concerning Membership
    1. Membership characteristics
        a. Naturalization and generation
        b. Occupation
        c. Ability to speak English
    2. Choice of language, either English or ethnic, demonstrated on the following occasions:
        a. At club meetings
        b. When playing soccer
        c. On social occasions

    3. Policy when accepting new members
    4. Policies for the actions taken to attract new members from:
       a. Other ethnic groups
       b. Core society
B. Policies Pertaining to Structure and Maintenance of Club
    1. Need for existence
    2. Election of officers
    3. Changes in organization
    4. Degree to which club perceives itself either as:
       a. Soccer club
       b. Social club
    5. Degree of organized social contact between the club and:
       a. Other clubs
       b. Core society

THE INSTRUMENT

Data collected in this investigation consisted of responses to a structured interview which was employed between April 7-23, 1967. The structured interview schedule consisted of two parts. The question for Part One were sent to the President of each club at least seven days before the date of the interview. These questions related to the club's history, the number of teams being sponsored, the size of the club, the age, and other details concerning members.

The questions for Part Two were answered spontaneously because it was considered that prior knowledge of them might have adversely affected the answers. The questions were related to club policy concerning membership: questions directed toward the assimilation of members; constitutional procedures; and the language used at club meetings, on social occasions and in the dressing room before a game.

The questions used in both parts of the interview were designed by the investigator. The assimilation variables in Part Two were culled from Gordon's paradigm.[33] An average of four committee members were interviewed from each club.

TREATMENT AND ANALYSIS OF DATA

This study utilized the responses of the club committees to the structured interview. Primarily, questions devoted to club policy formed the basis of the analysis. The study examined the relationship between

33. *Ibid.*

TABLE V

Degree of Assimilation of Ethnic Soccer Clubs in Milwaukee Based Upon the Model by Gordon

Club and Main Ethnic Group Represented[a]	Type of Assimilation[b]						
	Cultural		Marital	Identificational	Attitude Receptional	Behavior Receptional	Civic
	Intrinsic	Extrinsic					
"A" – Croatian	No	Partly	No	Partly	Yes	Mostly	Yes
"B" – Hungarian	No	Partly	No	No	Yes	Yes	Yes
"C" – German	No	Partly	Partly	Yes	Yes	Yes	Yes
"D" – German	Partly	Partly	No	No	Yes	Yes	Yes
"E" – Polish	Partly	Mostly	No	No	Yes	Yes	Yes
"F" – Serbian	No	Partly	No	No	Mostly	Yes	Mostly
"G" – Italian	No	Partly	Partly	No	Yes	Yes	Yes
"H" – German	Partly	Partly	Partly	Partly	Yes	Yes	Yes
"I" – German	Yes	Yes	Partly	Yes	Yes	Yes	Yes
"J" – Serbian	No	Partly	No	No	Mostly	Yes	Yes

[a]Clubs H and I were least representative of a single ethnic group. Club I was the smallest of the ten clubs by a substantial margin.

[b]Although Gordon identified seven types of assimilation, "structural assimilation" was omitted because it will be examined in the role of dependent variable.

the dependent and the independent variables and a logical analysis of that relationship.

The information accrued was analyzed in two stages: first, a measure of the level of assimilation already achieved by club members was determined by utilizing questions directly related to the six assimilation variables (excluding structural assimilation). Second, the effect of the policies of the clubs on structural assimilation was determined by utilizing the elements defined under the sub-heading "Independent Variable."

The hypothesis stated earlier, namely that ethnic soccer clubs in Milwaukee inhibit structural assimilation, was more specifically defined for this study as: club policy inhibits the structural assimilation of members.

The information was treated descriptively. In the first stage, the level of assimilation which had already occurred was analyzed deductively. In the second stage, each question was analyzed in terms of the independent variable. In conclusion, the relationship between certain

TABLE VI
Characteristics of Club Members:
Percentage Naturalized and by Generation

Club	Percent Naturalized	Percent by Generation[a]		
		First	Second	Third
A	90	50	15	5
B	75	90	10	0
C	90	60	20	20
D	75	80	19	1
E	75	75	20	5
F	50	80	15	5
G	70	65	25	10
H	75	90	7	3
I	98	99	1	0
J	65	90	10	0

[a]First generation, i.e., original adult immigrant.
Second generation, i.e., children of the original adult immigrant.
Third generation, i.e., children of the second generation.

elements of the independent variable and the dependent variable were deduced, and the hypothesis tested.

RESULTS

The hypothesis was tested by determining the degree of relationship between the dependent variable and the independent variable.

The results of this investigation showed that:

1. The perceived level of assimilation of soccer club members varied among clubs. (See Table V.) The two clubs whose members had

TABLE VII
Characteristics of Club Members:
Most Frequent Occupations[a]

Club	Most 1	2	3	Least 4
A	Unskilled Labor	Skilled Labor	Private Business	Professional
B	Skilled Labor	Unskilled Labor		
C	Skilled Labor	Private Business	Unskilled Labor	Professional
D	Skilled Labor	Private Business	Professional	Unskilled Labor
E	Skilled Labor	Unskilled Labor	Private Business	
F	Skilled Labor	Private Business	Unskilled Labor	Professional
G	Skilled Labor	Private Business	Unskilled Labor	Professional
H	Skilled Labor	Unskilled Labor	Private Business	Professional
I	Skilled Labor	Professional	Unskilled Labor	
J	Skilled Labor	Unskilled Labor	Private Business	Professional

[a]Homemakers and (high school) students not included.

assimilated most represented the German ethnic group, although they were less ethnic oriented than any of the clubs. The two clubs whose members had assimilated least represented the Serbian ethnic group.

2. In terms of three assimilation variables, namely civic, behavioral receptional and attitude receptional, the majority of club members were alleged to have assimilated in large measure. (See Table V.) In terms of three other assimilation variables, namely cultural, marital and identificational, the record of assimilation was poor. Of these, marital assimilation (amalgamation) had occurred least of all.

3. A review of the characteristics of soccer club members indicated that: (a) a large percentage were naturalized and first generation immi-

TABLE VIII
Characteristics of Club Members:
Ability to Speak English

Club	Very Good	Good	Fair	Poor	Very Poor
A	20%	20%	40%	10%	10%
B	10	60	20	10	——
C	40	50	10	——	——
D	15	40	40	5	——
E	50	10	35	4	1
F	25	25	25	20	5
G	30	30	20	10	10
H	30	40	20	10	——
I	100	——	——	——	——
J	15	40	30	10	5

Mean Percentage:

	33.5	31.5	24.0	7.9	3.1

Mean Percentage without Club I:

	26.1	35.0	26.6	8.8	3.5

grants (see Table VI); (b) their most frequent occupation was in the area of "skilled labor" (see Table VII); (c) they spoke English only moderately well (see Table VIII); and (d) approximately one-third were playing members and two-thirds were social members (see Table IX).

TABLE IX
Characteristics of Club Members:
Percentage of Playing Members and Social Members

Club	Percentage Playing	Percentage Social
A	45	55
B	65	35
C	12	88
D	25	75
E	45	55
F	25	75
G	40	60
H	35	65
I	65	35
J	20	80
TOTALS	37.7	62.3

4. When accepting new members, approximately half of the clubs had developed a clear-cut, if not rigid, policy, whereas the other clubs had a very open policy.

5. Half of the clubs took no action to attract new members, either from other nationality groups, or the core society (see Table X). Three clubs took action to attract players to their clubs, but otherwise ignored other potential members. One club encouraged players but discouraged non-players. One club took positive action to attract new members, whether players or non-players.

6. Seven clubs were identified with a specific ethnic group by their choice of name. Three had neutral names.

7. The language used at club meetings, when playing soccer, and on social occasions varied according to the club (see Table XI). Only two clubs spoke English exclusively. Four clubs spoke their own ethnic language for the most part. The remaining four clubs spoke their own ethnic language and English.

TABLE X

Action Taken to Attract New Members to the Clubs from
Other Ethnic Groups and the Core Society

Club	Other Ethnic Groups	Core Society
A	None	None
B	None	None
C	None (unless player)	None (unless player)
D	None	None
E	None (unless player)	None (unless player)
F	Players encouraged Non-players discouraged	Players encouraged Non-players discouraged[a]
G	None (unless player)	None (unless player)
H	None	None
I	Action taken to attract players and non-players, young and old.	Action taken to attract players and non-players, young and old.
J	None	None

[a]Unless parents of players.

8. There was little social contact between the clubs; with one exception, there was no contact between the clubs and the core society.

CONCLUSIONS

Within the limitations of this study, the following conclusions seem warranted:

With some exceptions, involvement in ethnic soccer is not conducive of furthering assimilation, and that more specifically, club policies of ethnic soccer clubs inhibit the structural assimilation of members.

TABLE XI
Language Used at Club Meetings, When Playing Soccer and on Social Occasions

Club	Club Meetings	Playing Soccer	Social Occasions
A	Croatian	Croatian and Others[a]	Croatian and Others
B	English and Hungarian	Hungarian	Hungarian
C	English	English	English
D	English	German and English	German and English
E	Polish	Polish	Polish
F	English and Serbian	English and Serbian	English and Serbian
G	English and Italian	English	English
H	English	English	English and German
I	English	English	English
J	Serbian	Serbian	Serbian and English

[a]This expression was used by the committee of Club A, presumably because English and other languages were spoken according to the ethnicity of those present.

THE NATIVE AMERICAN BALL GAMES

Jerald C. Smith

For a subject so basically "American," the Native Americans remain the most misunderstood people of America. The common assumption that they were generally a savage race intoxicated with murder and plunder has been widely projected. The native games of North America are virtually ignored in most texts, while others only mention the games in general, as it appears that the numerous "Indian experts and scholars" evaluated the games as an insignificant aspect of ethnology. This attitude is understandable considering the basic nature of most traditional research, which tended to treat the Native American people as "objects" of study, not as fellow human beings. Furthermore, under this scholarly form of racism, the black man was classified as a slave or work animal, while the Indian was merely a wild animal, which supposedly legitimized their non-human treatment and slaughter. Their classification as sub-human beings therefore may be recognized as affecting the non-consideration of their capacity to develop highly structured gaming activities. This viewpoint was of value only as a device to escape the guilt resulting from the treatment of our "red brothers."

For centuries after the invasion of their land the Native Americans suffered a long death which systematically repressed and ultimately destroyed various native religious institutions, perhaps the most vital of which effected a divorce of the people from the land. The path of recent Native American history has been a "Trail of Tears" along which much of their religion and life style has been lost. It is an inspiring tribute to the spirit and courage of these people that any of their culture has survived the long history of genocide. The areas that have survived are music and dance, crafts, and language; as a result a small part of Native American life style and religion remains. Unfortunately many of the unique gaming activities have not survived. Who can remember when these people experienced leisure, let alone the enjoyment of their leisure? With the recent movements in Native American unity and awareness, it is also important now that these people realize one of their most outstanding and richest sources of pride, their inborn sporting spirit. Accordingly, it is important to realize that the Native Americans were far too individualistic to be assigned any single description, as they shared no common language and few customs, and yet even in those groups classified as "warlike" much of their leisure time included the universal amusement derived from games and competitive activities. It is important to realize that in early times war functioned as an honorable game in which the highest score or coup was counted by striking an opponent. Within this structure therefore coups (pronounced *küz*) were awarded for touching, not killing an opponent. In later times various Native American cultures revised their scoring qualifications in accordance with the unsportsman-like conduct of their sharp-shooting enemies.

In considering the native games of North America it is not appropriate to think of sharp, independent divisions of activity or behavior. It should be not only recognized, but emphasized that the Native American life style was a physical and spiritual blending of the people with the earth. Hence, all activity, including games, may be thought of as religious and therefore not divorced from the total meaning of things. In this general life style the Native Americans developed a variety of games ranging from the quiet fireside sitting games involving two individuals, to the vigorous field games of ball with over one-thousand participants. Native American games were truly both as enchanting and spectacular as any ever played on the North American continent.

The most comprehensive study in the description and classification of Native American games was published in 1907 as "Games Of The North American Indians" by Stewart Culin (5). While Culin's study was primarily descriptive in nature, a classification of games was included. The two primary classifications of one, games of dexterity and two, games of chance were supplemented by a third group entitled "minor amusements." The activities classified as minor amusements included: "shuttlecock, tipcat, quoits, stone-throwing, shuffleboard, jackstraws, swing, stilts, tops, bull-roarer, buzz, popgun, bean shooter and cat's cradle." Running races were included in an independent classification. Figure 1 is based upon Culin's classification system for the games of detexerity and chance.

D E X T E R I T Y	B A L L	− SHINNY − RACKET − DOUBLE − BALL − FOOTBALL − BALL − RACE − FOOT − CAST − BALL − HAND − FOOT − BALL − TOSSED BALL − HOT BALL − BALL JUGGLING
		− ARCHERY − HOOP & POLE − RING & PIN − SNOW − SNAKE
C H A N C E	G U E S S	− HAND GAME − MOCCASIN − STICK GAMES − 4 − STICKGAME
		− DICE GAMES

FIGURE 1

Even though Culin's study must be recognized as invaluable, it offers very little information or theory pertaining to the possible origin and distribution of games throughout the North American continent.

It appears that structured gaming activities evolved with the various native cultures and institutions independently because of the lack of extensive cultural sharing. However, there were similar forms of what appears to be the same games found throughout the North American continent. It is this similarity which suggests the possibility of the distribution of initial gaming concepts from nuclear regions. Furthermore, it is important here to note that an accurate description of the evolution, distribution, variety and socio-cultural significance of native North

American games may never be established; however, an attempt will be made to present a general theoretical explanation.

The original population of North America may be directly identified through regional associations with forms of various related games from coast to coast. Just as the United States is recognized as the geographic home of basketball, baseball and football, the variations of Native American ball games were geographically unique. It is the similarity of many of these games, most notably the ball play, which suggests that various gaming concepts may have radiated from a common nuclear region.

Native Americans were playing ball games long before the time of Jesus Christ. By approximately 1 A.D. the highly structured ball court cultures were well established in Meso-America. The development and distribution of corn in Meso-America may have functioned as the transporting vehicle which carried various additional cultural concepts to the north, such as religion, political institutions, architecture, art and games. While it has not been determined how far north the ancient Meso-American civilizations extended, the excavation of apparent Hohokam "ball courts" in the southwestern United States is evidence of the possible northern boundary of these highly structured ball court cultures (14, 28). Another outstanding observation which may be utilized to emphasize the possibility of the widespread distribution of Meso-American cultural institutions is in the comparison of many Southeastern Woodland mounds with the stone pyramids in Yucatan, Mexico (34). Although the materials used in their construction varied, the basic architectural designs exhibit remarkable similarities. Accordingly, ball play varied throughout the Americas, yet one of the outstanding common characteristics was that the ball was not touched with the hands. According to Stern's research (*The Rubber-Ball Games of the Americas*), the use of rubber balls was limited to the highly structured "ball court cultures" of Meso-America and South America (29). Stern's findings, however, do not eliminate the possibility of the radiation of the "concept" of ball play to North America. Furthermore, the absence of rubber-bearing flora in the north must have limited the acceptance of the classic Meso-American form of play.

It is also important to consider the possibility that the ball play "concept" radiated from a form of ball play which preceded the rubber-ball game in the north and south, all knowledge of which has been lost. In this discussion the most meaningful consideration is not when, but if, how and where, the initial ball play concept reached the inhabitants of North America. It has been previously mentioned that various religious and political institutions, and artistic and architectural similarities link early North American cultures with those of Meso-America. It is the religious comparisons which are most evident in ball play. Many of the religions across the continent were based on the realization of the Sun as the center of the universe, with spherical objects and patterns symbolically significant. Hence, the possibility of religious symbolism as favorably influencing the popularity of ball play, regardless of when the initial concept radiated north.

It is apparent that each socio-cultural group or tribe in North America utilized the ball play concept in producing its own unique form of play. In this dimension the ball game may be recognized as an expression of tribal religious, socio-cultural, and economic structure. Hence, ball play in North America must be qualified by tribal identification, both cultural and geographic. While there are various generalizations to be recognized in the forms of ball play among tribes within common

West Coast	Southwest	Great Plains	Northeastern Woodlands	Southeastern Woodlands	
X	X	X			SHINNY
X		X	X		RACKET (single)
				X	RACKET (double)
X	X	X	X		DOUBLE–BALL
X		X		X	FOOTBALL
X	X				BALL–RACE
X					FOOT–CAST–BALL
		X	X		HAND–FOOT–BALL
X	X	X	X	X	TOSSED BALL
X	X				HOT BALL
X	X	X			BALL JUGGLING

FIGURE 2

cultural and geographic areas, it must be additionally understood that intra-cultural variations also existed. That is to say, it is not correct to classify American football with the game the British call "football" even though both groups speak English.

Figure 2 exhibits the general regional or geographic appearance of the major ball games of native North America (1, 5, 11, 16, 27, 29).

The socio-cultural influence on the development of unique ball games by Native Americans is evident when the geographic appearance of gaming implements is established. The following map offers a general representation of the wide variation of ball playing sticks and rackets, as well as footballs.

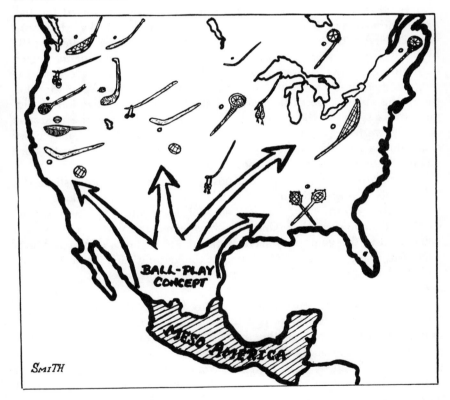

Note the variety of gaming implements on the West Coast, while the Northeastern and Southeastern Woodlands lack in comparison. The game of "shinny" is represented by the hockey-type curved stick. "Double-ball" games utilized sticks in propelling the two balls or billets joined by a thong. The "football" used in the game of "ball-race" is represented by the soccer-type balls.

A close survey of the numerous forms of ball play in North America indicates that the games of "shinny" and "racket" appear to be the most popular and highly structured. At present it has not been determined which of these games has the greatest antiquity.

The game of "shinny" was played throughout the continent at one time or another; however, it appears to have developed in the western regions. Culin, Baldwin, (1) and Stern associate shinny with those people who relied upon gathering natural foods rather than those who developed agricultural practices. It appears that those groups with a history of agriculture developed semi-permanent villages and preferred the ball game with rackets. These people living west of the Rocky Mountains were labeled with the derogatory classification of "Digger Indians" (18) by the white man because they harvested the bulbous roots of the region with a digging stick. It is possible that the shinny stick evolved from the digging stick used by these people's ancestors. The close association between the appearance of the game of shinny and the utilization of digging sticks supports the possibility. It is also known that the ancestors of many western people used curved sticks to club rabbits and other small animals (28). The shinny stick possibly could have been born when a hunter's swing sent a rock flying.

In an attempt to recreate the possible evolution of pre-historic developments it is essential to maintain an open mind while taking all of the possible contributing factors into consideration. The Zuñi of the southwest claim that the game of shinny came from Mexico long ago (30). Hence, the game may have been adopted from an ancient Meso-American brand of shinny. The origin of the gaming stick is not unknown and its development is uncertain, but shinny is an ancient game to be sure.

By the mid-nineteenth century shinny became widespread throughout the continent due to forced interaction between traditionally separated groups, as well as the increased range of trading capabilities resulting from the acquisition of the horse. When played in the west shinny was played by both men and women, but primarily men. When the eastern groups moving onto the Great Plains adopted the game it was primarily played as a women's field game. It is interesting to note that in most tribes women were not allowed to even touch the ball sticks and rackets (5, 6, 11, 12, 20, 26).

Shinny was played very much like contemporary women's field hockey. Each player was equipped with a single curved stick which was generally from 24 to 48 inches in length (5). The variation here was possibly due to the length of the players' limbs or individual preference. The buckskin ball was stuffed with deer hair or moss, and measured from 1 1/4 to 4 inches in diameter. The length of the playing field varied from 100 to 1,400 yards, depending on the number of participants (5). The goals consisted of either one post at either end of the field, or a pair at either end between which the ball was passed (1, 2, 5, 6, 20).

Unique variations in shinny play generally involved (1) sexual qualifications for participation, (2) the material used in the manufacture of sticks, and (3) the objectives of play. (The same factors identified variations in the game of rackets.) Shinny was played by men alone among the Assiniboin, Yankton, Mohave, and Walapai; by men and women alone among the Sauk and Foxes, Tewa, and Tigua; and by men against women among the Crows. Whereas a single stick or bat was the usual rule, the Makah (West Coast) used two, one for striking and the other for carrying the ball. In an unusual form of the game by the Miwok (West Coast) the objective was to pass the ball from station to station in relay fashion (5).

Shinny was a tremendously versatile athletic activity in that it could be played by two individuals or two hundred. It functioned both as an intra-village low keyed game, or as an inter-village or inter-tribal highly competitive and aggressive sport. When played among members of the same village or tribe it functioned as a supplemental activity in the celebration of a successful hunt, as with the Makah at the capture of a whale. (The Makah shinny ball was made from soft whale bone) (5). Another secondary function of inter-tribal shinny was the distribution of trade goods between the wagering parties. It should be noted here that heavy betting on the outcome of ball games was practiced extensively throughout the continent. Wagering may have been an expression of confidence rather than a careless obsession.

While shinny was played by both men and women, the game of "double-ball" was played exclusively by women. In fact, double-ball was generally known as the "women's ball game" (5). Double-ball appears to be closely related to shinny in both structure and objectives of play.

The ball games utilizing "rackets" were distinctly men's games. Hence, the pattern of sexual segregation in the ball games of shinny, double-ball and racket can be identified with the implements of each game. Accordingly, it may be concluded that the racket was definitely considered a masculine object. The segregation of the sexes in gaming activities therefore exhibited obvious correlations with the role of each sex in the given native culture. Among the Miwok (California) the women were identified strongly with their baskets, as baskets were used as seed beaters, storage containers, and as gambling trays. The basket became so basic in the role of the Miwok woman that it became part of their tribal costume as a hat, and hence, a true badge of womanhood. The appearance of the basket as a racket device was accordingly limited to the women's field game called "basket-ball" (2, 5). A survey of Culin's classification of ball games reveals that the Miwok game of basket-ball was also unique in that these women appear to have been the only group to have played the game as such in North America. In this game each woman was equipped with two large baskets, one being slightly larger than the other. The objective of the game was similar to that of both shinny and rackets. These baskets closely resembled the seed beating type and probably evolved from them. This would help explain the fact that the men were not associated with the game utilizing a clearly feminine implement (2, 5).

Racket ball play appears to have developed in the Eastern Woodlands and did not exhibit the wide distribution of shinny. In the Northeastern Woodlands the game was eventually to become known as "lacrosse," the national game of Canada. This form of ball play was engaged in at harvesting festivals, as well as political councils. The ball game was also prescribed by tribal shaman as a valuable means of combating sickness. The objective of racket play was to carry or hurl the ball through the opponent's goal using only the netted stick.

The most highly structured and popular form of ball play in North America was the double racket variety found only in the Southeastern Woodlands. Among the various confederacies of the region the ball game functioned as an inter-tribal activity symbolizing cultural and political unity. These games were played between "red" (war) and "white" (peace) towns. Hence, the ball game functioned additionally as a highly aggressive substitute for warfare. It is not surprising to discover that southeastern ball play was referred to as "the brother of war" (5, 19).

As an intra-tribal activity the double racket game was included in the annual harvest festival. During the spring festival the theme of annual renewing of the earth's productivity, as well as continued tribal harmony was celebrated. The climatic activity of the festival was the ball game.

An elaborate sequence of pre-game activities included: (1) the challenge; (2) purification through fasting and sexual abstinence; (3) erection of the goals; (4) the "ball play dance"; (5) wagering; and (6) the starting line-up (5, 21, 31, 32). Play was initiated with the center toss-up of the first ball by a noted member of the challenging town.

The sequence of a typical scoring play involved: (1) the toss-up; (2) the initial center scrimmage; (3) pass/carrying of the ball goal-ward;

and (4) the scoring drive through the goals (5). It is understandable that skilled players were those who possessed the combination of speed, strength, and jumping ability. The champion ball players must have been able to leap, catch, and whip-pass the ball away while still airborne. In this manner the ball could be quickly delivered to the players nearer the goals. The distance between the goals varied according to the number and ability of the participants.

Catlin's account of a Choctaw (Southeastern Woodlands) ball game is one of the most outstanding eye-witness accounts ever recorded. An estimated one-thousand young men competed ". . . with five or six times that number of spectators, of men, women, and children, surrounding the ground and looking on . . ." (5). Another eye-witness account by Capt. Basil Hall (Royal British Navy) while visiting the Creek (Southeastern Woodlands) noted that ". . . every one of them looked hard as iron and as agile as a puma" (13). Capt. Hall made these observations after being "treed" by the unpredictable flow of the scrimmage for the ball. While many historical accounts of ball play connote the wild free-for-all brawling image, it is important to note that although disputes did occur they were the exception rather than the rule. This general lack of bickering may have been due to the influence of the religious and legendary nature of respect for the rules of racket ball play. For example, the "no hands" rule apparently derived from the symbolic association of heavenly spherical bodies. This association is apparent in the following Native American explanation:

> The moon is a ball which was thrown up against the sky in a game long ago. Two towns were playing against each other, but one of them had the best runners and had almost won the game when the leader of the other side picked up the ball with his hand and tried to throw to the goal, but it struck against the solid sky vault and was fastened there, to remind players to never cheat. (5)

On June 4, 1763 an inter-tribal racket ball play was utilized as a stratagem of warfare. It was planned by the Chippewas and Sacs for a ball game to be played as a celebration for the birthday of King George III. As the racket game began and the players scrimmaged vigorously, the British soldiers came out of Fort Michilimackinac (Michigan). In their preoccupation with the game the soldiers left the gate of the fort open, and strangely enough the ball "accidentally" flew over the wall. Naturally the players rushed through the gate . . . in pursuit of the ball. Once inside the players became warriors, armed with war clubs and tomahawks which had been concealed under the blankets worn by the women spectators (27). The final score was indeed "hairraising!" Hence, in this dimension the ball game functioned as a Native American

"Trojan Horse" leading to an overwhelmng victory during the conflict known as Pontiac's War.

Even though the emphasis of contemporary American sporting activity does not outwardly reflect a Native American tradition, it is interesting to note that among the names of athletic teams are found the Chiefs, Braves, Redskins, Seminoles, Warriors, Blackhawks, Sun-devils, Indians, and many others. Hence, the Native American sporting spirit should be recognized as part of the rich sporting heritage of America. Native Americans have exhibited the ability to excel in the various gaming activities of contemporary America. The number of true "All-Americans," such as Olympic Gold Medal winners Jim Thorpe (Sauk-Fox) and Billy Mills (Sioux), has been limited.

If the Native Americans have not totally adopted the white man's games, perhaps it is because their sporting spirit is seeking identity. Accordingly, the exposure of the spectacular nature of Native American ball games emphasizes that the valleys, plains, mountains, and woodlands of this land were not lost in "savage" chaos before the arrival of the supposedly "civilized" invaders. Indeed this land has long echoed with the enthusiasm of the Native Americans at play.

Today in pow-wows across their land it appears that the Native American sporting spirit is experiencing a rejuvenation via the honorable competition of the "War Dance" contests. The nature of these contests rival the highest ideals of Olympic competition. Perhaps this atmosphere will render the possibility of additional rejuvenation in the area of Native American ball games, thus recalling a unique dimension to man's sporting capabilities.

BIBLIOGRAPHY

1. Baldwin, G. C. *Games of the American Indian*. New York: W. W. Norton & Company, Inc., 1969.
2. Barrett, S. A. *Miwok Material Culture*. Bulletin of Milwaukee Public Museum, Vol. 2, No. 4, March, 1933.
3. Catlin, G. *Episodes From Life Among the Indians, and Last Rambles*. Norman, Okla.: University of Oklahoma Press, 1959.
4. Culin, S. "American Indian Games." *The Journal of American Folk-Lore* 11 (October-December, 1898).
5. Culin, S. *Games of the North American Indians*. Twenty-Fourth Annual Report of the Bureau of American Ethnology. Washington, D. C.: Government Printing Office, 1907.
6. Grinnell, G. B. *The Cheyenne Indians: Their History and Ways of Life*. 2 vols. New York: Cooper Square Publishing Company, 1962.
7. Hassrick, R. B. *The Sioux: Life and Customs of a Warrior Society*. Norman, Okla.: University of Oklahoma Press, 1964.

8. Helm, J. C., and Lurie, N. O. *The Dogrib Hand Game*. Ottawa, Canada: R. Duhamel, 1966.

9. Hewitt, J. N. B. "Iroquois Game of Lacrosse." *American Anthropologist* 5 (April, 1892).

10. Hodge, F. W. "A Zuni Foot-Race." *American Anthropologist* 3 (July, 1890).

11. Hodge, F. W. *Handbook of American Indians*. Washington, D. C.: Bureau of American Ethnology, Bulletin 30, Part I, pp. 127, 483-486, 1907.

12. Hoffman, M. D. "Remarks On Ojibwa Ball Play." *American Anthropologist* 3 (April, 1890).

13. Hyrst, H. W. G. *Stories of Red Indian Adventure*. London: Seeley, Service & Co., 1921.

14. *Indians of the Americas*. Washington, D. C.: National Geographic Society, 1955.

15. Jones, W. *Ethnography of the Fox Indians*. Washington, D. C.: Bureau of American Ethnology, Bulletin 125, pp. 109-115, 1939.

16. Kroeber, A. L. "Games of the California Indians." *American Anthropologist* 22 (1920).

17. Kurz, R. F. *Journal of Rudolph Friederich Kurz*. Washington, D. C.: Bureau of American Ethnology, Bulletin 115, pp. 146-148, 1937.

18. LaFarge, O. *A Pictorial History of the American Indian*. New York: Crown Publishing Co., 1956.

19. *Life Magazine* 66 (April 18, 1969): 49-56.

20. Lowie, R. H. *Indians of the Plains*. New York: American Museum of Natural History, 1954.

21. Mooney, J. "The Cherokee Ball Play." *American Anthropologist* 2 (April, 1890).

22. Morgan, L. H. *League of the Ho-De-No-Sau-Nee or Iroquois*. Rochester, New York, 1851.

23. Parker, A. C. "Snow-Snake As Played By the Seneca-Iroquois." *American Anthropologist* 11 (1909).

24. Pennington, C. W. "La carrera de bola entre los tarahumaras de Mexico; Un problema de difusion." *America Indigena* 30 (1970): 15-40. Inter-American Indian Institute, Mexico, 1970.

25. Powers, W. K. *Indians of the Northern Plains*. New York: G. P. Putnam's Sons, 1969.

26. Reagan, A. B. "Some Games of the Bois Fort Ojibwa." *American Anthropologist* 21 (1919).

27. Schoolcraft, H. R. *The History, Condition and Prospects of the Indian Tribes of the United States*. Philadelphia, Penn.: Lippincott, Grambro & Co., 1854, Vol. II & VI.

28. Spencer, R. F., and J. D. Jennings, et al. *The Native Americans*. New York: Harper & Row, Publishers, 1965.

29. Stern, T. *The Rubber-Ball Games of the Americas*. New York: J. J. Augustin, Publisher, 1948.

30. Stevenson, M. C. "Zuni Games." *American Anthropologist* 5 (1903).

31. Swanton, J. R. *Source Material for the Social and Ceremonial Life of the Choctaw Indians*. Washington, D. C.: Bureau of American Ethnology, Bulletin 103, 1931.

32. Swanton, J. R. *The Indians of the Southeastern United States*. Washington, D. C.: Bureau of American Ethnology, Bulletin 137, 1946, pp. 674-686.
33. Underhill, R. *People of the Crimson Evening*. Lawrence, Kansas: United States Indian Service, No. 7, Haskel Institute, 1951.
34. Underhill, R. *Red Man's America*. Chicago, Ill.: University of Chicago Press, 1953, pp. 43.

PART III

BEYOND THE PEOPLE WHO PLAY: SYSTEMS WHICH CONTROL

People enter games and sport for many reasons and in various ways. These reasons for and patterns of involvement were considered under the previous topic of "People in the Process." Not only must the process be investigated and understood, but also the systems which shape and control the process must be examined. This third and last part is an effort to present several of the larger social systems as they affect the micro-system of sport.

SECTION

A

MEDIA AND THE
SPORTS MESSAGE

Does the media report sports news in a manner true to the reality of the happening or does it report as the editors, athletes, sports club owners and fans want to hear it? In this section, information and ideas about reporters, magazines and television are presented by several authors. Television is in a powerful position in relation to sport because of economic factors. Radio never got as deeply involved in the money market and power structure of sport.

The first article is by Edwards, who sees reporters as catering to public opinion in writing style and selection of content. He feels that the large majority of sports reporters (especially those who are white) have in no way demonstrated racial or social objectivity.

The content of mass circulation sports magazines is analyzed by Hart in order to find patterns in sports interest between 1889-1965. By recording the content of magazines with large circulation (such as the early magazine *Outing* or the contemporary *Sports Illustrated*), one can determine changes in reading interests by comparing issues of the same magazine throughout a defined time period. Changes in content patterns caused by quick coming and going of fads can also be detected.

Optowsky's article includes a look at both radio and television as they affect sport. Paying for rights to report and broadcast games was one of the main issues of conflict. It resulted in the paying of royalties by both media.

The influences of television on the number in attendance at sporting events is studied and presented by Bogart. How has television with the large money factor and increased exposure affected various sports? Although the answer is still being formulated, Bogart presents many pertinent facts.

Another source for the consideration of the controlling system of the media, not included in this collection, is Shecter's book. *The Jocks*. In it is revealed the orle of the sports writer as both journalist, sports enthusiast, and private businessman. Can the reporter be bought for a steak? Does he also become a fan of the team and write in that bias? Are the pressures and threats to please certain people so intrusive that honest reporting becomes difficult? Shecter answers *yes*. He says his book is about:

> ". . . the newspapers and the newspapermen who shill for sports. It's about television, the conscienceless and ruthless partner of sports. It's about the spoiled heroes of sports, shiney on the outside, decaying with meanness underneath. It's about the greedy professionals and posturing amateurs, the crooks, the thieves, the knaves and the fools."[1]

As a former sports reporter himself, Shecter has the ability to give the real inside story, and, as one who has left daily sports reporting, he looks back on it with considerable bias.

1. Leonard Shecter. *The Jocks* (New York: Paperback Library, 1970), p. 9.

SPORTS AND THE MASS MEDIA

Harry Edwards

The mass media in America, particularly television, have done a great deal to bring about a greater awareness on the part of whites regarding the problems and life circumstances of Afro-Americans. There is little doubt but that the various desegregation drives in the South would have failed were it not for the fact that through television the grim realities of "southern hospitality" were brought into America's living rooms. It is also true that, through all forms of the mass media, many Americans have become for the first time aware of the depths of the frustrations and anxieties suffered by black people in white America. This is not to say, however, that the newspapers, television reporters, and radio announcers have been unfailingly fair to Afro-Americans. In fact, with fortunately many individual exceptions, the mass media has on frequent occasions been harsh, insensitive, and indifferent to the plight of black people. It has acted upon many occasions as an unofficial arm of the establishment in America—particularly with regard to the phrasing of new stories and the general slant of the coverage. Rather than assessing or clarifying public opinion, the press, television, and radio frequently have catered to public opinion in phrasing and presenting news reports. A network television program on urbanization fixes on ghetto "riots" as its main theme, for example. And in a white racist society this practice can be and has been extremely detrimental to the interests of black people. Most news reporters in America, however, are towers of morality, ethics, and truth when compared to this country's sports reporters.

Reprinted with permission of The Macmillan Company from *The Revolt of the Black Athlete*, by Harry Edwards, Copyright © 1969 by The Free Press, a Division of The Macmillan Company.

THE WHITE SPORTS REPORTER

The large majority of white sports reporters in America have re-mained aloof from the problems of racial justice and injustice in the United States. As a group, they have seemingly been singularly unmoved by the frustrations and fate of black people, even of black athletes. With few exceptions—such as Howard Cosell and Jerry Eisenberg—many white sports reporters approved or stood mute as Muhammad Ali was immorally, unethically, and illegally stripped of his heavyweight box-ing title. Not a single white sports reporter to my knowledge ever both-ered to mention that John Wooten, in the incident mentioned in the last chapter, had been shunted aside.

The reasons behind this insensitivity on the part of white sports reporters are many. First of all, when a white American becomes a journalist, he does not all at once become a citadel of racial and social objectivity. A racist white man who becomes a journalist becomes noth-ing more than a racist white journalist, in much the same sense as a racist who becomes a cop becomes merely a racist cop. Reporters come from the same racially intolerant climate responsible for the denial of the American dream to black Americans for three hundred and fifty years, and in general their racial attitudes reflect that fact. These atti-tudes are inevitably reflected—either through omission or commission—in their work. I am not implying that all white sports reporters are dedi-cated racists. What I am saying is that many are simply insensitive to the magnitude and impact of the social problems that are festering be-neath their very noses. In short, many are either racist or ignorant. Or worse, they are indifferent.

Another factor that determines the present state of sports reporting in America is that sports reporters must be responsive to the desires and needs of the sports industry. This is roughly analogous to a situation where the jury is chiefly responsive to the needs and desires of the criminal. Unfortunately, in sports reporting, considerations of social justice and moral responsibility often are of secondary consideration or fall by the wayside completely. This is essentially because athletics still are regarded by most people as primarily recreational—as all fun and games. And the sports establishment would love to keep it that way. But the very word "establishment" belies the claim. Sports in America is big business, and has a significant social, economic, and political impact on both the national and international levels. To many white sports reporters, it is unthinkable that anyone would want to upset the "happy, socially peaceful, and racially tranquil world of sports" by exposing some of the racial or social injustices, the recruiting and slush fund scandals, or the naked exploitation that tarnish the fanciful picture. Even if he were so inclined, the average sports reporter would probably be dissuaded in the end by the fact that he must have access to sports figures—including coaches, managers, and owners—if he is to present anything more than box scores under his by-line. These captains of the sports industry have demonstrated upon many occasions that they can make the life of an unpopular sports reporter miserable. This in turn could affect the reporter's livelihood, because a sports reporter with no access to sports figures is of little value to any newspaper or network.

Along similar lines, many reporters are responsible, again not to society or to justice, but to their sports editors. These men, like the mass media they serve, tend to be of a conservative bent in social and political matters. Many a significant and worthwhile sports story has been "deep-sixed" because the slant of the story clashed with the political and social attitudes of the sports editor. The dictum handed down from above runs "Your job is to report the sporting news, not to initiate a crusade." So usually, the only element that detracts from the fun-and-games syndrome in most sports reporting is the sad fact that for every winner, there has to be a loser.

Public opinion studies have shown time and time again that people will not buy or read anything with which they disagree. Americans are no exception. We tend to read only what reinforces our own attitudes. Newspaper reporters, editors, and publishers are keenly aware of this tendency. They have to be. For most newspapers operate to make money. Most do, however, try to strike a happy medium between service and profit. (The results of this, in the case of sports reporting, is that significant social injustices in the athletic arena are typically slanted to minimize embarrassment to the sports establishment, are mis-stated, or simply are ignored.) For no segment of the American mass media, basically a capitalistic enterprise, is going to risk financial disaster for the sake of principle—not even when that principle is the basic right of all United States citizens to social, political, and economic justice. And in this racist society where the vast majority of American citizens see sports as primarily a recreational activity, not too many sports reporters are willing to risk their personal futures in an effort to bring those instances of injustice based upon race to the attention of the public. Consequently, the sports world in America (on the basis of a few exploitative "breakthroughs" such as Jackie Robinson's entering white-dominated professional baseball) has been portrayed as a citadel of racial harmony and purity, and this distorted image has been fostered primarily by sports reporters and by persons who control the media through which sports news and activities are communicated to the public.

The simple truth of the matter is that the sports world is not a rose flourishing in the middle of a wasteland. It is part and parcel of that wasteland, reeking of the same racism that corrupts other areas of our society.

Not all of the guilt, however, should be thrust upon the white reporter and his white employers. Negro reporters and Negro-owned media too are responsible, for they have deluded many of their own followers with fanciful myths that belie the truth about the world of sports.

THE NEGRO SPORTS REPORTER

Negro sports reporters in many ways reflect the same orientation—and hence the same inadequacies—as most white reporters. Access to sports personalities, economic considerations, and lack of control over what they can and cannot write are sources of constant frustration for many. But many others destroy their effectiveness completely through crippling individual and personal tendencies. Many simply are "Uncle Toms" who have been crawling and shuffling for white people for so long that they have misplaced completely all sense of responsibility and loyalty. Such persons categorically denounce any reporting about black athletes that is "social" or "political." Their chief concerns are to keep everyone happy, though deluded. Most of the time they are too busy looking the other way, keeping the boat steady, to report objectively and with conviction. Baleful the day when they find themselves in a position of having to side with black people against a racist or patronizing white establishment.

A publication, of course, is no better than the people who write for it—black or white. Many high-circulation magazines that purport to speak for America's blacks actually are more concerned with maintaining a "respectable Negro image," meaning the image that portrays black people striving as hard as possible to be like white folks. At the very best, such publications take a middle-of-the-road position when it comes to approaching and handling critical racial questions. Invariably, in their worst guise they fill their pages with irrelevant, defensive drivel about the social life of the bourgeois Negro, the latest wig crazes, the experiences of the "only big-time Negro hunting master," the only Negro airline pilot, and so forth. But when it comes to socially, politically, and economically relevant issues, most of them play it right down the middle, or worse. For they have their white advertisers to consider, who buy pages of space to advertise bleaching creams, hair straighteners, wigs, and other kinds of racially degrading paraphernalia. In the area of sports, one generally encounters innocuous stories about Willie Mays' ability with a bat or the speed of halfbacks Walt Roberts and Nolan Smith, little men in a big man's game. But seldom, if ever, has the truth about the sports industry in America and the situation of black athletes found its way to the pages of these publications. There is, however, a rising new face on the sports reporting scene—the sensitive, socially conscious black sports reporter.

THE BLACK SPORTS REPORTER

Unlike Negro and white reporters, the black sports reporter possesses certain qualities that tend to place him outside of, and in many instances in opposition to, the sports establishment. He differs significantly from his white and Negro colleagues in his attitude, philosophy, and guts level. And neither the designation "black" nor the differentiating qualities are necessarily directly related to skin color or racial heritage. On the contemporary sports scene, the black sports reporter is typified by Sam Skinner of San Francisco's *Sun Reporter*, Dick Edwards of the *Amsterdam News*, Bob Lipsyte of *The New York Times*, Jerry Eisenberg of the Newhouse syndicate, Pete Axthelm of *Newsweek Magazine*, and Dave Wolfe of the Life-Time syndicate. The last-mentioned four just happen to be white.

The black sports reporter writes not only about developments on the field of play, but also of those influences that might effect athletes off the field. He does not pause to consider how the sports establishment will respond to his story. If his editor refuses to print it, he may soften it, but he always presses to maintain its central focus. The black reporter is undeterred by risks to his job or personal attacks against his reputation. For him such considerations are secondary to justice, fair play, and personal character and conscience. For the black reporter actually believes in all the principles and ethical considerations supposedly fostered by sports. His fight is against those who have violated these standards and sought to profit from their debasement. It will be men of dispositions and pursuasions such as these who will write the true history of American athletics.

PERPETUATING THE MYTH OF THE
BLACK ATHLETE

As we intimated above, many Negro and white sports reporters in America have contributed to the conditions in the athletic industry that have prompted the revolt of the black athlete. Much of their influence comes through their omission of relevant social, political, and economic conditions within sports, but they also have been active perpetrators of discrimination and unfairness. (Although Negro reporters are less guilty in this regard, many Negro reporters have succumbed to pressures from above to color and dilute their stories. In some instances they have actually authored reports more biased than those that a white reporter would write in order to show that they are "part of the team.") Many black athletes have felt at one time or another that they were discriminated against. Aside from the money, prestige is the greatest incentive to professional sports participation. In amateur athletics, it is the main incentive, along with love of the game. Prestige is typically accrued and measured by the frequency and general tone of publicity that an athlete receives in the various reporting media. Black athletes as a whole feel that many sports reporters have not always given credit where credit was due. In a pro grid game not too long ago, a black flanker had scored on an end-around play and caught passes from his quarterback and halfback for two more scores. Next day he was outraged to find out that the reporter covering the game had heaped praise on the white quarterback for his masterful game-calling while the flanker himself was barely mentioned in passing. Were this an isolated case, we could dismiss it as merely the complaint of a disgruntled glory seeker. But it is not an isolated case. It reflects a state of affairs that exists at the high-school level and extends on into professional sports. This type of reporting perpetuates the myth that black athletes are not capable of leading or inspiring a team to victory. In the minds of many spectators, particularly white spectators, black athletes are excellent performers—once they are told what to do. But for them to spark a team to victory or, through their own individual performances to raise the competitive morale of their teammates, is simply beyond them. There have been very few black quarterbacks; therefore, blacks are not intelligent enough to play quarterback, or to coach, or to manage an athletic team, so the thinking goes and the myths are continued.

AMERICAN SPORTS MAGAZINES:
ONE PART OF THE MESSAGE

M. Marie Hart

How have the interests of American sports enthusiasts changed over the past 75 years? And how is this significant in understanding the changes in our culture during this time? Since the emergence of sport in its original setting cannot be directly studied, and since there are few studies related to this subject, one turns for information to the popular media of sporting magazines to look for indications of answers. Three sports magazines which covered a variety of activities and had sizeable circulation were chosen for the study.

The specific problems of this investigation became: first, to select general-circulation magazines devoted to the interests of sportsmen, each representing a different period within the years 1889*-1965; second, to analyze the manifest content of these magazines, utilizing the methods of content analysis described by Berelson (3); and third, to describe the patterns of interest revealed by these analyses in culturally-related terms. *Ayers Directory of Newspapers and Periodicals* was an invaluable aid for locating and establishing statistics and dates in the publication of magazines (2). A thorough analysis of this source led to the ultimate selection of *Outing, Sportsman,* and *Sports Illustrated* as magazines appropriate to the purposes of the study.

A review of *Outing,* a sport magazine of the general public in existence between 1882*-1923, showed a pattern of interest in non-organized and outdoor activities. More specifically, they were activities which: (1)

Adapted from M. Marie Hart, "An Analysis of the Content of Sports Magazines; 1889-1965," Ph.D. Dissertation, University of Southern California, 1967.
*The first few years of *Outing* were not available.

involved the individual in a relationship with the outdoors; (2) involved him in personal and active participation in non-organized activities; (3) expressed his interest in mechanization; and (4) evidenced little interest in spectator activity or highly organized team sports.

In the period of time from 1927-1937, *Sportsman,* a wealthy man's magazine, covered a content quite different from that in *Outing.* It reflected reader interest in activities which were characterized by: (1) substantial cost of money; (2) a show of ownership and possessions; and (3) involvement in individual and dual sports. Its readers, like those of *Outing,* showed little interest in team sports or spectator activities.

By 1955 the tide of interest seemed to have changed considerably, or perhaps it was just that a new magazine appealed to a different reading public than had been reached before. During the first ten years of *Sports Illustrated,* its content was increasingly characterized by: (1) interest in highly organized team sports performed by professional and amateur expert players; (2) interest in spectator activities; (3) an acceptance and promotion of professional sports; and (4) interest in international competition.

In all three of the magazines surveyed, there is evidence of sports fads which took precedence in content for a short while. The bicycle, car, airplane, and motorboat rose quickly into their own as sporting activities. There seemed to be an infatuated and intensely exaggerated use of this machinery (as with the snowmobile presently) for only a short period of time before interest stabilized. Most of these quick novelities involved mechanical power. This caused some concern to the editor of *Sportsman,* who commented in 1928:

> The philosophy of the machine in sport has yet to be studied by candidates for Ph.D. degrees, but it is worth their study and the intelligent appreciation of sportsmen who are neither afraid of a new thing because it is new nor so stupidly modern as to be slaves of novelty. All machines are means to an end and nothing more. It is for sportsmen as well as materialists to decide toward what goal our mechanical age is tending . . . (14:27)

Those patterns of sport interest that were indicated by the magazine coverage were examined in relation to other cultural patterns evidenced within the same time periods. One of these considered significant was the shift from rural to urban and then to suburban living which occurred during years under consideration. Another pattern of interest is that of the actual participation in sport and expenditures on sport during those years.

First, in relation to the population shift, Robert Boyle observed that:

The American interest in sport is not as some critics would have it the result of some flaw in national character. Rather it is in large measure the end product of a number of impersonal factors: industrialization, immigration, urbanization, increased leisure and income, commercial promotion and upper-class patronage . . . American sport is not of the people and the frontier, but upper-class and urban in impulse. (4:5)

The shift from rural to urban living has been described by many social historians. Morison, for one, has noted:

During the 1840's the population of the United States went up 36 percent, but the growth of towns and cities of 8,000 or more people showed a phenomenal 90 percent increase. Measured by numbers, the urban movement was stronger than westward migration; and its effect on the American character has been equally important. (10:483)

In the *Rise of Modern America,* Schlesinger has emphasized this shift in even stronger terms:

With only one out of every six people in localities of 8,000 or over in 1860 the proportion rose to one out of every three in 1900. . . . The effect on the agricultural sections of the East and Midwest was startling. Hill villages and farms were abandoned. The countryside was left silent and the age of the city was a reality. (12:45)

With reference to the later years of this period, Lerner has commented on the "civic renaissance" which began early in the twentieth century.

The emergence of the suburb as the characteristic form of American place, supplanting as well as supplementing the city, has been so rapid, with consequences so far reaching, as to be revolutionary. (9:172)

This very cursory examination of changes in the living and working patterns in the United States, mid-1800's to the present, suggests certain parallels between patterns of sport interest and the "way of life" for readers of sport magazines. The sport interests in the United States during the time of a predominantly rural population and first or second generation city dwellers from which *Outing* drew its readers reflect the independence of the frontiersman and his personal involvement with the forces of nature. The sport interests of the wealthy segment of an industrialized but temporarily depressed economy, as represented by the readers of *Sportsman,* reflect their preoccupation with personal symbols of wealth as well as their leisure to pursue time-consuming but non-involving activities. And the sport interests of the economically viable, urbanized, and industrialized population, represented by the readers of *Sports Illustrated,* reflect the organization, regulations, and expertness demanded by such an economy, as well as an acceptance of money-making as a primary goal.

A comparison between sport interests evidenced in analysis of content of sport magazines and actual participation in sport is of some interest. While there are very few accurate statistics, there are some general sources of information about participation. One of these appears in *Colliers* in 1924, within which Walter Hiatt commented:

> Is America enjoying itself? It is to the point of stupefaction judging by the figures as estimated by this writer. The motion pictures report 20,000,000 daily admissions. County fairs each year attract about 40,000,000 persons. The circus fans number 12,000,000. There are 10,000,000 fishermen, 2,200,000 golfers, 1,000,000 cyclists, 10,000,000 card players, 20,000,000 radio fans, 12,000,000 automobiles (exclusive of guests). More than 6,000,000 persons dance each day. About 1,200,000 children daily use our playground centers. More than 19,000,000 persons participate annually in Y.M.C.A. recreations. All this fun costs us at least six billion dollars a year . . . half as much as all the war debts, including unpaid interest, that foreign nations owe us. What does it signify? (8:19)

More tabulations are available for the years betwen 1946 and 1965. This data, as compiled from surveys by the Athletic Institute (1) and figures provided in *Sport: Mirror of American Life* (4) are presented in Table I.

Considering only the data for 1961 and 1965 (Table I) it becomes apparent that the patterns of sport participation are very different from the patterns of sport interest shown in the analysis of content of *Sports Illustrated*. Only two team sports, volleyball and softball, are listed as attracting more than 20,000,000 participants; and it may be noted that these sports are not commonly played by professional teams before large audiences of spectators. By the 1960's *Sports Illustrated* had made a transition to being almost exclusively a magazine for spectators of highly organized sport. In the early years of publication *Sports Illustrated* covered a greater variety of sports with more emphasis on the amateur athlete.

The other sports which attracted more than 20,000,000 participants seem to have more in common with the sport interests promoted by *Outing*, 1889-1921, as represented by cycling, boating, camping, fishing and hunting. The sports of bowling, roller skating, ice skating, table tennis, and billiards, which attracted little attention in *Outing*, have similar characteristics of individual involvement rather than complex team organization.

On the subject of money spent on sports equipment, Arthur Reeve wrote for *Outing* in 1910:

TABLE I
Total Sports Participation Survey*

Sport and Rank	1946	1956	1961	1965
1. Cycling	––	––	––	57,000,000
2. Volleyball	––	––	20,000,000	40,000,000
3. Boating	20,000,000	28,000,000	36,000,000	39,300,000
4. Bowling (ten pin)	12,500,000	20,050,000	30,000,000	39,000,000
5. Camping	––	––	5,500,000	37,000,000
6. Fishing	13,000,000	25,000,000	30,300,000	34,200,000
7. Swimming	––	––	33,000,000	––
8. Roller Skating	––	––	15,000,000	25,000,000
9. Softball (12″)	4,700,000	6,675,000	14,500,000	22,500,000
10. Ice Skating	––	––	––	20,000,000
11. Table Tennis	––	––	20,000,000	20,000,000
12. Shooting Sports	9,900,000	11,700,000	18,000,000	20,000,000
13. Billiards	––	––	––	20,000,000
14. Basketball	9,000,000	11,000,000	12,000,000	––
15. Shuffleboard	––	––	5,000,000	10,000,000
16. Horseshoes	––	––	––	9,000,000
17. Baseball	5,000,000	7,106,000	8,000,000 to 9,000,000	––
18. Water Skiing	––	––	6,000,000	8,750,000
19. Tennis	4,100,000	6,583,000	7,500,000	8,500,000
20. Archery (target)	1,700,000	4,600,000	5,500,000	8,000,000
21. Golf	4,300,000	5,100,000	6,000,000	7,750,000
22. Handball	––	––	5,000,000	6,000,000
23. Skin and Scuba Diving	––	––	5,000,000	––
24. Skiing	1,400,000	2,180,000	3,450,000	4,000,000
25. Football	1,500,000	1,725,000	2,000,000	––
26. Track and Field (schools only)	675,000	580,000	694,000 to 750,000	––
27. Bowling (duck pin)	––	––	560,000	––
28. Wrestling	150,000	170,000	300,000	––
29. Squash Rackets	––	––	50,000	––

*Based on survey prepared by the Athletic Institute (1:1-7) and Robert Boyle
(4:273).

Few of the hundreds of thousands who crowd the bleachers and grandstands ever stop to figure out in dollars and cents the size of the bills that America annually foots to carry on sport. . . . Never in the history of the world has a nation been so eager for athletics, cost what they may . . . . Our expenditure for this purpose literally runs into the millions every year, our investment into the tens of millions. (11:300)

He estimated the annual expenditure for sport at over $73,000,000 and the permanent investment in the sporting goods business at $105,000,000 (11:300).

In 1924, Hiatt stated that the public was spending approximately "a billion and a half in the field of sports" and six billion for "all fun" (8), during what Robert Boyle has called "the Golden Age of Sport in the Twenties" (4). The estimate included paid admissions to sport events as well as expenditures for sporting goods and permanent investment in sporting goods industry.

The distinction between sport interests represented by the content of *Sports Illustrated* and that represented by actual participation in sport is further emphasized in the data available on expenditures for sporting equipment between 1947 and 1965. This data, as shown in Table II, was compiled from *Trends in the Sporting Goods Market: 1947-65*, as prepared by Richard E. Snyder for the National Sporting Goods Association (13). His figures on expenditures for all sporting goods show a steady increase from $1,127,000,000 in 1948 to $2,857,200,000 in 1965 (13:9). Aside from the large increases in expenditures for gymnasium and playground equipment at the end of World War II, the greatest increases were in expenditures for tents, boats, sleeping bags, winter sports, photography. Expenditures for billiards also increased at a phenomenal rate in the years following 1958.

In an article in *Sports Illustrated* in 1964, Robert Boyle estimated sporting goods sales for the next decade. "In 1964 sales reached $2.6 billion, almost four times the 1948 figure ($746 million), and in another 10 years should near $4.5 billion. The average annual growth rate for sporting goods sales is 5.4%, which is greater than that of the gross national product" (5:40).

In writing about this phenomenon, Ray Cave has said: "There is only one constant: constant change. . . . No sport has gone untouched. Technology, leisure and jingling cash in the public pockets have led to a sports explosion unparalleled in history, one that has burst in an approximate pin point of time." Cave identified that time as the period from 1954 to 1961 (6:11).

The sport interest represented by this data on sport expenditures, as well as the data on sport participation, are in sharp contrast to the

TABLE II
Sporting Goods Expenditures
by Percentage of Change
from 1948 to 1963 and from 1958 to 1964*

	Dollars are in 1963	Figures the Millions 1948	% Change 1963/1948	Dollars are in 1964	Figures the Millions 1958	% Change 1964/1958
1. Archery	— —	— —	— —	$ 33.9	$ 20.0	+ 61.0
2. Baseball	$ 62.4	$ 35.0	+ 78.0	62.4	52.1	+ 20.0
3. Bicycles	204.6	138.8	+ 47.0	209.1	167.7	+ 25.0
4. Billiards	— —	— —	— —	73.0	8.8	+737.0
5. Bowling	— —	— —	— —	38.5	27.3	+ 41.0
6. Firearms	296.0	211.1	+ 27.0	278.1	241.3	+ 15.0
7. Fishing	172.3	111.4	+ 55.0	177.5	145.2	+ 22.0
8. Football, Basketball, and Boxing	53.0	33.2	+ 60.0	53.0	38.9	+ 36.0
9. Golf	174.3	62.0	+180.0	192.3	97.8	+ 97.0
10. Gymnasium Equipment	32.2	2.8	+1050.0	33.8	17.6	+ 96.0
11. Hockey	— —	— —	— —	7.6	3.9	+ 95.0
12. Balls (other than footballs, & basketballs)	— —	— —	— —	14.3	9.5	+ 51.0
13. Photography	440.0	160.5	+ 174.0	455.4	298.2	+ 53.0
14. Playground	65.0	9.1	+ 614.0	71.5	38.5	+ 86.0
15. Boats, Pleasure (no large yachts)	600.0	193.3	+ 210.0	620.0	479.7	+ 29.0
16. Skates (ice and roller)	33.8	21.3	+ 59.0	36.2	24.5	+ 48.0
17. Sleeping Bags	— —	— —	— —	41.2	19.5	+111.0
18. Tennis (lawn)	16.4	7.6	+ 116.0	17.6	12.0	+ 47.0
19. Tennis (table)	— —	— —	— —	5.5	3.2	+ 72.0
20. Tents	55.1	11.7	+ 371.0	60.5	34.4	+ 76.0
21. Winter Sports	25.0	12.7	+ 97.0	30.0	12.9	+132.0

*This table is based on information prepared by Richard Snyder (13).

Note: — — indicates no figures were available or it was not a sizeable enough item on the market to be treated individually.

interest revealed by analysis of the content of *Sports Illustrated*. The interests of the magazine readers became increasingly focused on highly-organized professional and amateur performance in team sports and in dramatic activities which have greater spectator appeal. The interests of those who buy and use sports equipment seem to be focused on a return to activities that provide for individual involvement with the forces of nature. How much spectators of sport also participate in sport would be an interesting relationship to pursue.

Perhaps this "return to nature" is a natural shift accompanying the population shift from urbanized centers to the open spaces of the suburbs, or perhaps it reflects the city dweller's need for personal involvement in activities which are not highly structured and crowd-dominated. In any event, it apparently served an important need for the suburban and urban population of an industrialized society.

In summary then, within the past 75 years some sports activities have been consistently represented in the media. Activities such as golf, tennis and yachting which have been of the upper class and participant oriented, are in this category. Other activities have to do with mechanical power (cars, boats, planes) and have taken on novelty or fad-like proportions for a short period of time. Auto racing as an outgrowth of one of these has developed into a high level spectator interest today. Another trend was the increasing emphasis in magazine content on the dramatic and physically demanding sports such as football and ice hockey.

This is the message of some of the media. However, there is other evidence in terms of people and dollars to indicate that the American public is also interested in family and out-of-doors activities such as camping, boating, billiards, and winter sports. There is a weekend bumper-to-bumper exodus to the mountains and waterways. Is spectator sport really "the cement of democracy," the integrating factor of our country, as some have claimed, or is it simply one aspect of the highly complex system of sports in the United States? Time will tell.

BIBLIOGRAPHY

1. The Athletic Institute. "Participation Survey." Chicago: Athletic Goods Manufacturers Association, 1965, pp. 1-7.
2. Ayer, N. W. and Sons. *Directory of Newspapers and Periodicals*. Philadelphia, Penn.: N. W. Ayer and Sons, Inc., Vol. 37, 1905 through Vol. 97, 1965.
3. Berelson, Bernard. *Content Analysis in Communication Research*. Glencoe, Ill.: The Free Press Publishers, 1952.

4. Boyle, Robert H. *Sport—Mirror of American Life*. Boston: Little, Brown and Co., 1963.

5. ———. "The New Wave in Sports." *Sports Illustrated* 21 (December 21, 1964): 40-45.

6. Cave, Ray. "The Fresh Face of Sport." *Sports Illustrated* 15 (August 21, 1961): 10-15.

7. Cozens, Frederick W. and Florence Scovil Stumpf. *Sports in American Life*. Chicago, Ill.: The University of Chicago Press, 1953.

8. Hiatt, Walter S. "Billions—Just for Fun." *Colliers* 74 (October 25, 1924): 19-42.

9. Lerner, Max. *America As A Civilization*. New York: Simon & Schuster, Inc., 1957.

10. Morison, Samuel Eliot. *The Oxford History of the American People*. New York: Oxford University Press, 1965.

11. Reeve, Arthur B. "What America Spends for Sport." *Outing* 23 (December, 1910): 300-308.

12. Schlesinger, Arthur Meier. *The Rise of Modern America: 1865-1951*. 4th ed. New York: The Macmillan Co., 1951.

13. Snyder, Richard E. *Trends in the Sporting Goods Market: 1747-65*. Chicago, Ill.: National Sporting Goods Association, 1965.

14. *Sportsman* 4 (December, 1928): 27.

TAKE ME IN TO THE BALL GAME

STAN OPOTOWSKY

"Sports is what TV was born to do best," says American Broadcasting Company program director Tom Moore. "There's no drama we can do on the stage that will match the drama on the ball field."

The result has been a revolution in sports. For all the ways that TV has touched upon national life, from entertainment to politics, no field has been so affected as sports. The lad who once begged his dad to take him out to the ball game a few afternoons a year now slumps beside Pop in the living room, following the fortunes of the local stalwarts.

From its earliest days, TV knew it had a vital stake in sports. NBC began experimenting long before it launched its commercial service. It brought both amateur and professional boxers into its Radio City studios for exhibition bouts that permitted the cameramen to study movement and lighting.

Within a month after regular TV service began in 1939, NBC went to Baker Field to telecast a Columbia-Princeton baseball game. It also went to Madison Square Garden for a six-day bicycle race and to Randalls Island for an intercollegiate track meet.

The first big boxing match to be telecast was that between Max Baer and Lou Nova in 1939. It turned out to be a dull fight, but the telecasts received in radio stores caused so much excitement that police ordered the sets turned off so they could get traffic moving again. In the Bronx a riot broke out when the cops tried to force entranced viewers out of a radio store during the fight.

There was immediate talk among promoters of banning the TV cameras from their arenas forever. Obviously no one would pay to see an event that could be viewed at home for free. This was not a surprising attitude. It had been expressed previously in the infant days of radio and, indeed, there was once consideration of barring newspapermen from sports events so that the fans would have to pay admission fees even to learn the final score.

But at the same time that the less-foresighted promoters built their barriers, clairvoyants like Mike Jacobs, then the Number One impresario of boxing, saw TV as the instrument of a great new age for sport. Jacobs predicted the day when there would be no arena at all, when sports events would be staged in a studio exclusively for the television audience.

Jacobs was not quite right, but boxing, his sport, was TV's first big hit. It was boxing that sold the television sets in the first years of mass production. Some decried this, as Gilbert Seldes subsequently wrote in reviewing that period of TV's growth:

> "The telecasting of sports was a turning point in the first phase of television history. It shocked the idealists who saw a great instrument of imagination and social significance turn to the mean estate of reporting not only a World Series, but phony wrestling matches and third-rate prize fights as well; and it shook the practical men, because for a moment it seemed that television was moving from the atmosphere of the home (an ideal place for selling clothes, soap, cars and other commodities supporting radio) to the saloon, where, according to persistent rumor, it didn't even increase the sale of beer, the spectators being so attentive to the sport that they forgot to order."

For all these qualms, sports stayed with TV and TV stayed with sports. Television moved out of the saloon and into the living room, carrying the fights and the wrestling and also the roller derby and the World Series and the Kentucky Derby.

The revolution was so great that it reached the halls of the United States Supreme Court. For generations organized sport has been free of federal antitrust laws. This was based on an old Supreme Court decision ruling that a party, such as a theatrical enterprise or a baseball team, that went from New York to Philadelphia for a performance or game was not in interstate commerce. No business was actually conducted across the state line, the court ruled; the business wasn't conducted until the performers arrived in Philadelphia.

Radio actually had changed that, but the stakes weren't high enough to worry about. TV's stakes were high enough, however, and it was an easy matter to prove that this ball game in Philadelphia actually was being played all over the United States if it was being televised. Thus sport was now in interstate commerce.

The International Boxing Club had enforced a monopoly of major professional boxing purely through its TV contracts. The money that television sponsors paid for the rights to exclusive broadcast of the fights was far more important than the money paid through the box office, and the IBC had exclusive contracts with both network boxing-match sponsors. The federal government, acting under the antitrust laws, consequently ordered the IBC to dissolve. It responded first by cutting itself in half, into "competing" organizations, and later by going out of business.

The fees sports promoters charged for TV rights rose fantastically. NBC's first contract for rights to the World Series was signed in 1947 for $65,000. Within two years the price jumped to $200,000. A year later it was $800,000. By 1957, ten years after the first $65,000 contract, the fee was $16,250,000. Today it is $20,000,000.

The Gillette Safety Razor Company, a natural sponsor for sports broadcasts, became synonymous with the nation's big events because it acquired a near monopoly on their sponsorship—the regular weekly fights, the World Series, the Kentucky Derby, the Rose Bowl. With the stars of these events often used in the commercials, Molly of "The Goldbergs" was moved to acknowledge her introduction to Mickey Mantle by saying, "I've never seen you play ball but I have seen you shave."

Sports promoters had to go to the United States Supreme Court to establish legally that they owned the radio and, subsequently, TV accounts of their games. Because newspapers have never paid for permission to report games, there were many radio stations that felt they need not pay either.

The major-league baseball teams and most college football teams succeeded in selling exclusive radio rights to their games, but this was challenged by Gordon McLendon, a radio-station owner of Dallas, Texas. He built an entire radio network on the piracy of major-league baseball broadcasts.

He thus set up the test case which eventually reached the Supreme Court. McLendon, who was the baseball announcer as well as the network president, was barred from the stadiums, but this did not deter him. He would set up his microphones in a hotel room and then subscribe to the Western Union play-by-play service, which is available to anyone. Using this telegraph report of the game, some appropriate sound effects, and a vivid imagination, McLendon broadcast the games to his network without paying a cent of royalty to the team owners.

He lost his case in court. The Supreme Court ruled that the sports promoter does indeed have a property right it could sell exclusively to a radio or TV station. The promoter could halt McLendon's type of piracy by a court injunction.

Television had great effect on the attendance of sports events. At first the matter seemed to boil down to whether the fans had to pay to see the event at the arena or whether they could remain at home and see the same thing for free. Actually, sports promoters learned that this was only one of many factors.

On one hand, they had to consider all the things that always affect sports attendance—the standing of the teams, the weather, the price of admission, the transportation to the stadium, and so on. On top of that they had to consider TV as competition—not simply their own ball game televised on TV, but the programs competing for attention. Would the people leave home to see a ball game on Milton Berle night? The Berle fans stayed home whether the game was televised or not.

Several major-league baseball teams made pointed tests to determine if televising their own games hurt attendance. The New York Yankees decided in 1952 that it did not. In the same pennant drive the Yankees played the Boston Red Sox in a game without television and the Cleveland Indians in a game with television. The no-TV game drew 59,212. The game that could be seen at home on TV drew 75,854. The Yankees thereupon decided upon unlimited television: they felt they could collect huge fees for the TV rights to their games and still not lose at the box office. The Washington Senators found practically the same thing. But some teams still balk at TV.

The National Collegiate Athletic Association, on the other hand, decided that television cut college football attendance by as much as 27 per cent. It adopted a plan whereby one game a week would be televised and the remainder would not.

The boxing promoters, characteristically perhaps, have their cake and eat it too. The routine fights that would scarcely draw a bridge foursome in the old days are presented for free to the TV audience. The big championship bouts certain to attract large paying crowds are staged without benefit of TV cameras.

Television has not only affected the attendance and finances of organized sport. It has affected the players themselves and their performance. In the first days of baseball telecasts the players had to be warned that because of the camera's telescopic lenses they should watch their language (the viewer may be able to lip read) and also be careful where they scratch. Professional football teams call a special time out every period to permit time for the sponsors' commercials.

But the effects of TV on sport went deeper than that. Dan Parker, sports columnist of the *New York Mirror*, wrote bitterly:

> "The various branches of sport which have had traffic with television because they couldn't resist the lure of fool's gold have furnished enough tragic examples of what happens once this electronic lamprey eel

sinks its fangs into the sports body. Little by little, the sport loses its identity and becomes merely a branch of the Television field. The worst example of all is provided by what happened to boxing. Television now runs the show.

"Its principal object is to build up program material, synthetically, well in advance, so that twice a week a main bout will be available to provide the framework for sales pitches as preposterous as some of the bouts, for the product that is footing the bill. Once, when boxing was its own master, there had to be an excuse for matching two boxers, besides the purely commercial one of making money. There was keen competition between rival promoters who operated in all the key cities where boxing was legal and this made for a healthy condition of the sport.

"There was a steady output of new talent, which had plenty of time to develop, promoters bid for the most attractive matches and thus the most deserving boxers in due time became the champions.

"Now there is no competition, except the synthetic type provided by two divisions of the outlawed IBC which still run the show. Virtually all the top-line boxers (most of whom would have been preliminary boys in the pre-television days) are managed by a criminal underworld syndicate which synthetizes the champions and supplies the 'talent' for promoters to line up for the TV people who have the last word. Boxing commissions accept their subservient role with a docility that is a sorry commentary on what is going on as the once-thriving sport is sold out to the hucksters at every turn. The National Basketball Association is another captive sport, run to suit television's demands.

"Baseball can no longer call its soul its own. The one-eyed lamprey eel has already drained the life blood out of the minor leagues but the TV show must go on and our so-called national pastime has become a mere advertising medium for beer, cigarettes, cigars, etc. Who can remember when baseball magnates wouldn't even permit such advertising to be pasted on their fences? Pro football is thriving on its TV arrangements which calls for time outs at intervals in every game so that TV sponsors can sneak in their commercials."

Sport is so tied in with television that the telecast of a baseball game is not a reporting job at all, but a package deal. The ball club owns the package. It makes the contract with the TV station and then sells its package to a sponsor. The "reporter"—the announcer—works for the ball club.

Insiders chuckle when they hear fans argue whether a Mel Allen broadcasting the Yankees or a Connie Desmond broadcasting the Dodgers games is too prejudiced in favor of the home team. It is not a matter of prejudice. It is a matter of salary. The announcer is on the same payroll as the players and manager. He is not the independent reporter sent to the game by a newspaper.

Yet TV has brought far superior sports announcers than those who held sway in radio's heyday. One of the most famous of radio's sports

announcers was known privately as "football's greatest lateral passer."
This was because of a little trick he devised to cover up his mistakes
in identifying the ball carrier. Jones would streak down the field, but
the announcer would mistake him for Smith and yell into his microphone,
"Smith is away, going for a touchdown!" Near the goal the announcer
would be prodded by a spotter and handed a note saying it's Jones, not
Smith, toting the ball. "Smith laterals to Jones and Jones scores the
touchdown!" the announcer would screech. Actually, Smith was on the
bench at the time, figuring out his withholding tax.

This sort of thing would not work on television, of course, because
the fan could see for himself that there was no lateral pass. The TV
sports announcer, despite his unfortunate loyalty to the team rather than
the fan, is far better versed in the intricacies of the sport than was his
radio predecessor.

The major-league baseball teams cannot decide among themselves
just what to do with television. The Yankees in New York televise all
of their home games and some fifty of their out-of-town games. The
Detroit Tigers televise far fewer games, but feed these occasional telecasts to eight other stations in the area as a promotional stunt. The Milwaukee Braves and the San Francisco Giants permit no television at all.

Most of the teams straddle the fence. They permit TV of an average of twenty home games a year, hoping that these will be an entice-
ment that will lead fans into the ball park. Baseball's big hope is that
pay television will someday permit huge TV audiences that shell out for
what they see on the ball field.

The greatest effect of TV has been on minor-league baseball. Once
these minor-league teams served two functions—they provided baseball
for the smaller towns as well as a proving ground for young players on
their way up to the major leagues. Today the minors are still proving
grounds, but they are supported as liabilities by their major-league parent clubs. Television has stolen away the paying customers to such an
extent that some minor-league teams play with fewer than one hundred
persons in the grandstand.

Minor-league owners have pleaded with the major leagues to prevent telecasts of big-league games from entering minor-league cities.
The majors have turned deaf ears to these pleas, or perhaps they did
not hear them at all over the jangle of the TV gold.

Boxing has been affected in somewhat the same way. The small
neighborhood clubs that profitably provided a place for a youngster to
break in have died off, unable to meet the competition of Milton Berle
and Desi and Lucy and Jack Paar over the years, not to mention the

competition of big-city fights coming over the networks twice a week.

The quality of boxing has also tumbled because of TV. Promoters with TV contracts must provide a show every week. If there aren't two good men to match, then the promoter must match two bad ones. The show must go on.

College football and basketball are based on intense local rivalries and followings, yet they have chosen a different road to TV. The NCAA controls all college football telecasts and generally permits only one game to be telecast live a week. A power such as Notre Dame can sell movies of its games for subsequent telecast the day after the game, but few teams have such box-office appeal to permit so synthetic a performance. College basketball is televised generally. Locally these programs are extremely popular, but ABC found it couldn't find a sponsor when it attempted to put together a national TV basketball schedule for presentation on the coast-to-coast network.

The participant sports have been affected little by TV. There are golf-instruction programs and telecasts of the tennis championships from Forest Hills and local fishing and hunting programs, but these have never been sports that lend themselves to great crowds; hence there is little interest in widespread television of their matches.

Horse racing is a natural for TV, and the big races draw large viewing audiences. However, television, so subject to government scrutiny, is wary of too close an association with a sport that is tied directly to gambling.

Because of its early interest in sports, NBC for years was the dominant network in sports. It had the best of the weekly fight programs and it also held exclusive contracts for the World Series, the Rose Bowl, the Kentucky Derby, and the NCAA football games. But ABC has now moved up.

ABC likes the idea of sports because it considers itself the network with a special appeal to young America, that part of the nation which is most often buying boats and cars and furniture and cigarettes and beer.

There's another thing about sports: The games are played at a time when the network has difficulty selling any other type of program. Saturday and Sunday afternoons are the key periods. ABC's Moore thinks TV eventually will be almost entirely sports on those days. The ratings aren't so high as those attracted by other shows, but the weekend daytime period goes begging anyway; and besides, sports moves advertisers' products out of proportion to the ratings. The only losers here are the intellectuals, who may soon face eviction from even their ghetto.

For the 1960-1961 season ABC got the boxing matches and NCAA football from NBC. However, these were things NBC was willing to give up. Officially, NBC said it was cutting itself loose from boxing because of the unsavory characters who dominate the sport. The inside story is a bit different. Gillette owned the fight contract, and NBC collected only its time charges for that hour each Friday night. Were NBC to rid itself of the fights and replace them with a network-owned show, it could collect both the time charges and the profit it derived selling the show to the sponsor. As is usual with big decisions in the TV industry, the guiding principal was money, not morality.

NBC retained the big sports extravaganzas—the World Series, the Kentucky Derby, and the Rose Bowl. These are the most valuable television properties in sports.

TELEVISION'S EFFECTS ON
SPECTATOR SPORTS

Leo Bogart

Television has brought outstanding athletic events within the reach of millions who would otherwise not see them. In 1955, the all-star baseball game in July, and the all-star football game the following month, were each viewed in nearly 14,000,000 homes.

Radio coverage of sports events has long been accepted and welcomed in college football and professional baseball both as an added form of income and as a stimulus to popular interest. By contrast, television was from the start regarded as a menace by organized athletics since it actually permitted the game to be watched and followed, play by play, much as it might be from the stadium. And these anxieties have been well justified.

While television has damaged attendance at baseball and football games, it has from time to time aroused interest in minor sports. The roller derby, a kind of roller-skating marathon, not only won a huge television audience for the few years of its popularity, but managed to attract a good many people to view the spectacle in the flesh. Wrestling, never one of the more popular spectator sports, developed, through television, a vast circle of devotees. In wrestling as in boxing, which has refused to permit championship bouts to be televised except in theaters, the small size of the screen does not cramp the view of the spectacle in the same way as it does in a football or baseball match where the camera must follow the action over a wide field.

The single outstanding piece of research on the subject of television's influence upon organized sports has not received more publicity and

Leo Bogart, *The Age of Television* (New York: Frederich Ungar Publishing Company, 1956), Chapter 9. Copyright © 1956. Reprinted by permission.

comment than far less substantial studies. Indications of television's effects are easier to trace in terms of attendance figures or gate receipts than in terms of actual public interest in the sports.

A few scattered reports are indicative:

1. Ruth Taylor, in a 1949 survey among 549 subscribers to *Television Forecast* magazine, found that 85% of the respondents said they had become interested in sports events which they had not been interested in before TV.

2. Stewart, in his 1951 survey of Atlanta, found that nine-tenths of the television owners said they had watched sports on TV. Two-thirds said their interest had increased as a result. About two-thirds said their attendance had not been affected. But one in three of the TV sports viewers said they had been going to fewer athletic events since they acquired television—and this was especially true of the better educated respondents who probably (since they also had the highest incomes) attended most frequently.

3. In McDonagh's Southern California survey, 39% of the television owners, and only 22% of the non-owners, reported that they were participating less in sports. This again suggested a decline.

4. In 1951, the New York *Times* interviewed principals of leading high schools in the suburbs of New York, and found a uniform picture of declining attendance. At White Plains, attendance at football games dropped from an average of 15,774 admissions in 1948 to 12,856 in 1950. In the same period basketball receipts dropped by $100 a game. The implications went beyond athletics, reported *Times* Radio-TV editor Jack Gould: "Football and basketball revenues formerly supported baseball, track and other sports, as well as activities such as the dramatics, riding and French clubs, and the school newspaper. With such revenues showing a $3,500 loss for the year, it was said, taxpayers ultimately would have to meet the deficit."

The story was exactly the same at New Rochelle High School, whose band was left with insufficient funds to buy new uniforms. The school's "big game" which produced gate receipts of three to seven thousand dollars before television, yielded only $700 in 1950. At Stamford, Connecticut, the high school stadium, with a seating capacity of 10,000, was only half-filled at many games. School sports, formerly self-sustaining, showed a deficit.

In contrast to these isolated case histories, Jerry Jordan, first in a college thesis and later in studies underwritten by the Radio-Television Manufacturers' Association, sought to assemble attendance histories for a number of organized sports, and supplemented this with several small-scale opinion surveys.

Rejecting the thesis that telecasting of sports events led automatically to a decline in attendance, Jordan drew attention to the variations and cycles in popularity which affected sports like baseball long before the advent of TV. He listed fifteen factors which could affect attendance: (1) economic conditions; (2) management; (3) performance (of both home and visiting teams); (4) publicity-promotion; (5) employment-working hours; (6) kind of games or schedules; (7) general population; (8) college population (at least insofar as college football is concerned); (9) weather; (10) accommodations; (11) ticket prices; (12) individual attractions; (13) competition; (14) radio sportscasting; (15) television sportscasting.

Seen in this light, television could be regarded as only a minor influence among many other influences. To illustrate that factors other than television might cause attendance to drop, Jordan cites a loss of 26,778 admissions per game in Los Angeles college football in 1948—at a time when only 2% of the homes in the area had TV. In 1949, when the number of sets had grown sixfold, the decline in admissions was less than half what it had been the previous year. (Jordon fails to underline a point, however, which is apparent from his accompanying data: that 1947 was an unusually good year.

In further support of his point Jordon quotes a newspaper column by Grantland Rice, who noted that in 1932 the Eastern Intercollegiate Association passed a resolution banning radio broadcasts of football games, and that much earlier there was talk of banning newspaper men from ball parks so that people would have to attend the game to find out the score.

The real secret of the attendance figures, Jordan believes, is in the quality of a team's performance record. He notes that baseball teams with good records increased attendance in 1949 over 1948, while attendance declined for teams with less satisfactory performance. On the other hand, he finds no relation between the attendance standing of the teams and the size of the television audience in their home towns. On days, nights and weekends, games which were good enough to attract large television audiences also drew crowds to the ball parks.

In football too, Jordan finds no evidence of TV's adverse influence on attendance. Of 106 colleges in TV areas, 56% showed an increase in attendance between 1948 and 1949, compared with 51% of the 88 colleges in non-TV areas. He reports the least improvement in the case of small colleges in non-TV areas.

Moreover, Jordan observes that (at this relatively early point in the history of television), the TV owners were especially apt to be represented among the crowd at the stadium. At a time when 17% of Philadelphians had television, ownership stood at 36% among season ticketholders of University of Pennsylvania football games. At a time when 19% of the city had television, Jordan interviewed 303 persons at two Philadelphia baseball games—one well- and one poorly-attended. In each case 27% said they had a TV set at home.

But in the light of his researches Jordan could not discount the effects of television altogether. He does find that it cuts into attendance, but he believes that this is the result of a novelty effect which wears off after a while. Interviewing 600 male heads of families in the Philadelphia area, in the fall of 1949, he finds that among the non-TV owners, 46% went to see a football game of some kind (high school, college, or professional). Only 24% of the new television owners (who had owned their sets for less than three months) had gone to a game, compared with 41% of those who had owned their sets between four months and a year, 45% of those who had owned their sets for one or two years, and 54% of those who had owned their sets for over two years.

Similar findings were produced in the case of baseball: 45% of the non-TV owners had seen a big-league game in Shibe Park in 1949, for an average of 4.4 games, 44% of the new TV owners (who had owned their sets for less than a year) saw at least one game, or 3.7 on the average. Of the old TV owners (who had owned their sets for a year or more), 58% saw an average of 5.9 games.

The new television owners were less apt to take other members of their families with them to the baseball games than were either the old owners or the non-owners. However, interviews at the ball park itself suggested that television was the most important factor stimulating other members of the family (mostly wives, no doubt) to attend a game.

Minor baseball league attendance reacts to performance more than to television competition from the big leagues, Jordan believes. However, this conclusion is not necessarily buttressed by his report on 300 interviews with television set owners in Wilmington, Delaware; 40% said they would prefer to see the Wilmington Blue Rocks play locally than watch the Philadelphia teams on television, but 53% said they would perfer TV; 7% had no choice.

Summing up his findings, Jordan says,

"There is a temporary decrease in football attendance during the first year of ownership. After the novelty wears off, attendance picks up again, and returns to normal in about one year. Owners of two or more years have higher attendance than non-owners. This temporary loss in attendance among new owners, indicated by the public opinion surveys, is not reflected in national attendance figures. There are three reasons for this: (a) The higher rate of long-term owners balances out part of the loss. (b) This temporary loss is not found among alumni, who represent a large proportion of the football crowd. (c) Television helps create new fans. The effect of these three factors just about neutralizes the loss among short-term owners."

The Jordan studies have been described here at some length not so much because of the inherent importance of the findings but because the surveys were widely publicized by the sponsoring Radio-Television Manufacturers' Association, which was understandably eager to discount the theory that TV posed a menace to any established American institutions. Accordingly these studies have had a disproportionate influence on discussion of the subject.

Actually Jordan's findings were largely based on small and unrepresentative samples, and most of the differences he reports (for example on the sports attendance of old and new set owners) are statistically not significant. As a devastating critique later pointed out in commenting on Jordan's prize theory of the novelty effect, "It is improper to conclude that the attendance of newer owners will ever reach the level of the older owners, since their prior or normal attendance was unquestionably lower. They are less well off economically and their average interest in college sports is less."

While Jordan in his reports discussed the whole broad area of TV's impact on athletics, without marshalling sufficient evidence to produce a completely convincing story, the most thorough investigation of the subject has confined itself to only one sport—inter-collegiate football. Since 1950, the National Collegiate Athletic Association has sponsored a series of studies made by the National Opinion Research Center and directed by Paul B. Sheatsley and Paul N. Borsky. Year by year, as the television-viewing area has been extended, NORC has carefully examined attendance statistics and has interviewed thousands of men about their interests in college football. The general conclusion has been that television cuts into sports attendance as seriously as into other activities.

These studies represent a clear-cut example of research influencing policy and action, for as a result of the first reports, the NCAA at its annual meeting in January, 1951, voted to restrict direct telecasting of its members' games. An experimental plan was set up which permitted only seven live games to be televised in a season in any one TV reception area, with each area shown an approximately equal number of nearby and distant games. No single team could appear on television more than once or twice.

In the 1950 season, the greatest decline in attendance occurred where a college's games were telecast. The next greatest decline was shown by other colleges in the same areas. The least effects were felt by colleges whose only television competition came from games in other areas.

Unlike Jordan, Sheatsley and Borsky began their researches by asking who the sports fans were. In a national survey they found that over half the adult public had never attended an intercollegiate football match. About the same number reported no interest at all in the game. Only one person in seven attends a game in any given season, and fewer than one in five can be classified as a fan. College football is therefore a minority sport, of particular interest to younger men, and particularly to those who have gone to college.

Interest in football develops early, and only one fan in a hundred said that television was responsible for arousing his interest in the game. By contrast, in two cities, 10% of the people who had gone to a game some time between 1947 and 1950 said they did not plan to attend any in 1951, but would watch televised games instead.

Like Jordan, Sheatsley and Borsky point to the factors other than television which might affect attendance, including "the weather, the calibre of the opposition, and special promotional efforts . . . the size of the stadium, the performance of the team . . . local interest in college football . . . the level of student enrollment, the pinch of inflation or the ready spending money of boom times."

Of these factors, the attractiveness of the game appeared to be most important, but competition from televised football made quite a difference regardless of how good the game was. To arrive at this conclusion, the 1947-8 attendance figures were taken as the "expected" norm, and comparisons were made in such a way as to carefully control for extraneous influences. The results of this analysis for the 1952 season are shown in Table 1. (Similar findings were obtained in 1951.)

It is clear that the more attractive games, particularly, did much better when they did not face TV competition. The explanation given by the NORC researchers is that these are the games which normally draw the largest number of less interested or "marginal" fans, who are more apt to accept a substitute on TV. The most enthusiastic fans, who don't consider a televised game a proper substitute, are also the ones who show up at the less attractive games as well as the big ones.

For the same reason, television has had a more serious effect on the big and middle-sized colleges than on the smaller schools. It is the big games which draw the general public, and consequently more of the marginal fans. At small college games, attendance is more apt

TABLE 1

Game Attractiveness and TV Competition as Factors
Affecting College Football Attendance

	Per Cent of "Expected" (1947-8) Attendance			
	All Colleges	No TV Competition	TV Competition	TV Differential
All games	93.1	110.5	83.8	26.7
More attractive	122.0	141.7	102.3	39.4
Less attractive	72.3	79.3	65.3	14.0
Attractiveness differential	49.7	62.4	37.0	

(Source: NORC-NCAA Report #3)

to be made up of loyal alumni and others with a very special interest. Because the small college games have a relatively heavy day-of-game sale (while the big colleges rely more on advance bookings) and because the public had no advance knowledge of which games would be telecast, the NCAA restriction on football telecasts aided the small colleges more than the big ones. This made the first findings of the NCAA experiment somewhat inconclusive.

The very fact that few fans knew in advance what games would be on the air meant that the size of the TV football audience remained surprisingly stable, regardless of the intrinsic quality or interest of the games themselves. As the fourth NORC report points out, "If 23% watched the average game, one might have thought that the less attractive telecasts would be watched by only 5% to 10% of the fans, and the most attractive ones by 70% or 80%. This is not at all the case. No game was lower than 17% and no game was higher than 35%." (The implication of this might be that home viewing of football is for the most part a kind of second-choice activity. Few of the viewers are people who have actively planned in advance to stay home Saturday afternoon and watch the game, in the same way in which a fan might plan ahead of time to *go* to the game.)

Under the NCAA plan of restrictions, the televised game of the week was not necessarily the one a given football fan was most interested in. However, radio continued to offer him a choice of the best games in the country. An NORC survey found that, in television areas, more fans (34%) listened to college football on the radio than watched it on television (23%) on the average Saturday afternoon in the 1953 season. Yet these figures contrast with a mere 3% of the fans who actually attended a game on the average Saturday. Sheatsley and Borsky conclude that if no games were telecast, the result would not be more listening to radio broadcasts, but an upward surge in attendance at the games themselves.

Watching football on television, they observe, actually breaks the habit of attendance. In support of this they point out that attendance is lower among those who have owned TV longest. In 1953, 84% of those fans who had owned their sets for four years or more did not attend a single game; this compares with 73% of those who had owned a set for two or three years, and with 69% of those who had owned their set for a year or less.

With these findings, the NORC researchers effectively dispose of Jordan's theory of TV's "novelty effect." In fact, their analysis leads them even further in the opposite direction. They note that strong interest in college football is heavily concentrated among the minority of college-educated. "The best seats are reserved for alumni and students, and a large part of the game's appeal lies in the songs and cheers, the campus associations and the pleasures of meeting old friends and classmates, which the non-college attender cannot fully appreciate."

But the select group who constitute college football's chief supporters were also among the first persons to acquire television. By contrast, those who bought sets later on were more apt to be "marginal" fans, if they were interested in the game at all. The last persons to acquire television had even lower incomes, and were less apt to have college ties. Such persons were far more ready than the TV pioneers to be wooed away from actual attendance, and less apt to have a strong attachment to a particular team. The result is that televised football would have a greater, rather than a smaller, effect as time goes on—if not for the NCAA restrictions on telecasting.

Actually the Sheatsley-Borsky analysis shows a fairly stable attendance pattern over recent years, at a level well below the pre-television norms of 1947-8, and with a clear-cut differential between TV and non-TV areas. Table 2 shows the results of this comparison for the years 1950-3. By 1954 there were practically no non-television areas left to measure.

The NORC studies not only reveal an unbroken array of evidence that TV cuts into attendance; they also fail to support the theory that telecasts stimulate interest in football among those who previously lacked it. "While televised games, just like radio and the sports pages, undoubtedly provide satisfaction to fans who are already interested, they

TABLE 2

Football Attendance in Areas With and Without TV Competition

	Per Cent of Expected (1947-8) Attendance		
Year	Colleges With TV Competition	Colleges Without TV Competition	TV Differential
1950	88.6	115.1	26.5
1951	85.1	103.7	18.6
1952	83.8	110.5	26.7
1953	81.6	109.3	27.7

clearly have not made many new fans for the game." Four fans of every five were found to have at least one strong favorite team whose fortunes they follow, and these attachments are based overwhelmingly on personal or geographic ties rather than on performance or quality.

To what extent are the conclusions of the NORC-NCAA studies applicable to other sports? The finding that television does not create interest probably cannot be made into a general statement. It seems likely that in the case of baseball, boxing and a number of other sports (and perhaps to a lesser degree even in the case of football), television combines with other media and channels of publicity to generate an atmosphere of interest and discussion which lifts the general level of awareness to the point where some people move from a position of apathy to one of marginal interest, or from the latter category to become true fans.

The major reason for hesitation in generalizing to all sports from the NORC findings is that college football and basketball are different from professional baseball and boxing in the degree to which their principal fans are drawn from a distinct social stratum. Because the professional sports have a broader mass following, it would probably be wrong to assume that the first owners of TV were also the most enthusiastic fans. Moreover, since baseball telecasts have not been restricted like college football games, it is impossible to trace the pattern of cause and effect in the exacting manner of the NORC analysis.

The period of television's growth has been a period of decline for professional baseball. Big league attendance fell from a high of nearly 21 million in 1948 to a low of 14 million in 1953. In 1954 it climbed back to 16 million.

A survey made in 1955 for the office of the Baseball Commissioner by the public relations firm of Stephen Fitzgerald and Company came

up with an optimistic view of the subject. Since the sampling and interviewing were not carried out by professionals, the findings cannot be
taken literally in spite of the 20,000 persons reportedly interviewed.
Seven out of ten reported that radio broadcasting and telecasting of
baseball games had increased their interest in the sport. Of those who
felt that broadcasts had increased the public interest in baseball, 39%
believed that they had decreased actual attendance, but 27% thought
that attendance had increased.

Half of those interviewed said they would favor a blackout of
home games if baseball were threatened by the telecasts. About one in
three indicated a willingness to pay 25-50 cents to see games on "pay-
as-you-see" TV.

Two major-league teams have taken the step of banning television.
The Braves, after moving from Boston to Milwaukee in 1953, showed
the biggest attendance increase of any team in either league. The Athletics, when they moved from Philadelphia to Kansas City, raised their
attendance by over a million. In both cases it is hard to say how much
of the improvement was wrought by the move, how much by the exclusion of TV.

However, television has provided the big leagues with some fresh
source of revenue. Television fees do not have to be split with the visiting club, which gets 25 cents for every customer at the gate.

TABLE 3
The Rise and Fall in Minor Leagues

Year	Number of Leagues	Number of Teams
1935	21	150
1937	37	249
1940	43	296
1943*	9	62
1946	42	310
1949	59	448
1952	43	324
1955	33	241

*Most minor leagues suspended play during World War II.
  1943 marked the lowest point.

(Source: *Sports Illustrated*)

In 1947, radio rights for the world series games were $175,000, TV rights $65,000. In 1949 radio cost $154,000, TV $200,000. By 1950 radio cost $175,000, TV $800,000. In 1953 radio cost $200,000, television $925,000. The National Broadcasting Company and a sponsor, Gillette, will pay $16,250,000 for TV rights to the World Series and All Star games for five years starting 1957.

By contrast, television has meant nothing but continued losses for minor leagues, which must compete with the majors on TV. *Sports Illustrated* mentions a number of other factors contributing to their decline, including the growth of other sports, outdoor movies, and miscellaneous summertime diversions. The story is told in Table 3.

In summary, the evidence suggests that unrestricted televising of sports events can cause attendance to drop *but* at the same time heighten popular interest in the sports themselves.

ECONOMICS OR EDUCATION:
DEDICATION AND DOLLARS

In the following section, the many facets of the profit explosion in pro football are examined by Mahoney. The economics of a pro team are considered by way of a mythical club, for, Mahoney states, the real ones guard their profits and losses too carefully to be examined. The analysis is thorough and the projections for new profit making in football are bigger than ever.

But dollars are only part of the picture. Also warranting consideration is the dedication of coaches like George Allen and Don Shula. Braucher tries to help us look at these men of intensity, drive and commitment. How do they affect the game of football and what do they derive from it?

How is sport in education affected by this profit explosion and the rising costs of events? Mathews turns the question around from "Student Unrest and Athletic Dollars" to "Athletic Unrest and Student Dollars." Students in colleges and universities are asking questions about priorities in budgets and numbers of people benefiting from the money provided. They are examining their own involvements and their social values. The questions are serious and the outcome unknown as it relates to intercollegiate sports.

The economics of the sporting goods market is not as widely publicized as other aspects of the business of sports. Richard Snyder, an economist, analyzed the market for the National Sporting Goods Association for many years. He reports that thirty or forty years ago the sporting goods market as an economic phenomenon was "hardly anything but a nothing" but now is "very much of a something." The sporting goods market, according to Snyder, topped one billion dollars for the first time in 1947. Twenty years later in 1967, it was over 3 billion dollars.

Although not specifically presented by any of the authors, it might be interesting to investigate who spends most in the sporting goods market. Gilbert, in an article in *Sports Illustrated* in 1965, stated: "In-

dustry buys more sport gear than all U. S. schools and colleges put together—at least, so say the representatives of sporting goods manufacturers, who are very, very high on industrial recreation."[1]

1. Bill Gilbert, "Sis-Boom-Bah! For Amalgamated Sponge," *Sports Illustrated* 22
(January 25, 1965): 54.

PRO FOOTBALL'S PROFIT EXPLOSION

STEPHEN MAHONEY

The love affair between the American public and professional football has had a number of interesting consequences. In millions of American households, the most noticeable consequence, no doubt, has been a total lapse in whatever it is the headman used to do on Sunday afternoon, as he now spends his time peering raptly at the television set. If his team's game is "blacked out" in the immediate area, he may well organize an expedition of some seventy-five or a hundred miles so that he can watch the game away from home; pro football is unique in being the only sport that moves people to travel long distances just to see a telecast. In several hundred thousand other households, of course, the headman leaves for the game itself. That vaulting red line on the opposite* page shows that attendance at National Football League games has passed the four-million mark; the young American Football League attracts another 1,300,000. These figures are for official league games. In addition, pro football derives a considerable revenue from attendance at exhibition games, since another of the sport's unique distinctions is that it can pack the house for mere "exhibitions." About 84,000 turned out early last September for an exhibition in Cleveland.

One natural consequence of the game's soaring popularity has been a breathtaking rise in revenues. In 1950, N.F.L. teams had gate receipts of less than $5 million and scarcely any television revenues at all. This year they should gross around $18 million at the gate (not counting those exhibitions) and they will take in another $16 million from TV.

Stephen Mahoney, "Pro Football's Profit Explosion," *Fortune* 70 (November, 1964): 153-230. Reprinted by permission of Time, Inc.
*Graph showing 1934 N.F.L. attendance at 493,000, climbing to 1963 N.F.L. attendance at 4,164,000 (not shown).

To the owners of the teams, perhaps the most interesting consequence of the new love for the game is that it has, at last, made pro football a real business. In one sense, of course, professional football has always been a business—by definition. Until quite recently, however, it lacked the ingredient of profits. Now the profits are rolling in: at least eleven of the fourteen N.F.L. teams earned something last year, with their average probably around $150,000 after taxes. (The most profitable team of all, the New York Giants, earned about $500,000.) This year the average may be around $400,000.

These profits have led the owners to relate football to some familiar business concepts that had previously seemed irrelevant to their own situation. For example, potential investors are now doing a great deal of fairly sophisticated analysis of the return available on pro football. The appropriate procedures for depreciating teams' assets are being closely examined by several clubs. And, as in many other kinds of business these days, there is intense concern about the pressure of demand on capacity. The Giants, who were assured of a sellout at the gate before the season began, are manifesting their concern by conducting an interesting new experiment with theatre television, at $6 a seat, for certain home games.

A CONTRIBUTION TO CULTURE

For the most part, this article will be concerned with the National Football League, which puts on the best ball games, draws the biggest crowds, has the most valuable clubs, and has been around for forty-five years. However, the pro-football boom has spawned a certain amount of competition and imitation. A second "major league" is the five-year-old, eight-team American Football League, most of whose outfits play in cities a bit smaller than those where N.F.L. teams play—e.g., in California the A.F.L. has San Diego, while the N.F.L. has Los Angeles. A "major league" in Canada has been in existence for fifteen years, and in the last few years several regional "minor leagues" have sprung up in the U.S.

New Money

Dan Reeves, fifty-two, has been an investor in pro football since 1941, and has controlled the Los Angeles Rams since 1961, when he and some friends paid $4,800,000 for two-thirds of the stock (he had earlier owned about a third). Reeve's money originally came from the sale of the New York-based Reeves grocery chain to Safeway Stores. "Why am I in football?" he mused recently. "But isn't it the dream of *every* American male to own a football team?"

Bill Ford, thirty-five, grandson of old Henry, younger brother of Henry Ford II, and vice president of the Ford Motor Co. in charge of styling, bought the Detroit Lions in 1963 for $6 million. Ford is a loud and emotional Lions fan who beats his players to the dressing room after a game, is the last person to leave it, insists that the players call him Bill, and occasionally has them to his home for dinner.

Art Modell, thirty-nine, had a background in advertising and show business (as an account supervisor and television producer) when he bought the Cleveland Browns in 1961 for $3,800,000. The price, he says, was "a steal." Finding the team underpromoted, Modell concentrated on press-agentry and such attention-winning shows as exhibition double-headers, and has built huge audiences for the team. The Browns are probably worth $10 million today.

Jerry Wolman, thirty-seven, a hustling Washington building contractor, who bought the Philadelphia Eagles this year, says he was moved by a strong yen to "have some fun for my money." Wolman says he is now worth close to $40 million, all of it made in the past decade. A Pennsylvania fruit wholesaler's son, he once went into the grocery trade and failed, was almost penniless as late as 1954, and clerking in a paint store. Today Washington is full of his shopping centers and commercial and residential buildings. Like some other owners, Wolman likes to get out on the field and toss the ball around with his players.

While the emergence of profits has made the game a many-sided business, it is clear that some teams are quite a lot more businesslike than others. In general, the owners fall into three categories. One sizable group may be thought of as essentially "millionaire sportsmen." These owners are immensely wealthy and under minimal pressure to make money out of football; sometimes they appear to view their involvement in the sport as a kind of civic philanthropy—i.e., as their own donation to the life and culture of their home towns. Many are the sons or grandsons of famous American entrepreneurs. One, for example, is Bill Ford, vice president of the Ford Motor Co., who bought the Detroit Lions last year. Another is Clint Murchison Jr., who owns most of the Dallas Cowboys. In the A.F.L., Conrad Hilton and his son Barron own 65 percent of the San Diego Chargers; K. S. (Bud) Adams, son of the chairman of Phillips Petroleum, owns the Houston Oilers; and Lamar Hunt, son of the famous H. L., is owner of the young Kansas City Chiefs.

A second category would be the "old-timers"—owners who have been in the game for three or four decades, typically starting out on a shoestring. George Halas, who owns (and also coaches) the world-champion Chicago Bears, is one conspicuous old-timer. Another is Art Rooney, who is sixty-three, has owned the Pittsburgh Steelers since 1933 and has yet to win a championship. The Mara family may be thought of collectively as another old-timer. The New York Giants were founded in 1926 by Tim Mara, a bookmaker who did business under a striped umbrella at New York State racetracks when bookmaking there was still legal; one persistent legend has it that a bettor gave Mara a marker for the Giant franchise, and when he was unable to redeem it Mara had the team. His sons Jack and Wellington have the Giants now, and could sell out for well over $10 million.

A third category includes some owners who have been successful promoters in other kinds of business. Carroll Rosenbloom, a Baltimorean who had made millions in textiles, land development, and electronics, put down $13,000 for a half interest in the Colts in 1953. Later he bought out his partners, bringing his total investment up to $1,300,000. The Colts today are worth around $9 million. Among the other "promoters" are Jerry Wolman, a young Pennsylvanian, now owner of the N.F.L.'s Philadelphia Eagles, who had earlier made a bundle in the construction business; and Arthur Modell, a former producer of daytime television programs for the American Broadcasting Co., who in 1961 bought the Cleveland Browns.

LIFE AND DEATH WITH THE LIONS

All three kinds of owners seem to get a lot of fun out of football. A few years ago Rosenbloom of the Colts was invited to play touch football at Robert Kennedy's old place in Virginia, and conceived the humorous notion of introducing some ringers into the game. Three Colt backfield stars, Alan Ameche, L. G. Dupre, and Billy Pricer, played incognito for Ted Kennedy's team, which beat Bobby's. According to some spectators, Bobby was a bit irritated when he found out whom he'd been chasing all afternoon. Rosenbloom combines football business and non-football business in other interesting ways. When the Colts won the championship in 1958, he steered a number of them into investing their windfall incomes in General Development Corp., the Florida real-estate firm (in which he was himself a big stockholder), promising that he would make good any losses they might have. In 1958-59, General Development shot up from $8 to $77.50, then turned down again. Most of the players got into the stock near the bottom and got out with nice profits. Two took losses and were reimbursed by Rosenbloom.

Of the other owners, several seem to live and die with their teams' fortunes. A friend who recently went to a Lions game with Bill Ford reported afterward that Ford's demonstrative cheering so unnerved him that he felt obliged to sneak away to a quieter spot. Jerry Wolman was so exhilirated by a recent Eagles victory over the Giants that he went out on the field before the crowd had left and ran around taking bows.

Lamar Hunt's enthusiasm is obvious to anyone watching him pass the ball around with the Chiefs.

Several reasons for the success of pro football may be discerned. One underlying reason seems to be that the game is wonderfully attuned to the pace and style of American life in the 1960's. To a nation of spectators, it offers an unsurpassed spectacle. In a time of mass education, it is an educated man's game; no other physical sport has so many elaborate and sophisticated strategies or requires such precise coordination of so many specialized skills. Sportswriters who seem to have had freshman psychology have also noted that the game mirrors the uncertainties of our age—i.e., in that any one contest's direction can be changed quite suddenly by a few big plays. (It may or may not be significant that fans refer to the long pass as "the bomb.")

Furthermore, football is a game ideally suited to television, which creates new fans who want to see the game in person. Television has also provided an important addition to the industry's "capacity." This year each N.F.L. club will get a bit more than $1 million from the league's sale of TV rights to C.B.S.; the figure is up from only $325,000 in 1963. To old hands in the game, television represents an incredible windfall. Rooney of the Pittsburgh Steelers remarked recently, "I can remember when we had to *pay* radio to broadcast our games."

The cost of the contract with C.B.S. is borne by advertisers, of course, and it is a testimonial to football's drawing power that the network has found commercial sponsors to carry that $16-million load. A one-minute commercial costs roughly $75,000, which means it is the highest-priced minute in the history of regularly scheduled daytime programing. (This year's N.F.L. championship game will cost advertisers $110,000 a minute.) Some special privileges come with these fancy prices. To ensure that the commercials are not deliverd while play is in progress, there is an "official's time out" midway in the first and third quarters of any game not otherwise interrupted by a score or a regular time out.

Still, the price seems to make football a dreadful buy. On a cost-per-thousand basis, the sponsor must pay almost $6 to reach a thousand people watching televised football; he could reach 1,000 weekday-evening viewers of Westerns for around $3.70. The case for paying the higher price lies in the quality of the football audience. It is well educated, high-income, and predominantly male, all of which makes it most desirable for manufacturers of big-ticket consumer items, such as automobiles. (Ford is the biggest single sponsor.) Furthermore, because football is so exciting, the audience stays in front of that television set; anyone rising from his chair during the commercials risks missing a play or two.

HOW THE HELLERS DO IT

To understand the economics of pro football, it will help to consider in detail the revenues and expenses of a mythical average club.
(Only mythical clubs can be examined this way; the real ones guard
their p. and l.'s closely.) We'll call our outfit the Cincinnati Hellers. The
Hellers, who play only average ball—winning seven games this year, and
losing seven—will take in gross revenues of $3 million. Costs will be
$2,200,000, income tax $385,000. After-tax profit: $415,000.

The chief source of revenues is, of course, the gate. Ticket prices
in the N.F.L. range from $2 to $6. The Hellers will charge an average
of $4.50 a ticket (including admission tax) to each of their seven regu-
larly scheduled home games, and, let us say, draw an average of almost
42,500 people to each. Thus they will gross a little more than $1,300,000
at home. They will also play seven games on the road, and in the
National Football League the visiting team gets 40 percent of the gate,
after certain deductions, with a guaranteed minimum of $30,000. One
of the games on the road will be with the Dallas Cowboys, who have
been a relatively poor drawing card at home; thus the Hellers will take
home only the $30,000 guarantee. The other road games will be much
more lucrative, averaging over $60,000 each, for a total of $400,000. The
"take" from pre-season exhibition games added another $150,000. Un-
fortunately, the Hellers will earn nothing this year from games following
the close of the regular season, for they will appear in neither the championship playoff (between the first-place teams in the N.F.L.'s eastern
and western divisons) nor the "consolation" playoff (between the di-
visional runners-up). Thus total revenues from paid admissions will
amount to approximately $1,900,000.

The TV proceeds add another big chunk of revenues. All fourteen
of the N.F.L. clubs will receive equal shares of the $14,100,000 paid by
C.B.S. for the regular-season games, which means that the Hellers' share
will be a little over $1 million. If the team played more inspired football
it might pick up extra TV revenues from exhibition games, post-season
playoffs, and closed-circuit showings in motion-picture theatres; however, the Hellers cannot yet count on any such extras.

Most clubs also take in something by selling game programs, and
the Hellers will gross $75,000 this way, including the programs' adver-
tising revenues. The sale of radio rights to home games will bring in
$40,000. The club stations employees around the stadium to peddle
pennants, miniature golden footballs to be stuck on lapels, and hats with
bright golden feathers on which is inscribed, "Go go GO Hellers." Another $6,000. Like most clubs, our team will derive no income from the

parking, food, and beverage concessions. The Hellers rent, rather than own, the stadium, and this concession money goes to the stadium owner.

This year the Hellers sold 30,000 season tickets—i.e., tickets good for all home games this fall—by June, long before most of the expenses began to eat into funds. The average ticket price was $35, and thus the pre-season total was over $1 million. The Hellers' business manager put this "float" into short-term governments, where they returned $13,000. (The float is obviously a more important matter to the New York Giants, whose pre-season sale in recent years has run around $2 million.)

THE HIGH COST OF STILEMEN

The chief cost set against this $3 million of revenues is for player salaries. Counting bonuses awarded rookies for signing with the club, the Hellers are paying their players $750,000 this year. The biggest single item is $25,000 for star quarterback Bull Diversitas. Because he commands an enthusiastic local following, and almost certainly gets people into the stadium who would otherwise stay home and mow the grass, Diversitas is a bargain at $25,000. (If he brings in only 1,200 extra customers per home game, he raises Heller season revenues by $37,800.) Note that Diversitas' salary isn't extraordinary, as N.F.L. salaries go. Two players, John Unitas of the Baltimore Colts and Jimmy Brown of the Cleveland Browns, are believed to be earning over $50,000 each this year. At $750,000, the Hellers' player payroll is up $75,000 from last year, $500,000 from ten years ago, and $635,000 from twenty years ago. The rising cost of top talent is eating up big hunks of those attendance revenues.

Aside from player salaries, the Hellers have six coaches, with combined salaries of $125,000. The administrative staff earns another $125,000, divided among the owner and president ($40,000), a general manager ($25,000), a business manager ($12,000), a press agent ($13,000), and sundry office workers ($30,000). Then the team has five regular and fifty part-time talent scouts who attend college games, thereby earning a total of $60,000. Other scouts attend the games of N.F.L. opponents, to report back on their strengths and weaknesses. Another $5,000. The Hellers pay ushers, ticket takers, special police, and stilemen (i.e., turnstile attendants) a total of $50,000. Total payroll: $1,115,000.

The big non-payroll expense is the sum paid to visiting teams for showing up and playing. Each home game this year will draw well enough to cover the $30,000 guarantee, and the total payout will be $416,000, or an average of over $59,000 to the seven visitors. The 10 percent federal admission tax will also bite $134,000 out of home receipts. Then the N.F.L.'s front office in New York takes a percentage of each gate in order to pay the salary and expenses of League Commissioner Pete Rozelle, thirty-seven, and of his staff. Rozelle is league arbitrator, schedule maker, and public spokesman—in short, "czar." His slice of Heller revenues: $21,000. The stadium owner collects a percentage of each gate (i.e., after the admission tax). This figure varies: the Cleveland Browns pay 6 percent, other teams up to 15 percent. The Hellers' stadium is owned, let us say, by Buckeye University, which drives a hard bargain and finally gets 12 percent; thus stadium rental costs work out to $145,000.

It also cost the Hellers a good sum to run their training camp this year. The team started working out at the end of July and continued in camp till mid-September. The owner rented two dormitories from Buckeye to house the team, fed it in the school's cafeteria. The university does not allow the Hellers to tear up its stadium field except during games, and so the team practiced at a prep school fifteen miles from the university. Bus transportation was required. The training-camp total: $52,000.

Travel is a fat item. Flying players, coaches, and other staff members to road games will cost $50,000. The team travels tourist class, but like a number of other clubs the Hellers have given up trying to squeeze 250-pound tackles three abreast on one side of an aisle; now it has the airline remove the center seats, and, of course, pays for the alteration. Hotel bills—two players to a room—will come to $20,000, restaurant bills to $15,000.

Insurance costs have been rising steadily, will total $25,000 this year. In the event of an aircrash, one policy will bring our owner enough money to form the nucleus of a new team.

Half-time entertainment, which the Hellers' owner suspects nobody watches, nevertheless costs $15,000. This is for busing in crack high-school bands from nearby towns, and such other talent as, say, a platoon of bagpipe players associated with the local chapter of the Ancient Order of Hibernians. The Hellers scrimp. The Washington Redskins, who play pretty poor ball but have traditionally put on a good show at half time, pay almost $25,000 for entertainment.

The scouts work with cameramen who take films of opponents' games for study by coaches and players. Cameramen, film, related expenses: $20,000. The services of two physicians, including a good orthopedist, cost $20,000. (The Hellers have to figure on five or six injuries a year requiring surgery.) Laundry costs $5,000.

Equipment and supplies will add still another $40,000 to the bill.

By the end of the season the team will have bought $1,500 worth of jerseys of three different weights, seventy-two dozen T-shirts, eighty suits of thermal underwear, eighty dozen socks, seventy pairs of uniform pants. It will also have bought at least 250 footballs at $17.95 each; as many as twenty may be kicked into the stands during a single game, and none of these is likely to be seen again unless they are presented to Diversitas, after the game, for autographing.

THE SHORT, HAPPY, USEFUL LIFE
OF A BALLPLAYER

A typical football team, then, grosses perhaps $3 million and gets to keep almost $800,000 of that before taxes, and $415,000 or so after taxes. What is this property worth?

The question is more complex than it sounds, and there are some imponderables not ordinarily faced in valuing conventional business enterprises. One imponderable has to do with depreciation. When a businessman buys a pro-football team, what he is chiefly buying (unless there is a stadium leasehold in the deal) are the contracts of his players. Yet there is no real agreement on an appropriate formula for depreciating such assets. Three of the four N.F.L. clubs sold within the past year have yet to settle on depreciation with the Internal Revenue Service. The fourth team is the Cleveland Browns, which does have an agreement with IRS and is writing off its players' contracts on the assumption that their "average useful life" is four and a half years. (Football is a wearing game.) Meanwhile, Clint Murchison is writing off the Dallas Cowboys' contracts over ten years. It's probably not just that the Cowboys are a young club. The stretchout may also be related to the fact that the Cowboys aren't making money now. It is hoped they'll be showing profits long before the ten years are up, and the remaining depreciation can be used to reduce federal taxes.

While it is still unclear what options a club owner has in writing off his contracts, it would seem that the *potential* of depreciation is considerable—and that it exerts some pressure for the purchase and sale of clubs. The main point is that once an owner uses up his depreciation he cannot renew it. Subsequent purchases of individual player contracts would be treated as expenses, not capital outlays. In any case, not many contracts are purchased individually; players are ordinarily "drafted" from college teams without any payments except salaries and bonuses. The Hellers today would pay federal taxes on the entire $800,000 difference between revenues and operating expenses. If they were sold, however, and the contracts written off in four or five years, the new owner's depreciation

would easily cover the Hellers' profits and he would pay no taxes at
all on the $800,000; if he paid more than $4 million for the contracts,
as he would probably have to do, he might well end up with a tax-loss
carry-forward. A proposition that generates tax-free cash this readily
makes it possible for businessmen to borrow money in order to buy,
which is what Modell of the Browns did.

THE OLD EQUALIZERS

The value of a pro-football team is further obscured by one aspect
of professional sports in general. Like a manufacturer, say, the football
owner is intent on maximizing profit. But he cannot go about it as the
manufacturer does, by trying to overwhelm the competition with a superior product. The product of a football team had better be good, but
not too good, lest the owner fail to put on a convincing contest. No
contest, no customers. The A.F.L.'s San Diego Chargers were in trouble
at one point when they trimmed their competition too often and too
easily. Baseball's New York Yankees had the same trouble for years
(although they managed to make things interesting in 1964). The fans
simply learned to stay home.

Thus to some extent an owner's success is contingent on the success
of his competition; in effect, his competition is also his co-exhibitor.
"Now isn't this a *strange* way to run a store!" marvels the treasurer of the
Green Bay Packers, Fred Trowbridge. "How much we earn when we
play in Los Angeles depends on how good a team Los Angeles has!"

In several respects, pro football has been more realistic than pro
baseball in recognizing this interdependence of the clubs. In football,
wealth is not allowed to monopolize talent. Each year the N.F.L. teams
pick their new players from the crop graduating from college—but they
make their picks in rotation. No team signs up a second player until
every other team has selected its first. Moreover, the order in which
teams make their picks is the reverse of their relative strengths. The
club that was last in league standings during the previous season will
have first crack at any superstars in the college ranks; the championship
team will have last choice. The leveling effects of this system prevent
the establishment of any self-perpetuating "dynasties" like the baseball
Yankees, and make it possible for relatively new teams like the Minne-
sota Vikings (who came into the league only four years ago) to develop
strength rapidly.

Another egalitarian measure is the remarkably generous 60-40 split
of the gate. (In baseball, the visiting team gets 25 to 30 cents a head,
which works out to an average of perhaps 15 percent.) The Dallas Cow-

boys, a league weak sister, played two games with the Giants last year, one at home and one in New York. The New York game drew a gate of some $200,000—after deductions for admission taxes, stadium rental, and the league-office cut—of which the Giants kept $120,000, the Cowboys $80,000. The Dallas game, on the other hand, had a net gate of $65,000, of which the Cowboys kept $35,000 while the Giants went home with just their $30,000 guarantee (and lost money on the trip). The gate in New York was more than 200 percent of the Dallas gate, yet for the two games the New York team took only 57 percent of the proceeds. The Cowboys earned more from their road games last year than from their home games.

Football's business men are also egalitarian in distributing their TV revenues: the total take is divided entirely equally. Thus the Giants, whose market is the audience potential represented by the more than 9,500,000 TV sets in and around New York, get no more than the Green Bay Packers, whose market is the 1,500,000 sets in Wisconsin. The Giants' rights might bring $4 million, if sold independently. The Packers might get only $100,000. (In baseball, the Yankees got roughly $1,700,000 from TV this year; some other teams earned less than $300,000.) Because of all these equalizers, then, anyone trying to value a pro-football team has to figure into the calculation a value for the *other* teams.

ONWARD TO SOUTH AMERICA!

There are some reasons for believing that the already interesting economics of pro football will become much more interesting in the years ahead. Some football businessmen think that the take for an average club may rise in ten years to $5 million, or even more. In that case, the capital-gain possibilities would be something to behold. A club like the Hellers, earning a before-tax $800,000, is today worth something between $6 million and $10 million; applying the same multipliers to those expected future profits gets you into the $60-million league.

A $5-million profit is not going to be derived from present income sources. Revenues at the gate will not rise much. Present stadiums are full, and bigger ones will not solve the problem. The ideal football stadium holds no more than 60,000 people. Ticket prices will rise, but owners are reluctant to hike them up too far and too fast, for fear of alienating fans. The publicity given the rise in TV revenues leads fans to suppose teams are enjoying fat profits already, and as Modell sagely observed a few weeks back, "You can't look greedy." Furthermore, the season can't be extended. To push it forward into August would create conflicts with baseball dates at stadiums. To push it back would be to require fans to sit through too many blizzards.

There is one big untapped source of revenue, however: pay television. What might pay TV be worth to football? Bud Adams, who owns the A.F.L. Houston team, suggests that in ten years the N.F.L. alone may be carving up $60 million or so a year in pay-TV receipts. This would itself guarantee a $5-million profit for each club, assuming costs do not rise much over present levels.

The estimate may, in fact, be conservative. At present over 15 million homes watch N.F.L. football on TV each of fourteen Sundays a year. The game has a lot of determined fans, and it is reasonable to suppose that at least a third of these homes would have their sets tuned in even if $3 had to be put into a slot. The total take then would be over $200 million. Allow the N.F.L. just half of that—the other half going to the pay-TV system—and revenues are up to $100 million.

To be sure, it is far from settled that pay TV in the home will ever exist at all. It is only a few months since the first serious pay-TV venture in the U.S. was launched in California. (The venture bought rights to home games of two California major-league baseball teams.) More recently, International Telemeter Corp., a subsidiary of Paramount Pictures Corp., announced plans to install pay-TV systems in Miami, Atlanta, Dallas, and Houston. Both enterprises intend to spread their wings in time. But the California venture faces large legal difficulties before it can expand. California voters will decide this month whether to outlaw pay TV in their state.

There is also the possibility of big-screen theatre television. This year three teams are putting home games on movie screens, via closed circuits, and charging prices comparable to those at the field. (The Giants' price is $6, and the initial disappointing attendance suggests it may be too high.) Modell says: "I envision the time when the league will be the exhibitor, the operator, the promoter. We'll hire banquet halls and meeting rooms for screening the games ourselves."

The rich prospects opened up by pay TV have led to some pretty dizzying talk among certain owners. Some foresee the day when it will be logical to spurn the advertisers' money and telecast *all* games via pay TV. And not just in the U. S. either. "We can send the games to England via Telstar," says Bud Adams, enthusiastically. "Send them anywhere! Europe! South America! We can create fans, and they'll pay to watch!"

PRO FOOTBALL'S 110% COACHES

BILL BRAUCHER

George Allen is forty-eight years old and looks as though he hasn't slept a wink of them. The tired, baggy appearance is promoted by Allen's habits of squinting and running a hand through wiry, graying hair.

Allen's hair evokes a sentence from Oscar Levant's observations of Phyllis Diller: "I treasure every moment I don't see her."

Don Shula is 40 years old and has a carved appearance, as if his flat-nosed face belonged on Mount Rushmore with the presidents.

Shula and Allen smile with approximately the frequency of a vernal equinox. This is not to say that they are humorless—only dedicated, with an intensity that does not admit distraction.

As a result, both are emininently successful in a pressurized and often grim business that in a past age of innocence was associated with frivolity, fun and band music—professional football. As practiced today in the 26-team National Football League, the struggle for the dollar is as ruthless as any competition being waged on Madison Avenue.

The physical strain involving the employes on Sunday afternoons can amount to child's play compared with the psychological brutality practiced in pro football's executive offices.

Allen and Shula, from their wary outposts on opposite corners of the country, share more in common than dedication of purpose. Let us examine:

The situations of Allen in Los Angeles and Shula in Miami furnish examples of the football Establishment at work. Football savants rank Allen and Shula as the Gog and Magog of their profession, head and

Bill Braucher, "Pro Football's 110% Coaches," *Aloft Magazine,* (Winter, 1970): 12-15. Reprinted by permission.

shoulders in savvy and intensity above exponents of the game even as successful as Kansas City's Hank Stram or Cleveland's Blanton Collier.

Yet when Shula left the Baltimore Colts for a head-coaching and part-ownership opportunity with the Miami Dolphins last February, after achieving the best winning record (71-23-4) in the NFL over his seven seasons guiding the Colts, he was publicly called "a loser of the big ones" and a "pig" by Carroll Rosenbloom, president of the Colts.

Rosenbloom had offered Shula no such opportunity in Baltimore. Nevertheless, the angry Baltimore owner also charged Dolphin president Joe Robbie with "tampering" by offering Shula the chance to improve his position.

Rosenbloom was so vociferous with his accusations and so powerful as an old, established NFL crony that Commissioner Pete Rozelle will give Miami's No. 1 choice in the upcoming college draft to Baltimore as "compensation."

Likewise, when Allen decided to upgrade his economic status by accepting the head-coaching job of the Los Angeles Rams in 1966, he was similarly castigated by his boss, George Halas of the Chicago Bears.

As Halas' first lieutenant, Allen was acknowledged to have built the mightiest defense in the business by prodding and plotting his men to utmost efficiency.

"People who don't want pressure deserve to be buried," Allen has said. The Bears responded fiercely. Allen's 1963 warriors carried the Bears to the NFL title by leading the league in 10 defensive categories and placing second in eight others. Following the world championship victory over the New York Giants—and in full view of a nationwide television audience—the Bears handed the game ball to Allen, their assistant coach.

In keeping with Allen's burial theme, Halas tried to inter his former employe when he left Chicago for Los Angeles without observing farewell amenities. Halas sued for breach of contract; he won a court decision but dropped the matter after proving his point, he said.

In Los Angeles, Allen shook up a team whose victories had not exceeded its losses since 1958. In his first season the Rams won eight of 14; the following year came a division title with an 11-1-2 record. In 1968 the Rams finished 10-2-1, only a notch behind Shula's Colts.

Allen and Shula shared NFL Coach of the Year honors in 1967. Shula won it in 1968; Allen in 1969 with an 11-3 mark and another division championship.

The binge of success, however, failed to elate Dan Reeves, the Rams' president and general manager. In fact, Reeves phoned his coach on the day after Christmas in 1968 to tell him he was fired.

"I haven't even told my children yet," Allen cautioned reporters at the time. "This came from way out in left field. He didn't even say 'Merry Christmas.' I guess when a guy owns a football team he can do what he wants."

Not quite, as it turned out. The firing heated an uproar among both the players and the customers. The theatrical reaction of 6-foot 5-inch Deacon Jones, the all-pro end, was typical: "This is the last time Deacon Jones will represent the Los Angeles Rams unless George Allen returns. I feel I owe this to myself and him, and I will not play if he leaves."

Richie Petitbon, the veteran safetyman Allen had obtained in one of his many trades to streamline the club, expressed shock: "If I owned the team and had a coach as capable as Allen, I'd want to lock the guy up."

Reeves, who likes to relax before and after a game with something heftier than the Coke or milkshake Allen prefers, apparently didn't mix like bourbon and water with his strong-willed coach. A "personality conflict" was Reeves' only description of his relationship with Allen.

Nevertheless, Reeves relented in less than two weeks, re-hiring Allen to serve the remaining two years on his contract. The contract may be taken up any day now, incidentally, despite the Rams' consistent success.

Reeves, by the way, has had eleven head coaches since taking over the Cleveland Rams in 1944. He even changes cities. After his Cleveland club won the NFL championship in 1945, Reeves took his franchise to Los Angeles.

Allen's position today might be considered as tenuous as Cleveland's was 25 years ago. He now communicates with his boss through Jack Teele, Reeves' assistant.

In the realm of security, Shula is far better off. He saw to his own security by investigating the young Dolphins thoroughly before dealing himself in as vice president, three per cent stockholder and head coach. Shula can operate without executive interference because he insisted on absolute autonomy before agreeing to leave an established contender in Baltimore for a rebuilding job in Miami.

"I had to have complete assurance from Mr. Robbie and the other owners that I would be the final authority on all policy matters relating to football, and that the owners were willing to make all the financial sacrifices and take all the risks necessary to produce a championship team," he says.

"We are aiming for a championship and nothing less. I don't care what this team has done in the past and I'm not interested in excuses. The past is for losers."

Shula is not likely to forget one ugly phase of his past, however. At the NFL executive meetings in Honolulu last March, Shula and Rosenbloom crossed paths for the first time since the coach changed jobs. (Rosenbloom's son and assistant, Steve, had given Shula the required permission to deal with Miami in February while Carroll was vacationing in Japan.)

As Shula started to exchange civilities with his former boss, Rosenbloom turned his back and stalked off.

Shula still seethes at the memory. Consequently, many who know the coach termed it sheer force of his will power when the Dolphins upset the proud Colts, 20-13, in an exhibition game this past August. It was the first confrontation of the rivals before a howling crowd of 76,712 in Miami's Orange Bowl.

Shula was aglow that Saturday night, even permitting himself a rare vodka-and-tonic at a post-game gathering. He had occasion to gloat. In halting Baltimore's string of twelve consecutive pre-season victories, Shula ended a string of achievements he began there himself in 1968.

"No miracle worker" by his own description, Shula has nevertheless performed a minor miracle by injecting his personality, drive and competence into the Dolphins, an outfit that had won only 15 of 56 games in four years. They immediately set a club record by winning their first four exhibition games under Shula last summer. They had won only four in the whole 1969 season—in twenty tries.

The players were elated. They apparently discovered they *could* win, just as the late Vince Lombardi's Green Bay Packers had discovered a decade ago after years of futility, or as the Rams found out when Allen arrived in 1966.

Larry Csonka, the former Syracuse All-American who is developing into a standout pro under Shula, made the discovery early.

"About the third day in camp we were running basic pass patterns," Csonka recalls. "We didn't even have a defensive line or an offensive line. Bob Griese was throwing long patterns while Jim Kiick (the other running back) and I would just sort of step up to where we were supposed to be.

"Shula was 40 yards downfield, understand. But he yelled, 'Csonka, what the hell are you doing?'

"I didn't know what was going on. I thought maybe one of my little boys had run onto the field, or my shorts had fallen off, or something.

"Then Shula came back and explained to me that I had moved out about a step too wide, and that if it had been the real thing and a linebacker had been coming, I'd have been too far out to block him.

"That's when it really dawned on me that I'd better be concentrating every second, because the time you least expect it, you're going to get Shula's foot in your rear."

While Shula and Allen practice similar dedication. Allen is more articulate and is not above dramatizing to make a point, as in a comment describing a stroll along the beach:

"Sometimes," says the coach, his pale face belying exposure to the outdoors, "I'll pick up rocks and throw them into the ocean. If one of the rocks is stuck in the sand, I won't just leave it there and keep walking. I'll stop and dig it out. I'm not going to let that rock defeat me. The same thing applies to my job."

The philosophy both coaches apply is perhaps epitomized in a series of remarkable observations which assistant coaches label "Allen's Ten Commandments," to wit:

1. Football comes first. (*During the off-season I tell my players that their family and church should be one-two . . . But during the six months of the season, the competition in the NFL is so tough we have to put football ahead of everything else.*)

2. The greatest feeling in life is to take an ordinary job and accomplish something with it. (*Fulfillment doesn't necessarily lie in accomplishing peace for all time or the total elimination of smog in California. Anybody can experience the joy of accomplishment.*)

3. If you can accept defeat and open your pay envelope without feeling guilty, then you're stealing. (*I've heard that the average NFL player draws a salary of $25,000, but I can't think of a thing this money will buy that a loser could enjoy. Losers just look foolish in a new car or partying it up . . . Life without victories is like being in prison.*)

4. Everyone, the head coach especially, must give 110 per cent. (*The average good American pictures himself a hard worker. But most persons are really operating on less than half power. They never get above 50 per cent, although they think of themselves as 100 per cent producers. Therefore, to get 100, you must aim for 110. A man who is concerned with an eight-hour day never works that long and seldom works half that long. The same man, however, when challenged by a seventeen-hour day, will just be warmed up and driving when he hits the eighth hour. Good things don't just happen to most men. You have to make them happen.*)

5. Leisure time is that five or six hours when you sleep at night. (*Nobody should work all the time. Everybody should have some leisure, and the early morning hours are best for this. You can combine two good things at once, sleep and leisure.*)

6. No detail is too small. No task is too small or too big. (*Winning can be defined as the science of being prepared. And I define preparation in three words: leave nothing undone. A loser is a man who's unprepared and doesn't know it.*)

7. You must accomplish things in life, otherwise you are like the paper on the wall. (*I see no difference between a chair and the man who sits in the chair if he is not accomplishing. Performance is the only thing that counts.*)

8. A person without problems is dead. (*The winner appreciates getting advice, but in the end he makes his own decisions; he solves his problems. The man swayed by someone else is a two-time loser. First he hasn't believed in his own convictions, and second he still lost.*)

9. We win and lose as a team. (*Nothing means less in football than the hero who catches seven or eight passes, or intercepts three—if his team loses. Better to drop seven or eight and win.*)

10. My prayer is that each man will be allowed to play to the best of his ability. (*The individual who uses the ability he was given when he was put on this earth, who works to the limit of that ability, is doing what the Lord intended him to do. This is what life is all about. This is my religion.*)

Allen has written six books on football, the gleanings of a coaching career which began with the Rams in 1957 after nine years of highly successful coaching at Morningside (Iowa) and Whittier (Calif., President Nixon's alma mater).

Following the 1957 season, Allen left the Rams and joined the staff of the Chicago Bears where he became Halas' most valued assistant as one-man boss of the Bears' defense.

Allen was born April 29, 1922, in Detroit. He attended Lake Shore High in Detroit, where he earned nine letters—three in football, three in basketball, three in track. He was captain and all-conference in basketball.

He went to Alma (Mich.) College in 1943, where he played right end; moved to Marquette and played football in 1944, and eventually to the University of Michigan, where he was too small for football but was on the wrestling and baseball teams.

He received his B.A. from Michigan in 1947 and was a member of Sigma Delta Psi, national honorary athletic and scholarship fraternity. While doing work for his M.A. in 1948, Allen coached junior varsity sports at Michigan.

Allen and his wife, Etty, live in Palos Verdes, Calif., with their four children: George, 18; Gregory, 16; Bruce, 13, and Jennifer, 9.

Shula, a native of Painesville, Ohio (about 30 miles east of Cleveland), was a steady defensive back for seven seasons in the National

Football League including two with Cleveland (1951-52), four with Baltimore (1953-56) and one with Washington in 1957.

He spent the next two seasons as an assistant college coach at Virginia and then at Kentucky before returning to the pros in 1960 as a defensive aide of George Wilson in Detroit, ironically the man he later replaced in Miami. After three seasons in Detroit, he was tapped by Caroll Rosenbloom to be, at 33, the youngest head coach in pro football.

Shula had been an outstanding running back for three years at Harvey High in Painesville and from 1947 to 1950 at John Carroll University in suburban Cleveland.

Shula and his wife, Dorothy, have five young children: David, Donna, Sharon Lee, Ann Marie and Michael; they live in Miami Lakes.

The two coaches have not yet met on the field since Shula took over the Dolphins. When they do, however, it should be memorable because their last meeting was disastrous for Shula. After guiding his 1967 Baltimore team through 13 games undefeated, Shula's championship hopes were ruined by a single loss, 34-10, in the final game to Allen's Rams. Both teams finished with identical records (11-1-2), but the Colts had to concede the NFL Coastal Division title because the Rams outscored the Colts in their two games that year. That was the year they shared Coach of the Year honors.

Shula and Allen's acquaintance is, as is the case with most pro coaches, polite and non-committal. Where the big boys play there is understandably little of the you-gotta-give-the-guy-credit palsiness of high school and college coaches. Nor is there likely to be.

As the so-called miracle workers of their profession, Allen and Shula have a lot to prove this season. And the next, and the next.

STUDENT UNREST AND ATHLETIC DOLLARS

ALFRED R. MATHEWS, JR.

I would like to begin by saying that the topic, along with the title, was given to me. The approach that I have taken is as though the title is "Student Dollars and Athletic Unrest." The "dollars" that I am going to talk about are those that belong to the students. The assumption that the money really belongs to us because we have received it in the past could be symptomatic and explain why the problem exists in the first place.

To say that the topic of "Student Unrest and Athletic Dollars" is a pertinent one to the people in this room is, of course, an understatement. Most of us are vitally concerned with some phase of the intercollegiate athletic program at our respective institutions, and most of these programs are financed at least partly by student body monies. In some schools a certain fixed percentage of this money automatically goes into intercollegiate athletics. In other situations, a budget must be presented yearly for review and approval. Other schools may handle the financing details somewhat differently, but the specific arrangements are not that important to this discussion. What is important is the fact that in the past several years there have been emerging problems with the granting of these monies by the student body governments. What has been almost an "automatic" thing in the past is no longer the case. Students the nation over are demanding to know where the money is going, why certain amounts are needed, and what the rationale is behind the entire program.

These demands have taken several forms: (1) Students have held referendums on campuses and voted against the granting of money to the athletic departments. It is also true that some student body elections

From a speech given at the annual conference of The National College Physical Education Association, Portland, Oregon, December, 1970. Printed by permission.

have voted in favor of intercollegiate programs, but not much has been heard about these. Obviously, it is better "copy" to write about the negative results. (2) There is at least one state college in California where the students voted to abolish all forms of student body government, and thus there are *no* student body fees. The financing of an intercollegiate program under these circumstances is almost impossible. Finally, (3) in several institutions an even more disruptive chain of events has taken place. The departments involved have presented budgets for the following year to the student body governments currently in office. After much discussion, and in several cases major budget cuts, the budgets were approved and the institutions began scheduling their programs for the following year. When the student body governments for the following year took office, they have refused to abide by the agreements made. In at least one instance, this refusal has even gone to the courts, and the courts have ruled that the agreement is a legal one and must be honored, but the students have appealed this decision to a higher court. What happens in the meantime? I'm sure that chaos has been the result. Programs have been cut back, certain vital parts of programs completely removed, and much time and effort spent in simply getting the funds that were legally allocated.

The questions that our profession must answer are: (1) why this surge of unrest in the area of athletic finance, and (2) what must be done by our profession so as to be able to continue our program?

First, why are our programs being attacked now more than ever before? Is it just a sign of the times? Is it fashionable to attack anything and everything? Or are there some things that we as a profession have done or are doing that make us especially vulnerable? A careful and critical analysis seems to indicate a combination of factors. It is true that student body governments have never really spoken for the majority of the students. Probably not more than 25 to 30 percent of eligible students have voted in student body elections over the country. The key difference now is that the small group interested in student government has changed. It used to be quite a social thing to engage in campus politics. The typical student body officers were students from organized living groups. Now, the small group of interested students is different in several ways. More than ever before in our history, young people are concerned with the problems of society. They are concerned with poverty, racism, war, as never before. They believe that society needs to change and some of them are even attempting to go out into the community to try to bring about change. The types of programs in which they are interested—help to disadvantaged students, child-care centers, political action—cost a great deal of money. It is only natural for these groups to look critically at programs where most of their money is presently spent. One of these is, of course, intercollegiate athletics. It makes no difference whether you have a good program or not. You are just "fair game." Most of these students know little about athletics. I have heard statements such as, "Why don't you play all your games at home?" "Do you really need more than $1.00 for dinner on the road?" "Why do you need insurance for the athletes?" The problem from the point of view of the students, can be summarized: You are there; you are established; you use a lot of money; we want the money; it is our money; why shouldn't we have it instead of you?

It also seems to be a time of student disenchantment with athletics. It is in this area that I feel we are more to blame than any other. There was a time when large universities made a lot of money from gate receipts and there was no need to justify programs. Programs were self supporting. Coaches were not hired as regular faculty members. Why? Because the successful ones could be paid thousands of dollars more than full professors. Now the athletic programs of most colleges and universities are losing money. Costs of recruiting, insurance, equipment, and travel have skyrocketed. The changes in the number of games that football teams can have, the fact that Notre Dame now goes to Bowl Games, and the possible limitation on the number of scholarships are both examples of recent attempts to make more money and cut down on costs. These rising costs now make student body fees more necessary than ever before. We have not cultivated or educated the general student. We have not sold him on the merits of our program. Now when we need his support, it is not always granted and I am not surprised.

Many times the student athletes are also "separate" from the rest of the college. They are selected for different reasons than other students. At times they live in dormitories completely apart from the rest of the students. They may have special privileges. Very few take part in student activities, other than the intercollegiate athletic program. Is it any wonder that students would question their money going to such a program?

Athletic programs are also considered to be part of the "establishment;" the establishment that certain groups would like to change, or worse than that, destroy. We, as a profession, have not done much to keep our program abreast with the changing ideas of society. Some of us are still concerned with length of hair, sideburns, beards, and dress, rather than performance during practice, in the classroom, and at games. Some of us still set arbitrary training rules based on modes of behavior accepted twenty years ago, and not those of today. When this type of thing continues to happen, it is no wonder to me that there is disen-chantment.

I hope that what I have just said will not be taken as an attack on athletics. There are enough of those every day. It is popular, for example, in certain magazines to have a new attack in every issue. This discussion is simply an attempt to explain why we seem to be having more prob-lems now.

What we need to do now, it seems to me, is to direct our energies and our abilities in the direction of making our programs more in tune with the needs of today. The things that need to be done are few and basic.

First, we need to evaluate completely our physical education pro-grams. We need to be sure what is happening is worthwhile, educa-tionally sound, and is what the students want today. If we offer a broad program, for both men and women at all levels, we will be less suscepti-ble to attack. In our service program we should offer a wide selection of individual activities that are popular today. Activities such as sailing, karate, judo, parachute jumping, water skiing, snow skiing, dance, circuit training, are taken more often today than the typical and traditional team sports. Excellent intramural programs are needed for both men and women, based on the assumption that if competition has educational value, then opportunities for competition must be available to more students. This means that people trained in intramurals must be hired, and they must be given a break in use of facilities and budgets. The natural extension of a service program and the intramural program is the intercollegiate athletic program for the highly-skilled performer. This program should be broad and deep and include as many teams as possible for both men and women. The program should have cross-campus appeal, and hopefully, include students from most academic disciplines.

Next, we need to be sure that our coaches and student athletes do not keep themselves separate from the rest of the student body. This means that athletes must run for student body office and be a regular student playing at athletics rather than an athlete playing at being a stu-dent. Our coaches need to be regular faculty members. Separate athletic departments are not needed. Coaches must be hired, promoted and granted tenure on the same basis as other faculty members. They need to be a part of the academic enterprise, complete with its benefits and restraints. As regular faculty members, the coaches need to run for faculty government offices, serve on faculty committees, and be active campus wide. What this, of course means, is that we must leave the friendly confines of the gymnasium and the playing field, and become involved with the rest of the faculty. It is time this happened on every campus.

Finally, and most important, is the point about how athletic programs should be financed. We all believe, and we have stated many times, that a broad program of intercollegiate athletics should be considered the same as any other instructional program in the college. If this is so, then why are student body funds needed? Why has the State College Board of Trustees in California recently passed legislation dealing with special funding of instructionally related activities and intercollegiate athletics. Did you notice the wording? Instructionally related activities *and* intercollegiate athletics. This seems to imply that athletics are not instructionally related. At least one Board of Trustees feels that they are not. If this is the situation, then maybe we have no place in an institution of higher education and should be separate from the academic enterprise. Perhaps programs should be financed by gate receipts, gifts from alumni, and whatever student body monies we can obtain.

I personally do not agree with this viewpoint of the California Board of Trustees. It is time for us to convince the legislators that athletics are a unique and worthwhile experience and so should be included in the educational environment, as is art and music. This convincing will take time as the legislators are no longer interested in our words. If we can succeed, then the programs could be financed out of the general fund and any gate receipts would return to that fund. This, of course, would mean submitting budgets through prescribed channels, carefully watching the dollars and making sure the money is well spent. It might mean a drastic reduction in athletic scholarships, or complete abolition of them. The athlete would become part of the regular student body and selected on the same basis. It might mean schedule curtailment— more local games and fewer inter-sectional games. It would mean that more programs would be student oriented, and less concerned with the community and alumni. The alumni would not be able to hire and fire coaches. Coaches would be retained because of their teaching ability and not because of their win-loss record. Coaches would be taken out of the fund-raising business. Interested students would pay to attend games, or possibly attend free because adequate financing would be received from the institution. Does it sound frightening to you? Not to me. It sounds exciting. It is the direction that we, as members of a profession, should be working toward.

TRENDS IN THE SPORTING
GOODS MARKET

RICHARD SNYDER

INTRODUCTION

A. History, Purpose, and Scope of this Report

This is the fifth edition of "Trends In The Sporting Goods Market."
The other four issues of "Trends" bear the year-dates: 1947, 1952, 1957,
and 1961. Beginning with the 1952 edition, these studies—as well as a
series of annual "interim" reports—have been issued under the auspices
of the National Sporting Goods Association. The "interim" report titles
and publication dates are listed below:

"The Sporting Goods Market In 1959"—Jan. 1959
"The Sporting Goods Market At The Threshhold Of The Sixties"—
Jan. 1960
"The Sporting Goods Market At The Turn Of The Cycle"—Jan. 1962
"Where Will The Sporting Goods Market Be In '63?"—Jan. 1963
"The Sporting Goods Market In The Mid-Sixties"—Jan. 1964

All these reports have served an essential single purpose, namely
that of tracing the progress of an economic phenomenon which was
(more or less literally-speaking) "hardly anything but a nothing" thirty
years ago, but which, today, is "very much of a something." It is doubtful
that there was, in this country, any area of business activity less well
documented than was the sporting goods market prior to—and for several years subsequent to—World War II, a point brought home to this
analyst during a four-year hitch of "researching" in the hallowed halls

From *Trends in the Sporting Goods Market: 1947-65*, pp. 2-16. Copyright © 1965
by Richard Snyder. Chicago, Ill.: National Sporting Goods Association. Reprinted
by permission.

of a major mail order concern. The basic assignment was that of figuring out the company's "share of market" (at retail, of course) on everything from Milady's boudoir trappings to farm machinery. Quite a range!

On sporting goods there was nothing except the company's own
sales figures and a few scraggly figures on output values, well buried
in the Census of Manufactures. But stay! *That* was the *secret* that
opened the door to needed enlightment. Mark up the national output
values properly and you get the national retail value counterparts for
the various products listed! (It used to be that simple.) And it was this
simple lever that was used to pry open the clamped-shut jaws of the
sporting goods market's statistical anonymity. The results of this *prying*
were set forth in the pioneer edition of "Trends," issued in 1947. That
work defined the essential product categorizations which have been used
in these reports ever since (with some additions), and also provided annual carryback consumer purchase estimates for the main categories to
and through the year 1929, thus establishing an historical frame of reference for the *1947* estimates, along with some indicative projections of
the total sales series.

Described briefly, the report now in hand, dated 1965, places primary emphasis upon the historical sales trend performances of the fifteen "major product groups" covering the period 1948 through 1964,
with preliminary estimates for 1965 also shown. (The year 1948 was
selected as the anchor point for these historical series because it was
the first "normal" year in our economy following the adjustments of the
immediate postwar period. For all of these "major" product groups,
annual total sales figures going back through 1929 are shown in the
1961 edition of "Trends.")

The post-1947 demand patterns for these series, as well as for a
number of other shorter-term product sales series, have been embellished
by projections of the sales levels that might be attained in the year
1970. The report also contains product line purchase estimates applying
to particularized items *within* seven of the major groups, covering the
seven-year span 1958-1964, inclusive.

A newly-developed schematic formulation of how the total sporting
goods market is "divvied-up" amongst various major types of retail outlets is presented. Regional and state breakdowns of total sporting goods
sales and sporting goods specialty store sales are shown.

On the supply side of the picture, the report emphasizes the part
played by manufacturers within the "total marketing concept" of the
sporting goods universe, detailing shipment value statistics from the
1963 Census of Manufactures, and providing a special "operating" analysis of the Sporting and Athletic Goods Industry (S.I.C. 3949).

In years past, many and varied interests have found our reports to be extremely valuable aids in the development of guidelines to effective marketing of sporting goods. We hope that this latest study will prove equally useful. All analyses, conclusions, and predictions set forth herein have been conceived in good faith and without any pretension to infallibility.

THE STATE OF THE SPORTING GOODS MARKET IN 1964-65

The sporting goods market is Everyman's market. In this usage we would have "Everyman" connote: (a) all those on the inside looking out (the sellers of sporting goods); (b) all those on the outside looking in (the end-use customers); and, (c) all those who may be said to be "just *looking on*" (the spectator group).

In the 1964-65 period there were more of all of them than ever before. On the basis of "presumptive" accountings ("—offering reasonable grounds for belief"), we estimate that, at the end of 1964, there were 2,500 manufacturers making at least one main-category sporting goods product line, and as many more making one or more supplementary or accessory items. Wholesalers of sporting goods numbered 2,100 according to our information. At the retail level, we estimate that there were 225,000 outlets handling at least one sporting goods product. The rate of expansion in the number of companies at all three of these operating levels during the 1958-64 period was well in excess of our domestic population expansion. Outlet-itis is now a chronic affliction of the sporting goods universe as is the growing intensity of product competition.

"Person participation" in actual "sports play" (i.e., *activity* involving the use of a sporting goods product) is estimated to have totaled 460,000,000 in 1964, but it must be understood that such a figure would include duplications for "multiple sportniks." If the enormous figures covering attendance at car, horse, and dog racing events are included, then 1964 also witnessed a new high in sports-spectating, estimated at 215,000,000 attendees (including multiple-goers). On the sales side, our revised estimate for 1964 shows that total U. S. consumer purchases of sporting goods reached $2,694,500,000, a new high, topping by 4 per cent the previous record total of $2,573,600,000 registered in 1963.

For 1965, we estimate that total U. S. consumer purchases of sporting goods will amount to $2,857,200,000. This would be another new high, topping the 1964 mark by 6 per cent. Whether this indication for the year 1965 is "high" or "low," there is nothing that appears more certain than the prospect of total sporting goods sales passing the 3 billion mark in *1966*.

Table 1 . . . sets forth our 1965 consumer purchase estimates covering twenty-four categories of sporting goods products. Comparative figures for 1964 are also shown.

Product groups that are expected to show 1965/1964 sales gains of from zero to 5 per cent are: baseball goods; bicycles; bowling balls; firearms and supplies; fishing supplies; football-basketball-boxing goods; photographic equipment; pleasure boat accesories; sunglasses and goggles; and lawn tennis equipment.

Increases of 5 to 10 per cent are predicted for: gymnasium equipment; inflatable balls; playground equipment; pleasure boats and equipment; skates; table tennis equipment; and tents.

Product groups with prospective 1965/1964 sales gains of more than 10 per cent are: archery equipment; billiard and pool tables and playing supplies; golf equipment; hockey goods; sleeping bags; winter sports equipment; and "all other" sporting goods.

The profit side of the sporting goods picture is not overly bright. Earnings of the few publicly-owned companies in the industry have shown considerable stickiness during the past several years. Random information suggests that sporting goods wholesalers have had it even tougher and, since 1960, the profits of sporting goods specialty stores have failed to match the average return realized during the decade of the fifties. In 1963 the "tradewide" gross profit margin on net sales, as represented by the performance of the NSGA retailers, dropped to a thirteen-year low of 28.9. The failure rate for the general run of sporting goods stores has been consistently higher than that for most of the other retail store categories over a rather lengthy period of years.

A rough-hewn measure of the "sporting goods universe" profit margin may be arrived at by construing total consumer purchases of sporting goods as "net sales," total sporting goods manufacturer shipment value as "cost of goods sold," and the difference as "gross margin." A tentative estimate of this "total field" gross margin for the year 1964 indicates a "return" of 31.95% on net sales. A similar computation for 1954—ten years earlier—shows 37.21%.

On the price side, the BLS wholesale price index covering "sporting and athletic goods" showed a reading of 100.5 for 1964 compared to 100.7 for 1963 (1957-59=100). A reading of 101.2 was shown for the month of January 1965. The *consumer price* index for sporting goods held closely to the 103.0 level during the 1962-64 period. But it is common knowledge that cut rate prices are readily available on many quality brand sporting goods products.

The day has passed when a *big sales volume* alone is the answer to all problems.

TABLE 1
Estimated Consumer Purchases of Sporting Goods, 1965 vs. 1964,
by Product Categories

Product Categories (Alphabetically Listed)	1965*	1964**	% Change 1965/1964
Archery Equipment	$ 37,600,000	$ 33,900,000(R)	+ 10.9
(Includes: Bows, Arrows, Quivers, Targets, Strings, Bowcases, and Accessories)			
Baseball Goods	63,100,000	62,400,000(R)	+ 1.1
(Includes: Hard & Soft Baseballs; Baseball Mitts & Gloves; Baseball Bats, incl. Softball Bats; Other Baseball Goods)			
Bicycles	216,000,000	209,100,000(R)	+ 3.3
Billiard and Pool Tables and Playing Supplies	83,700,000	73,000,000(R)	+ 14.7
Bowling Balls	38,500,000	38,500,000(R)	0
Firearms and Supplies	289,800,000	278,100,000(R)	+ 4.2
(Includes: Pistols & Revolvers; Rifles; Shotguns, Other Nonmilitary Small Arms; Cartridges & Shells— All Types; Equipment for Hunting and Shooting)			
Fishing Supplies	182,600,000	177,500,000(R)	+ 2.9
(Includes: Fish Line & Netting; Fishing Rods & Reels; Fishing Tackle Other Than Rods & Reels)			
Football, Basketball, & Boxing Goods	54,200,000	53,000,000(R)	+ 2.3
(Includes: Balls, Gloves, Helmets, and Other Gear)			
Golf Equipment	213,200,000	192,300,000(R)	+ 10.9
(Includes: Caddy Bags, Golf Clubs, Balls, Hand Carts, Motorized Golf Carts, Sundries)			
Gymnasium Equipment	37,000,000	33,800,000(R)	+ 9.4
Hockey Goods	8,800,000	7,600,000	+ 15.8
(Includes: Sticks, Gear, Goals, Pucks)			
Inflatable Balls Other Than Footballs and Basketballs	15,400,000	14,300,000	+ 7.7
Photographic Equipment	473,600,000	455,400,000(R)	+ 4.0
(Includes: Cameras, Cartridge or Roll Film)			
Playground Equipment	77,700,000	71,500,000(R)	+ 8.6

TABLE 1 (Con't.)

Product Categories (Alphabetically Listed)	1965*	1964**	% Change 1965/1964
Pleasure Boats and Equipment	$659,000,000	$620,000,000(R)	+ 6.3
(Excludes: Large Yachts) (Includes: Canoes, Rowboats, Sailboats, Sails, Motor Boats—Inboard & Outboard; Outboard Motors; Prefab. Boat Const. Kits and Other Boats)			
Pleasure Boat Accessories	48,100,000	46,900,000	+ 2.6
(Includes: Lifesaving equipment, fire extinguishers, signalling devices, navigational instruments, tools and spare parts, pumps, lines, fenders, etc.)			
Skates	38,100,000	36,200,000	+ 5.2
(Includes: Roller, Ice, and Hockey Skates)			
Sleeping Bags	46,200,000	41,200,000	+12.1
Sunglasses and Goggles	38,400,000	36,800,000	+ 4.3
Tennis (lawn) Equipment	18,400,000	17,600,000	+ 4.5
(Includes: Tennis Balls; Tennis Rackets; Other Tennis Eqpmt.)			
Tennis (table) Equipment	6,000,000	5,500,000	+ 9.1
Tents	66,300,000	60,500,000	+ 9.6
Winter Sports Equipment	34,600,000	30,000,000	+15.3
(Includes: Sleds for Children; Skis, Ski Poles, & Snowshoes; Sleighs, Bobsleds & Toboggans)			
All Other Sporting Goods	110,900,000	99,400,000(R)	+11.6
Total Sporting Goods	$2,857,200,000	$2,694,500,000(R)	+ 6.0

*Figures shown for 1965 are tentative advance estimates and are subject to revision.

**1964 figures accompanied by the symbol (R) have been revised from the original estimates for that year which appeared in "The Sporting Goods Market In The Mid-Sixties," published in January 1964.

DYNAMICS OF TOTAL SPORTING GOODS DEMAND OVER THE LONG PULL

A. The "Total Market" Series

The statistical data continued in Table 2 . . . portray quite effectively the salient aspects of the total sporting goods market expansion as reflected by our annual estimates of consumer purchases. (See Data Column 1.) (*Special Note*: On behalf of "keeping the record straight," may we repeat here our definition of the term "consumer(s)" as given in a previous report: " 'Consumers'—as applied to sporting goods—are small children, large children, young children and old children; men and women of all sizes, ages, stripes, and bents; educational and non-educational institutions; professional and nonprofessional teams, clubs, aggregations—religious and non-religious, inside and outside, on land, sea and in the air; at all points of the compass and all levels of society, vertical, horizontal, and radical.")

Taking the total consumer purchase figure for the year 1935 as a starter, let us examine the movement of the total market series by ten-

TABLE 2

Estimated U.S. Consumers' Annual Dollar Purchases of All Sporting Goods and Equipment, 1948 through 1965, with Chart Showing Annual Percentage Change Trend Since 1948

	Data Col. 1		Data Col. 2		Data Col. 3		Data Col. 4 % of Total Sporting Goods Sales	
Year	Consumer Purchases	Year	Index (1948 = 100)	Year	Year-to-Year % Change	Year	Percent	
1948	$1,127,000,000	1948	100.0	1948	+ 5.9	1948	100.0	
1949	1,115,200,000	1949	99.0	1949	− 1.0	1949	100.0	
1950	1,208,300,000	1950	107.2	1950	+ 8.3	1950	100.0	
1951	1,278,300,000	1951	113,4	1951	+ 5.8	1951	100.0	
1952	1,372,000,000	1952	121.7	1952	+ 7.3	1952	100.0	
1953	1,463,600,000	1953	129.9	1953	+ 6.7	1953	100.0	
1954	1,470,200,000	1954	130.5	1954	+ 0.5	1954	100.0	
1955	1,579,200,000	1955	140.1	1955	+ 7.4	1955	100.0	
1956	1,693,100,000	1956	150.2	1956	+ 7.2	1956	100.0	
1957	1,801,000,000	1957	159.8	1957	+ 6.4	1957	100.0	
1958	1,872,600,000	1958	166.2	1958	+ 4.0	1958	100.0	
1959	2,015,600,000	1959	178.8	1959	+ 7.6	1959	100.0	
1960	2,194,900,000	1960	194.8	1960	+ 8.9	1960	100.0	
1961	2,292,200,000	1961	203.4	1961	+ 4.4	1961	100.0	
1962	2,444,000,000	1962	216.9	1962	+ 6.6	1962	100.0	
1963	2,573,600,000	1963	228.4	1963	+ 5.3	1963	100.0	
1964	2,694,500,000	1964	239.1	1964	+ 4.7	1964	100.0	
1965	2,857,200,000	1965	253.5	1965	+ 6.0	1965	100.0	

Annual Growth Rate	*1970 Projected Total*
1955 Through 1964: + 6.3	A. $3,713,000,000
1960 Through 1964: + 6.0	B. $3,664,500,000

year jumps. In 1935, the total (as read from Table 1 in the January 1961 issue of "Trends") amounted to $215,900,000. By 1945, the total had more than doubled, to $449,000,000. The 1955 total of $1,579,200,000 was 3 1/2 times that of 1945. The estimated total of $2,857,200,000 for 1965 (subject to revision) represented an increase of about 81 per cent over the 1955 figure, this result being indicative of a slower pace in recent years, attributable not only to "inertia of large numbers" but also to the sporting goods market's arrival at the "maturity" stage in the business life cycle applicable to this sector of the economy. The chart . . . depicts the changes of pace in total sporting goods sales over the long pull *since 1947*, employing the percentage figures contained in Data Column 3 of Table 2. This clearly shows the slowdown that occurred after 1960.

When we appraise the performance of the total sporting goods consumer purchase series in terms of index numbers, using the 1948 total as base 100.0 (see Data Column 2), we find that the 1964 index reading of 239.1 represents a gain of 139.1 index points over 1948.

Interpreting the 1948-1965 trend performance of the total sporting goods consumer purchase series in terms of year-to-year percentages of change, i.e., rate of movement, as shown in *Data Column 3*, makes it possible to speculate about future prospects, in other words, to work with projections. In this connection, it should be noted that, inasmuch as the specified percentage change of +6 per cent for 1965 (over 1964) is a preliminary indication subject to revision, the two projected totals ("A" and "B") for the year 1970 have been developed from two separate series of growth rate percentages whose terminal year is *1964*. Thus, the "A" projection of $3,713,000,000 for 1970 is keyed to the average annual growth rate of 6.3% for the period 1955 through 1964, inclusive. The "B" projection of $3,664,500,000 is keyed to the growth rate of 6.0% for the period: 1960 through 1964, inclusive. The slower growth rate for the five-year period, 1960 through 1964, reflects those forces previously referred to as "the inertia of large numbers" and the sporting goods market's entry into the "maturity" stage of its life cycle. The higher rate of growth for the more extensive period, 1955-1964, encompasses the full effect of the uprush during the first six years thereof, which offset the slower pace of the early sixties.

Why give two different projections, one based on a ten-year span which overlaps the five-year span of the other? Answer: The two-projection approach allows a little "leverage" to take care of the contingencies that might arise if the basic economic conditions impinging upon the sporting goods market during the six-year period ahead, i.e., 1965-1970, inclusive, shifted in such a way as to form a "climate" pos-

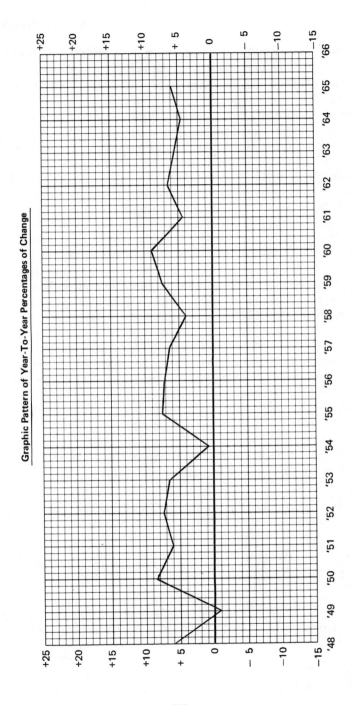

Graphic Pattern of Year-To-Year Percentages of Change

sessing a high degree of similarity to that which prevailed during the *first half* of the ten-year period, 1955-1964. Such a development would induce a step-up in the rate of growth during the 1965-70 period to a level exceeding that of the 1960-1964 period (6.0%) from which projection "B" was derived.

If, on the other hand, the impulse of the moving forces behind total sporting goods sales should slacken in the 1965-70 period to a pace *slower* than that laid down during the 1960-64 span, then projection "B" would prove to be an overstatement of the prospect now indicated.

On the subject of projections generally, there are these few further points to be made: No analyst in his right mind ever would contend that straight-line projections of any economic time series, based on past growth rates, could possibly give positive assurance that such-and-such a level will be reached at a specific point in future time. We would say that the main reason for this—of the 1,001 reasons which might be adduced—is simply that such projections ignore "the cycle." However, projections of this kind can be very useful—and are in wide usage today—as the *starting basis for long-term planning.* In the case of individual companies, a particularly startling projection may launch investigations along numerous lines of inquiry, such as: Will the projected increase in volume (dollars or physical) bring a concomitant large income in profits? How much would we have to spend to expand our plant facilities to accommodate that much additional volume? Where will we get the money to do this? How much extra operating and selling expense would be entailed in supporting the enlarged activtiy? Etc. Etc.

B. The Place of Sporting Goods in the National Market Basket

Despite the impressive growth of the sporting goods market over the long pull, this growth has not been "free and easy" and, moreover, when the total size of this entity—as measured for the year 1965—is viewed in relation to the "national market basket," it appears, in fact, quite puny. Construing the "national market basket" as the sum total of all consumer goods (both durable and nondurable) purchased by all U. S. consumers, we obtain the sporting goods share of such purchases, as revealed in Table 2a.

The percentage figures in this table, reflecting annual comparisons for a period of 19 years, show that sporting goods never accounted for less than 0.92% nor more than 1.17% of the total market basket. During the first five years of the nineteen-year period covered, the sporting goods share wavered between 0.92 and 0.93. Jumping to 0.95 in 1952, the sporting goods share then rose haltingly to 1.00, reaching that level in 1956, for the first time. Five successive new highs were recorded

TABLE 2a
Sporting Goods Share of All Consumer Goods Purchases

Year	Total U.S. Consumer Purchases of Sporting Goods*	Total U.S. Consumer Purchases of All Consumer Goods**	Sporting Goods % of Total
1947	$1,064,700,000(X)	$113,975,000,000(Y)	0.93
1948	1,127,000,000	121,460,000,000	0.93
1949	1,115,200,000	121,191,000,000	0.92
1950	1,208,300,000	130,152,000,000	0.93
1951	1,278,300,000	139,606,000,000	0.92
1952	1,372,000,000	144,199,000,000	0.95
1953	1,463,600,000	150,836,000,000	0.97
1954	1,470,200,000	151,726,000,000	0.97
1955	1,579,200,000	164,394,000,000	0.96
1956	1,693,100,000	169,900,000,000	1.00
1957	1,801,000,000	178,100,000,000	1.01
1958	1,872,600,000	179,300,000,000	1.04
1959	2,015,600,000	191,000,000,000	1.06
1960	2,194,900,000	196,723,000,000	1.12
1961	2,292,200,000	199,080,000,000	1.15
1962	2,444,000,000	210,380,000,000	1.16
1963	2,573,600,000	219,631,000,000	1.17
1964	2,694,500,000	234,300,000,000	1.15
1965(E)	2,857,200,000(E)	244,844,000,000(E)	1.17

*All data in this column are Richard E. Snyder's estimates.

**Total U.S. consumer purchase figures are Department of Commerce data.

(X)Sporting goods purchases topped the *1 billion* mark in 1947 for the first time.

(Y)Total consumer purchases topped the *100 billion* mark in *1946* for the first time. The total for that year (not shown in the above table) was $100,694,000,000.

E—Estimated by Richard E. Snyder.

during the 1957-1961 period. Since 1961 (when 1.15 was posted) the pointer has moved successively to 1.16, 1.17, 1.15, and now rests tentatively at 1.17, the 1965 figure which is an advance estimate subject to revision.

Table 2b provides a different slant on the sporting goods market's "market position"—this time using as the criterion the percentage share of the "total recreation dollar" accounted for by sporting goods. The "total recreation expenditures" series compiled by the Department of

TABLE 2b
Sporting Goods Share of the Total Recreation Dollar

Year	Snyder's Estimates of Total Consumer Purchases of Sporting Goods*	Dept. of Commerce Estimates of Total Consumer Expenditures for Recreation	Sporting Goods Share of Total Recreation Expenditures
1948	$1,108,000,000	$ 9,808,000,000	11.3%
1949	1,096,000,000	10,122,000,000	10.8%
1950	1,188,000,000	11,278,000,000	10.5%
1951	1,257,000,000	11,704,000,000	10.7%
1952	1,350,000,000	12,257,000,000	11.0%
1953	1,441,000,000	12,892,000,000	11.2%
1954	1,447,000,000	13,256,000,000	10.9%
1955	1,555,000,000	14,220,000,000	10.9%
1956	1,668,000,000	15,193,000,000	11.0%
1957	1,774,000,000	16,082,000,000	11.0%
1958	1,846,000,000	16,842,000,000	10.9%
1959	1,986,000,000	18,309,000,000	10.8%
1960	2,164,000,000	19,524,000,000	11.1%
1961	2,260,000,000	20,559,000,000	11.0%
1962	2,406,000,000	21,496,000,000	11.2%
1963	2,539,000,000	22,703,000,000	11.2%
1964	2,658,000,000	NA	NA
1965	2,819,000,000(E)	NA	NA

*Excludes sunglasses and goggles. See footnote to Special Supplement to Table 2b.

SPECIAL SUPPLEMENT TO TABLE 2b
Components of the Recreation Dollar and Percentages of Change
in Expenditures, 1963 over 1948

Item*	Dollar Figures Are in Millions 1963	1948	% Change 1963/1948
Total Recreation Expenditures	$22,703.0	$9,808.0	+ 131.5
1. Books and Maps (d.c.)	1,745.0	588.0	+ 196.8
2. Magazines, newspapers, and sheet music (n.d.c.)	2,778.0	1,374.0	+ 102.2
3. Nondurable toys and sport supplies (n.d.c.)	2,897.0	1,079.0	+ 168.5
4. Wheel goods, durable toys, sport equipment, boats and pleasure aircraft (d.c.)	2,544.0	980.0	+ 159.6
Sporting Goods Particularized—Total**	2,538.5	1,107.6	+ 129.2
(All figures based on Richard E. Snyder's exclusive sales estimates)			
Baseball goods	62.4	35.0	+ 78.3
Bicycles	204.6	138.8	+ 47.4
Firearms and supplies	269.0	211.1	+ 27.4
Fishing supplies	172.3	111.4	+ 54.7
Football, basketball, boxing goods	53.0	33.2	+ 59.6
Golf equipment	174.3	62.0	+ 181.1
Gymnasium equipment	32.2	2.8	+1050.0
Photographic equipment (cameras & film only)	440.0	160.5	+ 174.1
Playground equipment	65.0	9.1	+ 614.3
Pleasure boats and equipment	600.0	193.3	+ 210.4
Skates (roller and ice)	33.8	21.3	+ 58.7
Tennis equipment	16.4	7.6	+ 115.8
Tents	55.1	11.7	+ 370.9
Winter sports equipment	25.0	12.7	+ 96.9
All other sporting goods	335.4	97.1	+ 245.4
5. Radio and television receivers, records, and musical instruments (d.c.)	4,308.0	1,479.0	+ 191.3
6. Radio and television repair (s.)	1,008.0	174.0	+ 479.3
7. Flowers, seeds, and potted plants (n.d.c.)	1,159.0	483.0	+ 140.0
8. Admissions to specified spectator amusements	2,009.0	1,918.0	+ 4.7
a. Motion picture theaters (s.)	1,275.0	1,503.0	− 15.2
b. Legitimate theaters and opera, and entertainments of nonprofit institutions (except athletics) (s.)	433.0	182.0	+ 137.9
c. Spectator sports (s.)	301.0	233.0	+ 29.2
9. Clubs and fraternal organizations except insurance (s.)	837.0	438.0	+ 91.1
10. Commercial participant amusements (s.)	1,239.0	436.0	+ 184.2
11. Pari-mutuel net receipts (s.)	616.0	256.0	+ 140.6
12. Other (s.)	1,563.0	603.0	+ 159.2

*(d.c.) durable commodities; (n.d.c.) nondurable commodities; (s.) services.

**Excluding sunglasses and goggles. NOTE: Sunglasses and goggles are included in a Department of Commerce consumer expenditures sub-group labeled "Ophthalmic Products and Orthopedic Appliances" under the broad category "Medical Care and Death Expenses." Therefore, to obtain a net "pure sporting goods figure" to use in comparing total sporting goods sales with total recreation expenditures, we must deduct our sunglasses and goggles estimate from our total sporting goods sales figure.

TABLE 2c
Comparative Growth Patterns: Disposable Personal Income,
Total Recreational Spending, and Sporting Goods Sales

| Year | Disposable Personal Income | Year-to-Year Percentages of Change | | |
		D.P.I.	Total Rec.*	SG Sales**
1948	$189,300,000,000	+11.3	+ 4.9	+5.9
1949	189,654,000,000	+ 0.2	+ 3.2	-1.0
1950	207,655,000,000	+ 9.5	+11.4	+8.3
1951	227,481,000,000	+ 9.5	+ 3.8	+5.8
1952	238,714,000,000	+ 4.9	+ 4.7	+7.3
1953	252,474,000,000	+ 5.8	+ 5.2	+6.7
1954	256,885,000,000	+ 1.7	+ 2.8	+0.5
1955	274,448,000,000	+ 6.8	+ 7.3	+7.4
1956	292,942,000,000	+ 6.7	+ 6.8	+7.2
1957	308,791,000,000	+ 5.4	+ 5.9	+6.4
1958	317,924,000,000	+ 3.0	+ 4.7	+4.0
1959	337,145,000,000	+ 6.0	+ 8.7	+7.6
1960	349,889,000,000	+ 3.8	+ 6.6	+8.9
1961	364,684,000,000	+ 4.2	+ 5.3	+4.4
1962	384,558,000,000	+ 5.4	+ 4.6	+6.6
1963	402,472,000,000	+ 4.7	+ 5.6	+5.3
1948-63 Growth Rates:		+ 5.6	+ 5.7	+5.7
1964	431,852,000,000p	+ 7.3	NA	+4.7
1965	NA	NA	NA	+6.0E

*The Recreational Expenditures series used in computing these percentages is shown in Table 2b.

**The Sporting Goods Purchases series used in computing these year-to-year percentages is shown in Table 2. This series *includes* sunglasses and goggles which were excluded from the Sporting Goods Purchase series used in computing the sporting goods percentages of the Total Recreation Dollar, as shown in Table 2b. (See the footnote to that table.)

p—Preliminary   E—Estimated.

Commerce is employed for this comparison. The percentage figures in Column 3 tell the story. They say that sporting goods sales never have siphoned-off less than 10.5% (in 1950) nor more than 11.3% (in 1948) of the total recreation dollar. In 1963 (latest available reading) sporting goods accounted for 11.2%, same as in 1962. The sporting goods share had not been as high as 11.2% since 1953 until it reached that level again in 1962. (*Special Item*: Attention is called to the footnote accompanying Table 2b.)

Now, through the medium of Table 2c, we view the status-progress of the sporting goods market from a third angle which places it vis-a-vis an economic phenomenon of momentous sweep and significance, namely, the ubiquitous force of *buying power*. This tabulation sets forth the dollar amounts of disposable personal income as compiled by the Department of Commerce, along with year-to-year percentages of change not only for this series, but also for the total recreational spending series shown in Table 2b and the total sporting goods purchases series shown in Table 2a. The annual growth rate figures, as computed for the 1948-63 period, indicate that disposable personal income expanded at a rate of 5.6% while total recreational expenditures and total consumer purchases of sporting goods both rose at the slightly higher rate of 5.7%.

These various statistical measurements of the sporting goods market's performance *since 1947* make it quite clear that, although this economic entity has not lacked for support, neither has it lacked for competition in its role of "hurrier on the upward path."

THE SPORTING GOODS MARKET AT THE
THRESHOLD OF THE SEVENTIES
GENERAL INTRODUCTION

RICHARD SNYDER

This is our fourteenth annual report applying to the basic economics of the U. S. Sporting Goods Market, sponsored by the N.S.G.A. and truly reflecting "a rapidly expanding economic entity and social phenomenon," as described by a long-term observer of the "goings on" in this field.

"Selling Sporting Goods" in 1968 was more than just the name of a monthly magazine (i.e., the N.S.G.A.'s "official" organ of trade information).

"Yessir, selling sporting goods" in 1968 was a vast, record-breaking *human endeavor* which met the massive challenge posed by the title of our annual sporting goods market report issued early in 1968, namely: "The Sporting Goods Market Outlook For 1968—Is Great!" And it *was* just that! Total consumer purchases of sporting goods set a new record of $3,700,400,000! This was 9.7% above the 1967 figure of $3,372,100,000.

And now—at the threshhold of the seventies—the signs of other dramatic "new highs" are already clearly discernible. The *decade terminal year* of 1969 seems destined to take its place in the *Sporting Goods Market Hall of Fame* along with 1929, 1939, 1949, and 1959, (sequentially dubbed as: The "Roaring Twenties," the "Thwarted Thirties," the "Ferocious Forties," the "Frenetic Fifties," and the "Golden Sixties").

Following is a list of the titles in this series of annual reports:
"Trends In The Sporting Goods Market," 1947
"Trends In The Sporting Goods Market," 1952

"Trends In The Sporting Goods Market," 1957
"Trends In The Sporting Goods Market," 1961
"Trends In The Sporting Goods Market," 1965
"The Sporting Goods Market In 1959"—Jan. 1959
"The Sporting Goods Market At The Threshhold Of The Sixties"—
    Jan. 1960
"The Sporting Goods Market At The Turn of The Cycle"—Jan. 1962
"Where Will The Sporting Goods Market Be In '63?"—Jan. 1963
"The Sporting Goods Market In The Mid-Sixties"—Jan. 1964
"The Sporting Goods Market Outlook For 1966"—Jan. 1966
"The Sporting Goods Market In 1967"—Jan. 1967
"The Sporting Goods Market Outlook For 1968—Is Great!"—Jan. 1968

TOPIC I. THE ECONOMIC CHURN

As background to considerations of the 1969 general business outlook, it may be well to point up and review briefly the broad-gauge
aspects of how things were going during the preceding three-year period
of 1966, 1967, and 1968.

In 1966, the powerful leading forces of a superheated, inflationary,
guns-and-butter economy brought into being a slew of "new highs"
amongst the many foretelling statistical barometers which are used in
measuring dollar values, quantities, and rates of change in business
activity. For example, 1966 gains in Gross National Product, Disposable
Personal Income, and Personal Consumption Expenditures averaged 8.3%
over 1965. Total industrial output, as measured by the Federal Reserve
Board Index of Industrial Production, rose about 9.0%. Total retail sales
posted an increase of 7.7%. Slackened retail demand was felt in the
appliance, radio, TV, furniture and building materials categories due to
the bureaucratically-enforced sickliness of the home building industry.

In 1967, the general business picture was overshadowed and the pace
slowed by a dense fog of uncertainties, false starts and withdrawals, all
amidst threats, strikes, riots, and conflicting economic and political
philosophies.

The average 1967/1966 percentage gain for the three major dollar
volume indicators named above, i.e., GNP, DPI, and PCE, was 6.0%.
Total industrial output showed a drop of 0.6%. These divergences reveal
quite clearly the basic imbalance of the economy in 1967 which, in some
of its aspects, bore signs of an incipient recession.

Having plowed its way through the vicarious uncertainties of 1967,
the U. S. economy proceeded to chalk-up a lengthy list of healthy gains

in 1968 (dubbed by *Life* Magazine as "Incredible '68—, year of Shock and Discovery").

Table 1 (not included in this reprint) contains latest available (as of this writing, early January 1969) economic performance measures for 1968 over 1967. The stance is obviously bullish and reflects true progress across a broad enough front to justify a strong intimation of continuing prosperity in 1969.

Our own business cycle index, which we maintain for client use, suggests that the level of "business in general" in 1969 will be 5.0% better than in 1968. This index provides a broad measure of the total physical volume of goods produced, transported and sold in the United States. Our estimates for the year 1969, based on Department of Commerce figures, applying to Gross National Product, Disposable Personal Income and Personal Consumption Expenditures, are shown immediately below:

GNP .... +7.6   DPI .... +7.1   PCE .... +6.9

What this may mean to the Sporting Goods Industry is spelled out in subsequent sections of this report.

SPECIAL NOTE: The underlying purpose of the foregoing commentary is not merely that of calling attention to various and sundry statistical data. Instead, it is that of making clear to business executives that cyclical forces still operate in our economy in ways that can upset the best of planning.

Topic II. 1968 Was Great!
(Estimated Consumer Purchases of Sporting Goods, 1968 vs. 1967, by Product Categories)

As stated in the "General Introduction" section of this report, total consumer purchases of sporting goods in 1968 amounted to $3,700, 400,000. This was a new high of record, up 9.7% above the 1967 figure of $3,372,100,000 which, in itself, represented a rise of 7.9% over the 1966 recording of $3,126,000,000.

A resumé of annual grand total sporting goods sales figures is provided by the following text table, for the period indicated:

A year ago we pointed out, in a similar table, that "if our original estimate of $3,652,500,000 for 1968 proves to be accurate, and that, if total sporting goods sales in 1969 show a rise over 1968 of 6.8% (the average for the 1960-68 period), this market will attain the 4-billion dollar level in 1970, the first year of the 'Seventies' decade."

As things now stand, the first 1968 estimate of $3,652,500,000 has been revised to $3,700,400,000, and an original estimate of $4,077,500,000

Total Sporting Goods Sales, 1958-1969

Year	$ Amounts	Year-to-Year % Change	Index 1958 = 100
1958	$1,872,600,000	+ 4.0	100.0
1959	2,064,300,000	+10.2	110.2
1960	2,244,600,000	+ 8.7	119.9
1961	2,342,000,000	+ 4.3	125.1
1962	2,494,600,000	+ 6.5	133.2
1963	2,614,400,000	+ 7.0	139.6
1964	2,736,800,000	+ 4.7	146.1
1965	2,911,200,000	+ 6.4	155.5
1966	3,126,000,000	+ 7.4	166.9
1967	3,372,100,000	+ 7.9	180.1
1968	3,700,400,000(R)	+ 9.7	197.6
1969	4,077,500,000E	+10.2	217.7

for 1969 is already on the books as the first attainer of the 4-billion dollar level.

In Table 2 (not included in this reprint) we present comparative 1968-1967 dollar estimates of total U. S. consumer purchases of sporting goods classified by twenty-four product categories, in addition to the related 1968/1967 percentages of change.

These are the critically important basic market statistics which, in the last analysis, are most sought-after by the users of our reports, year in and year out.

Following is a summary of the 1968 product category sales performances by comparison with those for 1967, expressed in terms of percentages of change:

Two product categories showed 1968/1967 percentages of change ranging *from zero to +5.0%.* These were bowling balls, and sunglasses and goggles.

Thirteen product categories posted 1968/1967 sales gains in the +5.0% to +10.0% range. These were: archery equipment; baseball goods; bicycles; fishing supplies; football, basketball, and boxing goods; inflatable balls other than footballs and basketballs; photographic equipment; pleasure boats and equipment; pleasure boat accessories; sleeping bags; tennis (lawn) equipment; tennis (table) equipment; and tents.

Nine product categories registered 1968/1967 sales increases of *more than 10.0%.* These were: billiard and pool tables and playing supplies; firearms and supplies; golf equipment; gymnasium equipment; hockey goods; playground equipment; skates; winter sports equipment; and in this grouping we have included "all other sporting goods."

When appraising sales performance figures in terms of percentages of change, it is well to keep in mind that large percentages of change may reflect comparatively small amounts of money, and, conversely, that small percentages of change may be associated with large monetary commitments.

In previous reports we have referred to this phenomenon as an expression of the "volatility of small numbers" in the first instance and "the inertia of large numbers." For example, total sporting goods sales in 1968 amounted to $3,700,400,000, and this represented a 9.7% gain over the 1967 total of $3,372,100,000. Gymnasium equipment, however, showed a 1968 sales total of $63,000,000, and this was a 20.0% gain over the 1967 total of $52,500,000.

SECTION

C

POLITICS: NATIONAL AND INTERNATIONAL POSITIONS

In the section following, the political turmoil between the National Collegiate Athletic Association and Amateur Athletic Union is thoroughly investigated by reporter David Wolf. McIntosh, in his article, also comments on this power struggle in American sport. Wolf gives many examples of the effect such a struggle has on the individual athlete.

The article by Schollander and Savage looks especially at the problems of political activists, international political pressures and commercialism in the 1964 and 1968 Olympic Games. Schollander relates how he nearly called a press conference and resigned from the United States team the day before the 1968 Olympics started. Is there a way in this highly politicized and technical world to return to the Olympic ideal as stated in the Olympic Creed? Schollander makes some suggestions about how this might still be accomplished.

In "Sports and Politics" Lunn presents his view of the East-West political struggle as it affects sport. He illustrates the conflict with his experience in the Federation International de Ski. Lunn suggests forcing the political issue with a boycott of eastern block nations of any international sports event.

McIntosh takes the point of view that "very seldom has sport been free of politics." He looks into the effect of international politics on the Olympic Games, and also at the internal politics within one country, observing that sport can operate as a "cohesive agent" or as an agent of division when it is affected by the rivalry of governing bodies within the country.

Some of the many other directions that sport can take because of political views and demands are discussed by Hanna in an article called "The Politics of Sport: Indonesia as Host to the Fourth Asian Games." (This article is not included in this collection but is well worth reading.) In the late summer of 1962 Indonesia was host to some 1,200 athletes from seventeen countries for the "Fourth Asian Games." Hanna relates:

443

At the last moment, however, the Indonesian games committee and the Indonesian government deliberately excluded from the competition the teams of two charter members of the Asian Games Federation whose governments are not recognized by Indonesia thus stirred up an international controversy which, after almost stalling the games themselves, led to the decision by international sports bodies that the events in Djakarta did not qualify as the Fourth Asian Games at all but must be regarded as merely another international competition, and climaxed in an Indonesian riot at the Indian Embassy in Djakarta."[1]

In light of the present Third World organizations and their demands, the outcomes of this upheaval seem especially pertinent. Hanna continues:

They have also taken up a suggestion which originated, it seems, with the Minister of Sports and past president of the Asian Games Federation, who has proposed the establishment of a new international games organization. The "emerging nations," the argument runs, should free themselves of the "domination" of Western "imperialists" sportsmen who "discriminate" against Afro-Asians. They should form a new sports association of Asian, African and Latin American nations which takes account of the "realities" of the present world political situation."[2]

1. W. R. Hanna, "The Politics of Sport," *Southeast Asia Series*. New York: American Universities Field Staff, (1962), p. 1.
2. *Ibid.*, pp. 10-11.

THE GROWING CRISIS IN COLLEGE SPORTS

PART I

DAVID WOLF

Jack Ajzner had two dreams during his high school days in Paterson, New Jersey. One was to receive a basketball scholarship to a university; without financial aid, his chances of going to college were slim. The other dream was to represent the United States at the Maccabiah Games in Israel, because he once had lived in Israel. Little did he suspect that in 1969 those two dreams—seemingly parallel—would converge into conflict. He would have to choose between them, forcing him into the most agonizing decision of his life.

Ajzner, now a 6-9 center at the University of Cincinnati, was put in the same position as seven other Jewish collegians. All were caught up in the latest feud between the Amateur Athletic Union (AAU) and the National Collegiate Athletic Association (NCAA). Since 1967, the NCAA had tried to shake the AAU's hold on amateur basketball by barring collegiate players from all international competition except the Olympics and the Pan-American Games. That meant the Maccabiah Games were off-limits.

Ajzner tried desperately to get permission from the NCAA to play in the Games. And others tried for him. One man in particular was Harold Lefcourt, a Pennsylvania political figure and a leader in the U. S. Committee for Sports for Israel. Ajzner stayed at Lefcourt's home for a time, and together they tried to telephone Walter Byers, the Executive Director of the NCAA.

David Wolf, "The Growing Crisis in College Sport," *Sport* 49 (Part I, June, 1970) 24-92 and 50 (Part II, July, 1970) 30-74. Reprinted by permission.

"We called the NCAA office in Kansas City every day," Lefcourt says. "But Byers wouldn't even speak to us. They wouldn't listen."

Ajzner had no real choice but to decline the Maccabiah invitation. "My coach at Cincinnati told me that if I went, the NCAA would declare me ineligible for college ball and I'd lose my scholarship," Ajzner says.

Of the other seven Americans, only Jack Langer of Yale went to Israel—with the full support of the Yale athletic department. When Yale permitted him to play this past winter, the school was placed on two year's probation.

"I would have done anything to go," Jack Ajzner says now. "But I was up against the whole establishment. It makes you start to think about the establishment. You start questioning a lot of things. But I don't have to question the NCAA. I know about them. They don't really care about people."

The Ajzner-Langer case is not an isolated one for the NCAA. In recent years the NCAA's attempts to gain control of international competition have caused it to take stands against other athletes as well. In the past couple of years, close to two dozen college basketball teams have been prohibited from playing in foreign countries. International track star Jim Ryun was denied a world record in the half-mile when the NCAA refused to submit his time to the appropriate authorities. And the U. S. lost a track meet to the Soviet Union when the NCAA barred collegians from the team.

The timing of these recent events couldn't be worse, because the entire system of college athletics is fast approaching the crisis stage. There are major problems with financing, race relations and rules. At least one of these problems has affected every one of the 650 member schools of the NCCA. Some schools have been hit by all three. Worst of all, it is the individual athlete who ends up suffering most.

The financial problem is accelerating at the most rapid rate, particularly among the "big-time" schools. They have big-time gate and television receipts, to be sure, but they also have big-time expenses. At least half the schools in the Big Ten are operating in the red. Now athletic directors are talking about cutting the number of scholarships, or seeking financial help from state governments. The NCAA has tried to help by approving an 11th football game starting next season, but few schools believe that this will make much of a dent in the deficit.

In the matter of race relations between black athletes and athletic departments, there is a potential time bomb on nearly every campus. In the past three years explosions have rocked Indiana, San Jose State, Wyoming, California, Iowa, Wisconsin, Princeton, Washington, Oregon State and Texas (El Paso), to name a few. It is a problem that requires delicate handling, yet the NCAA has been largely insensitive. In the past year the Association has used its monthly newsletter to supply coaches and administrators with erroneous, simplistic and misleading information about the unrest among black athletes. The NCAA also left itself open to charges of racism when it punished only San Jose State—and the politically active blacks on its national champion track squad—for a violation also committed by eight other schools.

Finally, the NCAA rulebook is sprinkled with regulations that give the athlete—so long as he wants to remain an athlete—less political freedom and academic flexibility than the average student. And the rules often apply whether the student-athlete (a term found only in the NCAA's dictionary) is on an athletic scholarship or an academic scholarship or is paying his own way. Recently, more and more "student-athletes" have been rebelling against the inequity of some of these rules, challenging the right of the NCAA to restrict their freedom simply because they play intercollegiate sports.

Immersed in all these problems—the financial, racial and regulatory—is Walter Byers. He is a trim, aggressive 47-year-old Midwesterner and totally dedicated to his job as spokesman for the NCAA. He is at his desk 7:30 each morning, often working well into the evening, and he does an excellent job as an administrator.

Under his guidance the Association conducts 27 national championship events in 18 sports. It keeps official records, institutes surveys and research projects, promotes national events, negotiates network TV contracts and represents its members on the U. S. Olympic Committee. The Association also acts as a legislative and enforcement body. All this is done, says Byers, because "it is an important function of our American society to have good, honest competition by boys who want to play because they like to play. That's our principle in life."

In pursuit of this principle, however, Walter Byers and the NCAA have received some rather unpleasant press notices of late. The organization has been characterized as the worst thing that ever happened to college sports. Byers has been called power-mad and an egomaniac. None of this is fair or relevant. Byers and the NCAA operate under a mandate, and if you are looking for a villain, you must start first with the people who have delivered that mandate.

The NCAA represents the collective philosophy of the coaches and athletic directors. Often a university president will pick someone outside the athletic department as the school's voting representative, but this means little. "The kind of professor who'll spend time on sports legislation generally sees things our way," says a prominent athletic director. "It looks cleaner to have a law professor voting, but he votes the way we want him to."

The control within the NCAA is further compressed. It is the athletic departments of the *big-time sports* schools who runs things. This is true even though the majority of the NCAA's members are small schools which operate on a limited, or even non-athletic scholarship, basis. The president and secretary-treasurer, the vast majority of Council (which establishes policy between annual conventions) and the Executive Committee (which carries out policy) are from schools which conduct major athletic programs. So if Byers and the NCAA are conservative and seemingly preoccupied with money and power, it is only because—with some important exceptions—this is the state of mind in most athletic departments.

A strong example is a rule the NCAA passed in 1968. The rule was designed to intimidate athletes into staying away from demonstrations of any kind. It allows a college to "terminate the financial aid of a student-athlete if he is adjudged to have been guilty of manifest disobedience through the violation of institutional regulations or established athletic department policies and rules applicable to all student-athletes."

The NCAA defends the rule, stressing that the college's administration—not the athletic department—makes the final determination of a student-athlete's case. "The whole thing was a tempest in a teapot anyway," says Tom Hansen, the NCAA's public relations director. "The rule wasn't invoked once last year."

A prominent athletic director just laughs: "It didn't have to be invoked. We could hold it over the kids' heads. That was enough to keep them in line. That legislation got the job done."

If the NCAA's regulations are strict and inflexible, the members also feel such rules are necessary. Otherwise, so goes the argument, the orderly maintenance of the system would be jeopardized. And few of the big-time schools would want that to happen. After all, the theory behind the system is that successful (translate: winning) teams, especially in the revenue-producing sports of football and basketball, can do all kinds of wondrous things for an institution of higher learning. Winning teams can mean increases in gate receipts, TV contracts, alumni donations, university budgets and community acceptance.

In such a system, therefore, winning is a necessity; the coach who loses becomes an insurance salesman. That is why you have the University of Texas spending $50,000 a year to keep nine coaches in the field recruiting, and why Woody Hayes of Ohio State runs up a yearly phone bill of $27,000. It is also why the maximum NCAA grant-in-aid of tuition, room and board, books and $15 per month for laundry is often just a starting point in under-the-table bidding by a school. Columbia

All-America basketball player Jim McMillian says that before he chose the Ivy League, some schools promised him as much as $400 per month.

Coaches and administrators stress that they are offering plenty in return to the athlete, in addition to his free education. They are giving him the opportunity to learn the most essential American values: the endurance of pain, respect for authority and self-reliance. "Football's main feature is teaching responsibility," says Tom Hamilton, Commissioner of the Pacific Coast Conference and former coach at Navy and Pittsburgh. "This is what the military likes about sports. . . . I think football is the greatest thing we have in education today." The player may have to forego many campus activities—especially social and political—and he may have to wear his hair so short he looks like the eligible suitor for the coach's daughter, but the men who run the system see nothing wrong with this.

"As far as exploitation of the athlete, sure we're going to push them," says Indiana football coach John Pont, one of the more open-minded young coaches. "We want to win. We want to enhance the reputation of the University. We want to go to the Rose Bowl, but that's all within a football area, an athletic climate, and he (the athlete) wants to do these things. . . ."

While the majority are convinced that the big-time sports system is educationally valuable to both the schools and the athletes, there are some within the system who question that.

"If the athlete has a subsidy that the non-athlete doesn't have, he is being professionalized," say DeLaney Kiphuth, the athletic director at Yale, a school where athletes are recruited but where financial aid for *all* students is solely on the basis of need. "The athlete often can't drop sports if he wants to keep his scholarship. The scholarship comes from gate receipts. All this leads to the feeling that you are paying the student to be an athlete, and that you'd better get your money's worth."

Dr. Harvey Jessup, assistant athletic director at Tulane, wonders if the colleges, "because of our zealousness to please the alumni and show profits, push our athletic programs so far away from the education framework that they are entities unto themselves?"

In 1967, Harland Hatcher, then the president of the University of Michigan, articulated the dilemma. "A strong athletic program is a common denominator that brings together students, alumni and townspeople," he said. But "we are getting caught in a competitive system that is driving us to commercialism and undue pressure to win. I'd like to see sports pursued in a more relaxed way. But once a program like ours get started, it seems you just have to keep it going."

Now there is some question as to whether the system *works*, even by its own standards. Is the athlete's morality really being uplifted by sports? "You can't fool a kid today," says a coach in the Big Eight. "He knows you've recruited him primarily because of what he can do on the basketball court and that your basic interest in him is not how well he will fare in the classroom."

But as long as the system exists, it must be coordinated on a national level. That is where Byers and the NCAA come in, and by any standards Byers' administration, which began in 1951, has vastly improved college athletics.

Until 1948, the NCAA had restricted itself to writing playing rules and conducting tournaments. By then the public had become aware that "players" weren't necessarily students, that payments were lavish and open, and that the old story about the lineman who played for every team in the Southern Conference wasn't far from the truth. So the NCAA passed a "Sanity Code." This was supposed to eliminate athletic prowess as a basis for scholarship aid. But in 1950 a motion to expel seven members for violation of the Code didn't carry the NCAA convention. There was great bitterness and the NCAA seemed on the verge of breaking up.

By the time Byers took over, the Sanity Code had been repealed, allowing athletic factories to run wild again. A basketball fixing scandal didn't exactly help the colleges' image. And unrestricted football televising by some major schools was killing live attendance for almost everyone else.

Byers brought order and solvency from this mayhem. A new legislative and enforcement program was enacted in 1952. The obvious excesses of the system—massive payments and illiterate athletes—were attacked. Between 1952 and 1967, 104 schools were hit for recruiting and aid violations. How many more violators went undetected is another question. But at least the *image* of college sports improved markedly.

Byers also led a successful fight to restrict live TV coverage to selected games. The plan, administered by the NCAA's own TV Committee, has been a huge success for the colleges. Byers has sold TV rights for ever increasing sums. Next season the schools and conferences which appear on TV will split over $12,000,000. At the same time, college football's live attendance has risen markedly—to 27.6 million in 1969.

NCAA membership has almost doubled since Byers took over. There are now national championships in such sports as water polo, rebound tumbling, soccer and skiing. The NCAA and 100 of its members conducted a summer program last year—with extensive financial help from the federal government—that opened college sports facilities to 43,000 underprivileged youngsters. At the end of 1969, the Association had total assets of over $1,469,000—much of it coming from NCAA basketball tournament receipts.

The strides have been tremendous. But there also is considerable unrest among the members, particularly from those who do not feel the big time sports system is viable financially or educationally, and that some of the NCAA's rules are relevant to them. "They are clearly concerned with the heavy grant-in-aid program," says DeLaney Kiphuth. "Oberlin, Carleton and Yale have to try to figure out how these rules apply to us."

Many NCAA regulations are sincere attempts to protect the student from overzealous recruitors. For example, the organization recently voted to bar recruitors from contacting a prospect at the site of his competition. The NCAA also has some rules to guard the athlete against the unethical coach. At its convention in January, the members voted to require schools which grant one-year scholarships (as opposed to four-year) to inform returning athletes by July 1 that their grants will be renewed. Previously, many coaches had kept borderline players hanging all summer, then dumped them just before school started, if the coaches were sure they wouldn't need them.

There is even a movement within the NCAA, and backed by Byers, to do away with athletic scholarships and to make all athletic aid on the basis of need. This, of course, has a financial, as well as moral, motivation.

Too often, however, the NCAA regulations, designed to protect the colleges from each other, wind up punishing the athletes. One rule, designed to keep coaches from tampering with players at other schools, requires a transfer student to sit out one season before he's eligible for NCAA competition. Thus, the student, even if he isn't on scholarship, is barred from an extra-curricular activity simply because he decided to change schools.

Relevant here is the fact that the NCAA has no regulations against *coaches* jumping their contracts—as Doug Dickey of Tennessee did last winter when he moved to Florida. Yet the association forces the players the coach recruited to remain at the school he is leaving—or lose a year's eligibility.

Another NCAA rule punishes the athlete for accepting illegal aid. The penalty is loss of eligibility. But few youngsters know NCAA rules when they are recruited. When a "slush fund" scandal broke at Illinois several years ago, star halfback Cyril Pinder lost his eligibility because he had been receiving free plane trips to his home in Florida. An official report stated that "in his senior year in high school (Pinder) had offers of 90 football scholarships and thought trips home were a regular thing since all schools offered them."

Then there is the "Five Year" rule, which bars a student from intercollegiate athletics if five years have elapsed since he first enrolled in college. Even if the student has not completed his three years of varsity eligibility because of illness, injury or withdrawal from school, he is banned after five years of attendance.

The regulation is designed to prevent interminable "red-shirting." Only time spent in the Armed Services, Peace Corps or missionary work is exempted. "If the student applies himself," says Tom Hamilton, "he should be able to finish in five years. I think it's a fair rule."

It is also an inflexible rule, with no avenues of appeal. Consequently, it has sabotaged heroes and unknowns alike. One case was that of Bob Stiles, a 5-9, 170-pound defensive back. He started out at a school in the East. He dropped out after one year and spent the next two at odd jobs, trying to find himself. Finally he went to a junior college for one year, then transferred to UCLA. He capped a fine first season by being the defensive star in UCLA's upset win over Michigan State in the Rose Bowl. But there was no "next season" for Stiles. Five years had elapsed since he had first entered college, and he was no longer eligible for varsity competition.

Then there was Jerry Williams, a track sensation at Berkeley High in California in the early '60s. He enrolled at Texas Southern, but wasn't comfortable in the South. He returned to the Bay area and disappeared into the ghetto. Occasionally he'd attend a track meet. Once he watched world recordholder Tommie Smith of San Jose State in a sprint, then told Tommie: "I could get back in shape and whip your butt."

After several years of trying, Art Simburg, the sports editor of the San Jose student paper and who had known Williams in high school, convinced Jerry to leave the ghetto and try college again. Williams was admitted to San Jose State under a disadvantaged students program. He began working into shape. But he never ran for the San Jose varsity. The five-year rule was envoked. He was declared permanently ineligible although he had not spent even a full year in college.

It has occurred to a few NCAA officials that some of their rules might be contrary to civil law. 'If the reserve clause comes to the Supreme Court and is challenged," says Dave Nelson, Delaware's athletic director and chairman of the Professional Relations Committee, "we feel there could be some implications in intercollegiate athletics. We haven't taken a stand on any of this, but we are concerned."

Walter Byers isn't concerned. Actually, he's too busy battling the AAU.

The AAU and the NCAA have been fighting since before Byers was born. One of its more bitter battles came in 1928, when a squabble over the make-up of the Olympic squad necessitated the intervention of General Douglas MacArthur. His eventual settlement, which gave the NCAA considerable—but not majority—representation, kept things fairly cool until the 1950s.

By then, Walter Byers was running the NCAA. He took one look at the AAU's mismanaged tours and its politically motivated selection of coaches and athletes, and demanded a greater voice for the NCAA. In 1962 the NCAA (along with high schools, junior colleges and some club groups) set up national Federations in numerous sports to contest the AAU's authority.

The Federations were little more than front organizations for the NCAA, but the U. S. Track and Field Federation began holding meets in competition with the AAU. Both organizations refused to permit their athletes to compete in meets sponsored by the other. The result was a lot of lousy meets.

In 1965, the NCAA withheld collegians from an AAU-sponsored meet with the Soviet Union. The U. S. was soundly beaten. Later, when distance runner Gerry Lindgren of Washington State competed in a similar meet, the NCAA threatened to suspend him from college competition. But the national furor became so intense, the NCAA backed down.

The Senate Commerce Committee was so upset by the loss to the Russians that it created a Sports Arbitration Board headed by noted labor mediator. Theodore Kheel.

In 1968, Kheel's board introduced a seven-point peace plan that was very favorable to the NCAA. But Byers thought the USTFF should have still more power. The NCAA rejected the plan after the AAU accepted it. "I've rarely seen such intransigence," stormed Kheel. "Those people make the Teamsters look like undernourished doves."

After a moratorium for the 1968 Olympics, the battle is raging again. This time basketball has the center ring. The battle there actually began in 1963 when the NCAA-backed Basketball Federation of the USA (BFUSA) received permission from the International Amateur Basketball Federation (FIBA) to sponsor games between U. S. and foreign teams. This right had previously been limited to the AAU. But, after three years, the sole sanction returned to the AAU, which controls few top amateur players.

The NCAA was upset. To prove to FIBA that the Federation, not the AAU, had jurisdiction over almost all basketball players, the NCAA Council decided to bar college players from all international (AAU-sponsored) competition except the Olympics and the Pan-American Games. This was done by evoking the prohibition against a college player competing in organized summer basketball. The rule was never intended to be applied to international competition—its intent was to keep players from competing at gambler-infested resorts after the 1961 fixing scandals—but the NCAA used it for its own purposes.

"In 1965, under Federation sponsorship, more than 200 international games were played by Federation members," says Byers. "And in 1966 more than 400 games . . . there was more basketball competition than in the entire previous history of basketball since Naismith put the peach thing up."

The NCAA ruling, however, deprived hundreds of youngsters of an opportunity to travel abroad—an opportunity some might never have again. "Something like 20 NCAA colleges who had international trips arranged were denied those trips. There were high schools from at least seven states . . . ," says Byers matter-of-factly. "The United States Collegiate Sports Council, which is this country's governing body for the World University Games was denied. . . ."

Byers reasons that, in the long run, the NCAA action will give more collegians a chance to travel. "If you're going to accomplish something worthwhile, it takes sacrifice," says Byers, who neglected to ask the current college players if they wanted to forego their trips in support of this particular principle. "What about all the people who played basketball in the past years that because of AAU mismanagement and autocratic control were denied international trips? . . . Everybody was prepared to tighten up their belt and cut it out . . . so that the people who followed could have the freedom they deserved."

In 1969 FIBA tried to settle the dispute by setting up another group, the International Basketball Board, to mediate. A meeting was set on June 25 in Kansas City, but only half the AAU delegation showed up. The AAU people blamed bad weather. The NCAA blamed bad faith, and announced that its ban on foreign competition was still in force. This knocked out the Maccabiah Games.

"We thought the NCAA's grievances against the AAU were probably valid," says Kiphuth. "But we were shocked when they enforced the gambling rule in this instance. Still, we had no immediate concern because we had no one on the team. Then, when the other collegians were withheld, the Maccabiah Games Committee said 'could we invite your boy?' We said 'That's up to him.'"

Langer was invited. "We explained the risks to him," says Kiphuth, "but we told him that we weren't inclined to hold him back. It was bona fide Olympic-type competition. There was no threat of gambling contamination. Many boys paid their own way. It was *true* amateurism. And all collegians from other sports were permitted to go by the NCAA. Only the basketball players were barred. We felt this wronged the individual athlete. And we didn't feel we had that kind of power over a boy anyway."

Jack Langer went to Israel. In late December the Eligibility Committee of the Eastern College Athletic Association (ECAC), an arm of the NCAA, declared him ineligible. Yale defied the ECAC ruling and played Langer when the basketball season opened. Langer was only a substitute. The Yale team wouldn't have missed him very much. But Yale continued to support its student.

In January, the NCAA placed Yale on probation for two years. It was a stiff penalty for using an ineligible player. But Yale kept Langer on the team throughout the season. "We felt an obligation to the boy," said Kiphuth. "We advised him to go. In punishing Langer the ECAC was punishing the wrong party. We had to let him play. We weren't prepared to let him become a pawn in the NCAA's struggle with the AAU."

The probation kept Yale's fine swimming team out of the national championships. Several top track men were barred from competing in NCAA title meets. The University—because the probation will keep its football team off television for two years—lost about $300,000 in TV revenue.

Yale is considering suing the NCAA. Jack Ajzner of Cincinnati is doing more than considering it. He is going to sue, charging that the organization is a monopoly which deprived him of his rights.

But, as usual, the NCAA is already romping off into another new pasture. The latest preoccupation seems to verge on the political.

On November 15, 1969, when over 250,000 people demonstrated in Washington against the war in Vietnam, Walter Byers acted on behalf of the NCAA. It was a Saturday. ABC was televising the Purdue-Ohio State game. On each telecast the NCAA is permitted a one-minute announcement. Usually the blurbs tell what fun it is to be a student-athlete. But Byers wrote this one himself.

"As part of this week's salute to the United States' veterans," it began, "the National Collegiate Athletic Association expresses its deeply felt appreciation to the present and past members of the Armed Forces who have made it possible for this nation's people to work in safety and enjoy their leisure in freedom . . . and, for that matter, to make it possible for those who so choose, to carry on their dissent in unparalleled freedom. . . ."

Byers says he is shocked that many people think he was responding to the Mobilization Day in Washington. "This country is getting awful hung up," he says. "Golly, I don't know. It was just a Veterans' Day statement."

Chuck Howard, the ABC Executive who cleared the statement, didn't view it quite the same way. "We recognized it as the NCAA's response to the Mobilization. We put it on," he says, "because we didn't consider it excessive."

Then, last December, the NCAA News appeared with a lengthy article titled "Militant Groups Doing Great Dis-service to Black College Athletes." The article cited only the FBI and the McClellan Committee hearings on riots and disorders as its sources. Most of the information was undocumented. Most of the quotes were anonymous. The basic premise was that "a hard core revolutionary force designed to destroy the present government and educational system of the United States" was trying to gain publicity by using unwilling black athletes in unwarranted protests.

There was no attempt to deal with the very real problems and pressures that confront the modern black athlete in college. The article gave a gratuitous brushoff to the "several instances (when) black athletes have had legitimate complaints and concerns about which the athletic department management was not aware. . . ." It suggested that "the greatest improvement has occurred on an individual basis, athlete to coach. . . ."

The article ignored that fact that in 1968, black athletes at San Jose State, California and Washington, protested (with the support of the Black Students Union) against various practices. Among them were misleading recruiting, lack of aid in finding housing in virtually all-white campus areas, the channeling of black athletes into "Mickey Mouse" courses to keep them eligible, and sub-par treatment by trainers. The college administrations investigated and found that many of the allegations were true.

Most important, there was no discussion of the genuine concern for their people that has emerged among young black athletes. For the coach to deal with these concerns requires understanding. And he must also understand the symbolism inherent in mustaches, beards and "Afro" haircuts. These are manifestations of racial pride. Shaving them off—because a white man ordered you to do so—can be a form of emasculation.

Typical of the article's specific inaccuracies was the charge that due to "persuasion, coercion and threats of bodily harm to loved ones, some black athletes of the United States who wanted to compete in the Olympic Games did not do so." No athletes are named. In fact, none *could* be named. There weren't any. The only black athletes who actually passed up the games were basketball players Elvin Hayes, Wes Unseld, Lew Alcindor, Lucious Allen and Mike Warren. Hayes and Unseld didn't go to Mexico because they signed lucrative pro contracts. Alcindor, Allen and Warren have made it clear that their protest was political and very much their own choice.

The article also attempted to portray the black athletes' supporters as perpetrators of violence. It sighted a threat to the mother of an unnamed black athlete, a threat to disfigure the girl friend of a black college basketball player, the "cuffing and slapping of Washington coach Jim Owens' daughter and slashing the tires on Iowa coach Ray Nagel's automobile."

But these incidents would have been placed in a better perspective if the NCAA News had also noted that the life of Jim Owens' black assistant coach, Carver Gayton, was threatened when he broke with Owens, and that Harvey Blanks, the leader of the dissatisfied blacks at Washington, was warned over the phone that he would be shot if he ever put on a uniform again. The article could have added that Prof. Harry Edwards, Tommie Smith and Lee Evans received hundreds of death threats while they were leading the Olympic Boycott movement. One night, before the Olympics, Edwards' pet dogs were chopped to pieces and left on his porch, while feces was smeared on his car.

"They're getting into areas that are not within their competence," DeLaney Kiphuth says of the article. "They are somehow captured by the thought that athletics is a vehicle that promotes attitudes in kids that keep them from being bearded radicals. If they want to assure themselves that they aren't going to interest kids in athletics anymore, this is the way to do it: tell them it's the last stronghold of the things the younger generation doesn't believe in."

The younger generation would also be turned off by the circumstances surrounding the one-year probation currently in effect against San Jose State. Early last June, two San Jose trackmen, sprinter John Carlos and pole vaulter Sam Caruthers, competed in a Los Angeles *Times* charity meet in Orange County, California. A month earlier, the NCAA had sent a memo to all athletic directors noting, among other things, that the meet was not approved. "We wanted to be very careful," says San Jose coach Bud Winter. "We phoned the meet directors and asked for the number of their Federation sanction. Then, when Carlos went down there, he even demanded to *see* the sanction before he competed."

The meet was *sanctioned* by the Federation. But, San Jose discovered, it had not been *certified* by the NCAA. "We were under the impression that sanctioning meant certification," says San Jose athletic director Bob Bronzan, who is an NCAA representative to the Federation. "Several years before the last Olympics, the NCAA had a rule that meets had to be both certified and sanctioned. But that was put in the freezer for two or three years. Apparently they took it out. But we didn't know it. In fact, we took a survey of the schools which scored points at the NCAA track meet, and most of them didn't know about it. I certainly wouldn't have allowed Carlos to go if I had known."

That weekend nine colleges, including UCLA, LSU, SMU and Baylor competed in "uncertified" meets. But, when it came time for imposing penalties, eight schools received reprimands and San Jose State got a year on probation.

San Jose's acting president Herbert W. Burns angrily suggested that the school was being punished because it had tolerated the political activity of many black athletes, including the Olympic black glove protestors, Carlos and Tommie Smith.

Walter Byers bitterly denied that there was any ulterior motive. "The distinction is that San Jose had been up once before, in April, on what I'll characterize as a near violation of the same rule. The Council gave them the benefit of the doubt that time. When they came back the Council said 'These people had a warning, their case is separate and we've got to impress them with more drastic action.'"

But Winter disputes this. "The earlier case was concerning the fact that Carlos competed in meets unsanctioned by the NCAA while he was in school, but *before* he was a member of our team and before he was on aid. When we explained that he wasn't attached to our track team they didn't penalize us. The question of 'sanction' not meaning 'certification' never came up. We didn't willfully or knowingly do anything wrong. They hung us for what should have been a parking ticket, and they didn't hang anyone else.

"That meet was one week before the NCAA championships, which we won," he adds. "Do you think we would have jeopardized a national championship? We were breaking our necks to be right all along the way."

But the probation stands. A San Jose appeal was turned down and the school could not defend its title. "The kids are up in arms," Winter says. "This is the kind of thing the younger generation is talking about, the injustice of the establishment."

The fifty-seven-year-old coach pauses for a moment, then adds: "The NCAA sets quite an example for young people, doesn't it?"

PART II

The several hundred delegates to the National Collegiate Athletic Association's 1970 convention were assembled in a Washington, D. C., hotel ballroom. At the moment, they were listening with polite disinterest as a faculty representative from the Big Ten discussed the virtues of the athletic scholarship—the NCAA's version of true amateurism.

For the most part, the delegates were a homogeneous group: middle-aged, conservatively dressed, few sideburns threatening the earlobe and no hairs creeping over the collar. This was the physically-fit silent majority. Among them were the coaches, athletic directors and faculty representatives of the big-time, profit-oriented sports factories. These are the men who run the NCAA and control college athletics in this country.

The faculty rep now at the podium began to speak glowingly of the system which offers a high school athlete tuition, room, board, books and laundry money as an inducement to enroll at a particular school and participate in an extracurricular activity.

"Affording financial aid to the student-athlete enables him to get an education . . . ," the faculty rep said. "The student-athlete is a student first and an athlete second."

A man from Pomona College, a small California school, stepped to the floor microphone. "If we are concerned with the educational advancement of youngsters, how can we rationalize giving them a grant-in-aid, a payment, without calling them professionals?" he asked. Especially when many of the athletes who are brought in really have no chance of ever graduating."

One person applauded. The sound rang hollow through the room. Heads turned, casting disdainful stares at the visionary from Pomona. "The athlete is given a grant-in-aid because the figures show he has a reasonable chance, 50-50, to graduate," the faculty rep replied from the rostrum. "It could be better, but it's much better than it was. For the most part, it has been a system that has kept the athletic program in proper relationship to education, which is the primary function of the university."

If most faculty reps and the people at the NCAA really believe that, they might have an interesting discussion with Charles Owens. A few years ago Owens was an all-state fullback in Orange, Texas. He was also a fine student. Many colleges tried to recruit him. Owens finally was induced to turn down an academic scholarship to Yale and take a grant-in-aid at the University of Texas where, he was told, he could play big-league football and get a fine education at the same time.

Owens was injured as a freshman, red-shirted the next year, but played well in 1965, his first varsity season. The following spring, coach Darrell Royal said Owens might be All-American material. By then, however, football had turned sour for Charles Owens.

"I couldn't reconcile the role of the student with the role of the jock," Owens says now. "The coaches didn't tell me *not* to study, but periodically they'd explain what was expected. In a quiet moment before dinner you're told to give extra time to studying your plays. Next, they want an extra effort watching game films. When you add on the practice time, you realize you're just a football player. There isn't time to be a real student."

Owens also had become aware that when an athlete's playing eligibility expired, he usually had plenty of classroom work remaining. "Guys who had been stars, or near stars, didn't have anywhere near enough hours to graduate," he says. "They'd leave school without a degree and, if they didn't make it in pro ball, wind up selling insurance."

So Owens resisted the demands on his time. He was labeled an odd-ball. There was a falling out with the coaches. A year later Owens left the squad. Today he has his degree and is a Washington correspondent for McGraw-Hill. "I guess I couldn't come to an accord with the system," he says sadly. "I loved football, but I wanted to be a student too. That wasn't possible."

People at the NCAA might also be interested in the impression their system left on William Bradley of Crystal City, Missouri, currently employed by the New York Knickerbockers. Bradley's decision to attend Princeton came at the last minute. Before that he had become so confused by high pressure recruiting that he'd committed himself to Duke.

"We were taken in," says Bradley, who went on to become a Rhodes Scholar. "My mother made a big chart of the pros and cons of the different schools, but it was like playing cards with a rigged deck. It came out Duke. I'm very against the whole thing now, recruitment, scholarships, letters-of-intent. It's organized for adult men to manipulate 18-year-olds to come to a university and provide it with a winning team, some money and fame."

What happened to Owens and Bradley was hardly unusual. They were just quicker to recognize the flaws in the big-time college sports system. Now others, including administrators, are seeing the flaws too. And they are learning that the biggest problem is that the system often fulfills neither of its supposed objectives: 1) Making money for the university, or 2) giving the student-athlete an otherwise unobtainable college education.

Instead of raising revenue, many athletic departments are up to their shoulder pads in red ink. Now, in an ironic about-face, some sports administrators are turning to the student body, and even the taxpayer, for funds to cover expenses.

As for education, most student-athletes do get *something* out of college, whether they graduate or not. But they would get a far better, more rounded, education if they enrolled as normal students. (This is now increasingly possible, even for most underpriviliged youngsters, due to the growth of community and junior colleges, open enrollment, compensatory and remedial programs, and scholarship grants.)

In fairness, there certainly are student-athletes who prosper within the system. Some want stiff discipline, good training for professional sports careers and the campus glory that goes with being a sports hero. Others are so mature and intelligent that they can take advantage of the system's strengths, and not be hindered by its flaws.

But for many, even those who emerge with a degree, there are countless pitfalls. The traps are first laid, of course, in the intensive recruiting process, when even a sophisticated youngster like Bill Bradley might choose the wrong school. Recruiters may also needlessly inflate a boy's ego, or corrupt his values with under-the-table offers.

Once at school, the athlete may be exposed to excessive physical abuse or supplied with questionable drugs by coaches whose livelihoods depend on winning, not educating. The athlete may be channeled into "Mickey Mouse" courses to keep him academically eligible for sports. He will almost certainly be pressured to disassociate himself from that facet of the learning process which encompasses political involvement or contact with those different from oneself. In addition, like Charles Owens, he may discover that the demands of the playing field force a cursory approach to the classroom.

The details of the schools' financial dilemma began to surface at the 1970 NCAA convention. The NCAA now is conducting a survey on the matter, and no one expects the results to be encouraging. Some schools, to be sure, still make huge profits. But many others are in the red. Some of the latter continue to profit from football, but no longer make enough to cover the deficit in the rest of the athletic program.

At the convention, Michigan State's Athletic Business Manager, John Loetz, moaned about the huge expenses he has to meet before he can even begin to worry about more mundane things such as equipment, travel and medical bills. "I'm paying a half million in salaries, half a million in scholarships and I haven't taken a jock strap out of the bin yet," he said. "And expenses keep rising. Last year I paid $18,000 for football travel. This year it'll be over $30,000. And now I've got to pay for knee injuries, colds, warts and moles. I never had to do that before!"

Loetz, who is president of the College Athletic Business Managers Association, has a total budget at Michigan State of over $2 million. His problem is that the athletic program isn't taking in $2 million. "We've had three bad football seasons," he said. "After the second, people weren't so anxious to buy tickets. You've got to *win* to sell tickets."

Like many big-time administrators, Loetz sees a partial solution in cutting back the less prestigious, non-revenue-producing sports. Athletic departments used to justify the unsavory aspects of football by noting that it supported sports like golf, tennis and crew, which non-scholarship students participated in. But now Loetz says, "Football, basketball, baseball, hockey and track will remain, but the rest will probably have to go to a club basis, where we just give them a few thousand dollars and that's it."

Many colleges have decided to charge their students for the privilege of having a football team. This often amounts to an involuntary tax. Tuition at Purdue University, for instance, includes the compulsory purchase of a student ticket. At the University of California at Berkeley, a special student fee is charged upon registration. This gets the student an athletic activity card, but does not entitle him to a seat at many events. The money itself goes into a general fund controlled by the Chancellor, who last year gave $300,000 to the athletic department.

But forcing athletic fees on the student body isn't going to cover the deficits some schools are running up. John Loetz knows this, and feels he has a solution. "I would hope," he said at the convention, "that somewhere along the line, state taxpayers would help support athletic programs more."

Some state legislatures, like Wisconsin's, have already guaranteed to cover the tuition costs for many athletes, but government aid is hardly a long term solution. If the system is to retain its present form, schools will have to reduce the number of scholarships, increase schedules, and avoid empty seats. If you hear of a college business manager advocating topless cheerleaders, be understanding—he is under great duress.

Even if big-time college sports were lucrative for the vast majority of schools, the system still would be open to severe criticism on more significant grounds; that it is often incompatible with modern higher education. In recruiting, many colleges continue to view the NCAA rulebook as an obstacle course, not a road map. They are just not quite as blatant as Utah State was a decade ago when it actually paid one football star a weekly salary to make sure no one stole the scoreboard from the stadium, and another got paid to make sure no one stole the stadium.

"We've cleaned things up," insists Walter Byers, the NCAA executive director. "We whitewash no one."

The NCAA does place a few schools on probation each year for recruiting violations, and it privately reprimands many others. But the organization's investigative staff is miniscule, and it usually waits for a complaint to be registered before it goes into action.

"Things are better, but I doubt the NCAA catches one violator in fifty," says Dr. Harvey Jessup, the assistant athletic director at Tulane. "Things are just done more subtly. For instance, a school might have a third party establish a bank acount for a prospect in another town. Or a state university will put pressure on a gas station owner whose son is an athlete. If the kid goes to the school, the father gets plenty of state business. If the kid doesn't go, there won't be any state vehicles at the gas station."

A hustling young recruiter in the Western Athletic Conference says: "Of course we cheat. We have to compete. The head coach alters high school transcripts to get kids into school. We find jobs for fathers who are out of work. We make private deals with local people, so we can promise our recruits dental care for $1 and a car, if he's a blue-chipper, for not much more. As long as he pays *something,* it's hard to get caught."

Some schools simply offer money, period. Basketball star Heyward Dotson, who graduated from Columbia this spring after winning a Rhodes Scholarship, says: "St. John's and Michigan said I'd be taken care of directly. I wasn't interested in being paid. But some of my friends who went down to North Carolina, Duke and Davidson told me that they'd received the things I'd been promised."

Most schools which deal under the table couch their offers; things are implied, but never specified. This compounds the young recruit's confusion and often causes him to believe the school has double-crossed him. In 1967, Randy Smyth, an honorable mention All-American running back and an excellent sprinter at El Camino Junior College, was rushed hard by half a dozen schools. "Everywhere, the standard phrase is, 'We can work something out,'" says Smyth. "When I visited the University of Hawaii, they told me an alumnus had a car agency and 'something could be worked out.' They also told me they'd find a way to get me and my girl friend free transportation from the mainland, they'd get us both jobs, and they'd have her accepted in school. They never asked about grades. If I'd been a little younger it really would have snowed me." Smyth eventually enrolled at California and anchored a relay team for two years.

There are other ways girls are used by recruiters to induce a boy to enroll. At some schools, coeds are organized to date visiting prospects. The University of Florida labels its charmers the "Gator Getters," and at Kansas State they are called "Gibson's Girls," in honor of football coach Vince Gibson.

"I visited Wichita State with another junior college player," says Randy Smyth. "At ten o'clock they set up a couple of blind dates. The coach gave us his red convertible and two $20 bills, and told us to enjoy ourselves."

Even when the recruiting is totally within the prescribed framework of the NCAA code, there are evils, according to Dr. Jessup. "The system destroys the moral fiber of a teenager," he says. "Twenty leading coaches banging on his door, saying anything to please him. They kiss his rear until his self-image is totally out of touch with reality. Then they get him in school and kick his rear in the name of discipline."

"But the greatest sin in recruiting is to bring totally unprepared ghetto kids, put them in rinky-dink programs with plenty of badminton courses to keep them eligible, and then drop them cold when their four years are up and they aren't close to a degree," says Dr. Jessup. "With the remedial programs now available at some schools there's no justification for dumping a kid into a dead-end situation, just because you'd like to see him playing at your school."

Indiana's football coach, John Pont, is so genuinely concerned with presenting an honest picture that he suggests black recruits talk with the black players who boycotted his team last year. But Pont is an exception.

Samuel Barnes, the head of men's physical education at predominately black Howard University and a member of the NCAA's Council, estimates that over 60 percent of all black athletes who enter college on grants-in-aid never receive a degree. None of the five black starters who brought Texas Western the NCAA basketball championship in 1966 graduated.

Recruiting is just the beginning. Once the student-athlete has enrolled, he may find coaches responding in curious ways to the pressure to win. For instance, some schools are giving players access to drugs thought to improve performance. Recently, a University of California football player did a research project on drug use among his teammates. The athletic department successfully pressured him to keep silent. But there was a leak.

The player found that of the 50 athletes on the team 48 percent had used amphetamines to pep themselves up for games; 62 percent used depressants—either tranquilizers or muscle relaxers; 26 percent had been administered cortisone or Novocain to kill pain; and 28 percent had used anabolic steroids, male hormone derivatives that supposedly increase muscular size and strength but which have been listed as possible causes of muscular atrophy, change in libido, liver damage and edema. This is hardly a new phenomena, however. Ex-All-America George Connor says he was using pep pills when he played for Notre Dame in the 1940s.

You won't read about it in the *NCAA News*, but some schools conduct training programs which fall into the category of cruel and inhuman treatment. Like most excesses in college athletics, physical abuse occurs most often in the big money sport—football—where the pressure to win is greatest. A coach may simply want to toughen his players or instill a true killer instinct. Sometimes, however, at schools where four-year scholarships are awarded, another motive is to inflict such agony that a player who didn't pan out quits the team and gives up his grant-in-aid.

"Before spring ball," says a player from a Southern school, "we were *told* to volunteer for unofficial drills. There was running and agility work, but they also has this boxing session in the weight room. At the start of a session a coach would scream, 'I want you to beat the hell out of each other.' You'd have to try to kill the guy next to you, really beat his face in, make him bloody. We had no mouth protectors. Guys bled like crazy. One time a guy they were trying to make give up his aid was late for boxing. They told three of us to put on gloves and beat the guy. We fought him one after another till he could hardly stand. There was blood all over the place but if we tried to let up, they'd yell, 'Go easy and you change places with him.'"

The same player was confronted with something called "the cage drill" when regular workouts began. "They set up chicken wire in a square 30-feet-by-30-feet, and three feet off the ground," he recalls. "We'd line up in one corner and run diagonally across the square. Another group lined up in another corner and did the same thing. Two guys would criss-cross in the center and run over each other. If you didn't run into the guy hard enough, they made you do it again. But hell, I have a friend at another school whose coach dug a pit in the ground and covered it with chicken wire. He made two guys run down into the pit and collide at the bottom."

Such examples are the exception, not the rule. Most coaches are not sadists. But almost all athletes at big-time schools have at least one common problem—the control which the coaches and the athletic department exert over their lives. Otherwise progressive universities allow coaches to maintain a rigid, paternalistic relationship with student-athletes. This can circumscribe educational and social life in a manner no other department would consider imposing on its students.

Some psychologists believe coaches and sports administrators—who tend to be politically conservative and not especially tuned in to new trends on campus—suffer a sense of inferiority when functioning in an academic environment. Living among scholars, they feel a need to justify their existence by projecting themselves as more than teachers of games. Thus the coach becomes a builder of character, a molder of life-styles, a defender of traditions, or even a creator of patriots. The athletes are pressed to conform to *another generation's standards*—not those of their fellow students.

In varying degrees, coaches isolate their athletes from the rest of the student body. The extremes, of course, are athletic dorms, like the "Bryant Hilton" at the University of Alabama and the "Monkey House" at the University of Arkansas. Even without athletic dorms, athletes tend to be isolated by evening meetings, team trips, and training tables. Thus there often develops a kind of in-breeding.

This in-breeding, combined with the athletic department's influence over athlete's academic programs through tutors and advisors, can have an intellectually numbing effect. "You are subtly channeled into an educational rut," says Rick Sortun, who played at the University of Washington and put in six years in the National Football League. "Your advisers suggest fairly simple courses, like PE or business. The practices leave you too tired to study more than what you need to get by. You're definitely too tired to think on your own. You're told to be suspicious of hippies and radicals. You end up avoiding the kind of associations —the serious bull sessions, the intellectual give-and-take with people of various philosophies—that are really as much 'college education' as what you learn in the classroom.

"Increasingly, you accept the philosophy of the locker room," says Sortun, who has returned to Washington for graduate work, convinced his undergraduate years were a waste. "Physical strength and the ability to withstand pain are the most positive virtues. Women are things. Bookish people and little people are suspect. Finally, with the scholarship, the alienation, and the practice hours, you come to view it all as a job."

Since the primary "job" is athletics, the student-athlete often takes a minimal academic load the semester he competes. Basketball players, who compete during both semesters, are particularly prone to cutting academic corners. This past spring, at the end of the basketball season, Louisiana State stars Pete Maravich and Danny Hester were suspended for excessive class cuts. The coach, Pete's father Press Maravich, explained: "For the first nine weeks of the semester, Pete could only attend classes periodically because of the games."

Other faculty members usually believe students are responsible to them only while in the classroom. But most big-time coaches maintain that *their* responsibility for, and control of, the student-athlete extends far past the field and locker room. Indiana's John Pont often quotes noted sociologist Margaret Mead on the younger generation: "She makes the statement that 'it is not only the parents that are no longer guides but there are no guides.' Well, I'm still not to the point in my coaching career where I'm going to let an athlete do exactly what he wants to do. I feel there has to be discipline. There has to be somebody to guide this young man. I believe in tradition. I've had certain learning experiences that I think I can impart to our athletes . . . and I hope they're better people for having been in our program."

Pont's players can live off-campus and his dress code is flexible. But Pont believes it is his prerogative to impose discipline, even during the off-season. Thus, last February, with some of his stars graduating and a new personality to be molded for the squad, he ordered all players to wear their hair and sideburns short. Anyone who didn't conform immediately was off the Indiana football squad. All the players conformed.

This is relatively innocent until a passionately authoritarian coach uses the same reasoning to justify imposing his values on student-athletes. This happened at Oregon State. Dee Andros, aware that young blacks considered facial hair a sign of racial dignity, still threw a black football player off the team for refusing to shave his mustache more than a month before spring practice.

At the University of Wyoming, where coach Lloyd Eaton had an iron-clad rule against any political demonstrations by athletes, fourteen black football players were ousted. Their crime: they asked coach Eaton if they might discuss wearing black arm bands against Brigham Young to protest the Mormon racial doctrine.

At the University of Texas at El Paso, track coach Wayne Vandenburg kicked nine blacks off his team and cut off their scholarships when they refused to compete against Brigham Young several days after the death of the Rev. Martin Luther King.

Coaches wield such power because, unknown to most athletes when they are recruited, the majority of athletic scholarships are for *one year*, not four. This is the case in the Big Ten, Pacific Eight, Big Sky, and Western AC, to name a few. The coach need not tell the athlete until July whether his grant will be renewed for another year. If a coach, like Wayne Vandenburg, doesn't like an athlete's politics, he simply lets the aid lapse—often informing the student at the last minute, when it's too late to transfer. There is also the NCAA's "Manifest Disobedience" legislation which allows a school to withdraw the scholarship of athletes who violate "athletic department procedure."

In spite of all this, athletes are becoming increasingly independent and involved. On many campuses the "dumb jock" stereotype is evaporating. Athletes, particularly blacks, are in the forefront of various movements. The rollcall of schools hit by black athlete protests stretches across the country and reads like Lovejoy's College Guide. The Tufts University football team moved its practice time in order to participate in a Viet Nam Moratorium march. After the Cambodian intervention and the Kent State killings this spring, scores of athletes refused to compete in events. Stanford football players sat in at the ROTC building and the Columbia football team signed a petition supporting a nationwide strike. One motive, said Columbia guard Bob Hackett, was to "dispel President Nixon's image that athletes are all part of his famous silent majority." Black players wear Afros, most white athletes wouldn't be seen in a crewcut, and it's a rare ballclub that hasn't got some players who know that all "grass" doesn't grow on football fields. In short, the modern athlete is edging toward assimilation with his fellow students.

A few coaches seek an accord with the new generation. John Wooden of UCLA, once sought to impose his conservative, rather puritanical, values on his players. But he was deeply affected by contact with dignified black militants like Lew Alcindor. He was also affected by the way they played basketball. "I've had to do some compromising," says the man whose teams have won six national basketball titles in seven years. "I used to insist on coats and ties in restaurants; I don't anymore. I had a haircut code, which I've relaxed. I used to conduct bedcheck on the road. I rarely do anymore. I used to try control living off the court. Now I don't."

Wooden no longer tries to reshape his players philosophically. "The alternative is losing basketball," he says. "Compared to winning it's a poor choice."

In late April, twelve Yale trackmen (eight white and four black) passed up the Penn Relays to remain in New Haven for a student rally in support of a fair trial for the Black Panthers. Unlike Wayne Vandenburg at Texas El Paso, Yale's coach Bob Giegengack did not kick the athletes off the team for letting their moral convictions take precedence over a track meet.

"In fact," said Giegengack, who is over sixty years old, "I'm a little proud of them; they're doing something they believe in. They feel that they're trying to protect civil rights of fellow individuals. It would be hypocritical of me to deny them a means of expressing those feelings."

Unfortunately, few athletes get to compete for Bob Giegengacks or John Woodens. For most athletes at big-time schools, even those who pay their own way, it is a matter of substantially conforming or not participating in intercollegiate athletics. They are still blocked from real integration into the student body—and from the learning experience that would accompany it.

But the crisis in college sports won't subside. Instead, administrators can expect decreasing conformity as players become more aware of the system's flawed nature. "When I first came to Cal," says football captain Jim Calkins, "I'd do anything for the coach. I'd take what he said as the word, without question. Now, seeing athletics as a whole, I've come to the conclusion that I better start saying something."

In addition, the uncertain state of U. S. business indicates schools in financial trouble can expect more of the same. The NCAA can also look forward to increased internal turmoil as friction between big-time schools and those not bound by the grant-in-aid system becomes more acute.

But the situation is far from hopeless. The best things college sports has going for it are the sports themselves. There is nothing inherently wrong, for instance, with games like football or basketball. They are fun to play, promote fitness, and fulfill young men's competitive instincts. On an organized level they offer youths an opportunity to learn to work with others, perform under pressure, accept defeat, and to endure in adversity. The fact that coaches have perverted these learning experiences into a jingoistic ritual doesn't mean they aren't valid when removed from the red-white-and-blue wrapper.

There are numerous positive changes that can—and may—occur to ease the various aspects of the crisis. An important administrative suggestion was articulated by Arkansas football coach Frank Broyles at the NCAA convention. "Sometime there's gonna have to be a division in the NCAA, where those who award scholarships and participate in one brand of ball vote on rules that affect them," he said with more accuracy than he may have intended, "and those who play *students* vote on rules that affect them."

The big-time schools find the amateurs a nuisance. But the feeling is mutual. Ivy League schools—which recruit but don't give athletic scholarships—and the colleges which simply hand uniforms to the best players who happened to enroll, are drowning in a torrent of NCAA regulations they find irrelevent and restrictive.

"When you consider the Federation's inconsistency and self-interest in sanctioning meets," says DeLaney Kiphuth, Yale's outspoken athletic director, "when you hear that there's going to be another push for a national letter-of-intent (which would force a high school senior to irrevocably commit himself in writing to a recruiter many months before he enrolls), when you have the Langer case, pretty soon your patience runs thin. Unless there is a change in the general thrust of the NCAA's administering of its rules, and indeed in the form of the rules, I think the Bowdoins, the Yales, the City Universities, will want to form their own organization."

Dividing the NCAA, or setting up another organization, will help the non grant-in-aid schools conduct more meaningful programs. It will also give the better-informed high school student a clearer choice when he is recruited. But it does not get to the crux of the problem. The big-time schools operate the system. They must change, as must the system itself.

Recruiting must be de-escalated or even eliminated. Athletic scholarships should be granted only on the basis of real need—and quite possibly not at all. School administrations must break the hold athletic departments have over athletes. Coaches should get tenure like other teachers. But they should be asked to teach, not simply win.

This necessitates a movement away from the profit motive in college sports. "If athletics has educational merit," says Dr. Jessup of Tulane, "it should be truly supported by the school, like any other educational program. If athletics operated like an academic department, instead of an entertainment business and public relations office, the pressure to win would decrease and with it would go most of the cheating and hypocrisy we live with."

Too many schools still profit from sports, and too many administrators and alumni still equate the Rose Bowl with the Liberty Bell, for the system to change drastically overnight. Those who run the lucrative bowl games and men like Walter Byers, who uses the *NCAA News* to write complimentary articles about Spiro Agnew, think the system is fine the way it is.

But students and educators are becoming increasingly aware that there are alternatives. At many schools, especially where football for profit was a failure, students are returning to the original concept of college sports in America. In the 1860s, when intercollegiate athletics began, undergraduates ran the programs for themselves. It was only in the 1880s, when administraors and alumni saw the publicity and monetary potential of sports, that the present system evolved.

Today, student-run sports clubs in everything from judo to hockey and rugby are springing up all over the country. At close to seventy-five schools, club football is providing a reminder of the early days of the sport.

Some athletic departments supply funds for club football teams. More often the students raise the money themselves, sometimes even by selling stock. The essential principle is that the program is managed by the students. There are no scholarships, games are usually played on campus, and winning is a pleasant non-essential.

Club football has a national organization—to announce national rankings and All-America teams—but few restrictive rules. Transfers don't have to sit out a year before playing, freshmen are eligible, and any undergraduate not on academic probation may compete.

The NCAA has been understandably hostile to club football. Several years ago, when the clubs sought affiliation, Byers turned them down. "He said they didn't deal with students," says Roger Hacket, Fordham University's Sports Information Director and a leader in the club football movement. "He said that only when the athletic departments took over, when we became varsities, would they deal with us."

Several club teams have gotten permission from their schools to assume the label "varsity." But this is only to facilitate scheduling small college teams, which might be embarrassed losing to a "club." The principle remains unchanged. "At Fordham," says Hackett, "the students cherish the fact that they do it themselves."

There are top club teams from Loyola in Los Angeles to Manhattan College in New York. But Fordham is probably the best example of the club approach. Students print tickets, hire coaches, arrange trips, set schedules and administer a $50,000 budget. Revenue comes from gate receipts. "But we don't cater to gambling interests or subway almuni," says Hackett. "More than half our crowd are students, and that's enough to break even. If we didn't draw enough, we'd just spend less money next season. We don't fire the coach."

The Fordham players are real students. Last year the team's academic average was 3.1, high enough to qualify the *average* Fordham player for an NCAA scholar-athlete award. And Fordham doesn't play sissified football. Coach Jim Lansing is a former All-American with almost twenty years coaching experience in high school and college. Fordham has players who left athletic scholarships at TCU, Tulsa and Navy.

Eric Dadd, a 225-pound fullback, was recruited by Syracuse, Maryland, Boston College and Cornell. "I was more interested in getting an education," he explains. "I didn't want the regimentation of the schools that give athletic scholarships. Here you play club football because you like football, not because you get anything for it."

Dadd is so good he's already heard from NFL clubs like Dallas, Oakland and Cincinnati. But he doesn't regret passing up the big-time. "My friends at big-time schools aren't having much fun. Here all the players are known to the coach. But he doesn't try to impose his will on us. If a class conflicts with practice, you go to class. If he told me to cut my hair in February, he knows I might not bother playing football for him, so my hair stays long in the off-season. But I cut it pretty short in the fall. We take our team seriously. We like to be recognized as good football players. I think we can beat most small college teams. But the big thing is that we play because we enjoy it."

In the spring Dadd missed two practices. Fordham was in the midst of a student strike over issues of faculty tenure and tuition. Fullback Eric Dadd was on a picket line. "The coach didn't say anything about it," Dadd says. "He understands that this was part of a college education —just like playing football."

The NCAA and the big-time schools continue to turn up their noses at club sports and terms like "de-emphasis." But, as the crisis in college sport continues,they might give some thought to the words of Homer Babbidge, the president of the University of Connecticut: "We cannot justify intercollegiate athletics on any rational basis other than their value to the participants. And if spectators values continue to obscure these—and even threaten to eliminate them—then all is lost."

THE OLYMPICS THAT ALMOST WEREN'T

Don Schollander and Duke Savage

At the Olympic Games in 1964, when I was eighteen, I became the first swimmer in history to win four gold medals. Afterwards I talked at hundreds of banquets, high school assemblies and press conferences, but I didn't really have a great deal to say. I would just describe Olympic episodes and tell them stories about a few Olympic personalities.

Now, after two Olympics, I want to tell what it was like to be an Olympic competitor. I almost told it once, in a resignation speech I had prepared for delivery just before the opening of the 1968 Olympics in Mexico City. But I never gave that speech.

The reason I had intended to resign from the team was to draw dramatic attention to the serious problems of the Olympic Games. The fact is that the crowning event of sports is in danger of dying. The 1968 Olympics came very close to being cancelled and the diseases that threatened it have not been cured. They are all still there and the next attack may kill the patient—unless we do something about it, something to bring the Olympics back to its original objectives: "To demonstrate the principles of fair play and good sportsmanship. . . . To create international amity and goodwill, thus leading to a happier and more peaceful world."

The problems of the Mexico City Olympics began in February of 1968 when a biracial South African team was barred from competition because of its government's apartheid policies. In August Russia invaded Czechoslovakia and settled her tanks on the streets of Prague, and Sweden, following the spirit of the action against South Africa, protested that the Soviets should be barred from the Olympics. South Africa *was* banned; the U.S.S.R. was *not* banned.

A threatened boycott of the Olympics by American black athletes was finally called off on September 1, but the athletes, many of the finest on the U.S. team, were troubled and unhappy.

Before our arrival, rioting broke out in Mexico City, triggered in part by the impending Olympics. Student activists barricaded themselves on rooftops and, on October 3, nine days before the opening of the nineteenth Olympiad, Mexican troops opened fire on the students. According to official figures thirty-four people were killed and hundreds wounded, but the toll was in fact much higher.

Revolution . . . repression . . . racism . . . communism . . . imperialism. Before the Games even began the whole vocabulary of world dissension had attached itself to the one event designed to foster international goodwill.

There were other, less dramatic forces undermining the Olympics.

When I stepped off the plane in Mexico City, the foreign press bombarded me with questions. "How many gold medals this time, Don?" I replied that I was only swimming in two events, but on the bus into town I began thinking about those questions.

The emphasis on an individual gold medal count was already much more extreme that year than it had been in 1964. For two weeks the press had been talking up a gold medal count as though it were the only reason for the whole deal. And, at least in part, I was a cause of it because of those four gold medals I had won in Tokyo.

Then I thought about Karen Muir, the world-record holder from South Africa, who couldn't even come to the Olympics because of politics. I knew that these Olympics couldn't be the same for me. In a strange way, however, the 1968 Games did become very important in my life.

Perhaps it was because I was older now and because over the past four years I had seen so much. Perhaps it was because this time I knew what to expect and was looking for it. I know that it was partly because this time I was only swimming two events, in which I became increasingly less interested. At any rate I spent very little time thinking about myself and my races and a great deal of time thinking about what was obviously happening to the Olympics and where it would lead.

It came as no surprise to me that nationalism and politics were riding high again. With hardly a lost day the arguments began. The East Germans wanted to be called the Democratic People's Republic of Germany (the country's official name); West Germany didn't seem to care much what it was called. The men on the International Olympics Committee just called both sides Germany. The North Koreans, who were referred to simply as North Koreans, protested that they were the Democratic Republic of North Korea.

The pressure by nations on their athletes to win was running amok. For the first time that year, there were to be tests for drugs. The same as with a racehorse, that little pill can drive you harder and harder to win, win, win.

Also that year there were chromosome tests to decide whether the women competitors were really women. One Polish contestant failed the test and was said to be in a state of despair. There was a rash of scratched entries, especially among the women from the iron-curtain countries.

Mexico was caught in the gold medal fever. With the Olympics in their own country, it was a matter of saving face. They pinned their hopes on their swimming star, Guillermo Echeverria, who held the world record in the 1500-meter freestyle. He was swimming the 1500 and the 400, too, and the Mexicans believed that he would become their first Olympic gold medal winner in swimming. My teammate Mike Wall and I used to talk about how unfair this was because, according to our calculations, the guy just wasn't going to make it. But the Mexicans had pinned their hopes on him and the poor guy was under unbelievable pressure. Later, when he lost, it was terrible.

In short, the beautiful Olympic "spirit" was everywhere. East Germans were avoiding West Germans; Czechs were avoiding Russians. The press stepped up the gold medal predictions. There was a rumor —unverified—that a Japanese runner had committed suicide because his country was counting on him and he knew he couldn't win.

The biggest problem for the U. S. Olympic Committee had been the black athletes. At the time of the threatened boycott the USOC appointed a board of consultants to act as a liaison between the athletes and the committee. The board was made up of some very good men, including former Olympic athletes Jesse Owens, Billy Mills and John Sayers of *Pace* magazine. These men cared about the problems and were sensitive to the needs of the athletes.

Once the boycott threat had passed, there was no real reason for these men to be in Mexico except that they had already been invited. For their part, these consultants decided that they wanted to stay in touch with the athletes.

Many of them, especially Sayers, Owens and Mills, knew that the black athletes were still unhappy, and they knew that there were other problems, too. They decided to hear the athletes out—listen to all the complaints that no officials ever heard—and then make recommendations to the U.S. and International Olympic Committees.

Out of the thousands of people at the Olympics who should have known—officials, coaches, athletes—I felt that three consultants were the only ones who sensed, as I did, how wrong things were going and how close to the end it might be.

The men on the IOC honestly didn't know ahead of time about the problems that blew up in their faces. In the Olympic Village we knew that the black athletes were still searching for some way to express their feelings. They never did agree on a single plan and in the end they left it to each man to do his own thing. Some wore Afro-American clothes. Some spent a lot of time hanging around the entrance to the Village, to keep their protest in evidence. Some kept completely apart, segregating themselves from the rest of us. And later, Tommie Smith and John Carlos bowed their heads and raised black-gloved hands during the raising of the American flag.

Actually there wasn't nearly as much excitement about this in the Olympic Village as there was outside it. We knew how committed Smith and Carlos were to these problems. We knew that they were going to compete and try to win and we knew, too, that they felt they had to make some kind of a gesture. The public made a lot out of it and it was a big item with the news media.

But apparently the IOC had no idea that anything was going to happen. And when it did, the members were stunned. They got excited and said that Smith and Carlos had embarrassed not only the United States, but Mexico and the whole Olympic movement. In the Village we heard that all the fuss that followed originated with the IOC—that it told the U. S. Committee to kick out Smith and Carlos or the entire American team would be disqualified and sent home. That put the USOC in a bind. It ordered Smith and Carlos out of the Olympic Village and within three days the two guys were back in the United States.

When you come right down to it, whatever you may think about Smith and Carlos, if Russia could protest against South Africa and if the IOC respected the protest enough to keep South Africa out, then why couldn't Smith and Carlos protest? But the real tragedy was that both protests were dragging something into the Olympic Games that didn't belong there.

Another problem that blew up at the 1968 Olympics that the IOC men seemed to know nothing about was the payoffs. For days we in the Village had been hearing that Mexico City was crawling with manufacturers' representatives who were ready to make payoffs to athletes if they would agree to use their equipment in Olympic competition. We heard that they were slipping $500 in cash under the table to athletes of all countries. Later we heard that the sum was $1,500.

In the Village nobody doubted that money was changing hands under the table. The IOC, alone, did not know. When the rumors finally caught up with its members, they set up a howl of righteous indignation and announced that there would be a thorough investigation.

Did it ever occur to them, I wondered, to consider how much they had contributed to the situation by their failure to adjust to the times? Many of these athletes had jobs, especially the track men. Many were also married and had children. To compete in the Olympics, they had to leave their jobs for at least two months—six weeks of training and two weeks at the Games. That meant, in most cases, two months without pay. Add to that the money they had to shell out over the years just to keep up with their sport and the time they had put in for years, training twenty hours a week or more, when they could have been earning extra money instead. Even the college students have to sacrifice a semester of college to compete, plus spare time during which they could have been earning money. The Olympic Committee reimburses them for none of this—not even for lost salaries while they compete. And then it expects them not to take payoffs.

The simple fact is that when a man has worked so hard for so many years, with every legitimate opportunity to make money closed to him, and someone offers him $1,500 under the table, the temptation to take it is almost irresistible.

The IOC has a limited idea of just how much amateur sports have changed and the size of the personal investment the amateur and his family must make for years if he is to reach the top and stay there. The goal of the IOC is still the preservation of an amateurism that in my opinion no longer exists.

> "The most important thing in the Olympic Games is not to win but to take part, just as the most important thing in life is not the triumph but the struggle. The essential thing is not to have conquered but to have fought well."
>
> The Olympic Creed

Somebody had to call attention to what was happening to the Olympic movement. I decided that I was the one to do it.

My campaign in electing myself was based on four points. First, I was probably the best-known figure at the 1968 Olympics, so if I did something, people would notice. Second, for four years I had had the opportunity to see a great deal of the world of amateur sports. Less successful athletes do not have so much exposure to its problems, and sometimes the better athletes are beguiled by the preferential treatment they receive and fail to see the hard facts beneath the surface. I felt that I had the chance to see what was going on and that I understood it and cared. Third, I felt that in four years at Yale I had acquired enough mental discipline to think the problem through honestly, and that I had become articulate enough to say what had to be said. And, fourth, I felt that I had a debt to pay. The games had meant so much to me. I felt I wanted to do this as partial repayment for all the Olympics had given to me.

I found Mike Wall and told him, "I think I'm going to quit. I'm going to call a press conference tomorrow and make a speech to tell them everything I've been thinking about the Olympic movement." Mike knew what I was talking about; we'd been discussing it all week. "And then as a protest, I'm going to retire immediately, before the games begin."

I felt very strongly that I should make this gesture. I had had plenty of glory in 1964 and glory didn't mean much to me anymore. That night I started to write the speech. I stayed up until two o'clock that night and got up at six the next morning—Friday, the day before the opening ceremonies. I wanted to do it that day, before the Games began. I didn't want to steal the limelight from any individual performances during the Games, and I didn't think it would be nearly so effective if I waited until the Games were over.

When Mike got up we talked about it again—whether it was the right thing to do, whether it would possibly work, what the repercussions might be. I knew I would have to give my speech and leave Mexico City. I was concerned about the effect it would have on my parents; they had not yet arrived in Mexico City. I remember that Mike and I discussed whether people would see me only as someone who deserted the Olympic team the day before the Games began, or just as a dreamer who had thrown away his name, his career, his reputation for a totally unrealistic ideal. If I couldn't pull this off, I would have a very bad name. But I felt I could do it. And I felt I had to do it.

Then we talked about George Haines, the men's coach of the U.S. swimming team. I felt I owed it to George to tell him before I made the speech.

I found him in his room and handed him the speech. He was so tired he looked sick. I thought, "Why doesn't he get out of this business? Obviously he doesn't enjoy it anymore."

George read all the way through the speech twice. Then he looked at me and said, "Don, if you do this, I think I'll pack my bags and go home before the Olympics even begin."

As soon as he said that, I knew there was just no way I would be able to make that speech.

For a long time George talked to me, giving me the reasons why I shouldn't do it—that I would create such a sensation that the Olympics would end right then and there, that I couldn't pull this off alone, that I should work through the AAU and the Olympic movement. I hardly heard him; to me his reasons didn't make sense. The thing I kept thinking over and over was that George was tired, disheartened and sick and that he had said he would go home. I felt that this would be the final blow—and I couldn't do it to him.

This is the speech I didn't make:

"I have asked you to come here today—the day before the Olympics begin—in order to announce my retirement from the sport of swimming, from the United States Olympic Team and from the 1968 Olympic Games as of today, October 11. It is with deep personal sorrow that I announce this decision. Yet I feel this is something I must do. . . .

"Ever since the Tokyo Olympics I have been growing more and more disturbed about the direction in which sports and, especially, the Olympics movement are going. For almost a year, controversy and crisis have surrounded these 1968 Games. For two weeks here in Mexico City, I have watched the spirit of this nineteenth Olympiad and have compared it to the original spirit of the Olympic Games.

"The Olympic Games are intended to be an athletic contest for people from all over the world, competing against each other in the best spirit of competition, in the hope that politics, ideologies, racial and religious prejudices will be cast aside. It is intended that individuals will compete as individuals and come to understand each other as individuals, not as Russians or Americans or Africans.

"Mexico has intended to host a cultural and sporting event for the entire world to promote understanding and brotherhood, peace and goodwill. . . . What has happened and what is happening now is very far removed from this Olympic ideal.

"I am not trying to lead a rebellion. I am trying to bring about an honest, sincere reevaluation of the Olympic spirit which has been killed by people who have lost sight of its potential and its goals.

"I feel that the very future of the Olympics is at stake. . . . No matter how much we may disagree with any nation or sympathize with any people, the Olympics must not be used as an instrument of politics.

"As we get further and further away from the Olympic ideal, the risk of the Olympics being discontinued increases. The fault lies with nearly everyone—officials, national leaders, the athletes themselves who, too often, are concerned only with winning. I, too, have wanted to win. And I still have respect for excellence. I think the athletes are less to blame than anyone else. I have seen them at night in the international center, making attempts to communicate with each other in spite of language barriers. Every night they try to exchange pins, listen to each other's music and laugh together at the Village auditorium. They are at least trying—and this is what the Olympics is all about.

"You people of the news media, with your gold medal counts and trumped-up rivalries, are partly to blame. And the people who pay athletes to promote the sports products that they manufacture and even the general public are at fault. Everyone, to some degree, shares in the guilt.

"The Olympic Games should be open to everyone who qualifies, regardless of race, religion or color, whether professional or amateur, no matter what country he is from. This is a competition for individuals and the only person who is hurt by politics entering into the Games is the athlete himself. Many of you will say that I am naive to think that in the world as it is today we can still believe in an antiquated Olympic ideal. But somehow, something must be done.

"If we hope to contribute to world peace through sports and through the Olympic Games, we cannot permit the present trends to continue. We must act now to change the direction of the Olympic movement. We must recognize what is going on. We must rethink our purpose. We must put the Olympics back on course. It is the only way we can preserve the Olympics and the contribution it can make to international understanding and goodwill.

"My action is not intended as a boycott. It is not intended to embarrass anyone. I apologize to the people of the United States and to the people of Mexico. I am trying to save something that I truly believe is worth saving and that I feel is more important than any personal success I might gain. I only hope that something constructive will come out of my protest, and that my actions will not have been in vain."

I still think it's something that should have been said. Later it was too late and I was never able to say it until now. And I'm sorry.

The next day the nineteenth Olympiad began—with student activists in the fields around the stadium and armed soldiers in front of it.

Two weeks later I swam my first race as anchor man on the 800-meter relay team. I turned in a very fast time—1:54.6—and the event gave me my first and last gold medal. Even I was surprised at how fast I swam and by the next day, in the individual 200, I had slowed down. Also, by the next day I was telling myself with joy, "My last race." The race went to Mike Wendon of Australia: I came in second at 1:55.8.

I would have liked to go out a winner but at the closing ceremonies that was not very much on my mind. I kept thinking how glad I was that it was over. And then I began to think about all the other things while I looked at those blindly optimistic words: "Munich 1972."

I suppose it is unrealistic to think that the direction the Olympics has taken can be reversed. To do that nations and individuals—both athletes and coaches—would have to change. And how are you going to tell an individual to compete for the sake of competition when his government orders him or woos him to compete to win? How do you tell nations to be less nationalistic?

I think there are places to start. Certain things have crept into the Olympic ceremonies that shouldn't be there. When the medals are awarded, the flag of the winning country is raised and strains of its national anthem are played—every time. This has a propaganda effect which tends to intensify nationalistic rivalries. It should be eliminated and the medal should be awarded to the individual alone, not to his country. This would make it harder to squeeze propaganda out of the victory. Certainly the press could still find out the national origin of the winner and countries could keep tallies and publicize the news, but I think eliminating the nationalistic aspects from the ceremonies would have a psychologically cooling effect.

This would at least be a start. Once we recognized that this deflation of the nationalistic balloon was a healthy thing, we would begin to find other ways. Then victories wouldn't be worth quite so much to a nation and the Olympics might again become what it was intended to be.

SPORTS AND POLITICS

Sir Arnold Lund

The practice of the Free World, so far as sport and politics is concerned, bears much the same relation to the principles which they profess as the practice of the Allies when the war was won to the principles which they sonorously proclaimed while the war was being waged. The fate of Poland surrendered to a dictatorship as foul as that of the Nazis by Allies who claimed to be fighting to liberate Europe from tyranny is a case in point. Similiar sacrifices of principle to expediency are no less common in sport. My own examples are taken from skiing. It would be easy to parallel them from other sports.

The Federation International de Ski, usually referred to as the FIS, was founded in 1924 at a time when the dominant political fashion in Europe was Liberalism in the best sense of that much abused word. (I once defined a Liberal as a man who objects to the persecution of conservatives. There are few such Liberals.) Under the original rules of the FIS the Austrian Ski Association was declared ineligible to be the representative of Austria because that Association would not affiliate any club which admitted Jews, and Austria was therefore represented in the FIS by a delegation which included representatives of clubs which admitted Jews. When the Nazis came into power I circulated to the committee of the FIS, of which I was a member, a memorandum pointing out that under our rules the Nazi Ski organization was ineligible for membership of the FIS. The only effect of my memorandum was to expedite a rapid change of the FIS rule which penalized anti-semitism.

When the Nazis were in power the Olympic Committee paid them

From *Quest,* Monograph I (December, 1963), pp. 33-36. Copyright © 1963 *Quest* Board (The National Association for Physical Education of College Women and The National College Physical Education Association for Men). Tucson, Arizona.

the greatest of compliments by entrusting Nazi Germany, in which religious and racial persecution had begun, with the organization of the Olympic Games. I hated everything for which the Nazis stood, but not enough to stay away from the Games, in which the Slalom which I invented, was for the first time included, and which I had been asked to referee.

Two years later the Nazis marched into Austria just before the race meeting which I had founded with Hannes Schneider, the Arlberg-Kandahar, was to be held. Schneider was a great patriot who hated the Nazis and he was put into a concentration camp. The Kandahar Ski Club, the mother club of Downhill and Slalom racing, promptly cancelled the Arlberg-Kandahar. The Kandahar was the only ski club to break with the Nazis and the first ski club of any belligerent country to invite post-war Germans to compete. It was in the Arlberg-Kandahar of 1950 that Frenchmen first raced against German skiers.

The first post-war Congress of the FIS was held at Pau in 1946. The doctrine that politics must be kept out of sport was put into cold storage. Whereas the World of Sport had paid the Nazis the greatest possible compliment by holding the Olympic Games in Nazi Germany, the Germany which had repudiated the Nazis was excluded from the Olympic Games of 1948, and from the World Ski Championship of 1950; and it was not until 1951 that the Germans were once again admitted to the FIS. The FIS Congress of 1946 excluded Germany because the West Germans *had been* ruled by a dictator. The FIS Congress of 1951, and the majority of the leading international sport federations, admitted East Germany, which retained the worst features of Nazism. The creation of the East German puppet state was an act of aggression as naked and unjustified as Hitler's annexation of Czecho-Slovakia. East Germany was only admitted by the bare majority of one vote, and the three British votes would have been cast against admission *if* the British had been present at the FIS Congress of 1951. Why were they not present?

At the 1949 FIS Congress the Russians applied for admission to the FIS. The "application" was coupled with many demands of which the most impudent was that the Spanish Ski Association should be expelled. Here was an opportunity for those who really believe that politics should be kept out of sport to make a spirited protest, an opportunity of which only the Ski Club of Great Britain availed itself. Obviously if the Spanish Ski Association should be expelled because Spain is not a democracy, the Russians should be excluded for a similar reason. I therefore persuaded the FIS Council that we should admit no discussion of the Russian proposal to expel the Spanish Ski Association, and the

Russian delegate was duly informed by the President of our decision. He ignored our ruling and neither he nor the Czech, Hungarian, and Polish representatives were called to order when they made violent attacks on Spain. The Russian was subsequently elected to the Council whose ruling he had defied and, as I do not choose to belong to governing bodies which cannot govern, I resigned and as a mark of our displeasure there were no British at the next Congress.

I do not for one moment mean to suggest that the skiing world was more craven in its attitude to dictators than other sportsmen or, for that matter, than the Western world in general. What I have defined as "selective indignation," that is condoning in one group what one condemns in another group, is the dominant weakness of modern political thinking and the skiers were not unique in condoning in a dicatorship as vile as Hitler's what they had condemned in the Nazis after and only after the Nazis had been crushed.

The slogan "sport has nothing to do with politics" is always invoked to justify surrender to totalitarians, but it was not a *political* difference which separated civilized people from the Nazis and Communists. In civilized countries politicians are not divided into those who do and those who do not advocate genocide, as practiced both by the Nazis in their liquidation of the Jews and by the Communists in their liquidation of whole classes who opposed them, the Kulaks for instance. The gulf which separates civilized people from Nazis or Communists is the same gulf which separated the Hellenes from the Barbarians. The classic Olympic Games were restricted to the Hellenes, to those who in the words of Herodotus, had "common temples and sacrifices and like ways of life" for the Greeks knew that sport was part of a way of life. When I gave the Lowell Lectures on "Sport and Society" it was easy to show that sport does not exist in a vacuum and that codes of sport are the product of the prevailing philosophy, the Greek code *Aidos* being as organically related to Greek religion as Chivalry to Christianity and the sport code of Nazis and Communists to their revolting Philosophies.

In the modern world sport has a prestige and an influence comparable to that of the Church in medieval Europe and the Olympic Committee should have the same power as has the medieval Church to place a country which offends against the basic laws of humanity under an interdict. The Hellenes refused to compete against Barbarians and were right. While the last sparks of heroic resistance were being extinguished by Russian tanks in Budapest I saw a photograph in the Press of American and Russian athletes exchanging jokes during the Olympic Games in Australia. It made me sick.

The Dutch Olympic competitors and the Swiss gave the money which been collected for the teams to the Hungarian refugees and stayed at home. That is the kind of gesture which really counts. I am tired of people who merely *profess* a detestation of tyranny. Generous sentiments are two a penny, but a young athlete who gives up the glory of representing his country and a free trip across the world because he refuses to meet the Russians in sport has *proved* his devotion to those ideals which we all profess.

I know all the arguments for continuing to compete against the Communists and some have force, but only for those who acquiesce in the fact that nearly a third of the inhabitants of this planet are in the power of ruthless tyrants. I have been at pains to discover whether a boycott of Communist countries in sport until such time as they are prepared to show respect for human rights would achieve anything and all those who are in a position to know assure me that such a boycott would achieve surprising results. Unfortunately the overwhelming majority of my own countrymen and of Americans assume that they have paid their debt to the victims of communism by the correctness of their sentiments on the theme of democracy.

SPORT, POLITICS AND INTERNATIONALISM

Peter C. McIntosh

In 1956 the armed conflicts in Hungary and Suez caused six nations to withdraw from the Olympic Games which were to be held in Melbourne, Australia. Mr. Avery Brundage, President of the International Olympic Committe commented: "By their decisions these countries show that they are unaware of one of our most important principles, namely that sport is completely free of politics." A superficial glance into the past is enough to show that very seldom has sport been free of politics. Certainly Baron de Coubertin did not see sport completely free of politics when he founded the modern Olympic Games. On the contrary, he hoped that sporting activities might improve the political relationships between nations. He addressed a circular to the governing bodies of sport in January, 1894, expressing the hope that every four years the athletic representatives of the world might be brought together and that the spirit of international unity might be advanced by the celebration of their chivalrous and peaceful contests. If sport was to influence politics it was hardly conceivable that the interaction should be in one direction only and that politics should have no bearing at all upon sport. The naïveté of Mr. Brundage's statement, however, must not be allowed to obscure the relationship between sport and politics which is felt to exist by many people besides the members of the I.O.C.

The relationship may turn bad in at least two ways, by too much interaction and by the debasement of either one of the two agents. The injection of too much sport into politics might reduce the most serious of human activities to puerilism, while the seriousness of politics, if carried into sport in too great measure, could destroy its playfulness and so change its very nature. Again, corruption in sport might lead to corrupt pressure being brought to bear upon local or national politicians which could harmfully affect the life of the community. The greater danger, however, is from corruption acting in the opposite direction. If the political life of a community is corrupt or is organized for unworthy or inhumane ends then it will hardly be possible for sport to remain unaffected; it will be harnessed, however loosely, to the same unworthy ends. The ideals of sportsmen may for a while pull the polity back or slow down its regress but observation of Germany in the 1930s and of South Africa in the decades since World War II suggests that sportsmen share the corrupt political and social ideas of their community in about the same measure as other citizens. Even if they do not share those ideals they tolerate them and their application to sport in order to be able to continue to play. There is at least one noble exception to this generalization which ought not to pass unnoticed. When in 1848, the German State of Baden attempted to implement a liberal constitution, Prussia and the other big states at once invaded Baden. The provisional government appealed for help to oppose the aggressors. The *Hanau Turnverein* sent three hundred armed gymnasts, who increased their number to six hundred *en route*. For a time they held out against the best-trained army in Europe. The end was inevitable. Some escaped to Switzerland. The rest were killed in action or shot as rebels after capture. The collapse of the political movement for a united, free and democratic Germany caused many gymnasts to flee across the Atlantic. In America they reestablished their clubs. Their liberal ideals caused them to declare forcefully in favour of the abolition of slavery. They supported Abraham Lincoln politically and then enlisted in the armies of the North in considerable numbers.

Sport has certain characteristics which perhaps impel it more readily than other human activities towards an association with politics. Sport, especially competitive sport tends to identify the individual with some group and the individual welcomes this identity. Even the lone runner cannot escape his association with club or town, county or country. The member of a team inevitably sinks some of his individuality in the group. In the great age of sports development the extent to which the individual was submerged was an indication of merit in a game or sport. The young master in *Tom Brown's Schooldays* was made to say about cricket: "The discipline and reliance in one another which it teaches is so valuable, I think. It ought to be such an unselfish game. It merges the individual in the eleven; he doesn't play that he may win, but that his side may," to which Tom replies: "That's very true and that's why football and cricket, now one comes to think of it, are such much better games than fives or hare and hounds, or any others where the object is to come in first or to win for oneself and not that one's side may win."

The political significance of discipline, reliance on one another, and merging the individual in the group was not lost upon educators and statesmen in Victorian England. Furthermore, competitive sport fitted in well with the Victorian pattern of industrial and political rivalry. A belief in collisions, collisions of political parties, religious sects, industrial firms and teams of sportsmen was the light to illumine the broad road of social progress.

The merging of the individual in the group was not confined to the players themselves but to some extent was experienced by those who watched and those who shared a common club membership, a geographical location, or a racial affinity with the performers. In the later nineteenth century the growth of urban areas was so rapid and so amorphous as almost to smother the individual's sense of belonging to any group larger than the family, but on Saturday afternoons he could at least identify himself and his interest with those of eleven figures on the football field as he took his place on the terraces with thousands of others. Some transference of identity from local club to local government almost certainly helped the growth of civic sense and pride in cities such as Birmingham and Manchester. Local politicians who advocated measures to encourage or promote sport did so in the realization that they were helping the political development of their great towns.

In the United States the influence of sport on politics has been considerable. The line taken by German-American gymnasts has already been noted. In a broader sphere sport gave cohesion to a great variety of immigrants with different racial, religious and political backgrounds. It developed in America at about the same time as in Britain, in the latter part of the nineteenth century. Success quickly became an important matter of local prestige, and often the local representatives would be the high school or college; it thus united in rivalry different communities and townships. If the immigrants themselves retained some of their cultural isolation their sons found sport an easy avenue to the American way of life.

Success in sport was important to Americans and it is to their credit that in a community with a history of racial discrimination the racial complexion of the performer was not allowed to prevent his rise to the top in sport. He could represent his town, his state, his country if he were good enough. In boxing the negro Jack Johnson was heavyweight champion of the world from 1908 to 1915 at a time when the heroes of the American negro were almost all in sport because here could he meet and beat the white man on equal terms. Johnson himself in vaunting his superiority left a legacy of hatred. By 1937 the inarticulate and shy Joe Louis, the next negro heavyweight champion, was as beloved by white men as by negroes. In 1962 Floyd Patterson, the third of a great line, could write; "For myself I can truthfully say I feel no differently inside if I am fighting a white man or another negro." Later in that year he lost the world heavyweight title to the fourth negro to hold it, Liston.

In the Olympic Games many negroes have represented the United States with distinction. When in 1936 at the Olympic Games in Berlin Hitler refused to receive Jesse Owens because he was a negro after his great victories on the track, the action of the Führer was taken by Americans as an insult to them all.

North of the forty-ninth parallel the Canadians, with their federal constitution, provincial autonomy and large self-conscious minority population of French Canadians, have long experienced the lack of a sense of nationhood. In 1962 a government campaign for fitness and sport was launched by the Minister of National Health and Welfare who included this significant remark in his speech to Parliament: "Canadian participation in international competitive events is emerging as an important aspect of a growing spirit of nationhood."

Sport then has been found to be a cohesive agent and in countries where it is the policy of governments to keep a people divided as in South Africa or in Germany the community of interest in sport between different racial or political groups has been an embarrassment to the politicians.

In the planned societies of communist countries the interaction of sport and politics is deliberately carried a long way and the interaction is from politics to sport rather than in the opposite direction. At first, after the October revolution of 1917, the communist government in Russia took no official interest in sport. In 1925, however, sport was officially recognized and encouraged and in 1930-1 a number of tests in games and sports were instituted leading to the award of G.T.O. Badges ("Ready for Labour and Defence"). Sport was organized under an All Union Committee of Sport and Physical Culture, a government organ responsible to the Council of Ministers of the U.S.S.R. From then onwards there was no suggestion in communist countries that sport was or ought to be "free of politics." On the contrary, sport and training for sport were used extensively for political education so that it became impossible to train as a coach without instruction in Marxism-Leninism and it was impossible to compete in a stadium great or small without being bombarded with the political slogans and ideas of the government of the day. Many sports meetings were organized by political organizations for political purposes.

In countries where sport is organized piecemeal by voluntary bodies and is, to all appearances, independent of political organization and indoctrination, it cannot be inferred that interaction between sport and politics does not take place. The difference is rather in the pattern of organization rather than in the presence of absence of interaction. The pattern of sport in Eastern and Western Germany exemplifies extremes of political organization.

All the German sports organizations were dissolved by order of the Control Commission after the war ended in 1945. In East Germany the government party then decreed that anyone who wished to take part in sport must do so as a member either of the new political youth organization (F.J.D.) or of the workers organization (F.D.G.B.). In 1948 the *Deutscher Sportausschuss* was set up with an avowed political aim. This was followed in 1952 by a State Committee for Sport and Physical Culture.

By contrast, in the Western Zone the *Deutscher Sportsbund* was set up in 1950 with the stated object of solving its problems without reference to party political, religious, racial or military considerations. The establishment of the *Sportsbund* was the result of efforts to find an organization which would enable sportsmen to govern themselves and pursue their interests without control or interference from the government.

Whatever may have been the differing patterns of organization of sport the interest of government organs in West Germany has been no less than in the East. In 1960 the German Olympic Association published a *Memorandum on the "Golden Plan" for Health, Sport and Recreation.* The Golden Plan was based on nation-wide surveys of sports facilities and asked for expenditure of £568,900,000 (6,315,000,000 D.M.) over fifteen years. The first four years were to be used in building up a combined federal and provincial government expenditure of £28,000,000 in direct grants to local communities. By 1961 grant aid from government sources already totalled £13,500,000 (150,000,000 D.M.) or forty-eight per cent of the target for 1964.[1]

To a greater or lesser degree the governments of all western European countries and many others besides now finance sport for their people, all but three of the European countries drawing the revenue to do so from football pools. In Great Britain annual direct aid to sport from the government in 1962 still amounted to no more than £670,000 and that sum was reached only after the Chancellor of the Exchequer had announced an increase of £200,000 on the original sum budgeted. The Wolfenden Committee Report, comparable in some ways to the German Golden Plan but much more modest, had asked for £10,000,000.

Undoubtedly the parsimonious treatment of sport by the British Government has been largely the result of firmly held beliefs that financial aid would involve government interference and that interaction between politics and sport must stop well short of this point. The same beliefs caused the Wolfenden Committee to reject vigorously the suggestion that there should be established a new Department of State called the Ministry of Sport. Yet the Ministry of Education is already, within limitations, a Ministry of Sport. It accepts or rejects all plans for new schools and colleges and so determines the facilities which are provided there for sport in school and out. It provides some of the money for their construction; it sets limits on expenditure on sport by local authorities, it makes a small grant, already mentioned, to voluntary organizations. It helps to finance the coaching schemes of governing bodies of sport and it helps to maintain three national recreation centres. Where sport is educational, and, broadly speaking, is being taught or learned rather than played for its own sake the Ministry of Education already exercises the functions of a Ministry of Sport by permitting, assisting, controlling, inspecting and, some would say, by interfering. When sport is educational it is considered worthy of political direction and some measure of control, but when sport becomes an end in itself it has so far ceased, in Britain, to be an activity which is appropriate for political support.

There have been three occasions when the political disinterestedness of the British Government has been breached. In 1927 the Air Ministry entered an official team for the Schneider Trophy Air Race. It did so again in 1929 and 1931. The race was at this time an international sporting contest, nothing more, and the intervention of the British Government in a sporting event preceded similar intervention by any other government of whatever political complexion. In 1954 the British Government once again broke its principle of non-participation in the world of sport. Roger Bannister had just become the first man to run the mile in less than four minutes. The Foreign Office sent him on a "good will" visit to the United States in order to improve Anglo-American relations.

In January, 1963, the British Prime Minister, having rejected the recommendation of the Wolfenden Committee for a Sports Development Council with funds to allocate, assigned to Lord Hailsham the task of co-ordinating the aid given to sport and recreation by different Government departments, such as the Ministries of Education, Health, and Housing and Local Government. It looked as if Lord Hailsham was to be in fact but not in name a Minister of Sport. At almost the same time there appeared on the horizon a cloud no bigger than a man's hand in the form of a small sum in the estimates of the Commonwealth Relations Office, a government Ministry, to meet a deficit which had been incurred by the British Empire and Commonwealth Games organization in participating in the Games in Western Australia in November, 1962. Whether this was a precedent of political significance was not clear at the time.

It is in the international sphere that the modern development of sport has most significant political implications, for it is here that the hazard to the true nature of sport is most acute and it is here that sport may make its most significant contribution to human welfare and sanity. The rise of international sport has been meteoric. The America's Cup race instituted in 1857 for friendly competition by yachts of different countries was probably the first modern international sporting contest of any consequence. Before the end of the century other international events had appeared, but at the first modern Olympic Games in 1896 there was only thirteen competing nations. In 1960 the number was eighty-four and it has been during the first sixty years of the twentieth century that international sport has come into real prominence.

One of the most considerable achievements has been the setting up of International Federations for the organization and control of individual sports. In sports where times and distances can be measured it soon became necessary to have a body to ratify records so that the claimant to a record could enjoy world-wide acceptance and recognition. In all competitive sports, however, as competitors from one country met those from other countries it became necessary to agree upon the rules and the eligibility of competitors to ensure even competition. The desire for this international competition at all levels of ability became so strong and so widespread that differences of language, of local practice, of social and educational background and of political outlook were not allowed to stand in the way of agreement on an essential basis for competition. Federations were set up for athletics, football, swimming, lawn tennis and many other sports. From the start the decisions of these bodies enjoyed a remarkable acceptance and obedience from constituent bodies all over the world. Whatever defects there may be in international sport there have at least been forms of democratic world government which have had tolerable success within their own limited jurisdictions. Since 1960 there has also been an International Council of Sport and Physical Education under the aegis of UNESCO which was already in 1962 beginning to bring together the international federations and organizations of teachers, coaches and leaders in a further limited world organization.

The desire for international competition is not confined to the richer and more highly developed countries but is shared by these countries which might be thought to be preoccupied with the basic needs for survival. A complete analysis of participants in the Olympic Games of 1952 was carried out in Helsinki and showed that one hundred and sixty competitors came from countries so poor that the annual *per capita* income was less than $100. Rich countries with a *per capita* income of more than $750 sent one hundred and ninety-four competitors.[2]

The best performers anywhere want to test their skill against the best from elsewhere, but because at international level the best performer emerges some of his identity in the nation itself, whether he wants to do so or not, success in sport has political importance. This is true for the emergent nation as well as for the more highly developed countries. In February, 1959, the Indian Parliament debated a motion expressing concern at the deterioration of Indian sports, especially cricket. The motion was provoked by the previous failures of the Indian cricket team in the West Indies. One Member of Parliament suggested that no Indian team should be sent abroad for five years, to enable them to improve their standards. Canada, at the other end of the national income scale, launched a government campaign for fitness and amateur sport in 1962 in full recognition that "those who compete in the Olympic Games, the British Empire and Commonwealth Games, the Pan American Games and other international championship games are ambassadors of good will for Canada." The Prime Minister expressed the hope that the programme would add not only to the happiness and health of all people of Canada but to the international athletic prestige of Canada.

Direct intervention by a Head of State in sport because of its international and political significance took place in December, 1962. At that time in the United States disagreement between two rival governing bodies of sport, the Amateur Athletic Union and the National Collegiate Athletic Association, reached a climax. The Attorney-General failed to reconcile the two bodies. President Kennedy himself warned the American People in a Press conference on 12th December that the United States might not be represented at the next Olympic Games if the two factions refused arbitration. He said: "The governing bodies of these groups apparently put their own interests before the interests of our athletes, our traditions of sport and our country. The time has come for these groups to put the national interest first. Their continued bickering is grossly unfair. On behalf of the country and on behalf of sport I call on the organizations to submit their differences to an arbitration panel immediately." These were strong words, but the political importance of the statement lay not so much in the words used as in the fact that directions were given by the President of the United States to voluntary sports organizations which realized less clearly than he did their own inescapable political responsibilities.

Communist countries have long openly regarded their sporting representatives as political emissaries who can do more than diplomats to recommend the communist philosophy and way of life to those who have not adopted it. East and west sportsmen, whether they like it or not, are "ambassadors of good will" and are under pressure to vindicate not merely their own prowess but the ideology of their country. There are few governments in the world which do not now accept the political importance of success in international sport.

The desire to win is sometimes so strong that sport cannot contain it; when this natural human desire is reinforced with political pressures it is small wonder that on occasion the structure of the sporting event bursts assunder. It was argued in an earlier chapter that play is an essential element in all sport if it is to retain its intrinsic value, and that play implies a defined area of unreality in which the rules of ordinary life are superseded for the time being. It is possible for very great tension to be built up in a game or contest without the illusion of unreality being shattered. Often, however, it is shattered in international sports. A game of ice hockey may develop into an unregulated fist fight as it did in the Winter Olympic Games at Squaw Valley in 1960. A game of water polo may turn into a bloodbath as it did in the Olympic Games in Melbourne in 1956. Cricket or football matches may be destroyed as sporting events by bottles thrown by spectators. On these occasions the illusion is shattered and the contest has all the aggression, humiliation and bitterness of real life.

On the other side of the balance sheet there are many occasions when "strife without anger and art without malice" are maintained in the most intense competition. There have been numerous occasions at the Olympic Games when competitors from different ideologic blocks, even from countries in open hostility with each other have stood on the victor's rostrum, to receive their medals. Their nations' flags are flying, while the whole crowd stands to do honour to them. These moments and many honourable and friendly contests, unnoticed by the Press of the world, nevertheless enhance the dignity of man.

While competitors and spectators sometimes fail to sustain the unreality of sport, there are from time to time political forces which seek to destroy it. There is no reason in any sport why those who know and accept agreed rules and who have the necessary skill should not play together, yet in South Africa black and white races are not permitted to play together for fear of breaching the political doctrine of apartheid. In Europe, too, the political division of Berlin and the tension there in 1962 led to restrictions on movement between communist and non-communist countries which implied that no international sport would be possible between the two blocks.

In both these situations there was interaction from sport to politics as well as from politics to sport. The South African Olympic Committee was warned that it would be suspended by the International Olympic Committee if the South African government persisted with racial discrimination in sport. In the European situation the I.O.C. in March, 1962, stated that the Olympic Games would be held only in cities which would guarantee free access for all recognized teams. As no city in a country of the North Atlantic Treaty Organization would be permitted to admit East Germans, all these countries were debarred from holding the Olympic Games until they agreed to recognize the special and "unreal" nature of sport. The International Council for Sport and Physical Education urged UNESCO to try urgently to secure that the youth of the whole world and its officials might meet freely in sport. The Council cancelled its own general assembly which was to be held in Manila because the Government of the Philippines would not guarantee entry to delegates from communist countries.

The essential nature of sport is in danger internationally not only from restriction but also from domination by the two great power blocks, the U.S.A. and the U.S.S.R. It is inevitable in the present situation that they should be more than anxious for success and that this anxiety should be shared by their citizens and allies. In 1962 both global and local wars are likely to be suicidal ways of influencing people and winning support, and sport as a means of influence has assumed correspondingly greater political importance. The situation was analyzed in essence by Arnold Toynbee in 1948. In *Civilization on Trial* he wrote: "Communism is a competitor [with the West] for the allegiance of that great majority of mankind that is neither communist nor capitalist, neither Russian nor Western but is living at present in an uneasy no man's land between the opposing citadels of two rival ideologies. Both nondescripts and Westerners are in danger of turning communist today, as they were of turning Turk four hundred years ago, and, though communists are in similar danger of turning capitalist—as sensational instances have shown—the fact that one's rival witch doctor is as much afraid of one's own medicine as one is afraid oneself, of his, does not do anything to relieve the tension of the situation.

"Yet the fact that our adversary threatens us by showing up our defects, rather than by forcibly suppressing our virtues, is proof that the challenge he presents to us comes ultimately not from him, but from ourselves."

It may be that sport will provide opportunities for all people to meet this challenge but it may also happen that the Olympic Games and other top-level international competitions will change their character. There are indications that the U.S.S.R. will press for more and more sports to be included in the Olympic programme, for instance, parachuting, aerobatics and motor-racing, so that the Games become too vast for staging by any city other than one supported massively by a wealthy central government. The Russians may also press for the enlargement of the I.O.C. to such dimensions that it will be too unwieldy to exercise effective control and be a happy hunting ground for big powers. What could then happen is that the Olympic Games would be no more than a testing ground for two great political units. There would be no difficulty in training *élite* teams of participants whose efficiency and skill would be superb but who would cease to be sportsmen, just as the professional athletes of the Mediterranean arenas ceased to be sportsmen during the last five hundred years of the ancient Olympic Games. The competitions would be keenly contested but as predominantly political occasions they would cease to share with humbler events that playful unreality which is essential to sport. It remains to be seen whether the international bodies can so frame their regulations that a limit can be set to the political and financial exploitation of the best performers which will preserve their character as sportsmen. Most of these bodies have not so far shown signs of recognizing the problem and the International Olympic Committee, which has begun to see it, has not been markedly successful in finding a solution.

International sport is like an iceberg; a small part consisting of the Olympic Games and other world championships is seen, but most international contests go on unnoticed by Press or people. It is at this level that sport may have its greatest impact on world affairs. In his *Reith Lectures* in 1948 Bertrand Russell argued that the savage in each one of us must find some outlet not incompatible with civilized life and with the happiness of his equally savage neighbour. He suggested that sport might provide such outlets and that what was wrong with our civilization was that such forms of competition formed too small a part of the lives of ordinary men and women. Men must compete for superiority and it is best that they do so in contests which yield utterly useless results. This is not to say that the results do not matter. They matter supremely and if they do not they will not satisfy man or nation, but in sport victory is never for all time nor is defeat irreparable. The individual, the team, the nation, even the ideological block lives to fight another day.

The enormous growth of sport as a World-wide phenomenon may herald the birth of a new Olympic ideal and a new asceticism, an asceticism which looks to achievement and prowess in play as an end in itself. The final conclusion then is a paradox; sport, if it is pursued as an end in itself, may bring benefits to man which will elude his grasp if he treats it as little more than a clinical, a social or a political instrument to fashion those very benefits.

BIBLIOGRAPHY

1. MOLYNEUX, D. D., *Central Government Aid to Sport and Physical Recreation in Countries of Western Europe* (University of Birmingham, 1962).
2. JOKL, E. *et al.*, *Sports in the Cultural Pattern of the World* (Helsinki, 1956).
3. COZENS, F. W. and STUMPF, F., *Sports in American Life* (Chicago, 1953).

SEE ALSO

INTERNATIONAL OLYMPIC COMMITTEE, *Bulletins*.
RUSSELL, BERTRAND, *Authority and the Individual* (London, 1949).
TOYNBEE, A., *Civilization on Trial* (London, 1948).
UNESCO, *The Place of Sport in Education* (Paris, 1956).

POSTSCRIPT

So many factions of political interest and rivalry are operating at the present time that agreement on any one philosophy as a guide for international sport seems only a remote possibility. In exemplification of the persisting relationship between sport and society, the ideal of uniting the world at and through its games resides with the idealism of the socially involved and active youth of today in their quest for world peace.

Is it possible that a culture supporting sport in its present form, with its present means and ends, can attain peace? What kind or form of sport will it be that can exist and thrive in a world at peace? And finally, is it possible that the answer will be the one necessary to negate the present theory that sport and war are of the same family?

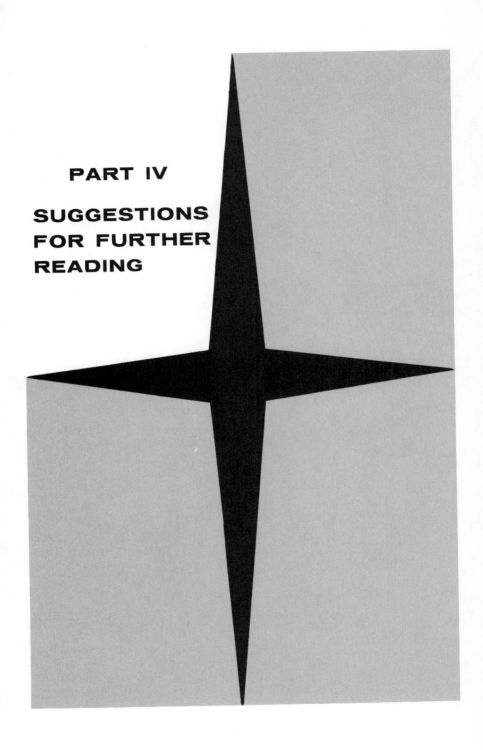

PART IV

SUGGESTIONS FOR FURTHER READING

PART I—CULTURAL CONTEXT

Section A. Theories and Definitions

Daniels, A. S. "The Study of Sport as an Element of Culture." *International Review of Sport Sociology* 1 (1966): 153-165.

Erbach, Günther. "Enlargement of the Sphere of Social Influence of Physical Culture." *International Review of Sport Sociology* 1 (1966): 59-73.

Kane, J. E. and Murray, C. "Suggestions for the Sociological Study of Sports." In *Readings in Physical Education,* edited by J. E. Kane and C. Murray, pp. 111-127. London: Physical Education Association, 1966.

Kenyon, Gerald S. and Loy, John W. "Toward a Sociology of Sport." *Journal of Health, Physical Education and Recreation* 36 (1965): 24-25, 68-69.

Section B. Sport and Social Organization

Caillois, Roger. *Man, Play, and Games.* New York: The Free Press of Glencoe, 1961.

———. "The Structure and Classification of Games." *Diogenes,* 12 (Winter, 1955): 62-75.

Huizinga, Johan. *Homo Ludens: A Study of the Play Element in Culture.* Boston: The Beacon Press, 1950.

Kenyon, Gerald S. "A Conceptual Model for Characterizing Physical Activity." *The Research Quarterly* 39 (March, 1968): 96-105.

Maheu, René. "Sport and Culture." *Journal of Health, Physical Education and Recreation* 34 (October, 1963): 30-32.

Wenkert, S. "The Meaning of Sports for Contemporary Man." *Journal of Existential Psychology* 3 (1963): 397-404.

Whyte, William. "Bowling and Social Ranking." In *Street Corner Society,* pp. 14-25. Chicago, Ill.: The University of Chicago Press, 1943.

Section C. Technology—A Perspective

Betts, John Richards. "Organized Sport in Industrial America." Ph.D. Dissertation, Columbus University, 1951.

PART II—PEOPLE IN PROCESS

Section A. Sport and Games: American Style

Theories of Meaning

Kenyon, Gerald S. "A Conceptual Approach for Characterizing Physical Activity." *Research Quarterly* 39 (1968): 96-105.

Metheny, Eleanor. *Movement and Meaning.* New York: McGraw-Hill Book Company, Inc., 1968.

Slusher, Howard S. *Man, Sport and Existence.* Philadelphia, Penn.: Lea & Febiger, 1967.

Stone, Roselyn Elizabeth. "Meanings Found in the Acts of Surfing and Skiing." Unpublished Ph.D. Dissertation, University of Southern California, 1970.

Thomson, Patricia Louise. "Ontological Truth in Sport: A Phenomenological Analysis." Unpublished Ph.D. Dissertation, University of Southern California, 1967.

Individual Meaning (Most available in paper back)

Bannister, Roger. *The Four Minute Mile.* New York: Dodd, Mead & Co., 1955.

Dixon, Peter. *Men Who Ride Mountains.* New York: Bantam Books, 1969.

Gibson, Althea. *I Always Wanted to be Somebody.* New York: Harper & Row, Publishers, 1958.

Gibson, Bob. *From Ghetto to Glory.* New York: Popular Library, 1968.

Kramer, Jerry. *Instant Replay.* New York: Signet Books, 1969.

Meggyesy, Dave. *Out of Their League.* New York: Ramparts Books, 1971.

Russell, Bill. *Go Up for Glory.* New York: Berkeley Medallion Books, 1966.

Sillitoe, Alan. *The Loneliness of a Long Distance Runner.* New York: Signet Books, 1959.

Section B. Rites of Passage and Sexual Identity

Blyth, Myrna. "Girl Athletes: What *Makes* Them Skate, Fence, Swim, Jump, Run?." *Cosmopolitan,* October, 1969.

Dattner, Richard. *Design for Play.* New York: Van Nostrand-Reinhold Co., 1969.

Hart, M. Marie. "Factors Influencing College Women's Attitudes Toward Sport and Dance." Masters Thesis, University of Southern California, 1963.

Manville, W. H. "The Locker Room Boys." *Cosmopolitan,* November, 1969.

Piaget, J. *Play, Dreams and Imitation in Childhood.* (Translated by C. Cattegno and F. M. Hodgson.) New York: W. W. Norton, 1951.

Roberts, John M. and Sutton-Smith, Brian. "Child Training and Game Involvement." *Ethnology* 1 (1962): 166-185.

Sutton-Smith, Brian; Roberts, John M.; and Kozelka, Robert M. "Game Involvement in Adults." *The Journal of Social Psychology* 60 (1963): 15-30.

Section C. Ethnic Group Patterns

Bennett, Bruce L. "Bibliography on the Negro in Sports." *Journal of Health, Physical Education and Recreation* 41 (January, 1970): 77-78. Supplemental bibliography *J.O.H.P.E.R.* 41 (September, 1970): 71.

Blalock, H. M., Jr. "Occupational Discrimination: Some Theoretical Propositions." *Social Problems* 9 (1962): 240-247.

Cady, Susan. "Bibliography of the Negro in Sports." *Journal of Health, Physical Education and Recreation* 42 (February, 1971): 70-71.

Edwards, Harry. *The Revolt of the Black Athlete.* New York: The Free Press, 1969.

Fox, J. R. "Pueblo Baseball: A New Use for Old Witchcraft." *Journal of American Folklore* 74 (1961): 9-16.

Frederickson, Florence Stumpf. "Sports and the Cultures of Man." In *Science and Medicine of Exercise and Sports,* edited by Warren R. Johnson, pp. 633-646. New York: Harper & Row, Publishers, 1960.

Henderson, Edwin B. *The Negro in Sports.* Washington, D. C.: Associated Publishers, 1969.

Henderson, Edwin B., and the Editors of *Sport, The Black Athlete—Emergence and Arrival.* Washington, D. C.: Associated Publishers, 1969.

Olsen, Jack. *The Black Athlete—A Shameful Story.* New York: Time, Inc., 1969.

Ribalow, Harold U. *The Jew in American Sports.* New York: Bloch Publishing Co., Inc., 1948.

Rosenblatt, Aaron. "Negroes in Baseball: The Failure of Success." *Trans-Action* 4 (September, 1967): 51-53, with a reply by Whitehead, 4 (October, 1967): 63-64.

Ruffer, William A. "Symposium on the Problems of the Black Athlete." *Journal of Health, Physical Education and Recreation* 42 (February, 1971): 11-15.

Russell, William. *Go Up for Glory.* New York: Coward-McCann, 1966.

Thompson, Richard. *Race and Sport.* London: Oxford University Press, 1964.

Young, A. S. *Negro Firsts in Sports.* Chicago, Ill.: Johnson Publishing Company, 1963.

PART III—BEYOND THE PEOPLE WHO PLAY: SYSTEMS WHICH CONTROL

Section A. Media and the Sports Message

Hart, M. Marie. "An Analysis of the Content of Sports Magazines, 1889-1965." Ph.D. Dissertation, University of Southern California, 1967.

Hastorf, A. H. and Cantril, H. "They Saw a Game: A Case Study." *Journal of Abnormal and Social Psychology* 49 (1954): 129-134.

Jordan, J. *Long Range Effects of Television on Sports Attendance.* Washington, D. C.: Radio and Television Manufacturers Association, 1950.

Schecter, Leonard. *The Jocks.* New York: Paperback Library, 1970.

Tannenbaum, Percy C. and Noah, James E. "Sportugese: A Study of Sports Page Communication." *Journalism Quarterly* 36 (1959): 163-170.

Woodward, Stanley. *Sports Page.* New York: Simon & Schuster, Inc., 1949.

Section B. Economics or Education: Dedication and Dollars

Andreano, Ralph. *No Joy in Mudville.* Cambridge, Mass.: Schenkman Publishing Co., 1965 (Chapter 8).

Flood, Curt, and Carter, Richard. "My Rebellion." *Sports Illustrated* 34 (February 1, 1971): 24-29.

Gilbert, Bill. "Sis-Boom-Bah! for Amalgamated Sponge." *Sports Illustrated* 22 (January 25, 1965): 54-65.

Gregory, P. M. *The Baseball Player: An Economic Study.* Washington, D. C.: Public Affairs Press, 1956.

Jackson, Myles. "College Football has Become a Losing Business." *Fortune Magazine* (December, 1962): 119-121.

Kraus, Richard G. "Recreation for the Rich and Poor: A Contrast." *Quest,* Monograph V (December, 1965): 48-58.

Murray, Thomas J. "The Big, Booming Business of Pro Football." *Dun's Review and Modern Industry* 84 (September, 1964): 38-40, 55.

Neale, Walter C. "The Peculiar Economics of Professional Sports." *The Quarterly Journal of Economics* 78 (February, 1964): 1-14.

Raiborn, Mitchell. *Financial Analysis of Intercollegiate Athletics.* Kansas City, Mo.: The National Collegiate Athletic Association, 1970.

Robinson, W. Clyde. "Professional Sports and the Antitrust Laws." *Southwestern Social Science Quarterly* 38 (1957): 133-141.

Ryan, Pat. "A Grim Run to Fiscal Daylight." *Sports Illustrated* 34 (February 1, 1971): 18-23.

Scott, Jack. *The Athletic Revolution.* New York: Free Press, 1971.

Section C. Politics: National and International Positions

Eagan, P. F. "Athletics—Medium for International Good-Will." *Journal of Educational Sociology* 28 (1954-55): 266-267.

Ganefo, I. "Sports and Politics in Djakarta." *Asian Survey* 5 (1965): 171-185.

Green, A. W. *Recreation, Leisure and Politics.* New York: McGraw-Hill Book Company, 1964.

Hanna, W. R. "The Politics of Sport." *Southeast Asia Series.* New York: American Universities Field Staff, 1962.

Heinilä, K. "Notes on Inter-group Conflicts in International Sport." *International Review of Sport Sociology* 1 (1966): 29-40.

Natan, Alex. "Sport and Politics" from *Sport and Society.* London: Bowes & Bowes, 1958.

Washburn, J. W. "Sport as a Soviet Tool." *Foreign Affairs* 34 (1956): 490-499.

GENERAL READINGS

Andreano, Ralph. *No Joy in Mudville.* Cambridge, Mass.: Schenkman Publishing Co., 1965.

Beisser, Arnold. *The Madness of Sports.* New York: Appleton-Century-Crofts, 1967.

Berne, Eric. *Games People Play.* New York: Grove Press, Inc., 1964.

Boyle, Robert H. *Sport: Mirror of American Life.* Boston, Mass.: Little, Brown and Company, 1963.

Caillois, Roger. *Man, Play, and Games.* New York: The Free Press, 1961.

Cowell, C. C. "The Contributions of Physical Activity to Social Development." *Research Quarterly* 31 (May, 1960): 286-306.

Cozens, Frederick, and Stumpf, Florence. *Sports in American Life.* Chicago, Ill.: University of Chicago Press, 1953.

Cratty, Bryant J. *Social Dimensions of Physical Activity.* Englewood Cliffs, N. J.: Prentice-Hall, Inc., 1967.

Daley, Robert. *The Bizarre World of European Sports.* New York: William Morrow & Co., Inc., 1963.

de Crazia, D. *Of Time, Work, and Leisure.* Garden City, N. Y.: Doubleday and Co., Inc., 1962.

Dulles, Foster Rhea. *A History of Recreation: America Learns to Play.* 2nd ed. New York: Appleton-Century-Crofts, 1965.

Dumazeder, Joffre. *Toward A Society of Leisure.* New York: The Free Press of Glencoe, 1967.

Gallico, Paul. *Farewell to Sport.* New York: Alfred A. Knopf, Inc., 1938.

Huizinga, Johan. *Homo Ludens: A Study of the Play Element in Culture.* Boston, Mass.: Beacon Press, 1950.

International Review of Sport Sociology. vol. 1. Edited by Andrzej Wohl. Warsaw, Poland: Polish Scientific Publishers, 1966.

Jokl, Ernst. *Medical Sociology and Cultural Anthropology of Sport and Physical Education.* Springfield, Ill.: Charles C. Thomas, Publisher, 1964.

Kaplan, M. *Leisure in America: A Social Inquiry.* New York: John Wiley & Sons, Inc., 1960.

Kenyon, Gerald S., ed. *Aspects of Contemporary Sport Sociology.* Chicago, Ill.: The Athletic Institute, Proceedings of Symposium on the Sociology of Sport University of Wisconsin, 1968.

Larrabee, E. and Meyersohn, R. *Mass Leisure.* New York: The Free Press, 1958.

Loy, John and Kenyon, Gerald. *Sport, Culture, and Society.* New York: The Macmillan Company, 1969.

Lüschen, Günther, ed. *The Cross-Cultural Analysis of Sport and Games.* Champaign, Ill.: Stipes Publishing Co., 1970.

McIntosh, P. C. *Sport in Society.* London: C. A. Watts & Co., Ltd., 1963.

Metheny, Eleanor. *Connotations of Movement in Sport and Dance.* Dubuque, Iowa: Wm. C. Brown Company Publishers, 1965.

———. *Movement and Meaning.* New York: McGraw-Hill Book Co., 1968.

Miller, Norman P. and Robinson, Duane M. *The Leisure Age.* Belmont, Calif.: Wadsworth Publishing Company, 1963.

Morton, Henry W. *Soviet Sport: Mirror of Soviet Society.* New York: Collier Books, 1963.

Natan, A., ed. *Sport and Society.* London: Bowes and Bowes, 1958.

Sage, George H., ed. *Sport and American Society.* Reading, Mass.: Addison-Wesley Publishing Company, 1970.

Sapora, Allen Victor, and Mitchell, Elmer D. *The Theory of Play and Recreation.* 3rd ed. New York: The Ronald Press Company, 1961.

Scott, Jack. *Athletics for Athletes.* Oakland, Calif.: An Other Ways Book, 1969.

Slovenko, Ralph and Knight, James A., ed. *Motivations in Play, Games, and Sports.* Springfield, Ill.: Charles C. Thomas, Publisher, 1967.

Slusher, Howard. *Man, Sport, and Existence: A Critical Analysis.* Philadelphia, Penn.: Lea & Febiger, 1967.

Tunis, John. *The American Way in Sport.* New York: Duell, Sloan and Pearce, 1958.

Unminger, Walter. *Superman, Heroes, and Gods.* London: Thames and Hudson, 1963.

Veblen, Thorstein. *The Theory of the Leisure Class.* New York: The Modern
    Library, 1934.
Weis, Paul. *Sport: A Philosophical Inquiry.* Carbondale, Ill.: Southern Illinois
    University Press, 1969.

BIBLIOGRAPHIES

Cratty, Bryant. In *Social Dimensions of Physical Activity.* New York: Prentice-
    Hall, Inc., 1967. (474 items).
Lüschen, Günther. "The Sociology of Sport." *Current Sociology.* vol. 15. Paris
    and The Hague: Mouton Publishers, 1968. (900 items annotated.)

This book may be kept
FOURTEEN DAYS
A fine will be charged for each
day the book is kept overtime.

APR 0 4 1992			